Pavel Basinsky

LEO TOLSTOY
FLIGHT FROM PARADISE

Glagoslav Publications

LEO TOLSTOY

FLIGHT FROM PARADISE

by Pavel Basinsky

Translated by Huw Davies and Scott Moss

Book Created by Max Mendor

© 2010, Pavel Basinsky

© 2015, Glagoslav Publications, United Kingdom

Glagoslav Publications Ltd
88-90 Hatton Garden
EC1N 8PN London
United Kingdom

www.glagoslav.com

ISBN: 978-1-78267-127-5

A catalogue record for this book is available
from the British Library

This book is in copyright. No part of this publication may be reproduced, stored in a retrieval system or transmitted in any form or by any means without the prior permission in writing of the publisher, nor be otherwise circulated in any form of binding or cover other than that in which it is published without a similar condition, including this condition, being imposed on the subsequent purchaser.

CONTENTS

Chapter 1. Departure or Flight? 5

Chapter 2. Paradise Lost 43

Chapter 3. Sonia and the Devil 83

Chapter 4. La Tête à Bonnet 141

Chapter 5. The New Russian 189

Chapter 6. A Dear Friend 273

Chapter 7. Whose Fault Is It? 315

Chapter 8. The Beautiful Idol 367

Chapter 9. Excommunication and the Will 403

Chapter 10. Ice-cold Rain 489

Epilogue 515

List of Sources 521

Chapter 1

Departure or Flight?

On the night of October 27, 1910, an unbelievable event took place in the Krapivensky District of the Tula Province, one that was exceptional even for such an extraordinary place as Yasnaya Polyana, the ancestral estate of the internationally acclaimed writer and thinker Count Lev Nikolayevich Tolstoy. The eighty-two year old Count fled from his home in secret, his destination unknown, escorted by his personal physician, a man named Makovitsky.

The eyes of the press

The news media of that time did not differ greatly from the media today. News of the scandalous events spread like wildfire throughout Russia and across the world. On October 29th, urgent telegrams from Tula began arriving at the Petersburg Telegraph Agency, to be reprinted in the newspapers the next day. "News has come in that has surprised everyone, to the effect that L.N. Tolstoy, escorted by Dr. Makovitsky, has unexpectedly fled Yasnaya Polyana and gone away. On leaving, L.N. Tolstoy left a letter, in which he declares that he is leaving Yasnaya Polyana forever." Tolstoy's fellow traveler, Makovitsky, didn't even know about this letter, written by L.N. for his wife, who was asleep, and handed to her in the morning by their youngest daughter, Sasha. He learned of its existence from the newspapers, like everyone else.

The Moscow-based newspaper *Russkoye Slovo* ("Russian Word") was quickest off the mark. On October 30th, it published a report by its own correspondent in Tula, containing detailed information about what had happened at Yasnaya Polyana.

"Tula, 29, X (*urgent*). Having returned from Yasnaya Polyana, I announce the departure of Lev Nikolayevich, with the details.

Lev Nikolayevich left yesterday, at 5am, when it was still dark.

Lev Nikolayevich went to the coachman's quarters and ordered that the horses be hitched to the cart.

The coachman Adrian did as instructed.

When the horses were ready, Lev Nikolayevich, together with Dr. Makovitsky, taking a few necessary items, laid out earlier that night, went to the Shchekino Station.

The postman Filka went in front of them, lighting the way with a torch.

At the Shchekino Station, Lev Nikolayevich bought a ticket to one of the stations on the Moscow-Kursk railway line and left on the first train that came along.

When it became known at Yasnaya Polyana that Lev Nikolayevich had upped and left, there was a terrible fuss. The despair of Lev Nikolayevich's wife, Sofia Andreyevna, defies description."

This report, which the whole world was talking about the next day, was printed not on the front page of the newspaper, but on the third. The front page, as was customary at that time, was reserved for advertisements for all manner of products.

"San Rafael wine – the stomach's best friend." "Medium sturgeon. Twenty kopecks a pound."

After receiving the nightly telegram from Tula, "Russian Word" immediately sent its correspondent to the Tolstoys' Hamovniki House (today this building is the house-museum of L.N. Tolstoy, between the "Park of Culture" and "Fruzensky" subway stations). The newspaper was hoping that the Count had perhaps fled from Yasnaya Polyana to his home in Moscow. But, as the newspaper put it, "Tolstoy's lordly old house was quiet and calm. There was nothing to suggest that Lev Nikolayevich might soon be coming back to the old hearth and home. The gates were locked. Everyone inside was fast asleep." The reporter sent off in pursuit along the supposed route of Tolstoy's flight was the young journalist Konstantin Orlov, a theatre critic and the son of one of Tolstoy's followers, the teacher and populist Vladimir Fyodorovich Orlov, who was portrayed in the stories *Dream* and *There Are None that are Guilty in the World*. He caught up with the fugitive in Kozelsk and accompanied him in secret as far as Astapovo, from whence he informed Sophia Andreyevna and Tolstoy's children by telegram that their husband and father was seriously ill and was currently at the central railroad station, at the home of the station master, I.I. Ozolin.

If it wasn't for Orlov's initiative, the family would not have found out about the whereabouts of the gravely ill L.N. until the newspapers all announced where he was. Need it be said how painful such a thing would have been for the family? Therefore, by contrast with Makovitsky, who felt that "Russian Word" had been behaving like "detectives on a manhunt", Tolstoy's eldest daughter, Tatiana Lvovna Suhotina, according to her memoirs, was grateful "till her dying day" to the journalist Orlov.

"Father is dying somewhere not far away, and I don't know where he is. And I can't take care of him. It may be that I will never see him again. Will they at least allow me to see him on his death-bed? A sleepless night. Genuine torture," Tatiana Lvovna later wrote of what she and her family were going through after Tolstoy's "flight" (to use her word). "But a man was found whom we did not know, who understood and took pity on the Tolstoy family. He sent us a telegram: "Lev Nikolayevich is at Astapovo at the station master's house. He has a temperature of 1040."

Generally speaking, it has to be said that in their attitude toward his family and, first and foremost, toward Sofia Andreyevna, the newspapers behaved in a more controlled and delicate manner than they did toward the fugitive from Yasnaya Polyana, whose every step was tracked mercilessly, even though all the journalists knew that in his farewell note Tolstoy had asked: don't search for me! "Please... don't come after me, if you find out where I am," he had written to his wife.

"In Belevo, Lev Nikolayevich got off the train and had some fried eggs in the station dining room," the journalists reported, savoring this indulgent act on the part of the frugal Tolstoy. They interrogated his coachman and Filka, the servants and peasants from Yasnaya Polyana, cashiers and waiters at the stations, the driver who took L.N. from Kozelsk to the Optina Monastery, the hotel monks and anyone who might be able to tell them the travel plans of this eighty-two year old man, a man whose sole desire was to run away, to hide, to become invisible to the world.

"Don't search for him!" the "Odessa News" exclaimed cynically, addressing the family. "He's not just yours – he belongs to all of us!"

"His new place of residence will of course be revealed very soon," the "Petersburg Gazette" coolly announced.

L.N. was not fond of the newspapers (although he kept an eye on them) and made no secret of it. Not so with S.A. The writer's wife understood well that her husband's reputation and her own reputation, like it or not, would be shaped by what people read in the press. She was therefore always willing to talk to journalists and give them interviews, explaining away the latest oddities in Tolstoy's behavior or the things he said and never forgetting, when doing so (this was her weakness) to outline her own role alongside the great man.

The journalists therefore treated S.A., with warmth, in the main. The tone was set by a piece in "Russian Word" by Vlas Doroshevich, entitled "Sofia Andreyevna", in the issue dated October 31st. "The old lion has gone off to die in solitude," wrote Doroshevich. "The eagle has flown away from us, so high; how then can we track his flight?!"

(Yet track him they did – and how!)

He compared S.A. with Yasodara, the young wife of Buddha. This was undoubtedly a compliment, because Yasodara was in no way to blame for her husband's departure. More malicious types, meanwhile, compared Tolstoy's wife not with Yasodara, but with Xanthippe, the wife of the Greek philosopher Socrates, who allegedly exhausted her husband with her peevishness and failure to understand his outlook.

Doroshevich rightly pointed out that without his wife, Tolstoy wouldn't have lived such a long life and wouldn't have written his later works. (Although how does this fit in with the Yasodara comparison?)

The piece concluded as follows. Tolstoy was a "superperson", and his actions could not be judged by any normal standards. S.A. was a simple, salt-of-the-earth woman, who had done everything she could for her husband whilst he was a mere mortal. In the realm of the "superhuman", however, he wasn't accessible to her, and in this was the tragedy of her situation.

"Sofia Andreyevna is alone. She is without her child, her old man-child, her titan-child, whom she had to think about and care for every minute of the day: is he warm enough, is he full, is he in good health? Now she has no-one to whom she can give her entire life, drop by drop."

S.A. read this article. She liked it. She was grateful to the newspaper "Russian Word" for both Doroshevich's article and Orlov's telegram. Thanks to these things she was able to overlook certain trifling matters, such as the unflattering description of Tolstoy's wife's outer appearance which the self-same Orlov provided: "Sofia Andreyevna's wandering eyes expressed inner torture. Her head was quivering. She was dressed in a cowl that had been carelessly thrown over her shoulders." She was also able to forgive the night-time surveillance of their house in Moscow, the very improper revelation about how much money the family had spent in order to hire a private train from Tula to Astapovo: 492 rubles and 27 kopecks, and Vasily Rozanov's transparent hint that Tolstoy had, after all, been fleeing from his family: "The prisoner has left his delicate dungeon".

A quick glance at the newspaper headlines covering Tolstoy's departure reveals that the word "departure" seldom appears in them. "SUDDEN EXIT…", "DISAPPEARANCE…", "FLIGHT…", "TOLSTOY QUITS HOME".

And this is in no way a reflection of the newsmen's desire to grab their readers' attention. This event was sensational enough already. The fact is that the circumstances surrounding Tolstoy's disappearance from Yasnaya Polyana are indeed far more reminiscent of an escape than a stately departure.

A nightmare at dead of night

Firstly, the event happened at night, when the Countess was sleeping soundly.

Secondly, Tolstoy's route was kept secret so carefully that the first she knew of his whereabouts was when she received Orlov's telegram on November 2nd.

Thirdly (and this is something that neither the reporters nor S.A knew about), the route in question – the final destination, at least – wasn't even known to the fugitive himself. Tolstoy clearly understood whence and from what he was running, but as for where he was headed and where his final refuge was going to be, not only did he not know; it was also something he tried not to think about.

In the first few hours after his departure, only Tolstoy's daughter Sasha and her friend Feokritova knew that L.N. intended to visit his sister, a nun named Maria Nikolayevna Tolstaya, at the Shamordino Monastery. On the night of the flight, however, this too was thrown into question.

"You'll stay here, Sasha", he said to me. "I'll summon you in a few days, when I've made up my mind once and for all where I'm going. And I'll go, in all likelihood, to visit Mashenka in Shamordino", - A.L. Tolstaya recalled.

When he roused Dr. Makovitsky from his slumbers, during the night, Tolstoy didn't even tell him this information. Most strikingly, he didn't even tell the doctor that he was leaving Yasnaya Polyana for good, as he had informed Sasha. In the first few hours Makovitsky thought they were going to Kochety, an estate owned by Tolstoy's son-in-law, M.S Suhotin, on the border of the Tula and Orlov provinces. Tolstoy had visited the estate on more than one occasion over the last two years, either alone or with his wife, to get away from the constant stream of visitors at Yasnaya Polyana. There he took, as he himself expressed it, his "vacation". His eldest daughter, Tatiana Lvovna, lived at Kochety. Unlike Sasha, she did not approve of her father's desire to leave their mother, although she was on her father's side in the conflict between them. In any case, it would be impossible to hide from S.A. at Kochety. His arrival at Shamordino would be less easy to predict. A visit to an Orthodox monastery by Tolstoy – a man who had been excommunicated from the church – would be an act no less sensational than the departure itself. And last but not least, once there Tolstoy could count entirely on his sister's support and silence.

Poor Makovitsky didn't realize straight away that Tolstoy had decided to leave home for good. Thinking that they were going to Kochety for a month, Makovitsky didn't take all of his money. He was also unaware that at the moment of flight, the only money Tolstoy had with him was fifty rubles in his notebook and some small change in his wallet. It was only during Tolstoy's parting with Sasha that Makovitsky heard about Shamordino. And only when they were sitting in the carriage did Tolstoy begin to ask his advice: where might they go, to get as far away as possible?

Tolstoy had certainly chosen his fellow-traveler well. One had to have the unflappable nature and devotion with which Makovitsky was blessed, in order not to be all at sea in such a situation. Makovitsky quickly proposed that they go to Bessarabia, to the home of a worker named Gusarov, who lived with his family on an estate that he owned. "L.N. gave no answer." They went to the Shchekino Station. The train to Tula was due to stop there in twenty minutes, and in one-and-a-half hours there would be a train to Gorbachevo. The route from Gorbachevo to Shamordino was shorter, but Tolstoy, hoping to throw anyone who might come after him off the scent and fearing that S.A might wake up and catch up with him, suggested that they go through Tula. Makovitsky talked him out of it: in Tula they were bound to be recognized immediately! They went instead to Gorbachevo...

All things considered, this bears little resemblance to a departure – in either a literal or figurative sense. Yet it is specifically this literal idea of Tolstoy leaving home that still serves as a heartwarming image for the locals to this day. In this image he will without fail be on foot, of a dark night, with a knapsack on his shoulders and a cane in his hand. And we are talking about an eighty-two year old man who, though strong, was nonetheless very sick, and suffered from fainting spells, memory lapses, heart failure and distention of the veins in his legs. What could possibly be said to be wonderful about a "departure" such as this? Yet the locals for some reason like to imagine that the great Tolstoy simply upped and left.

In Ivan Bunin's book *The Liberation of Tolstoy*, the words written by Tolstoy in his leaving note are quoted with admiration: "I am doing what old men of my age usually do. They depart from worldly life, in order to live out the last days of their lives in quiet solitude." *What old men usually do?*

S.A. noticed these words, too. Having barely recovered from the initial shock caused by her husband's running off in the middle of the night, she began to write letters begging him to return home, counting on the fact that third parties would help get these letters to him. In the second of these letters, which Tolstoy was never to read, she retorted: "You write that old men depart from the world. Where on earth have you seen that happen? Old peasant men live out their last days lying on the stove surrounded by their family and grandchildren, just like the nobility and everyone else. Surely it is not natural for a weak old man to depart from the care, concern and love of the children and grandchildren surrounding him?"

She was wrong. The departure of old men, and even old women, was a regular occurrence in peasant homes. They would leave home to go on pilgrimages or simply to live in isolated peasant huts. They would leave to live out their days, so as not to cause a nuisance for the younger ones, not to be reproached for having an extra serving of food, when it was no longer possible for the old man in question to take part in work in the fields or in the home. They would leave when "sin had taken root" in the home: drunkenness, discord, unnatural sexual relations. Old men did indeed leave. But they didn't flee at night from their ageing wife with the consent and support of their daughter.

Let us return to that fateful night of October 27-28th and retrace Tolstoy's departure, step by step.

From Makovitsky's notes:

"At 3 o'clock in the morning, L.N., wearing a robe, in slippers over his bare feet, and holding a candle, woke me up; the look on his face was one of suffering, and also expressed anxiety and determination.

"I have decided to leave. You are going to come with me. I'll go upstairs, and then you'll join me, only don't wake up Sofia Andreyevna. We won't take too many things – just the bare essentials. Sasha will come after us in three days' time and bring us what we need."

The "determined" look on his face did not signify that he felt calm and collected. It was the determination that comes before leaping from a precipice. Wearing his physician's cap, Makovitsky notes: "Nervous. I felt his pulse - 100." What are the "bare essentials" for an eighty-two year-old man who is leaving home? Tolstoy gave less thought to this than anything else. He was concerned that Sasha should hide his diary manuscripts from S.A. He took with him a fountain pen and some notebooks. Makovitsky, Sasha and Sasha's friend Varvara Feokritova packed up their belongings and provisions. It turned out that there were quite a lot of "bare essentials" after all, and they could have done with a large suitcase, which they couldn't retrieve without making a din and waking up S.A.

There were three doors between Tolstoy's bedroom and that of his wife. S.A. used to leave them open at night so that she would wake up if any sounds of distress were to come from her husband's room. Her explanation for this was that if the doors were kept closed, she wouldn't be able to hear him if he needed help during the night. The main reason was something else, though. She feared that he might run away one night. For some time now, this threat had been a real one. It is even possible to give the precise date when it first began to hang over Yasnaya Polyana: July 15th, 1910. After a heated row with her husband, S.A. spent a sleepless night and in the morning wrote him a letter:

"Levochka, my darling, I'm writing these words, not saying them, because after a sleepless night it's difficult for me to talk, I'm too anxious and might upset everyone again, and I want, so desperately want, to be calm and rational. I pondered over everything during the night, and here's what has become painfully clear to me: though you caressed me with one hand, in the other you brandished a knife. I had a vague feeling yesterday that this knife had already wounded my heart. This knife – it's a threat, and a very decisive one at that, to take back the promise you made and quietly leave me, if I go on being the way I am now… Does this mean that every night, just like last night, I will be listening out, in case you've left and gone off somewhere? Any absence on your part, even one that is slightly longer than expected, will torment me with the fear that you have gone away for good. Think about it, my darling Levochka, for after all your departure and your threat are tantamount to a threat of murder."

When Sasha, Varvara and Makovitsky had packed the things (they acted "like conspirators", Feokritova recalled, blowing out the candles on hearing the slightest noise from S.A.'s room), Tolstoy tightly closed all three of the doors leading to his wife's bedroom, and managed to retrieve the suitcase without making any noise. It turned out that even this case wasn't big enough, and they also had to take another bundle containing a blanket and a coat, and a basket with provisions. Tolstoy didn't wait around whilst they finished packing, incidentally. He hurried to the coachman's quarters to wake up the coachman, Andrian, and help him harness the horses.

Departure? Or flight…

From Tolstoy's diary:

"…I'm on my way to the stables to order that the horses be harnessed; Dushan, Sasha and Varya are finishing off the packing. The night is pitch black, I stumble off the path to the outbuilding, fall into a thicket, get stung, bump into trees, then I fall down, my hat falls off, I can't find it, I get to my feet with difficulty, go home, grab another hat and with the lantern in my hand I reach the stables and order that the horses be harnessed. Sasha, Dushan and Varya arrive… I'm shaking, expecting to be pursued."

What had seemed to Tolstoy, when he wrote these lines the next day, to be a "thicket", which he had struggled out of "with difficulty", had in fact been his orchard, which he knew like the back of his hand.

What old men usually do?

"It took us around half an hour to pack the things," Alexandra Lvovna recalled. "Father was already starting to worry, and was hurrying, but our hands were shaking, we couldn't fasten the straps and the suitcases wouldn't close".

Alexandra Lvovna also noticed the determined look in her father's eye. "I had been expecting his departure, expecting it to come any day, any hour, but nevertheless, when he said: 'I'm leaving for good,' I was stunned by it as if it were something new and unexpected. I will never forget the sight of him standing in the doorway, in his tunic, with a candle and an expression that was bright, beautiful and full of determination." "The look on his face was determined and bright," Feokritova wrote. But let's not get carried away. On a dark October night, when in rural homes, regardless of whether they're owned by peasants or nobles, you can't even see your own hand when you hold it in front of your face. An old man in bright clothing, holding a candle near his face, suddenly appears on the doorstep. This would be a pretty striking sight for anyone!

Of course, Tolstoy's fortitude was phenomenal. But this tells us more about his ability not to lose his cool under any circumstances. The musician Alexander Goldenweiser, a friend of the Yasnaya Polyana household, recalled one particular incident. One winter they had travelled in sleighs to village six miles from Yasnaya to help a peasant family in need.

"When we were approaching the Zaseka Station, a small snowstorm began, which got stronger so that in the end we lost our way and went off the road. Having strayed a bit, we noticed a lodge in the woods not far away and went toward it, so as to ask the forester how to get back onto the road. When we approached the lodge, three or four huge German Shepherds Dogs jumped out at us and surrounded the horse and sleigh, barking like mad. I felt pretty uneasy, I have to admit. With a decisive movement, L.N. handed me the reins and said: "Hold these" – and then he stood up, got out of the sleigh, gave a loud howl and bravely walked straight toward the dogs with nothing but his bare hands. And suddenly the terrifying dogs immediately stopped barking, moved aside and gave him right of way. L.N. passed calmly between them and walked into the lodge. At that moment, with his flowing gray beard, he looked more like a character from a fairytale than a weak, eighty-year old man..."

On the night of October 28th, 1910, this same self-control had not deserted him.. He met his assistants, who had brought along his things, halfway along the path. "It was muddy, our feet slipped on the path, and we found it hard going in the dark," Alexandra Lvovna recalled. "Next to the outbuilding there was a little blue light flickering. It was father coming to meet us.

'Ah, it's you,' he said, 'well, this time I made it safely. They're already harnessing the horses for us. Well then, I'll go ahead and light the way for you. Why did you give Sasha the heaviest things to carry?' he reproached Varvara Mikhailovna. He took the basket from her hands and carried it, and Varvara Mikhailovna helped me carry the suitcase. Father went on ahead, occasionally pressing the button on the electric lamp and then immediately releasing it, which made it seem even darker. Father was always trying to economize, and in this case, as ever, was reluctant to use up too much electricity." Sasha had talked him into taking this lamp after her father had got lost in the orchard.

Yet when Tolstoy was helping the coachman harness the horse, "his hands were shaking, they refused to obey him, and hard as he tried he couldn't fasten the buckle." Then "he sat down in the corner of the carriage shed, on the suitcase, and straight away his spirits sank."

Dramatic mood-swings were to accompany Tolstoy throughout the entire journey from Yasnaya Polyana to Astapovo, where he passed away on the night of November 7th, 1910. Decisiveness and consciousness of the fact that he had acted in the only correct way were to alternate with a lack of will and an extremely keen sense of guilt. No matter how prepared he was for this departure – and he had spent twenty-five years preparing for it! – it's understandable that he was not in fact ready for it, either mentally or physically. He could picture this departure in his mind's eye as much as he liked, but the first actual steps that he took, such as getting lost in his own orchard, brought surprises for which Tolstoy and his fellow travelers were unprepared.

But why had his decisive mood in the house suddenly given way to a sinking of his spirits in the carriage shed? All his things were packed (in just two hours – simply astounding!), the horses were almost ready, and only a few minutes remained until he was to be "liberated". And yet his spirits sank.

Besides the physiological reasons (he hadn't had enough sleep, was anxious, had got lost, and had helped to carry the things along a slippery path in the dark), there is also another circumstance, which can only be properly understood by thinking about the bigger picture. If S.A. were to wake up when they were packing the things, it would have resulted in an outrageous scandal. Yet it would nonetheless have been a scandal within the four walls of the house. It would have caused a scene merely among the "inner circle". Such scenes were something that nobody could grow used to, although lately they had been taking place with increasing frequency in the Yasnaya Polyana household. Yet the further Tolstoy was to get from home and hearth, the larger the number of people would get drawn into his departure. What happened was the very thing that he wanted least of all to see. Tolstoy was like a lump of snow, around which a huge snowball would gather, and this happened at every passing minute whenever he went anywhere.

It would be impossible to leave without waking up Andrian Bolhin, the coachman. And they also needed Filka (Filipp Borisov), the thirty-three year old groom, so that, sitting on horseback, he could light the way in front of the carriage with a lantern. By the time L.N. Tolstoy was in the carriage shed, the snowball had already begun to grow and grow, and with every passing minute it was becoming ever more impossible to stop it. The police officers, newspapermen, governors and priests were all still sleeping serenely… Not even Tolstoy himself could have imagined how many people were to become accomplices in his flight, whether willingly or otherwise – right up to ministers, the leading bishops, Stolypin and Nicholas II.

It goes without saying that he could not help but be aware that to disappear from Yasnaya Polyana without people noticing would be impossible. To disappear unnoticed was a feat that not even Fedya Protasov from Tolstoy's tale *The Living Corpse* could achieve: Fedya feigns suicide but is eventually exposed. Let us not forget, though, that besides *The Living Corpse*, he also wrote *Father Sergius* and *The Posthumous Papers of the Elder Fyodor Kuzmich*. And if, at the moment of departure, there was one thought that gave him solace, then it was this: a famous person, by disappearing, dissolves into the crowd, becoming one of the smaller forces that are invisible to everyone. The legend that was Tolstoy existed in its own right, and he himself existed in his own right. And it is irrelevant who you were in the past: a Russian tsar, a well-known miracle-worker or a great writer. What matters is that in the here and now you are the simplest and most common of people.

When Tolstoy was sitting on the suitcase in the carriage shed, in an old armyak, dressed in a padded coat and an old knitted hat, he was, it seemed, fully equipped to make his long-cherished dream a reality. And yet... That time of day, 5 A.M., "between the wolf and the dog". That dank end of October – the most disgusting of all the periods between the main seasons in Russia. That unbearable torment of expectation, when the groundwork for his departure has been done, the walls of the family home are abandoned and behind him, and there can be no going back, and yet... The horses are not yet ready, Yasnaya Polyana has not yet been abandoned... And his wife, with whom he has lived for forty-eight years, who bore him thirteen children, of which seven are still alive, and have produced twenty-three grandchildren in turn; his wife, on whose shoulders he placed the burden of all the housekeeping at Yasnaya Polyana, all his publishing matters concerning his literary works, who copied out his two main novels multiple times, section by section, as well as many other works, and who had stayed up through the night in the Crimea, when he had been at death's door nine years ago, because no one, besides her, could administer the most intimate care of all to him – this dear person might wake up at any second, find the doors all closed and see the mess in his room and realize that the thing she feared more than anything in the world had come to pass!

Or had it? It doesn't take an over-active imagination to picture the scene had S.A. suddenly appeared in the carriage shed, when her husband was buckling the harness to the horses with trembling hands. Things would rapidly have become more Gogolesque than Tolstoyan. It was not without good reason that Tolstoy both liked and disliked Gogol's short story, *The Carriage*, in which an aristocrat from the provinces, Pythagoras Pythagorovich Chertokutsky, hides from his guests in the carriage shed, but is discovered in extremely embarrassing circumstances. He considered this work a wonderfully crafted piece of writing, but an absurd joke. *The Carriage* was by no means a piece of comedy, by the way. When the general walks into the carriage shed, where the little Chertokutsky is curled up on the seat under the leather canopy, he represents Fate itself, catching up with a person at the very moment when he is less prepared for it than ever. How pitiful and helpless he is before it!

Sasha later wrote:

"At first father was chivvying the coachman, but then he sat down in the corner of the carriage shed, on the suitcase, and immediately his spirits sank:

'I sense that at any moment they'll discover us, and then all will be lost. There will be no leaving without a terrible fuss."

Tolstoy's weakness

Much in Tolstoy's mood at the moment of flight, before it, and after it can be explained by something so simple as delicacy.

By nature, Tolstoy remained an old Russian landowner, in the most wonderful sense of the word. This complex and, alas, long-lost mental and spiritual outlook incorporated such concepts as moral and physical purity, the inability to look someone in the eye and tell them a lie, or say spiteful things about a person behind their back, a fear of hurting anyone's feelings with careless words or simply of being in any way unpleasant for people. In his youth, due to his unbridled mind and character, Tolstoy sinned a lot against these spiritual qualities which were in the family by birth and upbringing and he suffered as a result of this. As he got older, however, besides the principles of love and compassion toward people he had acquired, his opposition to all that was ugly, dirty or scandalous became increasingly apparent.

For the duration of the conflict with his wife, Tolstoy was almost irreproachable. He pitied her, suppressed any attempts people made to say spiteful things about her, even when he knew these words to be just. He submitted as much as was possible, and even to an extent that was impossible, to her demands, occasionally utterly ridiculous, patiently put up with all her antics, occasionally monstrous, such as when she threatened to commit suicide. Yet at the core of this behavior, which surprised and even irritated his supporters, were not abstract principles, but the nature of an old landowner, and simply that of a wonderful old man, who found any strife, discord or scandal a painful thing to endure.

The strongest emotion that Tolstoy felt in the carriage shed, therefore, was fear. Fear lest his wife might wake up, run out of the house and catch him on the suitcase, beside the carriage which was not yet ready... And then it would be impossible to avoid a scandal, a painful, gut-wrenching scene, which would serve as the culmination of what had been going on in Yasnaya Polyana lately.

He never ran away from difficulties... Latterly, on the contrary, he had thanked God whenever He sent him trials. He accepted any "unpleasantness" with a humble heart. He was glad when people judged him. But now he passionately wanted to be spared such things. This was not something that was in his power.

Yes, Tolstoy's departure was a manifestation not only of strength, but also of weakness. He openly admitted as much to an old friend and confidante, Maria Alexandrovna Schmidt, a former teacher, who had believed in Tolstoy as in a new Christ, the most sincere and consistent Tolstoyan of all, who lived in a peasant hut in Ovsyanik, six versts away. Tolstoy often visited her whilst out riding, knowing that these visits not only brought her joy but were her *raison d'être*. He consulted her on spiritual matters on October 26th, just two days before the departure, telling her of his plans – at this stage he had yet to make up his mind once and for all – to leave. Maria Alexandrovna clasped her hands:

"My dear, Lev Nikolayevich!" - she said. - "This is weakness, it will pass". "Yes," - he answered - "it is weakness." Tatiana Lvovna Suhotina records this conversation, as recounted to her by Maria Alexandrovna, in her memoirs. The conversation doesn't feature in the diary of Makovitsky, who had accompanied L.N. on the stroll of October 26. Moreover, Maria Alexandrovna herself, when she spoke to a correspondent from "Russian Word", asserted that L.N. didn't say "a word" to her about his departure that day. This was a blatant lie, which can be explained by her unwillingness to wash her dirty laundry (dirty laundry that wasn't even her own) in public and reveal the conflict within the Tolstoy family to the rest of the world. In his secret "diary for myself alone", Tolstoy writes, on October 26th: "I am more and more oppressed by this life. Maria Alexandrovna forbids me to leave and moreover my own conscience doesn't allow me to do so." On October 26, Makovitsky, too, noticed that "L.N. is weak" and not with it. Along the road to Schmidt's house, Tolstoy committed a "foolish" act, as he himself put it: he rode through the "greenery" (winter crops), and this is something that mustn't be done in the dirt, because the horse leaves deep traces and destroys the tender greenery.

One wants to protest: he felt sorry for the "greenery", but not his old wife?! Unfortunately this is the typical way in which people judge Tolstoy. This is the kind of reasoning of those who see in Tolstoy's flight the act of the "father of mankind" and relate it to his "humane, all too humane ideas about the family. The strong Tolstoy left his weak wife, who was not compatible with him in terms of her spiritual development. It makes perfect sense, this is why he's known as a genius, but what a pity for poor S.A., of course! How dangerous it can be to marry a genius.

This widely held point of view, strangely, almost coincides with the one which is cultivated in intellectual circles, and, with a little help from Ivan Bunin, became popular.

Tolstoy left so as to die. This was an act of liberation for a spiritual titan from the material captivity which tortured him. The "liberation of Tolstoy". How wonderful! Synopsis: just as a strong animal, on sensing the approach of death, leaves the pack, so Tolstoy, feeling the approach of the inevitable end, fled from Yasnaya Polyana. There was also a wonderful heathen version which Alexander Kuprin set out in the newspapers in the first few days after Tolstoy's departure.

But Tolstoy's act was not the action of a titan who had decided to make a grandiose, symbolic gesture. Still less was it the reflex of an old but strong animal. It was the act of a weak, sick old man who had dreamed of leaving for twenty-five years, but, while he had had the strength, didn't allow himself to do so because he felt it would be cruel on his wife. And now, when he no longer had any strength, and the family rows had reached boiling point, he could see no other way out, either for himself or for those around him. He left at the very moment when he was utterly unprepared for the trip, physically. When it was late October outside. When nothing was prepared and when even the most ardent advocates of his departure, such as Sasha, couldn't imagine what it would be like for the old man to be in "the open countryside". It was at the very moment when his departure would almost inevitably mean certain death that Tolstoy no longer had the strength to remain at Yasnaya Polyana.

Did he leave in order to die? This explanation was proposed by Professor V.F. Snegirev, an obstetrician who treated S.A. and performed an emergency operation on her in the Yasnaya Polyana house. He was not only a wonderful doctor but also an uncommonly intelligent and delicate person. Desirous of consoling and comforting his patient, who, after her husband's death, was accused by all and sundry of having driven him to flight and to his grave, he wrote her a lengthy letter on April 10, 1911, on Easter Sunday, in which he tried to outline the objective and non-domestic reasons for Tolstoy's departure. He could see two such reasons.

The first was as follows. Tolstoy's departure had been a complex form of suicide – or at any rate, a subconscious acceleration of the process of death.

"Throughout almost all his life, he worked on and cultivated his spirit and body in an identical way, and due to his unquenchable energy and talents, he cultivated them equally strongly, binding them tightly together and merging them: where the body ended and the spirit began – it was impossible to say. Anyone who looked at his stride, the turn of his head, the fall of his foot, could *always* clearly see the deliberate nature of his movements: that is to say, every movement was worked out, developed, given meaning, and expressed an idea... On the death of such a fused combination of body and soul, the separation, the discharge of the spirit from the body could not and cannot be accomplished quietly, calmly, as is the case with those for whom the rupture between soul and body happened long ago ... to effect such a separation, it is necessary to have *inordinate* control over the body..."

Snegirev's other explanation was strictly medical. Tolstoy had died of pneumonia. "This infection is sometimes accompanied by manic seizures," Snegirev wrote. "Might not the night-time flight have occurred during just such a seizure, for sometimes the infection doesn't manifest itself until a few days before the illness, i.e. the organism is poisoned before the localized process begins. His hastiness and the fact that he changed direction so often during his travels fully support this theory..."

In other words, Tolstoy was already ill on the night of his departure, and the infection with which he was poisoned had affected his brain.

Let us not speculate to what extent Snegirev wrote this as a doctor and to what extent he simply wanted to comfort poor S.A. One thing is apparent: on the night of the flight and on the day before it, Tolstoy had been mentally and physically weak. This is confirmed by both Makovitsky's notes and L.N.'s diary. He had dreamed some "awful", confused dreams... In one of them, some kind of "struggle with his wife" had taken place, and in another, characters from Dostoyevsky's novel *The Brothers Karamazov*, which he was reading at the time, were mixed together with people who were real but had already passed away, such as N.N. Strahov.

Less than a month before his departure, he had come very close to dying. What happened on October 3 looked very much like the real end, right down to deathly seizures and sweeping hand movements that are sometimes observed immediately prior to death. This is how Tolstoy's last secretary, Valentin Bulgakov, describes this episode:

"Lev Nikolayevich overslept, and, having waited for him until seven o'clock, we sat down to dinner without him. After serving the soup, Sofia Andreyevna got up and went yet again to listen out to see whether or not Lev Nikolayevich was getting up. When she came back, she announced that at the very moment when she had gone up to the bedroom door, she had heard the striking of a match against a match box. She had gone in to see Lev Nikolayevich. He was sitting on the bed. He asked what time it was and whether they were having dinner. But it seemed to Sofia Andreyevna that something was wrong: Lev Nikolayevich's eyes seemed strange to her:

"His eyes had a nonsensical look in them... – That's what happens before his seizures. He lapses into semi-consciousness. I know what it's like. His eyes are always like that before an attack." Soon Tolstoy's son, Sergei Lvovich, the servant Ilya Vasiliyevich, Makovitsky, Bulgakov and Tolstoy's first biographer, P.I. Biryukov, had gathered in Tolstoy's room.

"Lying on his back, with the fingers of his right hand squeezed together as though he was holding a pen in them, Lev Nikolayevich began to run his hand over the blanket weakly. His eyes were closed, his brows were furrowed and his lips quivered, he was definitely experiencing something... Then... then the strange attacks of seizures began, one after another, causing his whole body, which lay helpless on the bed, to shake and tremble. He thrashed out violently with his feet. It was difficult to hold them down. Dushan (Makovitsky - P.B.) held Lev Nikolayevich by the shoulders, whilst Biryukov and I rubbed his legs. There were five attacks in all. The fourth was particularly powerful, when Lev Nikolayevich's body was thrown almost right across the bed, his head rolling off the pillow and his legs dangling on the other side.

Sofia Andreyevna threw herself to her knees, embraced those legs and pressed her head against them and stayed for a long time in that position, until we had positioned Lev Nikolayevich correctly on the bed again.

In general, Sofia Andreyevna made a horribly pitiful impression. She raised her eyes, hurriedly crossed herself with little crosses and whispered "Lord, don't let it be this time, don't let it be this time!..." And she didn't do this in front of the others: when I happened to go into the "Remington room" [in which the typewriter was housed], I found her uttering this prayer."After the seizure, L.N. became delirious, just as would later occur at Astapovo before his death, uttering a meaningless series of numbers:

"Four, sixty, thirty-seven, thirty-eight, thirty-nine..."

"S.A.'s behavior at the time of this attack was touching," Biryukov recalled. "She was pitiful in her fear and humiliation. Whilst we, the men, were holding L.N. down, so that the seizures wouldn't throw him from his bed, she threw herself to her knees at his bedside and prayed a passionate prayer, along the lines of: "Lord, save me, forgive me, Lord, don't allow him to die, I drove him to this, don't let it be this time, don't take him from me, Lord."S.A. also admitted in her diary that she felt guilty during the attack suffered by L.N.:

"When, as I embraced my husband's twitching legs, I felt that extreme despair at the thought of losing him, – remorse, pangs of conscience, a mad love and a prayer took hold of my entire being with incredible force. I would do anything, anything for him – just as long as he stayed alive on this occasion at least and recovered, so that in my soul there would be no more pangs of conscience for all the disquiet and worry I had caused him through my nervousness and painful anxieties." Not long before this she had had a horrible falling out with Sasha and Feokritova and effectively chased her daughter out of the house. Sasha went to stay in Telyatniki, not far from Yasnaya Polyana, in her own home. Tolstoy took this separation with Sasha, whom he loved and whom he trusted more than all his other relatives, badly. She was his invaluable assistant and just as good a secretary as Bulgakov. The rift between mother and daughter was one of the things that brought on the attack. They both realized this and patched things up the following day.

From Sasha's memoirs:

"When I went downstairs to the foyer, I found out that my mother was looking for me.

- Where is she?
- On the porch.

I go outside, mother is standing there wearing a dress.

- You wanted to talk to me?
- Yes, I wanted to take another step toward making up with you. Forgive me!

And she starting kissing me, saying over and over: forgive me, forgive me! I kissed her too and asked her to calm down...

We talked, whilst standing there outside. Some passerby looked at us in surprise. I asked mother to come inside the house."

It makes one wonder: isn't the theory that Tolstoy left in order to die, not only baseless, but also a very cruel myth? Why don't we look at the matter from a different perspective, the way L.N. saw it. He left, so as *not* to die. Or at least, if he were to die, then it would not be as a result of yet another attack of convulsions.

The fear that S.A. might catch up with him was not only a moral fear but also a very real, physical fear. This fear passed the further Tolstoy got from Yasnaya, although the voice of reason wasn't silenced in him.

When he and Makovitsky finally left the estate and the village and drove out onto the highway, L.N., as the doctor writes, "who up until then had been silent, melancholy and anxious, said, in a stilted voice, as if lamenting the situation and apologizing, that he had not been able to bear it any longer, and that he was leaving Sofia Andreyevna without telling her." And immediately after this he asked:

Where can we go, to get as far away as possible?

Once they were sitting in a separate compartment in the second-class car "and the train pulled out, he probably felt confident that Sofia Andreyevna was not going to catch up with him; he said happily that he was in good spirits." Once he had warmed up and drunk some coffee, however, he suddenly said:

What's going to become of Sofia Andreyevna now? I feel sorry for her.

This question was to torture him until the last conscious moment of his life. And for those who have some idea of Tolstoy's moral views in his later life, it will be very clear that for him there could be no justification for his departure. The morally correct thing to do, from his point of view, would have been to bear his cross until the end, whereas to leave was to free himself from this cross. All the talk about how Tolstoy left so as to die, so as to become one with the people, so as to free his eternal soul, holds true as far as his dream of twenty-five years is concerned, but not for specific moral practices. These practices left no room to pursue a selfish dream at the expense of real people.

This tormented him all the way from Yasnaya to Shamordino, when it would still have been possible to change his mind and go back. Yet not only did he not change his mind and not go back; he fled further and further, urging on his travelling companions. This behavior on his part was the biggest mystery of all.

We find a solution of sorts to it in three letters written by Tolstoy to his wife at the time of his departure. In the first of them, a "farewell" letter, he stresses the moral and spiritual reasons: "… I can't live any more in the luxury in which I lived, and am doing what old men of my age usually do: leaving the hustle and bustle of life behind, to live out the last days of my life in quiet solitude." This explanation was given as a way of taking pity on his wife. In the same letter he writes: "I thank you for your honest forty-eight years of life with me and I ask that you forgive me for everything of which I was guilty before you, just as I forgive you, with all my soul, for everything in which you may have been guilty before me." In addition to the fact that this letter is touching on a personal level, every word in it had been carefully weighed, on the off-chance that it might be discovered. Tolstoy wrote two draft versions of it the day before he left it – and with good reason. This letter was a sort of "safe conduct" for his wife. It was something that she could have no qualms about showing to reporters (and show it she did). Its meaning, roughly speaking, was this: Tolstoy had departed not from his wife, but from Yasnaya Polyana. He could no longer live in such lordly conditions, which did not chime with his worldview.

It's possible that Tolstoy believed S.A. would be satisfied with this explanation, and would not try to pursue him or doing anything crazy. But on learning that she had tried to drown herself in a pond in the Yasnaya Polyana Park, and on receiving her letter of reply, containing the words: "Levochka, my darling, come back home, save me from a repeated attempt at suicide," he realized that the threats on her part were continuing. And it was then that he decided to have it out with her directly, and express what he had omitted from his letter of farewell.

He didn't send the first version of the second letter, written in Shamordino. It was too harsh. "A meeting between us can only, as I wrote to you, can only worsen our situation: your – as everyone says, and as I think too, as far as I am concerned, for me such a meeting, let alone a return to Yasnaya, is completely impossible and would be tantamount to suicide".

There was a softer tone in the letter that he *did* send: "Your letter – I know that it is written with sincerity, but you have no power to do what you would wish. And it isn't about fulfilling any of my desires and requirements, but solely about your balanced, calm, reasonable approach to life. And until this is not present, for me, life with you is inconceivable. To return to you when you are in such a state, for me, would be to give up on life. And that is something I do not consider myself entitled to do. Farewell, dear Sonia, may God help you. Life isn't a joke, and we have no right to throw it away through our own will, and to measure it in terms of time is also unwise. It may be that those months that we have left to live are more important than all the years we have already lived through, and we must live them well."

Did he leave so as to die? Yes, if by this we are to understand his fear of an absurd, unconscious death, a death which, if he were to resign himself to it, would be tantamount to suicide as far as he saw it.

Tolstoy fled from such a death. He wanted to die with a clear mind. And this, for him, was more important than rejecting lordly living conditions or becoming one with the people.

When Sasha asked him in Shamordino whether he regretted that he had acted in that way in relation to her mother, he answered her question with a question of his own: "How can someone regret something if he could not act otherwise?"

He gave a more precise explanation of his act to his sister, a nun at the Shamordino monastery, in a conversation which was heard by her daughter,

Tolstoy's niece, and, oddly enough, also his daughter-in-law, Elizaveta Valeryanovna Obolenskaya (L.N.'s daughter Masha was married to E.V. Obolenskaya's son, Nicholas Leonidovich Obolensky). E.V. Obolenskaya left some extremely interesting memoirs about her mother, and one of the most important parts of them is dedicated to L.N.'s meeting with Maria Nikolayevna in her convent cell on October 29th, 1910.

"One could see just by looking at him to what extent this man was exhausted both physically and mentally ... telling us about his latest attack, he said:

"Another one like that and it will be the end; death is pleasant at such a time, because one is in a completely unconscious condition. But I should like to die whilst fully conscious.

And he started crying ... Mother expressed the idea that the Countess was sick; after thinking about it a little, he said:

"Yes, yes, of course, but what was I to do? One would have had to use force, and I couldn't do that, so I left; and now I want to make use of this fact to start a new life."

One must be extremely cautious and critical about words attributed to Tolstoy in the memoirs and diaries of other people. And we must be particularly critical when such people were close to him, and had an interest. It is only by comparing different documents that one can find the "point of intersection" and accept that the truth must lie here. Yet for all this, it must be remembered that Tolstoy himself didn't know this truth either. Here's an entry in his diary from October 29th, made after a conversation with Maria Nikolayevna:

"... I kept thinking about a way out of my situation and her (Sophia Andreyevna. – P.B.) situation and couldn't think one up at all, and yet, whether you like it or not, there will be a way out, and it won't be the one you expect."

Becoming one with the people

From the earliest days of Tolstoy's departure, the newspapers began to put forward their version of events, among which was this one: Tolstoy had left in order to become one with the people. In a word, it was described as follows: adoption of the *"simple life"*.

This theory was the one that prevailed in the Soviet era. It was the one instilled into schoolchildren. Tolstoy had rebelled against the social conditions in which he, and all of the nobility, lived. However, not having the Marxist world outlook, he had acted as an anarchist-populist: he had literally gone out to the people.

The fact that this hypothesis was adopted by the Communist ideology, which worshiped the hero of V.I. Lenin's article "Lev Tolstoy as a mirror of the Russian Revolution", does not necessarily mean that it is inaccurate. In any case, there is far more truth in it than in any of the romantic myths, like the one which claimed that Tolstoy had fled in order to meet death head-on. The desire to become one with the people, to be indistinguishable in their midst, genuinely was a cherished dream for Tolstoy. How happy he was during his walks along the Kiev high road, which ran alongside Yasnaya Polyana, and ceased to be a count, dissolving into a crowd of pilgrims who took him to be an ordinary old peasant. How many precious minutes and hours he spent in conversation with the peasants of Yasnaya, Kochety, Pirogov, Nikolayevsk, and other places where he happened to spend some time, and where he considered it his primary duty to speak with the local elders.

In the 20th century it became the norm among the intelligentsia, unfortunately, to snigger at Tolstoy's adoption of the "simple life". The following joke was repeated *ad nauseam*: "Your Lordship, the plow has been brought to the front door! Do you wish to go for a plow?" In reality, participation in peasant labor (plowing, haymaking, harvesting), in which he tried, with some success, to instruct his children as well (his daughters showed a particular aptitude for them), had a deep meaning for Tolstoy. It was part of a very complex package of self-education, without which the phenomenon that was the later Tolstoy would never have existed. In this image of the great sage and brilliant artist, humbly walking in peasant clothes behind a plow, there is something extremely important in terms of understanding the essence of being human, no less important than the image of the pyramids of Egypt or the sight of a simple village cemetery. It is no coincidence that this image doesn't require a "translation", it is clear to each and every national culture, because what it expresses is not some whim on the part of a Russian noble, but the way man is bound to the earth and a literal embodiment of the Biblical truth: "by the sweat of thy brow, thou shalt eat bread." "... A writer of great purity and holiness - lives among us ..." Alexander Blok had written in his article, "The Sun over Russia", on the occasion of Tolstoy's eightieth birthday. "The thought often occurs to me: nothing is so very important, everything is still simple and not terrible, relatively speaking, whilst Lev Nikolayevich still lives. After all, a genius, merely by being alive, seems to suggest that there are some firm foundations, some granite pillars: it's as though he holds his country and his people on his shoulders and feeds and nourishes them with his joy... Whilst Tolstoy is alive, and walks in the furrow behind the plow, behind his white horse, the morning is still dewy, fresh, not horrible, the ghouls are asleep, and thank God for that. Tolstoy is up and on the move – and it's as if the sun itself is on the move. Yet if the sun should set, if Tolstoy should die, if the last genius were to leave us, what then?" These words were written two years before Tolstoy's departure and death, but there is already a foretaste of these things within them. Sunset – departure – death – this was how Blok envisioned the end of Tolstoy's life. He could not have known that both the departure and death would occur at night, when the "ghouls" are *not* "asleep". Yet it is typical that, as he thinks about the death of Tolstoy, Blok could not picture him in any way other than as he appears in Repin's painting "Tolstoy behind the plow".

Blok would have had even less chance of knowing that initially, Tolstoy didn't plan to head in an unknown direction at all. In its first guise, his departure had a very specific destination. This destination was a peasant hut...

On the night of October 20-21, an acquaintance of L.N., Mikhail Petrovich Novikov, a peasant from the Tula Region, visited Yasnaya Polyana. The two met had met in 1895 in Moscow, when the twenty-six year-old Novikov had been working as a clerk at the military headquarters. His journey from revolutionary pursuits to an enthusiasm for Tolstoy's ideas was, on the whole, a fairly well-trodden one at that time. But Tolstoy took note of, and wrote an entry in his diary about this visit by a young man who was passionate, sincere and devil-may-care. He brought Tolstoy secret papers from the Military Headquarters about the shooting of workers at the Korzinkin factory in Yaroslavl. Tolstoy urged him to put the case files back where they belonged. Novikov was nonetheless arrested a month later, though not for stealing secret documents, but for the same reason for which Solzhenitsyn was to be arrested exactly half a century later: for discussing too brazenly, in private correspondence, the person of the head of state, who, at the time, was the Emperor Nicholas II. In later life, the peasant Novikov tilled the soil on a lean patch of land, wrote prose and articles, and met several times with Tolstoy. After the revolution, he sent bold letters to Stalin and Gorky about the difficult plight of the peasantry, was arrested again and was executed in 1937. For all his desperate courage, he was a surprisingly sensible peasant, sober and extremely hard-working, one of those who managed to turn Stolypin's agrarian reforms to his advantage, increase the size of his allotted patch of land and feed his family through his own labor.

It was on this man, specifically, that Tolstoy decided to rely. After visiting Tolstoy on October 20 and talking with him (in their conversation Novikov expressed regret that Tolstoy didn't call at his house, in turn), the peasant asked permission to stay the night because he was afraid he might bump into some drunk vagrants on the road. He was given Makovitsky's room. He had gone to bed, when suddenly L.N. came in. At first Novikov took Tolstoy for a ghost, "so light and soundless were his movements". He was struck by Tolstoy's appearance during this visit to Yasnaya Polyana: "... it was so bad that I wondered to myself, how can a person live, think and move around, when they are so exhausted and dried up?" Tolstoy sat on the edge of the bed and began a conversation with Novikov, which Mikhail Petrovich recounted in his memoirs, recently republished. To the uninitiated reader it may seem strange, but let's not forget that L.N. was trying to talk to the peasant in his own language, as he always did during conversations with the peasants and as he even spoke to Gorky when the two first met in Khamovniki, thinking that Gorky was a "real man of the people".

"Of course," said L.N., "if, when I was still young, I had yelled at my wife even once, and stamped all over her, she probably would have submitted just as your wives submit, but I, in my weakness, couldn't bear family rows, and whenever they started, I always thought that I alone was to blame, that I had no right to make someone who loved me suffer, and I always gave in.

"Whenever he spoke to me," Novikov recalled, referring to his repeated visits to Yasnaya Polyana, "he told me how painful it was for him to live at the manor house, where he was considered a parasite, a sponger, because he wasn't providing income to his family through his own labors." It hardly needs saying that no-one in Tolstoy's family considered him either a "sponger" or a "parasite". To do so would have been absurd; to say nothing of the fact that, although he had refused to accept the rights to his works, he had left Sofia Andreyevna the power of attorney to publish those of his works written before 1881 ("Childhood", "Boyhood", "Youth", "Sevastopol Sketches", "War and Peace" and "Anna Karenina" and, essentially, all the best material that Tolstoy ever wrote as an artist), and this brought the family real income. Yet Novikov could hardly have made up these words. The most likely explanation is that L.N. was playing the role of someone with a peasant's mentality, in order to explain, in rough and ready terms, the reason for his departure from the estate to a peasant who was working until his strength failed him on a worthless plot of land.

"I'm boiling in this house, as if I were in hell," he complained, yet people envy me, and say that I live like a lord, and no-one sees or understands how much I'm suffering here."

That night, Tolstoy outlined his plan to Novikov.

"I will not die in this house. I have decided to go to an unfamiliar place, where the people won't know who I am. It may be that I'll come and die in your hut. Only I know in advance that you'll start scolding me, because nobody likes strangers anywhere. I have seen as much in your peasant families, but I have become so helpless and useless... I'll merely get in your way and grumble as old men do."

"It took a lot of effort for me not to burst into tears on hearing these words..." recalled Novikov. "I was embarrassed that I had sort of forced him to confess in front of me, and at the same time glad that he, as a man, forgetting the differences between us, hadn't hidden from me his weaknesses and the sorrows of his soul, for which I had always loved him and had grown spiritually attached to him... Dear, kindly grandfather, could I ever have imagined at that moment that you were living out your last days in that house, and in this life? ..."

Even if we allow that Novikov quoted L.N. relatively accurately, it's impossible not to suspect an underlying irony in them (a poor wanderer, whom the peasantry were going to scold) and, again, an innocent game of playing the simple "peasant". It is significant that when L.N. recounted his conversation with Novikov to his daughter Sasha, he was chuckling a little.

"When I came to see him to collect the letters to the hall, he took me into the study, smiling happily and a little slyly, and then into the bedroom.

"Come on, let's go, I'll tell you a big secret! A very big secret!

I followed him and as I looked at him, I began to feel better.

'So this is what I came up with. I told Novikov a little about our situation and about how hard things are for me here. I'll go to his place. They won't find me there. You know, Novikov told me that his brother's wife was an alcoholic, and that if she starts to get really out of hand, his brother walks up and down her back, and she gets better. It helps.' And father laughed good-naturedly ... I had a good laugh, too, and told father that once, the coachman Ivan had been taking Olga somewhere (L.N.'s daughter-in-law, the first wife of his son Andrei - PB), and she asked him what sort of things went on at Yasnaya. He replied that things were bad, and then turned to her and said:

"Well what of it, your Highness, forgive me if I tell you. At our place we do things in the country-style, if a woman plays the fool, her husband takes a set of reins to her! It works an absolute treat!"

Obviously, one mustn't take this seriously. But the atmosphere in the Yasnaya Polyana household was such that "jokes" like this had become possible.

LN wrote matter-of-factly in his diary about the meeting with Novikov: "Mikhail Novikov arrived. I talked to him a great deal. A seriously smart fellow."

For some time, Tolstoy had been afraid to write the whole truth in his diary, knowing that S.A., who had got hold of the keys to his desk, would read his daily entries. He even started a special small notebook, in which he began to keep what he called a "Diary for myself alone", which he hid in the toe of his boot. On September 24, he writes: "I lost the little diary." He hadn't misplaced it, as it turned out. His wife had found it in the boot and taken it to her room. According to her later account, she had accidentally dropped some bed linen on the boot and lo and behold... But in this case it is neither here nor there. What is important is that the atmosphere in the Tolstoy house was such that it astonished the servants and peasants of Yasnaya Polyana, and L.N., in the conversations he had, had to somehow find ways to get out of awkward situations, including through the use of such "jokes".

His decision to go to Novikov's place turned out to be far from a joke, however. On October 24, he sends a letter:

"Mikhail Petrovich,

With regard to what I said to you before your departure, I am appealing to you once again with the following request: if it were really to happen that I were to come to your house, would you be so good as to find a hut for me, in your village – I don't mind how small it is, as long as it is isolated and warm, so that I would be inconveniencing you and your family for only the shortest possible amount of time. In addition I would like to tell you that if were to telegraph you, I would sign the telegraph not with my name but with the name T. Nikolayev.

I will look forward to receiving an answer from you, and I extend a warm hand-shake to you.

Lev Tolstoy.

Keep in mind that all this must remain known to you alone."

There certainly isn't much joking going on here! The secret code that Sasha, Tolstoy and Chertkov were to use during L.N.'s flight from Yasnaya Polyana to deceive S.A. and newsmen makes its first appearance in this letter. The great Tolstoy, who despised pseudonyms and had never been afraid to sign bold letters to the Tsars, to Stolypin or to Pobedonostsev with his own name, is hiding behind the shadow of a certain T. Nikolayev.

On receiving the letter, Novikov was at a loss as to what to do. It was one thing to pour out their hearts to one another, man-to-man, in the comfort of the Yasnaya Polyana house, and quite another to take on the responsibility before the whole world for having hidden Tolstoy as a fugitive.

"I can't forgive myself for the slowness," Novikov wrote in his memoirs, "which I allowed myself in replying to his letter, which, as it turned out later, Lev Nikolayevich had spent two days waiting for, and only after that, having decided that it is impossible for him to come to me, that I wasn't answering, headed south, to some acquaintances who lived there, and he only received my response when he was already ill at the Astapovo station. Who knows, perhaps through this his life could have been prolonged for a few more years, since the two-hour journey to our station from Yasnaya

Polyana would not have hurt him, all the more so given that the hut he was requesting, which was warm and clean, stood empty, exactly as if it was just waiting for someone to come and live in it. And there was a small, cozy room in my hut, too, where he could have taken shelter for a while without anyone noticing.

I will never forgive myself for this oversight!"

It was in vain that Novikov blamed himself. Tolstoy was no needle, and the Tula village was no haystack. With his world-famous appearance, and the network of reporters that existed at the time, along with both state investigators and private ones, L.N. was destined to be found very quickly.

What is curious is something else entirely. This hut itself, the "warm and clean" one, appeared in Novikov's memoirs later, after Tolstoy's death. In his letter of reply, not only was there no mention of any hut, but the letter itself was, essentially, a form of polite refusal. Therefore, even if this letter had not been delayed, and Tolstoy had received it not when he was terminally ill at Astapovo, but whilst he was still at Yasnaya Polyana, it wouldn't have changed anything. Tolstoy had nowhere to run, and Novikov had tried to explain as much to him.

"Dear Lev Nikolayevich, I received your letter and am very touched by your closeness and sincerity toward me. I couldn't answer immediately, so as not to act rashly. I have always been frank with you and said what was in my heart, and now have decided to tell you only what is in my soul concerning the request you made in the letter, without thinking about whether it will please you or not. That time when you ought, both for the benefit of the situation, and because of the force of the consciousness awakening within you, to have changed your outward conditions of life – has now passed, and now there would be no sense in changing them for any lasting period of time... As much as I'd like to see you conversing in freedom with all the ordinary people, nonetheless for the sake of preserving your life in such an old body, for the communication with you that everyone holds dear – I cannot have any serious desire to see this. My only wish is that what remains of your life here is not inhibited by external conditions for dialogue with those who love you, but for such temporary visits to see your friends for a day, a week, two weeks, or a month, my hut would be very uncomfortable. There is a bright little room in it that all my family will gladly give up for you, and they will serve you lovingly, all the more so given that I don't have any very young children who might make noise at the wrong time. The youngest is 5 years old. This is what I think, but if you think otherwise, let things be not as I wish them to be, but as you wish them to be, and in this case my little room will be yours for as long as you want. And particularly from April to October, you can live at my place without us getting in one another's way at all. We are not afraid that you will get in our way, but of the reverse...

With love from the peasant Mikhail Novikov."

In the post script there was a clarification concerning the separate hut.

"I think it would be impossible for you to live in a separate hut because of your weakness. Moreover peasants don't usually have completely separate huts. Usually there are cold second huts, which, although they can easily be adapted so that they are suitable for living in, by carrying out some repairs to them, they are nonetheless not separate, but will be accessed through a passage. My neighbor has just such a hut, measuring fourteen feet, and he wouldn't say no to the idea of giving it to you as an apartment. Or alternatively an elderly aunt of mine plans to have just such a fourteen-foot hut built next spring; she is lonely, and being an intelligent old woman, would also be glad to take you in and serve you."

It is clear that Tolstoy, with his extreme independence and at the same time delicacy, would not agree to these terms. And Novikov knew this, too... Just as he also knew that for a sick old man to change his place of residence in late autumn was madness, plain and simple! The thing to do was to wait until spring.

But Tolstoy could not wait.

It was not until November 3 that Novikov's letter was read out to Tolstoy in Astapovo by Chertkov, who had recently arrived there. L.N. listened attentively and asked him to write on the envelope: "Thank you. I went in completely the opposite direction."

"That Melancholy Road, the Railroad ..."

They travelled from Shchekino to Gorbachevo in a private compartment in a 2nd class car. They had now left behind them the estate and the village of Yasnaya Polyana, through which a surprising cortege had travelled two hours before. In a carriage drawn by a pair of horses had sat the aged count, in a quilted jacket and armyak, wearing two hats (his head was very sensitive to the cold); alongside him was the doctor, Dushan Petrovich, unflappable, with an unchanging expression on his face, in a shabby brown sheepskin coat and a yellow felt hat; in front, on a third horse, rode the groom Filya holding a burning torch (in Sasha's account) or a lantern (in Makovitsky's account). People who live in the countryside tend to be early risers: lights had already come on in the windows of some of the huts, and stoves were already being warmed up. At the upper end of the village the reins came loose. Makovitsky came down out of the cab to try to find the end of the rein, and at the same time checked to make sure that L.N.'s legs were covered. Tolstoy was in such a hurry that he began to shout at Makovitsky. At this, some of the villagers from the surrounding houses came out to see what was going on. A silent scene took place.

When Makovitsky bought the tickets in Shchekino, he initially wanted to name a different station as his destination, rather than Gorbachevo, in an effort to throw anyone chasing them off the scent. He realized, however, that lying would not only be wrong, but also pointless.

In Astapovo S.A. would later interrogate Makovitsky:

- Where were you planning to go?
- Far away.
- Well, where?
- First, to Rostov-on-Don; we wanted to get hold of foreign passports when we got there.
- Well, and after that?
- To Odessa.
- After that?
- To Constantinople.
- And then where?
- To Bulgaria.
- Do you have any money with you?
- There's enough money.
- Well, how much?
- ...

This conversation was put down on paper by A.P. Semenovsky, a senior doctor at the district hospital, who was summoned by telegram on November 1 to Astapovo from the nearby district town of Dankovo. He also wrote in his memoirs about a fascinating private conversation he had with Makovitsky, in which the doctor admitted that each time he had asked for the tickets at the stations, instead of paying for them, he had allegedly told the people at the ticket window that he was getting the tickets for Tolstoy. "We'll work out how much we owe later." And they had given him the tickets.

Tolstoy's skills as a conspirator left a lot to be desired. In Shchekino, walking into the station building ahead of Makovitsky, he immediately asked the bartender: is there a direct link to Kozelsk in Gorbachevo? He then asked the same thing of the station's duty officer. (The next day, S.A. already knew from the ticket office staff roughly in which direction her husband was headed.) While Makovitsky repacked their things, sending back anything they didn't need, he was wandering around 400 paces away with a boy who was on his way to school. The train pulled into the station.

"Let's travel with the boy," said Tolstoy.

On the train L.N. calmed down, took a nap for an hour and a half, then asked Makovitsky to get hold of a copy of "The Circle of Reading" or "For Every Day", collections of wise thoughts which he compiled. As it transpired, there were no copies on sale.

One of the most bitter aspects of Tolstoy's last journey was the fact that his long-standing habits were constantly coming into conflict with the new, unusual conditions in which the old man now found himself. One would have thought he needed so little, to such an extent had he simplified his life at Yasnaya Polyana ... And yet, lo and behold, it was the small, trifling things that seemed to be lacking all the time...

In this context, Sofia Andreyevna's exclamation about her husband's flight doesn't seem quite so absurd:

"Poor Levochka! Who on earth is going to give him his butter!"

And it is very touching that, when she set off to see her husband in Astapovo, S.A. didn't forget to bring with her a pillow, sewn by her own hand, on which L.N. was accustomed to sleeping. He recognized this pillow. But this was later.

Beginning with the loss of his hat in the garden, small, annoying frustrations troubled the fugitive from Yasnaya Polyana constantly, and all this placed a heavy burden on Makovitsky in the initial stages.

L.N. was determined to travel in the 3rd class car, with the common people, from Gorbachevo to Kozelsk. Once he had sat down in the car on a wooden bench, he said:

"How wonderful and free this is!"

But Makovitsky was the first to express some alarm. The "Sukhinichi-Kozelsk" train was a commercial one, a mixed train, with one 3rd class carriage, overcrowded and full of smoke. Due to how crowded it was, the passengers moved into the heated freight cars. Without waiting for the departure of the train and saying nothing to L.N., Makovitsky hurried to the station master to demand that he attach an additional car. The station master sent him to see another official, the second official pointed to the attendant on duty. At that moment the attendant on duty was in the car, staring at Tolstoy, whom the passengers had already recognized. He would have been happy to help, but it turned out that he was not the duty officer responsible for the cars. The "right" duty officer was also standing there, staring at Tolstoy. Makovitsky repeated his request.

"He said to a railway worker, somehow reluctantly and hesitantly (through gritted teeth), that the worker should pass on an order to the chief conductor to attach another third-class carriage," writes Makovitsky. "Six minutes later a locomotive brought the car past our train. The chief conductor, after coming in to inspect the tickets, announced to the public that another car was going to be hooked up and that there would be room for everyone, for at that point a lot of people were standing up in the train or on the gangways. But then the second bell was heard, followed by the third half a minute later, and they didn't hitch the car. I ran over to the official on duty. He replied that they didn't have a free car. The train started moving. I found out from the conductor that the car which had been brought over for hitching was needed in order to transport the station's schoolchildren."

"Our car was the worst and most cramped in which I have ever had to travel in Russia," Makovitsky recalled. "The entrance was not positioned in symmetry with the direction of travel. Anyone entering it whilst the train was starting to move risked hitting their face on the corner of the raised back, which was directly opposite the middle of the door; you had to walk around it. The compartments in the car were narrow, there was little room between the benches, and there wasn't enough room for the luggage either. Stuffy."

Makovitsky offered L.N a blanket to sit on. Tolstoy refused. "On this trip he was particularly reluctant to accept any of the services which he previously used."

Soon he began to suffocate due to the lack of air and the smoke, because half the passengers were smoking. After putting on a fur coat and hat, and deep winter galoshes, he went out onto the rear gangway. But there were smokers there, too. Then he moved to the front gangway, where the wind was blowing into his face, but there no one was smoking and the only people there were a woman and her child and some peasant..."

Makovitsky was later to describe the three quarters of an hour that L.N. spent on the gangway as "fatal". It was enough time for him to catch a cold.

After returning to the car, Tolstoy, as he was in the habit of doing, quickly began to get to know the other people; he chatted to a fifty year-old peasant – about his family, the housekeeping, carting, smashing bricks. L.N. was interested in every last detail. "Ein typischer Bauer" ("A typical peasant") - he said to Makovitsky in German.

The man turned out to be very talkative. He talked boldly about the vodka trade, complained about a landlord named B., with whom the community had refused to share the forest, on account of which authorities conducted a "flogging" in the village. A surveyor who was sitting nearby cut in to speak up for B. and began to blame the peasants for everything. The peasant refused to back down.

"We work more than you peasants do," said the surveyor.

"You can't compare the two things," objected Tolstoy.

The peasant assented, the surveyor argued back. It didn't bother him at all that he was arguing with Tolstoy himself. "I knew your brother, Sergei Nikolayevich," said the surveyor. According to Makovitsky, "he was ready to argue endlessly, and not in order to arrive at the truth in the conversation," but to prove his case at any cost. The argument spilled over onto wider issues: from Henry George's 'Single-tax' system, to Darwin, science and education. Tolstoy grew excited; he got to his feet and spoke for over an hour. The other passengers began to crowd in more tightly from both ends of the car: peasants, tradesmen, laborers, intellectuals. "Two Jews," noted Makovitsky, who had harbored an intense dislike of Jews ever since his youth in Austria-Hungary. A schoolgirl was noting down what L.N. said, then she stopped and began arguing with him herself...

"Man is already capable of flight!" she said.

"Leave it to the birds to fly," Tolstoy replied; "people ought to move around on the ground."

As it turned out, T. Tamanskaya, a graduate of the Belovo Gymnasium, was the only witness of Tolstoy's journey to Kozelsk who left a written record of it, which was published in the newspaper "The Voice of Moscow." She wrote that Tolstoy was "... dressed in a black shirt that reached almost to his knees, and high boots. On his head, instead of a round woolen hat, he wore a black silk skull cap."

Makovitsky, who idolized Tolstoy and was seriously concerned about his condition by this time, was unhappy with this familiarity in the way the people spoke to L.N. When Tolstoy dropped his mitten and lit his lantern so that he could find it on the floor, the schoolgirl did not miss her chance to point out:

"You see, Lev Nikolayevich, science came in handy that time!"

When Tolstoy, exhausted by the dispute and the tobacco smoke, once again went out onto the gangway to get some fresh air, the surveyor and the schoolgirl followed him "with fresh objections." When she got off the train at Belevo, the girl asked for an autograph. He wrote: "*Lev Tolstoy*".

The peasant heard L.N. say that he was planning to go to the Shamordino monastery, and that before doing so he wished to visit the Optina Pustyn.

"Well, father, you ought to settle on the monastery, the peasant advised him. "You ought to give up worldly matters, and save your soul. You ought to stay in the monastery."

"L.N. gave a kindly smile by way of reply."

At the end of the car someone began playing a harmonica and singing was heard. Tolstoy listened with pleasure and praised the musicians.

The train was traveling slowly: they covered one hundred and some miles in almost 6 and a half hours. Eventually L.N. grew "tired of sitting". "This slow ride on the Russian railways helped kill L.N." wrote Makovitsky.

About 5 o'clock in the evening they arrived in Kozelsk.

Ahead were Optina Pustyn and Shamordino. At this time, Tolstoy still didn't know what had happened at the estate after his night-time flight. S.A. had twice attempted suicide. The first time around, she had been pulled out of the pond, and on the second - they had stopped her as she ran down the path toward it. After that she struck herself on the chest with a heavy paperweight and a hammer, and shouted: "Break to pieces, my heart!" She cut herself with knives, scissors and safety pins. When these were taken off her, she threatened to throw herself out the window or drown herself in the well. Meanwhile she sent someone to the station to find out which destination they had bought tickets to. On learning that L.N. and Makovitsky had gone to Gorbachevo, she ordered a servant to send a telegram there, though not with her signature attached to it: "Come back at once. Sasha." The servant told Sasha about this, and she sent a neutralizing telegram of her own: "Don't worry, only telegrams signed Alexandra are genuine."

Mother had tried to outwit daughter, and daughter – mother.

"I'll find him!" shouted S.A. "How can you watch over me? I'll jump out of the window and go to the station. What will you do to me? If only I knew where he was! Oh, then I'd never let him go, I'd watch over him night and day, and sleep outside his door!"

A telegram was received on the evening of October 28 in Chertkov's name: "We'll spend the night in Optina. Tomorrow Shamordino. Address Podborki. In good health. T. Nikolayev."

Chapter 2

Paradise Lost

They arrived in Kozelsk on October 28 at 4.50 pm. L.N. got out of the train car first. While Makovitsky and the porter were carrying their things to the waiting room, Tolstoy disappeared, but soon returned and said that he had hired two coach drivers to take them to Optina Pustyn. He took the basket of provisions and led Makovitsky and the porter to the coaches. The coachman in the carriage in which Tolstoy travelled with the doctor was a man named Fyodor Novikov, by coincidence the namesake of the peasant to whose house LN had originally wanted to go. Soon Novikov was to give interviews to newspapers – something he had never done before. He had this to say about his passenger:

"I don't have any distinct knowledge about him, but I sense that his heart is not like everyone else's. I wanted to detach the hood of the carriage, but he didn't let me, he said, Fyodor, I'll do it, I have a pair of hands you know. He doesn't go to church, but goes around to the monasteries."

The luggage was transported in the second coach. On the way Novikov asked the master for permission to smoke. (Incidentally, at first he took Makovitsky to be the master; he took Tolstoy to be an old peasant.) Tolstoy allowed him to do so, but asked him how much money he spent on tobacco and vodka. It turned out that with his average annual expenditure on tobacco you could buy half a horse, and with the amount he spent on vodka – two whole ones. "That's how bad it is!" Tolstoy sighed. "Yeah, it's not good", the peasant agreed.

On the ferry across the Zhizdra, on which Optina is located, he got talking to the ferryman-monk and commented to Makovitsky that the ferryman was from among the peasantry. L.N. asked the monk Mikhail, whose hair and beard were ginger, almost red, and who served at the monastery hotel, "Are you able to put Count Tolstoy, who's been excommunicated from the church, up for the night?" The Monk Mikhail was greatly astonished and took the visitors to the best room – a spacious one, containing two beds and a wide sofa.

"How nice it is here!" Tolstoy exclaimed.

Made to feel at home

"I boil as though I'm in hell in that house," Tolstoy had complained to the peasant Mikhail Novikov before he left Yasnaya Polyana.

And these words had been spoken about the house in which he had spent the majority, and without question the better part, of his life; the house which was located on the estate where he himself had been born, as had all his brothers and sisters, most of his children and some of his grandchildren; the house where *The Cossacks*, *War and Peace*, *Anna Karenina*, *The Kreutzer Sonata*, *The Power of Darkness*, and most of his classic works, and more than 200 works in total, had been written; the house from whence even the patriarchal Moscow, not to mention St Petersburg, seemed to him to be a vain and noisy hell.

After all, his departure from Yasnaya Polyana was, in fact, an escape from Russia! "Without my Yasnaya Polyana," wrote Lev Tolstoy, "I can scarcely imagine Russia and my relationship to it. Without Yasnaya Polyana I will perhaps be able to see more clearly the general laws necessary for my homeland, but I will not love it with a passion."

How much must life at Yasnaya Polyana, or Tolstoy himself, have changed, such that residing at the estate where he was born had come to be like "hell" to him?

Having visited Optina Pustyn and on arriving in Shamordino, he said to his sister that he would be happy to settle in Optina and bear the heaviest obedience on one condition: that he did not have to attend church.

Monastic life seemed more appealing to him than domestic life. The eighty-two year-old found the prospect of life in a peasant hut, or a monastery, or a modest hotel more comfortable from a spiritual point of view than the comfort of his own home.

Since the summer of 1909, at least, he had felt better when he was staying with someone than when he was at home. When he went to

Kochety to see his eldest daughter Tatiana and his son-in-law M.S. Sukhotin, he found it resting for his soul, and far from hurrying back to Yasnaya Polyana, he delayed this return for as long as possible. Having arrived to stay at V.G. Chertkov's house in Meshcherskoye, a village near Moscow, in the summer of 1910, Tolstoy was reluctant to leave and only returned home after receiving a second alarming telegram about S.A. being in an abnormal condition.

"Lev Nikolayevich, apparently, feels very well," the secretary Valentin Bulgakov wrote in his diary on June 16th, 1910 in Meshcherskoye. "He is always lively, talkative. I think he is getting some good rest here after the constant fuss at home. And the comparative simplicity of Chertkov's practices, it seems to me, is much more in harmony with Lev Nikolayevich's whole spiritual condition than the "luxury" which he hates, and above all, the aristocratic isolation – it is not complete isolation, but it is nonetheless unmistakably there – of the house at Yasnaya Polyana."

Valentin Bulgakov was at that time too young and too much of a "Tolstoyan" to be able to assess the situation objectively. However, it isn't by chance that he puts the word "luxury" in quotation marks; he is hinting that this "luxury" probably existed in Tolstoy's mind, but not in reality. There was no "luxury" in sight at Yasnaya Polyana. But the myth of the allegedly "luxurious" conditions in which Tolstoy lived before his departure is still deep-seated in the Russian consciousness. Meanwhile, the Canadian political economist James Mavor, who was born and studied in Great Britain, and who visited Yasnaya Polyana in 1899 and 1910, wrote: "The standard of living at Yasnaya Polyana, besides the short intervals between meals, which is typical of Russia, was if anything slightly lower than the quality of life of a middle-class family in England."

There was no talk of "aristocratic isolation" at the estate, either – it was in fact more like a thoroughfare. Any penniless, drunk or crazy person could turn up at Tolstoy's house, bringing his problems with him. It is amazing that throughout all the time in which crowds of people flocked to Yasnaya, not a single one of them ever dreamt of making an attempt on L.N.'s life or otherwise assaulting him. And this was despite the fact that Tolstoy received a fair few letters and telegrams containing threats, packages containing ropes (hinting that he ought to hang himself), etc. Yet the openness and charm of L.N.'s personality disarmed any would-be hooligans and terrorists far more reliably than the police would have done.

It was only during the peasant looting and burning of 1905-1908 that S.A. appealed to the Tula governor to request that a police unit be allocated for the protection of Yasnaya Polyana. Yet even this step provoked strong opposition from her husband and youngest daughter.

In Kochety and Mesherskoye L.N. had been taking a break not from "aristocratism", but rather, on the contrary, from the excessive democratism of his later years at Yasnaya Polyana, the culprit of which was Tolstoy himself, with his teachings, which turned the consciousness of thousands of people – many of whom dreamed of talking face-to-face with the teacher himself – on its head. But there were even more people who, without having read a single one of Tolstoy's books, sought him out simply out of curiosity, so as to take a good look at this famous and approachable man. Others wanted to show off their own wit in front of him. Some came to complain about life. Others – to beg for money.

During a private meeting with Alexander III, Tolstoy's Aunt Alexandra Andreyevna Tolstaya said to the Emperor, "In Russia we have only two people who are truly popular: Count Lev Tolstoy and Father John of Kronstadt." The Emperor, after laughing at this comparison, agreed with her. But the well-known preacher John of Kronstadt, now canonized, preached in the great Cathedral of St. Andrew, and for personal meetings had a hospice in Kronstadt. Tolstoy didn't have any of this, nor could he have had it, on account of his beliefs. He could not hide himself away in a cell either, as the Optina Pustyn elders did, leaving their lay brother to deal with his visitors one by one.

"My dear father-in-law is leaving today," M.S. Suhotin, Tolstoy's son-in-law, noted on July 3rd, 1909 at the Kochety estate. "I wish to place emphasis on the word "dear", since his stay here did indeed leave the impression that there would be tenderness, delicacy and great ease in living together with him. If my mother-in-law were not jealous whenever it is convenient – or indeed inconvenient – for her to be so, continually insinuating in her letters to her husband that at Kochety he has found a place where he finds life better than it is in Yasnaya Polyana, then without question L.N. would have stayed here a lot longer."

"Papa left Kochety on July 3rd," Tolstoy's daughter Tatyana Sukhotina wrote in her diary. "It seems to me that he was happy with us: there were few visitors, no one interfered with the work to which he put his mind, nobody tried to goad him or order him around. He was completely free, and all around him he felt love and affection and the desire of each person to please him."

Here, though, is Makovitsky's entry on finding Tolstoy at Yasnaya Polyana, on July 26th, 1909: "Visitors. A young down-and-out told L.N. that he had set fire to a priest and then stabbed someone else with a dagger. He was facing hard labor. He was in hiding, on the run. There are a lot of curious people walking around today…"

"To consider one's own life alone to be all life is madness, insanity," Tolstoy wrote in his diary at around this time. And in Astapovo he was to utter a line that has become a kind of death-bed spiritual message from Tolstoy: "I advise you to remember just one thing: that there is an abyss of people in the world, and yet you are looking at Lev alone."

Nonetheless, one must admit that it was this "abyss of people", specifically, which arrived at Yasnaya Polyana in the 1900s, that seriously complicated his life and the lives of his loved ones.

Of course, among the "abyss of people" they also met people who were spiritually close and simply people of significance, like the young Alexei Peshkov, later known as Maxim Gorky, who came in 1889 on foot from Krutaya on the Gryaze-Tsaritsyn railroad line, so as to ask for land and money from Tolstoy for an agricultural commune, on behalf of some like-minded individuals. Among the pilgrims to Yasnaya Polyana were also lone spiritual seekers; serious religious sectarians, persecuted by the authorities; students, schoolboys, workers and servants frustrated in their search for the meaning of life; and sober men of sound character, who respected Tolstoy for his love of the peasants.

But there were other visits, too.

April 7, 1910. An unmarried female teacher, who has not completed her studies, but wishes to open "her own" school. It's quite simple: she must complete her education. And also she needs money, so as to be "of use to the people." L.N. talks to her about something, "but she doesn't need any of it." Asks for money for the journey home at least. Refused.

April 18. An old colonel, completely covered in medals, Orthodox, a monarchist. Travels to some of the troops, trains soldiers to read. L.N. talks with him for a long time. Having moved away from L.N., the colonel tells Tatiana Lvovna that he has a secret, and hesitates for a long time. Finally, he tells her that he wrote some poems against Tolstoy due to his apostasy from the Orthodox faith and Russian statehood. "What am I to do with them now? I'll have to burn them, and I just had two thousand printed..."

April 19. Two Japanese arrived.

April 30. Ivanov appeared, a retired artillery lieutenant who became a vagabond and sometimes helped to re-copy Tolstoy's works, with a promoter of the revolution, a weaver (about 55 years old), who lost his mind. For an hour and a half, the weaver says foreign words, mixed with Russian. L.N. lets him speak into the phonograph.

May 1. L.N. tells of a blind man from Svinok, who sometimes calls in to ask for help. He plows the fields with a boy, he has six children, poverty.

May 22. Zhilinsky, a student at Moscow University. He's travelling on foot to the Caucasus. Stopped by for some books. L.N. had a talk with him. In the evening, he expressed approval of him: "A true original." And he told of a merchant in Yelets who rides to Moscow on horseback, as he detests the railways: "I'm not a dog, that I should go running off at the sound of a whistle."

May 28. After lunch, a young peasant from 110 versts away arrived with some poems: they were illiterate, with no meter. L.N. told him the usual thing about poetry, and that he ought not to write poems. "I can come up with prose too," he replied. "What about Koltsov, could he, too? I have genius, inspiration."

May 29. Two Ossetians from the village of Khristianskaya in the Vladikavkaz District. Euphoric, enthusiastic... Have read little of Tolstoy, but believe in him as in a god.

June 12. Two young ladies. One – asking that a job be found for her, whilst the second brought the manuscript of a story about a cripple. For her own part she is unhappy and feeble, but she wants to live through work that is useful, in the Christian sense. The other girl had a limp, and came from the Orenburg Province, to ask questions about life. Both girls write...

This is a random selection of Makovitsky's diary entries chronicling the meetings which took place at Yasnaya Polyana in the spring and summer of 1910. But it must be taken into account that Makovitsky wasn't at Tolstoy's home throughout this period. He spent a considerable amount of time treating the peasants of Yasnaya Polyana and the surrounding villages.

Had Tolstoy been Chekhov, all this endless and motley string of characters would have been useful to him as an artist. At the end of life, however, Tolstoy practically renounced artistic creativity. He was entirely focused on thoughts about God and death. He was a horribly lonely thinker who needed peace and solitude above all else. This whole human river running through his soul, with the inevitable "garbage" it contained, was no longer turning the cogs of his creativity, but the "garbage" remained, a sediment that weighed heavy on his soul. He was not able to help these people. His hard-won and very personal truth was not comprehensible to them. Nor, indeed, had they come to Tolstoy in search of the truth. They had come to see Tolstoy. But he wasn't a confessor. He was a private man, with complex domestic problems aggravated by his poor health and the expectation of death.

Diary entry from July 9th, 1908: "A countless number of people, and all this would be a cause for joy if it wasn't poisoned by my consciousness of the madness, sin, vileness of the luxury, the servants and the poverty and the excessive strain of work all around. Without ceasing, I suffer tortuously from this, and alone. I cannot help but wish for death..."

These words were written a month and a half before his eightieth birthday. He celebrated this birthday in a wheelchair due to an aggravated disease of the legs, and this saved him from having to do too much talking to visitors.

For some time he had begun to love, or, at least, to value illness and, conversely, to have a negative attitude towards health. And it was not just the fact that illness brought him closer to death, but that death for him had become the main event in life. When he was weak, sick or even bedridden, he had a formal right not to meet with people, not to respond to letters (thirty to thirty-five arrived each day), entrusting this task to Sasha and his secretary. But his weakness would pass, a cheerful state of body and soul would return, and then, like flies to honey, these mysterious, vagrant individuals flew in, who considered it their right to "burden" Tolstoy with their own sins, petty passions, doubts and various mental garbage which a person who is settled, working and family-oriented would be too ashamed to discuss in public.

Diary entry of April 19, 1910: "Yesterday, a visitor: a spy, who had served in the police and shot at the revolutionaries, arrived, expecting to get my sympathy. And what's more he was the sort of person, who, apparently, wanted to share what priests would scold. It is very difficult, this, the fact that I cannot, that is to say I don't know how, humanely, that is, in God's way, lovingly and wisely to avoid all of them."

Jupiter and the Bull

When Bulgakov speaks of the "democratism" of Chertkov's summer house in Meshcherskoe, contrasting it with the "aristocratic reservedness" of the Yasnaya Polyana house, he neglects to mention an extremely interesting fact. Tolstoy went to visit Chertkov on June 12th, 1910. And the very next day, on June 13th, Chertkov sent his "Letter to the Editor" to the Moscow newspapers, in which he wrote that "Tolstoy does not wish to be visited here by people he does not know, who do not have a specific matter to see him about" and that "before making the trip, people should write to me to establish which day would be the most convenient for Lev Nikolayevich for their visit."

The letter was printed and provoked the wrath of S.A. "I read Chertkov's announcement today about how people who want to see you should ask his permission. What for? After all, you want to return on the 24th, and this will likely prompt visitors to come,"- she wrote to L.N. from Yasnaya Polyana.

This "Letter to the Editor" by Tolstoy's "spiritual executor", as Chertkov called himself, is curious for two reasons. First of all, if Chertkov had genuinely wanted to save L.N. from intrusive visitors at his dacha in Meshcherskoe, publishing this letter was the worst possible thing he could have done. Essentially, it merely redirected the flow of pilgrims from Yasnaya to Mesherskoye.

Secondly, the letter hurt S.A. What is permissible for Jove is not permitted for the bull. The bull in this case was Tolstoy's wife, who under no circumstances could have taken the liberty of making an announcement like that, even though she had far more right to do so. Yasnaya Polyana formally belonged to her. She was responsible for maintaining order on the estate, not to mention ensuring peace and quiet for her husband. Unlike Chertkov, she was not a supporter of Tolstoy's teachings and did not like the "dark lot", as she called Tolstoy's followers. But she never would have dared make a public declaration calling on visitors to Yasnaya to write to her in advance, so as to get a ticket for a meeting with Tolstoy.

Tolstoy's wife was supposed to know her place. Here is a diary entry she made on September 13th, 1908:

"Some red-headed, barefoot peasant or other came to visit Lev Nikolayevich and they talked for a long time about religion. Chertkov had brought him along, and he kept praising him for the fact that he had a good influence on those around him, even though he's very poor. I'd have liked to listen to the conversations they were having, but whenever I stay in the room in which L.N. is talking to his visitors, he looks at me in such a way, silently, questioningly, that, realizing that he does not want me to interfere, am forced to leave".

This offended her, without question. Three days later, she complains in her diary: "...L.N. is wise and happy. He has always worked by choice, not out of necessity. When he wanted to write, he wrote, when he wanted to plow the fields, he plowed the fields. He took it into his head to sew boots – and stubbornly went ahead and did so. He liked the idea of teaching children – and he did so. When he got tired of it – he dropped it. What if I were to try to live like that? What would become of the children, and of Lev himself?"

The Revolution of 1905-1908 sparked not only a wave of armed rebellions in both capitals, but also peasant unrest which V.G. Korolenko dubbed *grabizhki* ('little plunderages'). There were *grabizhki* at Yasnaya Polyana, too, although not to the same extent as at other estates, including estates in the Tula Province, during which the peasants simply set fire to the manor houses. The Behrs family, which S.A. came from, suffered in this revolution: on May 19, 1907, SR-terrorists killed her younger brother, a railway engineer named Vyacheslav Behrs. She suffered over her brother's death, but suffered even greater anxiety over the fate of her own family, the Tolstoys. She was a woman who did not scare easily: she had recently undergone an extremely serious operation herself, in the Yasnaya Polyana house, and displayed great bravery during it. But she was obliged to see to the external protection of Yasnaya Polyana, which was the home of her husband, famous throughout Russia, who inspired not only love and admiration in others, but also hatred. On Tolstoy's birthday in 1908, he received not only cards from well-wishers, but also "evil gifts, letters and telegrams," S.A. writes in her diary, "For example, enclosed with a letter signed "A mother", he was sent a rope in a box and the following message: that 'there is nothing left for Tolstoy to do but wait for and wish for the government to hang him, and he can save them the trouble.' This mother had probably lost her child due to the revolution, or the propaganda, the blame for which she laid at Tolstoy's door." Unrest had also begun inside Yasnaya Polyana, and Makovitsky writes about it on September 5, 1907: "The Yasnaya Polyana peasants were on strike for several days, five or six incited it, the others went along with it. They stopped working and have yet to come back, they aren't paying any rent, they're letting the horses into the garden, they come at night with carts for the vegetables, took pot-shots at the watchmen for two nights (is this right?), there's a complete lack of discipline ... Sofia Andreyevna called the guards to take away the guns and rifles and scare them... and LN submits to it..."

He may have submitted to it, but he made no secret of his irritation at the fact that his wife, through the Governor of Tula D.D. Kobeko, had organized police protection in the form of two guards at Yasnaya Polyana, whose duties, among other things, included checking the passports of visitors to Yasnaya.

"A difficult conversation took place with Sonia," Tolstoy writes in his diary on September 15, and this wasn't the first such conversation. Tolstoy was very unhappy that the guards had treated the peasants and visitors to Yasnaya rudely. Never mind the visitors, – when Tolstoy himself asked them not to check passports, they rudely replied that "the Countess wants to be protected from suspicious people." But the police position is understandable, too: after all, it wasn't the Count who had summoned them, but the Countess.

Tolstoy was unhappy, and his 23-year-old daughter Sasha was downright indignant.

"Does papa really need to be guarded by guards? How difficult this is for him! If it weren't for papa, I would leave right away!"

One can understand Sasha's point of view, too ... She was young, principled and wholeheartedly shared her father's convictions about "non-resistance", which he was setting out at this very time in his diary:

"Murders and brutality are intensifying by the day. What are we to do? How are we to stop it? Lock them up, exile them to Siberia, execute them. The degree of villainy isn't reduced – on the contrary. What to do? One thing, and one thing only: each and every one of us must put every effort into ensuring that they live as God intended. They will go on beating people and robbing them. And I, with my arms raised on their orders, will beseech them to stop living badly. They will not listen, they will go on doing the same thing. What to do? There is nothing else I can do."

There was nothing else he could do. All that was left for him, with his hard-won ideas, to do was, whilst not accepting violence, not resist it. Incidentally, Tolstoy's idea of "non-resistance" is often interpreted as acceptance of violence. This is a mistake, which Tolstoy always protested against. Don't accept it, but do not resist it either. All forms of resistance are also violence, and violence begets more violence.

But S.A. was no Lev Tolstoy. She was the mistress of the estate. Perhaps not the best, but she felt the responsibility that her husband had placed on her shoulders, and there was one thing she was sure of: the peasants must not be allowed to be willful. She herself could do nothing to prevent this. There was a need for guards. It was Tolstoy's wife who coined this aphorism, in which the helplessness of a weak woman is combined with the personal experience of managing an estate in those pre-revolutionary, heady days: "Running an estate is a struggle for existence with the people."

And she also knows that a man without a passport must be either a tramp or a fugitive from whom one can expect anything under the sun. And if something were to happen to her husband, they would never forgive her for it – her before all others. Why hadn't she protected the great Tolstoy? After all, it was to her that his life had been entrusted! And not only his life, but also those of Sasha, and Tanya Sukhotina, who had come to Yasnaya Polyana with her young daughter Tanya, the granddaughter of L.N. and SA, whom the old men all found so cute.

The complexity of the problem was in the fact that even the staunchest "Tolstoyans" didn't have passports either, because to hold a passport would mean to recognize the laws of a state founded on violence.

All these problems were *de facto* removed whenever L.N. was not at home but away visiting someone. Here, concern for his tranquility, that he should not be bothered by pesky visitors, was a normal thing. But at Yasnaya Polyana this wasn't the case. Neither visitors to the estate, nor even the peasants cared about the fact that the mistress of the estate was Tolstoy's wife, and not the Count. Passport-less "Tolstoyans" came to see him complaining that they had been insulted by the guards, and he received visits from the relatives of peasants who had been arrested for felling trees and stealing from the gardens. This situation was torturous for him and for S.A. as well. It was a Gordian knot which Tolstoy's wife was obliged to cut willy-nilly. It spoiled her character, exacerbated relations with her youngest daughter, which were already far from tender, and split the family into those who sided with their mother and those who sided with their father.

"... My mother not only didn't share father's negative attitude toward property, but, on the contrary, continued to think that the richer she and her children were, the better. She wasn't only a wife, she was a mother, and it is characteristic of mothers in particular to dream of earthly goods for their offspring," Sergei Lvovich, Tolstoy's eldest son, wrote in his "Essays about the Past".

But there was also another subtle circumstance that poisoned the last years of Tolstoy's life at Yasnaya.

Why did Father Sergius flee?

The story *Father Sergius* is one of Tolstoy's most deeply personal works. He wrote *Sergius* unhurriedly, with long breaks, over a period of nearly ten years, just as was the case with *Hadji Murat*. Both stories were published after the writer's death, and even on this formal basis may be seen in their own particular way as Tolstoy's artistic "testament".

Father Sergius is the story of a departure. This is its main subject, and it is all the more intriguing for the fact that its meaning took shape gradually, as he accumulated a personal spiritual experience of his own, which he was in no hurry to put down on paper, let alone publish.

The plot of *Father Sergius* was related for the first time in a letter to Chertkov in February 1890 - up to the point where the high society beauty

Makovkina comes to visit Father Sergius with the intention of spending the night in his cell, following a bet she had made. This was about one-third of the work. In many ways we are indebted to Chertkov for the fact that the story was written. Fearing that the plot would never be fleshed out, and wanting to draw Tolstoy into working on it, he copied out the letter he had received, leaving large spaces between the lines so that further work could be done, and sent back his copy of the letter along with the original. He often used this trick, stimulating Tolstoy into writing artistic works. This gives the lie to the widely-held belief that Chertkov was solely interested in the pedagogical aspect of Tolstoy's activities, at the expense of his artistic genius.

However, as was often the case with Tolstoy, the meaning of the story outgrew its plot. The hub of its meaning shifted from the story of the temptation of Father Sergius, formerly Duke Kasatsky, by two women – the beauty Makovkin and a merchant's daughter named Maria – toward the third female protagonist, Pashenka, whom Sergius visits after leaving his cell. Undoubtedly, the most important thing for Tolstoy, ultimately, was not the piquant story, but rather the story of Pasha, who only features in the last few pages.

Having seen off the devil as represented by Makovkina, at the cost of losing the index finger on his left hand, Sergius proves unable to resist what would seem to be a lesser temptation: he "falls", seduced by a feeble-minded maiden with well-developed female forms.

This contrast between the two temptations: the subtle, sophisticated one and the rude, insolent one ("What are you?" he said. "Maria. You are the devil." "Well, after all, it's nothing") provides the intrigue to the story, but is notits heart and soul.

The soul of the story, its main idea, isn't about why Father Sergius fled, but about why he *departed* – and from whom he was running when he did so.

After what happened with Maria, Sergius had no choice but to flee. But he had conceived of his departure much earlier, and what happened with Maria merely served as the pretext for his flight. One can assume that if it were not for Maria, Sergius would have required another excuse to get away, and that he would leave behind some sort of explanation for his actions. Such that his departure be perceived not as a new stage of his holiness, but as evidence that he was an ordinary, sinful man.

"There was even a time when he decided to leave, to escape. He even thought it all through, how he would do it. He prepared himself a peasant shirt, pants, coat and hat, saying that he needed them so that he would have something to give those who asked for help. And he kept these clothes in his room, and imagined how he would get dressed, cut his hair and leave. First, he would leave on the train, travel three-hundred versts, then get out and walk from village to village. He asked an elderly soldier which places he went to, what sort of food they served and where he was let in. The soldier told him where he would be allowed in and served food, and Father Sergius wanted to go through with his plan. One night he even got dressed and was on the point of leaving, but he didn't know what was the right thing to do: to stay or to flee. At first he was plagued by indecision, then the indecision passed, he grew used to it and surrendered to the devil, and the peasant clothes only reminded him of his thoughts and feelings."

This devil appears in the story before Maria does, and when he flees his cell it is from the devil that he is fleeing. He couldn't have fled from him without Maria's help. This devil represents human glory. To simply walk away would have meant increasing his renown, playing along with the devil and submitting to him once and for all. That's why Father Sergius tarried over his departure, as if waiting for this little fool to come along, who seduced him so easily because he had long been ready for this.

"Every day, more and more people came to see him and he had less and less time left for spiritual strengthening and prayer. Sometimes, in lucid moments, he thought that he had become like a place where there had once been a spring. "There was a weak spring of living water which flowed softly from me, through me ... But since then, the water has barely had enough time to gather when along come the thirsty, crowding together and pushing each other out of the way. And they have shoved everything aside, so that only the dirt remains ..."

Father Sergius' torment lay in the fact that "he was a burning lamp, and the more he felt this, the more he felt the weakening, the extinguishing of the divine light of truth which burned within him. "How much of what I do is for God, and how much is for the people?" – this was the question that constantly tormented him; it was not that he was not *able* to give himself an answer to it, but that he could not bring himself to do so. He felt in the depth of his soul that the devil had substituted all of the activities he did for God with the activities he did for the people. He felt this because, just as it had been hard for him in the past when he was torn from his solitude, so he now found his solitude hard to bear. He felt oppressed by his visitors, tired by them, but from the depth of his soul he rejoiced in them, glad of the praise which surrounded him."

It would be impossible to portray this devil on screen. He does not have one specific face, he has many faces. Ultimately, he is the crowd, the "mob". The fact that this devil would torment Tolstoy at the end of his life was something he predicted in *Father Sergius*, as was the fact that the only way to escape from this devil would be flight to nowhere in particular, into obscurity. The only way to flee from the crowd is to dissolve into it. Otherwise, sooner or later the crowd will catch up with you and demand answers to their questions. And no "Be off with you!" will save you then. In Tolstoy's case the situation was doubly desperate, because Pushkin's clearly defined concept of the "mob" didn't exist in his worldview.

"Judge others as you would be judged," writes Tolstoy in his diary on 13 February 1907. "Because after all – they are the same as you. And therefore be just as forgiving about their vile deeds as you have been, and are, in relation to yourself. And, just as you would in relation to your own sins, hope that they will repent and amend their ways." This is a deeply Christian thought, but in real life in Yasnogorsk it was impossible to identify oneself every day with the multitude of people who wrote to L.N. and came to see him fully convinced that they were the only ones for whom he existed on this earth. The vast majority of letters and oral questions he received were requests for money. It was in vain that he arranged for letters to be printed in the newspapers on several occasions, reminding people that he had relinquished ownership of and the rights to his works. This merely irritated the petitioners, making them think that the count was being disingenuous.

The second largest category of letters and appeals were the "appeal letters": these people were trying to bring Tolstoy back within the bosom of Orthodoxy and statehood, or, by pointing out mistakes and contradictions in his arguments, to set him on a truly "Tolstoyan" path, as they interpreted this to be.

It was only the third category – the smallest category of all – that wrote to Tolstoy or came calling with serious, honest questions about life and God. He described these letters and appeals simply as "good" ones. He included in this category even those in which there was no serious thought, but in which there was a sincere desire to talk, to express what was in the person's soul, or at least, without any second thoughts whatsoever, to remind him of their existence, just as Bobchinsky and Dobchinsky in Gogol's *The Government Inspector* asked Hlestyakov to remind the Emperor of their existence. The letters he would categorize as "good" would include ones like this:

"In the Name of the Father and of the Son and of the Holy Spirit, Amen. I dare to have recourse to the mercy of the Lord, that the Lord might send to a sinner such as me sufficient understanding to write this letter to Your renowned name, greatly respected by the peoples of the Russian land, and even famous abroad, – and I, sinful man that I am and the smallest, like a bug, wish to crawl, by means of a letter at least, up to your name, Lev Nikolayevich, Mr. Tolstov".

Tolstoy would make a point of answering such artless letters. It was the other people that tortured him. They wrote to him and came to him with convictions which they had adopted once and for all, regardless of whether these convictions were Tolstoyan or anti-Tolstoyan. These people were spiritual tyrants, and it was here that things became strained for Tolstoy and his "non-resistance".

Valentin Bulgakov tells of a dream Tolstoy had in February 1910. "He dreamt that he got hold of an iron stake from somewhere, and went off somewhere with it. And then he sees a man sneaking after him and slandering him to those around them: "Look, there goes Tolstoy! How much harm he has done to everyone, the heretic!" Then Lev Nikolayevich turned around and killed this man with the iron stake. But a minute later the man seemed to have been resurrected, because his lips were moving and he was saying something."

No, it was not merely due to family conflicts and a desire to simplify his life that Tolstoy left Yasnaya Polyana. One of the reasons for his departure or flight was the devil of earthly glory, the overly intense love and hatred that people felt toward him, which caused him suffering and of which he dreamed of ridding himself, by turning into an ordinary old man. In "Father Sergius", which he completed in 1898, more than ten years before he disappeared from Yasnaya Polyana, he thought out a version of this disappearance – one that at first glance seems so very original, yet which has in fact been tried and tested by centuries of idiocy. In order to disappear without multiplying your earthly glory, you need to commit some utterly indecent act which would wipe out your former greatness, your false holiness.

Regrettably, or perhaps fortunately, this model was just as impossible for Tolstoy as had been imitating suicide (*The Living Corpse*) or replacing one's body in a coffin (*The Posthumous Papers of the Elder Fyodor Kuzmich*). There were no templates for Tolstoy's departure at all.

And yet how nice it would have been! "Kasatsky spent eight months living like this; in the ninth month, he was detained in a provincial town, in a shelter where he had been spending his nights with wanderers, and since he had no papers he was taken in for questioning. When asked where his ticket was and who he was, he replied that he did not have a ticket, and that he was a servant of God. He was listed as a vagrant, tried and exiled to Siberia.

In Siberia, he settled in the lodge of a rich peasant and he now lives there. He works in the owner's garden, teaches the children and visits the sick."

A sinner whether he liked it or not

And yet there had been a time when Tolstoy not only gave no thought to leaving Yasnaya Polyana, but looked on any trip away from it as an unpleasant duty, as an annoying interruption to the natural course of his life. There was a time when, on the contrary, he left Moscow on foot for Yasnaya, making a sort of pilgrimage to his estate, just as he also made pilgrimages to the Holy Trinity monastery, Optina Pustyn and the Kiev-Pechersk Lavra.

When in 1847 Tolstoy's brothers, orphaned early in life, divided up their parents' legacy, Lev, as the youngest brother, was given Yasnaya Polyana. He was indescribably happy ... It is impossible to imagine what took place in the soul of this eighteen-year old boy, when he became the owner of the family estate, with which his purest and most sacred memories were associated.

"Oh the happy, happy, irretrievable time of childhood! How can one not love and cherish one's memories of it? These memories refresh and elevate my soul and serve for me as the source of my greatest pleasures...

After prayers, you would return to your blanket of a morning, a light, bright and heartening feeling in your soul; one set of dreams makes way for another set – but what are they about? They are elusive, but full of pure love and hope for pure happiness. You would recall Karl Ivanovich and the bitter fate that befell him – the only person whom I knew to be unhappy, and you will feel so sorry for him, you will feel such love for him, that tears will stream from your eyes, and you think: God grant him happiness; give me the opportunity to help him, to ease his grief; I am prepared to sacrifice everything for him. Then you take your favorite china toy – a bunny or a dog – and ensconce it in the corner of your fluffy pillow and admire how wonderfully warm and cozy the toy must be as it lies there. You also pray that God might give happiness to everyone, so that everyone might be content, and that the weather would be nice the next day so that you could go for a walk, then you turn to lie on your other side, thoughts and dreams are intertwined and get mixed up, and you fall asleep quietly, peacefully, your face still wet with tears.

Will it ever return – that freshness, carefree state, need for love and strength of faith, which you had in childhood? What time could possibly be better than that one, when the two best virtues – innocent cheerfulness and a boundless need for love – were your only *raisons d'être*?

Where are those fervent prayers? Where is the best gift of all – those pure tears of affection? The angel-comforter flew in, wiped away those tears with a smile and evoked sweet dreams for your unspoiled childhood imagination.

Can it really be that life left such heavy traces in my heart, that these tears and delights have left me forever? Are memories really the only thing left?"

These striking lines come from Tolstoy's first completed work –the story *Childhood*! They give us an idea not only about how he started out on life's path, but also how he dreamed of concluding it. Here, in essence, the whole spiritual vector of Tolstoy's life is reflected.

Life is happiness. The greatest happiness is attained through faith in God and love for all people. Faith and love – these are not even virtues.

They are the most urgent and, if you will, egotistical need of the soul. In childhood, if it is a happy one, this need is satisfied in and of itself. As we grow up, the egotistical needs of the body drown out and replace the main needs of the soul – a thirst for faith and love. But the more a person satiates the needs of the body, the more miserable he is. And the further he goes in satiating the egotistical needs of the body, the further away he is from the sources of happiness.

To return to these sources now requires a tremendous spiritual effort, difficult, meticulous work on oneself, and all for the sake of obtaining what is given to you for free in childhood.

Here, in condensed form, is Tolstoy's entire spiritual philosophy, which determined his spiritual practices. The paradox is that the spiritual practices themselves were as complex as the desired spiritual result was simple. "The point of life, the purpose of it – is joy," Tolstoy wrote. "Rejoice in the sky, the sun, the stars, the grass, the trees, in animals, and in people. And make sure this joy isn't disrupted by anything. If this joy is disrupted, then you must have made a mistake somewhere, so look for the error and rectify it." "All is within you and all is in the present," L.N. loved to repeat, quoting the peasant philosopher Vasily Kirillovitch Syutaev. But what a tremendous amount of work on oneself was required in order to achieve this state! Tolstoy's entire diary, from 1847 right up until his death, was devoted, in essence, to providing a continuous chronicle of this difficult work.

It's like an attempt to return to paradise. Or rather, to that heavenly state of the soul which is described in *Childhood*. The first reference to his work on *Childhood* came in January 1851; the novel was completed in the summer of 1852. Tolstoy starts keeping a diary in March 1847 at Kazan University Hospital, where he is being treated for *gaonaryi* (gonorrhea), which he got "from doing the thing it is normally caused by". Thus, the first entry in the diary bears witness to just how far he is from that "heavenly" state of the soul, the one experienced in childhood. His shameful physical uncleanliness is merely the outward manifestation of the terrible mortification of his soul, but it also signals that there is a need, before it is too late, to start working on himself. And it was to this major work that he was to devote his entire life, the objective and purpose of which he indicates in *Childhood*.

The need for love had always been present within Tolstoy. But the strength of his faith and his innocence were lost soon after he left his childhood paradise, Yasnaya Polyana. "I was baptized and brought up in the Orthodox Christian faith," he writes in *Confession* in the late '70s. "I was taught it when I was a child and all through my boyhood and youth. But when I turned 18 and completed the second year of university, I did not believe in any of the things I had been taught...

I wished with all my heart to be good; but I was young, I had passions, and I was alone, completely alone, whilst I was searching for something good. Whenever I tried to express what my most sincere wishes were: that I wanted to be morally good, I came up against contempt and derision; but as soon as I indulged in repulsive passions, I was praised and encouraged. Ambition, lust for power, greed, adultery, pride, anger, revenge – all these things were respected. As I yielded to these passions, I became like a grown-up, and I sensed that people were happy with me."

Tolstoy wrote these lines at a time when his consciousness was changing from one extreme to the other: everything he had previously considered white had become black, and vice versa. In actual fact, he wasn't as lonely as all that in his youth. His three wonderful older brothers, Nikolai, Sergei and Dmitry Tolstoy, studied at the same university as him – the University of Kazan. There was also his dearly beloved younger sister, Maria. He had two aunts: Pelageya Ilinichna Yushkova and Tatiana Alexandrovna Yergolskaya. The latter took over the role of mother for the younger children, Dmitri, Masha and Lev, at Yasnaya Polyana. Pelageya Ilinichna took in the Tolstoy brothers in Kazan.

The young L.N.'s loneliness lay rather in the fact that, fully "surrendering to his passions," he was nonetheless desperate not to become "like a grown-up". Accepting the external rules of the game among adults, he remained a "child on the inside". And it is telling, of course, that the first work which made him famous was called *Childhood*.

Tolstoy's diary from the period when he began work on *Childhood* paints a truly sad state of mind. This is in stark contrast to the childlike, "heavenly" mood which is shown in *Childhood*. The uninitiated reader might get the impression that it was written not by a healthy young man in the bloom of youth, who was soon to travel to the Caucasus as a volunteer and participate in combat operations against the Chechens, but by an effeminate wimp, a "decadent".

March 7, 1851: "... lack of energy."

March 9: "... lack of energy."

March 13-14: "Little pride ... gluttony ... laziness ... cheating yourself ... lies ..."

March 16: "Laziness ... cowardice ... lack of focus ... little resoluteness ..."

April 3: "Vanity ... cheating yourself ... weak ... sluggish ... untidy ..."

But this is a misleading impression. The ruthless scrutiny and punctuality with which Tolstoy recorded in his diary the slightest manifestation of pusillanimity or weakness of soul paint a different picture. From the first moment he starts to keep a diary, he commences the thorough work on himself, which was to result in the phenomenon of the later Tolstoy. A phenomenon of which Professor V.F. Snegirev, as you may recall, wrote: "Anyone who studied his movement, the way he carried himself, the way he turned his head, his gait, could clearly see *at all times* the deliberacy of these movements, that is, every movement was formulated, designed, given meaning and expressed an idea ... "

Tolstoy compared this work on himself to the exercises carried out by a sportsman: "Yes, just as an athlete rejoices every day, as he lifts increasingly heavy weights and inspects his ever-growing and increasingly strong white (biceps) muscles, so is it possible in exactly the same way, if only you put your life into it and begin working on your soul, to rejoice in the fact that every day, from now on, you have lifted a heavier weight than you did yesterday, and resisted temptation better" (Diary. November 9, 1906).

L.N. had spiritual and physical strength in spades. But genuine faith, love, the innocent sense of continuous happiness in communion with God, the world and other people had already gone. All that remained were the memories which he recreated so poetically in *Childhood*. In reality, it was an altogether different story.

"When I wake up, I feel what a cowardly dog must feel before its owner, when it's done something wrong..." he wrote in his diary in the Caucasus.

In the interval between assuming his rights as the master of Yasnaya and his flight (yes, yes, flight!) to the Caucasus, Tolstoy leads the typical life of a young, unmarried and well-off nobleman of that time. In other words, a lifestyle involving plenty of wine, cards, gypsies and prostitutes (let us call a spade a spade).

"I couldn't stop myself, I gave a signal to something pink, which, in the distance, looked very good to me, and opened the door behind me. She came in. I can't see her, it's nasty, repulsive, I even hate the fact that because of her I'm breaking the rules," he writes in his diary on April 18, 1851.

What are these rules, then? And then we see this: "In accordance with religious law, don't have any women" (diary entry from December 24, 1850).

Anyone who, driven by excessive curiosity, were to try to seek out evidence in Tolstoy's diaries of the terribly sinful lifestyle he was alleged to have led, does not quite have an accurate picture of the way the nobility led their lives at the time. In many ways this is due to Tolstoy, with his *War and Peace* and *Anna Karenina*, and also to the filtered film adaptations. We picture the landed gentry as being like Konstantin Levin, and the libertine city-dweller like dear old Stiva Oblonsky. But Tolstoy knew plenty of other types as well, which his pen simply refused to describe. For example, he was well aware of the life of his second cousin and the husband of his sister, Valerian Petrovich Tolstoy. Lev's sister-in-law, Tatiana Kuzminskaya, wrote to the literary critic M.A. Tsyavlovsky about Valerian Tolstoy in 1924: "Her (Maria Nikolayevna's. - PB.) husband was impossible. He cheated on her, even with the nurse-maids, scullery maids and so forth. In the attic at Pokrovskoe they found the tiny skeletons of one or two new-born babes."

Tolstoy's early diaries do indeed give the impression of some sort of unpleasant emotional and even physical impurity. Yet this stems from the fact that the man who wrote them had a very clear idea of what purity was, and described it in the novel *Childhood*. The young Tolstoy, as he emerges from the pages of his diary, fitted the bill as the continuously penitent sinner – a role that is extremely worthless from an aesthetic point of view. Hence this image of a dog feeling guilty before its master, and incidentally the master should of course be understood to represent God.

March 7, 1851: "Didn't get up for a long time in the morning, shrank from doing so, somehow deceiving myself. Read novels, when there were other matters to deal with; said to myself: look at you drinking all that coffee, as if it's impossible to do anything else whilst you're drinking coffee."

July 3, 1851: "... got caught up and lost 200 of my own money, 150 of Nikolenka's and the 500 I borrowed, i.e. 850 altogether. I'm restraining myself now and living in a deliberate way. Traveled to Chervlennaya, got drunk and slept with a woman; all this is very bad and tortures me a great deal ... I wanted it yesterday as well. It was a good thing she didn't let me have it. An abomination."

August 26, 1851: "Up since morning, writing my novel, doing tricks on horseback, studied Tatar and went with the girls."

Only occasionally did the "heavenly" feeling come back to him, as was the case in the Caucasus, in the village of Stary Yurt:

"Yesterday I couldn't sleep and was up almost all night, after writing in my diary, I began praying to God. The sweetness of feeling which I experienced whilst at prayer is impossible to convey. I uttered the prayers that I usually say: Our Father, Mother of God, the Trinity, Open unto me the doors of repentance, the appeal to the guardian angel – and then stayed for a further prayer. If prayer is defined as asking for something or giving thanks, then I was not praying. I wanted something lofty and good; but I cannot convey what it was; although I was clearly aware of what I desired. I wanted to become one with the all-encompassing being. I asked it to forgive my transgressions; but no, I didn't ask for this, because I sensed that since it was giving me this blessed moment, it must have forgiven me. I asked, and at the same time felt that I had nothing to ask for and that I was unable to ask and did not know how to do so. I gave thanks, yes, but not in words, nor in thought. I combined everything into one feeling: both prayer and gratitude. The feeling of fear completely disappeared. I couldn't have separated any one of the feelings of faith, hope and love, from the overall feeling I experienced. No, this is the feeling that I experienced yesterday – it is a feeling of love for God. It is a lofty love, incorporating all that is good within it and denying all that is bad ..."

"I spent the morning quite well," Tolstoy later notes, sleepily, "Was a little lazy, told some lies, though not sinful ones." And yet a few days later, he confesses: "Went to Chervlennaya, got drunk, slept with a woman... An abomination."

"Eternal bliss is not possible *here*," he writes, drawing a conclusion that is scarcely likely to console him. "Suffering is essential. Why? I don't know."

The Departing Count

The dividing up of the inheritance among the brothers took place on April 11, 1847, and on the very next day Tolstoy petitioned to be allowed to leave the University of Kazan and on May 1 arrived at Yasnaya Polyana, which now belonged to him. Henceforth, it becomes for him not just the family estate where he was born and spent his childhood, not just some property, but the Promised Land, to which he will return time after time, as he passes through each fresh stage of doubts and temptations. And on each occasion he will run to Yasnaya impatiently, like a child, turning his back on everything in the world: the university, the military, high society, literary circles and even his large family, when the family moves to Moscow.

His Excellency
The Rector of the Imperial University of Kazan
State Councilor and Cavalier
Ivan Mikhailovich Simonov
From an extern undergraduate of the 2nd year
Of the Faculty of Law,
Count Lev Nikolayevich Tolstoy

PETITION

Due to ill-health and family circumstances, not wanting to continue a course of study at the university, I humbly beg Your Excellency to draw up the order that is dependent on you for my omission from the roll of students and to return all my documents to me.

To this petition I set my hand
Student Count Lev Tolstoy.
The 12th day of April 1847.

Before Tolstoy resigned from the university, he received an administrative penalty – he was confined to a punishment cell for skipping lectures on history. From that moment on, Tolstoy begins to disparage history as a science, considering it to be collection of bizarre anecdotes about the immoral people, who, for some reason, are recognized as great leaders and even as saints. Sitting in the cell with another student, Nazarev, he mocks the science of history aloud:

"History is nothing but a collection of fables and useless trifles, peppered with a mass of unnecessary figures and proper names. The death of Igor, the snake which bit Oleg – what is this if not a fairy tale, and who needs to know that Ioan's second marriage to the daughter of John Temrük took place on August 21, 1563, and his fourth, to Anna Alekseyevna Koltovskaya, in 1572, and yet because they demand of me that I learn all this by rote, but I do not know it, they fail me."

It is significant that this diatribe, recorded in Nazarev's memoirs and confirmed by Tolstoy's biographer Biryukov, took place in the punishment cell of all places. From this episode onwards, Tolstoy was to get beside himself, literally becoming enraged, whenever he was affected by the merest trace of an administrative punishment or curb on his personal will.

Here, in confinement, he also pours scorn on the university's entire teachings:

"What do we take away with us from the university? Think hard on this and answer in good conscience. What do we take away from this sanctuary, when we return home, to the countryside? What are we qualified for, who needs any of this?

The spring of 1847 is a turning point in Tolstoy's life. He starts a diary, he becomes the master of Yasnaya and he quits the university. But above all – this is his first experience of taking flight. With this flight, he begins his own deliberate path in life, one that he will also conclude by taking flight.

"Lev Nikolayevich hurried in his departure from Kazan," writes N.P. Zagoskin, a historian of Russian law, in his memoirs – and didn't even wait for his brothers Sergei and Dmitry to finish their final university examinations. The day arrived when Tolstoy was to depart for Moscow, through which he was to pass to get to his Yasnaya Polyana. A small group of students gathered in the apartment of the Tolstoy Counts, in a wing of the Petondi house, who wanted to see Lev Nikolayevich off on his journey, one that would be long and difficult due to the state of the roads at that time... As might be expected, they drank toasts in honor of the traveller, wishing him well in all sorts of ways. Lev Nikolayevich's friends escorted him as far as the ferry across the Kazanka, which was at high tide, and here gave him a final farewell kiss."

All this seems strikingly familiar...

It's just like the start of the novel *The Cossacks*! "In one of the windows of Chevalier's, a light was shining illicitly from beneath the closed shutters. At the entrance stood a carriage, a sleigh and some drivers, huddled together. The three-horse postal carriage was there as well. The yard-keeper, furled up into a ball and pulling his coat tightly around him, stood around the corner of the house, as if hiding from someone...

"Dmitry Andreyevich, the coachman's impatient to get going," said a young serf, who came in wearing a fur coat and with a scarf tied round his neck. "The horses have been standing there since twelve and now it's four o'clock."

Dmitry Andreyevich looked at his serf Vanyusha. In the scarf wrapped around him, his felt boots, his sleepy face, he heard the voice of another life, calling him – a life of work, privations, and activity.

"Indeed, it's time I said good-bye!" he said, feeling for the unfastened hook on his overcoat.

Ignoring the pleas that he give the driver yet another tip so that he could buy vodka, he put on his hat and stood in the middle of the room. They kissed one another once, twice, then stopped and kissed for a third time. The one that was in the fur coat walked up to the table, drained the glass that stood on it ..."

Dmitry Olenin runs off to the Caucasus, after getting entangled in debt and relationships with women. Tolstoy fled to the Caucasus for exactly the same reasons. In the ideal scenario, of course, the basis for his flight would have been the thirst for "a life of work, privations, activity," which had initially driven L.N. from Kazan to Yasnaya. And at the most intimate level, the basis for it was the search for the Promised Land, the "paradise" which Yasnaya Polyana and the Caucuses – unspoiled by civilization – seemed to him to be. Before running off to the Caucasus, he came close to fleeing for Siberia, the place to which he subsequently sent several of his main characters: Father Sergius, the elder Feodor Kuzmich, and Stepan Pelageyushkin from *The Forged Coupon*.

Let us note with dotted lines the start of Tolstoy's youth. The clinic, where he receives treatment for a shameful disease and... starts to keep a diary, which will later become a global template for relentless work on moral self-improvement ... The punishment cell to which he is confined for the banal offence of skipping lectures and ... makes bold speeches about the history of mankind ... His rejection of his studies at university and... his happy acceptance of the yoke of owning an estate...

Ultimately, flight as a way of solving all his problems.

It is abundantly clear that Tolstoy was one of those people for whom it is not so much freedom that is important as personal *will*.

These people are ready to take on any circumstances, even the most difficult, only not whilst under pressure from the outside. Once the pressure from outside exceeds their strength and the capability of their personal will, they resort to flight.

Among Tolstoy's earliest diary entries in 1847 there is a very important one: "Will I ever reach a point where I do not depend on any extraneous circumstances? In my opinion, this would be a great perfection, for in a man who isn't dependent on any outside influence, the spirit must, by its needs, surpass the matter, and then the person will reach his destination."

When P.I. Biryukov, Tolstoy's first biographer, asked about his earliest experiences in life, he recalled the following:

"These are my first memories... Here they are: I am bound, I want to free my hands, and I cannot do that, and I scream and weep, and I my screaming is unpleasant to me myself; but I cannot stop. Someone is stooping over me, I can't remember who. And all this takes place in the semi-darkness. But I remember that there were two of them. My shouting has an effect on them; they are alarmed by my screams, but they don't untie me, as I would wish, and I scream even louder. They think that this is necessary (that is, that I be bound), whereas I know that it isn't necessary, and I want to prove it to them, and I pour out my screaming, which is repugnant even to myself, but I can't hold it back. I sense the injustice and cruelty not of people, because they take pity on me, but of fate, and pity for myself."

Here's my second memory from early childhood: "A visit by some, I don't know, cousin of mother's, the Hussar Prince Volkonsky. He wanted to stroke me and sat me on his knee, and, as is often the case, whilst continuing to talk to the other grown-ups, held onto me. I struggled to break away, but he only held me tighter. This went on for about two minutes. But this sense of captivity, of a curb on my freedom, of violence so angered me that I suddenly began to tear away, crying and hitting out."

And here's another memory: a French tutor named St. Thomas locks little Lev in a room, and then threatens to hit him with rods. "And I felt a terrible feeling of resentment, anger and disgust, not only toward Thomas, but also toward the violence which he wanted to use on me. This incident was probably the reason behind the horror and disgust I have felt for all kinds of violence throughout my life."

With his parents not around (his mother had died when Lev was not even two years old, and his father died suddenly before Lev reached the age of nine), his aunts played a huge part in his life. After his father's death, his sister Alexandra Ilinichna became the children's guardian.

Recalling this aunt, L.N. spoke about her husband, the Baltic Count Osten-Sacken, who suffered from unfounded jealousy. After becoming completely insane, the Count decided one day that "his enemies, wanting to take his wife away from him (she was pregnant at the time, moreover – P.B.), had surrounded him, and that the only salvation for him was to run from them. This happened in the summer. After getting up early in the morning, he announced to his wife that the only means of salvation was to run, that he had ordered that the carriage be prepared, and that they were now going to leave, and she should get ready. Indeed, the carriage was brought to the door, he put (Lev's) aunt inside and ordered the coachman to drive as quickly as possible. When they were on the road, he took two pistols out of a box, cocked them and, handing one to my aunt, told her that if his enemies found out about his escape, they would catch up with him, and then they would be killed, and that the only thing left for them to do was to kill one another… Unfortunately, along the country road which led out to the main one, a coach appeared; he cried out that all was lost, ordered her to shoot him, and for his part shot my aunt in the chest at point-blank range. Evidently, on seeing what he had done, and that the coach which had scared him had driven past them in the other direction, he stopped, carried my aunt's bloodied body out of the carriage, laid her on the road and rode away. Fortunately for my aunt, some peasants soon came upon her, picked her up and took her to the pastor, who bandaged the wound as best he could and sent for the doctor."

In this almost unbelievable story, it is not the plot of it that attracts attention, but the biased attention to detail with which L.N. conveys it in his memoirs. It is as though L.N. himself was a third party in all this, sitting in the carriage next to the mad Count and his unfortunate pregnant wife.

Interestingly, L.N.'s sister, Maria Nikolayevna, who had also heard this story from her aunt, retold it in a completely different way. There was no mention whatsoever of an escape "from enemies". The jealous graph had simply lured his wife into the park one night and shot her at point-blank range. Frightened by what he had done, the Count didn't flee at all, but took his wounded wife to the pastor himself.

If we suppose that the incredible story involving the escape was an invention on the part of little Lev, designed to add something to his aunt's story, then it's not difficult to see the direction his imagination was working in.

Little Lev's imagination came up with the most unusual things. For example, he would come into the room and do a backwards bow, throwing his head back and shuffling his feet. Once he shaved his eyebrows, which greatly disfigured his face.

"Another time," Maria Nikolayevna told P.I. Biryukov, "we were riding in a troika from Pirogov to Yasnaya. During one of the carriage stops, Levochka slipped out and started walking. When the carriage got going, they looked for him, but he was nowhere to be seen. From his seat at the front of the carriage, the driver saw his retreating figure on the road ahead; they pressed on, supposing he had gone on ahead, so as to get back in when the troika caught up with him, but no such luck. With the approach of the troika, he quickened his pace, and when the troika went at a trot, he began to run, apparently not wanting to get back in. The troika was moving very quickly, and he ran at full pelt, covering nearly three versts like that, until, eventually, his strength ran out and he gave up. They put him in the carriage; he was short of breath, drenched in sweat and exhausted from fatigue."

Were it not for the fact that Maria Nikolayevna talked about this episode from Tolstoy's childhood a few years before L.N.'s flight from

Yasnaya Polyana, and that it was even published in the first volume of the Biryukov biography, published in 1906, one might have suspected her of remembering it under the influence of this flight. The same goes for another episode, also related to Biryukov:

"One time we gathered for dinner, this was in Moscow, when grandmother was still alive, when a certain etiquette was observed, and everyone had to arrive on time, before grandmother came to the table, and wait for her. And therefore everyone was surprised to find that there was no sign of Levochka. When we sat down at the table, grandmother, noticing his absence, asked the tutor, St. Thomas, what this meant, and whether Leon had been punished; but the tutor shyly declared that he didn't know, but that he was sure that Leon would appear any minute, and that he was probably still in his room, preparing for dinner. Grandmother's anxiety was eased, but during dinner our tutor came up and whispered something to St. Thomas, and the latter immediately jumped up and ran from the table...

Soon the mystery was cleared up, and we found out the following: Levochka, for some unknown reason (as he now says, merely in order to do something unusual and surprise others), had decided to jump out of a little window on the second floor from a height of several *sazhen* ... On the lower basement floor was the kitchen, and the cook just happened to be standing at the window when Levochka plopped to the ground. Not realizing at first what was going on, she told the butler, and when they came out into the yard, they found Levochka lying in the yard, unconscious. Fortunately, he hadn't broken anything, and the only damage was a slight concussion; he passed from unconsciousness into sleep, slept for 18 hours straight and woke up completely healthy ..."

Listening to his sister's story, L.N. added that when he jumped out the window, he had not jumped down but up. He also said that when he was seven or eight years old, he had "had a terrible desire to fly in the air. He imagined that this was entirely possible, if you squatted and hugged your knees; moreover, the stronger you squeezed your knees, the higher you could fly."

There are many examples one could give of oddities in Tolstoy's behavior related to his striving for personal freedom and independence, with the pain he felt when experiencing any form of external violence.

But would we not be better off looking at which of these oddities he retained until the end of his days? First of all, the habit of going on ahead without waiting for the carriage. He remained loyal to this habit even after his flight from Yasnaya. When he and Makovitsky were leaving Optina Pustyn, Tolstoy went ahead on foot then as well.

Secondly, one can speculate that L.N.'s daily meanderings, both on foot and on horseback, along winding forest paths, during which he often got lost, were a kind of dress rehearsal, or, if you like, simulations of a departure. The unpredictability of the routes Tolstoy chose surprised everyone who accompanied him during the last year of his life, when it simply wasn't safe to leave the old man on his own. Bulgakov, his secretary, Goldenweiser, the musician, and Makovitsky, his doctor, all write about this. It is even conceivable that *departure and getting lost* were a passion of Tolstoy's, a mighty and invincible one, just as women, alcohol or card games are for other people.

What did this passion signify? Yes, we know that he spent this time in solitary prayer, addressing God with words known only to him. Indeed, in the last years of his life, the time he spent outside the walls of the house, was also a chance for him to take a break from the visitors and from the family rows. But even when he was no longer left alone, when he was accompanied on his walks by Bulgakov, Makovitsky, Goldenweiser or one of the more agreeable guests, he would still choose uncharted trails or steep ravines, as if deliberately forcing himself and his companion to get lost and be required to find a way out of a difficult situation.

"I had such a nice drive today with dear Bulgakov along the paths in the woods; we got lost," he said happily over lunch.

And on the last day before his departure, on October 27, he went out riding and strayed into a remote ravine along with Makovitsky.

The doctor was afraid that he would try to spur the horse out of the ravine, as he usually did, and asked him to get off his horse.

"... he did as he was told, which happened so rarely. The ravine was very steep, and I wanted to take each horse out individually, but fearing that while I led the first one out, L.N. would take care of the other one (L.N. didn't like it when people did things for him), I took the reins of both horses at the same time ... I got down in that way and jumped across the stream in that way. At that point L.N. shouted out in alarm, fearing that some horse would come crashing into my legs. Then I, with a great effort, climbed up the other side of the ravine. I waited there for a long time. L.N., having shoved the tails of his overcoat into his belt, and holding on carefully to tree trunks and the branches of bushes, made his way down. He came down to the brook and, sitting down, crawled across the ice, crawled ashore on all fours, then, arriving at a steep incline, reaching out to grab branches, he climbed up, taking long rests, and he was greatly out of breath. I turned my back so that L.N. wouldn't rush. I wanted to help him, but was afraid to bother him ..."

Even the doctor realized that it would not have been right to interfere with this process! To do so would only provoke the great old man's ire. It would be as sacrilegious as going into his study in the morning and trying to help him with his work. And who knows, perhaps, as he gazed at the greatest writer in the world crawling on all fours on the edge of a ravine, Makovitsky remembered the words he had uttered two months previously, over lunch:

"I watched some ants. They were crawling up and down a tree. I don't know what they might have been getting there? Only those who were crawling upwards, their abdomen was small, ordinary in size, whereas the ones going down had thick, heavy abdomens. By all appearances, they were collecting something inside themselves. And how he crawls, only knowing his own path. Along the tree are uneven patches, burrs, he goes around them and crawls further... in my old age I somehow find it particularly fascinating when I look at the ants, and at the trees. And what do all these airplanes mean alongside this! How coarse and tasteless it all is!"

In many of the photos of Tolstoy as an old man, we don't see this dynamic. Photos from the time could not always convey movement, it took a few seconds of exposure in order to take a picture. Fortunately, we are able to see Tolstoy in motion thanks to the newsreels. Especially impressive are the shots in which he is all alone on the "preshpekt", the birch-lined path leading from the manor house to the road. It is the movement of an extremely experienced walker. His legs are relaxed, half-bent at the knees, and his gait seems baggy. His feet point abruptly to either side. It creates the impression that his feet are moving separately from his body, like a rag doll.

But this is exactly how real walkers walk. In an absurd, relaxed way, wobbling from side to side idiotically, with an almost unnatural gait. They really do make maximum use of the inertia of the leg-swing.

It was an inability to pace himself while walking that did for the hero of Tolstoy's story, *How Much Land Does a Man Need*, a peasant named Pakhom. The Bashkirs told him he could help himself to as much land as he could walk around before sunset. Overcome by greed, Pakhom covers verst after verst, in an attempt to get around as much free land as he can, but when he arrives at the finish line, falls down dead. Of course, the moral of the story is that Pakhom was killed by his greed, and that ultimately the amount of land man needs is no more nor less than the amount taken up by his coffin. But the story also contains a sly, knowing glance at this little peasant, who decided that to walk around his land would be a trifling matter, and nothing like as hard as working on it. Tolstoy, who spent decades walking around his estate at Yasnaya almost on a daily basis and yet still got lost time and time again, knew the insidiousness of what looks like an unprotected expanse, stretching out before one's gaze; he knew how easily it could lead the inexperienced walker to stray from the right path, and even be the death of him.

And he also knew that fleeing (and Pakhom, before ending up in Bashkiria, runs from one plot of land to another in search of a better life) does not solve problems. And yet so many of his characters are forever leaving and running off somewhere, running off and departing.

The Tumbleweed

Olenin runs off to the Caucasus, and the young Nehlyudov in *A Landowner's Morning* escapes from the university to run off to the countryside. Count Turbin in Two Hussars suddenly turns up in the provincial capital, K., only to disappear just as suddenly. The main character of the story The Snowstorm gets lost in the wilderness. Bolkonsky flees from active service in the army. Natasha Rostova runs off with Anatoly Kuragin. Pierre Besukhov roams around the battlefields and around ransacked Moscow. Anna Karenina leaves her husband and Vronsky, after her death, can find no alternative but to flee to the Serbian war. The other Nekhlyudov, in the novel Resurrection, gradually departs to go after

Katya Maslova. Father Sergey runs from earthly glory, and the Emperor Alexander, in the form of the old man, goes into hiding in Siberia. The hero-villain from *The Forged Coupon* goes wandering and also turns up in Siberia. In the story *Two Old Men*, the peasants go on foot to Jerusalem. The merchant Vasily and the worker Nikita got lost in the steppes, in the novel *Master and Man*. The hero of *Diary of a Madman* gets lost while out hunting and experiences mortal terror. Hadji Murat dies after breaking out from encirclement. And this is far from a complete list of the characters who take flight or depart in Tolstoy's works.

But there is also a final form of escape – suicide. This is the path chosen by the third Nekhlyudov, in *Recollections of a Billiard-Marker*, Fedya Protasov in the *Living Corpse* and Yevgeny in the story *The Devil*. Anna Karenina throws herself under a train and Konstantin Levin thinks about suicide at what seems to be the happiest time of his life.

It would appear that flight has a happy and clear ending in only one of Tolstoy's works. It is a story written for children, entitled *The Prisoner of the Caucasus*. In the rest of his works, departure and flight do not solve problems, but open up a whole new list of them, with a clean slate. Not even death can save the characters from this. In *Recollections of a Billiard-Marker*, Nekhlyudov, before killing himself, suddenly realizes with surprise that death will solve nothing whatsoever.

"In the past I thought that the proximity of death would elevate my soul. I was wrong. In a quarter of an hour I will not exist anymore, but my opinion has not changed at all. I still see, hear and think in the same way; there is still the same strange inconsistency, unsteadiness and lightness in my thoughts, so contrary to the unity and clarity, which, God knows why, man is blessed with being able to think. Thoughts about what might await me beyond the grave, and about what sort of rumors about my death aunt Rtishchevo would spread the next day, assault my mind with equal force."

In *Polikushka*, the suicide of the protagonist, who has lost his mistress's money, proves to be a 'gateway' episode, after which events related to the lost money continue to evolve. Protasov's death does not solve the problems faced by his wife and her new husband. After all, the fact of bigamy has already been proven and Protasov's death by his own hand does not make it possible to argue before the investigators that this bigamy was not committed consciously. In fact, it is not clear how Protasov can be said to have done a "good deed" for his wife, or how his death will save her from disgrace, and, perhaps, exile in Siberia.

But if the ultimate flight from life doesn't solve the problems of said life, how can taking flight in a physical sense possibly be expected to do so? Deprived of a "heavenly" attitude to the world, man is doomed to "inconsistency, unsteadiness and lightness in his thoughts" and, as a result, to lose his way in life. He becomes a "tumbleweed". The wind carries it in unpredictable directions, until it finds a quiet place, sheltered from the wind, where the poor plant can at last put down roots in the soil.

Only Yasnaya Polyana could ever become such a place for Tolstoy, without question, and it is no coincidence that this was precisely the place to which he rushed off at the very beginning of his flight. But his first experience of managing a farmstead in the countryside was unsuccessful. He demonstrated the reasons for this failure perfectly in *The Landowner's Morning*. Due to his freedom-loving nature, Tolstoy was incapable of being a good slave owner, and until the emancipation of the serfs in 1861 there was no point in even thinking about establishing an isolated peasant paradise within serf-owning Russia. Yet almost all of L.N.'s future attempts to manage a rational farmstead, as a rule, ended in failure too. With the exception of gardens and forest plantations. He was too reckless as a master, and if he took up some project or other (whether beekeeping, pig breeding, a distillery or horse breeding), he would devote himself to it with a poetic passion; farming, though, is something that requires cold calculation and distribution of strength.

In May 1847, he travels from Kazan to Yasnaya, and in the autumn of 1848 is already running off to Moscow, where he lives "very carelessly, without service, without work, without a purpose". In February 1849, meanwhile, he leaves for St. Petersburg, drawn by an "indistinct thirst for knowledge". Two paths are open to him: he could either become a military officer or a civil servant. His "thirst for knowledge" trumped his ambition, and in early 1849 he passed two exams on criminal law and procedure at St. Petersburg University. But "spring came, and the charm of life in the countryside once again drew me to the estate".

So began a three-year period of constant confusion and vacillation. Now he dreams of serving in the Ministry of Foreign Affairs; now he plans to be a cadet in the horse-guards regiment, so that he can take part in the

Hungarian campaign; now, with the onset of spring, he dashes off to the "charms of rural life"; now he intends to take out a lease on a post office...

During this period he gives up the diary which he had begun in Kazan, but thanks to his letters to his older brother Sergei we are able to see what sort of things he was feeling.

February 13, 1849: "I am writing this letter to you from St. Petersburg, where I intend to stay forever ... I know you're not going to believe that I have changed, you'll say, 'that's the 20th time now, and still there's nothing to be made of you', 'the most trivial of fellows', – but no, I have changed in an altogether different way this time, than how I changed in the past; in the past I would say to myself: "OK then – I'll change", whereas now I can see that I have changed, and I say to myself, "I have changed".

May 1: "Seryozha! I bet you are already saying that I am "the most trivial of fellows", and you'd be right. God knows what I've gone and done. I went to St. Petersburg for no reason, didn't do anything useful there, merely spent a fortune and got into debt. Stupid! Intolerably stupid!"

May 11: "In my last letter, I wrote you various stupid things, of which the main one was that I was intending to join the horse-guard regiment; but now I shall only abandon this plan if I don't pass the exams and the war turns out to be serious".

That same spring, "without a penny to my name and owing money left, right and center", Tolstoy returns to Yasnaya Polyana with a German musician named Rudolph who liked a drink or two, and devotes himself passionately to music. He even commences, though doesn't complete, an article entitled *The Fundamental Principles of Music and the Rules governing the Study of It*. Pay attention to these key words: *fundamental* and *rules*.

Prior to his departure in April 1851 with his brother Nikolai to the Caucasus, L.N. leads a double-life which is torturous for him, torn between Moscow and Yasnaya Polyana. At Yasnaya he can enjoy strolls, gymnastics, music, the English language, Goethe, and his early work on *Childhood*. In Moscow he leads a life of cards, debauchery, gypsy girls, prostitutes, and debts piled upon debts... At Yasnaya he has a kindly guardian angel, his Aunt Tatyana Alexandrovna Yergolskaya, a pious old maiden, with whom L.N.'s father had once been in love, but had refused to marry him, nonetheless devoting herself to bringing up his children. He would spend the evenings with her, chatting over tea about their ancestors, about life in the olden days. In Moscow he led an "absolutely beastly" life, which he tried to put in order with the help of his "rules".

Diary entry, December 24, 1850: "*Rules*. Play cards only in extreme cases. – Talk as little as possible about myself. Speak loudly and clearly. –*Rules*. Take exercise every day. – In line with religious law, don't have any women."

January 17, 1851: "*Rule* ... 1) Get into a gambling circle and, if I have the money for it, play cards. 2) Get into high society and, if the conditions that are well known are satisfied, get married. 3) Find a place favorable for service."Tolstoy's dreams of a career ended in his enrollment in the Tula Province government as a clerical servant with the rank of a collegiate registrar. This was the lowest civil rank, the 14th class in Peter the Great's 'Table of Ranks'. It was a rank that was given the nickname "don't hit me in the face", because it conferred on people of non-noble descent hereditary honorary citizenship, thereby exempting them from corporal punishment. "And he messes things up just like a simple collegiate registrar, and not at all like a man with a star on his chest..." wrote Gogol in *Dead Souls*.

Meanwhile, the young Tolstoy was terribly ambitious! It's no wonder that he put ambition in the first place among the vices of his youth in *Confession*. But how was this ambition really reflected, other than in his vague career aspirations and an indistinct desire to go to war? Not in his flight to the Caucasus, that's for sure.

In a letter to T.A. Yergolskaya from Tiflis he describes this trip as "a fantasy which suddenly popped into my head". How suddenly such fantasies could come to him can be seen from the fact that in the fall of 1848, he very nearly left for Siberia with his future son-in-law, Valerian Tolstoy: he jumped into his coach without a coat and with no hat, and the only reason he didn't leave, it seems, was that he had forgotten his hat. (Oh, those hats! Fifty years later, when leaving the house at Yasnaya Polyana forever, he lost his hat once again and would have to go back for a new one. This was a bad omen, and L.N., though he did not recognize religious ceremonies, believed in omens.)

Interestingly, the flight to the Caucasus was also indirectly related to the dissolute Valerian Tolstoy, who by then was already married to L.N.'s sister, Maria Nikolayevna. The meeting of two brothers, Nikolai and Lev, took place on his estate of Pokrovskoye, on the outskirts of

Chern, on New Year's Eve (the new year in question was 1851), after a four-year separation. Nikolai had served in the Caucasus. Tormented by the split between his inner and outer life, entangled in debts as he was, and disillusioned by the farmstead and his career, the younger brother decides to follow him, without a plan of any kind, perhaps just to simply to go along for the ride, and unwind. There was all the more reason to do so given that the eternal inventor Nikolai had devised an unusual route: they would drive first to Saratov, then drift down to Astrakhan by boat. The trip turned out to be a magnificent one. Along the way Tolstoy found the time to fall in love with Zinaida Molostvova in Kazan, later writing some frivolous lines of verse about the experience in Syzran: "My wounds I lick as now I can, For we've arrived in old Syzran..." However, finding himself in the village of Starogladkovskaya on May 30, he writes with considerable amazement in his diary: "How did I get here? I do not know. What for? Don't know that either." From Starogladkovskaya he travels with his brother to the village of Old Yurt, admiring the view of the mountains and hot springs, where the eggs are hard-boiled in just three minutes and where the picturesque Tatar women stamp on their laundry as they wash it. His flight to the Caucasus was so hasty that he arrived there without the necessary papers, which he had been waiting for from Tula for four months, after which he presented himself in Tbilisi before Major General Edward Vladimirovich Brimmer, chief of artillery of the Separate Caucasus Corps. But the documents he received from Tula weren't sufficient: he had to wait for further documents from St. Petersburg. Tolstoy was officially appointed to military service in February 1852. This was no way to make a career. Nor had they gone to the Caucasus for the sake of his career.

Nevertheless, Tolstoy's ambition saved him from slipping into the abyss, from that "beastly" life in Moscow. No, it was not that life in the Caucasus, where he spent nearly three years, was any less "beastly", when judged by his elevated moral criteria. Gambling, debts, loose women – he wolfed all this down, with a little garrison vulgarity as an added ingredient: "Some officer said that he knows exactly what sort of things I wanted to show the ladies, and merely asserted, taking his short stature into account, that despite the fact that his were a little smaller in size, he could show them exactly the same thing" (diary entry from July 4, 1851).

But nature in the Caucasus, the air itself, as transparent as the relationships between the people here, along with his ambitious desire to loudly make a name for himself before the world and before his family, to prove he was not a "trivial fellow", were the perfect incentives for creativity. It was in the Caucasus that the writer in Tolstoy was born. And this writer was immediately a great one, the author of *Childhood* and *Boyhood*.

Looking back on his youth with a stern eye, Tolstoy admitted that he "began writing out of vanity, greed and pride" (*Confession*). Any serious writer, with hand on heart, knows the truth of this: the first works aren't written as a result of spiritual considerations or, at any rate, lofty considerations are strongly fueled by the desire for fame and money. But just as the Caucasus proved to be higher than L.N.'s childish bravado, the atmosphere of creativity was higher and deeper than his ambition. Above all, though – this was the place where the "tumbleweed" could come to rest and put down its first roots...

Chapter 3

Sonia and the Devil

"How nice it is here!" exclaimed Tolstoy when he saw the room provided for him in Optina Pustyn by the innkeeper Brother Mikhail. Spacious, with three windows, muslin curtains, ficus plants in pots, a large image of Christ the Savior in the corner, an ancient sofa and a round table in front of it, with a second soft sofa and yellow wooden screens fixed to the floor, hiding a comfortable bed – it was the best room in the hotel. When Tolstoy went to bed, he asked for another little table and a candle. Before going to sleep, he drank tea. Brother Mikhail brought him some Antonov apples. L.N. praised the apples and asked:

"You wouldn't happen to have a little honey would you, Brother Mikhail? After all, you haven't taken the mandyas yet, so I'll call you "brother".

Mikhail brought him honey as well.

His joy was premature, though... The night he spent in Optina proved to be a very restless one. This was despite the fact that Makovitsky, not wanting to break Tolstoy's habit of sleeping alone in his room, went to sleep in a different room across the hall.

Cats ran up and down the corridor all night long, jumping onto the furniture offset against the wall behind which Tolstoy was sleeping. Then some woman came out into the hall, wailing. Her brother, a monk and shopkeeper, had died that day. She came to see the Count early in the morning and begged him to adopt her babies. She fell to her knees in front of him. Tolstoy found it hard to bear when people got down on their knees before him. Whenever visitors to Yasnaya Polyana did this, L.N. would get down on his knees in front of them, too, to make them stop.

At 7 am, he left his room and bumped into Alyosha Sergeyenko, Chertkov's secretary and the twenty-four year old son of Pyotr Alexeyevich

Sergeyenko, whom Tolstoy knew, in the hallway. Alyosha was among a select few who were aware of the most closely guarded secrets of Tolstoy's life at Yasnaya Polyana, including the story of his conflicts with his wife. Alexei was therefore the one given the honor and at the same time the unpleasant mission of notifying Tolstoy about what happened at Yasnaya after his disappearance.

But how did Alyosha Sergeyenko know that Tolstoy was at Optina? It's all very simple. Whilst still at Shchekino, L.N. had sent Sasha a telegram that read: "We're probably going to go to Optina... Please, my dear, as soon as you find out where I am, and you'll find out very soon – let me know about everything: how was the news of my departure taken, and the more details you give, the better."

That's all there was to the conspiracy. But even if this telegram hadn't been sent... Everyone at Shchekino, the station near Yasnaya, from the station manager to the cashier, knew that L.N. and Makovitsky had gone to Kozelsk. And it wasn't difficult to guess that from Kozelsk he would go and see his sister at Shamordino, and not fail to stop off at Optina, which he had visited three times in his twilight years and where his aunts Alexandra Ilinichna Osten-Sacken and Elizaveta Alexandrovna Tolstaya were buried. It is unlikely that S.A. hadn't guessed as much too, after sending a servant to the station to find out where L.N. had bought his ticket to.

To send Sergeyenko as a visitor to the fleeing Tolstoy was an unkind decision in relation to S.A., taken by her daughter Sasha and Chertkov. Right from the outset, Tolstoy was surrounded by people who were unfavorably disposed towards her, finding out from them what was happening at Yasnaya Polyana without him.

Alyosha Sergeyenko's father was the author of "a dramatic chronicle in 4 parts", *Xanthippe*, about Socrates' shrewish wife, who poisoned his life just as effectively as the cup of hemlock. In this play, first published in a supplement in the journal *Niva* in 1899, one could clearly infer that the characters were based on L.N. and his wife, a fact which M.S. Suhotin, Tolstoy's son-in-law, wrote about in his diary. Whilst the general public may not have understood this, it was certainly picked up on in the Tolstoy family.

We don't know which words and expressions Sergeyenko used, or what comments he added, as he told of S.A.'s attempt to drown in the pond.

We only know that this story made a very bad impression on Tolstoy and gave rise not only to pity, but also to unkind thoughts in relation to his wife.

"I slept uneasily," Tolstoy writes in his diary on October 29, "in the morning Alyosha Sergeyenko... I, not having understood, greeted him cheerfully. But he brought terrible news. They figured out where I am, and Sofia Andreyevna asked Andrei (Tolstoy's son. - PB) to find me, no matter what. And now, on the evening of the 29th, I am awaiting Andrei's arrival... It was hard on me all day, and I'm physically weak." "Diary for me alone": "Sergeyenko arrived. Everything is as before, even worse. If only no sin could be committed. And no ill-will harbored. There's none now." The difficult feeling which he was struggling against, and which, as he thought, he had defeated, was ill-will toward his wife.

"... If anyone ought to be drowning themselves, it certainly shouldn't be her, it should be me," he complains in a letter to Sasha Tolstoy.

"...I only want one thing – freedom from her, from the lies, pretense and malice, with which her whole being is permeated... You see, my dear, how bad I am. I'm not hiding it from you".

When he entered the cell of his sister, Maria Nikolayevna, at Shamordino, he wept, for the first time since fleeing Yasnaya. His sister was pleased to see him, but expressed surprise that he had made the journey in bad weather.

"I fear things are bad for you at home."

"Things are awful at home!"

His conversation was interrupted several times by his sobs: "To think of it, what horror: into the water..." His niece E.V. Obolenskaya, who had arrived, offered him a drink of water... Tolstoy declined the offer...

The Drowned Woman

After her father's departure, Sasha sat in an armchair for a long while, wrapped in a blanket. She was shaking as if she had a fever. She counted the minutes and hours. The train from Shchekino left at eight. At eight o'clock in the morning she began to wander through the rooms. She happened to cross paths with the old servant Ilya Vasilevich. He had already worked out what had happened.

"Lev Nikolayevich told me that he planned to leave, and now I can tell by the dress you're wearing, that he isn't here..."

The other servants were already whispering, speculating, and S.A. was still asleep. She got up late, at 11 o'clock, and sensing that something bad had happened due to the servants' behavior, ran to Sasha's room.

- Where's Papa?
- He's gone.
- Where did he go?
- I don't know.

Sasha handed over her father's farewell letter. S.A. quickly ran her eyes over it... Her head shook, her hands were trembling; her cheeks flushed red.

She didn't read to the end, but threw the letter on the floor and, shouting: "He's gone, he's gone for good, goodbye, Sasha, I shall drown myself!" ran toward the pond.

This is how the scene looks in Alexandra Lvovna's memoirs. It is described in more detail in Valentin Bulgakov's diary.

"When I arrived at eleven in the morning at Yasnaya Polyana, Sofia Andreyevna had just woken up and had gotten dressed. She peeked into Lev Nikolayevich's room and saw no trace of him. She ran into the "Remington" room and then into the library. There she was told about Lev Nikolayevich's departure, and his letter was given to her.

"Oh my God!" Sofia Andreyevna whispered.

She tore open the envelope and read the first line of the letter: "My departure will upset you ..." She could not go on; she threw the letter onto the table in the library and ran to her room, whispering:

"Oh my God!.. What is he doing to me!"

She ripped the envelope of the letter open and read the first line: "my departure grieves you..." She couldn't continue, threw the letter on the table in the library and ran to her room, whispering:

"Oh my God!... What is he doing to me!..."

"Read the letter, maybe there's something in it!" Alexandra Lvovna and Varvara Mikhailovna shouted after her, but she didn't listen to them.

The next moment, one of the servants runs in and shouts out that Sofia Andreyevna has run into the park, toward the pond.

"Go and find her, you've got boots on!" Alexandra Lvovna said to me, and then ran off to put on her galoshes.

I ran out into the yard, to the park. Sofia Andreyevna's gray dress flashed in the distance between the trees: she was moving quickly down the linden tree-lined path toward the pond. Hiding behind the trees, I went after her. Then I started running.

"Don't run!" Alexandra Lvovna shouted from behind me.

I looked around. There were already a few people walking along behind me: the cook Semyon Nikolaevich, the footman Vanya and others.

At this point Sofia Andreyevna turned to the side, heading directly for the pond. She hid behind the bushes. Alexandra Lvovna flies swiftly past me, her skirts rustling. I too ran after her, as fast as I could go. We could not afford to dawdle: Sofia Andreyevna was already at the pond.

We ran up to the slope. Sofia Andreyevna glanced back and noticed us. She had already passed the slope. She's walking along the gangway (near the bathhouse), where they rinse out the laundry. She's clearly hurrying. Suddenly she slipped – and with a crash she falls onto the gangway, right on her back ... Clinging to the boards with her hands, she crawls to the edge of the gangway nearest to her and rolls into the water.

Alexandra Lvovna is already on the gangway. She falls over as well, on the same slippery patch, as she walks onto it ... I'm on the gangway as well. Alexandra Lvovna jumps into the water. I do likewise. I can still see the figure of Sofia Andreyevna from the gangway: face up, mouth open, into which water must have already come pouring, helplessly throwing up her hands, she is sinking into the water... And now the water has completely covered her.

Fortunately, Alexandra Lvovna and I can feel the bottom underfoot. It was a good thing Sofia Andreyevna fell where she did, when she slipped over. If she had thrown herself in directly from the gangway, we wouldn't have been able to stand on the bottom. The middle pond is very deep, people had drowned in it before. Near the bank the water came up to our chests.

Alexandra Lvovna and I drag Sofia Andreyevna up, hoist her onto one of the logs on which the gangway rests, then onto the gangway itself.

Vanya Shuraev, the footman, arrives. Together, he and I, with difficulty, lift up the heavy, wet-through Sofia Andreyevna and carry her to the bank.

Alexandra Lvovna runs off to change her clothes, prompted to do so by Varvara Mikhailovna, who came out of the house after her.

Vanya, the cook and I slowly carry Sofia Andreyevna toward the house. She complains about the fact that we pulled her out of the water. She finds it difficult to walk. At one point, she lowers herself helplessly to the ground:

"I just want to sit down for a bit..! Let me sit for a moment..!"

But this is out of the question: Sofia Andreyevna must change her clothes as soon as possible...

Vanya and I lock our arms together to form a seat, and with the help of the cook and others, we sit Sofia Andreyevna in it and start to carry her. Soon, though, she asks us to put her down."

After the first suicide attempt, they began to watch over S.A. They took her opium, a pocketknife and a heavy paperweight away from her. But she kept saying that she would find a way to kill herself. An hour later, she managed to run out of the house. Bulgakov caught up with her as she ran toward the same pond and brought her home by force.

"Like a son, like my own son..!" she said to him.

This story of a double suicide attempt cannot fail to inspire compassion. One must have too callous a soul to see in this only the desire to do something dramatic and scare the family, and through them – her husband, so as to make him come back.

What good to her now were his words, even if they were the best, kindest and most apt ones? What good to her now were his words, when set against his action, which the whole world would notice and which (she understood this full well!) would go down in history. But she too would go down in history, the woman that her great husband had, for whatever reason, left.

Even for ordinary women with ordinary husbands, a husband's departure is painful not only because he has left them, but by dint of the way it makes them look in the eyes of others. So she had been a bad wife, had she? All those years? Or perhaps she had become bad when she got old? And while she was young, he had been happy with her? While she was still strong, healthy and attractive?

A conflict between a husband and a wife is also a competition to be seen as the one in the right by others. No matter how great Tolstoy was, he too depended on this opinion. The fact that his wife did hardly needs stressing.

After L.N.'s departure, she was alone and "the guilty party, all round". The entire house, including her own daughter, was on the side of the unfortunate fugitive. As a woman, she was offended, as a person - insulted. As a man, her husband had acted forcefully and in a way that was beautiful in its own way (after all, no-one, except for two or three people, had seen him trembling in the coach house). As an individual, he had made the last choice of his life in favor of independence and spiritual freedom (after all, Tolstoy had yet to step off the train in Astapovo, supported by the arms, in search of a regular bed, where he could just lie down).

Before judging her for making too dramatic a suicide attempt (yes, it was possible to do it some other way, but who dares to judge this!), it's necessary to assess the full extent of her loneliness. The whole house and the whole civilized world were on her husband's side. On her side were only some of her sons, but at that moment, they weren't there. They arrived the next day, summoned by Sasha's telegrams. And it was primarily for them, entangled in debt as they were, that she was in conflict with her husband because of the inheritance. And there was no one to take her by the arm, except Bulgakov, who, overall, was foreign to her, like all of Tolstoy's secretaries sent into their house by Chertkov, whom she hated.

We cannot judge what happened in S.A.'s soul or how the hysterical condition coexisted with guile in her. Of course, she kind of played out the scene with the flight to the pond and the fall into the water (it was no coincidence, writes Bulgakov, that she looked back at her pursuers). But it was not at all to simulate suicide, as she had done repeatedly earlier, by shooting a cap gun in her room, or saying that she had drunk a whole bottle of opium, or lying down in just a dress on the cold ground in the garden. Now, she was done with simulation. She had intended to go through with the act with which she had scared the whole house during the conflict with her husband, and which she hadn't committed this time either, and she was now, perhaps, very sorry about that. Ah, if she had drowned before his departure, as she had often threatened! The one acting extravagantly in this story would have been him. He would thus have killed his wife, who had selflessly served him for forty-eight years, brought up his children, rewritten his manuscripts and nursed him when he was sick, feeding him with a spoon. He would then have been the *villain* of the piece, and she - the *martyr*.

One of the chapters of S.A.'s copious memoirs, entitled *My Life*, is called *The Male Martyr and the Female Martyr*. It would be more accurate to replace the "and" with an "or". In fact, who was the victim? Her, an ordinary woman whose fate was to serve a genius, or him, a genius, doomed to live with a normal woman? There can't be a verbal answer to this question. The answer which would convince everyone could only be an action. And it was L.N. who carried out such an action first. What was left for her to do? Accept defeat and go down in history as "guilty all round?" For this, she was too proud. Complain, make excuses? In the end, that's exactly what she had to do in Astapovo, when surrounded by reporters. But in the first moment, in a state of shock, she also tried to commit a beautiful (as it seemed to her) act, to put her own independent plot into the novel of her life with Tolstoy. If she couldn't drown in front of her husband, then she would do so in front of those who supported him, and condemned her.

We can't forget that she was the wife of the world's greatest novelist, the author of *Anna Karenina*. And if the Kursk railroad hadn't been a few versts away, but had passed close to the Yasnaya Polyana house, there is no doubt that the plot of the suicide attempt would have been different. She had already gone once to the railway, as Anna Karenina did, with the idea that "everything is a lie, everything a deception, everything is evil," but after she chanced to run into Kuzminsky, her sister's husband, along the way, he had brought her back home.

In the style of her behavior after her husband's departure, there was much that was unpleasant, much that grates on the ears and eyes. In general, there is little that is pleasant in the style of family conflicts. Is there any style in them at all, come to that?

The (Im)possibility of Paradise

But let's return to the past.

In this book, there is no point in dwelling in detail on the military period of Tolstoy's life from 1851 to 1855 in the Caucasus, the Crimea and Romania. Tolstoy was a good soldier and officer, however not outstanding and somewhat strange. He was brave, strong physically, was a wonderful companion, a gambler and a bit of a poet: he wrote the satirical *Song About the Battle at the Black River*, which the soldiers and officers liked to sing at the rest stops, and which has gone down in various forms into military folklore. His strangeness lay in the fact that he was often moody, was original in judgment and didn't want to use money from the pocket of the treasury, even when this was allowed under the officers' unspoken code. But above all - he was in some way *unloved*, to borrow Yeroshka's phrase from *The Cossacks*. This is a popular expression that cannot be translated into literary language without losing the meaning. *Unloved* by whom? By women, by destiny? Yes, by all these things at once! Tolstoy was awkward with women, unlucky in his career and at card games. But of course, this does not exhaust the meaning of the difficult word "*unloved*", which, nonetheless, the simple Cossack Yeroshka and Prince Olenin understood perfectly.

But it was thanks to this that the young Tolstoy succeeded as a writer, realizing in literature what was lacking in his life. Orphaned prematurely, he wrote the most poetic work in Russian literature about childhood. By no means a fan of war, he hymned the heroism of Russian soldiers and officers in the besieged Sevastopol, so much so that upon reading *Sevastopol in December*, the Empress, the strict literary connoisseur Ivan Turgenev and the adolescent tsarevich (the future Alexander III) were moved to tears, whilst the young Tsar Alexander II ordered that the story be translated into French, and, it was even rumored, sent a courier to the Crimea to relay the message that the talented writer-officer must be sent to a safe area.

Tolstoy was, as was said at the time, an honest officer, but not more than that. He wasn't attracted either by the dubious heroism of war, nor by the even more dubious career of an officer at the time of the conquest of the Caucasus and the failure of the Russo-Turkish campaign. At any rate, they didn't grab him completely. But Tolstoy was a very complete person, and if he wanted something, then he wanted it completely.

What did the young Tolstoy want? Love and happiness. He definitely wanted to settle down at Yasnaya Polyana and marry. Writing didn't appeal to him to the same extent as the entirely commonplace perspective of a landlord's life on an estate with a devoted wife and ancestral portraits on the walls of a stately home. Literary success quenched his vanity, but didn't subdue his mental strength. A literary career demanded compromise - with editors, publishers, censorship - and this wasn't consistent with his notion of the ideal, of perfection, and ultimately of "paradise".

Yasnaya Polyana + marriage were closest of all to the ideal. This was the objective, personified "paradise" which he portrayed in a letter from Mozdok to T.A. Yergolskaya in January 1852:

"Years pass, here I am no longer young, but not old in *Yasnaya* - my affairs are in order, there are no worries, nor hassles, and you're still living in *Yasnaya*. You've gotten a bit older, but you're still fresh and healthy. Life goes on as before, I do exercises in the mornings, but we are together most of the day; after dinner, in the evening I read out loud whatever you don't get bored listening to, then a conversation starts. I tell you about my life in the Caucasus, you tell me about your reminiscences of the past, about my father and mother; you tell me *scary stories* of the kind we used to listen to with frightened eyes and gaping mouths. We remember those who were dear to us, and are no longer with us; you cry, and so do I, only with peaceful tears... I'm married - my wife is gentle, kind and loving, and she loves you like I do. Our children call you "grandmother"; you live in the big house, upstairs, in the room where my grandmother used to live; everything in the house is still like it was before, in the same order as it was during papa's life, and we continue the same life, only having changed roles, you take the role of the grandmother, but you are still kinder than she was, I - the role of papa, but I hope someday to deserve it; and my wife – that of mama ..."

In this picture, which at first glance is idyllic, Tolstoy despotically paints all the roles that need to be taken on by the future inhabitants of *Yasnaya* or *Yasnogo* as it was acceptable in those days to call the estate, using the masculine form in a way that sounded patriarchal. 'He' referred to papa, that is to say, Nikolai Ilyich Tolstoy, who completed the work of his father-in-law, Nikolai Sergeyevich Volkonsky, on the construction of the Yasnaya Polyana estate complex. A distant relative, T.A. Yergolskaya was assigned a place of honor, as "grandmother", i.e., the father's mother, Pelageya Nikolayevna, née Princess Gorchakova, imperious, capricious, who slighted her servants, but adored her son Nikolai and didn't survive his death. His wife is assigned the role of mama, Maria Nikolayevna Tolstaya, née Volkonskaya.

This part of the letter is particularly important. If Sonya Behrs had read this letter before she became Countess Tolstoy, she would have guessed what sort of a role her future husband was preparing for her. To be his wife and mother at the same time.

Tolstoy remembered and loved his father, was proud of him and wanted to emulate him, whereas he barely knew his mother, yet he idolized her, and depicted her as Princess Maria in *War and Peace*. Tolstoy carried the cult of his mother throughout his life; as he neared old age, that cult even manifested itself in him with much greater force. The fact that he couldn't remember her face, and that there weren't any portrait images of her, only strengthened the cult, turning his mother from an earthly woman into the image of the Madonna. It is no coincidence that a reproduction which he loved of the Dresden "Sistine Madonna" by Raphael hung in his bedroom from 1862 to 1885, and then migrated to his office, where it can still be seen in the Yasnaya Polyana museum to this day.

His female ideal was embodied in his mother, and that was something he subconsciously demanded from his future wife. At the same time, she was also supposed to become a mother in the usual sense. And the kids had to play a role in this domestic "paradise", too. They had to repeat the childhood enjoyed by Maria Nikolayevna and Nikolai Ilyich when they were children. "...our children shall play our roles," he writes to Yergolskaya. And she also has to be the perfect hostess. "I imagine... how my wife will fuss about..." And yet... We will find out what else he was expecting from his future wife from the story *A Landlord's Morning*:

"I and my wife, whom I love in a way that no-one has ever loved anyone else in the world before, are always living in the midst of the calm, poetic nature of the countryside, with the children, perhaps with an elderly aunt as well; and we have our mutual love, our love toward the children, and we both know that our purpose is kindness. We help each other move towards this goal. I give overall direction, bestow general, just benefits, build up farms, savings banks and workshops; and she, with her pretty little head, in a plain white dress, lifting it above her slender legs, walks through the mud to the peasant school, the infirmary, to the unfortunate peasant, who doesn't really deserve her help, and provides comfort and help everywhere she goes... Children, the elderly, the old women adore her and look on her as on some kind of angel, as on Providence. Then she comes back and hides it from me that she went to see the unfortunate peasant and gave him money, but I know everything, and hold her tightly and firmly and gently kiss her lovely eyes, bashfully blushing cheeks and smiling red lips."

S.A. later transposed much of this image into reality. As a young woman, she wore plain, short dresses and helped to tend the village women. She was a wonderful mother and housewife. In the dreams dreamt by Nekhlyudov in *The Landlord's Morning* it is easy to detect erotic overtones as well. His wife must be an angel, but must have "slender legs", "a pretty little head", "rosy lips". S.A. was no great beauty, but everyone noticed her appeal when she was young and how youthful she seemed in her older years.

In his letter to Yergolskaya, Tolstoy assigns roles for his brothers as well. "Three new characters will appear from time to time on the stage – these are my brothers, and, most importantly, one of them - Nikolai, who will often be with us. The old bachelor, bald and retired, is, as before, kind and noble. I picture him, just like in the old days, telling the children his made-up stories. The children will kiss his hands, which are strong (but worthy of being kissed), and he will play with them..."

And finally - his sister Maria Nikolayevna, Mashenka. He gives her the role of both his father's sisters, Alexandra Ilinichna and Pelagea Ilinichna. Only she will not be "unhappy, as they are".

But the question arises: to what extent was all this serious? Perhaps, having fled to the Caucasus, Tolstoy was merely having a flight of fancy, after stopping off in Mozdok? He wanted to comfort his old aunt and himself?

Five years later, he writes to his brother Sergei: "It's in vain that you think that this love of family life is a dream that sickens me. I'm a family man at heart, all my tastes were that way inclined in my youth as well, and now they have long since been so. I am as convinced of that as I am of the fact that I am alive."

Of the four Tolstoy brothers (Nikolai, Sergei, Dmitri and Lev), only the last found familial happiness. This happiness ended in complete catastrophe, but the catastrophe had a prelude that lasted forty-eight years, the first fifteen of which, at least, were happy years. Nikolai and Dmitri died bachelors. Sergei spent his whole life with Masha, a woman bought from a gypsy camp, and although he loved her in his own way, it is probably fair to say that he lived with her more out of a debt of honor rather than out of love. The Tolstoys' only sister, Maria, proved unlucky in marriage, leaving her husband and children and giving birth to an illegitimate child in Europe, then becoming a nun in later life. All of Lev Tolstoy's children, except for those who died in infancy, became notable people, talented and original. Today, there are more than three hundred and fifty direct descendants of Tolstoy living in various countries, and they are all still in touch with one another. Isn't this evidence that L.N. and S.A.'s family project was successful?

But could a family paradise ever have been successful?

On scrutinizing the letter to Yergolskaya, one cannot but marvel at the way he masterfully painted this paradise in both real and mystical projections. God- the Father. In real terms – this was three generations of men from the Volkonsky-Tolstoy lineage: the grandfather Nikolai Sergeyevich (the model for old Bolkonsky in *War and Peace*), the father Nikolai Ilych (Nikolai Rostov) and son Lev Nikolayevich. He may still be a "trivial fellow" in the eyes of his older brothers. But Yasnaya belongs to him, and this alone gives him the legal right to continue the projection of God the Father. The Holy Virgin. In the mystical projection – the mother, and in the real one – the perfect, though as yet unknown, wife. The Holy Spirit. Of course, this is aunt Yergolskaya, the soul of the house, keeper of family traditions. The angels are the children. And the archangels are the older brothers.

There is one character missing from this picture. Jesus Christ. His attitude toward Christ was still uncertain in 1852. In *Confessions*, he assures us that at the time he was a confirmed atheist, but this isn't true. The Caucasian diary tells how he sometimes appealed heatedly and passionately to God the Father, the Creator of the world. As far as Christianity is concerned, though, it's all very vague.

On July 7, 1854, while in Romania, Tolstoy writes in his diary: "What am I? One of the four sons of a retired lieutenant-colonel, who was left at the age of seven without parents and put under the care of women and outsiders, who received neither a secular education nor an academic one and was set free into the world at seventeen, without great wealth, without any social status and, most importantly, without rules; a person who, after ruining his affairs to the utmost, after spending the best years of my life without purpose or enjoyment, eventually banished himself to the Caucasus to escape his debts and, most importantly, his habits, and from there, finding fault with some sort of ties that existed between his father and the army commander, obtained a transfer to the Danube army at 26 years of age, an ensign, almost without means, other than his salary (because what money he has, he must use to pay off his remaining debts), without patrons, without the ability to make a living in the world, without knowledge of the service, without practical abilities; but with a vast amount of pride!" This picture is complemented six days later with an important admission: "My prayer. I believe in a single all-powerful and benevolent God, the immortality of the soul and eternal recompense for our deeds; I wish to believe in the religion of my fathers and I respect it." He believes in God the Father, and wants to be an Orthodox Christian. Primarily, because it is the religion of his fathers. These are rules, but not sincere faith. Thirty years later, in 1881, he would keep a diary which would be called *Notes of a Christian*. His attitude toward Christ would become fully defined. Yet this would be the very thing that signified a break from the "religion of the fathers".

Podkolesin Syndrome

Looking at the story of Tolstoy's courtship and marriage to Sonya Behrs, one cannot escape the parallels between its protagonist and a character in Gogol's comedy *Marriage*, Court Counselor Podkolesin. The hastiness with which the wedding was prepared, and on the other hand - the groom's indecision and the fact that he is prepared to flee before the wedding, are reminiscent of the plot of *The Marriage*, in which Podkolesin flees from his bride by climbing out of a window before he can be taken to church.

Can it really be possible to compare the great Tolstoy to the insignificant Podkolesin? Let's look at Tolstoy's letter to his sister Maria Nikolayevna, written from the French resort of Hyeres.

Whilst in Hyeres, Maria Nikolayevna conceived of the idea of marrying off her brother Lev to the niece of the Vice-President of the

Academy of Sciences, M.A. Dondukov-Korsakov, made famous by an epigram by Pushkin:

> At the Academy, by some fluke,
> The sitting chairman's Prince Dunduk.
> It's said this honor ill befits
> Dunduk and that it's quite a farce;
> Why is it then that he now sits?
> Due to the fact that he's an a –.

Tolstoy was in Brussels at this time, and paid visits to the Prince's family, where he was introduced to his niece Yekaterina Alexandrovna Dondukova-Korsakova. He liked the Princess. At this time he was focusing on looking for a bride, and Maria Nikolayevna had made up her mind that he wouldn't find a better one.

After receiving a letter from her brother from Brussels (the letter didn't survive), in which he apparently asked her to ascertain from the princess, Aunt Katya, how the girl's heart was set, and whether it wasn't already taken by a certain Gardan, about whom he had some information, she wrote to him:

"For God's sake, don't run from your happiness; you will not find a better girl for yourself; and family life will tie you once and for all to Yasnaya Polyana and to your affairs.

Come and see us, Levochka, in matters of the heart, it's true, we (i.e. women) know best - if you start to reason, then all is lost ... If only someone from our family were to be happy! Don't think about it, just come... I am writing this letter fearing that you have already left for Russia." But what was M.N. so afraid of, that she had written the letter "in fear"? Why did she beg her brother not to flee from his happiness?

"But I am specifically afraid of the *Podkolesin*-like bent that is in you. If it is arranged, suddenly you'll see why I'm doing all this. K.A., if she's not in love with you, which I don't think is the case, will probably come to love you, after becoming your wife, and at her age, of course, it is probably fair to say that she won't fall out of love for you and has everything that's needed to be a good, understanding wife and assistant and a good mother. So, from this point of view, it's alright. But do you feel that you seriously want to get married and take care of a wife, to want the same thing that the other person wants, that is to say, not do solely the things you want to do, be less egoistic; such that *quiet hatred* toward your wife won't come to you one morning and the thought that "if I weren't married, then ..." that's what's scary! But for God's sake - don't over-analyze things, because once you start to analyze, you're bound to find a stumbling block in any ordinary matter, and then, not knowing how to answer the questions *what* and *why* to yourself, you'll resort to *flight*."Podkolesin syndrome is not a disease of frivolity. It is a disease of intellect. For Tolstoy, just as for Podkolesin, marriage was too serious a "project". So serious that when it comes down to it and you start to weigh up the "pros" and "cons", so many questions come up that one feels the urge to run away.

"P o d k o l e s i n. For one's whole life, for all time, whatever may happen, to bind oneself, and then only afterwards - no excuses, no remorse, nothing, nothing - it's all over, all done ... Hey, coachman!"

"After death in terms of importance and before death in terms of time, there is nothing more important, more irrevocable than marriage," - Tolstoy writes in his diary on 20 December 1896. "And, just as death is good only when it is inevitable, and every deliberate death is ugly, the same goes for marriage as well. The only cases when marriage is not evil are when it is insuperable..."

This is an idea of the later Tolstoy, one that he liked to repeat, as he did with the words of the Apostle Paul, to the effect that it is better to live in a marriage than to "burn with passion".

In this idea, though, there is another component – the *irrevocability* of marriage. Marriage is for life. There can be only one wife. This is in full accordance with Podkolesin's way of thinking and with the feelings of the young Tolstoy.

The finicky bachelor

After his childish infatuation with Sonia Koloshina, Tolstoy's first attempt to profess his love for someone occurred in Kazan. In 1851, on his way to the Caucasus, Tolstoy met an acquaintance of his at a ball, a friend and classmate of his sister Masha at the Kazan Rodionov Institute, Zinochka Molostvovaya. Zina was not a beauty, but she was a graceful and dreamy girl. When Tolstoy and his brother Nikolai arrived in Kazan, Zinaida was almost the bride of N. V. Tile, an official for special assignments under the governor of Kazan. Nevertheless, at the ball held at the house of a leading member of the nobility, she danced all the mazurkas with Tolstoy. It was doubtful she was as much in love with him as he was with her. She then confessed to him that it was "interesting but difficult" with him. But one innocent event took place in their time together – probably during Tolstoy's student days.

"Do you remember the Arkhiereisky Garden, Zinaida, on the path at the side? I was on the point of declaring my feelings, and so were you. My role was to start, but do you know why, as it seems to me, I didn't do anything? I was so happy that I had nothing to wish for, I was afraid to mess up my ... not my, but our happiness." This is not a letter to the girl, as one might suppose. It is recorded in Tolstoy's diary, in the Caucasus, at Stary Yurt. In the same section Tolstoy asks himself, "Can it really be that I will never see her again?... Shouldn't I write her a letter? I don't know her patronymic and for that reason, perhaps, shall be deprived of my happiness. How ridiculous ..."

These are the concerns of a young man who felt "grown up" for the first time, capable of deciding his own destiny independently. They can hardly be taken seriously. It is a different entry that must be taken seriously, made a year later and also in the Caucasus, when Tolstoy learned of the wedding of Molostvovaya and N. V. Tile: "I'm annoyed, and all the more so given that it didn't alarm me very greatly." Here Tolstoy's special spiritual egocentrism was already manifesting itself: he evaluated all people and events not in terms of their own importance, but of how they were reflected in his own soul, of the feelings they evoked in it. He wasn't annoyed that Zinaida had married someone other than him, but that it left him indifferent. Did this mean his feelings were somehow incomplete? That he had a cold personality? Did this mean he was not capable of love?

Compare this passage from an earlier diary with a later entry made in 1909: "After dinner, I called in on Sasha (his daughter. – P.B.), she is sick. If Sasha hadn't been reading, I would have written her something nice. I took something of Gorky's from her. I read it. Very bad. But the main thing is that it's not good that I find this false assessment unpleasant." The next "victim" (this time there really was a victim) of Tolstoy's family "project" was the provincial lady Valeria Arsenyeva. Her estate of Sudakovo was eight versts from Yasnaya Polyana. After the death of the Tolstoys' neighbor, V.M. Arsenev, L.N. was appointed guardian of his children. When at the end of May 1856, Tolstoy was traveling from Moscow to Yasnaya and called in at Sudakovo, the eldest of Valeria's children was twenty years old. "She's very sweet," he wrote in his diary. "Do I seriously love her? And is she capable of long-lasting love? These are two questions that I would like to decide for myself and am not able to." The 'Matchmaker' was the Tula landowner D.A. Dyakov, a friend of Tolstoy's. He was five years older than L.N.. Married, a thoughtful man, a perfect host. But Tolstoy, too, had changed a lot by that time. He was no young man, but a husband, who had been through two wars, become a famous writer and become disillusioned with both war and writers.

After arriving in St. Petersburg from the Crimea as a messenger in November 1855, Tolstoy didn't return to the army and a year later he resigned. Between the fall of 1855 and the summer of 1856 he got reacquainted with the best writers in Russia and became part of the most prestigious literary circle of the time, the circle of the journal *The Contemporary*, headed by Nekrasov. In St. Petersburg, he lived in Turgenev's apartment and spent time with the likes of Nekrasov, Panayev, Druzhinin, Ostrovsky, Maikov and other well-known authors, but he only made friends with Ostrovsky and Fet, having sensed in them the same lack of dependency on the fashionable trends of the time and the same obstinacy of character which were also in him. Relations with Turgenev, right from the start, were strained and scandalous. These two whales felt constrained by being in the same literary aquarium. After a few years, relations between them almost ended in a duel with guns...

To summarize what happened in one word, Tolstoy eventually *escaped* from the circle around *The Contemporary*, from this gathering of "warlocks", as he put it. *The Cossacks* and the two novels, *War and Peace* and *Anna Karenina*, were published in *Russian Journal*, edited by M.N. Katkov, who was initially a liberal, and then a reactionary journalist and publisher, and about whom Turgenev wrote the "prose poem" entitled *Skunk*. Yet Tolstoy got on with Katkov not because of his convictions, but for practical reasons. For example, he pre-sold *The Cossacks* to Katkov because he had lost a thousand rubles playing Chinese billiards.

The idea of marrying Arsenyeva took hold of Tolstoy in such a serious way that their "love affair" lasted more than six months and was reflected in the story *Family Happiness*, in which Tolstoy retroactively created a model of his prospective family life with Valeria.

In V.A. Zhdanov's remarkable book *Love in the life of Tolstoy* (1928), which was highly praised by no less harsh a judge than Ivan Bunin, the development of the relations between Tolstoy and Valeria are shown, and Tolstoy, it must be said, does not come out of it looking particularly good. He is cast as a malevolent, cerebral man who is not ashamed to put the object of his love to the test. –Yes, the object of his love, and not his love itself, which would be understandable and for which he could be forgiven. Valeria was a common provincial lady, brought up in the countryside. To her, L.N. was, needless to say, a very eligible bachelor – a Count, a military man, a famous author, whose book *Childhood* was read by all the young ladies...

In late summer, Valeria went to visit her aunt in Moscow and witnessed the coronation of Alexander II. She was struck by the splendor of the occasion, and wrote about it to her Aunt Yergolskaya at Yasnaya Polyana, probably knowing that her nephew would read the letter. Tolstoy's reaction startles with its cruel tone. Seemingly likening her to 'poor Liza' from Karamzin's famous work, Tolstoy immediately lets her know what kind of Erast she is dealing with.

"Why did you write this? You knew that this would go against the grain for me. Was it for my aunt's sake? Believe me, the worst way to make someone else feel, "this is what I'm like," is to come and say, "this is what I'm like!"... You must have looked horrible with your currants de toute beauté and, believe me, you would have looked a million times better in simple travelling clothes.

To love a haute volée, and not a person, is dishonest, and what's more it is dangerous, because they turn out to be good-for-nothings more often than those from any other volée, and it's not even in your interests, because you yourself aren't haute volée, and therefore your relations, founded on a pretty face and currants, aren't exactly going to be particularly enjoyable or rewarding... As for aide-de-camps, there are about 40 of them, it seems, and I know for a fact that there are only two who are not rogues and fools, so, there is no joy in this, either. - I am so glad that they crushed your currants in the parade, and how stupid that baron, who rescued you, was! If I were in his shoes, I'd have delighted in joining in with the crowd and I'd have smeared your currants all over your white dress... Therefore, even though I really wanted to come to Moscow, so as to get angry for a while whilst looking at you, I shan't come, and whilst wishing you all sorts of vain pleasures, along with their customary bitter ending, I remain your humblest, most unpleasant servant, *Count L. Tolstoy*." It appeared that this "romance" was destined to end before it had begun. But Tolstoy had set himself a goal: to get married! He writes in his diary: "Wandered around with Dyakov. He advised me on a lot of useful matters concerning the construction of the wing, and most importantly, advised me to marry V. Listening to him, it seems to me too that this is the best thing I can do..."

Podkolesin syndrome, sufferers of which can be talked into getting married, is to be found in Tolstoy's desire to build his life according to rules. For a few months he studied Valeria, recording his impressions in a diary, in which his cold, Pechorin-like mind is combined with an indecision reminiscent of Podkolesin.

June 16. "V. sweet."

June 18. "V. chatted about the outfits and the coronation. It seems that her frivolity isn't a transient passion, but a constant one. "June 21. "I didn't talk very much to her, all the more so given that she had an effect on me. "June 26. "V. wearing a white dress. Very sweet. Had one of the most enjoyable days of my life..."

June 28. "V. awfully badly brought up, ignorant, if not stupid."

June 30. "V. is a great girl, but I decidedly don't like her. And if we go on seeing each other this often, before you know it you're married."

July 2. "Wearing an ugly, foppish bonnet again... I caused her serious hurt yesterday, but she spoke out about it frankly, and after a slight bit of sadness which I experienced, everything went away ... Very sweet. "July 25. "For the first time I caught her *without dresses*, as Sergei likes to say. She is ten times better, and more importantly, she's natural ... I think she is active and loving by nature. Spent the evening *in happiness*. "July 30. "V. went all out, in a negligee. Didn't like it very much."

July 31. "V., it seems, is simply stupid."August 1. "V. was in a confused state of mind and was cruelly melodramatic and stupid."

August 10. "V. and I talked about getting married, she isn't stupid and is extremely kind." August 12. "She was extremely simple and sweet. I should like to know whether I am in love or not."

August 16. "I am spending more and more time thinking about dear little Valeria." September 24. "V. disgusts me." In order to test his relationship with Valeria, Tolstoy leaves for Petersburg and in November-December 1856 he writes her long letters in which there is no passion, only admonitions, interspersed with hesitant declarations of love.

"Please do not waste your evenings... not so much because evening studies will be useful to you, but so as to train yourself to overcome evil tendencies and laziness... Your main flaw is weakness of character, and all the other minor flaws flow from it. Cultivate willpower. Take it upon yourself and fight stubbornly against your bad habits... For God's sake, go for walks and don't sit for a long time in the evenings, take care of your health." "You say that for a letter from me, you're willing to sacrifice *everything*. God forbid that you should think like this, and you shouldn't say such things either. Included in that *everything* is *virtue*, which mustn't be sacrificed, either for a good-for-nothing such as me or for anything in the world. Think about it. Without respect, above all, for *kindness*, you cannot live well in the world... Work on yourself, be strong, and be brave." But there are two very cruel places in these letters. The first: Tolstoy, in spite of everything, confessed his love for her: "... I simply love you, *am in love with you*..." And the second, far more important... He invents a couple: Khrapovitsky and Dembitskaya. They "supposedly love each other" and intend to get married, yet at the same time they are people with "contradictory inclinations". He describes their future lifestyle, giving details, such as the figures for their income and outgoings, the number of rooms in their imaginary house, and so on. Essentially, he is inviting Valeria to play along in his family "project". At the same time, he carefully examines not only her flaws, but also the flaws of her former flame – the French pianist Mortier de Fontaine, by whom she had been attracted in Moscow. He writes: "Do not become discouraged from making yourself perfection." He advises her to put on her stockings and corset without the aid of servants. And there is a great deal more in the same vein, the sort of things one can only write to one's bride.

In early 1857, Tolstoy goes abroad and writes Arsenyeva a farewell letter, bringing the curtain down on their "romance": "That I am guilty before myself and terribly guilty before you is beyond doubt. But what am I to do? ... Goodbye, dear Valeria Vladimirovna, Christ be with you; there is a big, beautiful road ahead of you, just as there is one ahead of me, and God grant that you go along it toward the happiness that you deserve 1000 times. Yours, *Count L. Tolstoy*."

A year later, Valeria married Captain Talyzin; she bore him four children, but later divorced him and remarried. In 1909, she passed away in Basel, where she was buried.

"Tyutcheva, Sverbeyeva, Shcherbatova, Chicherina, Olsufyeva, Rebinder - I was in love with them all," Tolstoy wrote a year after breaking up with Arsenyeva, but it's fairly hard to believe in this love. And also, the Lvov sisters, Baroness Mengden, Princess Dondukova-Korsakova, Princess Trubetskaya...

After Arsenyeva, the one who occupied his thoughts the longest was Yekaterina Fyodorovna Tyutcheva, the daughter of his favorite poet.

29-31 December 1857. "Quietly beginning to take a liking for Tyutcheva."
January 1, 1858. "K. very sweet."
January 7. "Tyutcheva, nonsense!"
January 8. "No, not nonsense. She is taking hold of me seriously and wholly, albeit little by little."
January 19. "T. occupies my mind relentlessly. I would even say it is annoying, all the more so given that this is not love, it lacks love's charms."
January 20. "I spoke to M. Sukhotin with sarcasm about K.T. And I can't stop thinking about her. What rubbish! Regardless, I know that I only passionately desire her love, but feel no pity for her."
January 21. "K.T. only loves people because God commanded her to do so. In general, she is bad. But I'm not indifferent to this; it annoys me."
January 26. "I went to Tyutcheva's, with my love prepared. She was cold, shallow, aristocratic. Nonsense!"
February 1. "With Tyutcheva there is already a certain force of habit."
February 8 - March 10. "I was at Tyutcheva's. Neither one thing nor the other, she avoids me." March 28. "Alas, cold towards T. Everything else is utterly disgusting, I would go so far as to say." March 31. "I positively don't like Tyutcheva." In September 1858 he undertook his last sincere attempt

to marry Tyutcheva. "I'd almost be willing without love quietly to marry her, but shegreeted me with deliberate coldness." At the end of that year, an event took place in Tolstoy's life, which, of course, had no bearing on his courtship, but which accurately illustrates his attempts to procure a happy family life against all the accepted rules of normal society. In December, he went to Vyshny Volochyok on a bear hunt. Dropped off at a certain place, he didn't trample down the snow around him, as one ought to do, and very nearly paid for this mistake with his life. A female bear ran into the clearing and jumped right at L.N. He missed the bear with his first shot; the second hit it in the mouth, so that the bullet got lodged in its teeth. At first the bear flew over him, then she came back and started biting his head, tearing a piece of skin off his face. A hunter came to the rescue and shot the bear dead. The hide of that bear, killed by someone else's hand, later lay in his house at Yasnaya, and then at Khamovniki.

The Sense of the Deer

On the road to family happiness, to earthly paradise, as was to be expected, a number of temptations lay ahead of him.

As regards one of the main temptations, which he wrote about in *Confessions*, namely vanity, it wasn't so much that he coped with it easily, but that this sin, in and of itself, this sin had not for the time being come into conflict with the family idyll painted by his imagination. He hadn't turned out to be an outstanding military man; his first disappointment in his efforts at managing the estate was behind him, but there was the promise of a successful second attempt, along with the Yasnogorsk landlady. As for his literary success, however, this was undeniable and, in addition to real money, it also gave him a guarantee of a very attractive life in the country, free from the inevitable seasonal boredom that usually afflicted him. The combination of agriculture and literary work – work that was practically bringing him a profit, at that – what more could one ask for!

The main stumbling block on the route to his 'paradise' was another sin: lust. In this sin, as it seemed to him, he got caught up to such an extent that it was driving him crazy, having become an ever-present theme in his diary.

Apparently, the feeling of lust was very well-developed within him, yet hardly exceeded what is felt by any healthy, young and unmarried man. The wives of peasant-soldier's, maids in European hotels, and, finally, prostitutes were at his disposal, but his relations with them gave him nothing but irritation and moral torment. The servicing of his lust, for him, not only could not be his goal in life, but more than that it literally interfered with living. "Those darned girls have knocked me off course," "girls are getting in the way", "...because of the girls...I'm killing the best years of my life" – such comments are a constant refrain in the diary of his youth. In terms of his moral nature, Tolstoy was an undoubted 'monk' who did not consider there to be anything bright and joyous about sexual passion whatsoever. But the main thing was that he had nowhere to run from that passion, it caught up with him everywhere: at Yasnaya, in Moscow, in Petersburg, the Caucasus, and abroad, and there is even a suspicion that his almost happy state in Sevastopol, when it was under siege, is largely due to the fact that the cannon balls and buckshot dispelled thoughts of girls better than anything else. Fear of death was more acute than the "sense of the deer".

"The sense of the deer" is an expression used by Tolstoy in his diary. It is a very powerful definition of lust! But the very fact that Tolstoy so accurately defined it proves that this feeling did not take up his entire inner being, and that L.N. was able both to see and to condemn the "deer" within him. The deer is not capable, either during or after the rut, to reason about it, but Tolstoy's reflections about lust were far more debilitating than the "rut" itself.

His foreign journal from 1857 may give the impression that Tolstoy was an erotomaniac. He travelled first to Paris, then to Switzerland. He writes sparingly about the beauty and attractions of Geneva, Clarens, Bern. The event that makes the strongest impression on him in Paris is a demonstration of the death penalty by the guillotine. What he never fails to take note of, though, are the "pretty girls".

"A saucy lady, I froze with embarrassment." "... flirted with an Englishwoman". "A pretty, blue-eyed Swiss woman." "The maid has me flustered." "Beauties everywhere you look, with white chests." "Yet more beauties..." "A beauty with freckles. I want a woman badly. A good one." "A beauty on parade – a nice plump one". "*Girls. Two girls* from Stanz flirted with me, and one of them has wonderful eyes. I thought some impure thoughts and was immediately punished by becoming shy. A glorious Church with an organ, full of *pretty women*. Gulf between the *sociable* ones and the *half-pretty ones*... A meeting with a handsome young German in an old house at the intersection, where there were two *beauties*." "I met a small one, but ran away from her."Let's set all this in its proper context, though. Paris, Switzerland, Lake Geneva ... And what's more – in the spring, for the first foreign journal was written down in March, April and May. Tolstoy's flight abroad is somewhat reminiscent of his flight to the Caucasus six years earlier, which also took place in the spring. He had left behind in Russia his debts and his 'intrigue' with Arsenyeva, for which he was ashamed. His dreams of getting married had not left him, however, and in Dresden he was ready to fall in love with the Princess Yekaterina Lvova ("beautiful, intelligent, honest and of a sweet nature"), but even in her he found there to be something lacking. "What kind of a monster must I be?" In Geneva he even came dangerously close to being in love with his great-aunt Alexandrine, Alexandra Andreyevna Tolstaya, maid of honor, who corresponded to his spiritual ideal more closely than all the other women. And had she not been ten years his senior...

This is not yet Lev Tolstoy, the old man of Yasnaya Polyana, whose every gesture and word was to attract the attention of the whole world. But this is a man who is already very complicated, and of whom Turgenev, having met with him in Paris, was to write to P.V. Annenkov: "... he is a strange man, I haven't met anyone like that and I don't quite understand him. He is a mixture of poet, Calvinist, fanatic, nobleman's son – something reminiscent of Rousseau, but more honest than Rousseau – highly moral and at the same time an unsympathetic being."

"Pretty little girls", "little ones", "wonderful" – this is just an additional hue in the complex, colorful perception of the world for which Tolstoy has always been known. This is not yet the "rut". But Tolstoy himself already sees in it the devil's temptations and that is why he records it so meticulously in his diary. In his old age, re-reading the diary and thinking about how to publish it after his death, he first proposed that these parts should be discarded, but then nevertheless recommended that they should be kept in as evidence that even such a vile and sinful man as he had not left God.

And God was to provide a reminder of His existence very soon. In July 1857, he lost at roulette in Baden "down to his last penny", so he had to write to Turgenev and ask him to send five hundred francs at once.

And soon news came from Russia that his sister Masha had fled with her children from her husband, having found out about his dissolute life. "This news suffocated me," Tolstoy writes in his diary.

In this same diary, in late July – early August, he complains suspiciously of some kind of "illness". It was the same "illness" that he had had when he began keeping a diary in Kazan, in the spring of 1847. It was venereal disease.

Turgenev, having rushed to Baden-Baden as a matter or urgency, found him in a terrible state. He was sick, he had lost all his money, and he felt aggrieved about his sister. Besides that, her husband Valerian was the de facto in control of Yasnaya Polyana in Tolstoy's absence, because his brother Sergei had refused the task. Feeling crumpled and crushed, Tolstoy leaves for Russia.

And when he arrived, the devil caught up with him once and for all.

The Devil

Tolstoy wrote the tale with this title in November 1889, in one go, in just ten days. However, not only did he make no attempt to get it published, but he also hid it from his wife in the upholstery of an armchair. This is the most intimate work that L.N. ever wrote about himself. It is even more intimate than *Childhood*.

This "skeleton in the closet" (or rather, in the chair) stayed where he had hidden it for 20 years, until it was discovered by his wife.

"Sofia Andreyevna is in the grip of evil today," Makovitsky writes on May 13th, 1909 – she has been furiously, angrily reproaching L.N. for the story...a story about which he couldn't even remember what he had written or when he had written it."

He couldn't remember? On February 19 of that year, Tolstoy writes in his diary: "Looked over *The Devil*. Difficult, unpleasant."

The story of *The Devil* touches on one of the most intimate and painful chapters of their family life. It was about Tolstoy's relationship with Aksinya Bazykina, a married peasant woman from Yasnaya Polyana, the longest and most painful relationship he had with a woman before his marriage. It resulted in an illegitimate son, of whose existence S.A. was aware.

On April 26th, 1909, Tolstoy's son-in-law, Sukhotin, writes in his diary:

"I went with L.N. to Chertkov's. On the way we stopped by a peasant woman, at whose place an unknown wanderer had died during the night. The deceased was lying on the floor on some straw, his face covered with some kind of cloth. LN ordered that the cloth be removed and stared at the dead man's face for a long time. The face was comely, at peace. A few peasant men were sitting there. L.N. addressed one of them:

"Who are you?"

"The village elder, Your Excellency."

"What's your name?"

"Timofei Anikanov."

"Oh, yes, yes," said L.N. and went out into the hall. He was followed by the lady of the house.

"Who is this Anikanov?" L.N. asked.

"Why, he's Timofei, Aksinya's son, Your Excellency."

"Oh, yes, yes," said L.N., lost in thought.

We got into the carriage.

"But you used to have a different elder, Shukayev," LN said, addressing Ivan the coachman.

"He was dismissed, Your Excellency."

"What did they dismiss him for?"

"He began to behave very poorly, Your Excellency. He drank far too much."

"And this one doesn't drink?"

"He drinks too, Your Excellency."

I observed Tolstoy all this time and didn't notice any sign of embarrassment in him. The thing is, this Timofei was L.N.'s illegitimate son, and bore a striking resemblance to him, only he was taller and more handsome. Timofei was a wonderful driver, who lived by turns with each of his three legitimate brothers, but never got along with them due to his addiction to vodka. Whether L.N. had forgotten his passionate love for the peasant Aksinya, about whom he writes with such frankness in his old diaries, or whether he found it necessary to show his complete indifference to the past, I do not presume to decide."

Timofei Bazykin was born in 1860, less than two years before L.N. and S.A.'s wedding. When the newlyweds settled at Yasnaya, he was a baby. This is the very baby that S.A. writes about in her diary, recounting a dream that she had four months after the wedding:

"Our Yasnaya village girls and women had come to see us in a huge garden of some kind, all dressed up like proper ladies. They all come from somewhere, one after the other; the last to come out was Aksinya, dressed in a black silk dress. I spoke to her, and such a fury overcame me that I got hold of her child from somewhere and began tearing it to shreds. I tore off everything – its feet, its head – and I was in a terrible rage. Levochka comes over, I tell him that they will exile me to Siberia, and he picks up the feet, the hands and all the other parts and says don't worry about it – it's a doll." This was nothing more than an "unpleasant" dream. But what an expressive one it was! S.A. was very jealous. But jealousy was not the only thing at play here. The diary entry was made in January 1863, when she was already pregnant. The name of their first child had already been decided upon: if it was a boy, it would be called Sergei, if it was a girl – Tatiana. Does it not go without saying that the very idea that this would be her first-born child, but by no means his first-born, could not but torment the heart of this young wife and future mother?

Rumors that the Count had had an illegitimate son who was living in Yasnaya Polyana had spread among the peasants and reached S.A. When her and L.N.'s own children grew up and began to take part in the work in the fields, following their father's example, they too heard the rumors.

The Yasnaya Polyana 'paradise' was desecrated right from the outset. The devil had left traces in it which could not be erased.

Tolstoy began his relationship with the peasant Aksinya a year after returning from abroad. It happened on the Trinity, in May 1858. "A wonderful Whitsunday. Withered bird-cherry in gnarled hands, the choking voice of Vasily Davydkin. Caught a glimpse of Aksinya. Very pretty. I waited with fond feelings all this time. Today in a big old wood, daughter-in-law, I am a fool. A beast. Her red tanned neck…I'm in love like never before in my life. I can think of nothing else. I am tormented. *Tomorrow – all my efforts.*" The summer of 1858 was one of the most difficult of Tolstoy's life. "I aged terribly, grew tired of living that summer," he writes in his diary. His relationship with Aksinya lasted two years and broke his spirit far more powerfully than all his previous relationships. This relationship was "exceptional" and led to him sensing something in this married peasant woman that he hadn't found in the provincial ladies or the ladies from the capital: not just a woman but a *wife*. And not someone else's wife, but *his own*.

Whereas a year after the beginning of this relationship, he "recalls" Aksinya "with disgust, thinking of her shoulders," in October he writes that he is seeing her "exclusively". Six months later he realizes that he is thoroughly confused. "She was nowhere to be found – I looked for her. It was no longer the sense of the deer, but the feeling of a husband toward his wife. It's strange, I am trying to recapture that former feeling of satiation and I cannot." This was a serious revelation for Tolstoy and the first frightful blow to his family "project".

Had it really been such a terrible thing though? A young nobleman had sinned with a peasant woman whose husband was in the city, working hard to provide for his family and pay the nobleman rent. It was a sorry situation, of course, but a fairly commonplace one.

This wasn't the first time he'd fallen in love with a commoner. The famous Cossack Mariana from the novel *The Cossacks* was most likely based on a real prototype called Solomonida. He writes about her in his diary from the Caucasus: "the drunk Epishka (Uncle Eroshka in the story – P.B.) said yesterday that matter with Solomonida is going smoothly. I would love to take her." Returning from Sevastopol, and living by turns in Yasnaya and in Moscow, he observes in himself "something that is already not a tendency towards," but "a habit of debauchery". "Terrible lust, reaching the point of physical pain." "Hung around in the garden with a vague, lascivious hope of catching someone in the bushes. Nothing interferes more with my work than this. I have therefore decided, no matter where or how, to get a mistress for these two months." "A very pretty peasant, with a very becoming beauty. I am unbearably disgusting in this powerless, feeble crawl toward vice. It would be better to have the vice itself." Well, this time he had got "the vice itself", and an ever-present lover, and not for two months but for two years.

Why is it that his lust for the Cossack woman Solomonida gave rise to the extremely poetic *The Cossacks*, whilst his relationship with the peasant woman from Yasnaya Polyana resulted in the terrible, hopeless *Devil*?

The reason was Tolstoy's family "project". In a letter to Yergolskaya and in *A Landowner's Morning*, he had developed an entire program for his future family life, and at the end of the 50s he was already consciously seeking candidates for the role of landlady at the Yasnaya Polyana paradise. And if he had only thought everything through like a normal, rational person... But he was a brilliant artist. He had painted this paradise in his imagination with such clarity and at the same specificity that in essence, he was already living in it. He initially looked on the relationship with Aksinya as a temporary state of being.

And then suddenly it seemed to him as though she might indeed be his wife. Lust and her satisfaction was not a temporary phenomenon, not an "ebb" and "flow", not a matter of physiology, but the foundation and the very "heart" of family life.

In *The Devil*, the landowner Evgenii Irtenev (almost the namesake of Nikolenka Irtenev from *Childhood*) undoubtedly represents Tolstoy himself, with some reservations. Tolstoy didn't even bother to hide it. Evgenii graduated from the Faculty of Law. Tolstoy tried to get a law degree from St. Petersburg as an external student. Evgenii received his share of an inheritance after it had been divided up among his brothers, just as had been the case in Tolstoy's life. Evgenii began his service in a ministry (probably the Ministry of the Interior), and the young Tolstoy wanted to serve in the same place. Evgenii settles in the countryside, hoping to "resurrect that form of life that had existed not in his father's time – his father had been a bad landlord, but during his grandfather's time". Tolstoy's father was not a bad landlord, but in all he did at Yasnaya, he was continuing the course steered by his father-in-law, Prince Volkonsky, a course which, as can be seen from the letter to Yergolskaya, the son and grandson, Lev, also wanted to follow. Evgenii was very strong physically, "of medium height, well-built with muscles that had been toned through his gymnastics, sanguine with bright rosy cheeks and bright teeth and lips." Tolstoy was an avid gymnast. From his youth to his old age, he lifted weights and spun on the high bar.

These are trifles, though, by comparison with the main point. The main thing that torments Evgenii and distracts him from estate management is lust. "He wasn't a libertine, but was no monk either, as he admitted to himself. And he gave in to this only as much as was necessary for his physical health and mental freedom, as he used to say..."

Who did he say that to? L.N. himself wrote in his diary: "Nothing interferes with my work as much" (as lust).

Evgenii, like the young Tolstoy, is a man of the program, the "project". He set himself the goal of turning the estate into a model farm and marrying a virtuous girl. Not out of financial considerations, nor due to a casual feeling, but because to do so would be in accordance with his inner convictions and ideas about family paradise.

But alas! "Involuntary abstinence began to have a bad effect on him. Did he really need go to town because of this? And if so, where would he go?"

And at that point Stepanida appears in Evgenii's life. Her name itself is a compound of Solomonida and Aksinya, the mathematical mean of the two names. It's a folksy name, but not a common one. And it has a distinct "male" element.

At the end of the story, when Eugene starts to become more mature, he says of Stepanida: "After all, she's the devil. The devil himself. After all, she captured me against my will." An alternative version reads as follow: "Heavens above! There is no God. What does exist is the devil. And she's it. The devil overwhelmed me. And I don't want this, don't want it. The devil, yes, the devil." In the first version of the novel, Evgenii shot himself. In the second – he killed Stepanida. In both versions, he was thought to have temporarily lost his mind. In both versions, the last couple of lines are almost identical. "And indeed, if Evgenii Irtenev was mentally ill, then all people are just as mentally ill as he, and the most mentally ill are without doubt those who see signs of insanity in other people which they don't see in themselves."

Thus, in Evgenii's story, just as in Aksinya's, Tolstoy saw a universal situation. It is the fate of all men. And those of them who don't understand this are far more mentally ill than Irtenev.

The story *The Devil* was written later than the *The Kreutzer Sonata* (1888), but at the same time as the "Afterword to *The Kreutzer Sonata*", in which Tolstoy made a moral judgment not only about sexual love, but also about marriage: "There cannot be such a thing as a Christian marriage and there never has been one..."

Kreutzer Sonata was written earlier, but in terms of plot is a continuation of *The Devil*. After Evgenii killed Stepanida, he was declared mentally ill and sentenced to repentance within the church. He returned from prison and the monastery a hopeless alcoholic. The protagonist of *The Kreutzer Sonata*, Pozdnyshev also goes free thanks to the jury. During a conversation with a fellow traveler, Pozdnyshev constantly drinks the strongest tea, which is "like beer". This is a man with a shattered psyche, but who is convinced that he is mentally much healthier than those around him. Pozdnyshev realizes (but does so too *late*) that there is no fundamental difference between sexual intercourse with his wife and with any other woman. Marriage is a hidden crime.

The attitude of the later Tolstoy toward marriage wasn't one that was entirely negative. According to his conviction, though, the first woman with whom a man "falls into sin" must also become his wife. He expressed this idea more than once and did not shy away from saying it in S.A.'s presence. He remained loyal to this idea until his dying day.

Therein lay the discovery that was made by Tolstoy-Irtenev-Pozdnyshev. And if Tolstoy, at the end of the 50s, had carried this idea through to its logical conclusion, his fifty-year marriage with Sofia Andreyevna would never have happened, and there would have been no *War and Peace* or *Anna Karenina*.For now, though, perhaps frightened by this thought, he was to write feverishly in his diary on January 1, 1859: "I must get married this year – or never."

The Behrs

At the end of May 1860, Tolstoy admits, in his diary: "I didn't see her (Aksinya – P.B.). But yesterday ... I'm even starting to become horrified at how close she is to me." At the same time, he experiences fresh disappointment in his efforts at agriculture: "Agriculture, in the amount in which it is conducted at my place, oppresses me" (from a letter to Fet).

In July, Tolstoy goes abroad with his sister Maria, to Soden. He makes a brief diary entry on the road, in Moscow: "Moscow. The Behrs". In Soden their brother Nikolai is dying of consumption. He passed away in Hyeres, in France, on September 20th. This event had a frightening effect on Tolstoy.

"Why bother making an effort and trying, if, of what was once N.N. Tolstoy... there is nothing left," he writes to Fet.

The irrevocability of death and the impossibility explaining it rationally overwhelms him so much that he decides to abandon literary work. What purpose does it serve? After all, "the suffering of death will start tomorrow, with all the abominations of meanness, deceit, self-deception, and will end in nothingness, zero, for oneself." The only thing that remains is this "foolish desire to know and speak the truth", "only not in the form of your art. Art is a lie, and I am no longer capable of loving a beautiful lie."

At the same time, he convinces himself that he, too, is coming down with tuberculosis. He rushes through Europe, as if trying to get away from the disease. Hyeres - Paris - Nice - Florence - Tuscany - Naples - Rome - London - Brussels – Frankfurt-am-Main - Eisenach - Weimar - Dresden - Berlin - this is the map of Tolstoy's flight, during which he nonetheless manages not to waste time in vain, studying the European teaching practices in schools. In May he returns to Yasnaya Polyana and gives in to a new passion: pedagogy, which he called his "last mistress".

What exactly does Tolstoy think of himself on the eve of his marriage to Sofia Behrs in September 1862?

1) He thinks he's sick, despite being generally physically fit and healthy.

2) He is suffering from a panicky fear of death.

3) He is afraid of physical relations with women, yet is in the grip of a heightened sensuality.

4) He is second only to Turgenev as a recognized leader in Russian literature, but is prepared to give up writing for the sake of his new hobby – teaching.

5) He had not turned out to be a wonderful landlord.

6) He is a passionate man, but not a spontaneous one, a man of the "project".

7) He is undeniably egocentric man, whose view is constantly directed towards the interior of his soul, yet at the same time he has a heightened awareness of the outside world and seeks to learn as much as he can about people with his greedy eye.

8) He believes in God, though he is not a Christian.

9) He is very eager to get married.

This was the unimaginable "bouquet" his chosen one would be lumped with. It's hardly surprising that he was in no hurry to give it away to the first weak hands that came his way. Finally, his gaze came to rest on the Behrs family...

Everything here was wonderful and at the same time practical. The mother of Tolstoy's future wife was a childhood friend of his, with whom he had almost been in love as a child, and rumor had it – a rumor denied, admittedly, by his future mother-in-law – that he had once, in a fit of jealousy, pushed little Lyuba from the balcony of the Yasnaya Polyana home.

The father of Lyubov Alexandrovna Behrs, née Islavina, Alexander Mikhailovich Islenev, had been a neighbor of Nikolai Ilyich Tolstoy. He was a real Russian gentleman, and the papa in *Childhood* was based more on him than on Tolstoy's own father.

The Islenevs' estate, Krasnoye, was thirty-five versts from Yasnaya Polyana. Nikolai Ilyich and Alexander Mikhailovich constantly hunted together and visited each other's families for weeks at a time, bringing their cooks, footmen and maids. All these servants huddled in the rooms and corridors and slept on the floor on felt and burlap.

Lyubov Alexandrovna was the illegitimate daughter of Islenev's third, unregistered marriage to Princess Kozlovskaya, who had fled from her first husband and secretly married Islenev in the village of Krasnoye. This incident caused a great scandal in high society, because Princess Kozlovskaya had been a maid of honor at court when she was a young girl. On the basis of an appeal by Prince Kozlovsky, the marriage was declared illegal, and Islenev's children from his third wife were forced to have the "corrected" surname of Islavin.

In the history of Tolstoy's wife's family on her mother's side, there was a great deal that was poetic, truly Russian, ancient, which could not fail to warm the soul of the author of the novel *Childhood*, in which the Behrs-Islavin family rightly recognized their relatives; they idolized this story with an almost religious degree of ecstasy. Little Sonia Behrs learned whole chunks of it by heart.

Thus, Tolstoy became related to a family in which his cult as a writer was already established. On the other hand, he used the familiar form of "you" with the mother of his future wife and called her 'Lubochka', whilst she called him 'Levochka'. This eliminated the possibility of strained relations between mother-in-law and son-in-law in advance. For the most important person besides him in the Yasnaya Polyana household, Aunt Yergolskaya, too, Lyubov Alexandrovna Behrs was someone who was very familiar: she had known her since her early childhood. That provided a certain confidence in the idea that her daughter, too, would get along with Tatiana Alexandrovna.

It was agreeable to spend time with the Behrs family. Tolstoy was awkward in conversation and considered himself ugly, "shocking" (big nose, big ears, bushy eyebrows, small, bluish, deep-set eyes).

Yet at the Behrs' household, everything was simple.

As a childhood friend of the lady of the house, Tolstoy would come to their house for dinner when he was in Moscow; he would also drive or go on foot to their summer house in Pokrovskoye, stay overnight, and then the next morning, Lyubochka's extremely kind husband, Andrei Yevstafievich Behrs, would drive him to Moscow in their carriage on his way to the Kremlin.

Andrei Yevstafievich worked as a doctor at the Kremlin. He too came from an ancient bloodline, – in his case, a German one. On his mother's side, he was one of the many members in Russia of a noble family from Westphalia. His father had been a wealthy Moscow apothecary who went bankrupt as a result of the great fire in Moscow in 1812 but subsequently returned to relative prosperity. Two of his sons, Alexander and Andrei, attended the Schlözer school, Moscow's best German private boarding school, and then the medical school at Moscow University. On completing his studies, Andrei Yevstafievich Behrs travelled to Paris as the family doctor to Sergei Nikolayevich and Varvara Petrovna Turgenev and their little son Vanya, who would go on to be one of the greats of Russian literature. After returning from Paris, he began serving in the Senate. He was given an apartment in the building of the Kremlin Palace. During the reign of Emperor Nikolai Pavlovich, he received the title of court physician. He then petitioned for the restoration of his family's noble title and coat of arms (all the documents were burned in 1812), which was indeed returned to both brothers, though the bear on the coat of arms was now missing ('Behrs' was derived from the German for 'bear').

Andrei Yevstafievich had been a womanizer in his youth. Varvara Petrovna Turgeneva even had an illegitimate daughter with him, who was thus a half-sister to Turgenev and to Tolstoy's wife. Varvara Zhitova left some extremely interesting memoirs for posterity. Rumor had it that the leader of the Russian anarchists, Prince Peter Kropotkin, was also, in fact, the child of the Kropotkins' family doctor – Behrs.

Andrei Yevstafievich was a practical and sentimental man. This deep-rooted German trait was passed on to his middle daughter Sonia, in whom practicality coexisted with heightened sensitivity, often passing into hysteria. He was a stubborn man, who could sometimes be hard work for those around him at home, but was an infinitely loving, caring father to his "daddy's girls" and, as it later turned out, a superb father-in-law, whose letters to S.A. and L.N. at Yasnaya, after their marriage, cannot fail to elicit a benevolent smile.

September 24, 1862: Did you somehow make it home, my dear, sweet friends? I can imagine what kind of welcome you were given. Please pass on my respects to Tatiana Alexandrovna and give a friendly bow to Sergei Nikolayevich (Tolstoy's elder brother. – P.B.) from me. I embrace you, dear Sonia, and you must shower your husband in kisses from me. Your mother kisses and blesses you. We talked about you all day. Farewell, your sincerely loving Daddy."

September 27: "Do you kiss your kind, dear husband hard? – kiss him from me too and give him a good shake of his beard." Immediately after the young couple's departure for Yasnaya he insistently, though gently, calls on them to come back to Moscow, promising to provide them with an apartment at the Kremlin or find them inexpensive but comfortable rooms near the Kremlin. He's prepared to go to Hunter's Row to purchase provisions for them, which is quite easy for him, because he already does this for his own family. Having been the first, as a physician, to work out based on the descriptions of Sonia's ailments that she was pregnant, it is not her that he seeks to calm, but L.N. As for Sonia, he strongly urges her not to ride on a sled, not to eat heavy foods, which put pressure on the uterus, and to ward off nausea with the help of a failsafe French medicine called 'tranche de citrone', which translates simply as 'a slice of lemon'. Only – God forbid! – don't swallow it with the rind.

When he took away their middle daughter from the Kremlin to Yasnaya Polyana, almost immediately after the wedding, Tolstoy left the Behrs a difficult inheritance in the form of their eldest daughter, Liza, who, until the last moment, had been considered L.N.'s bride and had convinced herself that she was in love with him.

There were three sisters in the Behrs family: Liza, Sonya and Tanya. And of course, all three of them were in love with him! He may have thought he was ugly, "shocking", with his nose, ears and eyebrows. But to young girls from the modest family of a court physician, the son of a pharmacist, to whom even the illegitimate Lyuba Islavina had been given in marriage grudgingly ("You, Alexander, will soon be giving your daughters away to musicians" their grandmother Daria Mikhailovna Isleneva had angrily said to her father, mindful of with the fact that they were related to the Sheremetyevs, no less), for these "pretty girls", as Tolstoy casually described them in his diary, he was the most interesting man they could ever have imagined.

At that time he did not yet wear the famous "Tolstoy shirts", which S.A. would later sew him, along with baggy trousers. He had his clothes made by the best and most expensive tailors in Moscow and Petersburg. He was a famous writer and military officer, whom the royal family was prepared to show a lot of consideration for, were it not for his character. The cult of the imperial family, in the family of the palace doctor, was unconditional. S.A. did not get free of it even when she was Tolstoy's wife, when he became a bitter enemy of the autocracy. But, of course, it was not in the gleam of high society, which shone on Lieutenant Tolstoy, that his charm lay for the "pretty girls". Wherein did it lie, though? Perhaps in the fact that he sang and played music well? The fact that, being the same age as their mother, he danced with her daughters as if they were adults? Or in the fact that the youngest of them, Tanya, simply used him as a riding horse, riding around the room on his back with a triumphant shout?

"Someone will go on horseback around the hall at our house," Andrei Yevstafievich Behrs wrote to the Tolstoys at Yasnaya, trying to coax them into coming to Moscow. "Little Tanya can't wait to climb on your husband's back." Of course, Tolstoy became an idol to all three sisters, these little girls' hearts, so unlike one another, were united in the delight they felt before the magnificent L.N., whose every visit to the Kremlin or to Pokrovskoye, before he left for the army or to go abroad, was an event of incredible happiness, which they talked about all the time until he came to visit once again.

Tolstoy himself understood this, and sensed and breathed in this air of universal love for him, the kind of air without which any artistic nature suffocates.

Wouldn't anyone find it agreeable to receive an "invitation letter" such as this on their birthday:

"At the head of all writers, I bring to you, my dear Count Lev Nikolayevich, my heartfelt congratulations on this your birthday, and I ask you to join us today for dinner and to spend the night here. On Wednesday morning, I undertake to drive you to Moscow, if you should agree to come with me. I hope that the kindly Lev Nikolayevich won't turn down this opportunity to comfort all of us – particularly on such a day, a day which has brought comfort to so many as a result of your coming into the world and being among us today. – And thus, I shall say 'so long', in the hope of seeing you soon. Yours with sincere affection, Behrs".

On the back of this piece of paper, incidentally, was a postscript written in a different hand, which could hardly have been pleasing to the prospective groom:

"In the olden days, Levochka and Lyubochka danced on this day; now, in old age, it wouldn't be a bad idea for us to dine together in a somewhat calmer fashion, at Pokrovskoye, and to recall our youth and childhood in the company of my family. L. Behrs".

A reminder of his age from his future mother-in-law couldn't have pleased L.N. Especially in August 1862, when *his fate was sealed*. And it had been resolved not in favor of the eldest daughter, Liza, but of the middle one – Sofia.

Tolstoy came into the Behrs family on a legitimate basis as an old friend, but among the young maidens in the family his arrival had the destructive impact of a lawless comet.

The story of Tolstoy's search for a bride, at first glance so entangled, almost like a piece of vaudeville, can be divided into several stages. In May 1856, on the road from Sevastopol to Yasnaya, he stops off in Moscow, visits his childhood friend Lyubov Alexandrovna Behrs at Pokrovskoye and, for the first time, notices that she has three lovely daughters growing up. Due to their being temporarily absent from the house, the servants of these girls (Liza – aged twelve, Sonia – eleven, Tanya – nine) had entrusted them with the task of setting the table for their dear guests (Tolstoy, and their uncle Konstantin Alexandrovich Islavin) and take care of them. How happy they were!

The middle sister made far more of an effort than the others. According to an unwritten family rule, the middle sister was always given more things to take care of. The eldest sister was intelligent, well-read, "proper", but, as is often the way, was not the favorite. The youngest was a flirt, "dressed in feathers", spoiled and adored by everyone. The middle one had to combine within her the liveliness of the younger sister with the thoroughness of her older one, without expecting much respect or admiration in return. Most of the matters that had to be taken care of naturally fell on her shoulders, because the eldest was forever sitting around with her books, whilst the youngest was forever doing headstands.

The Behrs family was, in all respects, a classic family. Papa, needless to say, spoiled his daughters, whilst mama, of course, brought them up to be real women and future wives. Tanya was spoiled the most, whilst Liza and Sonia were taught about managing the household from early childhood. "Besides our lessons," S.A. recalls, "we, two sisters, had to sew and mend the linen ourselves, and embroider... Household chores were also partly in my sister Liza's and my hands. From the age of 11, we had to get up early and make coffee for father. Then we would give the cook what was needed from the pantry provisions, then by 9 am, we prepared everything for class... Overall, our father spoiled us and loved to get us not only what we needed, but even what was luxurious. Mother had her own rather peculiar views. She was afraid to bring us luxury, afraid lest we might become accustomed to it; she made us sew clothes for ourselves, embroider, mend, do the housework, clean everything ... And yet she could not imagine that we, as little girls, might go for a stroll without a footman or ride in a carriage." "Dined with Lyubochka Behrs," Tolstoy writes in his diary on May 26. "The children waited on us. What kind, fun girls."

Ten days earlier, there is an entry in his diary: "Never let opportunities for pleasure slip by and never go looking for them. – I am giving myself the rule of never setting foot in any tavern or any brothel..." However, in February of that same year, while in St. Petersburg and seeing to work and literary matters, he writes, "quarreled with Turgenev and now I've got myself a whore." One cannot help but sense what a huge psychological distance there was between this experienced man and the "nice, cheery girls" who waited on him at the table. Six years later, one of these girls would become his wife. In order to get an idea of her internal character, let us examine an incident from her memoirs:

"When I was 15 years old, a first cousin, Lyuba Behrs, came to visit us, whose sister Natasha had just gotten married. This Lyuba, as if divulging a great secret, told my sister Liza and me all the secrets of marital relations. This discovery, for me, a little girl who idealized everything, was simply horrible. I became hysterical, and I threw myself on the bed and began to sob such that my mother came running in, and in response to her questions about what had happened to me, I could only say one thing: "Mama, make it so that I forget it all..."

"... and so I decided at that moment," S.A. continues, "that if I ever got married, it would only be to a man who was as pure as I was..."

There is one note that does not quite ring true in the way she presents this subject. She began writing her memoirs in 1904, when she already knew absolutely everything about her husband, including his diary of 1856, in which the "nice girls" coexisted openly with "whores". *Resurrection* had already been written by that time; its main character, so highly praised by S.A.'s husband, was, for all that, a prostitute. It was for precisely this reason, and not because of its artistic shortcomings, that S.A. didn't like the novel. "... I hate to read the details of the lives of prostitutes, these creatures, whom our husbands, sons, fathers and men in general visited. And we, pure, innocent girls found ourselves the heirs of these fallen creatures, and L.N.'s description of them was a painful reminder to me of his own repeated visits to brothels, which he himself told me about and which he wrote about in his diaries as a young man. And at that time, (when *Resurrection* was written – P.B.) I was diligently transcribing L.N.'s diaries, so that one copy could be kept in the museum, and another at Yasnaya Polyana. It was a great torment for my soul." But then, at Pokrovskoye, in the spring of 1856, seated before the enraptured little Sonya was not the author of the "young diaries" and *Resurrection*, but the author of *Childhood*. And on top of that he was also the author of the patriotic "articles" in *The Contemporary* about the defenders of Sevastopol, which had pleased the Emperor so much.

This was the beginning of the first stage. Two years later, in September 1858, he came to Lyubov Behrs for her name-day party and then repeats almost verbatim his diary entry from 1856: "Nice girls!" But again – everything is still very vague. They are simply "nice girls", three sisters. But there was already an exclamation point, something that was not infrequent in Tolstoy's diaries, by the way. Sonia was 14 at that time, teenager fairly grown-up girl by the standards of the day, but Tolstoy still doesn't see her as a separate part of this "nice" trinity. He is already in love, incidentally. Only not with Sonia, but with the Behrs.

Let's run our eyes over his diary from 1858, to get a sense of how this man was feeling.

"Tyutchev ... cold, shallow, aristocratic. *Nonsense*!", "Alexandrine Tolstaya has aged and ceased to be a woman to me." "I was at Tyutcheva's; neither one thing nor the other..." "A wonderful day. Women in the garden and by the well. I'm possessed..." "Nadezhda Nikolayevna was alone. She was angry at me but her smile was nice. If it were't for her peacock-like hands." "My Auntie and I are having a grand time of it." "Caught a glimpse of Aksinya. Very pretty... I'm in love with her as never before in my life. I think of nothing else." "I had Aksinya ...; but she repels me." "Turgenev is treating dear Masha abominably." "I saw Valeriya – don't even miss the feelings I had for her."

One can trace three main points in these entries. True love and even tenderness break out in Tolstoy only in relation to those close to him – toward Auntie Yergolskaya, toward his sister Masha, who at this time is in love with Turgenev and desperately hopes to develop a romance with him. But this tenderness rapidly turns into anger toward those who offend his family. "Garbage" – he writes of Turgenev, whose only fault was his eternal indecision in all things related to 'romances' with women. Another vector is his vibrant, strong, yet animalistic feeling toward the peasant women in general, and toward Aksinya Bazykina in particular. And the third is his cold feeling, devoid of life, toward his potential brides – Yekaterina Tyutcheva and Valeria Arsenyeva.

But can it really be said that Tolstoy every really loved women at all? This is a very difficult question.

On the one hand, the 'sexism' of the later Tolstoy, which the family laughed about and which angered S.A. greatly, is well-documented. The harsh things that L.N. had to say about emancipation, and about the fashion, rife among young women, for becoming teachers and midwives are also well-documented. He famously said that he would only tell the truth about women when he was at the edge of the grave: he would jump into the coffin, tell the truth and slam the lid shut, and the phrase has almost gone into common parlance. On the other hand, Tolstoy loved his daughters, Tanya, Masha and Sasha, with great affection, and that, besides giving them the joy of interacting with their father, also created problems for them: adoring his daughters as he did, he was often jealous of their suitors.

One can't define his attitude toward women simply by using the word 'sexist'. Indeed it would be strange to talk about the man who created Natasha Rostova, Maria Bolkonskaya, Kitty Levina, Katyusha Maslova as a 'sexist'...

Yet regardless of that, Tolstoy's attitude toward women cannot be called love either. From his youth and for the rest of his days it was a mixed feeling of fear, intense interest and difficult thoughts about the diabolical nature of sexual love.

Tolstoy's 'sexism' inevitably gave rise to the myth that he was a latent homosexual in the 20th century. Unfortunately, he himself provided plenty of fodder for those who love suggesting that our classic authors were gay. I am referring to one of his diary entries, which we shall quote in full, because at the end of the day it's an admission by Tolstoy himself.

"I've never been in love with women. I experienced one strong feeling akin to love when I was just 13 or 14 years old, but I don't want to believe that it was love, because the object of it was a fat maid (albeit one with a very pretty face), besides, the age of 13 to 15 is the most disorganized time for a boy (adolescence): you don't know what to rush toward, and sensuality in this period acts with unusual force. I very often fell in love with men, the 1st love was for the two Pushkins, then the 2nd – for Saburov, the 3rd – Zybin and Dyakov, 4 - Obolensky, Blosfeld, Islavin, and also Gautier and many others ... I fell in love with men before I had the concept of the possibility of *pederasty* – but even after I found out about it, the thought that intercourse might be possible never even entered my mind. A strange example of a fondness that I couldn't explain – that's how it was with Gautier. Without having had any kind of relationship with him whatsoever, besides buying his books. I was thrown into a fever when he came into the room. My love for Islavin spoiled an entire 8 months of life in St. Petersburg for me. Though I was not conscious of it, I didn't care about anything else other than that he should like me. All the people I loved could sense this, and I noticed that they found it hard to look at me. Often, not finding the moral conditions which reason demanded that I find in the object of my love, or after some unpleasantness with him of some sort, I felt aversion toward him; but this aversion was based on love. I never felt this kind of love for my brothers. I was very often jealous of women. I understand the ideal of love: the total sacrifice of oneself toward the object of one's love. And that is precisely what I experienced. I've always loved those who treated me coolly and did no more than appreciate me. The older I get, the less frequently I experience this feeling. When I do experience it, it is not as passionate, and I do not feel it for those who love me, i.e. the opposite of how it was before. Beauty has always had a lot of influence in the selection; the example of Dyakova comes to mind; but I'll never forget the night when he and I left Pirogovo, and I wanted to duck beneath my bag, kiss him and weep. There was sensuality in this feeling too, but as for why it crept in, it's impossible for me to determine; because, as I said, my imagination never painted any lubricious pictures, on the contrary, I have a terrible aversion."

This admission relates to the year 1851. It is amazing to see how ruthlessly the twenty-two year-old Tolstoy analyzes his experiences.

In 1858, the year in which he writes of the Behrs sisters: "Nice girls!" with an exclamation point, he also writes in his diary about a strange dream featuring his brother Nikolai Tolstoy, who was still alive at the time: "... I saw in a dream that Nikolenka, dressed in a woman's blue dress with a flower, was riding to the ball." Tolstoy took dreams seriously, was forever recording them in his diaries, devoted some space to them in his works, and even wrote entire works about them (*The Dream of the young Tsar, What I Saw in a Dream...* etc.).

This suggestive dream from 1858 just begs to be interpreted according to the aesthetics of the Silver Age, as did another one from the beginning of 1859: "I had a dream – strawberries, an alley, her, immediately recognized, though never seen before, and Chapyzh in fresh oak leaves, without a single dry twig or leaf ..."

But this is the Stranger, "recognized" half a century before she appeared in Blok's poem! This forces us to reexamine the image we have of Tolstoy the groom.

When Tolstoy's visits to the Behrs family became too frequent and it became obvious that he was making them as a suitor, the eldest sister decided that she was L.N.'s chosen one. Who else could it be? After all, by the time he began to differentiate between the three "nice girls" as individuals, Elizaveta Behrs was the only sister of marriageable age. And besides that, etiquette required that the eldest sister should be the first to get married.

However, it wasn't in vain that the Behrs sisters' great-aunt, their father's aunt Maria Ivanovna Wulfert, spoke of Sonia, whom she loved more than anyone else: "Sophie a la tête abonnée." This is a play on words, with two meanings: "Sonia's wearing a bonnet" or "Sonia's been earmarked." This meant that Sonia would marry first.

The elder sister Liza lacked something. She was a sweet girl, serious, but uncommunicative. She was constantly to be seen with a book in her hands.

"Liza, come play with us," her younger sisters and brother Alex would call out to her, trying to distract her from her reading.

"Wait, I want to get to the end."

"But this end always lasted a long time," T.A. Kuzminskaya recalled, "and we would start the game without her. She wasn't interested in our childish lives, she had her own world, her contemplation of everything, so unlike our childish one. Books were her friends, she seemed to have read absolutely everything that was available to someone of her age."

One would think that this seriousness ought to have attracted Tolstoy. After all, what annoyed him most in Arsenyev? Coquetry, love of finery, balls and mental vacuity. Liza was the polar opposite of her. Tolstoy noted this too, at first, and even managed to get her to collaborate on his pedagogical journal *Yasnaya Polyana*.

Everything seemed to suggest that in the elder sister he had a ready-made wife and collaborator for his life as a writer. At this point, the second stage of his entry into the Behrs family begins, and a sort of separation of powers occurs among the three sisters. He collaborates with Liza, makes music with Sonia, mercilessly criticizing her for any notes that are out of tune, and with little Tanya he would sing and mess around.

And at this same time, Tolstoy tells his sister Maria, who was very friendly with Lyubov Behrs:

"Masha, I like the Behrs family, if I ever got married, then it would only be to someone in their family."

He does not yet know whom he'll marry, but he already knows *where* his bride is to be found. These words, which were overheard by the governess of Maria Nikolayevna's children and related to her sister, the governess of the Behrs children, were interpreted by the Behrs family in their own special way. The only potential bride in the household was Liza. Sonia was still just a "healthy, rosy-cheeked girl with dark brown eyes and a dark braid" as her sister Tatiana recalled her. As for little Tanya, she was just a child.

Judging by the diaries, Tolstoy closely scrutinized all three sisters, with interest and even some amazement observing the process of their growing up, which at their age is a rapid one: a child in a short dress one day, a bride at the altar the next. These observations didn't stop even after his marriage to Sonia, in relation to Tanya, who was the main prototype for Natasha Rostova. It is specifically of the character of Natasha Rostova that most clearly reflects all the complexity of Tolstoy's attitude toward the Behrs sisters. "I took Tanya, melded her with Sonia and Natasha emerged," L.N. joked.

He also said jokingly, in the presence of his wife and sister-in-law: "If you were horses, then they would have given a lot for such a pair at the mill; you go together surprisingly well, Sonia and Tanya." Artists are forgiven much. But S.A. can hardly have been pleased to read the confession made in her husband's diary three months after their wedding: "I keep gazing intensely at Tanya.. And three days later: "Fear of Tanya – sensuality." Tatiana Andreyevna Kuzminskaya wasn't happy in her family life. Perhaps the main reason for this was the Tolstoys. They were extremely interesting, charismatic men after all, next to whom everything else somehow faded. L.N. was Tolstoy was number 1. And he chose Sonia. But there was also his wonderful older brother, Sergei Nikolayevich, with whom Tanya fell in love the year after her sister's wedding, when she herself was a girl of marriageable age. However, Sergei Nikolayevich, who served as the prototype for Andrei Bolkonsky, was, in real life, bound to a gypsy woman named Masha, lived with her in Pirogovo and had illegitimate children. Having fallen in love with Tanya ("You gave a beggar a million," he said of her love for him), he nonetheless didn't dare leave Masha and the children, tormented both with his "um-ing and ah-ing" and ended up staying with the gypsy, behaving honorably toward her, but, in essence, shooting Tanya down at the very moment when she was in her prime.

With his frequent visits to the Behrs and having told his sister that he would like to find a wife in this family, Tolstoy gave Liza a reason to hope that this wife would be her. Her two sisters and the governesses of the Behrs and of Maria Nikolayevna, one after another, "began telling Liza how much Lev Nikolayevich liked her." In turn, Maria Nikolayevna sang Liza's praises to her brother, telling him what a wonderful wife she would make. She wanted very much to find him a wife!

Liza was at first indifferent to this, but then, according to Tatiana, "a cross between a woman's self-esteem, and her heart, or something, began to make itself felt within her... She became more animated, kinder, paid more attention than before to her make-up. She would sit for a long time before the mirror, as if asking it: "What sort of girl am I? What impression do I make?" She changed her hairstyle and her serious gaze would sometimes stare dreamily into the distance." Whilst Tanya sympathized with her, Sonia made fun of her. She knew that in a competition with her older sister, feminine charm and appeal were on her side. Fourteen year-old boys and thirty-five year old men, who had called in at the hospitable Behrs household, had already fallen in love with her. There was a funny incident that occurred at Pokrovskoye. The Perfilevs, friends of the Behrs', came to visit with their fourteen year-old son Sasha, an "underdeveloped, naive boy". "He was sitting next to Sonia," writes Kuzminskaya, all the while gazing fondly at her. Suddenly, taking hold of the sleeves of her dress, he began to rub them intensely with his fingers. Sonia smiled shyly, not knowing what this might mean.

"Pourquoi touchez-vous la robe de m-lle Sophie?" the sharp voice of Anastasia Sergeyevna, Sasha's mother, suddenly rang out.

"Must be love."

Everyone laughed in concert, and all eyes turned to Sonia, who was even more embarrassed than her admirer." Nothing like that could have happened to Liza. Take the thirty-five year old professor Neil Alexandrovich Popov, "staid, with sluggish movements and expressive gray eyes" – he fell in love with Sonia. –As did the teacher of Russian, Vasily Ivanovich Bogdanov, who, as a result, had to leave the house. And the son of the court pharmacist. And the son of the famous partisan and poet Denis Davydov. And Yanihin, son of the famous obstetrician.

There was something in Sonia that attracted men of all ages. This "something", in a word, is called "femininity". It was a combination of a lively character, momentary sadness and a maternal instinct which appeared early. Little Sonia was a woman *par excellence*. She was a wonderful actress in the plays they put on at home, and could even portray men, with a subtle feeling for their characteristic weaknesses.

"For some reason, Liza always related with slight contempt toward the family, everyday concerns," wrote Kuzminskaya. "Young children, feeding them, changing diapers – all this made her feel either disgust or boredom. Sonia, by contrast, often sat in the children's playroom, playing with her little brothers, kept them entertained during their illnesses, learned to play the harmonica for their benefit and often helped her mother with the household chores." At the same time, Sonia had a trait of which other men would have been wary, but which couldn't fail to attract Tolstoy, with his dream-like ideas about the Ideal Wife.

"She had a very lively character," writes Kuzminskaya, "with a touch of sentimentality, which easily passed into sadness. Sonia never gave herself over fully to the fun and happiness, to which her young life treated her … She didn't seem to trust happiness, didn't know how to take it and use it to the full. It always seemed to her as though something would come along at any moment and get in the way of it… My father knew this trait in her character and used to say: 'Poor Sonya will never be completely happy.' Only a complex character such as this, though, could completely satisfy Tolstoy. Let us not forget that at this time, and then for the rest of life thereafter, he was very fond of music. In Sonia there was "musicality"!

To be sure, she had certain problems with tone and with her talent as a performer. But "musicality" was to be found in her very nature, in her actions and in the different tones of her moods.

Here's an example of an event which, though seemingly insignificant, paints an expressive picture of the "balance of power" within the kind trio in L.N.'s eyes. The scene is Pokrovskoye, in the spring. Liza, Sonya, Tanya and their brother Petya went for a walk with L.N., Professor Popov and the French teacher Georges Paco. As was his wont, Tolstoy took them along an unknown path, and soon on their way there was a cross between a stream and a deep puddle. What to do? Tanya jumps on L.N.'s shoulders, and he carries his "Madame Viardot", as he jokingly called her because of her beautiful voice, to the other side. Liza gradually crosses the stream, lifting her dress, walking across some branches which Paco brought over for her. Little Tanya looks at her and thinks, "But no one offered to carry her. Why? She's completely different from us." And what about Sonia? Popov offered her his services.

"Sofia Andreyevna, you can't make up your mind where to cross. I will help you, I'll carry you across."

"No!" cried Sonia, blushing all over and apparently fearing his intentions. She immediately stepped into the water and quickly ran across it, sending spray in all directions.

"Popov is without flair," Tanya notes to herself, "Sonia can't be carried – she's big, and he wanted to do what Lev Nikolayevich had done. It's different with me, I'm small enough to carry." On the face of it, what sort of conclusion can be drawn from this? None whatsoever. Yet, all the same, before going to bed, Sonya and Tanya (without Liza, she wasn't directly involved) debate this "event" fervently. And we suddenly find out that this "event" excited Tolstoy too.

"He approved of me very much, for not allowing Popov to carry me across," said Sonya. 'This is what I've come to expect from you,' he told me. Then he asked lots of questions about what I had been doing all this time and how I had been spending my time."

There are some things that cannot be explained. For example, why it was that all the arguments "for" in Tolstoy's eyes were on Sonia's side, and all the arguments "against" were on Liza's side. Little Tanya understood this well. That was why she was "in on it" whereas Liza was "out of the loop".

"Sonia, tu aimes le Comte?" Tanya once asked her sister.

"Je ne sais pas," she replied quietly, not at all surprised by the question.

"Oh, Tanya," she said after a short pause, "he has two brothers who died of consumption..."

This was the beginning of the third stage of Tolstoy's entry into the Behrs family, which could not finish any other way than in his marriage to Sonia.

Tolstoy isn't yet in love, and Sonia isn't yet in love. Or rather, she is ever so slightly in love with someone else – a cadet named Mitrofan Polivanov, a friend of her brother Sasha. "He was a tall, fair-haired young man, smart, handsome, very eligible." Sonia was secretly "engaged" to Polivanov, just as Tanya was to her cousin Sasha Kuzminsky.

These childish, though completely serious and promising connections, which, in different circumstances (that is to say, to put it bluntly, if Tolstoy had not been around) would probably have resulted in successful family love stories. Sasha Kuzminskiy was a relative and "one of their own" in the Behrs family. Mitya Polivanov, the son of a general of the Imperial stables, and who himself later became one, was more suited in terms of his social status to the Behrs, with their "bourgeois", "apothecary" pedigree. Tolstoy's marriage to Sonya was, it must be said, a mismatch. Sonya wasn't a countess and there wasn't a penny of a dowry for her.

After the disaster with Sergei Nikolayevich, Tanya married Kuzminsky, who became a legal activist and then even a senator, but it was no longer possible that this might become a happy family situation. From the very beginning, their life had been poisoned by her husband's jealousy toward Tolstoy. And not only toward Sergei Nikolayevich, whom Tanya loved all her life, but toward the Tolstoys in general, to their breed itself, too prominent and talented, to the fact that his wife was utterly in love with Yasnaya Polyana and couldn't imagine her life without it, and, by extension, without the Tolstoys. And of the fact that she couldn't detach her own self from Natasha Rostova.

Sonya and Tanya guessed at the Count's love for Sonia earlier than their parents or Liza. Lyubov Alexandrovna and Andrei Yevstafievich were initially sure that if the Count were to make a proposal, then it would surely be to Liza. There were already rumors in Moscow of Tolstoy's impending marriage to Liza Behrs. But Tolstoy himself not only didn't feel as though he was in love, but was also sure in advance that he would never marry Liza.

On September 22, 1861, he writes in his diary: "Liza Behrs tempts me; but it will not happen." After this, he breaks off the diary for six months and resumes in May of 1862, when he flees to the steppes of Samara to be treated with mare's milk. He is indeed seriously ill at this time, losing weight, even "withering" visibly. He is harassed by the specter of consumption, which killed two of his brothers, despite the assurances of A.E. Behrs, who said that this wasn't consumption, but merely "phlegm in the blood".

But the flight to Bashkiria in the spring 1862 is also very reminiscent of the flight from Arsenyeva to Petersburg. On the steamship, Tolstoy is "reborn to life" and "to an awareness of it." "... I was allowed to go free a little," he writes, referring to the strained relationship with Liza, who was expecting a marriage proposal. And again, as had already happened in the love story with Tyutcheva, he was almost ready to get married. But in a cold way, without love. "Oh my God! How beautifully unhappy she would be if she were my wife," he writes, a week before proposing to Sonya. "I'm beginning to hate Liza with all my heart," he writes two days later, when his attitude toward Sonia has been defined once and for all: "I'm in love, as I never believed it was possible to love." And Sonya? This is no longer the same little girl who, blushing with shame and admiration, served tea to the author of *Childhood*. Sonia is fully aware that the Count is possibly suffering from consumption and may leave her a widow before she can enjoy family happiness. She is already capable of condemning his vices – his passion for gambling, for example.

And L.N.? In the last few days before he proposes to Sonya, he can't sleep at night and suffers terribly! Tolstoy is afraid for the first time. Not of making the wrong choice, but of being turned down. He feels at once unimaginably old and like a "16-year-old boy". He carries a note with him with a declaration of his love, crumples it in his pocket in Sonya's presence and can't make up his mind to give it to her. He is even willing to resort to using little Tanya as a go-between. Yes, I am old, he tells himself, "but I'm wonderful in my love." Simply put, he's going out of his mind. "I'm crazy, I'll shoot myself, if things go on like this."

'Yes', of course!

It seems so simple and natural to us that the love story between L.N. and Sonya Behrs went into the novel *Anna Karenina* virtually "unedited". In fact, the courtship and marriage of Levin to Kitty, down to the smallest details, was exactly the same as it was between Tolstoy and Sonya.

But there we have the great mystery of Tolstoy-the artist, the incomprehensible "sleight-of-hand" of his artistic genius. How is it that a living-and-breathing life, in essence utterly unchanged, flows into the flesh of the novel and becomes fixed in it for all time? It is just as mysterious as the birth of a person from banal intercourse, with the difference that, in the case of Tolstoy, we don't see the transition from the one state to the other. Everything happens suddenly and immediately. There is no boundary and no overcoming thereof.

The secret probably lies in the fact that the story of the courtship and marriage of Levin, like the other pages of *Anna Karenina* and *War and Peace* which deal with family matters, were created by Tolstoy *before* they were put down on paper. A half century later, the symbolists, the futurists, and other representatives of radical movements in Russian art would dream about the artist-demiurge, who fuses art and life together. Tolstoy did this much earlier. To some extent, the real stories which he "played out" in life or which were "played out" under his supervision, were even fuller and bigger than the "paper" versions. For example, the famous scene in *Anna Karenina* when Levin writes the first letters of the declaration of his love for Kitty on the card table, in real life, had a number of details which were not included in *Anna Karenina*.

Firstly, there is no rivalry between Liza and her middle sister in the novel. There isn't this exciting moment of feminine competition, in which the person at stake is not just anybody, but Tolstoy himself.

Secondly, the scene is missing a third party. The ubiquitous, fleet-of-foot Tanya, the future Natasha Rostova. When Tolstoy is in the hamlet of Ivitsa, Islenev, the Behrs sisters' grandfather, wrote: "Y.y.a.n.f.h.t.v.r.m.o.m .o.a.a.t.i.o.h." on the table, ("your youth and need for happiness too vividly remind me of my old age and the impossibility of happiness"), they weren't alone in the living room. Tanya was sitting under the piano, hiding from the adults who had been forcing her to sing. This obnoxious spy witnessed what Tolstoy chose to conceal in his novel. Namely, that Sonya, unlike Kitty, was unable to decipher this complex abbreviation. "My sister, under some kind of inspiration, read… Lev Nikolayevich told her what a few of the words were," writes T.A. Kuzminskaya. And if the whole truth really must be told, Sonya later confessed to her sister that she couldn't work out what *le comte* had written on the card table at all.

But Tolstoy hadn't intended to test Sonya's aptitude. He felt obliged to let her in on a *secret*. To make her bow together with him over the card table and make her complicit in the conspiracy against her older sister. Yes, a conspiracy! Unlike the kindly Levin, Tolstoy-the-groom behaved in a way that was far from impeccable. Having given Liza grounds to dream of getting married to him, he realized that proposing to the middle sister, bypassing the elder, was, to put it mildly, not *comme il faut*. It would not only cause her emotional trauma, but seriously undermine the girl's reputation as a potential bride.

In reality, the lofty words about "the impossibility of happiness" were not the only thing that Tolstoy wrote on the card table. He also wrote that misconceptions about his relationship with Liza had developed in the Behrs family. And he asked Sonya, together with little Tanya (she was there, close by, but they didn't know it) to help get him out of this awkward situation.

So if Sonia deciphered, based on the first letters, this indirect declaration of love, she must also have deciphered the suggestion that she enter into a conspiracy against her sister.

Was this cruel on Liza? Of course it was! A month later, having become the mistress of Yasnaya Polyana, Countess Tolstoy repents in her diary: "But how I made poor Liza suffer, it makes me feel so sick, it's so sad, how awful…"

Before going to Ivitsa, the Behrs stayed at Yasnaya Polyana. It was in August 1862. The girls were given "the room under the arches", where there used to be a storage room, but which now housed Tolstoy's study. One bed wasn't enough, and the host suggested that they use a sliding chair.

- I'm going to sleep here –Sonya immediately announced.

— I'll prepare everything for you now — said the host.

And Tolstoy began... to make Sonya's bed. In T.A. Kuzminsky's memoirs, this is described with humor, as Tolstoy, with "unaccustomed, inexperienced hands began to unfold the sheet, put down the pillows, and how touching he looked when dealing with material, domestic matters." In S.A.'s memoirs, however, this scene has a different significance.

"I was making the bed with Dunyasha, the old maid, when Lev Nikolayevich suddenly entered, and Dunyasha addressed him, saying that the sofa bed had been made up for three of them, but that the fourth had nowhere to sleep. "Someone can sleep in the chair," Lev Nikolayevich said, and, having pulled a long chair out, placed a stool next to it. "I'll sleep in the chair," I said. "And I'll make the bed for you myself," Lev Nikolayevich said, and began to unfold the sheet with awkward movements. I felt both ashamed, and also there was something pleasant, intimate, in this joint preparation for the night..."

But when Tolstoy left, Liza gave Sonya an earful. But it was too late.

It may well be that Sonia herself wasn't expecting such a turn of fate, either. In the summer of 1862 she writes a short story called *Natasha*, which, after serious doubts, she showed to Tolstoy. It is a pity that this story was destroyed after the wedding, as were the diaries she had kept as a young girl. This is especially sad because *Natasha* made a strong impression on Tolstoy and gave him some of the character traits and even the names of the Rostov family in *War and Peace*. In essence, before she had even become the writer's bride, S.A. had written a draft for him of some of the pages of his work in which the family appears.

We know the content of the story thanks to T.A. Kuzminskaya's memoirs.

There are two main characters in the story: Dublitsky and Smirnov. Dublitsky is middle-aged, not blessed with good looks, energetic, intelligent, with changeable views on life. Smirnov is young, twenty-three, with lofty ideals, a positive, calm character, trusting, making a career for himself.

The heroine of the story is Yelena, a young girl; she is beautiful, with large black eyes. She has an older sister, Zinaida, a cold, unsympathetic blonde, and a younger one — Natasha, fifteen years of age, a thin and high-spirited girl.

Dublitsky visits their house without any thoughts of love in his mind.

Smirnov is in love with Yelena, and she is fascinated by him. He proposes to her, she hesitates about whether or not to say yes. The parents are against the marriage, on account of how young he is. Smirnov leaves to serve in the military. There is a description of the torment he feels in his heart. There are a great many secondary characters. There is then a description of Zinaida's fascination with Dublitsky, various diseases suffered by Natasha, her love for her cousin, etc.

Dublitsky continues to visit Yelena's family. She is at a loss and cannot decide how she feels, she doesn't want to admit to herself that she is beginning to love him. She is tormented by the thought of her sister and Smirnov. She struggles with her feelings, but she isn't strong enough for the struggle. Dublitsky is interested in her, not her sister, and this, of course, attracts her even more.

She is aware that his fickle views on life wear her out. His observant mind embarrasses her. She mentally compares him to Smirnov and says to herself, "Smirnov loves me simply, sincerely, without demanding anything of me." Smirnov arrives. At the sight of his distress, and at the same time feeling attracted to Dublitsky, she decides to leave for the monastery.

The tale ends with Yelena arranging the marriage of Zinaida to Dublitsky, and then marrying Smirnov.

Thus the sensible creator of *Natasha* arranged for Dublitsky to marry her older sister, whilst choosing the softer version of a woman's fate for herself – with Smirnov. The real S.A. destroyed *Natasha*, and chose for herself the role of serving a genius. She didn't forget about this victim of hers, however. Marriage to a genius is always a mismatch, always a union of unequal partners, but who in this inequality is "more equal" as far as being a "victim" is concerned? This problem was incorporated into the foundations for the Tolstoys' family paradise even before the wedding, though it could not be seen. But it would take a lot of time for this seed of a problem to grow into a real conflict.

Tolstoy's attitude toward *Natasha* was a complex one. The tale, on the one hand, puzzled him, and on the other – spurred feelings for Sonya, which from that moment on became irreversible.

There is no better way to rekindle the flame of passion from a smoldering twig, than to make it "a little jealous".

S.A. recalled that L.N. returned *Natasha* to her "coldly". As it happens, he had asked her to show him her diaries, but she had refused, and then they had agreed on the story. "What great energy of truth and simplicity," Tolstoy writes in his diary.

It need hardly be said that the character of Dublitsky affected Tolstoy. "I read it all without a sigh, with no trace of jealousy or envy, but the "extremely unattractive appearance" and "fickle judgments" affected me pleasantly. I calmed down. All this isn't about me..."

The possibility of family happiness with Sonia "isn't about him." He is old and ugly, she is young and beautiful. "You fool, it's not written about you..." "Not about you, you old devil, – write critical articles!" "Dublitsky, don't poke your nose in where there is youth, poetry, beauty, love – there, my brother, the cadets." "Nonsense – the monastery, work, that's your business, from the height of which you can calmly and joyfully look at someone else's love and happiness..." "Oh, Dublitsky, stop dreaming!" "Lord, help me, teach me. Mother of God, help me." "I'm in love, as I never believed it was possible to love." How remarkable! Tolstoy dreamed of marriage for almost twenty years, from the age of fifteen. He lived for nearly half a century with his wife. But the period of his courtship lasted just a month. And what sort of courtship was it anyway? Until the last moment, no one in the Behrs family, not even Sonia, knew which of them L.N. would choose. On September 16 he proposed, and on September 23 the wedding took place. That same evening, the young couple left for Yasnaya.

Tolstoy didn't really have time to properly experience the feeling of being a fiancé, nor did Sonia have time to experience the feeling of being his betrothed.

How different it was from her father's courtship of her mother. That had included an age-old poetry: there had been fortune-telling servant girls with a saucer of water and sticks thrown over it to form a "bridge". Placed under Lyubochka Islavina's bed for the night, this "bridge" was supposed to appear to the girl and to Andrei Yevstafievich in their dreams, and, of course, it did. We know nothing about any bridal dreams Sonya may or may not have had. The only dream which Tolstoy records in his diary at this time does not augur well: "In my dream, a pathetic sick hound dog." S.A. recalled her week as a bride without enthusiasm. "They took me shopping and I tried on underwear, dresses and hats, feeling indifferent.

Lev Nikolayevich came along, and his excitement, the kisses, embraces and touching of this impure, experienced man bothered me horribly and infected me with a bad feeling. It was as though I was completely crushed; I felt sick, abnormal. I couldn't eat anything except pickled gherkins and rye bread…"

On September 16th, Tolstoy came to the Behrs house, clutching the letter of proposal which was in his pocket. "The proposal was written on a dirty folded square of plain typing paper, and Lev Nikolayevich had carried it in his pocket for a week, unable to make up his mind to give it to me," SA writes.

"Sofia Andreyevna!

It's becoming unbearable for me. Every day, for the last three weeks, I have said, "today I will say everything," and I leave the house with the same longing, remorse, fear and happiness in my soul. And every night, like this one, I go over the past, I suffer, and I say: why didn't I say it, and how, and what I would have said. I'm carrying this letter with me so as to give it to you, in case once again I shan't be able or shall lack the heart to tell you everything. The false view that your family has of me, as it seems to me, is that I am in love with your sister, Liza. This isn't fair. Your story stuck in my head because, after reading it, I was convinced that I, Dublitsky, ought not to dream of happiness, that your outstanding poetic requirements of love… that I was not jealous and will not be jealous of the one that you love. It seemed to me that I might delight in you as one delights in a child. In Ivitsa I wrote: "Your presence too vividly reminds me of my old age, and the impossibility of happiness, and you, specifically…"

Both then and thereafter, however, I was lying to myself. Even then I could have broken off everything and gone back to my monastery of solitary labor and engagement in my work. Now, I cannot do anything, and I sense that I have confused things in your family, that the simple, dear relationship I have had with you as with a friend, with an honest person, is lost. But I cannot leave and I do not dare to stay. You, honest person that you are, hand on heart, without rushing, for God's sake don't rush, tell me what I am to do. Don't laugh at others, you'll only end up getting laughed at. I would have died laughing, if a month ago someone had told that it was possible to suffer as I have been suffering, as I have happily been suffering, this past month. Tell me, as an honest person, do you want to be my wife? Only if, with your whole being, you can boldly say "yes", for it's better to say "no" if there is a shadow of a doubt within you.

For God's sake, consider it thoroughly. I'll be scared if I hear "no", but I can foresee it and shall find the inner strength to bear it; but if I'm never to be loved as a husband as greatly as I love now, that would be more horrible." Sonia, so practical and sensible, had another quality which her older sister lacked. She wasn't only an understanding girl, but also a girl of spontaneous outbursts, of passion, capable of taking life-changing decisions at lightning-quick speed. After receiving the letter from the Count, she went to the girls' room and locked the door behind her. Her elder sister went after her and began knocking on the door.

"Sonya!" she cried. "Open the door, open it now!"

The door opened. She stood there in silence, holding the letter in her hand.

"Tell me what le Comte wrote to you!" Liza shouted.

- Il m'a fait la proposition.

- Say no! Say no immediately!

Sonia went through to her mother's room, where Tolstoy was awaiting her answer.

"'Yes', of course!" she said.

A few minutes later the congratulations began. Liza was in the girls' room, sobbing.

Later, after learning of Sonya's "betrayal", the cadet Polivanov was to beat his chest in hysterics in the children's room. He was very ashamed of himself, but he couldn't help it. When Sonya and L.N. tied the knot in the church at the Kremlin, Polivanov was the one holding the wreath over the bride's head. "Polivanov drank the glass to the bottom," S.A. recalled.

As they saw Sonya off, the whole Behrs family sobbed. Except, that is, for Andrei Yevstafievich, who was ill and out of sorts, because the Count's somersaulting act, in marrying the middle sister and bypassing the elder one, was not to his liking. The young couple went to his room to say goodbye separately.

Tolstoy bought a brand new travelling carriage especially for the journey, a huge coach in which there was enough space to lie down flat. Let us now quote from L.N.'s diary:

"On the wedding day fear, mistrust and a desire to escape. The festivity of the ceremony. She began to cry. In the carriage. She knows everything and it's simple. In Biryulyevo. Her timidity. Somehow painful. Yasnaya Polyana. Sergei (his brother. – P.B.) is all affectionate, Auntie is already preparing for suffering. Night, a difficult dream. Not her." Not *her*? Not the one he dreamt about in Chepyzh, "immediately recognized, although never seen before?" And what about Sonia? "She's like a wounded bird," Tolstoy writes about his impressions of his bride after she agreed to marry him.

He also writes about the strange vision which arose between them when they were left alone, as bride and groom by now. "It's unclear how it can be that a week has passed. I don't remember anything; only a kiss at the piano and the appearance of Satan…"

On the evening of September 24, 1862, Count Lev Nikolayevich Tolstoy and Countess Sofia Andreyevna Tolstaya arrived at their Yasnaya Polyana paradise.

Chapter 4

La Tête à Bonnet

Tolstoy spent, on the face of it, only a short time at Optina – until just before 3 pm on Saturday, October 29. That's not counting the previous evening and night at the hotel from the 28th to the 29th, however. Don't forget, either, that Tolstoy had a bone to pick with time.

Tolstoy woke up early, at 7 am. He thus spent a total of 8 hours up and about at the monastery – a full working day. During this time he tried to help a petitioner, the peasant widow Daria Okayemovaya and her children, handing her a letter with a request for help to the family of his son Sergei Lvovich; he dictated to Chertkov's young secretary, Alexei Sergeyenko, who had come to see him, an article on the death penalty entitled *An effective means*, the last one he ever wrote, written at the request of Korney Chukovsky, and twice tried to meet with the elders of Optina.

Although it is not clear why, in this case, we usually speak of "elders". There was only really *one* elder that mattered – Iosif, a disciple of St. Ambrose. Ambrose (after his death – Iosif) was the confessor of Tolstoy's sister, the nun Maria Nikolayevna Tolstoy, whose cell in the nearby monastery, near the village of Shamordino, was built as a personal project by Ambrose.

It is quite astounding, really! The writer who was most at odds with the Russian Church was tied to it by the most intimate ties, ties of blood. The very fact that having fled from Yasnaya Polyana, Tolstoy specifically made tracks for Optina and Shamordino, speaks volumes. It was his choice.

And it was a heartfelt, and not an intellectual choice on the part of Tolstoy. There can be no question of mind-games or of pride, here! He is on the run. He's all tangled up in family discord. Chertkov, S.A., the "Tolstoyans", heirs and petitioners are all grappling for a piece of him… He is weak, sinful, sick and well aware of it. And in this state of utter despair, Tolstoy makes the only heartfelt and human choice he could make. To go to his sister, in the monastery! It wasn't possible for him to settle down in Shamordino – it was a women's convent. But he is willing to rent a hut in the village. That would be even better, because he dreamed so much of living with the people! But let's look at things rationally. An 82-year-old man living in a hut, in a village?

The correspondent from the newspaper "New Time", Alexei Ksyunin, questioned the Shamordino village peasants, after Tolstoy's death, about where the fugitive had tried to rent a house.

"In winter, the snow blows in briskly," the peasants told the Count, complaining about their unhappy lot – it was eighteen versts to the town, sometimes they couldn't get there.

"Snow is nothing, there's no sin in it," Tolstoy reassured the peasants. "When the spring comes, it melts."

But before spring came, he had to survive another winter. And at that time he already had a cold after standing in the open area of the train car in the icy wind.

And so, no matter how one looks at it, the most natural way out for Tolstoy at that moment was to stay at Optina. At least for a while, in order to collect his thoughts and come up with some new decision. After all, it's clear that after the departure from Yasnaya, he had been carried without a rudder and without sails. Tolstoy, accustomed to decades of sedentary life at Yasnaya, had no serious experience as a traveller. There cannot be any doubt about the fact that Tolstoy wanted to stay at Optina. During his conversation with his sister in Shamordino, her daughter, and Tolstoy's niece, E.V. Obolenskaya, was present:

"Over tea mother began asking about Optina Pustyn. He liked it very much there (he'd been there many times before), and he said:

"I would gladly stay and live there. I would bear the heaviest of monastery duties, as long as they didn't force me to get baptized and go to church."

This conversation with his sister is reported to Bishop Veniamin of Kaluga and the abbess of the Shamordino monastery:

"At 6:00 pm the Count arrived in Shamordino at his sister's cell; the meeting was very touching: he embraced his sister and kissed her, and sobbed on her shoulder for at least five minutes; after that they sat together for a long time, and he told her of his sorrow: the discord with his wife. Then there was dinner. His doctor and a nun N had been invited to it... All four dishes, namely potatoes, mushrooms, kasha and soup, were mixed together for them on one plate; he ate a lot, talked a lot, here's what he said:

– Sister, I was in Optina; how nice it is there, how gladly I would now put on a cassock and live, performing the most menial and difficult tasks; the only condition I would set would be: don't compel me to pray, I cannot do that.

His sister replied:

– That's good brother, but they would give you this condition: do not preach or teach anything.

The Count replied:

– What would I teach? There one must study; in each of the inhabitants I met, I saw only teachers. Yes, sister, things are hard for me now. How about for you? Is it like Eden here? I would shut myself in my cell and prepare for death here as well, after all, I'm 80 now, one can't go on forever!"

Maria Nikolayevna herself, in a letter to S.A., which was written sometime after L.N.'s death, told of his desire to stay at Optina or Shamordino in a more reserved manner:

"When Levochka came to see me, he was very anxious at first, and when he started telling me how you threw yourself into the pond, he wept bitterly, I could not look on him without the tears coming, but he didn't tell me anything about himself, he said only that he had come here for a long time, that he was thinking of renting a hut from a peasant and living here. It seems to me that he wanted privacy, he felt weighed down by life at Yasnaya Polyana (the last time he told me this was when I was with you) and all the conditions, repugnant to his beliefs; he simply wanted to organize everything to his liking, and live in solitude, where no one would bother him."

In a letter to Tolstoy's translator into French, Charles Salomon, dated January 16th, 1911, Maria Nikolayevna wrote the following: "You would like to know what my brother was looking for in Optina Pustyn? An elder-confessor or wise man living in solitude with God and his conscience, who might understand him and be able to alleviate some of his great sorrow? I don't think he was looking for either of these things. His sorrow was too complicated; he just wanted to settle down and live in a peaceful spiritual environment."

Tolstoy clearly wanted to stay at Optina. He liked Optina. There could be no discussion, however, of ecclesiastical repentance, or a formal return to Orthodoxy.

An elderly Buddha had come to the Orthodox monastery. It sounds crazy, but let's not forget that this was a Russian Buddha. Buddha's sister was living in the neighboring, "affiliate" monastery, his closest relative and in fact the only person who could accept him simply as the person he was.

- I'm so happy here! - Tolstoy told A.P. Sergeyenko in Shamordino. - My sister has understood me completely.

The old Buddha doesn't want to teach anyone. He's tired, he thirsts for peace, seclusion. And, if possible, wise, leisurely conversations with wise people, the kind of people he sees the Optina elders as being.

Was that possible?

"No," the zealous defenders of Orthodoxy shouted in the past and still shout today, of the "fearsome" Count Tolstoy. – "Oh, what has he come up with! To live in the monastery, but not go to church! Who does he think he is! He ought to have gone crawling on his knees to the elders!"

But let us listen to the voices of the spiritual hierarchy, which were heard at the time. The newspaper "Russian Word", on October 31st, 1910, two days after L.N.'s departure from Optina, published opinions of the Orthodox Bishops on whether it was possible or impossible for L.N. to stay at the monastery.

Bishop Makarios: "We need to find out where he has gone, – to Orthodox Christianity or to Buddhism. If it's the Orthodox Church, the church will happily accept its wayward son, although this would require Tolstoy to renounce his anti-christian doctrines in a manner as solemn as his excommunication."

Bishop Arseny: "Tolstoy's recognition of the official church, his departure for the monastery will bring, undoubtedly, a huge benefit to the church."

Bishop Nikon: "After all, Tolstoy isn't only against the church, he is against Christ himself."

Bishop Eulogius: "My deep conviction is that the monastery can take L.N., even if he didn't go there for repentance, but simply seeking rest for his soul."

As we can see, not even in the higher church hierarchy was there a single, shared view on whether it was possible for L.N. to live at the monastery. The Bishop of Tomsk and Altai, Makarius, was categorical, but the Bishop Eulogius of Kholmsk and Lublin Eulogy (whose secular name was Vasily Georgiyevsky, the future Metropolitan of Western European Russian churches, who passed away in 1946 in Paris and was buried in the cemetery of Sainte-Genevieve-des-Bois) assessed the situation more loyally.

Eulogius was an admirer of Pushkin and Leskov, and loved Melnikov-Pechersky and Tolstoy.

The opinion of the enlightened bishop surprisingly fully coincided with that of the simple novice Mikhail from the monastery. In the "Annals of the Monastery of St. John the Baptist, located at Kozelskaya Optina Pustyn", the details of Tolstoy's conversation with brother Mikhail are reported:

"And they arrived," said Father Mikhail, "the two of them. They knocked. I opened the door. Lev Nikolayevich asks, "May I come in?" I said, "Please do." And he said: "Perhaps I'm not allowed, I'm Tolstoy." "Why," I say, "we welcome all who have a desire to come to us." He then says, "Well hello, brother." I answer, "Hello, Your Excellency". He says, "You're not offended that I called you brother? All men are brothers." I answer: "Not at all, and it's true that all are brothers." Well, and they stayed with us. I took them to a better room. And early in the morning I sent a servant to the head of the skite, Father Varsanophy, to warn them that Tolstoy was coming to the skite."

Mikhail behaved like the Biblical figure, Martha: first he provided shelter, and then everything else. But if for Eulogius Tolstoy was Tolstoy first and foremost, for Mikhail he was Count Tolstoy. One mustn't forget that the Optina monastery, in the early XX century, although it was known among the faithful, from the penniless to the rich patrons, was nevertheless an ordinary provincial monastery. It was possible to get to it from the road only by ferry across the Zhizdra, and when the river overflowed in the spring, the monastery was sometimes cut off from the world. There were all of 50 inhabitants in the monastery in 1910: one was the head of the skite, Abbot Varsonofy, one was the Elder Iosif, 6 were hieromonks, 8 were mantle monks, 17 were rassophore monks and 17 were rassophore novices. The nearby town of Kozelsk was an ordinary district town. The unexpected appearance of the "excommunicated" Tolstoy was an incredible event in the quiet life of the monastery!

And yet there had been a time when Tolstoy was accepted at Optina as a guest of honor. Everyone wanted to meet and talk with the famous writer – from the Archimandrite to the simple monk.

The memoirs of Tolstoy's servant Sergei Arbuzov, with whom he walked to the Optina monastery in 1881, and S.A.'s memoirs as well, probably written down based on what the servant and her husband told her, clearly show the hierarchical attitude toward pilgrims at the monastery.

First Arbuzov recalls how L.N. prepared for the journey: "…with my assistance, the Count put on his sandals, according to all the rules of peasant art, with leggings, and tied them to his legs with string… then we had the bags containing our things were tied to our shoulders; in the Count's bag were pajamas, two pairs of socks, two towels, a few handkerchiefs, two linen shirts, a sheet, a small pillow and leather boots."

A drunken sergeant-major ran after Tolstoy along the road in one village, hoping to get from the simple, and possibly undocumented, wanderer a bribe for his release, but seeing from the documents that it was Count Tolstoy, he was terribly frightened, and tried in every way to be of service.

They arrived at the monastery in the evening, in time for the evening meal. "The bell rang for dinner, and we went into the dining hall with knapsacks on our backs, we weren't allowed into the clean dining room, they sat us down to eat supper with the poor… After dinner, went for the night to the third-class inn… The monk, seeing that we had sandals on our feet, doesn't give us rooms, and instead sends us to the general rooming hut where there is a lot of dirt and insects."

As S.A. tells it, it looks even more unpleasant. "In the monastery inn, they took Lev Nikolayevich, dressed in a blue peasant shirt, jacket and sandals, to be a commoner, and Yefim, the innkeeper-monk, spoke rudely to him:

"This is the xenial house, you'll sleep here. You've stuffed yourself, and I haven't even eaten yet. Sit down here!"

Even the servant Sergei, who was wearing a bowler hat, was treated with more respect."

For a ruble, he was given a dirty, small room with bedbugs, where a third man was already asleep, a shoemaker, who was snoring loudly.

"The Count jumped back in fright," writes Arbuzov, "and said to me:

- Sergey, wake the man up and ask him not to snore.

I walked over to the couch, woke the shoemaker up and said:

- My dear man, you are snoring an awful lot, you're scaring my old man; he doesn't like it when there's a man sleeping in the same room as him and snoring.

- What's this, are you ordering me not to sleep all night because of your old man?"

But two days later, everything changed.

An Optina monk, a former serf from Yasnaya Polyana, caught sight of him. He was surprised to see his Count looking like this:

- Your Excellency, why ever did you put up with it!

They began to look for a new room for Tolstoy on the orders of the Archimandrite, and Elder Ambrose. "Two monks come," Arbuzov recalls, "to take the Count's things and ask him to go to the first-class inn, where everything is upholstered in velvet. The Count refused to go there for a long time, but in the end decided to do so."

The Archimandrite's reception lasted three hours. Tolstoy then went to see Father Ambrose and stayed in his cell for four hours. Arbuzov recalls that throughout that entire time, nearly thirty people were waiting near the Elder's cell. "Some of them said they had been there for five or six days and each day in the monastery are at Father Ambrose's cell and cannot see him and get a blessing. I asked why it was that Fr. Ambrose couldn't see them? They say that it isn't Fr. Ambrose's fault, but that his attendant doesn't announce them to him."

After Tolstoy, Ambrose also opened his door to the servant Arbuzov, and lamented very much: didn't the Count rub his feet while walking? At the hotel, a reception of the highest order awaited them. "The door opens, a monk comes in and asks, would His Excellency like to have dinner... The monks ask in surprise whether we had really travelled all the way there on foot…" And this time they had dinner "in the first-class hotel where he (Tolstoy. – P.B.) was served by the monks."

Servility in the monastery was commonplace. For example, in 1887, the Grand Duke Konstantin Konstantinovich Romanov visited for the first time. The "Annals" of the Optina hermitage report the event as follows: "Having met all the brethren at the Holy gates of the monastery, the Grand Duke proceeded to the rector's quarters, which the rector had made available to His Highness. It was evening – the eve of a holiday. In accordance with the monastery's custom, dinner was served to the honored guest, to which the rector was also invited. But the latter, in his simplicity, refused this honor, saying that he would be serving tomorrow, and that in such cases he was not in the habit of dining. This simplicity on the part of Father Isaac, by the way, made a pleasing impression on the Grand Duke, who repeatedly said that he had never seen such people as him."

Monastic receptions were notable for the special monastic etiquette. The rector may have taken the liberty of passing up the chance to have dinner with the grand duke, by citing the fact that he cannot eat food before the service. But at the same time, the dinner was held in his chambers, which he had given up for the distinguished guest.

In May 1901, Grand Duke Konstantin's children also visited the monastery. Their father was at that time at the estate of the landowner Kashkin in the village of Pryski; in anticipation of his arrival, the walls of the house were painted to look like marble. "At the request of Their Highnesses," the "Annals" report, "there was no solemn reception either at the monastery or at the hermitage. There was only the ringing of all the bells…" May 21 was the Prince's name-day, and "the Father Hegumen, along with Hierodeacon Father Theodosius, went to the Pryski village to bring greetings to the most August name-day celebrant, to whom Father Hegumen brought an icon of the Presentation of the Blessed Virgin in a gilded silver chasuble and the book *A Description of Optina Pustyn*."

This apparent unfairness had its own particular kind of order and tradition. What was unusual and offensive to the monastery was the "disguised" Count's behavior. Everyone is equal before God, but not before the rector, who was responsible above all for the internal, rather complicated administration of monastic life, which included regulating the influx of visitors, especially in summer.

The "disguised" Tolstoy had grossly violated monastic etiquette and was in breach of the rules.

The situation in 1881 was almost a mirror-image of Tolstoy's visit to the monastery in 1877, when he arrived there, albeit as a Count, with a friend, the renowned critic N.N. Strahov, but nonetheless wanted to stay at the third-class hotel like a simple pilgrim. He had every right, of course, to do so. But word of this spread like wildfire around the monastery, and Tolstoy and his companion were urged to move to the nice hotel. He was received by the Elder Ambrose, they had a long talk, and Tolstoy, by his own admission, was very pleased with the conversation.

Why was it that, four years later, he played out this spectacle, so strange in all respects, at the monastery? Why does he suffer in a room with bedbugs and a snoring shoemaker, imposing silence on Figaro-Arbuzov, who, a few years later, was to publish openly mocking memoirs of his master's visit to Optina? Why put the monastery administration in an awkward position?

There were many reasons for this. Tolstoy genuinely wanted to mingle with the people and see the monastery with his own eyes, not through the eyes of an important landowner. He genuinely found it unpleasant to live in a luxurious environment and take food from the hands of obliging monks. It was also a sign of the famous "wildness" of the Tolstoy breed, which refused to be guided by the generally accepted norms, and the stubbornness of the Tolstoys, though this was by no means "pride", as is commonly thought. Rather, it was purely the writerly curiosity of the future author of *Father Sergius* and *The Posthumous Papers of the Elder Feodor Kuzmich* Tolstoy wanted to 'live' his future works in as 'flesh-and-bone' a manner as possible.

Tolstoy was a foreign body at the monastery. And the monastic organism naturally sensed this and compelled him to act according to their rules, not according to the writer's "script".

If he had been nothing more than an eccentric landlord, that is. But he was a great writer, whose every word, nay every gesture, echoed throughout Russia and all over the world. To take an example, he had seen an old woman in the monastery store. The old woman could not find an inexpensive gospel for herself. Tolstoy bought her an expensive Gospel. One might well think, what of it? But you see, this gospel wasn't bought merely by a generous landlord, but by a man who had set himself the task of saving the evangelical doctrine from church dogma. And this ordinary gesture immediately became a symbol.

In October 1910, it was not only the Count and writer Lev Tolstoy that appeared at the monastery, but also the Tolstoy who had been "excommunicated from church". We may be able to understand, today, the intricacies of the synodal designation in 1901, according to which Tolstoy became persona-non-grata within the framework of the Orthodox Church. We may be able to debate, today, as to whether or not this "excommunication" really was an excommunication. Back then, however, it was precisely as an "excommunicated" person that he was received in the monastery.

We might think of it in terms of a family... the husband has left his wife and lives apart from her. The wife puts up with it, and then files for divorce, which is formalized accordingly. After that, the husband may go back to his wife, only no longer as a husband, but as a lover. And they may formalize the marriage again, but it will be awkward, difficult, and painful.

This uneasiness is felt in every step Tolstoy takes around Optina in the autumn of 1910, in every word he utters, every gesture he makes.

His own feeling is that he should have been thrown out. But Mikhail is welcoming, flinging open the door of the best hotel room. "I'm Lev Tolstoy, excommunicated from the church, I've come to talk to your elders and tomorrow I'm leaving for Shamordino," Tolstoy quickly explains just in case there has been a misunderstanding. But Mikhail brings apples, honey, and arranges everything in the room to his liking.

And Tolstoy feels his soul being thawed... At this time, he surely remembers that his Aunt Alexandra Ilinichna Osten-Sacken, his father's sister, spent the last few years of her life at Optina and passed away there – the aunt who, after the death of her brother Nikolai Ilyich, became guardian of the young Tolstoy children. She was buried there, too. She had once been a brilliant society lady, a real "star" at court. But... an unsuccessful marriage, her husband's mental illness... "My aunt was a truly religious woman. Her favorite activities were reading the Lives of the Saints, talking to pilgrims, holy fools, monks and nuns... Aunt Alexandra Ilinichna was not only outwardly religious, observing fasts and praying a lot... she also lived a truly Christian life, trying to avoid all forms of luxury and servants, and instead trying, as much as possible, to serve others," wrote Tolstoy.

He first visited Optina in 1841, when Alexandra Ilinichna's funeral took place. Lev was thirteen at the time. Later her nephews put a modest memorial with a touching epitaph on her grave:

> Asleep to this life here on earth,
> You have passed away into the unknown,
> Among the abodes of the life in heaven
> Enviable is your sweet repose.
> In the hope of a sweet reunion
> And with faith in life after death,
> Your nephews this mark of remembrance
> Erected, the ashes of the deceased to honor.

Elizaveta Alexandra Yergolskaya, the sister of Tolstoy's most beloved "auntie" Tatiana Alexandrovna Yergolskaya, also lived, died and was buried here. Neither Alexandra Ilynichna nor Elizaveta Alexandrovna had been nuns. They had simply lived at the monastery. And they found eternal peace there.

On the way to the hermitage, Tolstoy happened to meet another hospitaller, Father Pahom, a former soldier in the Guards.

Father Pahom, already knowing that Tolstoy had arrived at the monastery, went out to meet him.

- What is that building?
- A hotel.
- I'd like to stay here. Who is the hospitaller?
- I am, the sinner Father Pahom. Is it you, your Excellency?
- I am Lev Nikolayevich Tolstoy. I'm on my way to see Father Iosif, the elder, I'm afraid to disturb him, they say he's unwell.
- He's not unwell, but he's weak. Go, your Excellency, he will receive you.
- Where did you serve in the past?

Pahom named some Guards Regiment in St. Petersburg.

- Oh, I know them ... Goodbye, brother. Forgive me for calling you that. I call everyone that now. We are all brothers of one king.

And there was another encounter, with a boy at the hotel. "Lev Nikolayevich spoke to me too," the boy said proudly. "He asked if I lived far away or close by, who my parents were, and then he gently patted me and said: "What brings you here then, come to become a monk, have you?"

From the moment he arrived at Optina, people greeted the "excommunicated" Tolstoy was as if he was their own father: the ferryman, the hospitallers, the boy... Everyone was pleased to see this extraordinary man, a famous writer and at the same time such a simple, approachable "grandfatherly" character. And this time, Tolstoy wasn't "disguised" at all. After all, he was a grandfather. And he always knew how to find the shortest path to the heart of the common man, asking him about the details of his life and taking an interest in every detail.

Everything was fine until Tolstoy arrived at the hermitage.

Here it is – the most worrisome moment of Tolstoy's last visit to Optina! Why didn't he meet with Iosif, for whose sake, in fact, he had come to the monastery, not expecting at all the kind reception that the simple inhabitants gave him? Why didn't Iosif summon Tolstoy, whom Ambrose himself had invited to his cell?

It is in their assessment of this event that the opinions of the zealots of Orthodoxy and its opponents are diametrically opposed. "Pride!" say the former. "Pride!" say the latter.

In fact, on the face of it, this was a clash of two authorities, the ecclesiastical and the secular. Two elders. One didn't send a summons, the other didn't go. What if he had sent a summons? What if Tolstoy had gone of his own accord? Perhaps there would have been a reconciliation between the Church and Tolstoy, not a formal one, not for the sake of the Synod, not for the sake of the tsar, and Stolypin, who, incidentally, had an interest in such a reconciliation under the gaze of Europe, for all sorts of reasons. Not for the sake of the letter, not for the bishops, not for the sake of the state. For the sake of the simple hospitallers Mikhail and Pahom, for the sake of the boy Kiryushka, who, had he been an adult monk, would have been proud of his meeting with the great Russian writer. For the sake of those simple monks who, according to Makovitsky, crowded around the ferry when Lev Tolstoy, empty-handed, set sail from Optina forever toward some eternity of his own, as if eternity in Russia is not the same for everyone.

"It's a pity for Lev Nikolayevich, oh Lord!" the monks whispered. "Yes! Poor Lev Nikolayevich!"

Tolstoy, meanwhile, standing at the railing, was talking to a gray-haired old monk wearing glasses, of pleasant appearance. As old men do, he asked him sympathetically about his vision. He recalled an anecdote from his youth in Kazan when, as a student, a Tatar had said to him: "Buy some glasses." "I don't need any." "What do you mean you don't need them! Every respectable landlord is wearing glasses these days."

"The crossing was short," writes Makovitsky, "one minute." All of one minute, and one of the most important spiritual issues of pre-revolutionary Russia, the conflict between Tolstoy and the Church, was, with a Russian carelessness, left "for later". Although at that time, nothing should have been left "for later". By the time "later" arrived, it was already too late to fix anything.

When Tolstoy died and was buried at Yasnaya, on the edge of a ravine in Stary Zakaz wood, the fool Parasha came to the burial mound and sang a funeral song in her own special way, in a folksy way:

Oh wither, you dimwit, have you gone,
Oh wither did you want to go,
Along some little path or other,
Oh, with whom have you left us, with silly fools,
With whom have you abandoned us...
With whom have you left us...

The peasant women made fun of Parasha. That fool, performing a funeral service for the Count! But the fool was, of course, a thousand times wiser than the "stupid" and "unsophisticated" participants in the awkward scene that unfolded on October 29 in Optina. This fool was precisely the sort of person who was missing: someone who might have taken Tolstoy by the hand and brought him to the Elder.

Everyone behaved just a little too smartly, as if everyone was right in their own way. The monastery Rector, Archimandrite Xenophon, was sick. A few days earlier, he had returned to the monastery from Moscow after an operation. And the abbot of the monastery couldn't meet with a heretic on such a scale as Tolstoy, without having received permission from the Bishop of Kaluga.

"I think it's my duty to respectfully inform your Grace that on 28 October, Count Lev Nikolayevich Tolstoy, accompanied, in his words, by his doctor, arrived on the 5pm train from Belevo at the monastery entrusted to me... on October 29 at 7 o'clock in the morning, some young man came to him from the station; they spent a long time writing something in the room, and then with the same coach driver his doctor went to the city of Kozelsk. At 8 o'clock in the morning on this day, Tolstoy went for a walk; on both occasions he walked alone. The second time he was seen passing near an empty building, which is outside the monastery wall, known as the "Consular", which he had visited during the life of the late Elder Ambrose, with the late writer Leontyev; he then passed near the hermitage, but he didn't call in on any of the elders, or on me, the rector. He didn't come inside the monastery or the hermitage. Tolstoy returned from this walk at 1pm, had lunch and left for Shamordino at 3pm, where his sister, the nun, lives. In the hotel's visitor book, he wrote: "Lev Tolstoy expresses his thanks for the reception."

This is from the "report" made by Hegumen Xenophon to Bishop Veniamin. From it we can ascertain the following... not only did Tolstoy not visit the hermitage, he didn't visit the monastery either. In fact, on carefully reading Makovitsky, Sergeyenko, Ksyunin and Tolstoy's diary, we do not find any mention of Tolstoy having stepped through the Holy gates and going into the grounds of the monastery. Tolstoy literally walked "around the church walls" as V.V. Rozanov would have put it.

The hermitage and hotel were outside the grounds of the monastery. "Lev Tolstoy went for a walk to the hermitage," writes Makovitsky. "He went to its south-western corner. He walked along the south wall... and went into the woods... At 12 o'clock, L.N. again went for a walk to the hermitage. He left the hotel, took a left, went to the holy gates, came back and went right, came back again to the holy gates, then set off and turned at the tower toward the hermitage."

It was seemingly an ordinary walk... Tolstoy held a folding cane-seat in his hands, which he always took with him on walks at Yasnaya Polyana. But "L.N. never went for two walks in the morning." Makovitsky emphasizes the strangeness of Tolstoy's behavior. "L.N. visibly had a strong desire to speak to the elders."

But something was preventing him from doing so. When he returned from the second walk, he said:

"I won't go to the elders of my own accord. If they themselves were to summon me, I would go."

Many see the manifestation of Tolstoy's "pride" in these words. Indeed, why did he not just knock on the door of Iosif's house, the porch of which extended beyond the wall of the hermitage precisely so that any pilgrim going past could ask for a reception with the elder, via his cell-attendant? Why insist on waiting for them to "summon" him? Even if Makovitsky has not conveyed his words accurately, even without words it is clear that Tolstoy was waiting for an invitation and that without one he was unwilling to take the first step. But did Iosif know this?

Yes, he did. Here is what the Elder Iosif's cell-attendant says in the "Annals":

"The Elder Iosif was sick, I was sitting next to him. The Elder Varsonofy walks in and tells us that Father Mikhail had sent him to warn us that Tolstoy was coming to see us. 'I asked him,' he says, 'Who told you?' He says, 'Tolstoy himself.' The elder Iosif says: "If he comes, we'll receive him with affection and reverence and joy, even though he was excommunicated; since he has come here of his own accord, no one forced him, we cannot do any different." Then they sent me to look over the fence. I saw Lev Nikolayevich and reported to the elders that he was walking close by the house, coming up to it, then walking away. The elder Iosif says: "It's difficult for him. He came to us for living water. Go, invite him, since he came to visit us. You go and ask him." I went, but he was no longer there, he had left. He hadn't gone very far at all yet, but he was on a horse after all, I couldn't have caught up with him..."

However, the latter explanation contradicts what actually happened and was scrupulously recorded, minute-by-minute, in Makovitsky's diary. After the second walk, Tolstoy returned to the hotel on foot and had a hearty lunch ("It seemed to L.N. that the monastery's cabbage soup was very tasty and the buckwheat porridge with sunflower oil was well cooked; he ate a lot of it," – Makovitsky writes). He paid the hospitaller ("What do I owe you? – What you are willing to pay. – Is three rubles enough?"). He signed his name in the visitors' book for distinguished guests and walked to the ferry, where Sergeyenko and Makovitsky caught up with him in two carriages. At the ferry Tolstoy was accompanied by fifteen monks, according to Makovitsky's estimate.

There was no need to catch up with Tolstoy. All that needed to be done was summon him. He didn't go to Iosif himself because he knew about his illness and simply didn't want to disturb a sick old man without being invited. He clearly said as much to his sister Maria Nikolayevna in Shamordino. And he also said he was afraid that he, as someone who had been "excommunicated", would not be received. Tolstoy was let down in the most elementary of ways by his own aristocratic delicacy. For his part, Iosif didn't know for sure why Tolstoy had come. Iosif knew only by hearsay that he wanted to talk to him. And lastly, Iosif could not yet have known anything about the most important thing of all – Tolstoy's flight. No-one, other than those closest to him, knew anything about it yet. There weren't any newspaper reports about it yet, as these only appeared the following day.

Later, after Tolstoy's death, in the presence of Makovitsky, who visited the monastery in December 1910, a certain abbess scolded Father Pahom: why hadn't he taken Tolstoy to the elder, knowing as he did that the Count wanted to talk to him? "I somehow couldn't make up my mind to do so..." Father Pahom said in his defense. "I didn't want to be obtrusive."

It's impossible to read this after the fact without feeling a little bitterness. Everyone, on the face of it, is doing the right thing. One might even say they are behaving nobly. And yet they are all... somehow sick, showing weakness. And no one dares to make the first move so that they can meet in the middle. As a result, the great Russian writer wanders around like a castaway, "beside the monastery walls".

In Shamordino Tolstoy told his sister that he planned to return once again to Optina and talk to Iosif. By then, though, it was too late. Some unknown force was driving Tolstoy further and further away.

All of a sudden

In Tolstoy's biography, one can single out three events which not only influenced the course of his life, but radically altered it, turned it 180°.

These are his marriage, his spiritual upheaval in the late 70's - early 80's and his departure from Yasnaya Polyana.

The last of these, however, is too close in time to the tragedy in Astapovo and Tolstoy's death, effectively merging with it into one event. Moreover, it only lasts ten days, so one cannot talk about this as a new stage in Tolstoy's life. Thus, as far as the most important events in his *life* were concerned, there were two: his marriage and his spiritual upheaval.

There were no other events – neither his departure from the Caucasus, nor the Sevastopol campaign, nor the death of his beloved brother Nikolenka, nor the "Arzamas horror", nor the premature death of his children, even the most beloved, Vanya and Masha, that changed the very structure of Tolstoy's life to such an extent, transforming him *suddenly* into a fundamentally new man.

Tolstoy before his marriage and Tolstoy after it are two fundamentally different people, and the same goes for Tolstoy before the spiritual upheaval and Tolstoy after it. *Suddenly* absolutely everything changes! The world appears to him in a completely new light, and the meaning and significance of certain people, things, emotions, situations – changes from a "+" sign to a "-" sign or vice versa.

Tolstoy before his marriage is an unhappy man! And an impossible man, in the opinion of others. He simultaneously gets mixed up with prostitutes, gambles with the last of his money and lives with another man's wife as though she is his own, and quarrels with Turgenev, bringing the scandal nearly to a duel...

It is clear that there couldn't be any talk of a harmonious structure to his life in these conditions. And Tolstoy understands this. In no way does he try to look for the causes of this mental disorder in his surroundings. Only in himself! He calls himself every name under the sun in his diary on the eve of his marriage. "Fool", "pig", "beast", "old devil", "madman", etc.

"Often with horror I find myself asking myself: what do I like? nothing..." "I feel sickened with myself, embarrassed..." "Stuffed myself with Vasinka (Perfilev. – P.B.) just now and started wheezing, lying opposite one another ..."

And everything goes wrong... Before the wedding it transpires that his clean dress shirt was left behind in the coach with the things and he had nothing to wear for the wedding. It's quite a hitch. Everyone is waiting in church for the groom, but he's not there. Sonya already thinks he has done a runner, like Podkolesin. Well, it's not surprising... After all, in the past he had effectively run away from her older sister Liza to the Samara Steppe, just as he had fled from Arsenyeva to Petersburg... There is an entry in Tolstoy's diary, incidentally: "On the wedding day fear, mistrust and a desire to flee." If we recall that Tolstoy was also a superstitious person and believed all his life that putting on a shirt inside out in the morning was a bad omen, the lack of a shirt on the day of the wedding might well have a fatal role to play.

On the morning of the wedding day, L.N. unexpectedly turned up at the Behrs' house and went straight to the girls' room. Liza wasn't home, but Tanya retreated from the room and ran to report to her mother the sudden arrival of the groom to see Sonya. Her mother was surprised and unhappy: such things weren't supposed to happen on the wedding day. She went to the girls' room and found them together "between vases, suitcases and unpacked things." Sonya was crying. It turned out that L.N. hadn't slept all night, and was now "asking lots of questions of her about whether she loved him", "perhaps, her memories of the past with Polivanov were troubling her" and "whether it might not be better to break up in that case." Sonya had tried to convince him that this is not the case. In the end, her mental strength had been exhausted and she had begun to cry.

A shirt turned up, though, and the wedding took place, and yet there was no joy, there just wasn't.

The public, gathering at the wedding, noted the difference in age between the bride and groom and her tear-stained eyes and drew their own conclusions. "So, they're forcing her to marry him..." "Just look how young she is, and him so old..." "But he's a Count, they say he's rich..."

The husband wasn't happy with the tears Sonya shed upon parting with her family. "He didn't understand at the time," wrote S.A., "that if I loved my family so passionately, so ardently – then I'd transfer that same ability to love to him and to our children. And that was indeed what happened."

They were on the road for almost a whole day ... The night in the dormeuse was excruciating for the young wife. "It only cost embarrassment!" she exclaims in her memoirs. Besides that, she didn't remember anything else from the trip: where they stayed, what they talked about.

The first night spent at Yasnaya, according to Tolstoy, was "difficult." Over their morning coffee, the husband and wife felt "uncomfortable".

But *suddenly* a miracle occurs! On the very same day, September 25, 1862, he writes in his diary: "Unutterable happiness… It cannot be that all this could end only in life."

Tireless Sophie

Sonia, accustomed to the Kremlin family life of loving parents, was troubled by the "wildness" of her husband's habits – those of a bachelor and at the same time of an aristocrat of the old school. The lack of silverware when the table was set was something she found strange. The lack of silver was the least of it… the Tolstoy Brothers had grown used to sleeping in the house on straw, without sheets. There was a smell of hay all over the house and weeds were growing rampantly around the house. The paths weren't cleared, the servants were dressed slovenly. Never mind the servants… the master of the house himself covered himself up during the daytime in an old long robe fastened with flaps, which also served as pajamas.

Tolstoy's cook, Nikolai Mikhailovich, who, during Volkonsky's time, had been transferred to the kitchens from the musical staff because he lost the *embouchure* (a mouthpiece for a flute), was, according to S.A., "extremely dirty". He often drank, although he "cooked adequately". Once, over lunch, S.A. burst into tears, on finding a "disgusting parasite" in her bowl of soup. The old iron forks pricked her mouth, and the sight of her husband sleeping under a quilt, his head on a pillow without a pillowcase, was horrible.

The atmosphere of having been orphaned at a young age, the absence of paternal and maternal care, that is to say everything that surrounded S.A. in her own childhood and adolescence, was another thing that was acutely felt in the life of Yasnaya Polyana. It's no coincidence that her husband had an especially soft spot for the Lower Park with its sentimental nooks, little bridges and gazebo, reminiscent of the touching strolls his father and mother would take on their own. This circumstance, together with Tolstoy's "wildness", was something that the eighteen-year-old S.A. had to experience, accept with her heart and make sense of in her mind. She was required to display practicality and sensitivity as she mastered spiritual territory that was new to her.

"The Tireless Sophie", as Alexandra Andreyevna Tolstaya called her, not only coped with this task, but, essentially, remodeled life at Yasnaya Polyana so that it was to her liking. If the Natasha Rostova that we see at the beginning of *War and Peace* is the youngest of the Behrs sisters, Tanya, then the married Natasha is, of course, Sonya.

Charming looks, without garish or irritating beauty. Comeliness of body. A lively mind which grasped and absorbed everything quickly. She was not spoilt – the Behrs family never spoiled their daughters. A strong maternal instinct and an undoubted talent as an educator. And at the same time – an unfeigned, ardent interest in her husband's creative work … In his creative work mind, not the agricultural work which fired L.N.'s passion for a while, when he dabbled in bee-keeping, rearing Japanese pigs and building a distillery. S.A. didn't like agriculture and made no secret of it.

Her Yasnaya Polyana notebook, in which she wrote down in detail what she "loves" and what she "doesn't like", has survived.

What I love:

Peace in my soul.
Dreams in my head.
Love of people toward me.
I love children.
I love all kinds of flowers.
The sun and lots of light.
The forest.
I like to plant, trim and tend to trees.
I like to portray things, i.e. to draw or photograph things
  or play a role; I like to create things - even if it's just sewing.
I love music, with some limits.
I love the clarity, simplicity, talent
  in people.
Costumes and decorations.
Fun and festivity, glitter, beauty.

I love poetry.
Affection. Sentimentality.
I like to work productively.
I love honesty, truthfulness...

What I don't like:

Hostility and discontent in people.
Emptiness in my soul and thoughts, even if it's temporary.
Autumn. Darkness and night.
Men (with a few exceptions).
Gambling.
People mired in wine and vices.
Secrets, dishonesty, secrecy, unfairness.
The Steppe.
Roaring, noisy songs.
The process of eating.
I do not like any kind of agriculture.
I do not like: lack of talent, cunning, hypocrisy and lies.
I do not like being alone.
I do not like mockery, jokes, parodies, criticism and caricatures.
I do not like idleness and laziness.
I find it hard to bear disorder of any kind.

It's impossible to imagine Tolstoy writing something like this. The style of his diaries is more subtle, if anything, more "feminine". Tolstoy made every effort to understand and accept that which was "foreign", to find a justification for it and, conversely, never found justification for him himself. For him, there were no rigid boundaries between the "familiar" and the "foreign". If he felt them, he tried to overcome them. Generally speaking, the categorical phrase "I don't like" is not something that is in Tolstoy's vocabulary.

L.N. and S.A. were very different, in fact, diametrically opposed, in terms of their nature.

She embodied, relatively speaking, the "bourgeois" female type, with all its flaws and virtues, perfectly reflected in the novel by Charlotte Bronte, *Jane Eyre*, S.A.'s favorite novel.

S.A. was in the mold of the *pragmatic believer*. The diary she kept as a girl, an excerpt from which happened to survive and is quoted in her memoirs, contained this interesting entry:

"...Character and morality – it all depends on the organization of the brain, nerves, veins, intestines ... Depends on warm, clear weather, on good food, warm housing. Matter, the ideal, the soul ... Oh my God, what chaos! What important issues, and who will solve them? Is there something mysterious in the world?"

As a little girl, she had visited a monastery in the Moscow suburb of New Jerusalem and been taken aback by a life-size crucifixion of Christ "...a full-length statue, all painted, dressed in a black velvet gown, with chains on his hands ...and it was horrible to look on this doll, and immediately the idea came to me that this was idolatry, and that everything – especially religion – must be idealized, and that one's attitude toward Christ must remain in the abstract."

SA was a life-long believer and church-goer, who brought her children up to be the same and was angered by her husband's statements against the church. By contrast with L.N., however, there was no mysticism in her religiosity. God existed, of that there was no doubt... but He was so far away and so incomprehensible that one must live by the rules here on earth, which also include the laws of the church.

L.N. embodied a very different, so to speak, "lordly" type, a type that is best portrayed in Goncharov's novel *Oblomov*.

Tolstoy was an idealistic believer. God is not somewhere far away... He is all around us and, ultimately, within us. Hence the inscrutable and mysterious laws of earthly life, which must be understood not in the abstract, but with all one's heart and mind, conforming to the direct will of God, as revealed in the world.

S.A. was practical in household affairs. She composed a menu a month in advance, so as not to spend any more than was necessary when buying provisions. And at the same time, she loved high society, balls and fashionable outfits. Her husband was not practical in household matters and could not stand high-society entertainment, felt oppressed by the chic décor of the Khamovniki home, was sparing in his use of writing paper and even the batteries for the electric flashlight, but not because he was a spendthrift, but rather because this had been someone else's labor, which he would be ashamed to expend without good reason.

S.A., who had a bourgeois temperament in the way she conducted domestic matters, was, at the same time, sentimental, sensitive to details, never hesitating to express her feelings.

L.N. was, perhaps, equally sentimental. He was extremely stingy in the outward expression of feelings, though. He was ashamed to caress the children, and couldn't bear the tantrums for which his wife, alas, had a tendency.

S.A. was direct in her behavior in public, saying everything she thought and felt straight to one's face. L.N. was extremely tactful when talking to strangers, he was afraid of offending them with a careless word. Only he could have come up with one particular family game, known as "Numidian Cavalry". Having awaited (calmly awaited! – no more than that) the departure of an unpleasant guest who had become a bore, he and all the members of the household would form a chain and canter around the table, shaking their hands over their heads. This was how they got rid of the tension which the unpleasant person had brought into the house. It would have been unthinkable, though, to give the guest any sign that he was unpleasant or that it was time for him to leave.

S.A. adored nature, but didn't like the countryside or the peasants, being a city person. While in Moscow or St. Petersburg, she didn't miss a single important concert, show or exhibition. L.N. didn't like the city, not even Moscow, where people didn't say hello to one another, and was exclusively a man of the countryside. After his spiritual upheaval, he didn't recognize the value of concerts, and had an extremely unconventional attitude toward the theater, even when he became a famous playwright, as the author of *The Power of Darkness*; he was narrow in his interpretation of painting, not only refusing to acknowledge new trends, but also refusing to acknowledge, for example, the significance of landscapes.

It seems incomprehensible that two people so very different from one another could have fallen in love.

But love it certainly was! And not just love, but "unutterable happiness". It's wrong to assume that this love left L.N. along with sexual desire, with the "sense of the deer", as S.A. herself sometimes thought. Tolstoy's very last diary entries contain the kind of expressions of such love toward his wife which cannot be faked.

In April 1863, S.A. writes to her younger sister in Moscow, at Easter: "I was bored celebrating the holidays, you do understand that at such times one always feels it more and more, and sure enough I felt it, that I wasn't with you, and I became sad. We didn't have any fun dyeing of eggs, no all-night vigil with the tedious 12 Gospels, no shrouds, no Trifonovna (the Behrs' housekeeper – P.B.) with a giant Easter loaf on her belly, no waiting for matins – nothing ... And such melancholy fell upon me on Good Friday evening that I began to spill over, crying uncontrollably. I was bored because the holiday was not happening. And I was ashamed before Levochka, and there was nothing that could be done... On Bright Sunday, I calmed down, and Lev and I began to look at everything from the *critical* <side>... Our priest, Father Konstantin, orated and uttered such nonsensical lies that I had to have a truly Christian patience to listen to him..."

Her husband's lack of religious ritual didn't irk Sonya too much, though. Not as much, at any rate, as she would later suffer from his "new Christianity". Rather, she just missed her mother and sisters, the Kremlin lifestyle, recalling, in this regard, how they used to celebrate Easter in Moscow. She asks Tanya in the same letter: "Tanya, my dear, write to me too about what you are all wearing and are going to wear. Which materials, what colors, what kind of hats..."

On the other hand, the entire life of the Yasnaya Polyana estate was filled with ancient legends and a religious pietism, reminiscent of Tolstoy's mother. Ancient black images hung in the room of Auntie Yergolskaya and her old sponger Natalia Petrovna. In the neighboring wing there lived a remarkably old creature – the former maid of Tolstoy's grandmother, Pelagea Nikolayevna Tolstoy, Agafiya Mikhailovna. Forever clad in an old jacket, from which tufts of wool stuck out, she used to gather up the stray dogs in the area, which would then live in her wing, as equals. They called her the "dog governess". Like Auntie Yergolskaya, Agafiya Mikhailovna was a "girl" and she lived only for the sake of others. But she also had her pride, about which the Tolstoys' eldest daughter Tatyana Lvovna writes:

"Once, my Aunt Tatiana Andreyevna Behrs, my mother's younger sister, got sick while visiting us. As usually happened in such cases, Agafiya Mikhailovna was sent for.

"I had just come home from the bathhouse," Agafiya Mikhailovna said, "drank some tea and laid down on the stove. Suddenly I heard someone knocking at the window. 'What do you want?' I shout. 'Tatyana Andreyevna sent me to get you – she's sick, so they're asking you to come over.' And I had just gotten warm on the stove and didn't want to get off, get dressed in the cold to go to the house. So I answered, 'Tell them Agafiya Mikhailovna can't come, she's just gotten back from the bathhouse.' The messenger left, and I lie down and think, "Oh, what I'm doing is not good, I'm pitying myself and not taking pity on a sick person.' I got my legs down off the stove, began putting on my shoes. Suddenly I heard knocking on the window again. 'Well,' I ask, 'what is it this time?' – 'Tatyana Andreyevna sent me to tell you to come without fail - they will buy you a dress.' –'Ah! ah,' I say, 'buy me a dress... Tell her that I said I'm not coming, and I shan't come.' I took off my boots, climbed back on the stove and for a long time could not fall asleep. It's not because of new dresses that I take pity on the sick... I loved Tatiana Andreyevna, and how she had offended me..."

The pious Agafiya Mikhailovna was capable, however, of turning a holy icon around to face the wall, if it the "help" it provided had been substandard. At the same time, she had "existential" consciousness and had once left L.N. struck by a story, which he liked to recall till his dying day:

"I was lying here once all alone, all was quiet, with only the clock ticking on the wall, seeming to say: "who are you, what are you? who are you, what are you?" And it set me thinking: indeed, I think to myself, "Who am I? What am I?" I lay awake all night thinking about it."

Agafia Mikhailovna took pity on flies and cockroaches and fed the mice, which almost become tame in her wing. "Agafiya Mikhailovna died when none of us were home at Yasnaya Polyana," recalls Sukhotina-Tolstaya. "She died quietly, without fuss or fear. Before her death she requested that they convey her thanks to all our family for our love. It was said that when they carried her to the graveyard, all the dogs, with the kennelwoman, escorted her far beyond the village on the road to the cemetery, howling."

"There were some strange people living in the house..." adds Sukhotina-Tolstaya. "The monk Voyeikov lived there for a long time. He was the brother of the guardian of my father and his brothers and sister. Voyeikov walked around in monastic dress, which was not in keeping with his passion for wine. A dwarf also lived there. It was his duty to chop firewood, but, in addition, he always played an important role in various amusements and masquerades at Yasnaya Polyana. There was an old wanderer, Maria Gerasimovna, who went around in men's clothing. She was the godmother of my aunt Maria Nikolayevna."

Of course, this is a far cry from the Kremlin life of the Behrs family, where girls, during walks, were accompanied by a footman in a helmet with a "zishagge". At Yasnaya, on the other hand, one might see gypsies with a bear.

- Mikhailo Ivanich, bow to the audience.

The bear groaned, got up on his hind legs and, jingling his chain, gave a low bow.

- Show us how the kids steal peas from the priests.

The bear lay on the ground and crept toward the imaginary peas.

- Show us how the ladies put on their make-up.

The bear sat on his hind legs, a mirror was held up in front of him, and he stroked his muzzle with his fore-paws.

- Die!

The bear, groaning, fell down and lay motionless.

"It all ended as it usually did" wrote Sergei Lvovich, the Tolstoys' eldest son – everyone, including the bear, was brought vodka. Having drunk it, the bear became good-natured, lay down on his back and seemed to be smiling..."

This domestic poetry of Yasnaya Polyana, which left such indelible enchantment on the Tolstoy children that they all remembered their Yasnaya Polyana childhood as a paradise, left an impression on their mother, aged eighteen or nineteen, that was by no means unambiguous. In the end, she just got used to it.

"In the early days of my marriage," S.A. recalled, "they came to congratulate us: servants, peasants and schoolchildren. My mother had given me 300 rubles for my expenses, so that I wouldn't need to take money from my husband straight away, and I gave almost all of it away to the well-wishers. It seemed to me then that everyone was so kind, how much they loved us, and this pleased me, although I was greatly embarrassed by these congratulations. There was the old wife of Uncle Nikolai Dmitriev – Arina Ignatyevna, with her daughter Varvara; the cowgirl Anna Petrovna with her girls Annushka and Dushka, the elder Vasily Ermilin, the confectioner Maxim Ivanovich, the old maid of grandmother Pelageya Nikolayevna – the dull, austere Agafiya Mikhailovna, the cheerful laundress Aksinya Maximovna, with her beautiful daughters Paula and Marfa, the coachman, the gardener and *many other foreign and strange people with whom I had to live for a long time after that.*" (my italics. – P.B).

All these incomprehensible people, who fed the creative imagination of her husband, the author of *Childhood* and *Boyhood*, *Polikushka* and the late story *Alyosha Gorshok*, brilliant in its poetic simplicity, remained alien to S.A. The attitude of Tolstoy's wife toward the real prototype for Alyosha Gorshok, a village idiot who actually lived in Yasnaya Polyana, was telling. "For example, a simpleton came over from the village, nicknamed Alyosha Gorshok, and they made him make indecent sounds, and everyone laughed, and I felt disgusted and wanted to cry," she recalled, at about the same time that Tolstoy was writing the story *Alyosha Gorshok*.

For the uninitiated reader, S.A.'s memoirs may create a false impression, namely that a refined, metropolitan young lady had been brought to a "wild" rural wilderness full of bears and deranged people, with "dog governesses" and farting half-wits. In fact, it wasn't like that at all...

Her husband was the one who was an aristocrat. But Tolstoy's aristocratic nature wasn't ostentatious, but ancient, tied to the estate. "By his birth, education and manners," wrote Tolstoy's son Ilya Lvovich, "father was a true aristocrat. Despite his worker's blouse, which he always wore, and despite his complete disdain for all the prejudices of the nobility, he was a gentleman, and remained a gentleman until the end of his days."

Sophie was well educated, understood French and German, had a university degree as a home tutor obtained as an extern, could draw and play the piano and had an undoubted literary talent, enabling her to write children's stories (in a book called *Skeleton-dolls*) and translate the philosophical writings of her husband into French. In later years, she was fond of painting and achieved great success in this.

Her main talent, though, was for running the house and for her children. No wonder her grandmother said: "Sonya's head is in a bonnet." It was precisely this bonnet, the symbol of the housewife, that was the first detail highlighted by L.N. in his first letter from Yasnaya, in which he talks about his familial bliss.

"...God grant you the same happiness that I feel, there is none greater" – he writes on September 25, 1862 in Moscow to Tanya Behrs. "She (young Sonya – P.B.) is now wearing a bonnet with crimson – doesn't matter.

And how well this morning she played at being a grown woman and the lady of the house, she looked the part and was excellent."

It was the first day of their life together. Three days later, Tolstoy would turn thirty-four, and one month earlier Sonya had turned eighteen. Sonya is still on her "tippy-toes" in front of him. He's a great, brilliant person! He owns a whole estate. And not just one: a hundred versts away was the wonderful Nikolskoye, the estate left behind after the death of his brother Nikolai. He is a writer, a teacher, a passionate hunter and the chosen international mediator in the matter of the abolition of serfdom. Finally, he was physically a very strong man. When some passer-by began ogling his wife as she bathed in the pond, he chased after him and gave him an almighty thrashing. There could be no talk of any "non-resistance" at this stage. This was the *furious* Tolstoy. How enraged he was when, before the wedding, the police came to Yasnaya and searched his house, trying to find banned books and imagining they might find a printing press with the writings of Herzen hot off the press. It was fortunate that at that time he was in the steppes of Samara, or else L.N. would certainly have shot the warrant officer!

He weighs down on Sonya with his authority, his physical strength: "Brilliantly talented, intelligent and more elderly and experienced in his spiritual life – he suppressed me morally." "Physical might and the experience of a man who has lived a bit in the sphere of love – animal passion and brute force – weighed down on me physically."

It might seem as if she had very little on her side: youth and the "bonnet". Young, beautiful, she is always right, even when she's wrong.

Tolstoy's letters from 1862-63, are simply infused with the dumb happiness of the newly-wed.

"Tanya! You know that in moments of friendship Sonya calls me *belly button*. Don't tell her to call me "belly button", it's offensive. And how I love it when you and Sonya call me Drysinka... Tanya! Why did you go to St. Petersburg?... You will be bored there. There..."

The letter is then continued by Sonya, in accordance with the habit they had formed of writing letters together.

In the exciting duel between husband and wife, Sonya's youth and attractiveness were far stronger than his physical strength. Tolstoy's letters and the diary from his first few years of marriage create a sense of some kind of drunken happiness.

"... as I write I can hear the voice of my wife, who is talking to my brother upstairs, and whom I love more than anything in the world," he tells A.A. Tolstoy. "I've lived to the age of 34 and didn't know it was possible to love like this and be so happy... Now I have the constant feeling that I have stolen a happiness which is undeserved, illegal, not intended for me. Here she comes now, I can hear her and it's so wonderful."

"Fetushka, dear old chap and simply dear friend, Afanasy Afanasievich. I have been married two weeks and am happy, and a new, completely new person."

To E.P. Kovalevsky: "...it's been a month since I got married and I'm happy in a way that I never would have believed people could be happy."

M.N. Tolstoy: "I am a great pig, my dear Masha, for having not written to you for so long. Happy people are selfish."

To I.P. Borisov: "We have everything at home, thank God, and we live in such a way that we mustn't die."

He had temporarily parted company with his "last mistress", teaching. Not just because the pedagogical journal *Yasnaya Polyana* hadn't attracted serious public interest. Not just because the peasant children, whilst working in the fields, had not time for studying. Perhaps the main reason was the incompatibility of teaching and his young wife. For example, the rural teachers who came to Yasnaya for a kind of "training" or "exchange of experience", used to smoke in the living room, and Sonia, who in no time at all was pregnant, couldn't tolerate the smoke at all.

"All of these young people," recalls S.A., "were very ill at ease due to my presence, and some looked at me with hostility, sensing that their close interaction with Lev Nikolayevich would now come to an end, as he shifted all his interests onto family life."

Thus a conflict arose for the first time: for whom did Tolstoy exist? For his family or for everyone? Sonya won the first battle easily because L.N. himself was bored of pedagogy at the time, and his new "mistress" was agriculture: bees, pigs, horses and the little distillery. But the question had been asked, and in L.N.'s life there was no happenstance.

But what does this "new man" signify, about whom he writes to Fet? It is indeed a new Tolstoy. And at the same time, a transitional Tolstoy as it were. A Tolstoy between youth and old age. A Tolstoy between the period of all-out flight (from Kazan! to the Caucasus!, to Sevastopol! Abroad! To the Steppe in Samara!) and greedy pursuits of happiness, and a period of devastating spiritual upheaval.

This is *the happy Tolstoy*. In fact, this is the only period of his life when he was happy, and when it seemed as if there was nothing more to wish for. It lasted about fifteen years of his life... That's a lot! Of course, it wasn't completely unadulterated happiness. The first time he quarreled with his wife was on the fifth day after their arrival at Yasnaya. "Today there was a *scene*" he wrote in his diary on September 30. There were both scenes and tantrums, and an extremely difficult argument over the issue of feeding the children... But still, if we compare this time to the torments of the young Tolstoy and those that he experienced after his spiritual upheaval, then this was a time of joy, almost paradise. And of course, it was only in this period that the novels *War and Peace* and *Anna Karenina* could have been written.

The main driving force behind these works was *love*. Not love for people in general, not even love toward those "close" to him, but love for a woman. A love which, temporarily at least, had created, in some mysterious way, an elemental force by the name of 'Tolstoy'. It had brought this force to the shore. It had placed on his head its invisible cap, on which lay the reflection of the crown which had been held above L.N.'s head in the Kremlin church.

The first thing Sonya did as mistress of Yasnaya Polyana was to issue all the cooks with snow-white caps. Thenceforward, no "disgusting parasites" appeared in her soup. It was a matter of basic hygiene. But what a remarkably precise symbolic gesture, too! After that the paths were cleared, the weeds and nettles were torn out by their roots, white sheets were stitched together under a silk blanket, which replaced the cotton one, pillowcases were put on the pillows and silverware was put on the table at meal-times. But the first thing had been the caps! At any rate, these were the things she recalled first of all, when describing her first steps as lady of the house in *My Life*.

And Tolstoy, who laughed at the lackey in a helmet with a "zishagge", who accompanied the Behrs girls on walks, had not only reconciled himself to this life, but was happy as never before...

"I love her when, at night or in the morning, I wake up and see that she is looking at me and loves me. And no one – least of all, me – is stopping her from loving, in the way she knows how, in her own way. I love when she sits close to me, and we know that we love each other as best we can, and she will say: Levochka – and then she stops – why are the pipes in the fireplace upright, or why don't horses have long-drawn-out deaths, etc. I love it when we are alone for a long time and I say: what shall we do? Sonya, what shall we do? She laughs. I love it when she gets angry with me, and suddenly, in the blink of an eye, she sometimes has a sharp thought and a sharp word: leave me alone, I'm bored; then a minute later she's already smiling at me shyly again. I love when she can't see me and doesn't know it, and I love her in my own way. I love it when she's a girl in a yellow dress and thrusts out her lower jaw and her tongue, I love it when I see her head thrown back, serious and frightened, and childlike, and a passionate face, I love it when..."

"Today I woke up, she is crying and kissing my hands. What? You died in my dream... I love you all the better and all the more."

"We recently felt that our happiness was scary. When death comes, everything is finished. Is it really finished? God. We prayed."

And finally, on February 8, 1863, an entry appears in his diary which puts everything into perspective: "She doesn't know and won't realize that she is transforming me incomparably more than I am transforming her. Only not consciously. Consciously both she and I are powerless."

Interestingly, shortly before this there was a diary entry by S.A. herself: "Sometimes I want so much to free myself from his influence, which is a little difficult... The reason it is hard, I think, is that I find myself thinking with his thoughts, look at things through his eyes, I get annoyed, I shan't become him, I am losing myself."

There you have it.

Gashes

No marital happiness can be complete without arguments, jealousy and reconciliation, however. Both L.N. and S.A. were jealous. Tolstoy was jealous because of the young teacher, whilst she was seriously jealous not only because of Aksinya, but also... because of her own younger sister.

Tanya Behrs is forever visiting Yasnaya and going out hunting with Tolstoy. The two sisters love each other endlessly. But Sonya writes in his diary: "My sister Tanya is worming herself into our lives too much." And how... The younger sister, dressed in a tight-fitting riding habit, graceful and sexy, goes out riding with her husband in the woods and fields, whilst the older one, pregnant and boring, stays at home. Tanya becomes a kind of 'model' for Tolstoy. He creates the character of Natasha for *War and Peace* literally in her image. And Sonya has to transcribe the whole thing many times over. Tanya has one unhappy love affair after another: with her cousin Anatole Shostak (Anatole Kuragin in the novel), and with Tolstoy's brother Sergei Nikolayevich (Andrei Bolkonsky), because of whom she nearly poisoned herself to death. And Sonya had "affairs" of her own –she suffered from bleeding in the chest, the children came down with diarrhea, the cook had hit the bottle and she had to roast a goose herself, whilst pregnant... Yet despite all this Tanya was cast as the "unfortunate" one whilst Sonya was the "fortunate" one. How unfair!

"I remember once, in the summer," recalls S.A., "everyone had gathered together to go riding: the horses were saddled, carriages were harnessed – rollers and buggy: Olga Islenova was there, with her sister Tanya and some guests. I went out onto the porch, timidly waiting for Lev Nikolayevich's instructions, as to where I would be seated, because he was arranging everything. But when everyone had taken their places, and without even having asked me what I wanted to do, Lev Nikolayevich turned to me and said, "You, of course, are staying at home?" I could see that there was no more room, and, barely holding back the tears, I didn't say anything. But as soon as they all drove off, I started to cry so bitterly, the way children cry;

I wept long and torturously, and I haven't forgotten those tears even now, though more than forty years have passed since that time."

"*Nobody, neither a man nor a woman, must ever be allowed to get close to the intimate life of spouses, this is always dangerous,*" S.A. would write forty years later.

But it wasn't jealousy toward Tanya or even toward Aksinya that was the main reason for the "gashes" that the family suffered. Sometimes her husband begins to inwardly toss and turn, as if he feels some kind of uneasiness, a lack of external and internal freedom. Although what more freedom could anyone want? He had wanted to run a school – he did so, got bored – and quit. He had developed an interest in bees, spent whole days in the apiary, and his wife had meekly brought him his lunches. He had wanted some special breed of Japanese pigs, a special kind of apple tree – and they were ordered. The pigs died, but the orchard lasted. In the spring he went out almost every day to hunt woodcock; in the fall and winter he drove out with the greyhounds to hunt foxes and hares. Writing was starting to bring in a significant amount of money. From the fee for his novel *War and Peace*, he gave ten thousand rubles to each of his nieces, Liza and Varya, to be put toward their dowries. And his wife understood and approved of this generous gesture.

And yet ... "All the conditions of happiness came together for me. I have often missed one particular thing (all this time) – the knowledge that I have done everything I was supposed to do, in order fully to enjoy what is given to me, and to give to others *everything*, through my labor, for what they have given me."

In the spring of 1863 he starts writing *Kholstomer*, a strikingly "humane" story about a horse which was ridden too much and which ultimately gives up everything, down to the last bone, down to the last piece of skin – to *others*. At the very peak of happiness, when all the conditions for it had come together, he suddenly starts work on a story which is the apotheosis of Russian asceticism, comparable only to Turgenev's *Relics of the Living*. Why?

But *Merin*, as the story was called at the time, "wasn't coming easily". Yet *The Cossacks* was coming easily. *War and Peace* is coming easily. And *Anna Karenina* would come easily – and how! It is as if he himself wasn't serious about his second novel, as if he was surprised about why it had provoked such strong interest in readers. Yes it is clear why this was. Because people all over the world want *happiness*, not suffering. And to attain that happiness they'll do anything – even jump under a train!

But something in this happiness starts to irritate Tolstoy. "Where am I – that I, whom I myself loved and knew, who sometimes comes out to the surface and makes me happy and scares me? I am small and insignificant. And I've been like that since I married the woman I love." This diary entry appeared less than a year after the wedding.

Suddenly, at the peak of family happiness, Tolstoy's pen creates a dialogue between Prince Andrei and Pierre Bezuhov in which Pierre urges Andrei: my dear friend, don't get married! Don't get married until you have become old and useless to everyone. Suddenly infinitely happy with his charming Kitty (who is almost Sonya), Konstantin Levin in *Anna Karenina* begins to think seriously about a strong rope and the secure crossbar beneath the ceiling. And his creator himself, meanwhile, is hiding ropes from himself and is afraid to go out hunting alone with a gun. What happened?

Not in the diaries, but in Tolstoy's notebooks, in which he put all sorts of things, it is worth paying attention to the entries he made when he was interested in the natural sciences: "Hydrogen falls upward, that is, from the sphere of air it strives to get into the sphere of hydrogen." The "hydrogen" is Tolstoy and the "air" is the family. For the time being, this "air" is perfectly breathable. More than that – he cannot live without it. But some kind of incredible force is pushing him further and further into a different space, and he cannot resist it, because it belongs to a different "sphere". Tolstoy's observations about natural gravitation and the influence of the planets on one another are even more interesting:

"The moon revolves around the earth, because it is lighter, and is one of the visible objects orbiting the Earth.

The Earth rotates with the other planets around the sun. That is, by the measure of its density with respect to the sphere of the sun, it finds its path in one of the spheres. The direction of its rotation is defined by the sphere of the sun, directly in contact with its sphere and the spheres of other planets."

This is also the "model" of family life according to Tolstoy. The wife is the moon, which revolves around the husband, the Earth, along with other small satellites – the children, subordinate to its "sphere". But the Earth isn't independent and is subordinate to the solar "sphere", which, in turn... etc.

Jealousy toward Aksinya, jealously toward her sister... Too much of Tolstoy's wife's attention is focused on this in her later memoirs. The issue of feeding their first child, Sergei, became a very serious "gash". S.A. had a painfully aching chest, she couldn't produce enough milk, but L.N. even got angry about the fact that the doctor (another man!) was allowed to examine his wife's chest. He's behaving like a Muslim. "He left me and drove away, to have a fun time with my cheerful, healthy sister Tanya..."

L.N. was convinced that there could no question of giving up feeding the child herself and taking a wet-nurse. "I'm losing heart horribly," S.A. writes in her diary after ten months of marital bliss. "I instinctively seek support, in the same way that my child looks for my chest. The pain oppresses me terribly. It is more deadly than Lev." "The pain intensified, I shrank into myself like a snail and made up my mind to tolerate it to the extreme." "It is monstrous not to look after one's child; who would deny this? But what can one do against physical weakness?" "I can't fix the situation, I will look after the boy, I'll do everything I can, not for Lev, of course, he deserves wickedness for the wickedness he is doing to me."

In the end they got a wet-nurse, but the "gash" remained. "Once he expressed a wise thought to me about our quarrels, which I remembered all our lives, and often told others about. He compared the two spouses to two halves of a sheet of white paper. If you start to tear or cut them apart from the top – more, and more ... and the two halves will separate altogether."

Something's wrong...

S.A. looked on these "gashes" from her female point of view. L.N., with his male stubbornness, was sometimes cruel toward his young and inexperienced wife. At the same time, he too was inexperienced, inconsistent, and even before his spiritual upheaval he changed the "rules of the game" on more than one occasion. "One minute he was striving for simplicity, ferrying me around in a wagon, demanding that his first-born son be given coarse linen. The next, he was making me swear that

I would go 1st class, not in 2nd, as I wanted to, and buying me bonnets and dresses from Madame Minangoy in Moscow – the most expensive milliner in Moscow at that time, and golden shoes from Pinet; one minute a dirty, Russian nanny was looking after the children and the next they were hiring an Englishwoman from abroad..."

Four years later, when Sonya was pregnant for the umpteenth time, there was a row between them which neither he nor she could explain, a "senseless and merciless" one. "Sonya told me," writes T.A. Kuzminskaya, "that she was sitting upstairs in her room on the floor, near the dresser drawer, and sorting out some parcels containing rags. (She was expecting a baby.) Lev Nikolayevich went in to see her and said:

- Why are you sitting on the floor? Get up!
- I will in a moment, I'll just clean everything up.
- Get up at once, I tell you, - he shouted loudly and went to his study.

Sonia didn't understand why he was so angry. It offended her, and she went into the study. I could hear their irritated voices from my room, I listened in and didn't understand anything. And suddenly I heard something fall, the sound of broken glass and a raised voice:

- Go away, get out of here!

I opened the door. Sonya had already left. Some crockery and a thermometer, which had always hung on the wall, lay broken on the floor. Lev Nikolayevich was standing in the middle of the room, pale, with trembling lips. His eyes were staring fixedly in one direction. I felt both pity and fear – I'd never seen him like that. I didn't say a word to him and ran to find Sonya. She was very pitiful. Like a madwoman, she kept repeating: "For what? What's happened to him?"

She told me a little later: - I went into the study and asked him, "Levochka, what's up?" – "Go away, go away!" - he shouted angrily. I walked up to him in fear and disbelief, he pushed me away with his hand, grabbed a tray with coffee and a cup on it and threw it all on the floor. I grabbed his arm. He went into a rage, tore the thermometer off the wall and threw it on the floor."

"This event caused a miscarriage..." S.A. writes in *My Life*.

The year 1867, when this happened, was a critical year in Tolstoy's life. All winter, he had been trying to finish, "irritated, with tears and anxiety", the third volume of *War and Peace*, whilst suffering from severe headaches.

In March, the entire greenhouse established by his grandfather Volkonsky burned down in one night. L.N. only just managed to rescue the gardener's children from the flames. In March, his best friend's wife, Dolly Dyakova, dies. At the funeral in Moscow, he learns of the absurd death of A.A. Tolstoy's sister, Elizaveta Andreyevna, in Italy – she had choked on a bone. "There are times when you forget about her – about death, but there are times, like this year, when you're sitting with your loved ones, hiding away, scared to recall those you have lost, and you hear with horror that somewhere or other she [death] aimlessly and cruelly, is doing away with sometimes the best and most needed" he writes to A.A. Tolstaya. Finally, he himself in this year becomes particularly paranoid about his own ill health. A suspicion that he has consumption forces him to consult one Dr. Zaharin in Moscow. He awaits the verdict with trepidation. All they find are stones in his gallbladder.

Tolstoy often travels to Moscow in this year: to attend Dolly's funeral, to arrange matters for the printing of *War and Peace* and to see Zakharin for the examination.

During these absences, he and his wife write to each other every day! In this correspondence from 1867 there is something incredibly touching and... abnormal, as there is in all of Tolstoy's correspondence with his wife, which ended with the terrible "one-sided" correspondence when he fled home.

"I'm afraid I won't have time to write you tomorrow, dear Levochka, and therefore I'm starting my letter in the evening, at 11 o'clock, when the children are asleep and when it is especially sad and lonely. And tomorrow auntie will send Ivan, and I cannot send him when it is late. In the morning, anyway, I'll write to tell you whether everything's OK with us. For now we are all healthy, the children seem to have completely recovered now, the pain that I had in the morning has also passed, and nothing special has happened to us. I tried to drown out all the gloomy thoughts I had today by doing something unusual, but the more I tried, the more persistently sad thoughts came into my head. Only when I sit down and transcribe your work, then do I unwittingly pass into the world of your Denisovs and Nicolas (characters of *War and Peace.*" – P.B.), and it is especially pleasant for me. But I have done little transcribing, I never seem to have the time for some reason.

Tomorrow, I shan't be able to get a letter from you at all, and I await this letter with painful impatience. After all, just think, I don't know anything other than the content of that laconic telegram, and my imagination has already started torturing me. You know, I have been walking around the whole day like a madwoman, I can't eat anything, nor can I sleep, and all I do is wonder how Tanya is, how the Dyakovs are, and I call Dolly to mind, and I feel sad and scared, but also, above all: you aren't here either, and I keep thinking about you, about what might happen to you. Come home as soon as possible."

L.N.'s responses are infused with just as much tenderness and concern, only they are perhaps more sensuous and passionate.

"I'm sitting alone in the room right at the top (of the Behrs' apartment –P.B.); I've just read your letter, and I cannot describe to you all the tenderness, tenderness that brings tears, which I feel toward you, not only now, but every moment of the day. My darling, my dearest, the best in the world! For God's sake, don't stop writing me every day until Saturday... Without you feel not exactly sad, horrid, although sometimes I feel that way too, but above all – I'm dead, I'm not a living person. And I love you too much when you are absent."

It was precisely this ardent passion of her husband's that, incidentally, S.A. didn't much like. "Although it comes to my mind that the reasons for your greater tenderness stem from reasons that I don't like; but then I don't want to spoil my joy immediately and I console myself and say to myself, no matter what the reasons may be, he loves me, and thank God for that," she wrote.

The result of this passion were children, one after another. S.A. loved her children infinitely, her main life's talent was manifested in how she cared for them and brought them up. But the fact that she is constantly pregnant, almost without a break, begins to weigh on her, and, moreover, she soon notices that her husband is no different from the majority of ordinary men: he loves his wife when she's healthy, not when she's sick.

"Of the thirteen children she bore," wrote Tolstoy's son Ilya Lvovich, "she breast-fed eleven of them herself. Of the first thirty years of married life, she was pregnant for one hundred and seventeen months, that is to say ten years, and she spent more than thirteen years breastfeeding..."

But what S.A. especially resented was the fact that her husband, who had a passionate masculine temperament until old age (the last child, Vanya, was born in March 1888, shortly before Tolstoy's sixtieth birthday and S.A.'s forty-fourth), nonetheless had a strikingly negative attitude toward sexual relations, considering them to be sinful and unworthy of a spiritual being. Surprisingly, this attitude hadn't changed at all since the time when he was suffering from the "sense of the deer" toward prostitutes and peasant women. "But what to do?" he would say to his wife in such cases, implying that if he had no control over the "sense of a deer", which he had already felt in his relations with her, this did not mean he was willing to justify this feeling morally. Some of his diary entries, such as "I slept *criminally*" made S.A. explode with rage. They hinted that she was not only an accomplice in this "crime", but also the main motive which provoked it. But what enraged her most of all – most of all! – was the fact that her husband couldn't see any fundamental difference between her and the women who came before her.

Tolstoy considered the birth of children to be the only justification for sexual intercourse. "The bond between husband and wife," he writes in his notebook, "is based neither on a contract nor on carnal union. There is something horrible and sacrilegious in carnal union. This sacrilegious element is absent only when it produces fruit. But it is still horrible, just as horrible as a corpse. It's a mystery." And then he writes about the inextricable, "deathly" bond between husband and wife, pointing out that cases of near-simultaneous deaths of brothers and sisters are extremely rare, but that for old couples, such cases abound. And in this one must feel the subtlety of Tolstoy's attitude toward sexual relations. He saw it not only as a sin but also as a mystery, as great a mystery as death. Death always fascinated Tolstoy. He couldn't have failed to understand that the first link in the chain 'birth - life - death' is a sexual relationship. It was for this reason that it frightened him. If sexual intercourse does not result in fruit – birth and life, then the union signifies "corpse".

S.A. didn't understand this subtlety in her husband's attitude toward carnal union. Far be it from her to think about such things. For her, this union meant specific things: the difficult condition of pregnancy, the pain of labor, breastfeeding, sleepless nights, her husband's aloofness toward his sick wife and her jealousy of young and healthy women, like her sister... "I admit that I was beginning to deteriorate, became more selfish than I was before. I'm thankful for the fact that, besides me, Lev Nikolayevich didn't love anyone else, and his strict, impeccable loyalty and purity in relation to women was striking. But this was in the Tolstoy breed…"

S.A., at some time, sensed that there was a border, before which she could understand her husband and beyond which it wasn't worth worrying her head, concerning herself instead with what God had put her there for: the inner life of the family and the children.

But this position of hers had a subtlety of its own, too. Tolstoy, after all, wasn't a physicist or an astronomer. He wasn't even a "man of letters" in the usual sense, who earns a living through his creativity in a straightforward way. Tolstoy was a *creator of life*. The very life which flowed freely and organically from the life of Yasnaya Polyana into *War and Peace* and *Anna Karenina* and back again. And she, his wife, was an accomplice in this creative process, and moreover he himself insisted on this, giving the marriage not only a pragmatic, but also an idealized, creative meaning. How was she to determine the precise point beyond which her authority ended and his exclusive sphere began?

Whilst this sphere remained no bigger than her husband's study, everything was more or less clear. The idea that papa's study was a sanctuary, and that the time he spent writing or reading was the most important time of all, for the sake of which, indeed, Yasnaya Polyana existed – Tolstoy's wife not only understood this, but also firmly instilled it in her children.

To disturb papa while he was working was unthinkable! It was unthinkable to enter his study at this time, to cross the border of this "sphere". But even when Tolstoy left the study, the creativity didn't stop. He didn't turn into a regular husband and father. He continued to remain a "sphere", but one that was now interacting with the "spheres" of the other people in the household. And how could one find the boundaries?

"How wonderful everything which you left me to transcribe is," she writes to her husband during one of his trips away from home. "How I like Princess Maria! That's just how one imagines her. And such a nice, pleasant character. I will be your critic for all of it. Prince Andrei, in my opinion, is still not clear. You don't know what kind of person he is. If he's smart, then how come he can't understand or make sense of his relationship with his wife."

"I'm sitting in your study, writing and crying. Crying about my happiness, about you, the fact that you're not here..."

"In terms of my spirits, your novel has had a very uplifting effect on me for some time. As soon as I sit down to transcribe it, I'm transported to some poetic world, and it even seems to me that it's not that your novel is so good... but that I'm so clever."

"I'm sending you, my dear Levochka... a holy picture, which, as always, was with you wherever you went, and therefore let it be with you now as well. You may be surprised that I'm sending it to you, but I'll be glad if you take it and keep it."

Prince Andrei's unclear attitude toward his wife, the holy picture which Princess Maria begged him to take with him to the war and which he took, in surprise, to please her – all this either flowed from Yasnaya Polyana life into *War and Peace*, or came back the other way, from the novel into life. It was like a system of blood vessels, rather than a rigid delineation of spheres.

S.A. was despotic in her love for her husband. This despotism of hers was a continuation of her main virtue – selflessness. That was how she had been raised by her father and mother, and it's not clear which of the two contributed most to this.

She also had subtleties of her own in her understanding of relations between married couples, which her mother and father had instilled in her when she was a child, but which didn't work in the ideal world order of the Yasnaya Polyana paradise. She writes in her diary: "Sometimes there is an anger in me, I feel it's not necessary, don't love him like that, if he can't love *me*, and most importantly, anger over the fact that, why do I love him that strongly, humbly and painfully. Mama often boasted about how papa had loved her for so long. It wasn't that she knew how to make him so attached, it was that he knew how to love like that. This is a special ability. What does one need in order to make another so attached? There are no means with which this can be done. I was taught that one must be honest, one must love, one must be a good wife and mother. This is what's written in the ABC book – and it's all nonsense. One must be able *not* to love, one must have cunning, one must be smart and be able to hide all that is unpleasant in one's character, because there have never been and will never be people who have nothing unpleasant about them. But above all, one must not love. What have I done by loving so strongly, and what can I do now with my love? It will only bring pain on myself and be humiliatingly awful. And this seems so stupid to him."

This is the diary from that same year, 1867, which seems to be dripping with a foreboding of disaster. But it is as if only S.A senses this. Tolstoy is completely absorbed in *War and Peace* and his illness. He consults with Zakharin and paces the fields of Borodino, in the certainty that he will write a battle scene which not even Stendhal, the leading authority for him among all the "battle writers", could have dreamed about. But S.A. is forever "sensing" something at this time.

Something's wrong ... Something's wrong...

Marginalia

It's remarkable: Sonya Behrs destroyed the diaries she kept as a girl, which must have been innocent in the extreme, without showing them to Tolstoy. But as for the notes he made during his life as a bachelor, which were far from innocent, not only did he show them to his bride, but he *forced* her to read them. How so?

No clear explanation for this act is to be found in any of his diaries, nor in *Anna Karenina*, in which Konstantin Levin does the same thing. But some of the reasons are obvious.

First of all, he wasn't sure that he, as the man he really was, was worthy of his bride, and he wanted her to know that he was unworthy of her, and that she wasn't taking a shot in the dark but making a conscious decision. This is a noble motive.

Secondly, since he intended to bring his wife and the future mother of their children to Yasnaya Polyana, he knew she would inevitably come face to face with Aksinya and his illegitimate son there. It was better to reveal this abscess before the wedding than to traumatize his young wife, who, by the time she heard this "pleasant news", might already be pregnant. Not the most noble of motives perhaps, but not a bad one either. Yet for all that, why would he show her the diary?

Tolstoy had done something that went against the rules. It was a "wild" act that left Sonya and her parents stunned. The parents put it down to the groom's "strangeness", though: they already knew about some of his foibles. But as for little Sonya, she would have to live with this "truth".

"...All the impure things that I learned about and read in Lev Nikolayevich's past diaries, *was never erased from my heart and stayed with me as suffering for my entire life,*" S.A. writes in *My Life*.

"All of his (her husband's – P.B.) past was so horrible for me that I will never, it seems, make peace with him," she complains in her diary during the first year of marriage. "Perhaps when there are other goals in life, children, whom I wish for so much, so that I'd have a whole future, so that I could see in my children this purity without a past, without nastiness, without everything that I now find it so bitter to see in my husband. He doesn't realize that his past is an entire lifetime, with thousands of different feelings, both good and bad, which can never belong to me, in the same way that his youth will never belong to me, spent on God knows whom or on what..."

By giving Sonya the diary, Tolstoy thought he was testing the strength of her feelings and showing her the 'mines' which might await her at Yasnaya Polyana. In reality, he was laying so much dynamite under his future family life!

All of S.A.'s shortcomings stemmed from her virtues, and vice versa. Her selflessness in family life was accompanied with despotism, and her devoted love for her husband – with reckless jealousy. His diaries awakened in her the dark side of her nature, and forced her to suffer not only from jealousy, but also from an awareness of how powerless she was before the dark side of her personality. If it was a spiritual lesson, it was a very cruel one.

What upset her most, of course, was what Tolstoy had written about Aksinya as a *wife*. "In love like never before!" S.A. always attached special meaning to particular words spoken or written by her husband. She clung to these words, inflating them with an additional significance only she could understand. This was the illness she had.

"It seems to me that I will lay hands on myself one day out of jealousy," she writes in her diary three months after the wedding, after seeing Aksinya in her home. 'In love as never before!' And she's just a peasant, fat, white, horrible. I looked with such pleasure at the dagger, the guns. One blow – it would be easy. Whilst I'm not yet pregnant. And she's here, a few steps away. I'm like a madwoman ... If I could kill him, and then create a new version of him, an exact replica, I would gladly do that as well."

By making the diaries of his youth transparent for his wife, he was also making another mistake, which he undoubtedly regretted bitterly in his old age, before his departure. He had given her the right to consider herself a "victim". Having awakened the dark side in her – jealousy, he was also giving her grounds for her family despotism as well, because there is nothing more despotic than a victim's love. She cultivated this sense of "victim" within her from the very beginning of their life together. L.N.'s diaries would "come back to bite him" throughout the entire duration of their forty-eight years of family relations. This "skeleton in the closet" gradually acquires flesh, fills up with blood and will be a constant presence in the household during the most difficult conflicts.

And all for what?

The very beginning of the Tolstoys' life together assumes a strange marginal character. The diary (in essence simply words written on paper) suddenly begins to play the role of a *third* character in this life. Both of them keep diaries, as if competing to see who could be more frank. More importantly, though, both of them not only allow the other to read these diaries, but do so as an important component of the completeness of their family happiness. There shall be no secrets!

What do they read in these diaries?

HER:

"He is loathsome to me with these people of his..."

"For him, the physical side of love plays a big role. This is terrible – for me it doesn't play any role at all, by contrast..."

"What makes him a bad man is that he doesn't even have the kind of pity which every person, who is kind in the slightest degree, has toward any suffering being..."

"There is no love, no life..."

"Good weather rolls in, health returns, there will be order, and joy in the household, there will be a child, and physical pleasure will come along too – how disgusting..."

"I'm going to sacrifice myself for our son..."

"He shan't have any more children..."

"I'm spent. Neither day, nor evening, nor the night. I am gratification, I am a nanny, I am a familiar item of furniture, I am a *woman*."

HIM:

"I cannot work. Just now there was a *scene*. I felt sad because we have everything, just like the others do. I told her she had upset me in my feelings for her, I started to cry..."

"This idleness is becoming difficult for me. I cannot respect myself... I am irritated about my life, and even about her. *It is essential that I work...*"

"I was very unhappy with her, I compared her to others, almost felt regret, but knew it was temporary, and sat it out, and it passed..."

"Tanya – sensuality..."

"Since morning – the dress. She was trying to provoke me into saying something against it, and I was against it, I said as much – and there were tears and vulgar explanations... We masked over it somehow. I am always dissatisfied with myself in these cases, especially with the kisses, it is a deceptive mask... Over dinner the mask slipped, there were tears, hysterics..."

"Her character is being spoiled with each passing day ... I looked over her diary – pent-up anger at me breathes out from under words of tenderness..."

"In the morning I came in happy (after a walk – P.B.), cheerful, and see the *countess*, who is in a rage and who is having her hair combed by that *maid Dushka*... and I'm like a scalded cat, *afraid* of everything and I see that only there, where I'm alone, is it nice and poetic."

"It's already 1am, and I cannot sleep, much less go to sleep in her room with that feeling that suffocates me, and she will moan when she knows it can be heard, but for now is snoring quietly."

The notes made by Tolstoy in his wife's diary, some humorous, others remorseful, leave one in no doubt that he read the diary carefully. And as for him, he certainly doesn't have any right to hide his diary, after having thrust his past on his bride. By making his own past her spiritual burden, he had opened the door to the hiding place of his soul, and no longer dared to close it again.

Among S.A.'s external symbols as lady of the house was not only her bonnet, but also a heavy bunch of keys, to the entire house and the annexes, which she always carried on her belt, around her waist, even when she was pregnant. But in order to penetrate the hiding place of her husband's soul, she didn't need a key. Everything was unlocked.

Could things continue like this for a lifetime? Why was it that two adults, who had dinner at the same table and slept in the same bedroom, had to carry on this strange, ambiguous "correspondence"?

S.A. liked this game. At any rate, she got into the spirit of it, and always demanded the utmost frankness from her husband. As for Tolstoy, however, the absence of any secrets between them soon became annoying. In the summer of 1863, he exclaims in his diary: "Everything written in this book is almost lies – it's false. The thought that she's reading even this, over my shoulder, reduces and spoils my truth."

In the end, the diaries, which, according to Tolstoy's original idea, were supposed to unite the spouses into a single and indivisible spiritual flesh, became one of the main causes of the marital conflict that ended in the disaster of 1910...

"Life had become broken"

This is the title of one of the chapters in S.A.'s memoirs. An event which had a serious impact on the couple's relationship even before Tolstoy's spiritual upheaval and was the reason for the first fracture – no longer just a 'gash' – in their family life, was the birth, on August 12, 1871, of their second daughter and fifth child – Maria. This was the first child who would subsequently be on her father's side in the conflict with her mother, denoting a split between Tolstoy's children. Maria, who passed away at a young age, was, in many ways, a very unusual and not quite earthly being, like the last child of all – Vanya. And she was Tolstoy's favorite daughter.

After Masha's birth, S.A. came down with puerperal fever and nearly died. The doctors advised her not to have any more children. But Tolstoy couldn't contemplate family life without bringing children into the world. After Masha, his wife gave birth to eight children, of which the first three – Pyotr (b. 1872), Nikolai (b. 1873) and Varya (b. 1875) – died in infancy. It was only with the birth of their son Andrei in 1877, followed by Mikhail in 1879, that the Tolstoy clan began to gain momentum again. But Alexei, who was born in 1881, died at the age of five, and Vanya, who came into world in 1888, died when he was seven. Yet a daughter who was born in 1884, against her mother's wishes, went on to become the longest-lived member of the Tolstoy clan. Alexandra Lvovna lived to the ripe old age of ninety-five.

In Tolstoy's procreative strength there was something almost biblical. And every child was unlike the one before and the one after it. Each had his or her own unique character and even some exaggerated personality trait. All the children were gifted in a variety of ways.

Tolstoy did not keep a diary in 1871, but an entry has survived from his notebook, in which he condemns the natural sciences for having identified natural laws with the mystery of human procreation: "The natural sciences is the desire to find commonality in the life of the outside world with the life of man. A person is born from a fertilized egg. Let's look for an egg in a polyp and for fertilization in a fern…"

For Tolstoy, procreation is a mystery that cannot be controlled. But for S.A. this mystery entailed more concrete things. Here is a diary entry she made in 1870:

"Today is the 4th day since I weaned Levushka (Lev - the Tolstoy's fourth child – P.B.). I felt sorry for him almost more than all the others. I blessed him, and parted with him, and wept and prayed. It's very difficult, that first complete break with one's child. I must be pregnant again."

Tolstoy, at the beginning of the 70s, continues to live an incredibly intense intellectual life. The desire to teach returns, and he composes an ABC book for children (S.A. transcribes it). He studies Greek, so that he can read Homer and Xenophon in the original. He gathers material for a novel about Peter I. In 1873, work begins on *Anna Karenina*. At the same time, Tolstoy goes twice to the Samara steppes – by mare.

Family life gets back on track. However, there is no longer any "unutterable happiness". All the fault lines along which the Tolstoys' family life was to split in the future, had appeared. But some sort of external jolt was required in order for the split to begin.

The jolt came when the family moved to Moscow.

In 1871, when the breakdown in the family occurred, Tanya Behrs, Yasnaya Polyana's winged angel – and demon at the same time – who visited her sister every year from spring to autumn, left the estate. After an unsuccessful and tedious 'romance' with Tolstoy's brother Sergei

Nikolayevich, she married her cousin Kuzminsky after all and went with him to the Caucasus, where her husband had been given a posting. This was a cause of great grief for S.A. Her sister was her only confidante in her family problems, and she had confided to her all her joys and sorrows in her relations with her husband. With Tanya's departure, her lively and constant connection with her previous family, with the Behrs, was broken. From then on, she was only Countess Tolstaya...

And at the same time, Tolstoy is thinking about going to Optina. The trip didn't take place, it was to happen six years later. But when talking about this many years later to his first biographer, Pavel Biryukov, Tolstoy suddenly confuses two dates in his memory, 1871 and 1877, and talks about that first "trip" as if it actually took place. He will tell Biryukov that he travelled to Optina to speak to the Elder Ambrose about his family problems.

Chapter 5

The New Russian

Alyosha Sergeyenko, Chertkov's young secretary, who arrived at Optina on October 29, the day after Tolstoy's departure, was immediately asked by L.N. to sit at the table to write Tolstoy's response to Korney Chukovsky's inquiry about the problem of the death penalty. Whilst doing this, Sergeyenko saw a narrow piece of paper on the opposite side of the table, on which something was written in Tolstoy's large handwriting. He really wanted to take a sneaky look at it, but couldn't find the right moment.

"When he had finished dictating, Lev Nikolayevich went up to the little wash table, on which stood a large earthenware bowl and a large earthenware pitcher. He poured water from the pitcher into the basin and began washing his hands. Suddenly he exclaimed in dismay:

- Oh, how annoying!
- What's annoying, Lev Nikolayevich?
- I forgot my nail brush...
- I'll try, Lev Nikolayevich, to get you one.
- No, no, there's no need. I'll write and ask them to send me one from home..."

The agony of Tolstoy's moral well-being after leaving home stemmed from the fact that, though desiring more than anything else not to burden other people with his person, this was all he was doing. And the more he tried not to be a burden on them, the more he created problems for them.

When Tolstoy went out for a walk, Sergeyenko immediately pulled the piece of paper toward him and read:

"Soap
Nail brush
Notebook."

If "scalpel" had been on this list, instead of "notebook", there could have been no doubt that this was a note sent home by a surgeon who was constantly at work and had temporarily gone away somewhere. But this was a request from a writer, for whom soap and a nail brush were probably no less important, because the writer's main tool – his hands – should be kept meticulously clean. To say nothing of the fact that Tolstoy was noted for his extraordinary general cleanliness.

In a letter to Sasha which she never received, having already left for Shamordino, Tolstoy asked her to send or bring "the thingy for loading ink" (he hadn't forgotten the ink itself), and also "small scissors, pencils and a bathrobe." The soap he needed had to be vegetarian, incidentally, not made from animals. To the list which Sergeyenko saw on the table the following were later added: "coffee, a sponge". In the letter to Sasha, he asked her to send him books by Montaigne and Nikolayev and the second volume of *The Brothers Karamazov*. Having left at night, he hadn't brought the books he needed with him, and no sooner was he on the first train than he began to be tormented by their absence. He particularly missed *Circle of Reading* and *For every day*, which he had compiled himself, and in which he had collected the works and thoughts of the great and not-so great writers and thinkers, considering this to be his primary occupation at the end of his life. He would later spot some of these collections on his sister's bookcase in Shamordino and promptly "pinch" them, with Maria Nikolayevna's consent.

L.N. required all this – books, soap, brush, the "thingy" for ink, scissors, notepad, a robe – in the first two days after his departure. Their absence spoiled his mood, which was heavy enough as it was, no matter how hard he tried to convince himself and others that he felt "free" and "good". Yes, in his diary and letter to Sasha, he wrote that the trip in the third-class carriage to Kozelsk, together with the common people, "instructive" and "pleasant" for him. But when they left Kozelsk and suddenly there was the prospect of travelling on the same train again, in the same third class carriage (and there simply weren't any other types on the train), Tolstoy got very scared, and Makovitsky noticed this and recorded it in his diary...

And there were a lot of little things like that... In fact, the entire trip from Yasnaya to Astapovo consisted of them. For example, what and where to eat? Not always at the stations, surely? In Yasnaya Polyana there was a special, fairly complex diet for the vegetarian, who suffered from a bad liver and intestines. This diet was the result of a long search by S.A., who was unusually pedantic in compiling the menu at home. There were a few family tricks, such as adding, unbeknownst to L.N., a few spoonfuls of beef broth to the mushroom soup that was prepared especially for him. There was a whole problem with cauliflower and brussel sprouts, with kissel puddings, of which L.N. was a great fan, and with something else, which we won't talk about, so as not to annoy those who believe that the later Tolstoy led a 'lordly' life. It wasn't a 'lordly' life, but the life of an ascetic, who paid extremely great attention to the precious vessel which would transfer his immortal soul from one eternity to another – his body. It was a special kind of asceticism, with neither lice nor fetters.

But what to do with this precious vessel in nasty Russian trains and hotels, on the potholes of our eternally impassable roads?

"The road was horrible, dirty, uneven, and the coachmen veered off to the left, through the meadows of Kozelsk, and several times had to pass through ditches. It wasn't very dark, the moon was shining through the clouds. The horses were going at walking pace. At one point the driver whipped them, they tore ahead, and there was a terrible jolt, L.N. groaned," – Makovitsky writes, describing the road from Kozelsk to Optina.

Sasha and Feokritova arrived in Shamordino, bringing oatmeal, dried mushrooms, eggs and an alcohol lamp with them. Tolstoy, in true old-man fashion, ate heartily and abundantly at Optina, in Shamordino and then on the train, before lying down – everyone who was with him noticed this. There was probably some physiological explanation for this: nerves or weakness, or perhaps his organism was simply preparing itself for a difficult death?

All this was a burden first on Makovitsky alone, and then on Sasha and Feokritova. And when Tolstoy wrote to Sasha from Optina Pustyn: "Dushan is breaking down and physically I feel wonderful", he only meant that he greatly appreciated the care shown by his companion, but was also suffering as a result of the fact that he was giving others so much trouble.

There was one person, however, whom he not only wasn't afraid to put to any trouble, but to whom such trouble would undoubtedly be pleasant. This was his sister Masha, the nun Maria Nikolayevna Tolstaya.

Masha and Levochka were the youngest children in the Tolstoy family and had therefore been particularly attached to one another since their early childhood. Maria Nikolayevna was only a year and a half younger than L.N. The correspondence between them covers half a century, and going by their letters alone one can already see how tender the brother and sister's feelings for one another were. She took an active part in his affairs, both affairs of the heart and creative ones as well. He was godfather to her daughter Varvara, his niece, to whom he gave a dowry of ten thousand rubles from the royalties for *War and Peace*. After L.N.'s failed romance with Arsenyeva, Maria Nikolayevna tried to play the role of matchmaker and marry off her brother to Princess Dondukova-Korsakova. She knew her brother's psychology well, and was the first to identify in him the "Podkolesin" syndrome of the fugitive.

In turn, since Masha was the only one in the family who was younger than him, he demonstrated a particularly touching concern for her, experiencing her personal misfortunes as his own. Many misfortunes had befallen her, and her fate was in some ways reminiscent of that of Anna Karenina.

Married off at sixteen to her cousin Valerian Tolstoy, she settled at the estate of Pokrovskoye near Chernya in the Tula Region and bore him four children. She loved her husband with devotion and was outraged when she learned of his many love affairs, including affairs with nurses and governesses (in this regard, her fate, in its own particular way, foreshadowed that of Dolly Oblonsky). Being proud and independent by nature, Maria Nikolayevna left her husband in 1857. This news was crushing to L.N., who at that time was in Baden-Baden. He dropped everything and rushed to Russia to rescue his sister. Tolstoy rented a house in Moscow, where he settled together with Maria and her children. But his sister's misfortunes didn't end there.

She set off with the children abroad, where she met a man who was young, handsome, but unwell, Hector Victor de Kleen. Before long, their friendship turned into a passionate love. They spent three winters in Algeria. In 1863, Maria Nikolayevna bore an illegitimate daughter, Elena. She took her patronymic, Sergeyevna, from her godfather, Maria and Lev's elder brother, Sergei Nikolayevich Tolstoy.

Lev took an active part in this drama in his sister's life and even offered to raise her illegitimate daughter himself. In 1873, when *Anna Karenina* was printed in the *Russian Gazette*, de Kleen died, and Maria Nikolayevna thought seriously about suicide. Not yet knowing how her brother's novel ended, she wrote to him: "The thought of suicide has begun to haunt me, yes, positively to harass me, so relentlessly that it has become like a disease or insanity... Oh, Lord, if only all Anna Kareninas knew what was in store for them, how they would run from fleeting pleasures, because everything that is *illegal* can never be happiness..."

After returning to Russia with Elena, who by now was a young girl who could think for herself, brought up in the European style and speaking Russian poorly, Maria Nikolayevna was at first afraid to admit to people that she was her daughter and passed her off as her ward. Her brothers Sergei and Lev didn't understand this; they openly referred to her as their niece. The daughter's attitude toward her mother was therefore far from straightforward. She left her at an early age, lived on her own and then married a lawyer, a court official in Voronezh, then in Novocherkassk, Ivan Vasilievich Denisenko. It was to this man, Denisenko, that Tolstoy headed when he fled from Shamordino.

After the dramas in her personal life with Valerian Tolstoy, de Kleen and her daughter Elena, Maria Nikolayevna settled at the Belevsk women's convent in the Tula Province, from whence she wrote to her brother in 1889:

"You're interested, after all, in my inner, spiritual life, not in the *arrangements* I have made, and want to know whether I have found in myself what I sought, that is, the moral satisfaction and peace of mind, etc. But that is the very thing that is difficult for me to explain to you, of all people: for if I say that I haven't found it (it's too soon), but that I hope to find what I need, then I would need to explain how I will do so and why it must be *here*, and not somewhere else. You won't acknowledge any of this, but you must admit that one must renounce everything that is empty, vain, superfluous, that one must work on oneself so as to correct one's shortcomings, overcome one's weaknesses, and attain humility and calmness, that is to say, the indifference that is possible to everything that might disrupt one's spiritual peace.

I cannot achieve this in the world, it is very difficult; I tried to give up everything that distracts me – music, reading extraneous books, meetings with various extraneous people, empty conversations... Too much willpower is required in order, whilst surrounded by all of this, to organize one's life such that nothing that might disturb my spiritual peace comes into contact with me, after all I cannot measure up to you: I'm the most ordinary woman; if I were to give up everything, I'd need to join someone, and work hard, that is, live by my labor, and I cannot. What am I to do? What sacrifice will I bring to the Lord? Without sacrifice, without labor, one cannot save oneself; so for us, weak and lonely women, in my opinion, the best, the most decent place, is the one in which I am living now."

This admission by a future nun (she left society once and for all in 1891, settling at the newly created Shamordino monastery, in a house-cell, specially designed by her spiritual father, the Optina Elder Ambrose) is very interesting. It tells us how close L.N. and his sister were in their understanding of faith, in spite of how differently this faith had manifested itself in their paths through life. Both of them were practical in their attitude toward faith. If faith is happiness, i.e. "complete moral satisfaction and spiritual peace", then one must look for the path toward happiness that is the shortest and most accessible for you personally. For Tolstoy (in his understanding) this path lay outside the church, for his sister – it was through the monastery.

Of course, Maria Nikolayevna, who had already set off firmly down the monastic path, was worried about her brother, and suffered for him. "... I love you very, very much, I pray for you, I sense what a good person you are, how much better you are than all your Fets, Strahovs and the others. Yet what a pity that you aren't *Orthodox*, that you don't want to be united with Christ in a *tangible* way ... If you only desired to unite with Him ... what *enlightenment* you would feel and peace in your soul, and how much that is not clear to you now, would become as clear as day to you! Tomorrow, if my strength allows it, I will take communion in church", she wrote to her brother in 1909.

Tolstoy responded to his sister's attempts to bring him back into the bosom of Orthodoxy in his diary: "Yes, monastic life has much that is good: mainly in that it eliminates temptations and fills one time with harmless prayers. That's fine, but why not fill that time with the labor of feeding yourself and others, characteristic of man."

Tolstoy's stubbornness in defending his religious path, and his denial of the church, often led to disputes between brother and sister, but these arguments never even came close to the possibility of a break in relations. They always ended with... a joke. Both of them appreciated wit. Once, having visited his sister in Shamordino, Tolstoy joked, "You are seven hundred fool-nuns over there, doing nothing." It was a nasty joke, in bad taste. The Shamordino monastery was indeed overcrowded, with girls and women from the poorest, most undeveloped classes, as Ambrose, the organizer of the monastery, before his death, had ordered that all those who wished to come must be given sanctuary. In response to this cruel joke, Maria Nikolayevna soon sent a little pillow that she had embroidered herself to Yasnaya with the inscription: "One of the seven hundred fools from Sh.." And Tolstoy not only appreciated this answer, but also felt ashamed of the words he had spoken in the heat of the moment.

This pillow still lies in Tolstoy's bedroom at the "Yasnaya Polyana" Museum-Estate to this day.

Maria Nikolayevna herself was not quite an ordinary nun. She certainly stood out from the crowd, at any rate. Just before she died, after she had taken the schema, she began raving in French. Accustomed to living by her own will, it was hard for her to resign herself to this life, and she was always asking permission for things from the confessor or abbess. She missed talking to people with a similar level of education to her own, and read newspapers and modern books. "In her cell," recalls her daughter E.V. Obolenskaya, "in every room in front of the images and in the bedroom in front of the icon case, lamps were burning, she was very fond of them; but she never put candles in church, as the others did, didn't venerate the images, didn't serve at prayers, but prayed simply and quietly in her place, where she had a chair and a mat was made up as a bed. In the beginning, some scoffed at this, and others condemned it, but then they got used to it."

"I once went to see my mother with my daughter Natasha, who suffered from malaria. Mother assigned her a young, very kind nun, who went with her everywhere on her walks, but when she wanted to take her to the holy well, assuring her that if she poured water on herself, the fever would immediately pass, mother said:

'Well, Natasha, the water may well be holy, but it's nonetheless better not to pour it all over yourself.'

The young nun was terribly scandalized by these words."

Once a year, for two months in the summer, she came to visit her brother at Yasnaya Polyana. Getting permission for this wasn't easy, she had to address the Bishop of Kaluga. The last time she was in Yasnaya was the summer of 1909 and, according to her daughter, she cried bitterly on leaving, saying that she would never see her brother again.

However, his sudden arrival in late fall was, for her, not entirely unexpected. Even on her last visit to Yasnaya, she had seen that in her brother's family an irresolvable conflict was brewing, and she was, when all was said and done, on his side.

Their meeting at Maria Nikolayevna's home was very touching. Having arrived in Shamordino with Makovitsky and Sergeyenko on October 29 late in the evening, Tolstoy didn't even take a cursory glance at the hotel room in which they were to be staying. He immediately went to see his sister. This directness on his part, after his absent-minded wandering near the hermitages of Optina, speaks volumes. He rushed to his sister to pour out his soul, to cry, to hear words of support. Perhaps even to hear justifications for his departure from the family...

It was a very delicate moment. As a nun, his sister ought, of course, to have reprimanded her brother for refusing to carry his cross to the end. As for Maria Nikolayevna, she criticized her own past actions, for having divorced Valerian out of pride and thus condemned herself to a further fall into sin. Yet she didn't speak a single word of disagreement with L.N.'s act and on the whole supported it.

Her daughter, Elizaveta Valerianovna Obolenskaya, and the Mother Superior were in Maria Nikolayevna's cell at the time. They witnessed the extraordinary, melodramatic scene when the great Tolstoy, alternately weeping on the shoulders of his sister and niece, told what had been happening at Yasnaya Polyana lately... How his wife had watched his every move, how he had hidden his secret diary in his boot and discovered the next morning that it was gone. He told of how S.A. had snuck into his study at night and rummaged through his papers, and if she noticed that he lay awake in the next room, she would come to him and pretend she had come to inquire about his health... With horror he told of what Sergeyenko had said to him at Optina: of how S.A. had tried to commit suicide by drowning herself in the pond...

To his niece, Tolstoy seemed "pitiful and old". "He was covered by his brown hood, from beneath which his gray beard stuck out somehow pitifully. The nun who had accompanied him from the hotel told us afterwards that he had nearly toppled over on the way."

His daughter Sasha, who arrived the following day in Shamordino, also noted her father's pathetic appearance. "It seems to me that papa is already regretting the fact that he left," she told her cousin Liza Obolensky.

In the hotel, L.N. was sluggish, sleepy, distracted. For the first time, he mistakenly called Makovitsky Dushan Ivanovich (instead of Dushan Petrovich), "which has never happened before." After looking at him and feeling his pulse, the doctor concluded that his condition resembled the one which had preceded his seizures.

And once again, Tolstoy constantly loses his way ... The next day, on leaving his sister after his second visit to her, he got lost in the hallway and couldn't find the door out. Before this, his sister had told him that during the night some "enemy" was coming to her, wandering along the corridor, feeling the walls, looking for the door. "I got lost, too, just like your enemy," Tolstoy said with dark humor, during the next meeting with his sister, referring to his own wanderings in the corridor. Subsequently, Maria Nikolayevna suffered greatly from the fact that these were the last words her brother ever said to her.

After the second visit, on October 30, Tolstoy returned to the hotel and found out that Sasha had arrived and gone to see her aunt, in hopes of finding her father there. They had missed one another because Makovitsky had led Tolstoy back via a short-cut. Tolstoy immediately turned back, but Makovitsky, already sensing something was wrong, went after him, following at a hundred paces. "And sure enough, L.N. went past Maria Nikolayevna's house and headed further to the left. I caught up with him and brought him back and then, together now, we went in to see Maria Nikolayevna."

It seems that everything pointed to the fact that Tolstoy was at death's door, at the absolute limit of his mental and physical strength. He could not go any further! To go further would be suicide!

But, as at Optina, everyone is gripped by some sort of stupor. Just as at Optina there wasn't a single person who thought to take Tolstoy by the hand and bring him to the elders, so, in Shamordino, everyone basically understands that to go further would be mortally dangerous and that Shamordino was the last haven of common sense, but not only do they do nothing to stop L.N., but rather they effectively push him into further flight. Even though his beloved sister lives here. Here, Tolstoy is loved by everyone. Having been to Shamordino on several occasions, he is someone for whom the simple nuns of the monastery feel affection. There is a hotel here. There is a village nearby where L.N., on the morning of October 30, looked at the house of the widow Alyona Khomkina, in which there was a clean and warm room with a wooden floor, available for five rubles a month.

Tolstoy, as before, was insatiably curious. He wants to examine the state of affairs at the monastery, explore the workshops and print shop. In his diary are plans for four works, which he wrote down back at Optina: "1) Feodorit and the Dead Horse; 2) The Priest Faced With a Convert; 3) The Strahov novel. Grushenka the housekeeper, and 4) The Hunt; duel and head-on clashes." After finding some books from M.A. Novoselov's *Religious and Philosophical Library* in his sister's collection, he studies them with interest at the hotel, especially Herzen's article on socialism, remembering that he had left an unfinished article on the very same subject at Yasnaya. He dictates a friendly letter to Novoselov and dreams of continuing his own article. There was still strength enough for thought and creativity in Tolstoy.

When Sasha arrived to see her father with Feokritova, he had almost made up his mind to stay in Shamordino. Otherwise, he wouldn't have discussed renting a home in the village, thus deceiving a poor widow in need of money. The widow was not particularly on the ball, admittedly: she didn't come to the hotel that evening for the final agreement. But Tolstoy, as Makovitsky writes, would have been happy with the hotel, too – for a ruble a day.

His daughter's arrival ruined his mood. Sasha was still too young and resolutely opposed to her mother and brothers. In addition, she was excited by the journey to Shamordino, via a circuitous route through Kaluga. Why? So as to confuse the trail for S.A.

Like all stubborn people, Tolstoy was extremely fickle in his moods and prone to sudden external influences. It was almost impossible to change his view of the world, it took him years and years of mental work, an enormous accumulation of positive and negative emotional experiences for that. But it wasn't difficult to change his mood. Especially at a time when he was terribly unsure about whether he was doing the right thing, and had even written to Sasha that he was "afraid" of what he had done. At that point, he was akin to Tsar Saltan, whom the least messenger could perturb with bad news.

The first to play the role of the messenger bringing bad news was Sergeyenko, also a young person and also hostile to Tolstoy's wife. It was from him that L.N. first heard that S.A. planned to come after him. And not alone, but with their son Andrei. On arriving at Shamordino, Sasha confirmed this and, with her agitated appearance, brought an additional nervousness to the prevailing atmosphere.

One mustn't blame her for this. Sasha had to put up with more than anyone else in the conflict between her father and mother. Unlike Tolstoy's other children, who lived with their families and visited Yasnaya Polyana when they themselves wanted to, or when they needed to, Sasha lived at Yasnaya permanently. Boundlessly loyal to her father, for whom she was both the secretary and the main confidant of his secrets (to the extent her youth allowed), she, of course, loved her mother deep in her soul, and felt sorry for her, but because of her youth and dramatic nature, behaved cruelly towards her when the conflict boiled over. She assured herself (and worst of all – tried to convince father) that her mother wasn't sick, but was merely being cunning and pretending to be sick. Judging by the diary of her friend Varvara Feokritova (who, by the way, had been taken into the home by S.A. herself to transcribe her memoirs), Feokritova was sure of this. And now they had both come to Tolstoy's rescue in Shamordino, but in fact it was their arrival that was the impetus for his further flight and inevitable death.

Sasha's visit and her excited state, of course, could not have changed Tolstoy's decision to stay in Shamordino on their own. After living with his wife for forty-eight years, he knew far better than Sasha what could be expected of her. And if the day before, and even on the day of his daughter's arrival, he intended to stay near her sister, that meant he was hoping for some other sort of solution to the conflict and was expecting some other sort of news from Sasha, and not the news which she actually brought.

For example, let us consider why it was that S.A. chose Andrei as her travelling companion.

Having heard this name from Sasha for the second time now, Tolstoy couldn't help but experience a heavy feeling. But not because Andrei would have been unpleasant to him, but rather because of all Tolstoy's sons, he loved Andrei the most. This sometimes surprised even S.A. The most dissolute of the children, Andrei Lvovich had turned out to be Tolstoy's most beloved son. This is despite the fact that all his son's habits were irreconcilably at odds with the way his father lived and what he preached. Andrei Lvovich was very partial to wine, revelries and women. His relations with the peasant women of Yasnaya Polyana reminded L.N. of the shameful sin from his own youth. Andrei Lvovich chose a military career, the only one of Tolstoy's sons to do so, and even went to fight in the Russo-Japanese war as a volunteer. And this was at a time when hundreds of people, under the influence of his father's teachings, were refusing to do their military service and being sent to prison or penal battalions as a result. Tolstoy's son passionately and openly supported the use of the death penalty by Stolypin during the suppression of the Revolution of 1905-1907. He helped his mother to organize the armed guard at Yasnaya Polyana and even instigated searches of the peasant households to look for cabbage that had been stolen from their garden.

Finally, Andrei Lvovich had not only left his first wife, Olga Konstantinona (also Chertkov's sister-in-law) with two children, but had left her for the wife of the Governor of Tula, Artsimovich, who had six children. The sin of Anna Karenina and Vronsky was an innocent literary joke compared to what Tolstoy was confronted with in the behavior of his own son, which Tolstoy was forced to account for in writing to the Governor of Tula, whom he knew well.

–And yet in spite of all that... "How incomprehensible it is that Andrei – the worst in life of all his children – is his father's favorite" exclaimed S.A. in a letter to T.A. Kuzminskaya.

"It's surprising, why do I love him so?" – L.N. himself, struck by this fact, wrote in his diary. "To say that it's because he is sincere and truthful would be wrong. He's often untruthful... But I feel at ease and good when I'm with him, I love him. Why?"

Andrew Lvovich believed that his father had based Fyodor Protasov from *The Living Corpse* on him. Fyodor Protasov is a pathological fugitive, a sort of quintessence of all of Tolstoy's fugitive protagonists, from Prince Dmitry Olenin (*The Cossacks*) to the elder Father Sergius (*Father Sergius*). Protasov was Tolstoy's most artistically written dramatic character. And if Tolstoy's son was right, we find a curious fact. Tolstoy didn't portray any of his many other children in a character anywhere near aseye-catching, vivid or affecting as this one. This despite the fact that Tolstoy based many of his characters entirely on his wife, brothers, sisters-in-law and other distant relatives, friends and just random people. Of his children, only Andrei proved worthy of this. In any case, Andrei's fate is also reflected in *Anna Karenina*, completed in 1877, the year of Andrei's birth, and *The Living Corpse*, written in 1900, when his twenty-three-year-old son's character had already been determined. It is fair to say that of all the writer's children, Andrei Lvovich was the most "literary".

At the same time, Tolstoy had every reason not only not to love Andrei, but to hate him.

Andrei made no bones about calling his great father a "crazy old man". Of all the sons, he was more like his mother than any of the others in terms of his bluntness, and not surprisingly, in the conflict with his father Andrei was openly on her side. He considered his father's rejection of the copyright in his works as nonsense, and didn't hesitate to say that the aristocratic life was to his liking, and that he didn't want to abandon it. When he was just fifteen, Andrei openly expressed scorn for the "dark ones" – the common people who came to visit Tolstoy – and said that the servants didn't like them because they never gave them any tips.

Yet, strangely enough, it was Andrei that his father considered to be the most "kind". "You have a kind heart," he wrote to him. "You have the dearest and most important quality, which is dearer than anything else in the world – kindness." "You are kind at heart."

And this wasn't a paradox on his father's part... Apparently, Andrei, for all his bluntness and rudeness, was indeed "kind at heart". After all, there must have been a reason why women loved him and forgave him for the things he did. His first wife, Olga Konstantinovna, not only forgave her husband, but even made friends with his second wife, Yekaterina Artsimovich. When Andrei Lvovich died suddenly in 1916 from a rare blood infection, some of his mistresses, inconsolable, were in the funeral procession along with his wife and his mother.

It's easy to see what Andrei's sudden arrival with his mother in Shamordino would have meant for Tolstoy. The whole set of family relations, so difficult to bear, all the 'gashes' and adhesions would have to be experienced again. But this was the very thing from which Tolstoy was fleeing. This was the very thing that he not only didn't want, but feared more than he feared death.

What's more, Sasha had brought her father a letter from Andrei, from which it was clear that he was unwavering in his condemnation of his father. Andrei Lvovich's letter was the rudest and most tactless of the four letters from his children which Sasha brought to Shamordino and which Tolstoy read immediately in his sister's cell. But at the same time it was also the most direct letter, without any attempt to somehow soften the family problem in his father's eyes, the problem which had now reached its full dimensions. The main problem was the fact that their father had left his children a mentally ill mother, who was continually threatening to kill herself, and it was by no means out of the question that she would do so, even if it were to happen by accident.

Let us return, though, to Yasnaya Polyana, where all the Tolstoy children had arrived, having been summoned by telegram, with the exception of Lev Lvovich, who was in Paris.

Six of Tolstoy's children (Sergei, Tatiana, Ilya, Andrei, Mikhail and Sasha) were forced to discuss an issue that was not that of their father. The problem of their father would arise a few days later, when he was to die in Astapovo. For now, it seemed to the children (except, of course, to Sasha, who was infinitely loyal to her father), that Tolstoy had chosen a path which, though perhaps not the easiest, was nonetheless a path towards liberation from the family problems which had accumulated at Yasnaya Polyana. And that they, the children, were now bound hand and foot to their sick mother, with whom it was not clear what they were to do.

"Mother came to see us in the hall," Sergei Lvovich recalled. "She was undressed, unkempt, in some kind of hood. I was struck by her face, which had suddenly grown old, wrinkled and trembling, with shifty eyes. It was an expression that was new to me. I felt both pity for her and horror. She talked incessantly, sometimes crying and saying that she would certainly kill herself; that they had not let her drown, but that she would starve herself to death. I told her pretty sharply that her behavior would have the opposite effect on father and that she needed to calm down and soothe her nerves; then father would come back. To this she said, "No, you don't know him, you can only influence him through pity" (i.e. by arousing pity in him). I thought this was true, and although I objected, I could sense that my objections were weak. I said that since father had left, he couldn't come back soon, and that it was necessary to wait, and after a while, he might return to Yasnaya. What was especially difficult was the fact that she had to be kept under observation all the while. We didn't believe she would make a serious attempt at suicide, but, in simulating suicide, she might fail to take into account the degree of danger and actually do herself some harm..."

The main discussion revolved around their mother. This is understandable: after all, she was there, and her life was in danger. Well, and what about their father? His whereabouts were unknown, and he was eighty-two years old! To this, Andrei "said quite rightly that there was no sense in searching for their father, that the governor and the police probably already knew where he was, that it was naive to think that Lev Tolstoy could hide anywhere. The newspapers, too, evidently, would soon get wind of his whereabouts. It was even becoming a kind of sport: who would be the first to find Lev Tolstoy."

This whole situation was interpreted by the sons thus: their father had left their mother. Only Sasha and, to an extent, Tatiana, knew what suffering this had cost him and what he must be going through now. Tolstoy was always more frank with his daughters than with his sons. And the daughters were always on their father's side, in contrast to the sons. This was the dynamic that had emerged in their family, in which their mother was the real head, but their father was the substance and *raison d'être*. With their father's departure, the family had lost its meaning, but the problems which their mother used to solve on her own remained. And these now fell on the sons... together with their sick mother...

Here it is necessary to take into account the psychology of the children in terms of their relations with their father. Since their childhood they had grown accustomed to the idea that their father was a "thing unto itself". He was an immutable being, a constant, an independent planet.

Or rather, he was the star around which all the planets in the 'Tolstoy' system revolved, though they couldn't come into direct contact with it, so great was its energy field. Any attempt by the sons to bond emotionally with their father ended in failure, sometimes tragically, as was the case with Lev Lvovich. As a teenager, he had become interested in his father's ideas and befriended his main disciple – Chertkov; he had listened eagerly to the conversations with "the dark ones" in the Khamovniki house and, ultimately, he tried to become a writer himself, signing his works "Count Lev Tolstoy-the son". This ended in severe depression, which nearly led to an early death, debilitating medical treatment in Russia and abroad, and extremely unfriendly relations with his father. "Tiger Tigrovich", as they jokingly called Lev Lvovich, sometimes without even realizing how offensive this was for him, probably loved his father more than all the other sons and was at the same time the most unloved of his sons.

After reading the letters which Sasha had brought with her, Tolstoy was extremely upset. It was specifically these letters, and not Sasha's arrival or the things she said, that became the major cause for Tolstoy's onward flight.

S.A.'s letter was truly frightening, written in an insanely talented way, such that even today it's impossible to work out where the talent ends and the madness begins.

"Levochka, darling, come home, dear, save me from a second suicide. Levochka, friend of my whole life, I'll do everything, everything that you want, I'll give up all luxury completely; I'll be friendly to your friends, I will seek treatment, I will be gentle and sweet, darling, come back, after all, you have to save me, after all it's said in the Gospel that one should not under any pretext abandon one's wife. Dear one, darling, friend of my soul, save me, come back, come back even if it's only to say goodbye to me before our eternal separation.

Where are you? Where? Are you well? Levochka, don't mistreat me, darling, I will serve you with love both with all my being and with my soul, come back to me, come back; for God's sake, for the love of God, of which you speak to everyone, I will give you the same humble, selfless love! I promise you honestly and firmly, darling, and we'll forgive everything in friendship; we'll go away, to wherever you want to go, we'll live the way you want us to.

Well, farewell, farewell, perhaps forever.

Your Sonya.

Did you really leave me forever? But I won't survive this misfortune, but you'll kill me. Darling, save me from sin, for you cannot be happy and at peace, if you kill me.

Levochka, my dear friend, don't hide from me, where are you, and let me come to see you, my dear, I won't upset you, I give you my word, I am humble and loving in my attitude toward you.

All my children are here, but they won't help me with their arrogant despotism; I only need one thing, I need your love, I need desperately to see you. My friend, let me at least say goodbye to you, and say for the last time how much I love you. Call me or come yourself. Farewell, Levochka, I'm ever looking for you and calling for you. What torment for my soul."

A scary letter! From its verbose insanity, however, Tolstoy couldn't fail to draw two very specific conclusions for himself. The first conclusion was that his wife was not going to leave him alone. She would either catch up with him, or harass him from Yasnaya Polyana with the constant threat of suicide. The second conclusion was that the children wouldn't be able to solve the problems of their ill mother. "... they will not help me with their arrogant despotism", writes S.A., clearly letting him know that his hopes as regards the children are in vain. The children will not be able either to isolate her or to cure her nerves, or even to provide a firm guarantee that she will survive. "... I need one thing, I need your love."

Along with S.A.'s letter there was a letter from Chertkov. "I cannot express in words how joyous the news was for me that you had left... I am sure that because of this action on your part, everyone will be better off, first and foremost poor S.A., regardless of what the outward effect on her might be."

This self-assured tone could not reassure L.N. He understood perfectly well that one couldn't just "joyfully" curtail a forty-eight year relationship with the person closest to you.

The most pleasant letter of all was the one from Sergei Lvovich. The eldest son chose a loyal tone with regard to his father, realizing how difficult the departure had been for the man himself. "I think that mama is in a nervous disposition and is in many ways not compos mentis, that you had to part (perhaps a long time ago), however hard it might be for both of you. I also think that even if something were to happen to mama, which I don't expect to be the case, then you shouldn't reproach yourself for anything. The situation was hopeless, and I think you chose a genuine way out..."

Tatiana Lvovna was the only one who, in her letter to her father, promised to prevent her mother from taking fatal steps, through "fear or power".

Ilya Lvovich expressed regret that his father "had not carried this cross to the end." "Both of your lives are at journey's end, but you must die well." In effect he was absolving himself of responsibility.

Andrei Lvovich made no secret of the main reasons why the sons could not take full responsibility for their mother upon themselves. "The only way is to protect her through constant supervision by hired people. She will, of course, oppose this with all means and, I am sure, will never submit to it. For the brothers, our situation in this case is impossible, because we cannot leave our families and jobs so as to be by our mother's side at all times."

The situation in which in which Tolstoy must have felt himself to be in was hopeless. He had had pointed out to him what was, in fact, the case, but in which, until the last moment, he perhaps simply did not want to believe, reserving himself the right to a beautiful illusion. His night-time departure had solved nothing. How right his sister had been back in 1873, when she wrote to him, just when he was starting to type out *Anna Karenina*: "everything that is *illegal* can never be happiness."

Early in the morning, Tolstoy fled from Shamordino.

In his prime

From the mid-1860s to the end of the 1870s, L.N. barely kept a diary, having recourse to it only sporadically. A sure sign that no dramatic changes were occurring in his soul, but that instead a slow process of the accumulation of a new spiritual experience was taking place, such that later on, these changes were already irreversible.

The image of Tolstoy in the seventies was perfectly reflected in the famous portrait of him painted by Ivan Kramskoy. The powerful forehead of a thinker, strong features, the unrelenting gaze of his small but piercing eyes. Large, powerful arms extending from broad shoulders and ending in hands which are also big but at the same time soft and elastic. A large ear, barely covered by a lock of unruly hair, as if everything is concentrated in his hearing, as in a hunting dog. There is something suggestive of the hunt in the flared nostrils, too, and in the mustache, combed vertically. A shaggy, lush and evenly trimmed beard envelopes the entire lower part of the face and neck, like gates made of valuable fur going gray along the edges. And below the collar – a shirt with soft, flowing folds and large buttons on the vent. And of course, the energetic center of the portrait is the deep vertical furrow between his brows, which draws the viewer's gaze away from his eyes, which are staring too insistently, as if testing the beholder's honesty. This small furrow speaks of an incredible concentration of will and thought, capable of gathering together in one point, so as, like the lever of Archimedes, to turn the whole world upside down.

Tolstoy as he appears in Kramskoy's portrait is a *bogatyr* (a heroic character akin to a knight-errant), at once both specifically Russian and yet clearly transcending national borders. No wonder Repin compared this portrait to the works of the Dutch painter Van Dyck.

In the 1870s, *Anna Karenina* was written, about which Vladimir Nabokov said that it was the best Russian novel, and then, after a moment's thought, added: "And, come to that, why only the best Russian one? It's the best novel in the world, too."

Also written in this period, in the seventies, was *The Prisoner of the Caucasus*, which initiated the radically new, folk style of the later Tolstoy. It was at this time that he created his *ABC* textbook-reader, intended, by the proud design of its creator, for children from all social strata – from imperial children to the children of peasants and shoemakers.

During these years, Tolstoy started, no fewer than thirty-three times – like something out of a Russian fairy tale – a historical novel about Peter I, having collected a huge amount of documentary material. Not one of these alternative beginnings was ever continued, however. To this day, researchers still wonder why he gave up such a fruitful idea, which half a century later his namesake and distant relative, the "Red Count" Alexei Nikolayevich Tolstoy, would bring to fruition? One of the most plausible explanations is that Tolstoy did not feel capable of literally putting himself, body and soul, into the everyday life of the ordinary people of that era.

The war of 1812, depicted in *War and Peace*, wasn't all that far removed in time from his own life, whilst putting himself into the life of the characters in *Anna Karenina* had not presented any difficulty. All it took was the secret mechanism of the Tolstoyan imagination, which in those years was working like clockwork. Thus, the character of Anna Karenina was made up of various people, from Pushkin's eldest daughter, the wife of a colonel, Maria Alexandrovna Hartung, whose "Arab curls on the back of her head" stuck in his mind at the provincial ball, to Anna Stepanovna Pirogova, the housekeeper and mistress of his neighbor, the landlord A.N. Bibikov, who threw herself in front of a train at the Yasenka Station on the Moscow-Kursk Railroad to avenge her treacherous cohabitant, who had made up his mind to marry the governess.

The main reason for rejecting the work was probably something different, though. He simply loathed Peter I as a person. In this case one would have needed an artist who was less morally judgmental, without meaning any disrespect to the "third Tolstoy". The first Tolstoy could not, without a sense of disgust, write about the debaucheries of the "All-Joking Synod" and about how Peter, drunk and with unskilled hand, personally cut off the heads of some of the condemned. Having conceived of his Peter in the same vein as *War and Peace*, as the conductor of an impersonal will, whose role was to turn Russia toward the West, Tolstoy couldn't quite get away from his own sense of horror at his actions. Work on the novel did not come easily right from the outset, and, in contrast to the planned novel about the Decembrists, which excited him throughout his life, he did not return to the subject of Peter I in the future. "The drunk syphilitic Peter with his jesters" – this was how he described the character of the Tsar in *The Kingdom of God is Within Us*, and in 1905 he would tell his secretary N.N. Gusev: "In my opinion, it was not that he was cruel, but that he was simply a drunken fool. He visited the Germans, he liked how they drank there…"

During these years, from his idea for a novel about the Decembrists, which had already given rise to *War and Peace*, yet another grandiose idea was to take seed. The fate of the Decembrists led him to Siberia, where he never ended up going in his lifetime, but which excited him greatly. In the late 70's, he conceives of a work about "the overpowering force", about the great migration of Russian tillers to Southern Siberia and on to

China. The idea that the main calling of Russians is the peaceful conquest of the immense eastern expanse has already been stated twice in *Anna Karenina*, by the author and by his alter ego Konstantin Levin. Thus, from the Western aspirations of Peter I, Tolstoy's thoughts slowly turned to the East, like the needle of a giant compass. Yet it did not linger long here, either (the idea never came to anything), but continued its onward movement toward some point predetermined from on high.

At the same time, the 1870s were a settled period in Tolstoy's life. Apart from the annual summer trips to Samara Province for courses of treatment with mare's milk, he lives only in Yasnaya Polyana, and has almost no contact with the neighbors, with the exception of Bibikov. He and the family live together in the same house, which is already becoming cramped due to the burgeoning family, and the building has to be extended. In this decade, truly fruitful in every way, Maria, Andrei and Mikhail were born, following on from Sergei, Tatiana, Ilya and Lev who were already growing up; Pyotr, Nikolai and Varvara were born and died in infancy.

Children require constant care and worry, and all of this falls on S.A. For a while, Tolstoy, with his specific views on the feeding, upbringing and education of children, wavers, but he eventually gives in to his wife. In their home, as in all manor houses, nurses, nursery-governesses, governesses and home teachers appear. The children formed almost familial relations with some of them, including a wonderful English girl, the daughter of the gardener at Windsor Palace, Hannah Tardsey, sent for by Tolstoy from London. Their father teaches the children geography and arithmetic, but mostly takes care of their physical and moral culture. In Tolstoy's family one mustn't be a puny wimp and one mustn't lie or be a hypocrite. One mustn't do a job badly – it's better not to do it at all. One mustn't shift one's responsibilities onto others. The punishment for this was father's disfavor, something which all the children are acutely afraid of, because for them their father is an unquestioned authority. Even as teenagers, however, they don't realize that their father is a great writer. To take pride in this is not the done thing in the family. Had the children been asked to name a great writer, therefore, they might well have said Jules Verne, whom they and their father read in French, looking at the illustrations that went with his book, specially drawn by their father.

Tolstoy had some sort of secret key to the hearts of little children. By way of example, it is impossible to explain how the games and stories that he invented held such infectious fascination for them.

"There was one game which papa played with us and which we loved dearly. It was a game he invented," recalls T.L. Suhotina-Tolstaya. "This is what it was: without any warning papa would suddenly pull a frightened face, he would start looking around in all directions, grabbing two of us by the hand and, jumping to his feet, on tiptoes, raising his legs high in the air and trying not to make any noise, ran off and hid somewhere in the corner, pulling any of us who happened to be in his way along by the hand.

"It's coming... It's coming..." he would say, in a frightened whisper.

Of the three of us, the one whom he hadn't managed to take with him would rush headlong toward him and cling to his blouse. All four of us would then huddle in a corner, waiting with beating hearts for "it" to pass. Papa would sit with us on the floor, on his haunches, and pretend that he was nervously watching some imaginary person, the "it" whose arrival he had sensed. Papa would follow "it" with his eyes, and we would sit in silence, terrified and huddled together, fearing lest "it" might see us.

Our hearts were pounding so much that I thought "it" would hear this beating and thus find us.

Finally, after several minutes of tense silence, papa's face would become calm and cheerful.

"It's gone!" he would tell us.

We jump up happily and go with papa from room to room, when suddenly... papa raises his eyebrows, his eyes start to stare, he pulls a scary face and comes to a stop: it turns out that "it" has appeared again from somewhere.

"It's coming! It's coming!" we all whisper, and start darting from place to place, looking for a secluded place in which to hide from "it". Again, we huddle into some corner and once again wait anxiously whilst papa follows "it" with his gaze. Finally, "it" leaves again, having failed to find us, we jump up again, and it all starts over, until papa gets bored of playing with us and sends us off to Hannah.

It seemed to us that one could never get bored of this game."

It is also impossible to explain just how he managed to fascinate all children, without exception – his own and other people's – with 'the tale of the seven cucumbers'. "He told it to me, and to other children in my presence, so many times in my life that I know it off by heart," writes Suhotina-Tolstaya. Here it is:

– A boy walks into the garden. He sees a cucumber lying there. It's this big (he shows how big the cucumber is with his fingers). He grabs it and – munch! gobbles it up! (This is told in a calm, rather high-pitched voice.)

- Then the boy moves on – he sees a second cucumber, it's thiiiiiis big! He grabs it and – munch! Gobbles it up. (At this point the voice gets a little louder.)

- He goes on – and sees a third cucumber: it's thiiiiiiiiiis big (and papa shows with his fingers a distance of about half an arshin) – munch! – and he gobbled it up. Then he sees a fourth cucumber – it's thiiiiiiiiiiiiis big! He grabs it! and gobbles it up.

And so it goes on until the seventh cucumber. Papa's voice is getting louder and louder, stronger and stronger...

- The boy keeps going and sees a seventh cucumber. It's thiiiiiiiiiiiiiiiiiiiiiiis big! (And papa stretches out both his arms as far as he can.) The boy grabs it: munch! munch! and gobbled it up.

When papa shows how the boy eats the seventh cucumber, his toothless mouth opens up so wide that it's scary to look at him, and he pretends with his hands that he can hardly stuff the seventh cucumber in... And all three of us are watching him, and involuntarily, just like him, we open our mouths and sit there with gaping mouths, never taking our eyes off him."

During this period, the boys adore their father just as much as the girls do, if not more. After all, their father stood for hunting, fishing, exercise. He stood for frequent races against one another, with rolling laughter, which prevented the more spirited kids from overtaking their weighty father. He stood for cleaning the rink in winter on the Big Pond – an activity that the children liked even more than ice skating, at which their father excelled. He stood for pas-de-geant ("Giant Steps"), sent by father from Moscow, when he was on his way to Samara. He represented a lot of other pleasures which the boys associated with their father.

Reading Tolstoy's sons' memoirs about their Yasnaya Polyana childhood, one cannot but come to the conclusion that if he had dreamed of turning Yasnaya Polyana into a paradise, then he certainly achieved this. Only not for himself and his wife, but for the young children.

It's no coincidence that the best work his son Lev ever wrote was a story entitled *Yasha Polyanov*. In this remarkable name and title, it is as if the child's character and the character of the estate are combined. They become a single whole. Tolstoy's children, in their childhood and adolescence, were all, to some extent, Yasha Polyanovas.

Here's how Lev Lvovich Tolstoy described his Yasnaya Polyana childhood: "Mother, father, brothers, sisters, nannies, governesses, servants, guests, dogs and on rare occasions a bear with a cub, horses, hunting with my father and brothers, Christmas holidays, the Christmas tree, Shrovetide and Easter, winter – with snow, sleds, bullfinches and skates; spring – with muddy streams and gleaming carpets of silvery melting snow, with the first birch leaf and currants, with a thrust, with the first flowers and the first 'coat-free' walk, summer – with mushrooms, bathing, all kinds of games, riding on horseback and fishing; autumn – with the start of much studying and work for all the family, with yellow leaves in the garden paths and delicious Antonov apples, with the first snowfall – there it is, the happy life of my childhood..."

And it wasn't his alone, but also that of the other children – Seryozha, Tanya, Ilya, Maria, Andrei, Misha, Sasha, and the Tolstoys' beloved son – Vanyechka, who only lived to the age of seven. And of course, the largest share of this inexpressible happiness came in the 70s, which were not clouded by their father's spiritual crisis or by the deep crack which split the family. That is an undeniable fact. The most well-grounded and morally stable of Tolstoy's children were the older ones – Sergei and Tatiana. Their awkward age came in the 70s. Their childhood and adolescent souls weren't affected by the storm which broke out in the family in the late 70s and early 80s. Their souls had had time to grow stronger and weathered the storm without breaking.

But was everything wonderful for L.N. and S.A. themselves in the '70s? And can one describe this as a time full of domestic bliss?

– The answer, of course, is no.

The sun may hold the planets in its orbit, but this doesn't mean that it exists only for them. The sun may warm the Earth, but this doesn't mean that when it goes behind the clouds, it's not there. Those pas-de-geant (giant steps), with which Tolstoy, in the '70s, moves in a direction that he himself has yet to fully understand, could in no way fall into step with the process of life that was taking place in his family. The tragedy of the '80s therefore had its origins in the seventies.

Everything that Tolstoy does in the 70s is somehow excessive. There are more grandiose plans than there is real strength for making them a reality. The *ABC* textbook he conceived requires, in his opinion, at least a hundred years of work, yet the first version is done and published in a single year. It's impossible to say how much time the average person would need to learn ancient Greek. Tolstoy learned it in six weeks, in the winter of 1870-1871, when S.A. was a month away from giving birth to Masha. "My whole being is in Athens; at night I speak in Greek," he writes to Fet a few days before his wife gives birth, a difficult birth which very nearly results in her death. And Tolstoy himself undermined his own health with the incredible effort he put into the study of Greek, such that in June 1871, he had to leave for the Samara steppes to take mare's milk, with his brother-in-law, S.A.'s brother, the law student Stepochka Behrs.

Who were the '*kumysniki*', that is, the people who came to be treated with mare's milk? They were mainly pulmonary patients, people with consumption, most of them doomed to an early death. One can imagine the mood of these people. Yet Tolstoy and Behrs live like primitive Bashkirs, in a tent with an earthen floor, and enjoy a free and easy steppe life in the village of Karalyk. Tolstoy goes hunting at every opportunity (wild game beware!), goes on walks in the wilderness without a coat and is drunk all day long because of the mare's milk. To him, the steppe "smells like Herodotus," whom he is translating for himself, no matter how many times S.A. tries in her letters to talk him into quitting the study of this "dead language", which will be the death of him. He plays draughts with the Bashkirs and invites other *kumysniki* to go riding with him. He and Behrs travel more than ninety versts to the fair in Busuluk, to admire the herds of horses from the Urals, Siberia and Kyrgyzstan. He has a look round an estate that he will decide to buy the following year.

At Yasnaya Polyana he returns, after a ten year break, to his "last mistress", teaching. More than thirty village children assemble each day in the Tolstoys' small house, to be taught reading and arithmetic by L.N. himself, his wife and the older children, Sergei, Tatiana and Ilya. But Ilya is too young and also cocky. In the end, this particular 'teacher' simply ended up fighting with his students.

Add to that Peter I... and the Decembrists... and the vast human landscape of *Anna Karenina* ... And also the article on military reform, written then torn up. And his passion for the natural sciences, physics and astronomy. "Levochka would look at the stars the whole night until dawn" S.A. writes in her diary. And agricultural work, in which Tolstoy is as passionately engaged as in everything else, and once again he is prepared to quit literature, and says as much in a letter to Fet. In the spring and fall he goes hunting almost daily... There was also the rebuilding of the Yasnaya Polyana home. The article *On Public Education*.

During yet another trip for mare's milk, Tolstoy organizes some grandiose horse races over a distance of fifty versts for the Bashkirs, to revive in them the spirit of the ancient, free and easy life. People from many villages come together for the event, and the entire steppe is suddenly enlivened by nomadic tents. Before the races, Tolstoy organizes a competition, a fight "on a stick". The competitors sit facing one another, pressing the soles of their feet against the other man's; they then take hold of either end of a stick and try to lift the other man up in the air. "Father beat the lot of them," his son Sergei recalled, "except for a sergeant, and the only reason he couldn't pick him up was that the sergeant weighed at least ten poods."

On the Samara estate, which he expanded to more than 6,000 desyatins, Tolstoy organized a large stud farm. From the confluence of cultured blood of Russian and English trotters with scrubby steppe mares one had to get fast and sturdy horses, suitable for the cavalry. Ten years later, the Tolstoyan idea which brought the family significant losses, became an external motivation for family quarrels that nearly led to L.N.'s departure from the family.

All Tolstoy's ideas are grandiose. In this period, when he's alone, without assistants or secretaries, supported only by a wife who is constantly pregnant, he does an unheard of number of things. Yet it's strange ... To read S.A.'s diaries and letters, one would think her husband was very sick.

And not just sick, but in a state of severe depression.

"... Constant worry about Levochka's health. The mare's milk, which he has been drinking for two months, hasn't cured him; the illness is sitting in him, and it's not my mind that tells me this, I sense it in the indifference to life and all its interests, which has manifested itself in him since last winter."

"Levochka had chills in the evening for the last three days and can't seem to get well."

"Levochka has chills all through his spine and keeps being unwell."

"Despondent, downcast, he sits idle, without work, without energy, without joy for days and weeks on end and seems to have reconciled himself to this state. It is some kind of moral death, and I don't want it to be in him, and he cannot live for long like this either." (Diaries.)

"Levochka is unwell, and you have gone." (From a letter to her sister.)

The correspondence between L.N. and S.A. during Tolstoy's treatment in Bashkiria is an invaluable psychological document.

Whereas the first trip to the steppe was, without question, dictated by necessity (he was literally collapsing under the strain of studying Greek), then the subsequent annual trips and the purchase of the estate in Samara (which did not engender any enthusiasm in S.A.) suggested that L.N. felt better in the wild steppes than at home, at Yasnaya Polyana. The steppe air, mare's milk, lamb, riding on horseback, the remains of the ancient nomadic life – all this had a beneficial effect on Tolstoy and restored him to life. Perhaps, as he took the ferry from Nizhny to Samara, he recalled his first flight, to the Caucasus, when he and Nikolai had sailed from Kazan to Astrakhan. Be that as it may, the persistence with which L.N. set off for the steppes each year suggests that the spirit of the 'runaway' had not yet disappeared in him in the first ten years of settled family life. His soul was reaching out for the point from which the marriage had begun: after all, he had made his proposal to Sonia after returning from Samara.

S.A., with her extreme sensitivity to such "signs" in her husband's moods, could not help but be agitated about this. She couldn't go with her husband, being sick after having given birth. (In 1873, she would make the journey with an infant in her arms.) There could be nothing obviously offensive about this, but offence was nonetheless caused. All of L.N.'s trips were hard for his wife to take. It's worth recalling the terrible quarrel that occurred between Kitty and Levin, when he made plans to visit his dying brother without her. When, in the fall of 1869, Tolstoy set off for the Penza Province to look for an estate to buy, he received a letter from Yasnaya Polyana:

"There are already moments when I am in utter despair because you aren't here, and I wonder what's going on with you, dear Levochka, especially when the day ends and I am left alone in the evening with my dark thoughts, imaginings and fear. It is such hard work to live in the world without you; nothing is right, everything seems all wrong and not worth it. I didn't want to write you anything like this, it just all came out... and it's not good for you to leave me, Levochka; the evil feeling of the pain your absence causes me, remains in me. I'm not saying that because of this you shouldn't go away, but only that it is harmful; in the same way that I do not say that we shouldn't have children, I merely say that it hurts."

The hint about giving birth here is quite transparent. It is a hint that any departure by L.N. is a small injustice in relation to S.A., bound hand and foot as she is by the pregnancies and the children.

In her letters from the summer of 1871 she persistently tries to persuade her husband to stay in the steppe as long as necessary. There is a lot of touching tenderness and concern for his health in them. "Be strong, please, live on mare's milk as long as you can and, above all, don't let fear or sadness into you, because that would interfere with your recovery ... Goodbye again, I kiss you on the head, lips, neck and hands, how I love to kiss, when you're here. God bless you, take care of yourself as much as possible."

She nonetheless gives L.N. indirect hints about the abnormality of his long absences from the family, but she does so through the words of his best friend Dyakov. "Dyakov and Masha came over for lunch on Friday. He kept preaching about the principles of marriage and reproached me and Tanya for having parted with our husbands for two months. He didn't embarrass me. For me it is too serious a matter, and it was too painful for me to make up my mind on this, for me to discuss this matter lightly with Diakov. If we both decided on it, then, it seems, it must have been necessary. Diakov upset me a little, nevertheless, and I didn't like it."

But the most important part is at the end of the letter.

"Goodbye, my dear friend; I am not advising you on anything now, am not insisting on anything. If you feel sad, then it is harmful. Do whatever you want, as long as you feel good. Try to be sensible and see clearly what might be good. You were tired, you suddenly changed your whole way of life; perhaps after a little more living, you'll be in condition once again, to be not one-tenth of yourself, but your whole self. God bless you, my dear friend, I embrace and kiss you. If only I could give you at least a small part of my own health, energy and strength. I never grow numb. My strong love for you is enough for me, in order to support all my spiritual and vital strength. Farewell, it's two in the morning, I am alone and yet it's as if I'm with you. Sonia."

In the first fifteen years of the marriage, at least, she didn't want to feel weak or as if she were the suffering party. Of course, her husband was for her out of reach in terms of creativity, but at a human level, she wanted to be, if not higher, then at least stronger. And indeed she was, in a sense. It's hard to imagine how his wife must have suffered when, in February 1875, her one-year old son Nikolushka died in her arms.

"There were three weeks of painful vomiting, a week when little Nikolushka was unconscious, and for three days there were continuous convulsions. Thinking that he was dying, I stopped breast-feeding him for a week and spoon-fed him water. But he grabbed the spoon so eagerly that I was afraid the child would die of hunger. I started breast-feeding him again. I cannot recall without a sense of horror how this child, having already lost all signs of consciousness, like a little animal, grabbed my breast and clenched it with his 7 sharp little teeth. Then he began to suck greedily. The appearance of this expired human consciousness and the idiocy in the eyes, which had, not so long ago, looked at me cheerfully and affectionately – was horrible. And I went on feeding him like that for nearly a week. One day before his death, all of Nikolushka's tiny digits froze in a stationary position, his little fists clenched, his face contorted."

When the baby was buried in the Kochakovsky Cemetery, there was a "terrible blizzard". "I feared for Lev Nikolayevich, he feared for me."

Nevertheless, grief, illness and separation brought the spouses closer together, more so than their calm, measured life, when L.N. gave himself up entirely to his work, as was the case during the writing of *War and Peace* and *Anna Karenina*." S.A. cherished this time and seemed to dream about it. But it wasn't by chance that there was so much anguish and sorrow in her diaries and in her letters to her husband and sister. Her husband was too excessive a man for her, such that she was not always able to feel her kinship with him. It was another matter altogether when he was weak, sick and in need of her…

This was a very complex family happiness. Tolstoy wasn't completely right when he began the novel *Anna Karenina* with the assertion that "all happy families are alike." They are similar to one another – yes, but only superficially, and not deep down. After all, the example of his own family showed that every family happiness has a lot of deeply individual components, which would not be suitable for a different family. Yet Tolstoy hit the nail on the head when he said that "every unhappy family is unhappy in its own way." What happened with the Tolstoy family in the late 70's - early 80's was indeed unparalleled.

Tolstoy's Renunciation

Tolstoy's contemporaries and later biographers described the spiritual crisis which he experienced from approximately 1877 to 1884 (any exact dates, of course, are bound to be imprecise), and which ended in his first attempt to leave the family, in various ways. For some it was a "crisis", for some it was an "evolution", for others a "revolt", and Tolstoy's first biographer P.I. Biryukov calls it "enlightenment". But one thing is clear: Tolstoy changes incredibly in this period, and much more than he does after the marriage.

In place of "the decrepit man", as he saw it, a "new man" had appeared. And this wasn't simply a new man, but a *new Russian* man, because everything that happens at this time to Tolstoy is of a very national character and outwardly resembled the behavior of the Russian Slavophiles in the 40s and 50s, who wore beards and kaftans and by so doing shocked public opinion in high society. On the cusp of literary success and family happiness, Tolstoy suddenly showed all educated Russians a hitherto unprecedented style of behavior, but most importantly – an unheard of system of views on the world in which everything was "the other way round". White became black, black became white. A new Russian.

Tolstoy himself didn't consider this a revolt. "In one of his autobiographical works, Lev Nikolayevich himself states that there was in fact no crisis, no turning point in his life, that he always strove to find the meaning of life and it was only challenging external conditions and events, as well as his own passions and hobbies, that pushed to one side the matter of solving the questions of life and condensed his hidden forces into one powerful inner impulse, which overturned the dilapidated building," P.I. Biryukov observes. This is, of course, true, but only as regards Tolstoy's own self-actualization. For his family, it was indeed a revolt, a natural disaster, because the "old building" that was overthrown by the "powerful inner impulse" was not only the man himself, but also his family life, built up so painstakingly over a decade and a half.

It's no wonder that S.A. observed Levochka's lethargic state so intently during those "cessations of life" to which he became prone in the '70s. She sensed trouble. She had an amazing ability to sense it! But it still wasn't good enough for her to recognize immediately how serious and irreversible were the changes that occurred in L.N. from 1877 onwards.

In that year he travelled to Optina Pustyn, accompanied by Strahov.

But here we are dealing with a mystery, the solution to which split two of Tolstoy's most authoritative biographers – Nikolay Gusev and Vladimir Zhdanov. The fact is that he first intended to visit a monastery (not counting the childhood trip for the funeral of Aunt Osten-Sacken) back in 1870.

This is evidenced by his phrase from a letter to Fet on November 20, 1870: "Having received your letter, I immediately decided to come to you ... had it not been for Urusov, whom I summoned to me for a trip to Optina Pystin..."

This phrase wouldn't seem to be significant, given that this trip did not take place. Many years later, though, in a conversation with Biryukov, Tolstoy spoke about this trip as if it had really happened and associated it with his falling outs with his wife. Here is what Biryukov says: "Around 1906, for my biographical work, I asked Tolstoy in Yasnaya Polyana, at the round table, about some of the events of his life. We were alone in the room. I asked him, among other things, what the purpose of his first visit to Optina Pustyn had been. Lev Nikolayevich's answer was something like this: 'I wanted to talk with the then-Elder Ambrose, whose moral qualities I held in high regard. I had a huge doubt in my soul, the reason for which was the breakdown in my family relations. My wife, after a serious illness, influenced by the doctor's advice, had refused to have children. This development was so hard for me, turned my whole concept of family life upside down, that I couldn't decide for a long time in what form it should continue. I even put to myself the question of divorce. And so in order to resolve this doubt, I decided to consult the Elder Ambrose.'"

According to Biryukov, Tolstoy wasn't satisfied by this "trip" (which did not in reality take place).

In fact, he went to Optina in the summer of 1877, and he was very pleased by his conversation with Ambrose. "Apparently," another biographer, N.N. Gusev, rightly tells us, "Lev Nikolayevich combined a number of episodes from his life, which took place at different times, into one memory."

"His first visit to Optina Pustyn occurred on July 22, 1877," continues Gusev. "There is no evidence either of a breakdown in his family life at the time, or of a conversation with Ambrose about his family affairs, or even of him having been left dissatisfied with Ambrose after the first meeting with him." There is no evidence that in the first half of 1877 (Tolstoy was preparing for the trip ahead of time, starting in the winter), L.N. had any serious quarrels with his wife, let alone that he was thinking about divorce. But then, even in November 1870, when he wrote to Fet about the proposed visit to Optina, the real conflict still hadn't happened. S.A. had just got pregnant with Masha, and there couldn't as yet have been any advice from the doctors about no longer giving birth. It appears that the desire to visit the monastery was always, in Tolstoy's mind, somehow linked to family problems.

But who can know all the reasons why Tolstoy decided to visit the monastery? Or why, after many years, he mistakenly linked this visit to the family situation in 1871?

Unlike Gusev, the author of a book about Tolstoy's family life, V.A. Zhdanov, is convinced that family reasons were among the reasons why he went to the monastery in 1877. After all, no one knows what Tolstoy spoke about with Ambrose for the several hours when they were alone together. The conversation with Ambrose remained a mystery. From his wife's memoirs about Tolstoy's four visits to Optina, however, we know from his words that this meeting left him "very satisfied, after recognizing the wisdom of the elders and the spiritual power of Father Ambrose."

Incidentally, in the summer of 1877, S.A. was again pregnant, with her son Andrei. Both husband and wife awaited this birth in fear, with far more fear than the birth of Masha in '71. The deaths of three babies in a row – Pyotr (in 1872), Nikolai (in 1874) and Varvara (in 1875) – couldn't but prompt Tolstoy to think that if the justification for sexual intercourse was continuing the bloodline, then God was depriving him of this justification. Or was something other than God doing so? And was there a God, after all?

The Tolstoy family was not the result of a random connection between two people in love. But it wasn't a "marriage contract" either. It was a *happiness project*. This project had religious bases and reflected the state of Tolstoy's faith, as it was in the 60s and the first half of the 70's. It was a fairly long experiment in creating heaven on earth on a particular plot of land, which in the seventies was also added to by the very extensive Samara estate. But it is significant that precisely at the time when Tolstoy begins to expand the geographical expanse of this "paradise", obviously less out of economic need than because he was captivated by the primitive, untouched steppe of Bashkiria, this "paradise" ceases to satisfy him. Tolstoy's very soul feels constrained within its borders (hence the desire to expand, the search for new spaces unspoiled by civilization), and the project itself in his eyes suddenly loses all meaning.

By the time of the spiritual crisis he had turned forty-nine. He had lived for half a century. The thought of death had worried Tolstoy earlier too, but he had always run away from it, saving himself by means of war, running the household, literature, and family life. But he couldn't lie to himself, and the damned question of "why?" finally catches up with him and overshadows all other issues. A "cessation of living" takes place.

S.A. looks on with growing concern as her husband, the *raison d'etre* and mainstay of the family, which was created by his will, but mostly by her efforts, slowly but surely "departs" from them, not physically as yet, but mentally. One cannot read her diaries and letters to her sister from this time without a sense of compassion for this intelligent and self-sacrificing woman, who cannot fully understand what is going on, but already feels that something that is not quite right and is obviously horrible is taking place. Her husband is changing in front of her eyes, even externally. She desperately tries to put this down to his painful ailments, because how else can she be made to understand what she cannot fathom in her husband if not as a "disease". She records any return to literary interests on his part with hope, because these interests are "embedded" into their family project, unlike her husband's new interests. This was, to put it bluntly, what she had "signed up to" by marrying him. She was also prepared, albeit reluctantly, to agree to his acquisition of land in the Samara Province, although she didn't like the steppe, the heat and lack of sanitation. But Bashkiria, for her husband, was a breathing space, and the main problems began at Yasnaya.

"Levochka is gloomy for some reason; either he spends whole days out hunting, or he sits in the other room, in silence, and reads; if he argues, he openly says that he's gloomy and not happy."

"Levochka keeps on saying that everything's over for him, that he'll die soon, nothing makes him happy, there is nothing more to expect from life. What sort of joys can I have, alongside him."

"...very busy with his thoughts about the new novel, and I can see that it will be something very good, historical, set in the time of the Decembrists, like, perhaps *War and Peace*. May God grant him only to get better soon, he has begun to be sick often, but apart from that the work is progressing."

"Levochka... has now completely departed into his writing. His eyes are halting and strange, he barely says anything, has become not of this world, and is resolutely unable to think about the matters of everyday life."

"I sew and sew, *ad nauseam*, to despair; spasms in the throat, headaches, depression, yet all the while I sew. Work is death, and I see no end in sight; seven people and I'm the eighth..."

Her husband's spiritual crisis coincides with her mental crisis, when the reclusive life in the countryside, for a woman brought up in the city, begins to weigh heavily on her. After fifteen years of selfless marriage, continuous pregnancies, painful childbirth, miscarriage, the deaths of three children and the daily hassle of running the estate and bringing up children, S.A. suddenly remembers that there is another life – outside the sphere of her husband's interests.

From the very beginning of their life together, though, she was never fully allowed into the sphere of his interests. "I would like to just grasp all of him, to understand him, so that he might be the same with me as he was with Alexandrine," she writes in her diary a year after her marriage, feeling jealous not only of the simple peasant woman Aksinya, but also of his cousin and spiritual confidante A.A. Tolstaya, "and I know that this cannot be, and do not feel offended, and reconcile myself to the fact that

I'm too young and stupid for this, and not sufficiently poetic. And so as to be like Alexandrine, excluding innate qualities, one should be older and childless, and even unmarried."

S.A. begins to be jealous of her younger sister, who, having married Kuzminsky, can lead a normal social life. "We are living a very secluded life this winter, and I often grow bored and begin to tire of the solitude of the countryside," she wrote to her sister. "To keep myself entertained I have begun embroidering a large rug, four arshinas long and three and a half wide, in the Persian style. It will require three years' work. It was in just this way that, in the olden days, hermits in palaces would work on big projects, so as to keep themselves busy in their solitude."

In 1875, she confesses in her diary: "Village life is too secluded and is finally becoming unbearable for me. Dull apathy, indifference toward everything, and today, tomorrow, the months, the years – always the same thing again and again. You wake up in the morning and don't get up. What will get me out of bed, what awaits me? I know: the cook will come, then the nanny will complain that people are unhappy with the food and that there's no sugar, that we must send someone for it, then I, with a pain in my right shoulder, will sit silently embroidering holes, then teach grammar and scales, which, though I do it with love, I also do with a sad awareness that I'm not doing it well, not the way I would have wanted. Later in the evening the same embroidery of holes and the endless laying out of solitaire for auntie, which I find hateful, with Levochka,. Reading affords me a brief pleasure – but are there all that many good books? Sometimes, as happened today, one is alive in one's dreams. You are really living, not just dozing. One minute I'm going to some church for vespers and praying, such as I never pray when I'm awake; the next I can see some wonderful art galleries, then beautiful flowers, then a crowd of people whom I don't hate, and don't shun, but for all of whom I feel sympathy and love."

As their joint life at Yasnaya Polyana flows on, L.N. and S.A. gradually begin to experience a seasonal mismatch of moods. He especially appreciates the autumn and winter, when they sit at Yasnaya as complete recluses and he can calmly give himself over to work. In the spring and summer begins the influx of guests who entertain S.A. and annoy her husband. Tolstoy even built a hut in the forest of Chepyzh, to hide from the guests. With the beginning of autumn, L.N. perks up for his work, and S.A. writes in her diary: "I have finally lived through to my autumnal, painful longing. Silently, I stubbornly embroider a rug or read; I'm cold and indifferent toward everything, bored, sad, and darkness lies ahead."

But everything would have been avoidable, and life at Yasnaya Polyana would have flown in its own normal course, had it not been for the fact that, starting in 1877, when L.N. visits Optina and when his son Andrei is born, Tolstoy began consistently denying – for the time being only in his soul – everything that he himself had taught his family: the importance of literary pursuits and the purposefulness of life at Yasnaya Polyana.

In *Confessions*, Tolstoy described this internal process in detail:

"That was how I lived, but five years ago (in 1874. – P.B.) something very strange started happening to me: I began to experience moments first of bewilderment, of a cessation of living, as if I didn't know how I was to live, what I was to do, and I got lost and fell into despair. But this passed and I continued to live as before. Then these moments of bewilderment began to recur more and more often and all in the same form. These cessations in life were always expressed in the same questions: Why? Well, and then what?...

These questions seemed to be such stupid, simple, childish questions. But the moment I touched on them and tried to answer them, I immediately became convinced, first, that these weren't childish and stupid questions, but the most important and profound questions in life, and, secondly, that I cannot, cannot, however much I might think about it, answer them. Before taking on the Samara estate, educating my son, writing books, it is necessary for me to know why I am going to do these things. Among my thoughts on running the estate, which greatly preoccupied me at the time, a question suddenly came to mind: 'Well, OK, you'll have 6000 desyatins in the Samara Province, 300 horses, and then...?" And I was completely taken aback and didn't know what to think thereafter. Or, when I started to think about how I was bringing up the children, I would say to myself: 'Why?' Or, when talking about how people can achieve well-being, I suddenly said to myself, 'But what does it matter to me?' Or, when thinking about the fame which my writings will bring me, I said to myself, 'Well, OK, you'll be more famous than Gogol, Pushkin, Shakespeare, Molière, all the writers in the world – well, what of it?..."

And there was nothing, nothing I could say in response.

My life had stopped. I could breathe, eat, drink and sleep, and had no choice but to breathe, eat, drink and sleep, but there was no life...

If a sorceress had come along and offered me the chance to make my dreams come true, I wouldn't have known what to say. Though I have desires, or rather the habit of former wishes, in moments of intoxication, in sober moments I know this is a deceit, that there is nothing to wish for. I couldn't even wish to know the truth, because I could guess what it was. The truth was that life is meaningless."

In *Confessions*, Tolstoy relates the parable of the traveler caught in the steppe at the mercy of a furious beast. Fleeing from it, he jumps into a well, only to see a dragon with gaping jaws at the bottom. After grabbing on to the branches of a bush growing in a crevice in the well, he sees that two mice, one white, the other black (day and night), are slowly but surely walking around the trunk of the bush and gnawing away at it. Soon he will inevitably be in the jaws of the dragon (death). But while he's hanging there, the traveler looks around him, finds some drops of honey on the leaves of the bush and licks them up with his tongue.

"The two drops of honey which kept my gaze away from the cruel truth longest of all – love for my family and writing, which I called art – are no longer sweet to me," Tolstoy admits.

It's interesting that he puts family in first place. For him, renunciation of it was the most difficult moment of the crisis.

It was not a speculative crisis, but "a stoppage of life", the result of which could have been either suicide or an answer to the questions which Tolstoy was asking himself. One can tell how close he was to committing suicide by looking at the finale of *Anna Karenina* (not the one everyone knows about, where Anna throws herself under a train, but the real one, where Konstantin Levin, though happily married, is also close to suicide), and by his admission in *Confessions*: "And it was then that I, a happy man, took the rope out of the room in which I was alone each evening, when I got undressed, so as not to hang myself on the crossbar between the cupboards, and stopped going out hunting with a gun, so as not to be seduced by a way of getting out of life that would be all too easy ... "

In the early 70s, Tolstoy begins, but doesn't finish, two stories which revolve around a fictional death as a means of escaping one's former life.

He will return to this plot later in his *Living Corpse* and *The Posthumous Notes of the Elder Fyodor Kuzmich*. In the first, untitled story, a landowner, Zhelyabuzhskiy, kills his unfaithful wife, flees arrest with the help of his valet, arrives at a river crossing, where a crowd of common people are standing, gets undressed and walks into the water. The development of this story was the second story, entitled *Stepan S. Prozorov*, in which a wealthy landowner, having squandered all his money and his children's money, also flees, arrives at a river, takes off his clothes and walks into the water. On coming out of the water, he puts on some peasant clothes which are lying on the shore and sets sail on a boat in a 3rd class cabin; at first, out of habit, he tries to enter a first class one, but he gets kicked out of it.

The idea of a fictitious death undoubtedly seemed to Tolstoy to be, if not the most appealing option, then at the very least an acceptable way of solving intractable problems. When all's said and done, it's better than the sin of suicide. In life, however, he would only bring this idea to fruition in part, when, in the early 90s, he renounced all property so that his wife and children could have it, "as if I were dead."

In the mid 70's an incident occurred with Tolstoy that prefigured what would later happen at the time of his departure from Yasnaya Polyana. Tolstoy got lost ... in his own house.

"Before bed, father usually got undressed and washed in the room under the hall, his former study, and then, in his bathrobe, walked upstairs to the bedroom, the one he shared with mother," recalled Sergei Lvovich Tolstoy. "My brother Ilya and I at that time slept in a room located between the dining room and the room with the vaulted ceiling. One autumn day I woke up around midnight to hear the desperate cry of my father: 'Sonia, Sonia!' I glanced outside. In the foyer it was completely dark. He repeated his cry. I went out into the hall and heard my mother quickly run over to the stairs with a candle in her hand.

In a very worried voice she asked, 'What is it, Levochka?'

He replied: 'It's nothing, I got lost' ... "

At the end of 1879, when Tolstoy was writing *Confessions* and his spiritual upheaval was irreversible, the Tolstoy family grew larger. A son, Mikhail, was born. The diary entry SA made two days before the birth paints a grim picture of the heavy, airless atmosphere at Yasnaya Polyana, when nothing brings any joy any longer to this large and once united family:

"I sit and wait for the birth to come at any moment – it is late. The new baby brings a feeling of depression, the whole horizon has shifted, it has become dark and cramped to live in the world. The children and the whole household are in a state of tension ... Horrible freezing temperatures. Levochka has gone to Tula ... He writes a great deal about religious matters."

Inexpressibly painful

His infatuation with the Orthodox Church can be traced to 1877 and the beginning of his spiritual crisis. It was exactly that, an infatuation, to which he devoted himself with a passion, as he did with all his hobbies, but it left an extremely unpleasant aftertaste in his soul.

Tolstoy was brought up in such a way such that his worldview could not be penetrated by the spirit of the church's ritual poetry. His mother and father were religious people, who carried out all the customary religious rites, and his two aunts were also deeply religious, both of whom lived at Yasnaya Polyana during his childhood, A.I. Osten-Sacken and T.A. Yergolskaya (the second had a strong influence on him), but one cannot talk of a deeply religious upbringing for the boy.

In the story *Childhood*, the protagonist prays often and does so fervently, especially before going to sleep. This need for solitary interaction with God persisted in Tolstoy always, even in his period of atheism as a young man.

Idealizing the image of his mother, whom he barely knew, Tolstoy depicted her in Princess Maria Bolkonskaya. Tolstoy's biographer N.N. Gusev believes, however, that the real Maria Nikolayevna Tolstaya was not so exaltedly religious and that there was no significant difference of views between her and her unreligious father. "There is no trace of any enmity between father and daughter on account of their worldviews, such as we see in *War and Peace* (for example, in matters of religion), in the diary of Maria," says Gusev. We know, however, that she was well-educated, spoke four European languages and knew Russian very well, which was a rare thing among society women of that time. Brought up by her father, Tolstoy's grandfather Tolstoy N.S. Volkonsky, an enlightened 18th-century aristocrat, she strove to develop in her children, too, not so much the beginnings of a good heart, but will and the ability to reason.

Great importance was attached to the boys' intellectual development, to getting them into the habit of reading at a young age, to teaching them courage and even patriotism, but we don't know of any serious attempt by their mother to instill in them a love of the church.

Tolstoy's father was an ordinary aristocrat of his time, for whom, as it had been for Tolstoy's grandfather, the church was nothing more than a civil institution. Yes, it was necessary for weddings, baptisms and so on, but in no sense was it a "pillar of truth and proof of the truth". The enlightened Russian aristocracy in the 18th century had an attitude toward the church rites that was condescending at best. One recalls the beginning of *War and Peace*: after all, both the old Prince Bolkonsky and his son Andrei are atheists through and through, for whom the devout piety of Princess Maria can only be explained by her unpleasant appearance and inability to find a handsome groom. The prototype for Prince Andrei was L.N's older brother Sergei Nikolayevich. Right up until the time of his death he was an atheist and made fun of the monastic robes worn by his sister Masha, when she came to visit Yasnaya or Pirogovo, referring to her hood in jest as a 'top hat'. When the question arose as to whether or not he should take communion before his death, his devout wife, the former gypsy, appealed to L.N. with a request that he ask his brother not to refuse this act, especially since Sergei Nikolayevich himself wanted to do this before his death. L.N. supported their outburst, and his brother confessed his sins and took communion.

"Tolstoy's aunts had a different attitude to the church," writes Gusev, "especially his aunt Alexandra Ilinichna. Unhappy in her personal life, she sought solace in religion. Her favorite pastime was going to church, her favorite company – pilgrims, monks, nuns, holy fools. When her mother was still alive, strangers and pilgrims found a hospitable refuge in the house at Yasnaya Polyana; now, their numbers had increased greatly. There was the semi-nun Maria Gerasimovna, there was also Olga Romanova, Feodosiya, Fyodor, Evdokimushka and others. Nikolai Ilyich didn't prevent his sister from taking in strangers and pilgrims, but he himself, with his innate common sense, didn't share her enthusiasm for these people." And in this Levochka was in agreement with his father, whom he greatly respected. His aunt's religious inclinations instilled in him a certain fear of God, however. In an autobiographical passage, *What am I?* he tells of the time when, as a child, he ate some communion bread sent by the priest, not on an empty stomach, as one was supposed to, but having drunk some tea. This tormented him greatly afterwards, and he said that "God punished" him for this.

The deepest religious influence on Tolstoy was exerted by Aunt Tatiana Alexandrovna Yergolskaya. She has lived in his house until the mid-70's, enjoying cordial relations with her nephew, his wife and their children. T.A. Yergolskaya's religious views were very specific though, and, oddly enough, prefigured religious modernism. She accepted all the dogmas of the church, except for one: the doctrine of torment in the afterlife. That is, she denied hell. She used to say: "God, who is kindness itself, cannot wish for us to suffer." The religious philosopher N.A. Berdyaev wrote the same thing in the early twentieth century. We find this same denial of hell beyond the grave in Tolstoy's religious views. "Ever since I was a child, I have never believed in torment in the afterlife," he wrote in 1884 to V.G. Chertkov.

At the time of his adolescence and youth, Tolstoy departs altogether from the church, and not so much on account of his religious nihilism, but on account of not being in the habit of going to church and performing the rituals, a habit which was characteristic of the young unmarried men in his circle. Prior to his marriage, it simply didn't occur to him that it was necessary to go to church, stand through long services, prepare for communion, take confession and take holy communion. We remember the embarrassment that Konstantin Levin feels when he walks into church for the wedding. He feels a deep emotion, admittedly, but this is because is the scene seems to be happening to him in a dream, in some sort of new reality.

In the late 70's, in his search for the meaning of life and a strong faith, Tolstoy appeals to the ordinary Russian people, finding in them the only thing that cannot destroy his analytical mind. Tolstoy was always struck by the relaxed attitude of the Russian peasant and soldier toward death. And in this he wasn't alone: one recalls Lermontov's *Borodino*, Turgenev's *A Living Relic*, Nekrasov's poetry. But if the common man doesn't fear death, then he must know some answer to the most important question of all: the meaning of human existence. This mystery always troubled Tolstoy and was the main reason for his "wanderings among the people". Having appealed to the common people for an answer about the meaning of life, he had also to admit that the Russian people were an Orthodox people. Hence Tolstoy's attempt in 1877 to turn to the church and to hagiographic literature.

"How many times I envied the peasants their illiteracy and ignorance," exclaims Tolstoy in *Confessions*. "From those provisions of faith, which for me led to conclusions that were nonsense, for them nothing false came out; they could accept them and could also believe in the truth in which I believed. Only for me, unfortunate one that I was, it was clear that the truth was interwoven by the tiniest of threads with lies, and that I could not swallow it in that form."

S.A., herself a believer and a church-goer, was somewhat surprised by the passion with which her husband suddenly turned to the church.

"He observed lent so strictly that at the end of Holy Week, he consumed only rye bread and water, and spent most of his time in church," she wrote, recalling the events of 1877. "He infected the children with this approach too; and I too, even when I was pregnant, kept a strict fast ..."

The daughter of a priest from the Kochaki church, close to where the Tolstoy family cemetery is, told Makovitsky: "Occasionally my father would go to the morning service in the morning, and Lev Nikolayevich would already be there, sitting in one of the pews. My father often visited Lev Nikolayevich at home, and would return at two o'clock in the morning. He and Lev Nikolayevich spoke a lot about faith."

V.R. Chayevsky, the District Superintendent of Police, heard the following story from the peasants: "Our masters, that is, the Count and his family, are in church for the Kazhinny festival; the large family arrives, the Count himself always comes on foot ... He comes before the beginning of mass. Us men are sitting on the steps of the church, watching – and the Count comes and sits down with us, and starts chatting away merrily, talking about his business or of things divine..."

The servant Sergei Arbuzov, who in 1881 went with Tolstoy to Optina, recalled that in 1877, starting out early in the morning to church, the Count saddled his horse himself so as not to wake the stablemen.

Tolstoy understood religion in the strict sense of the word as a 'connection'. The ritual aspect of orthodoxy, though, signified something to him that was clearly not a connection with God, but, as it were, a 'horizontal' connection – with his ancestors, who once performed the very same rites, and with millions of Russian peasants.

"When performing the rituals of the Church," he wrote in *Confessions*, "I calmed my mind and subordinated myself to the devotion which all mankind had. I was at one with my ancestors, with those whom I loved – my father, mother, grandpas and grandmas. They and all those who came before them had all believed and lived, and they had brought me into the world. I was also at one with all the millions of people from the population whom I respected."

Tolstoy's stubborn mind, however, could not stop at the fact that he was acting like everyone else, and therefore acting correctly. The first experience of communion after many years of refusing, provokes spiritual rejection within him.

"I'll never forget the painful feeling I experienced that day, when I took communion for the first time after many years. The service, confession, the rules – all this was clear to me and caused a joyful awareness within me that the meaning of life had been revealed to me. I explained away the sacrament of communion itself, as an action to be taken in remembrance of Christ, signifying purification from sin and full acceptance of the teachings of Christ. If this explanation was artificial, I did not notice its artificiality. I was so happy, demeaning and submitting myself before the confessor, a simple, timid priest, to shake all the dirt in my soul loose, repenting for all of my sins, I was so glad to merge my thoughts with the strivings of my forefathers who had written the rules of prayer, so joyful was this coming together with all those who believed and who believe, that I did not feel the artificiality of my explanation. But when I went up to the royal doors and the priest made me repeat what I believed, that what I was about to swallow was the true body and blood, it pained my heart; it was something like a false note, it was the cruel demand of someone who obviously had never known what faith was."

At that point, Tolstoy was "inexpressibly hurt". But "I found a feeling in my heart which helped me overcome this. It was a feeling of self-abasement and humility. I reconciled myself to it, and swallowed the blood and the body without feeling sacrilegious, with the desire to believe, but the blow had already been dealt. And knowing in advance what awaited me, I could not go again," he writes in *Confessions*.

Neither the fasts, nor prayer, nor confession, nor the sacrament of communion itself provoked rejection in him, but, on the contrary, they evoked a joyful feeling (one remembers his definition of life as "a joy"). He experienced joy from reading hagiographic literature, too, especially the 'Menaion Reader'. Yet the priest's demand that he confirm his belief that the bread and wine were the blood and body of Jesus was "unspeakably painful". Here Tolstoy's intellectual conscience hits a stumbling block and cannot accept this.

The second important factor that pushed Tolstoy away from the church was the requirement to pray in church for those in power and for the army. Not only could Tolstoy not find this requirement in the Gospel, but he saw in it something quite the opposite. And once again, Tolstoy's intellectual conscience revolts, resists external pressure to take what he cannot see or understand on faith.

"Father's Orthodoxy came to an abrupt end," recalled his son Ilya Lvovich Tolstoy. "It was lent. At that time, a lenten meal was prepared for my father and those wishing to observe the fast; for the young children, teachers and governesses, meat was served. The servant had just taken away the plates, put down a dish with the leftover meat cutlets on it on the small table and gone downstairs for something else. Suddenly, my father turned to me (I always sat next to him), and, pointing to the dish, said:

'Ilya, pass me some of those cutlets, won't you?'

'Levochka, you're forgetting that it's lent,' my mother intervened.

'No, I haven't forgotten, I shan't fast any more, and please, don't order anything lenten for me any longer.'

To the dismay of us all, he then ate the meat and said how good it was. On seeing our father's attitude, we too soon cooled toward fasts, and our prayerful mood was replaced with complete indifference to religion."

The Enfant Terrible

It seemed like the mature, family-oriented Tolstoy had moved away from the mischievous habits of his youth, but during his spiritual crisis he again returns to them. In Moscow, he will defiantly stay home stitching boots when his wife and daughter go out to balls. In the presence of literary fans he, he will talk in mocking terms about *War and Peace* and

Anna Karenina, as happened in the office of Polivanov, the director of a private school, where he went to help secure jobs for his sons Ilya and Lev. In the office were the director's wife and a man named Markov, a former teacher from the Tula school and an old friend and admirer of Tolstoy.

"Markov asked Tolstoy whether it was true that he wasn't writing anything at the moment?

'It is true,' Tolstoy said defiantly. 'So what?'

'But how is this possible?' exclaimed Markov, an ardent admirer of Tolstoy's works. 'To deprive society of your works?'

Tolstoy replied calmly:

'If I've done bad things, surely that doesn't mean I have to continue doing them? In my youth I visited Gypsy girls, drank champagne, do I really have to go back and do it all again?'

Deeply offended, Evgeny Markov said reproachfully:

'How can you make such a comparison?'

And once again he hears Tolstoy's calm response:

'Well, what if I think that my works are just such nonsense and that 'artistic' pursuits are an unworthy thing?'

One can infer from the memoirs of Polivanov's wife that Tolstoy's works were not the only thing he described as "nonsense".

"Take Pushkin for example. He wrote a lot of nonsense. They put up a statue of him. There he stands in the square, just like a butler reporting that dinner is served ... Go and explain the significance of that statue to the ordinary peasant, and why Pushkin deserved it."

In March 1881, he writes a daring letter to Alexander III, asking that the murderers of his father, Alexander II, be spared, after the notorious events of March 1. We don't know the content of the letter, in the form in which N.N. Strakhov tried to pass on to the tsar through Pobedonostsev.

A draft version of it has survived, however. The mere fact that a nobleman was advising the tsar not to execute regicides, no less, would have had very serious consequences for any other nobleman. S.A. understood this perfectly and was strongly opposed to the letter, getting into an argument with her husband right from the outset because of his 'dissident' sentiment. She threatened to "kick out" the home tutor V.I. Alekseyev, who agreed with her husband. She was afraid for her family and for the children. For Tolstoy, however, such reasoning did not hold up as an argument. The letter was passed on by Strahov but got no further than Pobedonostsev.

In response to Tolstoy, he wrote: "… don't hold it against me that I declined to carry out your instructions. In such an important matter everything must be done through faith. And after reading your letter, I saw that your faith is of one kind, and my own faith and that of the church is of another kind, and that our Christ is not your Christ. I know mine as a man of strength and truth, who heals the weak, whilst in yours I seemed to see the traits of a weak man who himself demands to be healed. This is the reason why I, according to my own faith, could not do what you asked me to do. Yours respectfully and devotedly, K. Pobedonostsev."

The allusion to "weakness" and the need for "healing" by a member of the State Council and the recently appointed chief procurator of the Holy Synod was quite clear. The case of Chaadaev's letter (not even to the tsar), for which he was declared insane, was still fresh in the memory. Tolstoy's path as a dissident begins with the writing of this letter to Alexander. The letter didn't reach the tsar, but he was aware of its content.

Tolstoy is setting off down a dangerous path, where his only guarantee of immunity is his famous literary name. Yet this name is the very thing that he now appreciates the least. And at the very same moment when his daughter Tanya, as can be inferred from her diaries, is faithfully reading *War and Peace*, like all educated girls of the time, her father is troubled by the fact that the censors won't allow his anti-church *Confessions* to be published. "If I want to describe how a woman fell in love with an officer, that's allowed; if I want to write about the greatness of Russia and sing the praises of war, that's most definitely allowed", but a book "in which I talk about what I lived through and thought about – I can't even think about publishing such a book in Russia."

He no longer even hopes to publish the new philosophical-religious treatise, *What I Believe In* (1884) after "Confessions" had been "cut" from the May 1882 issue of the journal "Russian Thought". The treatise is printed at Tolstoy's expense in fifty copies on Kushnereva's printing press, and after the ban and arrest imposed on the publication by the spiritual censors, came out in print in St. Petersburg and changed hands in high society. This was an early form of "samizdat".

S.A. was frankly frightened by the prospect of being the wife of a dissident. Marakuyev (the publisher. - PB) said that the secular censor transferred your new book to the spiritual censors; that the Archimandrite, chairman of the censorship committee, read it, and said that in this book are so many higher truths that they cannot be denied and that from his side he doesn't see any reason not to let it through – she said in January 1884. "But I think Pobedonostsev, with his tactlessness and pedantry, will ban it again."

Needless to say, he banned it. But in this case, it is Tolstoy's wife's attitude toward the book that is much more important. At this time she is preparing for publication a collection of her husband's works and is distinctly unhappy that his new "works" are being published and distributed without her involvement.

"I found Kushnerev (the owner of the printing press. - P.B.) sick, in a dressing gown; he apologized profusely, but I had to get the copies, and I asked him. He said - here's my card, ask Marakuyev. But last night I sent Seryozha (her son. - PB) over to Marakuyev's place; but Marakuyev very simply declared that since everyone is very interested in this work, he had given all of them away for reading and correspondence. I was so angry that I went today myself and told him that "the copies are not yours, but the Count's, and he neither asked you nor authorized you to distribute them. And you must grant that the Count's relatives, his nearest and dearest, have, if not more right, then at least the same rights to be interested in his works." He promised to bring me two tomorrow; but don't be angry at me, I have obtained even more evidence that he is an extremely insolent man, and I have to be more careful with him," she writes home indignantly in January 1884. This is already the cry of the soul of a writer's wife, who for the first time is having to confront the fact that strangers are meddling in the family's concerns, claiming some sort of rights of their own to her husband's new works.

"What served Tolstoy well has now turned into a bad thing for him," says Vladimir Zhdanov. "What made the family happy – Lev Nikolaevich's spiritual, creative side – is now making the family unhappy. Before, he and the family mutually fed each other, and now their interests are opposed, the link is broken, and they have joined battle, each defending their right to life, sometimes growing embittered, sometimes becoming reconciled only to have a fresh outburst again."

Ilya Lvovich, who was 13-14 years old at that moment, explained the Tolstoy family drama more frankly than anyone, in his memoirs. He was at the most difficult adolescent age, the so-called 'transition'. And perhaps because of this, the fracture which had taken place in his father was so vividly felt by his son, that L.N. himself in this period behaves like an adult teenager.

"A man who had idealized family life, lovingly described aristocratic life in three novels and created his own, similar set-up, suddenly started to condemn and denounce it severely; a man who had prepared his sons for school and then university using the program that existed at the time, began denouncing modern science; a man who had gone to Doctor Zakharin for advice and sent for doctors for his wife and children from Moscow, began to renounce medicine; a man who had been a passionate hunter, a hunter of bears, who loved hunting dogs and fired arrows at game, started referring to the hunt as "dog-chasing"; a man who for fifteen years had saved up money and bought up cheap Bashkir land in Samara began calling property a crime and money debauchery; and, finally, a man who had dedicated his whole life to elegant literature, began to repent of his activity and almost quit it for good."

"But what my mother had to endure at that time!" Ilya Lvovich continues. "She loved him with all her being. She was almost created by him. From the soft and good-quality clay that she had been when she was the eighteen-year old Sonechka Behrs, my father fashioned for himself a wife such as he wanted to have, she gave herself to him completely and only lived for him – and now she sees that he is suffering terribly, and as he suffers, starting to move further and further away from her, her interests, which had once been their common interests, no longer interested him, he begins to criticize them, begins to tire of their life together. Finally he begins to scare her with talk of separation and a decisive split, and at that time she had a large and complex family on her hands. She had children ranging from infants to the seventeen-year old Tanya and eighteen-year old Sergei.

What to do? Could she have followed him then, given away all of their fortune, as he wished, and condemned the children to poverty and starvation?

My father was at that time fifty years old, and she was only thirty-five. Father was the repentant sinner, whereas she didn't even have anything for which to repent. Father had his enormous moral strength and intelligence, whilst she was an ordinary woman; he was a genius, eager to cast his eye over the whole horizon of world thought, she was an ordinary woman with conservative instincts of the female of the species, building herself a nest and protecting it.

Where is the woman who would have acted differently? I don't know of any, in real life, in history, in literature.

In this case, one can feel sorry for my mother, but one cannot condemn her. She was happy in the early years of her married life, but after the 1880s, her happiness faded and never came back.

The one who suffered most of all though, of course, was father himself."

At this time, S.A. writes to her brother: "If you could only know and heard Levochka now. He has changed a lot. He has become the most sincere and fervent Christian. But he has turned gray, his health has weakened and he has become quieter, more melancholy than he used to be."

"Levochka works all the time, as he puts it," she writes to her sister, with alarming irony, –"but, alas, he is writing some sort of religious discourse, so as to show how the Church is incompatible with the teachings of the Gospel. One would struggle to find ten people in Russia who might be interested in it. But nothing can be done, I only wish one thing, that he might finish it as soon possible and that it might pass, like an illness."

It is easy to catch S.A. out based on her words, to prove how ill-attuned she was to her husband's spiritual quest and how mistaken she was in her forecast about the "ten" people who might be interested in such things. But Tolstoy's search at this time left Fet and Turgenev bewildered, too, and even those closer to him in spirit, like Strahov, disagreed with him about many things. Ultimately, the spiritual upheaval caused a serious conflict between L.N. and his aunt A.A. Tolstaya, the very one whom S.A. was used to considering a cut above herself.

S.A. was supported by her relatives. On March 3, 1881 (two days after the assassination of the tsar, after which Tolstoy set out on an openly dissident path) she writes to her sister that their brother, Alexander Behrs, who was visiting Yasnaya Polyana, had found in L.N. a "turn for the worse, that is to say he fears for his sanity." From herself she adds that "religious and philosophical inclinations are the most dangerous of all."

The prisoner of Moscow

Now here's a thought: what would have happened if in 1881 the Tolstoy family had not moved from Yasnaya Polyana to Moscow?

Perhaps the irreversible discord within the family would not have arisen? And Tolstoy's views wouldn't have changed to such an extent that they came into irreconcilable conflict with those of his loved ones?

The move was motivated by need. The older children, Sergei and Tatiana, had grown up. Sergei planned to enroll at Moscow University. Tatiana was already a grown woman, it was time to bring her out into society. In addition, Tatiana showed progress in painting and wanted to go to the School of Painting and Sculpture. Ilya and Lev needed secondary education. Sergei's home schooling, with annual examinations in Tula, had proved to be troublesome. The publishing interests of Tolstoy and his wife required that they make the move to Moscow, too. Not only did S.A. understand this, but so did Tolstoy himself. He anticipated the move with great fear, was homesick. But he resigned himself to it.

Tolstoy didn't like Moscow.

We find the first signs of this dislike in the story "Childhood". After visiting Moscow, Nikolenka Irtenyev was unpleasantly surprised by the look of the city's inhabitants: "I couldn't understand why they all stopped paying attention to us in Moscow – no one took off their hats as we passed, some even gave us some unfriendly looks." This is the view of a child, but let's not forget that by the time they moved to Moscow, LN had started asking himself "stupid, simple, childish questions."

The big city aroused an aesthetic and moral aversion in him. It is difficult to say which of the two had the greater share. For example, Tolstoy's aesthetic sense was bothered by a policeman who was standing in the middle of the street with a big gun. It seemed to him to be just as absurd as the footman in the helmet "with a feather in it," who had accompanied his future wife in the Kremlin when she was a little girl.

Moscow in the 1870-80s was a colorful city where the achievements of urban civilization were strikingly combined with archaic rural life.

Except for a few main streets, it was a conglomeration of many aristocratic estates, joined one to another willfully and haphazardly. In any case, that was how Moscow must have seemed to Tolstoy, with his years of visual acumen and having been brought up on the Yasnaya Polyana estate, with its infrastructure and landscape. It must have seemed like an extremely large village.

"A part of Moscow, stretching from the banks of the Moscow River and roughly to Malaya Dmitrovka and Karetny Ryad, the part of it, on which the radii are Ostozhenka, Prechistenka, Arbat, Povarskaya, Bolshaya and Malenkaya Nikitskiye, with a confusing labyrinth of alleys between them, was mainly the aristocratic and the bureaucratic side," wrote the historian M.M. Bogoslovsky about Moscow in the 70-90s. "Here, on the Sadovaya ring road, and here and there outside this ring, large aristocratic mansions were located along the main streets – palaces with columns and pediments in the empire style. Here, both on the main streets and in the side streets, there were many aristocratic mansions, small in size and often wooden, one-story buildings with a mezzanine, often also with columns and pediments, on which could be seen coats of arms with prince's caps and robes or noble crowns, helmets and suits of ostrich feathers. These large and small aristocratic mansions were very reminiscent of similar aristocratic homes in suburban and more distant estates, especially since most of the forecourts adjacent to them, containing all manner of service buildings and outhouses – sheds, cellars, stables, wells – were not much different from the rural estates that belonged to the same owners. The average Moscow street back then didn't yet have the look of two tall, continuous façades, facing one another and elongated in boring fashion, with one building merging into the next unnoticeably. Back then it wasn't the façades of the homes that bordered one another, but individual property, in the form of estates, separated one from another by wooden fences. In these properties there were mostly wooden gates, very often left open to provide access from the street to the front porch. The similarity to the rural estates was only enhanced by the mass of green. It was rare for any of these mansions not to have at least a small garden. The gardens at other houses were enormous, they were really as big as parks."

Such was the appearance in the 1880s of Moscow, the city to which Tolstoy was about to move. It is one thing to move from the country to the city. It's quite another to move from the family estate, from one's fortress where one is at liberty, into the throng of other people's fortresses.

The urban part of the city could not satisfy Tolstoy's aesthetic taste either, though. "Tverskaya Street, and especially the Kuznetsky Bridge, have made significant progress in terms of the exterior of the shops located there, but the majority of the commercial establishments and shops on the other streets have preserved their former, antediluvian signs, with ungrammatical, often funny signs and pictures depicting in a naive way the nature of the commercial enterprise; among the signs which particularly jumped out at me were the ones for "tobacco shops", in which there would always be an Asian-looking man in a turban, smoking a pipe, on one side of the front door, and on the other, a black man or mestizo (in the latter case – in a straw hat), sucking his cigar; hairdressers' signs usually depicted, besides coiffed ladies' and men's heads, glass jars of leeches, and even scenes of blood-letting; on the signs for bakeries there were images of rolls, loaves and pretzels, whilst on the signs for 'colonial' shops there were sugarloaves, candles, fruit, or else boxes and bundles attached to the road, with steamships sailing away in the distance; on the signs for tailors all kinds of items of clothing had been drawn, whilst the shops selling Russian dresses had signs showing a coachman's cloth coat and jerkin; one would see pictures of hats, tea-trays, dishes with a piglet and sausages on them, cold cuts, cheeses, boots, suitcases, spectacles, watches – in short, the traders weren't relying on the literacy of the public or by what was in the shop window, but were presenting their wares to the customers in roughly drawn and painted form, and moreover the signs themselves were very clumsy and utterly ugly ... " another memoirist, N.V. Davydov, recalled of Moscow at that time.

Besides that, the big city had a big problem in terms of sanitation. "Moscow to this day (1914. - PB), despite the water supply and plumbing, cannot achieve clean air," wrote N.V. Davydov, "and it's best not to go into other courtyards even now, but in the sixties a stench of varying degrees entirely held sway over Moscow. This is to say nothing of the numerous primitively organized sewage convoys, often made of tubs which are not covered, and spill their contents when they move, or at best, made of simple barrels with tall buckets sticking out of them, whose movement through the streets, which begins after midnight, or even earlier, lasted until the morning, poisoning the whole neighborhood for a long time, even in winter – the stench, to a greater or lesser extent, existed in all courtyards, which often lacked not only specially adapted cesspits, but cesspits of any kind whatsoever. Designated parking for carriage drivers, courtyards for "lodgers", taverns, folksy restaurants and similar establishments, and finally, almost all street corners, even those boarded at the bottom with planks, different backstreets (and there were many!) and roofed gate houses, despite the notice "strictly forbidden", were focal points for polluted air ..."

The first conflict arose when the children were being enrolled at school. At first, LN wanted to send Ilya and Lev to a regular public school. But there he was required to give a signed statement about the "trustworthiness" of his sons. This angered Tolstoy! "I cannot even give such a signed statement about myself, how can I give one for my sons." As a result, they chose the Polivanov private school, where no "signed statement" was required.

Another thing that made the Polivanov Gymnasium a good and convenient choice was the fact that the house of Princess S.V. Volkonskaya on Denezhny Lane, between Povarsky and Ostozhenka, which S.A. found and which the Tolstoy family rented in the fall of 1881, was right next door to it. One of the main reasons that Tolstoy resigned himself to move to Moscow was *fear for the children*. There could be no talk of Ilya and Lev going to private school, or of the already fully-grown Sergei being in Moscow alone, without constant parental supervision. Tolstoy's patriarchal convictions about how to run a family had not been shaken by his antichurch and anti-state sentiments.

One of the reasons for moving to Moscow was Tolstoy's fear that his sons might be influenced by nihilistic-minded youth at high school and university. He remembered his student years in Kazan well, when in his first year of study he had landed up in the clinic with a venereal disease. On the other hand, Tolstoy, with his new religious worldview, in general had no reason to love the university, and especially the faculty of natural sciences, in which Sergei enrolled. A confirmed anti-Darwinist (in this sense he was an ally of Strahov, who wrote a book against Darwin), Tolstoy, to the end of his days, couldn't forgive his eldest son for that choice. Shortly before his death, in Astapovo, he dictated a letter to Sasha for Sergei and Tatiana, which contained these words: "I would also like to add for you,

Sergei, some advice, namely that you should think about your life, about who you are, what you are, what is the meaning of human life and how any reasonable person ought to live it. Those views you adopted about Darwinism and evolution and the struggle for existence do not explain to you the meaning of your life and do not give you guidance in your actions, and a life without an explanation of its significance and meaning, and without the constant guidance that ensues, is a pitiful existence. Think about it, loving you, I'm telling you this, probably on the eve of my death."

Commenting on the letter, Sergei Lvovich writes that by 1910 his views "had changed in many ways." His father, it would seem, was just remembering their arguments from the time when he was a student.

The father didn't like his son's choice, didn't like the university in general, but it was he, more than anyone else, who took the trouble to make sure that Sergei prepared himself adequately for the university exams.

It was L.N. that sought out the home tutors for the children, just as he had sought out their nannies and governesses. He negotiated it so that Sergei, who had undergone home schooling, nevertheless sat the annual examinations at the Tula school along with the ordinary students. The results of these examinations worried Tolstoy a lot, as is evident from his letters.

And suddenly, having moved to Moscow, the father begins to berate the university in front of his son and express negative views about science in general. In his memoirs, Sergei Lvovich records some of the things his father said about science and scientists during their disputes:

"Science is concerned with anything it pleases, only not with questions about what one needs to know and about how to live."

"Scientists do not distinguish between useful knowledge and unnecessary knowledge, they study unnecessary subjects such as the genitals of the amoeba, because by doing so they can live like a lord."

"All these scientists receive an allowance from the state and not only are they unable to speak the truths that the government doesn't want to hear, they must also dance to the government's tune ..."

Not a single nihilist, not a single Bazarov could have uttered anything like this in Sergei's presence. The destructive power of his father's denial was so great that the 18-year-old boy became confused. When was his father in the right? When expending money and emotional strength so as to prepare him for the university, or when cursing science and scientists?

In Notes of a Christian, a kind of confession by Tolstoy in the early 80's, his eldest son is mentioned frequently. Tolstoy, undoubtedly, felt guilty before him, yet couldn't rid himself of an unamicable attitude toward his son. From the diary it is apparent that they constantly argued, moreover it was the father who would hector him and provoke the argument and the son who had to fight back. "Seryozha has admitted that he loves the carnal life and believes in it," writes Tolstoy. And he coldly observes: "I am delighted the problem has been stated so clearly."

And what of Tanya? A seventeen-year-old girl, she of course dreamed of moving to Moscow! And not just because she wanted to study at the School of Painting and Sculpture. After all, Moscow meant dances and costumes, admirers. Tanya was not indifferent to all of that. Intelligent, well-educated, with an undoubted talent for painting, she was nevertheless an ordinary provincial young lady, and a somewhat rhapsodic one at that, who longed for romance.

She was secretly in love with one Kolya Kislinsky, her own age and the son of the chairman of the Tula district council. She was being courted by the slightly older Anton Delvig, a friend of her brother Sergei, nephew of the famous poet and friend of Pushkin, and son of the Delvigs, acquaintances of the Tolstoys' from Tula. She had read *War and Peace* and her sympathies lay with Natasha Rostova, not Princess Maria. Her female idol was her aunt Tanya Kuzminskaya.

She herself wrote some remarkable lines about what was happening in the head of this charming girl in her memoirs. The best evidence of all as regards her state of mind and soul, however, were reflected in two diary entries from 1879 and 1880.

"Around the Christmas tree I was given a pair of binoculars and some writing paper with my monogram on it, costing 4 rubles. 50 kopeks. Grandma sent me a ring from St. Petersburg. Mama also gave me papa's works, two vases and a vial for cologne and the English novel *Jane Eyre*."

"I know what he (her father. - PB) wanted: he wanted me to be Princess Maria, so that I didn't think at all about having fun, about Delvig, about Kolya Kislinsky, and, if it were possible, so that I didn't go anymore to Tula. But it's too late: why did they take me there the first time?"

A startlingly full portrait of the young Tanya is painted by these short lines. One can see her mind, her charm, her education, her ability to count money; one can sense her gratitude for the gifts from her family, her powers of psychological observation, and an early aptitude for self-analysis. And all of this was the result of a long and careful family upbringing, in which her father's role was no less prominent than that of her mother. "The paternal influence was stronger in the home than the maternal one," T.L. Suhotina-Tolstaya later admitted. "Everyone realized this."

When Tanya broke her collarbone after slipping on a waxed floor, her father took her to Moscow, to the best surgeon, and asked him whether there would be any trace of the injury left after the operation? "He wanted to make sure that there wouldn't be any noticeable bulge when I would have to appear in the restroom at the ball…"

In Moscow, Tolstoy took his daughter to her first ball in person and presented her to a circle of society people, with whom he retained old connections.

Reading Notes of a Christian, we see a very different attitude on the part of the father toward his daughter. But we have to be aware that this diary is in fact a chronicle of endless suffering by the people. Tolstoy's eyes have been opened. He sees around him what he had seen before but never really noticed. The common people are poor, sick with all sorts of diseases, dying "from melancholy", of consumption, lasting the last people who provided for them, don't know what to give their young children to eat, are subjected to corporal punishment for the slightest offense and tolerate all this in silence.

"A peasant from Shchekino. Consumption. Sneezing blood, sweat. Has been bleeding for 20 years now."

"The daughter-in-law of Yegor, who has no arms. She came to ask for money for a horse."

"A drunk man tied the bandages too tight, broke his nose."

"A boy, Kolpenskoy, 12 years old. The eldest, the others are 9 and 6. Their father and mother died."

"Soldier from Shchekino, in a fever."

"Pogoreliy, Ivan Kolchanov."

"A woman from Sudakovo: 'They set fire to my place. I ran out as I was.

My son went into the flames. I've lost everything. I haven't got a horse. The horse was taken by the judges."

"A sick woman from Shchekino, with a little girl, walked for 3 days to see me."

"A man from Podyvankovskoy whose sister is sick. The sister's nose is sweating."

"Peasant from Salamasov. His cow died."

"A lame, well-dressed girl. Her cousin is driving her away."

"A woman who was burned, lower-middle class, with a child, the boy was burned, her husband got burned ..."

This is just a small part of the human misery and universal evil with which *Notes of a Christian* are packed, turning them into painful reading. Tolstoy's view has become selective. He sees around him nothing but grief and suffering. He is like Buddha, who in his childhood and adolescence was carefully protected from the sight of human suffering, but when he saw them, he was no longer able to see anything else.

And against this backdrop –was his family. There is a feast day to celebrate. Everyone is going on a picnic. "We're having a huge lunch with champagne. The Tanyas (his daughter and Tatiana Kuzminskaya. - PB.) got dressed up. 5-ruble belts on all the children. They have lunch and already the picnic wagon is moving amidst the peasant carts, carrying the people exhausted by their work."

All this is happening not in Moscow, but still at Yasnaya Polyana. But Tolstoy can no longer look at those close to him as he looked at them before." Sonyahad a fit. I endured it better, but it was still bad. We must understand that she is amiss, and feel sorry for her, but we cannot turn away from evil. - The talk with Tanya about education lasted until morning. - They're not people."

This new attitude toward women, on the part of a man who would go on to write *The Kreutzer Sonata*, ricocheted onto his daughter, who at this time was impatiently preparing to become one. Whilst still at Yasnaya, Tolstoy, to use an expression from his diary, is "making a stink about" his wife and daughter, bullying them, provoking them into arguments and suffering from their reactions.

But now here they are in Moscow...

"The stink, the stones, the luxury, the poverty. The debauchery. A group of villains have gathered together, having robbed the people, and brought in soldiers and judges to protect their orgy, and now they are feasting. The people have nothing else to do, besides, taking advantage of the passions of these people, entice the stolen loot back from them. The men are more adept at this. The women are at home, whilst the men rub the floors and their bodies in the bath houses, where they are taken by the carriage drivers."

And at home? "The arrangements are still being made. When will they finally start to live? Everything is being done not so as to live, but so that things might be as they are for most people. How miserable they are! And there is no life."

The house on Denezhny Lane, which S.A. had found, was noisy, "as if it were a gambling den." The partitions between the rooms were so thin that you could hear everything that was being said and done in the next room. Wanting to please her husband, SA chose a large room for his study, overlooking the courtyard and located away from the other rooms. "But this magnificent study," she wrote in her memoirs, "subsequently led Lev Nikolayevich to despair, because it was too spacious and luxurious."

Almost twenty years previously, when L.N. had brought Sonia to his bachelor house in Yasnaya Polyana, for her, a woman from the city, it had been difficult to get used to and adjust to life in the country. Now their roles had been reversed. "Finally, we had an explanation," S.A. writes to her sister. "Levochka says that if I loved him and thought about his state of mind, I would not have chosen this huge room where there is not a moment's peace, where a seat of any kind would bring joy to a peasant man, that is, these 22 rubles would get him a horse or a cow, that he wants to cry, and so forth."

"For the first two weeks I cried continuously and daily," she writes to her sister again, "because Levochka isn't only discouraged, but even in some desperate apathy. He hasn't slept and hasn't eaten, and he too has literally cried sometimes, and I just thought I'd go crazy."

In order to work in a familiar environment, L.N. rents an additional two small rooms in the wing for 6 rubles a month.

But what does he write? The only work he completed in 1881 was the story *What Men Live By* for a children's magazine.

That same autumn of 1881, when he finished the story *What Men Live By*, a new addition came to the Tolstoys' home in Moscow. Their eighth child (not counting the three that died) was born, their son Alexei. The trouble was that S.A. had already reached a point where she didn't want this child. While still at Yasnaya she had written to her sister: "Misha spits up what little milk he sucks, every time, and I feel bad. So it seems, to my utter dismay, that I am probably pregnant again."

She was *tired*. Her husband was not reckoning with her physical and psychological capabilities. He was engrossed in his new world view and his search for people who might respond to these views, or who might at least think that he wasn't insane. On her shoulders were two babies, two small children, two schoolboys, a student and a girl of marriageable age. And at that time her husband, for the first time, suggests that they should abandon all property, all the income from his works, all aristocratic habits, and give everything to the poor and the peasants, and live by the fruits of their labor on a small piece of land.

And it's *not just words*.

In Tolstoy's diary of 1884, we find a whole program for a new family life, as it appeared to Tolstoy and as he, apparently, suggested that it should be to his wife and children. We shall quote this passage from beginning to end, keeping in the bits which he crossed out as well.

"Live at Yasnaya. (*Crossed out*: In the first instance use the income from Yasnaya Polyana.) Give away the Samara income to the poor and to schools in Samara, for (*crossed out*: the founding) disposal and monitoring by the payers themselves. With the Nikolsky income (after giving the land to the peasants) – exactly the same thing. For myself (*crossed out*: maintain), that is, for my wife and I and the small children, maintain for now the revenue from Yasnaya Polyana, from 2 to 3 thousand. (Maintain it temporarily, but with the sole desire of giving it all to others, and satisfy ourselves through our own efforts, i.e. limit as much as possible our own needs and give more than we take, towards which all our efforts should be directed and in which we should see the goal and joy of life.) The three grown-up children should be given the choice: either to take from the poor the next portion of the Samara or Nikolsky money, or, whilst living there, to help ensure that this money is put to good use, or, whilst living with us, to help us. The younger ones should be brought up in such a way that they grow used to demanding less from life. Teach them the things they want to learn, but not only the sciences, but science and work. We should only keep as many servants as we need in order to help us make the transition and teach us, and even then only for a while, as we grow accustomed to doing without them. We should all live together: in the men in one room, the women and girls in another. A room should be set aside for a library for intellectual pursuits, and there should be a working room, a shared one. Because we are spoilt there should also be a separate room for the weak. (Crossed out: And) Besides keeping ourselves and the children fed and the teaching, there should also be work, farming, the giving away of food to the needy, provision of medical care and teaching. On Sundays there should be dinners for the needy and the poor, and reading and conversation. Life, food, clothing (crossed out: art, science and so on), all the simplest things. (Crossed out: and close to our hearts.) All extraneous things: (crossed out: to be sold) the piano, the furniture, the carriages – to be sold, given away. Science and art should only be taken up in a form in which they can be shared with everyone. The way one talks to all people – from a governor to a pauper – must be the same. One goal – happiness, one's own and that of the family – knowing that happiness consists in being content with little and in doing good to others."

It was a labor commune on the basis of a single family. Of course, S.A. didn't agree to this. It wasn't just the fact that neither she nor the children, nor, ultimately, L.N. himself, had any skill at living in such conditions. It was the fact that Tolstoy was proposing that his wife erase and destroy everything that she had created over twenty years by his say-so. She was being asked to start family life all over again. A new husband, new concerns, new quarrels and reconciliations.

She had neither the mental nor the physical strength for this. The birth of Alexei was the last drop in the cup of her female patience. Whilst still breastfeeding Misha, she wrote to her sister from Yasnaya: "Sometimes I would just fly to you, to my mother, to Moscow – anywhere, anywhere, to get away from my half-darkened bedroom, where, bending down awkwardly over the little red face of the new boy, I express milk 14 times a day and faint from the pain in my nipples. I have decided to be consistent, i.e., to feed this *last* one too, and put up with those pains yet again, and I am putting up with it fairly patiently."

Not only was Misha not the *last* one, but neither was Alyosha. The last one would be Vanya. But before him there would be Sasha, whom S.A. almost got rid of, by going to see a midwife in Tula and asking for an artificial miscarriage. This was in the very same year, incidentally, that Tolstoy wrote out his project for their family commune.

The mismatch, no longer just in terms of their interests, but simply in terms of their rhythms of life, between husband and wife is becoming catastrophic. Tolstoy's life in the late 70's and early 80's seems to slow down, at times even coming to a stop ("there is no life"), and his wife, who is bearing children and breastfeeding them almost without a break, doesn't have time to think about or analyze their new family situation. In this period, Tolstoy behaves very cruelly towards his wife and children. He would later feel a lot of guilt over this time in his life, when, through stubbornness, bluntness, he tried to bend the family over his knee, making demands on it which it was in no condition to satisfy.

Searches and reconciliation

Yet what a strikingly strong and sturdy family the Tolstoys were! Even in 1881, in one of the most desperate periods of their family life, the thought of "separating" himself off from his family never once enters L.N.'s mind.

"One's family is one's flesh and blood," he writes in his diary in 1881. "To ditch one's family is tantamount to the second temptation – to kill oneself. A family is one body. But do not give in to the 3rd temptation – serve not your family, but God alone."

There we have it: to abandon one's family means to *kill oneself*. And the point here, of course, is not about physical survival, without having the care of one's loved ones. It's about the fact that Tolstoy still doesn't think of his spiritual life as something that is separate from his wife and children. The death of the family is one's own death, not a physical one, but a spiritual one. Therefore Tolstoy cannot "leave the dead to bury their dead." It is not "the dead", but rather the spiritual body which is at one with them, that is sick, but that cannot simply be divided into "sick" and "healthy" parts. And Tolstoy is trying to cure this "body" together with himself. Hence the intense passion in his arguments with his loved ones.

Tolstoy's behavior in Moscow, at first glance, seems very inconsistent. He renounces property, but in the spring-autumn of 1882 throws himself energetically into searching for, acquiring and designing a new home in Moscow. Volkonskaya's "gambling den" house on Denezhny Lane doesn't suit him. He doesn't want a temporary refuge, but a safe and comfortable family nest, just like the one in Yasnaya Polyana.

It's no coincidence that the search for and finding of the house was preceded by multiple flights by Tolstoy to Yasnaya in February-April 1882, when he was able to simultaneously rest his shattered nerves, and to do something akin to assessing the possibility of living without his family. His hurtling between Yasnaya and Moscow was also the first test of strength for the family, and the search for a new format for family life. S.A. wisely didn't interfere with his trips, but didn't try to pretend that all was well either. She gave her husband *carte blanche* to choose a new format for family life in accordance with his new convictions. And she couldn't have acted in a better way than that.

They write to one another almost every day, sometimes writing two letters a day. In her first letter, S.A. makes her feelings abundantly clear. Yes, she infinitely loves her husband. She would be happy to live with him quietly and peacefully at Yasnaya Polyana. She doesn't like city life, either. But she won't sacrifice the interests of her children, not even for the sake of her husband's peace of mind, and it's his right to choose how he sees fit to live from now on.

"I have just come down from upstairs, from Andryusha's room, where he was screaming violently in his dreams. When I looked out through the window, I saw a beautiful, starry sky and thought of you. What poetic and melancholy mood did this sky evoke in you at Yasnaya this evening, when you went for a walk, as you used to do. I felt like crying, I missed that quiet life, I cannot cope with the city, and here I am left to languish, more in the physical sense, perhaps, but it's not good for me here."

This letter honestly and thoroughly describes the confusion and bustle of life in Moscow, with the carriages, stage shows at the fair, the Maly and Bolshoi Theaters, balls, relatives, friends' children. "There's a dance at the Olsufyevs on Saturday and on Friday Obolenskaya is inviting us over. One of us needs a dress, another needs shoes, another needs something else." And she is suffering from "spasms in her throat and chest," and at night – nightmares. "I saw a woman last night in a print dress, her bare legs and shoes dragged and shuffled, and I wasn't afraid when she came to my bedside. I asked, "Who is it?" She turned around and went out the living room door ..."

She reminds her husband about the child she is breastfeeding, Alyosha. "My little one is unwell all the time and is very dear to me and pitiable. You and Syutayev may not especially love your children, but us mere mortals are not able not to love them, and perhaps, indeed, we do not want to mutilate ourselves and justify our lack of love for anyone by citing some kind of love for the whole world."

She doesn't use up a single line trying to "smooth over" the family dispute, to put the brakes on it. "I am disgusted, I am not feeling well, my life is hateful to me, I cry all day long, and if some poison was at hand, I would probably drink it. I am not calling on you to share this life and I shall not lie again. Your presence upsets me too, especially since I cannot soothe and comfort either you, or myself. Goodbye."

In response, she receives a "quiet, humble" (in her words) letter, from which it follows that no matter how good life is at Yasnaya Polyana, L.N. nonetheless misses his family, and he is waiting for the call to return home. "I am writing to you, my soul, from Yasnaya, in Alexei Stepanovich's room, where I like to spend time ... Peter Shintyakov slept here, on the stove. Maria Afanasyevna and Agafia Mikhailovna came for tea and conversation yesterday, and today I went out riding, drank lots of coffee and started working, but couldn't do much – my head aches because of a migraine, and I feel weak. I am not allowing it to trouble me, and have been reading old Revues and thinking. I have been reveling in the silence. I have been avoiding visitors. I'd very much like to write what I have thought up. They're heating auntie's room in the house. I'll only move in if the air is very warm and light. I will stay for as long as God intends and as you shall instruct me."

"No, I won't summon you to Moscow," S.A. responds, "live there as long as you want, let me burn alone, why should we both do so: you are more needed than I am, for everyone and everything. If I get sick again, I'll send a telegram, then there will be nothing to be done. Enjoy the silence, write to me and don't worry; in essence, everything is the same whether with or without you, only there are fewer guests. I rarely see you even when you're in Moscow, and our lives have grown apart. What kind of life is this, by the way – it is some kind of chaos of labor, fussing about, absence of thought, time and health and all the things by which men live... Goodbye, dear Levochka, be healthy. Where have you gone? that is, you, as you once were in relation to me. That you is now long gone. Goodbye, it's already 2 am, and I still have a lot to do."

In this letter there is an unambiguous "dig", a hidden quote taken from the title of his new story, *What Men Live By*.

In the letter S.A. again lists the ways in which the children entertain themselves in the city, although, of course, she knows how he feels about these things.

"Today, the boys, Ilya and Lyolya, went to the opera, along with Kolya Obolensky, Ivan Mikhailovich and Seryozha. Lyolya started crying, apparently, when one character killed another in a duel in *Faust*. In the evening they went to the circus with Keller, the Lyarskys, the Obolenskys and Olsufyevs. They paid for five boxes. Tomorrow morning I'm taking the girls and Andrusha to the circus, and in the evening to a party at the Obolenskys. On Saturday they're going to a party at the Lyarskys: the Olsufyevs canceled their party."

In the next letter there is another description of balls: "We've just got back from the Obolenskys, dear Levochka, we're tired, and the kids seemed to have fun. Tanya danced too, and Tanya Olsufyeva was there, and the two Lyarskys, and the Kellers –there must have been 15 couples there. Even old Olsufiev was there, and he kept saying: 'How much fun I'm having!'. ... We were at the circus during the day: a wonderful circus, and I had fun watching Andryusha, although I admit that such amusements are harmful to children. But he kept saying his thoughts on it out loud, laughing, and even applauding a boy on a pony." There is also a complaint about being overworked: "I had to break off my letter, I fed the children, got undressed, finished everything I was doing and now it's nearly three o'clock in the morning, the time I always go to bed." And there's a line advising him not to rush to return: "restore yourself to full health, live in Yasnaya as long as you want, write to me and enjoy yourself. If life has separated us, then we must each arrange things as best we can, which is what I shall try to do for us, that is, for me and the children. It's still very difficult and unfamiliar for me, but people can get used to anything."

Almost all of S.A.'s letters to L.N. in this period are constructed like this: the fun times being enjoyed by them (the children), the tiredness and sleepless nights suffered by her (the wife and mother), the peace and enjoyment afforded to him (the husband and father). And she agreed to all this. And that was how it should be. If *life had separated them*. But she doesn't hide the fact that it hurts her.

Sometimes, she admits that her letters are "evil" and "bad". Sometimes she dreams herself of moving to Yasnaya. But she doesn't ask her husband to return to Moscow. On the contrary: "For the first time in my life, dear Levochka, today I wasn't overjoyed by your imminent return. You write that you'll be leaving on Monday or Tuesday: thus, perhaps tomorrow you'll come back and start to suffer and be bored and be a living, albeit tacit, rebuke about my life in Moscow. Heavens, how that grieved me and how it tormented my soul! Perhaps you won't get this letter; but if you do, don't think that I strongly desire your return; on the contrary, if you are healthy and working, and especially if you feel good there, then why come back? The fact that I don't need you for any worldly affairs is beyond doubt. I'm keeping everything in order and in balance for the time being: the children are obedient and trusting, my health is better, and everything is going as it should in the house. As for my spiritual life, it is so deeply buried that it can't easily be got at. And let it be like that for the time being, I'm scared to dig into it and bring it into the light of God, what would I do then? This inner, spiritual side of life is so out of kilter with the outer side."

Later, at the end of their life together, she will do anything and everything to try to bind her husband to her. She won't let him go out alone anywhere, not even to see his own daughter and son-in-law, let alone Chertkov. She will try with all her might to prevent his departure to Stockholm. And as a final argument in their quarrels she will utter promises to the effect that she will share completely his spiritual life and live with him anywhere, even in a peasant hut. And he, for his part ...will flee from Yasnaya Polyana. In a letter to her husband after his departure, she will agree to anything, to any demands he might make, if only he will come back. And he will flee from Shamordino.

But now, at Yasnaya, as he receives letters from home which have apparently given him the freedom to act as he sees fit and the moral right not to participate in the "vanity of vanities" of life in Moscow, where his grown-up daughter is tapping her heels at the balls, and his little son is clapping his hands at the circus, where his wife isn't waiting for his return, and even writes that she is living more easily without him – he not only returns, but starts organizing their family nest in the most energetic way imaginable. S.A.'s victory in this epistolary battle between the spouses to assert their rights was complete. This was precisely because she didn't encroach on *his* rights. But she also let him understand that the family would be able to go on living without him.

Incidentally, L.N.'s replies contained a few "digs", too. For example, he reminded her about Arsenyeva. "Agafia Mikhailovna has just been amusing me with stories about you, and about what I would be like if I had married Arsenyeva. 'And now you've left, you've abandoned her there with the children, – saying do as you please, and as for you, you sit around stroking your beard.' It was good."

On the whole, though, the tone of his letters was sad. The calm of life in the country has a favorable effect on him, but it is amid that quietness that he realizes that he cannot live without his family. It's more specific than that – he cannot live without S.A.

"I cannot live apart from you ... I need urgently for everything to be together... You say to me, 'I love you, but you do not need that now'... But it's the very thing I need. And nothing can revive me like that, and your letters revived me."

This is his humble reply to a letter from his wife, in which she, whilst expressing pity for her husband, nevertheless reminded him that the reason for the family conflict was his new beliefs:

"You ought to get treatment. I say this without a second thought, I think it's clear. I'm awfully sorry for you, and if you could think about my words without getting annoyed, and about your situation, you might, perhaps, find a way out. You were in this sad state once before, long ago; you used to say, "you wanted to hang yourself due to unbelief." And now? – after all, you aren't living without faith, why are you unhappy? And can it really be that in the past you didn't know that there were people who were hungry, sick, unhappy and malevolent? Take a closer look: there are also people who are happy, healthy, fortunate and kind. If only God might help you, but what can I do? Goodbye, my dear friend; how am I to comfort you, my dear, I can only do one thing –love and pity you, but you don't even need this now. What is it you want? If only I knew."

The trouble was that he himself didn't know at that time what he wanted, either. The idea, that was clear to him, about the injustice of the living arrangements had not had a positive outcome. He couldn't publish *Confession*. He didn't have any friends or like-minded associates. His writing wasn't coming easily...

On S.A.'s side were the children, her relatives and all of Moscow's high society. On L.N.'s side there was *no one*. Even those closest to him in his literary sphere, Fet and Strahov, didn't understand the meaning of the upheaval happening to Tolstoy. At this time, he fell out with his spiritual correspondent Alexandrine Tolstoy, as well. When they met in St. Petersburg in the winter of 1880, an argument broke out between them. A.A. Tolstaya was an ardent supporter of a church-based understanding of faith. On leaving the capital, L.N. wrote to her: "I'm not coming to see you, I shall leave today. Please forgive me if I offended you, but if I caused you pain, then I shan't ask forgiveness for that. It is impossible not to feel pain when you start to feel the need to break away from a lie to which you have become accustomed and with which you are at ease."

In the next letter he tried to find a path to reconciliation, writing that although he did not think that a man with her level of education could believe in church rituals, "but as for women I don't know."

The older children, Tatiana and Sergey, cannot support their father. They are too young and caught up in the pleasures of the city. In addition, Sergei, like any good student, is in love with Pisarev and Chernyshevsky, attends student gatherings, spreads anti-government proclamations, and so on. He is a positivist and believes that only math and the natural sciences are true knowledge. He resents his father over the latter's contempt for university studies.

Tatiana was somewhat warmer in her attitude toward her father. All the daughters, as they grew older, became dedicated co-workers of their father, performing secretarial duties for him with joy and even jealousy ... until they got married.

In the early 80's, though, Tanya simply couldn't share in her father's works and ideas. Tanya was becoming a society lady, and she liked this very much, by contrast with her father's tedious moralizing.

"Recently, papa argued with mama and Aunt Tanya in the evening and spoke very well about how he considers one can live in a good way, about how wealth prevents one from being good – mama was already sending us up to bed, and Manya, Aunt Tanya and I had left, but he caught us and we stood and talked for almost an hour. He says that we are spending the most important part of our lives trying to be like Fifi Dolgorukaya, and that we are sacrificing the best feelings of all for some silly dress. I told him that I agree with all of this and that I understand it all in my mind, but that my soul remains completely indifferent to all that is good, yet starts getting so excited when I am promised a new dress or a new hat ..."

The position of "Aunt Tanya" (T.A. Kuzminskaya) was not favorable towards Tolstoy, either. She idolized him as a writer, particularly as the author of *War and Peace*, for which she had served as the prototype for the main female character. In the 1880s, she herself wrote stories about everyday peasant life, under his influence and guidance, and had them printed in the "Journal of Europe". Her habits and attitudes did not coincide with Tolstoy's new beliefs, though.

"Tanya – the charm of naiveté in egotism and intuition... – Tolstoy wrote in his diary in 1863, brilliantly expressing his sister-in-law's inner world. "I love her and am not afraid of her."

Her clashes with Tolstoy at Yasnaya were the talk of the town. Once, Tolstoy, already a vegetarian and having infected his children with vegetarianism too, to mark the arrival of 'Aunt Tanya', who did not believe in vegetarianism, ordered that a chicken be tied to a chair at the dining table and that a knife be placed on the table. "You'd like some chicken? Then grab it and slaughter it."

'Aunt Tanya' wasn't easily embarrassed either, though.. Tolstoy's son, Lev Lvovich, recalled an episode from Yasnaya Polyana life:

"For example, one morning, on the 'croquet' lawn – the little square in front of the house – two tables were laid for the morning coffee. One table was for the Tolstoy's, the other – for the Kuzminskys. Footmen and maids could be seen in the distance, carrying delicious coffee, fresh buns, hot bread with raisins and thick cream, from the kitchen, and putting it all down on snow-white tablecloths. Their masters stood up, strolled around, went for a dip and started getting ready for the meal. Lev Nikolayevich arrives at the croquet lawn as well...

"So you aren't ashamed, either?" Lev Nikolayevich suddenly asks "auntie", "so you too, Tanya, aren't ashamed to sit like that and stuff your face, whilst you watch the peasants carrying hay past us? And you're not ashamed that the laundry women wash these tablecloths for you in the pond?"

"No, not at all," Aunt Tanya answered gamely, "one has to drink coffee! I cannot do otherwise."

Lev Nikolayevich then fell silent, and after a while sat down at the table to drink a cup of coffee."

In her letters to her elder sister, Kuzminskaya protested against her overly submissive attitude toward her husband. S.A. wrote back: "Men are constantly straining their mind and, consequently, their nerves, therefore it's necessary to protect their heads and nerves above all; and in return for this silence, for looking after their nerves, after work, they come home to the family in good spirits…"

Thus there could be no support, either from the children, or from 'Aunt Tanya'.

Perhaps, though, Tolstoy might get some support from his own relatives, from his sister and brother?

No, he couldn't hope for support from them, either. Rather, his sister and brother were themselves in need of his support, both spiritually and in a material sense. "Uncle Seryozha", Sergei Nikolayevich Tolstoy, was a wonderful person, but in life he was unable to achieve stability. His relationship with his children, especially his son Grisha, didn't go well, nor did his running of the Pirogovo estate, which didn't bring in enough revenue. The only thing he was really good at was hunting, and a row of wolves' teeth next to a path in the park at Pirogovo bore witness to this in picturesque fashion. He was a man of conservative view, he read the "Moscow News" and then "New Time", and he read English novels as a hobby, even learning English in order to read them in the original. He was extremely knowledgeable about Russian songs and gypsy songs, and after moving with his family to Moscow at the same time as his younger brother Lev, Sergei Nikolayevich once took his nephew Seryozha to Strelna – to listen to the Gypsies.

"My Uncle spoke to the Gypsies in an aristocratic manner" recalled Sergei Lvovich Tolstoy – "when addressing the famous conductor Fyodor

Sokolov, whom we, the youth, treated with respect, he used the familiar form of 'you', and he requested ancient songs and scolded the gypsies for forgetting the real gypsy songs and Russian songs. The gypsies treated him with great respect, Fyodor Sokolov tried his best to please His Excellency. That night, I understood the charm of gypsy singing better than ever before."

Here, Sergei Nikolayevich was really in his element. The correspondence between the brothers in the early 1880s suggests that the elder brother was constantly in need of funds and asking for money from the younger one, whose financial affairs were going well.

"In 1881, our family's financial affairs were in a brilliant condition. I say the financial affairs of our family, not of my father, because father always believed that his fortune didn't belong only to him, but also to his entire family, and he never thought twice about giving mother as much money as she needed. At that time he had accumulated a lot of money. He sold the mill at Nikolskoye-Vyazemskoe for 9,500 rubles, sold part of the forest (Stary Zakaz) in Yasnaya Polyana, I don't remember how much he got for that, and he received 25,000 rubles from the Salayev brothers for a complete collection of his works."

"I had heard ever since I was a child," Sergei Lvovich also recalled, "that my uncle was an excellent manager, but I later became convinced that this wasn't true. He knew all the terms and conditions of management as it was in those days, but he wasn't thrifty, wasn't business-like, and ran the estate in a lordly manner... He was suspicious, but often didn't suspect those whom he ought to have suspected. As a result, his financial situation got worse every year." After spending four winters in Moscow, the older brother did not take a liking to urban life, not due to his inclinations and beliefs, but simply due to a lack of money. And he locked himself up once again in Pirogovo.

"After all, you live off the money received for your father's writings," Sergei Nikolayevich liked to say to his famous brother's offspring. "Whereas I have to count every kopek. If your father's steward steals 1,000 rubles, but then renders an account for it and gets 2,000 rubles for this accounting: that's a thousand rubles of profit ... I cannot run things in that way..."

Tolstoy tenderly loved and respected his handsome and independent brother, this real Russian lord of the manor, all his life, but he couldn't count on his brother's support in his search for something new.

He couldn't count on any support from his sister, either. Her own life was rapidly going downhill. After her divorce from her husband and her unhappy romance with de Klein, she received treatment from a homeopath named D.S. Trifonovsky and befriended this "good-natured, slightly eccentric, unselfish and religious" man. He had a religious influence on her, as did the popular archpriest of the Archangel Cathedral, Valentine Amfiteatrov, but it wasn't the influence that her brother Lev could have had on her. She, like Sergei Nikolayevich, had serious problems with children. She had a difficult and capricious nature. She never could never quite settle anywhere, neither at her estate of Pokrovskoye, nor in Moscow, nor abroad. She tried to live at Yasnaya, but there she didn't get on well with S.A. She was headstrong and witty. Once, in Moscow, a womanizer in the street tried to solicit her. She led him up to a streetlamp, lifted her veil and said, "Take a look at me, and then you'll probably leave me alone." When a group of holidaymakers asked her, near Yasnaya Polyana, to take them to see Lev Tolstoy, she replied: "They aren't showing the lion today, they're only showing the monkeys." In the end, the monastery was the only place where her proud and independent nature could find peace and harmony.

Thus, whichever way you look at it, the only person in Tolstoy's inner circle who could somehow understand him was his wife.

In the vast literature about Tolstoy which came out during his lifetime, a widespread opinion took root that in the early 80s, S.A. didn't understand her husband, and that this was the reason for their marital conflict. This isn't true. In fact, his wife was the only person who understood him. And *this* was the reason for their marital conflict.

Firstly, S.A. was a very intelligent woman. As it seems to us, she was much smarter than not only her younger sister, but also than Maria Nikolayevna, and even Alexandra Andreyevna Tolstaya. Her intellect wasn't one-sided, did not lie solely in the sphere of material interests. In his letters from the early 80s, Tolstoy almost never discussed spiritual issues with his wife, not because they didn't concern her, but because they had plenty of time to discuss them without needing to do so in their letters. The intensity of the disputes that occurred at Yasnaya Polyana and at the Tolstoys' home in Moscow suggests that S.A. took a tough, independent line on these issues. They concerned her too much from a personal perspective. She couldn't but take into account the consequences of her husband's spiritual upheaval for their family, and saw clearly that these consequences were the death of the family as it had once been, in its prosperous state. For her, these issues were not merely theoretical, as they were for Alexandrine, but literally questions of life and of the future happiness or unhappiness of the family.

She explained her own place in her husband's spiritual upheaval as follows: "I probably wasn't smart enough to understand my husband's whole spiritual worldview, at which he had arrived by a difficult, lengthy and complex path; and I wasn't foolish enough to blindly follow him, without thinking, with dumb obedience. And there was no time for reflection."

Secondly, S.A. knew the origins of this new spiritual worldview. Its birth had taken place before her very eyes, in the writings which she had copied out, in the draft versions of them, in L.N.'s diaries, which she had read and which were written in the knowledge that his wife was going to read them. Lastly, she knew, and this is also important, about his physical weakness and malaises: his unstable psyche, diseased liver and persistent headaches. She knew the secret reasons behind his mood swings, including those which had been caused by the intimate conjugal life of a man who was old, but still very biologically strong, and a woman who was still young, but constantly bearing children and breastfeeding them.

And Tolstoy knew that she knew this. There is therefore a lot more subtext in their letters than there is text itself. Sometimes a small detail, like a sentimental forget-me-not, put into a letter which the 60-year-old Tolstoy sends from Yasnaya to his wife in Moscow, says more than words.

When a man and a woman are so in love with each other and when they are connected by such a large number of children whom they love, they will, sooner or later, even with all the differences of opinion which arise, be required to find some new format for their family relations which might suit them both completely.

At times one gets the strange feeling that this ideal format was the correspondence between the spouses during L.N.'s trips to Yasnaya Polyana, or to the Samara Province. Tolstoy's letters to his wife fill two entire volumes in the full collection of his letters. There is only one other correspondent who merited a similar exclusivity. This was Vladimir Grigorievich Chertkov.

Among the several hundred letters sent by Tolstoy to his wife, we do not find a single message that was cruel or harsh, nor indeed any that are offensive. Even in the letters he wrote during the departure in 1910, there isn't a single offensive line.

"My dear", "darling", "dear friend" – these are all common ways in which Tolstoy addresses his wife in the letters. All the quarrels and disagreements take on a different, more intelligent character in his letters.

"There is a lot of strength within you, not only physical but also moral", he writes to his wife on September 26, 1896, after thirty-four years of living together, "only something is missing, something small but all-important, which will nonetheless come, I'm sure of it. I will only be sad in the hereafter, when this thing comes along after my death. Many are upset that fame only comes to them after death; I have no reason to desire this; I would have given up not only a lot of my fame, but all of it, if it meant that you, during my lifetime, might coincide with me, in terms of your soul, as you will coincide with me after my death."

This admission, in the first place, is startling in that Tolstoy acknowledges his personal immortality and the possibility of someone being able to look down from the next world on his loved ones, who remain in this world. This is so inconsistent with Tolstoy's religious philosophy, which denied any individual immortality, that it casts doubt on his notorious 'Buddhism'. Secondly, Tolstoy was absolutely right! After his death, S.A. did indeed start to adopt his views, and the whole of the last nine years of her life were devoted to this difficult "spiritual consensus".

In their letters, husband and wife understand one another better, more clearly and more precisely. It's as though the veil slips from over their relationship, and the quarrel itself suddenly acquires a different, more profound meaning.

It would seem that their ideals are diametrically opposed. He calls her to the future, she calls him to the past. He suggests burning bridges and not being afraid of anything. She takes on the responsibility of safeguarding the old hearth and home. He calls her to come roaming, she calls him to stay in the same place.

When these stances manifest themselves in the letters, they cease to be just family disputes.

Her: "When I think about you (which is almost all day long), my heart aches because the impression that you are making now is that you're unhappy. And I'm so sorry for you, but at the same time perplexed: because of what? why? Everything around us is so good and happy."

Him: "One man lives by begging, another has epilepsy, this one has consumption, that one lies crouched, that one beats his wife, this one abandoned his children. And there is suffering and evil everywhere, and people's acceptance of the idea that this is the way it must be."

Her: "... I feel all the tragedy of your position..."

Him: (about a fire at Yasnaya Polyana, in which 22 courtyards burned down): "I feel very sorry for the peasants. It's difficult to imagine everything that they suffered and will suffer yet... I've just taken a walk among the buildings that burned down. And it's pitiful, horrible, and majestic – that strength, that independence and confidence in their strength, and peace of mind."

Her: "Yes, we have been on different paths since childhood: you love the countryside, the people, you love the peasant children, you love all of this primordial life which, by marrying me, you left behind. I am a *city-dweller*, and no matter how much I reasoned, and sought to love the countryside and the people – I cannot love it with all my being and I will never be able to; I *don't understand* and will never understand the people in the countryside... When you depart into that countryside atmosphere, morally, I suffer for you and track you jealously, and see that here we are *probably* not together; and not because I don't have the *will*, but because, less than at any other time, I do not have the *ability*."

It may be that S.A. didn't understand her husband either, at a time when very few people did. But she never allowed her children to doubt, in her presence, that their father's actions and writings were dictated by a higher understanding. "Farewell, dear Levochka", she wrote to her husband, I want Tanya (their daughter. - PB) to write to you, but she says, "He writes three lines, and in return there will be three of us writing three pages each to him." And I say, "But he then writes 300 pages for the whole world." Kissing you!"

"*Your* goodness and kindness is enough for the whole family," she admits in another letter, "or, as Urusov put it last Sunday, 'you all live in his rays and don't appreciate it!' Well, without you there are no rays, and I have to shine a light myself, weak as that light is."

The First Departure

On July 14, 1882, the senior notary of the Moscow district court signed the deed of purchase for Tolstoy's purchase of the house at 15 Dolgo-Khamovnichesky Lane for 27,000 rubles in installments from the collegiate secretary I.A. Arnautov. Tolstoy's wife's uncle, Konstantin Islavin, had urged him to buy the house. He wrote: "....there are more roses than in the gardens of Hafiz; there is an endless number of strawberries and gooseberries. There are tens of apple trees, there will be around 30 cherry trees; 2-3 plum trees, many raspberry bushes and even a few barberry bushes. There's water right there, almost better than the water in Mytishchi! And there's fresh air and quietude! And all this right in the middle of the hustle and bustle of the capital. You mustn't miss out on it."

It seems that the quietude and the huge orchard, in which one could get lost as one might in the woods, did indeed appeal to Tolstoy. The house itself was very old and not sufficiently spacious. Built in 1808, it had survived Napoleon's invasion of Moscow and the only reason it didn't burn down was that the houses in the Khamovniki Region were few and far between and surrounded by large expanses of greenery. The house had no electricity, which already existed at that time in Moscow. Lastly, its fence rested against the brick wall of a brewery. And the whole area was industrial, suburban. The Olsufyevs, the neighbors, were very nice.

The Tolstoy family returned to Yasnaya from Moscow in the summer. And it was there that the event which S.A. feared most occurred, in August. Perhaps anticipating it, she tried to dissuade her husband from making too hasty a return to Moscow. But it was at Yasnaya, not in Moscow, that he first expressed a desire to get away from the family.

In Moscow, he felt a terrible weakness and the desire to die. Tolstoy wrote to Strahov: "I am terribly tired and weak. The whole winter passed idly. That which I think people need most of all, turns out not to be needed by anyone. I want to die sometimes. For the matter in which I am concerned, my death will be useful..."

At Yasnaya, on the twentieth anniversary of their wedding, the storm broke out. S.A. wrote in her diary:

"For the first time in my life, Levochka ran away from me and spent the night in his study. We had an argument about nothing, I attacked him because he doesn't concern himself with the children, doesn't help look after the sick Ilyusha and sew him a jacket. But it wasn't about the jackets, it was a matter of his cooling toward me and the children. Today he shouted out loudly that the most passionate idea he had was to get away from the family. I will die before I forget this sincere exclamation on his part, but it seems as though he has cut my heart out. I pray to God for death, it's horrible for me to live without his love, I clearly felt that then, when that love went away from me. I cannot show him the extent to which I love him strongly, as of old, and have done for 20 years. This humiliates me and he gets fed up with it. He is full of Christianity and thoughts of self-improvement. I'm jealous of him... I shall not lie down tonight on the bed which my husband abandoned. Help me, Lord! I want to take my life, my thoughts are confused. The clock is striking four o'clock. I said to myself: if he doesn't come, it means he loves someone else. He hasn't come."

L.N. has been transformed from a "quiet, humble" husband into a caged beast, and S.A. – from a wise, confident lady of the house into a madwoman who is afraid that her husband will abandon her. What seems superficial when they are apart in fact turns out to be the most important thing of all. Some stupid "jackets" very nearly become the grounds for a divorce. Let's try to imagine what S.A. meant by "little jackets". In Moscow, Tolstoy sawed wood and sewed boots. This was his manly, *peasant man's* work. Well then, why wouldn't he sew jackets for his children?

They later patched things up. S.A. writes in her diary: "He came back, but we only made up the following day. We both cried, and I saw with joy that the love for which I wept on that terrible night hadn't died. I will never forget that delightful morning, clear and cold, with a gleaming, silvery dew, when I came out after a sleepless night along the path through the woods to the bathing pool. I hadn't seen such triumphant beauty in nature in a long time. I sat for a long time in the icy water with the idea of catching a cold and dying. But I didn't catch a cold, returned home and took to feeding Alyosha, who was overjoyed to see me and smiled at me."

There is an alarming obsession with the idea of suicide in this entry. In the letter, she hinted about "poison"; now, while swimming in the pond, she dreams of catching cold and dying. S.A.'s suicidal tendencies can be attributed to a large extent to her pregnancies, the problems of being a breastfeeding mother, her children's continuous illnesses and the premature deaths of three of them (two more such deaths would follow). They were also associated with her husband's difficult behavior. But there were also some inherent traits in her character from the outset. Tolstoy's wife was, so to speak, an *extremist* in love. This is evident in all her diaries, including the early ones. The jealousy she had felt about Aksinya, when she dreamed about "tearing her child to pieces", and about all the women from her husband's past in general, cannot be put down to anything other than the inherent characteristics of her character as a woman.

"All of his (my husband's) past is so horrible for me that I, it seems, will never make peace with it."

"I have so much foolish pride that if I see the slightest lack of trust or misunderstanding of me, then all will be lost. I shall get angry. And what he does to me; little by little, I shall withdraw into myself, and I shall be the one poisoning *his* life."

"He kisses me, and I think, 'This isn't the first time he's got carried away.'"

"The poor thing, he looks for entertainment everywhere, so as to somehow get away from me. Whyever am I alive in the world."

"... I almost laughed with joy when I ran quietly out of the house, alone."

"I would have gone, gone somewhere far away, would have looked in to see what was going on at home, and then would have come home again, back here."

"One can die of happiness and of humiliation with such a man ... I find it easier when he's not here."

"If I could kill him, and then create a new one, an exact replica, I would gladly do that as well."

"There is only my husband, i.e. Levochka, who is everything, and this is an achievement on my part as well, because I love him terribly, and nothing is dear to me, besides him."

"I was in bad spirits just now and got angry about the fact that he loves everyone and everything, whereas I want him to love me alone."

"... so that he lived, and thought, and loved – all for me."

"My woe is jealousy."

"I cried like a madwoman and then afterwards couldn't think what I had been crying about, as is always the case – and yet I knew and understood so well that there was something to cry about, and that I might even die if Lev does not love me as he once did."

"For Lev I don't exist."

"There is no life. There is no love, there is no life. Yesterday I ran into the garden, and I thought, can it really be that I won't throw him out."

"Nothing exists for me, except him and his interests."

All of these citations are from her diary from before the birth of their first child. They were written not by a tired, exhausted woman, but by the eighteen-year old Sonia.

She always wanted to be with her husband all the time. "Since Ilya was born," she writes in her diary in 1866, "he and I have been living in different rooms, and it shouldn't be so, because if we were together, I wouldn't have held back, and would have said to him all the things that have been boiling up inside me this evening, whereas now I won't go to see him, and it's the same on his side, too."

But is it true that Tolstoy did not show concern for the children on the eve of the argument with his wife in August 1882? In Tanya Tolstoy's diary we read: "Ilya was severely ill. The doctor was sent for, and he said that he had typhoid. He was moved upstairs to the balcony room. I, too, had a gumboil, and papa took care of me – he made me a poultice of vinegar, salt, alcohol and bran, which helped me a lot... I was lying there at one point in Ilya's room in terrible pain, and Ilya was groaning too because of the fever, and suddenly papa comes in; he asked how we were, and says, "it's so bad it's almost funny". And all of a sudden all three of us began laughing, so much so that papa sat down and almost fell over on the floor with laughter, and I don't remember ever laughing so hard in all my life, and Ilya, too."

In the eyes of the children, their parents' quarrel looked different than it did in S.A.'s diary. "The other day papa and mama quarreled terribly over nothing, and mama began to scold papa for not helping her, and so on, and it all ended with papa spending the night in his study, as if to ensure that his sleep wouldn't be interrupted by mama, who was constantly getting up to check on Ilya. But reconciliation followed the next day. Lyolya says he accidentally walked in on them in the study and saw that they were both crying. Now they are more affectionate and gentle with one another than they have been in a long time. Papa promised to get more involved in all family affairs and to express his will, which is what mama wanted as well."

On September 10, having left the family at Yasnaya, Tolstoy went to Moscow to work on the renovation and improvements on the home in Khamovniki. He throws himself into this project with such reckless abandon that the family was amazed. He goes to the Sukharev Market to a shop selling old furniture and selects a furniture set made entirely of different types of mahogany, and together with the architect he helped to plan the rooms for all the members of the family. To put it in modern terms, he is preparing a 'turnkey' home, and dreaming of the moment when the family will see this majesty.

It is as if he is picking up the baton from where his wife left it twenty years ago, when, arriving at her husband's aristocratic lair in Yasnaya Polyana, she brought some 'bourgeois' order to it. Now he wants to show her his own taste and his own choices.

His wife even starts to get anxious...

"I've just received your letter, dear Levochka, and it confused me. From the tone, I see that the house is completely unready, and that we'll be moving God knows when. But from the content one wouldn't know it at all. What exactly isn't ready upstairs, are the two rooms off the corridor ready, and the girls' room, and the kitchen? You somehow always forget people. And then if the furniture is taken downstairs, where would we live? After all, there is a lot of furniture, it's cumbersome, and it will all get broken if we're all living in close quarters. In general, I cannot say anything about what I think, and when I will move; I need to know everything in greater detail."

Tolstoy himself buys and chooses everything: from the carriages to the color of the wallpaper. He gets personally involved in everything: from the re-surfacing of the Russian oven to the transportation of furniture and things from the house in Denezhny Lane. He was obviously in a hurry to make his family happy. It took him only a month to furnish the new home. "How stupid it was of the architect to say that we should have the floors painted in the autumn," his wife nags at him in a letter. "It would be better than the damp floor we have now, to which everything will stick, and the smell of paint will be a torment."

Finally, on October 10, the family moves into the new home. This episode is recorded in Tanya Tolstaya's diary as a magnificent holiday:

"We arrived at Arnautovka in the evening. The porch was lit, the hall was too. Dinner had been served and there was a vase containing fruit on the table. In general, the first impression was a most magnificent one: it was light everywhere, it was spacious and in everything one could see that papa had thought everything through, and tried to arrange everything in the best possible way, which he had fully succeeded in doing. I was very touched by the trouble he had gone to for us; and it was all the more sweet given that this was not like him. Our house is wonderful, I cannot find any flaws in it that need addressing. And as for my room and the garden – what a delight!"

From that moment on, it is as if a bright new period begins in the life of the Tolstoy family. It's certainly not the paradise of Yasnaya Polyna, but it's pretty close to it. In Opulsky's book *The House in Khamovniki* the family's daily life in Moscow is described as follows:

"The Tolstoys had lunch at 1pm, dinner at six and gathered for evening tea at nine. The table would be laid for 12 people for dinner. There were Viennese chairs around the table and beside the walls. The lady of the house, Sofia Andreyevna, sat at the head of the table, her back to the window. Opposite her was the eldest son Sergei Lvovich, to her left – the youngest son Vanya, to her right – the youngest daughter Sasha. Lev Nikolayevich usually sat next to Vanya, next to him were their daughters Tatiana and Maria, and across from him – their sons Ilya, Lev, Mikhail and Alexei. They rarely sat down together just as a family, though: they always had guests.

During lunch, a tureen of meat soup was put in front of Sofia Andreyevna, and on the left was a stack of deep bowls. Standing up, she poured the soup into the bowls, and the servant carried the bowls round and placed them in front of those sitting at the table, on small plates …

wine was never served at the family table, but there was always a carafe of water and a glass pitcher of homemade kvas..."

When Tolstoy became a vegetarian, cereals, vinaigrettes, jellies and compotes were specially prepared for him... In the nut dish next to the silver dinner service there was always a white enamel coffee pot. Early in the morning it was filled with barley coffee. Every morning, L.N. collected it, along with a glass and a roll, and took it up to his study.

It was almost always lively at the table. The publisher L.Y. Gurevich recalled:

"I can picture him (Tolstoy. – P.B.) so clearly, when he was sitting at the long dining table, chewing bread with his already toothless mouth, saying something and laughing ... When everyone was gathered together, it was fun and noisy at dinner. They would joke and tease each other and play 'Post'. The older children would laugh so loudly, until they screamed... Sometimes a serious argument of some sort would break out the next moment."

And the sheer number of guests that visited Khamovniki! The artists Ge and Repin, the sculptor Troubetzkoy, the writers Fet, Grigorovich, Chekhov and Gorky, the philosophers Strahov and Solovyev, the composers Rubinstein, Rimsky-Korsakov, Arensky, Rachmaninoff and Scriabin. And they all commented on the extraordinary warmth and hospitality of the Tolstoys' home. On one occasion, in the dining room, Paolo Troubetzkoy was sculpting a bust of L.N. whilst Nikolai Ge painted a portrait of S.A. The original portrait was kept at Yasnaya, but a copy of it hung in the couple's bedroom, over a mahogany sofa upholstered with pale yellow satin. The master bedroom opened out onto the terrace. At the exit stood S.A.'s writing-desk, also made of mahogany, on which she copied out *Resurrection* and her husband's plays and articles.

Repin wrote about her with the rapture of an artist: "A tall, well-built, beautiful, plump woman with black, energetic eyes."

Once it had been renovated, the Tolstoys' house in Moscow was large and comfortable. There was a hall, a dining room, small and large living rooms, a master bedroom, L.N.'s study and a separate work room where he stitched boots, the children's room, the boys' room, Tanya and

Masha's room, and besides those – a corner room and a room for washing the dishes, and bedrooms for the housekeeper, seamstress and room valet.

Near the main house were outbuildings, a barn, a caretaker's house, kitchen and gazebo. There was a huge garden. In winter there was an ice rink in front of the house.

But let's take a look at Tolstoy's diary… It gives us the impression that he's living not in paradise, but in hell.

In 1882 and 1883 Tolstoy barely kept a diary, but from 1884 onwards he starts to make regularly entries.

March 17. "Downstairs in the morning I seemed to hector my wife and Tanya over the fact that their life is bad."

March 18. "–There are lots of people at home. It's awkward and seductive. Music, singing, conversation. Just like after an orgy."

March 23. "I went riding. To travel by coach is boring. Silly – vacuous. Tried to talk to my wife after dinner. It's impossible. One thorn and she's in pain. Went to see the cobbler. One walks into a working household and it's enough to make the soul feel uplifted. Stitched shoes until 10. Again I tried to speak, again there was evil –a lack of love. Went to see Sergei. Spoke with him eye to eye. It was hard, difficult, but I seem to have moved forward."

March 24. "Twice I began to talk to my wife – impossible."

March 31. "I was left alone with her. We had a conversation. I had the misfortune and cruelty to wound her self-esteem, and it all kicked off. I couldn't keep quiet. It turned out that I had irritated her three days ago, in the morning, when she had come to disturb me. She is mentally ill in a very serious way."

April 24. "Why won't I talk to the children: to Tanya? Sergei is impossibly obtuse. The same castrated mind that his mother has. If the two of you ever read this, forgive me, it hurts me terribly."

April 26. "Started out for the bookstore, but didn't reach it, no-one in the tram could change 10 rubles. Everyone thinks I'm a crook. Came home, ate dinner alone… Went to the store, for some reason bought some cheese and cakes. As if in a dream – weakness… At home I spoke to Madame Seuron (the governess. – P.B.) and Ilya. He was seeking a dialogue with me. I thank him for that. It made me very happy. Then our family arrived. Deadly."

May 3. "... Found a letter written by my wife. Poor woman, how she hates me. Lord, help me. If this is my cross, let it be a crest, so that it puts pressure on me, and crushes me. But this wrenching of my soul – not only is it horribly oppressive and painful, but it's difficult. Help me!"

May 4. "Lord, deliver me from this hateful life, pressing down on me and ruining me. The one good thing is that I want to die. It is better to die than to live like this."

May 5. "I saw that my wife loves me, in a dream. How easy it was for me, everything became clear! There's nothing like that in my waking life. And this is what is ruining my life. I am not even trying to write. It is good to die!"

May 6. "At home is the chatter of the Kislinskys. Melancholy, death."

In the spring, as usual, they return for the summer to Yasnaya Polyana. But there is no joy for Tolstoy there either.

May 28. "I am trying to be clear and happy, but it is very, very hard. Everything I do is bad, and I am suffering horribly from this badness. It's exactly as if I am the only sane person at a lunatic asylum run by madmen."

On June 18th, 1884, Tolstoy went out to mow the grass near the house, then go swimming in the pond. He returned home vivacious and cheerful. Suddenly his wife began reproaching him over the horses from Samara which he had reared, and which were now bringing in nothing but losses, some had been euthanized, and he wanted to get rid of them altogether. The dispute took on a vicious, hysterical character. Tolstoy went to his study, collected his knapsack, the one with which he walked to Optina Pustyn, and headed down along the tree-lined avenue. His wife caught up with him and asked him where he was going. "I don't know, somewhere, perhaps to America, for good. I can no longer live at home!" he shouted, with cruel intent and tears. S.A. reminded him that she was pregnant and would be giving birth at any moment. He merely walked faster and soon disappeared from view.

Having walked half-way to Tula, he turned back. "At home some bearded peasants are playing *vint* – my two young sons" he writes with hostility in his diary. He heads off to go and sleep on the couch in his study. His wife wakes him up at 3 am. "Forgive me, I'm giving birth, there's a chance I might die." That night, their daughter Sasha was born.

Neither the father nor the mother were particularly pleased about it.

Chapter 6

A Dear Friend

Tolstoy's departure from Shamordino in the early morning of October 31 re-enacts his flight from Yasnaya three days earlier with surprising accuracy.

Those same witnesses and accomplices of the event, Sasha, Feokritova and Makovitsky, must have experienced a sense of déjà vu, when the pale, excited and determined Tolstoy suddenly woke them up at the hotel just after 4 o'clock in the morning.

"Soon after 4 o'clock L.N. came into my room and woke me up; he said that we would set off, though he knew not where to, and that he had slept for 4 hours and could tell that he wouldn't be able to get off to sleep again (and therefore) had decided to leave Shamordino on the morning train and move onwards. Again, just as he had done before dawn on the morning when he left Yasnaya, L.N. sat down to write a letter to Sofia Andreyevna, and after that he wrote to Maria Nikolayevna as well. I began to pack my things. After 15 minutes L.N. woke up Alexandra Lvovna and Varvara Mikhailovna," writes Makovitsky.

The same sequence of steps. The same people. The same atmosphere. The middle of the night, turning into early morning. Complete darkness and silence. Besides the fugitives, there wasn't a single guest at the monastery hotel. There was the same suddenness in the decision taken by L.N., who had not even said goodbye to his sister the previous evening. On leaving her cell, he had left Maria Nikolayevna in no doubt whatsoever that they would meet again the next day. There were the same negotiations with peasants about renting a home, shortly before the flight. In the first case it had been the peasant Mikhail Novikov, but the second time around it was the widow Alyona Khomkina from the village of Shamordino.

And finally, the most important and frightening shared detail of all: the complete uncertainty as to where they were actually going to go. Just as at Yasnaya, L.N. didn't tell his loved ones exactly where he was going, so too in Shamordino he seemed to hide it from them as well.

A strange suspicion arises that he deliberately confused them, didn't allow them time to come to their senses, and despotically subordinated them to his will. That's exactly how the elders behave, stunning their students with the most unexpected of instructions, without explaining to them the meaning of their words and actions, which are sometimes wild and even blasphemous at first glance. It was Tolstoy's cherished dream to become a holy fool. Might he not therefore have been trying to put this model of behavior to the test in his actions?

This theory must be rejected, though. One senses even less assuredness in Tolstoy's behavior in Shamordino than when he was leaving Yasnaya. Above all, however, just as at Yasnaya, a fifth person is present – S.A. It is she, in fact, who is guiding all of Tolstoy's eccentric actions. And moreover she is doing so not only against her will, but without knowing it.

What S.A. wants is the exact opposite: to stop her husband, to keep him near her. But all of her actions cause the opposite effect: Tolstoy takes off and flees. Had she been able at that time to take into account a fundamental character trait of her husband's, of which she was perfectly well aware, namely his fierce internal resistance to any force from without, she would of course have behaved differently. But to discuss, let alone condemn S.A.'s behavior, is, in the first place, immoral, and secondly, nonsensical.

P.I. Rastegayev, the psychiatrist who examined her immediately after Tolstoy's flight, came to a conclusion which, though cautious, due to the short duration of the examination, was nonetheless very definite: he wrote that S.A. was "suffering from a psychopathic organization (hysterical)", and that this, "under the influence of certain conditions, may cause such fits that we could be talking about a short-term transient mental disorder." Facts are facts. Tolstoy, both at Yasnaya and in Shamordino, was terribly afraid of his wife, or rather afraid of suddenly encountering her. At Yasnaya he feared that she would wake up and witness his flight. In Shamordino he feared she might suddenly arrive there, the possibility of which he had grasped from her letters and those sent by the children. "My father would have stayed in Shamordino," A.L. Tolstaya recalls. "He had already taken a look at an apartment in the village... But the news and letters that I brought alarmed him. We sat in Aunt Masha's warm, cozy cell and talked. My father listened in silence. And suddenly, leaning his hands on the arms of the chair, he stood up with a brisk movement and went into the next room. It was evident that he had made some firm decision."

Even in her later memoirs, Sasha focuses on the letters from home, trying to absolve herself of responsibility for her father's flight from Shamordino, which was sheer folly. In actual fact, though, she herself had made a considerable contribution to the instilling in Tolstoy of fear of the specter of her sick mother, toward whom she was hostile at the time. Makovitsky paints the scene of the conversation in Maria's house somewhat differently in his diaries.

"Alexandra Lvovna said that Sofia Andreyevna wanted to come after L.N. immediately; that she was trying to scout out (through the Governor, through her own servant and through the correspondents of "Russian Word") where L.N. was, that they assumed he was in Shamordino and that the arrival of Sofia Andreyevna and Andrei Lvovich was to be expected.

L.N. said that he'd be glad of Andrei Lvovich's arrival; that he would convince him that he could not go back, could not be together with Sofia Andreyevna, for her sake and for his sake.

When Alexandra Lvovna expressed her concern that Sophia Andreyevna might already be on her way here; that she might arrive in the morning; that they needed to gather their things and depart for another place in the morning, L.N. said:

- I have to think about it. Shamordino is a good place to be.

He told us about an apartment in the village where he might be able to settle:

- I don't want to second-guess myself.

Varvara Mikhailovna (Feokritova. - PB) came in, a great deal was said about Sofia Andreyevna's condition and about the consternation at Yasnaya Polyana.

One could tell by looking at her, and particularly by looking at Alexandra Lvovna, that they were panic-stricken with fear.

Alexandra Lvovna and Varvara Mikhailova insisted that it was necessary to get further away, and to be quick about it. She (Alexandra

Lvovna) had left her coachmen until morning, so as to go with them to catch the 5 o'clock train to Sukhinichi-Bryansk."

Tolstoy's sister and her daughter, Elizaveta, were against the idea of a hasty flight. Makovitsky adopted the neutral position of the doctor, whose task was to monitor the health of the fugitive, and everything else was for Tolstoy himself to decide.

Later, when putting his notes and jottings in order, Makovitsky reproached himself frankly for having failed to see the onset of Tolstoy's illness, and for having replied to Elizaveta Valerianovna's direct question of "is he fit to travel?" by saying: "Yes, the weakness has passed."

Perhaps a role was also played by the fact that Tolstoy didn't wait for the woman from the village, who was supposed to come and confirm that the hut for rent was ready. L.N. repeatedly asked Makovitsky about her, the last occasion being in the evening, on the way from his sister's place to the hotel. But the woman didn't come. It's entirely possible that word had already reached the village of exactly who it was that wanted to move in there (Count Tolstoy, no less!) and they simply got scared. If that was the case, then it once again replicates with precision L.N.'s attempt to move into Mikhail Novikov's village home, or into the building next door.

The main reason for his flight, though, was the specter of S.A. Why was he so afraid of this meeting that his fear woke him up in the middle of the night and forced him to leave a place he clearly loved and where he wanted to stay and, presumably, to die?

This is a telling moment! Tolstoy wasn't hell-bent on fleeing. All the theories which suggest that he was guided by some sort of irrational desire to flee, either from death or toward it, or that at the end of his life a romantic spirit of pilgrimage was awakened in him, a desire to visit the places of his youth, such as the Caucasus – all of these are completely unfounded, in our opinion. They do not take into consideration the most important aspect of the spiritual mood of the later Tolstoy. His exact location didn't matter to him at all. All he wanted was to be left alone with his thoughts, with his God. All he wanted was for the external conditions to be sufficiently austere that they did not rankle his conscience or divert his attention away from thoughts about God, about his imminent reunion with Him.

He was ready to live in Optina, in Shamordino, in the monastery hotel. He was ready to become a novice and do menial work. His only wish was that there might be no external violence against his soul, that they wouldn't force him to pretend, to pray and confess in a way that he did not consider it possible for him to do.

His spiritual self-absorption reaches its climax at the end of life. He no longer wishes to compromise with the external demands of life and wants to serve only that inner "I", that "Lev Tolstoy", who will be standing before God any time now.

The hut which he wanted to rent in Shamordino consisted of only two rooms, two "halves", one of which housed two women, two widows. There wasn't even a decent bed, only a cot. Yet Tolstoy agreed to this option without hesitating for a moment. When the woman from the village failed to come, he decided to settle at the hotel.

In a letter to Chertkov, written before he fled from Shamordino, he wrote: "We're going south, probably to the Caucasus. Since it's all the same to me where I am going to be, I decided to choose the south, especially since Sasha has a cough." For his daughter's unhealthy lungs, the best place to be was the Crimea, where she had recently been successfully cured of tuberculosis. It was specifically the route to the Crimea, rather than to the Caucasus, that they had initially thought about the day before, at the hotel, as they leant over Bruhl's railroad map. "We planned for the Crimea," writes Makovitsky. "We rejected the idea because there is only one way to get there, and nowhere to go once you're there. And moreover it's a resort area, and L.N. is looking for a wilderness." There we have the two requirements which L.N. had in mind for his new and, self-evidently, final place of stay. It must be a "wilderness", yet it must be possible to flee even further from this wilderness, should it become known that S.A. has decided to pursue him after all.

How will he find out for sure, though? He touched on this in that same letter to Chertkov, the final one. "The most important thing is to keep tab's, with someone's help, on what is happening at Yasnaya, and let me know once you've found out where I am, let me know by telegram, so that I might leave. A meeting with her would be horrible for me." And again we ask the question: why was he so afraid of this meeting that instead of going to the more favorable destination of Crimea, he chooses the wild Caucasus, where it would be easier to hide from his wife?

Here, besides Tolstoy's spiritual mood, it is necessary to take into account another of his fundamental character traits. Unable to endure any external violence against him, he could not stand quarrels or hysterics either. In critical domestic situations, and even more so in ones which involved arguments, he always gave in to his wife. In addition to his inherent sensitivity, this was also a manifestation of his escapism, his 'fugitive syndrome'. It was easier and simpler for him to give in than to try to prove he was in the right. It was easier to bring the row to an end with outward agreement than to stand up for himself with brutal stubbornness. During the forty-eight years he spent with S.A., he was continually giving in to her, again and again. Even in the first fifteen years of happy married life, when, as a mature and experienced man, he was educating his young wife, he admitted that his wife had a far greater influence on him than he had on her. Gradually, he conferred on her the full range of the man's rights and responsibilities. She managed Yasnaya, she took charge of disposing of the income from the works he wrote before 1881 (Chertkov did this for the later works), she hired guards for the estate, and she withstood the onslaught of her sons, who were constantly in need of money.

By making outward concessions and absolving himself of responsibility, he bought himself the right to spiritual solitude, his need for which, at the end of his life, being a philosopher, was far greater than his need to interact even with those dearest to him. He even conceded Chertkov to S.A., or rather, the possibility of interacting with him. There was one thing, though, that Tolstoy could not yield to her – that inner 'Lev Tolstoy', which he had prepared with the utmost care for a reunion with God.

Take careful note of this: the only thing that Tolstoy didn't concede to his wife during their frightful rows in the last month before his departure was his diary. On this he stood firm literally unto death, risking a heart attack.

On all other things, he was prepared to make whatever concessions were needed. And if S.A. had caught up with him – in Shamordino, in the Crimea, in the Caucasus, or on the moon – he would, of course, have returned to Yasnaya Polyana. He wouldn't have been able to put up with her tears and hysterics. And it would have been a shameful return. Besides the external absurdities (she had brought home the crazy old man who had escaped), it would have signified such colossal violence against his body and soul that it would have been far, far worse than dying during the journey.

The night before, at the hotel, Tolstoy had not firmly made up his mind to leave. Yet he and Sasha, Feokritova and Makovitsky nevertheless discussed the possibility. They spread the big blue map drawn up by the popular railway mapper Bruhl on the table. It was a wonderful guide to all the pre-revolutionary routes in Russia, which came out twice a year – in April and October. 'The Official railroad, steamship and other passenger services map' came out in two editions, a summer one and a winter one. It was cheap: it cost 85 kopecks without a hard cover and 1 ruble 15 kopecks in a binder. Despite its convenient, almost pocket-sized format, it was still able to contain two huge maps, each of which, once unfolded, covered a small table. One map showed not just Russia but the whole of Europe, South Asia and China. But the fugitives were probably interested in the second map – the more detailed one.

Having rejected the Crimea as a dead-end route, "they talked about the Caucasus, about Bessarabia. They looked at the Caucasus on the map, then at Lgov." "We didn't make up our minds on anything definitive" recalls Makovitsky. "The most likely option was Lgov, which was 28 versts from where L.F. Annenkova lived – she was a friend of L.N.'s and a kindred spirit. Lgov seemed very close to us, though – Sofia Andreyevna might make the journey..."

It appears that Sasha had also had Lgov in mind, when, as Makovitsky reports, she "retained her coachmen until morning, so that she could go with them to catch the 5-o'clock train to Sukhinichi-Bryansk." Sasha herself, however, recalling their evening vigil over the map, says that Novocherkassk was the place they had in mind. "It was proposed that we would go to Novocherkassk. In Novocherkassk we'd stay at Elena Sergeyevna Denisenko's place, try to get passports there with the help of Ivan Vasilievich and, if possible, go to Bulgaria. If that wasn't successful then we'd go on to the Caucasus, to stay with some of those who espoused father's views."

Each new alternative was as bad as the last one. It would have been impossible to hide from the reporters and from S.A. in Lgov. And this is despite the fact that Lgov was a provincial town in the back of beyond, which, according to the Brockhaus Encyclopedic Dictionary, had only a little more than five thousand inhabitants in 1895. It was about sixty versts from Kursk, on the Seym River. The estate of Leonila Fominichna Annenkova, an admirer of Tolstoy, was located twenty-eight versts from the city and, of course, Tolstoy would have been welcomed there with open arms. "What a religious woman!" Tolstoy exclaims about Annenkova in one of his letters. Annenkova had visited Tolstoy's house in Moscow a number of times, and Yasnaya Polyana too. S.A. disliked her, just as she disliked all the other "dark ones". What's more, Annenkova had been overly intimate in the attentions she had shown to Tolstoy, sending him articles which she had stitched and woven herself: warm socks, handkerchiefs, towels and a summer hat. In doing so, she had invaded S.A.'s territory. In September 1910, she visited Yasnaya for the last time and was made well aware of how serious the conflict between L.N. and S.A. was. In a letter to Tolstoy written after his departure, she urged her idol not to give in to his wife. Tolstoy replied with a sympathetic letter, as an "old friend".

If L.N. were to go and stay with Annenkova it would be a cruel blow to S.A. But Tolstoy had no intention of staying there forever. It would only have been to "get some rest". If they opted for the Sukhinichi-Bryansk railway line, though, their onward journey would have taken them to Kiev, and L.N. had no intention of going there. The only alternative, then, would be to retrace their steps and risk being caught up with by S.A. at any moment.

The other problem was that it would be impossible to reach Lgov on the Sukhinichi-Bryansk line. On Bruhl's map, Lgov was mistakenly shown as being on the Bryansk-Artakovo line, and the fugitives did not grasp this straight away.

The other problem was that this might be the very train that S.A. might take to get from Gorbacheva to Kozelsk. This was what Sasha had in mind, when she insisted on a speedy departure from Shamordino. And if everything had indeed happened like that, L.N. would almost certainly have come face to face with his wife in Kozelsk, when boarding the train on which she had come after him. As far as it was serious (at least in the minds of the fugitives) can be understood from Makovitsky's diary. When they set off in the early morning from Shamordino to Kozelsk, and it became clear that they were not going to make the 5-o'clock train, they were terribly afraid of running into S.A. along the way. Tolstoy rushed the coachman a lot, and Makovitsky proposed that they pull the hood over the coach. L.N. didn't agree to this (how shameful it would have been!), and at that point the doctor said to the coachman, "if anyone coming from the opposite direction asks who's in the coach, you're not to answer them." It was in this tense state that they drove to Kozelsk.

In order to get to Lgov, they had to go not toward Sukhinichi (to the west, the wrong direction), but to Gorbachevo (to the east) and only then to the south: to Orel-Kursk. In this case, however, their onward journey would take them to Kharkov and Simferopol, i.e. to the Crimea again, where L.N. didn't want to go. In addition, there wasn't a direct connection from Kozelsk to Kursk through Gorbachevo. They would have to wait at Gorbachevo for eight hours for a transfer, again constantly risking an encounter with S.A. at this junction station – her journey from Shchekino to Kozelsk would take her through Gorbachevo.

Thus the spiritual journey to Optina and Shamordino, via the remote town of Kozelsk, turned into a real trap for L.N.: the only way of escaping it was to go through Gorbachevo again, the town from whence they had travelled to Kozelsk, but to which, if she were to set off in pursuit of her husband, his unfortunate wife would inevitably journey.

And now, driven by fear, Tolstoy picks a route that is the fastest, in terms of the railway timetable, but also the longest in terms of geography: Kozelsk-Gorbachevo-Voronezh- Novocherkassk.

It was the inexorable laws of the Russian railways, and not a romantic love of the Caucasus, that formed the main, determining reason as to why Tolstoy decided to flee neither to the west nor to the south, but to the south-east, through the endless Don steppe.

This is why it is so ludicrous and painful to read that Tolstoy died "at a God-forsaken station". Astapovo wasn't a "God-forsaken station" at all – far from it. It was a large, junction station between Dankov and Ranenburg. If Tolstoy's illness hadn't developed so quickly and they had been able to pass quickly through Gorbachevo, Dankov, Astapovo, Bogoyavlensk, Kozlov, Gryaz, Grafskaya, and finally Voronezh, without changing trains, the way forward would lie across the empty steppes, across hundreds and hundreds of versts, to the first large village – the Cossack village of Millerovo.

The East is far from a straightforward place…

Not quite a desert

In the previous chapter, we said that in the early 1880s Tolstoy was alone in his quest. This is not entirely accurate. Tolstoy felt alone, having lost the support of the family: "… you cannot even imagine to what extent I'm alone, to what extent that which is the real *me* is despised by all around me," he wrote to Mikhail Engelhardt at the end of 1882, confessing to a young man he didn't know who had shown compassion for the way he was feeling. In reality, though, as early as the fall of 1881, just after the Tolstoys move to Moscow, people had begun to appear around him, who, although they weren't "Tolstoyans", were nonetheless kindred spirits whose company he enjoyed.

One such person was the philosopher N.F. Fyodorov, who served as a librarian at the Rumyantsev Museum. He was the same age as L.N., but even then looked like a thin, old man of small stature, who wore the same short jacket all year round. He was known as "the Socrates of Moscow". He was the epitome of the ascetic: he lived in a cramped little room at the library, sleeping on the bare boards, which he covered with his jacket, and the considerable salary he received as chief curator of the library was spent on books for the library and given away to the poor. He was timid and shy, but he burned with the inner fire of a fierce protector of world culture – especially of books. Tolstoy's son, Ilya Lvovich, on seeing him, declared that "if there are such things as saints, that is exactly how they ought to be." As a thinker, as the author of "Philosophy of the Common Task", published after his death by Peterson, and as a former teacher at Tolstoy's Yasnaya Polyana School, Nikolai Fyodorov influenced Tsiolkovsky, Vernadsky and Chizhevsky. He also influenced many Soviet writers of the 20-30s: from Andrei Platonov to Vladimir Mayakovsky. His main idea was that it was necessary to physically resurrect all the people who had died, the "generation of the fathers", using the latest breakthroughs in science. During Fyodorov's life, and also after it, this seemed like quasi-scientific utopian nonsense. Today, though, in the era of the fashion for "cloning", it does not sound so very far-fetched. In order to make room for those who were resurrected, he proposed that mankind should explore space and find places to settle there. At the end of the XIX century, this too seemed like utopian nonsense.

Tolstoy first laid eyes on N.F. Fyodorov in 1878, when he was working at the Rumyantsev library with some material about the Decembrists. In October 1881, after the first month he spent in Moscow ("... the most agonizing of my life", he complains in his diary), he met him once again and saw him in a completely different light. "Nikolai Fyodorovich is a saint," he writes in his diary on October 5. "A tiny little room. Do this please! It goes without saying. He doesn't want a salary. No bed-linen, no bed."But Tolstoy couldn't have anything in common with the "philosophy of the common cause". The very idea of the material resurrection of the "fathers" went completely against what Tolstoy was looking for in the spiritual realm. He was looking for the kingdom of God *within*, and not outside man. And Fyodorov could only be attractive to him as a man who had found the kingdom of God within himself. Tolstoy was a spiritual egomaniac, Fyodorov – a practical man with utopian ideas. For Tolstoy, the forcible returning of a person by any means other than the will of God to his sinful, earthly incarnation would not only have been wrong, but a horrific act. Finally, they had diametrically opposed interpretations of the "common cause". In Tolstoy's understanding, the "common cause" was the most natural thing of all, the thing the peasants did. Fyodorov called on people to serve a single idea, and in this respect he was a spiritual communist.

Fyodorov was delighted with *War and Peace*. Why so? "In *War and Peace*," he wrote, "Tolstoy himself resurrects his forefathers, as much as his strength allows him, putting all of his great talent into this cause and only verbally, of course." After getting to know the author of the novel, Fyodorov hoped that, whilst he might not go so far as to promote his idea of resurrecting people, he might at least continue this verbal "resurrection" of his forefathers in his creative work. "Every time he met my father," Tolstoy's eldest son Sergei Lvovich recalled, "he demanded that my father spread these ideas. He wasn't asking, but insistently demanding, and when my father expressed his refusal to do so in the gentlest of ways, he was upset, offended and unable to forgive him."

Just at this time, though, Tolstoy effects a departure from historical prose, and hides his dreams of writing "in a poetic way" deep within himself, admitting this only in letters to his wife. More than that, at this time the book culture makes him feel revulsion. On one occasion Tolstoy went to the Rumyantsev library. Fyodorov invited him to the repository, so that he could choose the books he needed himself. Tolstoy looked at the long rows of tall bookcases with glass doors, full to bursting with books, and in a soft voice said thoughtfully:

"Oh, if only we had a stick of dynamite!"

Fyodorov's indignation knew no bounds! "Always calm, good-natured and friendly, this time he was burning all over, seething and indignant," a mutual friend recalled.

The final split between them was caused by Tolstoy's article 'On Hunger', which for censorship reasons couldn't be published in Russia, but was printed in the British newspaper *The Daily Telegraph* on January 14, 1892. Tolstoy wrote this article whilst feeling dejected by scenes from the peasant famine of 1891-92, during which he and his elder children were directly involved in providing famine relief. Fyodorov was angered by the radical tone of the article, which on top of everything else had been translated into English in an anti-government spirit. Perhaps he recalled that "stick of dynamite" and decided that Tolstoy was calling for rebellion and violence against the government. G.P. Georgievsky, Head of the Department of Manuscripts at the Rumyantsev Museum, described the meeting between Tolstoy and Fyodorov after the article was published as follows:

"On seeing Tolstoy hurrying toward him, Fyodorov abruptly asked him: "What do you want?"

"Wait," Tolstoy said, "let's say hello to one another first... I haven't seen you for such a long time."

"I cannot shake your hand," said Fyodorov. "We're through."

Nikolai Fyodorovich nervously held his hands behind his back, and, moving from one side of the corridor to the other, tried to move as far away from the other man as he could.

"Explain to me, Nikolai Fyodorovich, what is the meaning of all this?" Tolstoy asked, and there were some notes of nervousness in his voice, too.

"Was it you that wrote that letter they published in *The Daily Telegraph*?"

"Yes, I wrote it."

"Aren't you aware of what feelings it is dictated by, and what it calls for? No, I have nothing in common with you whatsoever, and you can leave."

"Nikolai Fyodorovich, we are old men, let's at least say good-bye..."

But Nikolai Fyodorovich refused to do so, and Tolstoy, with visible irritation, turned around and left..."

The way Tolstoy felt about Fyodorov as a person, however, didn't change. In letters to various people he called him "dear, unforgettable," "a wonderful person", for whom he had always felt, and still felt, "the most profound respect".

Another remarkable man whom Tolstoy encountered in 1881 was the peasant philosopher-sectarian Vasily Kirillovich Syutayev. Syutayev became the first of the "dark ones", who used to visit the Tolstoys' house in Moscow and opened up a new stage in the life of this family which, much as it irritated S.A., could not now be imagined without the meddling of outsiders in everyday family life.

Unlike Fyodorov, Syutayev shared Tolstoy's views almost completely in spiritual matters, and as for the practical solutions to these problems he can even be described as Tolstoy's teacher.

A.S. Prugavin, who did some research into Russian sectarianism, left some wonderful memoirs about Syutayev, a peasant from the Novotorzhsky District, Tver Province. "In 1880," he writes, "the newspapers, quoting the *Tver Messenger*, reported that a new religious sect had come into being, known as 'Syutayevsky' after its founder, a peasant from the village of Shevelin, Vasily Kirillovich Syutayev."Prugavin made the journey to Tver province to become acquainted with the new sect and its leader. Here is how he described his outward appearance:

"... A small, frail man of fifty-five, dressed in a worn, woolen kaftan with narrow sleeves, tightly buttoned, beneath which one could just make out some blue, striped linen ports and big, heavy, clunky boots; in his hands he held the sort of cap which is usually worn by workers in the cities... A cross between reddish and flaxen, thin hair, always stuck together, always wetted with something and brushed forward onto his bulging forehead. A thin face with a pink tinge, with a thin, small nose and two hard lines running from the corners of his mouth, ending in a sharp chin, from which there stuck out a beard that was wedge-shaped, or rather, shaped like a washcloth, a small, always crumpled, pale reddish beard."

Not the most attractive appearance... And, of course, one that would have surprised any intellectual from the city. A peasant who didn't dress like a peasant, a worker who didn't dress like a worker?

We find an interesting explanation of this type in an article by another researcher of Russian sectarianism – M.V. Muratov. He calls people like Syutayev the "people's intelligentsia". "The opinion that there is one uniform Russian people is nothing more than a preconception. It would be truer to say that there are two different peoples: on the one hand, Russian society, on the other hand the mass of workers and peasants. These peoples have different lives, different ideas and even different languages: even the most ordinary newspaper articles are incomprehensible to the common peasant. But it doesn't end there: each of these peoples has its own intelligentsia, its own fighters for truth, its own heroes and martyrs."

In 1876, a case was brought against Syutayev after he was denounced because he was not going to baptize his grandson. During the interrogation, Syutayev said that he "did not plan to baptize his grandson because the Scripture says, 'Repent, and may every one of you be baptized' – but a child is not yet able to repent." One of the justices of the peace in charge of the Syutayev affair was the younger brother of the famous anarchist Mikhail Bakunin, A.A. Bakunin. The Bakunins' estate, Pryamukhino, was located in the same place, the Novotorzhsky District. So, in reality, this was a clash between two intelligentsias, the intelligentsia of the 'people' and the intelligentsia of the 'masters'.

According to Syutayev, the main thing is not to believe, but to "organize one's life", "one must watch over one's life". One must organize "life according to the truth," so as "not to do harm to one another" – that is the "law of God," which he set out to A.S. Prugavin on meeting him.

Syutayev was no ordinary sectarian. An ordinary sectarian, Muratov writes, is "neither cold, nor a hot-head". His "religious feeling is manifested with a certain degree of measure... He knows that he will be saved, knows this even when he says that no-one knows this in advance, and his soul is clear and calm." Syutayev was a sectarian-"enthusiast". "The faith of an enthusiast", writes Muratov, "on the contrary, has no boundaries. He devotes himself to it with all his heart and is always ready to consider his religious experiences as every bit as real as what he sees and hears..."

"Seek out the truth, Alexander!" he said to Prugavin as he bid him farewell. "Seek out the truth, the truth, so that everyone might live well on the land! We must find out whether the Savior will come!"

"Everything is within you and everything is now" – Syutayev's interpretation of God as being within each person was particularly close to L.N., who at the time was feeling disillusioned about all those who would be intermediaries between man and God.

Tolstoy heard about Syutayev in July 1881, when, whilst he was in the Samara Province, he met A.S. Prugavin. Prugavin told him about an unusual peasant who was preaching "love and brotherhood among all peoples and nations and complete communism of property." Tolstoy said: "All this is so interesting that I'm prepared to go and meet Syutayev at the first opportunity, to get to know him." And he wrote to his wife: "There are some smart people out there, of surprising audacity." In late September, Tolstoy set off for the Tver Province to meet Syutayev. Along the way, though – and how symbolic this is! – he stops off at Pryamukhino, to pick up that same man, Alexander Bakunin, who was in charge of Syutayev's case, to escort him. Tolstoy knew all three Bakunin brothers, Pavel (a writer), Alexander, with whom he had served in Sevastopol, and Mikhail, an anarchist, who once escaped from Siberia and fled to Paris, where the first thing he did was to order oysters and champagne; when revolutionary Dresden came under siege, he suggested that Raphael's *Madonna* should be put up on the city wall, saying that the royalists would not dare shoot at such a treasured painting.

L.N. was delighted by Syutayev and his family. There is no doubt that in the plan for a communist dormitory for his own family, which Tolstoy recorded in his diary in 1884, there were echoes of what L.N. had seen and heard in 1881.

There was no personal property in Syutayev's rather large family. The women's trunks were used by all of them. Syutayev's daughter-in-law was wearing a headscarf. "Well, what about that scarf you're wearing – is it yours?" the Count asked her. "No, indeed it isn't," said the woman, "it's not mine, it's my mother's, I don't know what I've done with mine." Syutayev took him to see an ex-soldier, to whom he had given his daughter away in marriage. "When we decided on it and gathered together in the evening, I gave them instructions on how to live, then a bed was made ready for them, we said goodnight and the fire was put out, and that was it, that was the wedding," said Syutayev.

Syutayev and his followers didn't keep icons in their homes, didn't believe in the holy relics and didn't go to church. They buried their dead wherever they liked: underground, in the open field. "They say," preached Syutayev, "that the cemetery is a hallowed place, and other places are not consecrated. This isn't true: the whole earth is sanctified, the land is the same everywhere." In earlier times, incidentally, he used to manufacture gravestones and had a shop where he sold them. But one day he stopped selling them, gave his money away and tore up the IOUs.

Syutayev renounced the right to own land, the righteousness of wars and everything that divides people. Everyone must work on commonly owned land "collectively". The masters should give the land to the peasants, and the peasants should stay with the masters out of charity. Syutayev was a Christian Communist through and through, and everything that Tolstoy later proposed to Stolypin concerning land fell pretty much within the scope of Syutayev's project. The main thing that attracted him about Syutayev's sermons, however, was the idea of *love* as a new driving force for civilization. When Syutayev renounced the oath, people said to him: "Well, what if, for example, the Turks were to capture us – what then?" "He'll take us," Syutayev replied, "when the time arrives when there is no love among us. The Turks will take us, but we'll put them on the path of love. And we will have unity, and we'll all be in consensus. And then good will be done to all and all will be well."

Again – in Tolstoy's sermons that is fundamentally new in comparison with Syutayev's simple idea. Do not resist evil by evil, offer love to evil and evil will cease to be evil. God, in the soul of each person, will tell us the route to universal unity in love, all we need do is refrain from interfering with God.

In Syutayev, Tolstoy was shocked by the fact that all the thoughts at which he had arrived via a difficult and painful path, as set out in *Confessions*, sounded as simple and obvious from the lips of this peasant from Tver as two times two. The main thing was that Syutayev was a perfect match for the form of Russian peasant that Tolstoy would have liked to see in the peasant populace, and for whom he begins to search in the early 80s. If in the city he not only sees, but also actively seeks out every possible evil and injustice, if in the countryside he sees (and searches for) this evil and injustice in everything that stems from ownership of land by the nobility, from "aristocratic luxury", then in the deepest depths of the country he dreams of finding a pearl-like grain of truth, which in and of itself might embody a specific type or national character.

At the end of January 1882 Syutayev pays a return visit to Moscow. He stays at the Tolstoys' house on Denezhny Street and through his speeches, but even more so through his exotic appearance, manages to attract high-society guests to the house. In Moscow, a real craze forms over him. Photographs of him are sold at the Avanzo art salon on the Kuznetsky Bridge. Repin paints a portrait of him. This painting, called *The Sectarian*, was acquired by Pavel Tretyakov, on Tolstoy's recommendation. L.N.'s sister, Maria Nikolayevna, also takes an interest in Syutayev, and even meets him.

At this time, Tolstoy is actively involved in putting census data about the population of Moscow into tables – he chose one of the lushest neighborhoods, along Protochny Pereulok between the Beregovy passage and Nikolsky Pereulok. He writes an article, 'On The Census in Moscow' and calls on society to provide charity for the downtrodden. Syutayev doesn't support it. He proposes a different plan for eradicating poverty.

"Let's divide them up between us. I'm not rich, but I'll take two right now. Another ten people will take the same number – and eventually we'll house all of them. You will take some, and I'll take some. We'll go and work together, too – he will be able to see how I work, to learn how to live, and we'll sit down together at the same table, and he'll hear what I have to say and what you have to say. Now that is charity."

It hardly needs saying that Syutayev's appearance did not please S.A. Just at the time when her husband was starting to "move away" from the family, people who were strangers and were clearly dangerous, and whom she described as "the dark ones", had begun to appear in their home.

But what did she mean when she described them as "dark"?

"Yes, they were indeed dark people as far as I was concerned," S.A. later recalled, "about whom one often knows absolutely nothing, neither who they are, nor where they come from, nor who their parents are, where their homeland is, or what they want. And my family's life suffered because of them, and I avoided them and was afraid of them."

There were other people as well who responded to Tolstoy's new spiritual aspirations. There was Vladimir Fyodorovich Orlov, for example. The son of a village priest from the Vladimir Province, a former adherent of Nechayev who had spent two years in prison before being acquitted, Vladimir Orlov worked as a teacher at a railroad school outside Moscow. He was very close to Tolstoy, both in terms of his spiritual quest and in the books he liked to read. He pleased L.N. as a person of stamina and patience in the face of hardship and suffering, although he was not without flaws, such as his fondness for drink, the classic Russian flaw. He used to visit the Tolstoys' home in Moscow and stay overnight, and L.N. happily wrote in his diary about how he had personally prepared Orlov's bed and even brought him a chamber pot. This was the care and concern one might have for a brother, a *little brother*, a concern that had something monastic or sectarian about it, something akin to the "washing of the feet", which would inevitably have been painful for the family to behold and yet at the same time seemed quite natural to L.N. Another person who was close to Tolstoy was the resident tutor Vasily Ivanovich Alexeyev, who left some interesting recollections for posterity.

Tolstoy was bound by a deep attachment to Prince Leonid Dmitrievich Urusov, "the first Tolstoyan" as L.N.'s son Sergei Lvovich dubbed him. Urusov, who served as Vice-Governor of Tula, in contrast to the "dark ones", was a close friend of the Tolstoy family. S.A. became friends with him and even made him the hero of her short story, *Who's to blame?* Prince Urusov was delighted by L.N.'s religious writings. He translated his treatise, *What I Believe*, and *The Prince was Loved by the Children, and Even the Servants* into French (and helped to get them published in Paris), recalls S.A.

Impossible Tolstoy

Shortly before Tolstoy's spiritual upheaval, his wife had a terrible dream, which she recounted to Alexandrine:

"She saw herself standing outside the Cathedral of the Savior, not yet finished in those days; in front of the cathedral doors stood a huge cross, and on it was the crucified Christ, still alive... Suddenly this cross began to move, and, after completing three laps of the church, stopped in front of her, Sofia Andreyevna... The Savior glanced at her – and, raising his hand, pointed at a gold cross, which was already gleaming on the cathedral's cupola." "The clashes with Levochka have become more frequent," she complains to her sister – "I even felt a desire to leave home. I am sure it is because we have begun to live *the Christian life*. But I think that before, when we were without Christianity, it was a lot better." This frank admission accurately reflects S.A.'s religious consciousness. When faced with Christianity of that sort, she'd far rather do without it altogether!

One can't say that SA was completely deaf and indifferent to the religious needs of her husband. She was brought up in an Orthodox family, after all. A family, what's more, with ties to the court, albeit from a distance. Her father was a court physician, let's not forget. For S.A., Orthodoxy was what it was in Russia in the 19th century – a connection between religion and the state. So when her husband turned out to be a religious dissident, this frightened her infinitely more than if he had been an atheist, but been loyal to the monarchy.

For a while she tried not to reveal the differences of opinion between her and her husband, and even in letters to her sister, managed not to air their dirty laundry in public. "Lev is very calm, he is working, writing articles of some sort; occasionally he bursts into speeches decrying city life and *lordly* life in general. This hurts me sometimes, but I know that he can't be any other way. He is a leader among men, he is walking ahead of the crowd and pointing the way that the people should go. And I am the crowd, I live with the movement of the crowd, along with the crowd I see the light of the lantern which is carried by any leader and by Levochka, of course, also, and I admit that it is *light*, but I cannot go faster; the crowd is pushing me, and so are the surroundings, and my habits. I can picture you laughing at my *in the highest degree* words, as the children like to say, but this will clarify it for you a little as to how we relate to each other."

One day, though, she makes a fatal mistake. Whilst copying out her husband's religious work, *A Critique of Dogmatic Theology*, in her room, she can't hold back the rising feelings of protest within her, and takes the manuscript back to L.N.'s study, putting it down on the table and refusing to copy it out. She is effectively refusing to be his assistant any more, after fifteen years of creative collaboration in which there has been tenderness and gratitude on both sides. Her motivation for this decision is remarkable! She tells L.N. that she gets "too anxious" when she copies it out.

If she's "anxious", does that mean she understands?

A Critique of Dogmatic Theology is Tolstoy's earliest religious work, along with *Confession*; he began writing it back in 1879. And it was the most destructive of his works, in relation not only to the Orthodox faith, but to the entire Church-based interpretation of Christianity. In terms of its destructive power, *Criticism*... can only be compared to Nietzsche's *Antichrist*, which subjected Christianity itself to a merciless analysis. But what Tolstoy is doing is defending Christianity. However, he does it in such a way as not to leave any stone unturned in the thousand-year tradition of teachings by the church fathers.

What prompted the article was a book by the Moscow Metropolitan Macarius (Bulgakov), *Orthodox Dogmatic Theology*, published in Russia and in mass circulation as the main textbook for spiritual training. As he analyzes Macarius's textbook, Tolstoy consistently overturns all the cornerstones of the Christian faith: the Trinity, the divinity of Jesus, the story of the Fall of man, redemption through the sufferings of Jesus, the rite of communion, etc. In fact, the article is not a criticism of a specific book, but a negation of the entire history of church-centered Christianity, which, under Tolstoy's pen, turns into a terrible drama, now of naive delusion, now of deliberate fraud.

The redeeming feature of this article it's the childish view of things. What does it mean to say that God is "three in one"? After all, one isn't equal to three. And why is there such a complicated formula for the One God? Why did God forbid Adam and Eve to eat the fruit from the tree of knowledge of good and evil? Did He want people to be like animals, or something? God promised the first people that they would die if they ate from this tree. But this didn't happen. Does this mean that God lied?

To argue with Tolstoy is just like arguing with a child who shouts out that the king is naked. If the king isn't naked, the child should just shut his mouth. And if he is naked, you just have to agree with the child.

"The Orthodox Church?" asks Tolstoy. "I cannot now connect any other concept to this word now, other than a few people who have let their hair grow long, who are very arrogant, misguided and uneducated, dressed in silk and velvet, with diamond panagias, and known as bishops and archbishops, and thousands of other long-haired people who are obscenely servile to these few dozen people, whose job it is, under the guise of carrying out sacraments of some sort, to cheat and rob people. How can I believe in this church and believe it when, in response to the deepest questions about one's soul, it responds with pathetic lies and absurdities, and even claims that no one should dare answer these questions in a different way, that in everything which is most precious in my life, I should not dare to be guided by anything else other than its instructions. I can choose the color of my pants, I can choose a wife, I can build a house to my taste, but in everything else, in the very thing in which I feel myself to be a man, in all that I have to ask for instruction from them – those idle, cheating, ignorant people. In my life, in my shrine, I have a guide – a shepherd, my parish priest, who graduated from the seminary, who goes around in a stupor, a semi-literate boy or drunken old man, whose only concern is to collect as many eggs and kopecks as he can. They decree that, during prayers, the Deacon should spend half the time shouting about the harlot Catherine II, who was Orthodox and pious for so long, or that pious rogue, the murderer Peter, who blasphemed against the Gospel, and I have to pray about it. They are ordered to curse and burn and hang my brothers and I have to yell anathema at them; they decree that I should consider my brothers as damned, and I scream anathema. I am told to go and drink wine out of a teaspoon, and swear that this is not wine, but the body and blood, and I have to do it.

But this is horrible!"

In Tolstoy's words, the church exists only for the "feeble-minded", "rogues" and "for women". It's not surprising this article "bothered" S.A. so much.

She knew her husband well. She knew that the snooty, impossible tone of the article didn't reflect L.N.'s true attitude toward Orthodoxy, the clergy, particularly the rank and file, and even more so to popular church-based faith. The target and at the same time the recipient of the article could only be the higher clergy and the government, which her husband made fun of just like a teenager. She knew that side of his character all too well, one that was so characteristic of the entire Tolstoy clan. The sharpness of Tolstoy's statements and his "fickle judgments" frightened her even before the marriage. What must it have been like for her to discover that after almost twenty years of marriage, that old yeast had fermented in her husband?

Ultimately, S.A. simply got scared. Unfortunately, her husband's spiritual upheaval comes at a time when the family has reached its upper limit and has nine (!) children. S.A.'s maternal feelings were uncommonly developed, and Tolstoy himself thought highly of them. Meanwhile, beginning in the spring of 1881, after Tolstoy's letter to Alexander III, the issue of L.N.'s conflict with Russia's chief ideologue – Pobedonostsev – rears its head. Pobedonostsev is the umbilical cord of state and spiritual power. And he made his attitude toward the "new" Tolstoy clear immediately and unequivocally, when he decided that it wasn't even necessary to pass the letter on to Alexander. His attitude toward the sectarian movement was also very clearly expressed in his decision to exile "without the right to return" the retired Colonel Vasily Pashkov – the founder of the "Pashkovite" sect –in 1884.

By the beginning of the '80s, S.A. was not a high-society lady. She was a provincial landowner, a noble lady. However, thanks to her open and confident character, experience in interacting with society people and even with the powers that be was something that S.A. acquired fairly quickly. In 1885, she met Pobedonostsev, whilst trying to defend her right to print Tolstoy's banned articles *What I Believe* and *What Then Must Be Done?* in his collected works, which she wanted to publish.

By going to meet Pobedonostsev, S.A. was trying to kill not two, but three birds with one stone. She was showing her husband that she felt sympathy for his new views, she was trying to turn his new works into a source of income for the family and at the same time to remove the "dissident" stigma from them, for not a single moral censor would dare to ban anything to which Pobedonostsev had given the green light. Pobedonostsev refused Tolstoy's wife request without a moment's hesitation. But the mere fact that she had a personal meeting with him, which took place in a polite and even sympathetic atmosphere, could not fail to appease S.A. She later looked back on this visit with pride.

In *My Life*, she relates the conversation she had with Pobedonostsev: "I have to tell you that I am very sorry for you, I knew you as a child, loved and respected your father very much, and I consider it a misfortune to be the wife of such a person."- "This is new to me," I replied. "Not only do I consider myself fortunate, but everyone is jealous of me because I am the wife of such a talented and intelligent man." "I must tell you," Pobedonostsev said, "that I don't even profess to see any great intelligence in your husband. Intelligence is harmony; your husband is all extremes and edges."

"Maybe," I replied. "But Schopenhauer said that intelligence is a lantern which a person carries in front of him, whereas *genius* is the sun, which shines brighter than everything else."Tolstoy was indifferent about his wife's meeting with Pobedonostsev, and if anything was hostile to the idea. This was not at all the sort of thing he expected of her. He wanted her to share his new beliefs, but not to try to smooth over the inevitable conflict between him and the government. He needed a companion, not a lawyer.

In December 1885, when he departs for a visit to the Olsufyevs' estate, Nikolsky-Obolyaninovo, 60 versts from Moscow, where he often escaped from the bustle of city life and enjoyed sojourns as an honored guest, L.N. leaves a lengthy letter to S.A. at their home in Moscow. She read it and then, picking up her husband's archive, made a note at the beginning: "A letter by Lev Nikolayevich to his wife, which he neither gave her nor sent to her." This letter is a cry of the soul! It breaks off on a terrible line: "There is a struggle to the death between us – Godly or not godly." This letter isn't addressed to S.A. alone, but to the whole family, which L.N. once again wants to leave.

"What has already happened so many times has happened again," S.A. writes to her sister. "Levochka came home in a very nervous and gloomy mood. I'm sitting there writing, he comes in, I look at him – there's a terrible expression on his face. Until then, we got on wonderfully, not a bad word was said, well, absolutely nothing. 'I came to tell you that I want to get divorced, I can't live like this, I'm going to Paris or to America.' You understand, Tanya, if the whole house came down on my head, I wouldn't be as surprised as I was then. I ask in amazement, 'What happened?' 'Nothing, but if you keep piling more and more into the cart, the horse will stop and won't pull it.' As for what was being piled in – I know not. But then the shouting started, the accusations, coarse words, everything got worse and worse, and in the end I just put up with it, I put up with it, I barely said anything at all in response, I see that the man before me is crazy, and when he said, "wherever you are, the air is infected," I ordered that the trunk be brought in and began to pack my things. I wanted to come and see you, if only for a few days.

The children came running in, roaring. Tanya says, 'I'll go with you, what's this about?' He began to beg, 'Stay'. I stayed, but suddenly he began sobbing hysterically, it was simply horrible; think of it: Levochka – all shaking and jerking with sobs. At that point I felt sorry for him, the four children – Tanya, Ilya, Lyolya and Masha – all roaring, shouting. It was as if I had lockjaw, I couldn't talk or cry, all I wanted was to talk nonsense, and I'm afraid of this and kept quiet and am silent for three hours, do as you like, kill me – I cannot speak. That's how it ended. But the anguish, sorrow, tears, a painful condition, alienation – all this is left in me. You know, I often ask myself to distraction: well, what's it for this time? I don't step outside the house, I work with the edition until three in the morning, in silence, I so loved everyone and remembered that time like no other, and for what?"

Tolstoy's hysterics cannot be explained in any other way than by the fact that the irritation that had accumulated within him over the days, weeks and months suddenly and for no apparent reason came flooding out. Had he argued with his wife every day, even that would have been easier to bear. But that wasn't in Tolstoy's nature. As he departs with his daughter Tanya, after the hysterics, for Nikolskoye-Obolyaninovo, "in a tiny sled", he tries to explain the reason for his "madness" in a letter.

"Imagine that I were to chance upon your diary, in which you express your sincere feelings and thoughts, all your motives for this or that activity, how interested I'd be to read it all. As for all my works, which have been nothing other than my life itself, have been and continue to be of such little interest to you, that you'll read them merely out of curiosity, as a literary work, should you chance upon them; and as for the children, they aren't even interested in reading them at all. You think that I exist in my own right, but it is my writings that exist in their own right.

My writings are my whole self. In life I couldn't express my views fully, in life I make concessions to the need to live together as a family; I live and in my soul I renounce all of this life, and this life – this one that isn't mine – you consider to be my life, whereas my life, as expressed in writing, you believe to be mere words, devoid of a reality of their own."

The "writings" in question are Tolstoy's spiritual works after the upheaval: *Confession, Critique of Dogmatic Theology, What I Believe, Connection, Translation and Study of the Four Gospels*. And also the poignant article, *What Then Must Be Done?*, the end of which he was working on in 1885. In this article, which describes the appalling state of European civilization, in which a caste of "educated" people cynically exploit the hard work of millions of "uneducated" people, Tolstoy gives his verdict the entire political and economic development of the world. This article was the culmination of the renunciation by Tolstoy of the life of the educated classes, and those of the nobility and the clergy and figures from science and the arts. All of them, in his opinion, were parasites on the body of the nation, "freeloaders", and the only way out for any of the representatives of these classes was to take a fearless look at their situation and attempt to live on new bases, rejecting property, excessive amounts of money and all caste privileges, and earning their daily bread through menial labor. Should this not happen, Tolstoy predicts a revolution:

"...we are only just keeping our tiny boat afloat on the sea, which is already raging and inundating us, and might at any moment angrily swallow us up and consume us. A workers' revolution, with the horrors of destruction and murders, not only threatens us, but is something we have been living in for 30 years already, and only deferring the moment when it breaks out for the time being, by means of various cunning tricks."

The finale to this article is remarkable. In it, he addresses women who are mothers. It is these women, even the ones from the privileged classes, who know what hard work it is to give birth to, feed and bring up children. Tolstoy appeals to their natural inner sense of duty and justice; in them he sees the light of a new, unifying humanity.

But this finale is the least convincing part. He doesn't account for the natural selfishness of mothers when it comes to the interests of their families. No normal mother would wish hard work and deprivations on their children, the path to which Tolstoy was calling them. One would have thought that the experience of living with S.A. ought to have forced Tolstoy to question the correctness of the chosen target for his spiritual propaganda. On the other hand, when reading this finale, it is impossible not to realize that, whilst appealing to women-mothers in general, Tolstoy had a specific person in mind. That person was his wife.

"Such an (ideal – P.B.) mother *gives birth by herself*, she *feeds* them herself, she will, above all else, feed and cook food for the children, and sew, and wash, and teach her children, and sleep with and talk to them, because it is in this that she sees her role in life to be. Only a mother such as this wouldn't seek for her children security from without, in her husband's money, in her children's diplomas, but would encourage in them that same ability to perform God's will selflessly that she knows she has herself, the ability to bear hard work despite the costs and danger of life, because she knows that therein – in this single security – lies all that is good in life. Such a mother would not ask others what to do – she will know everything and fear nothing."

The conflict between L.N. and S.A. had deep and ancient roots. We encounter this same conflict in Gogol's *Taras Bulba*. It is the conflict between *the mother and the father*. The father, like Abraham, is aware of values that are higher than his child's life, and is willing to sacrifice his son for these values. It doesn't matter what these values are: God, "Cossack comradeship" or "good", "the business of life", as Tolstoy understood Christianity. It is important that in this matter, no mother would *naturally* take the father's side.

In December 1885, Tolstoy tries to leave the family, and on January 18th of the following year, Tolstoy's youngest son, Alyosha, dies at the age of four. He dies in Moscow, which raises the question: where to bury him? At the cemetery of the Devichy Monastery, the price quoted is outrageous – 200 silver rubles. The problem there, however, isn't so much the money, but the fact that there are too many graves, "one on top of the other," as S.A. writes to her sister.

In the end, she chooses a cemetery herself, the new one near Pokrovsky, where she had spent her summers as a child, on the high bank of the Khimka River. "Today," she writes to her sister, "we loaded the little coffin into our big sleigh, in which I just recently took him to the Zoo, and the monkey theater; the nanny and I took our places... We arrived; a priest met us there and a few local people... They found out that I was the daughter of Andrei Evstafevich Behrs, and I was surrounded by such an atmosphere of love, sympathy, happy memories of father, that I understood what a good man he was, and I was pleased. Everyone helped carry the coffin; all of them did so tenderly, carefully, like a loving woman (though in fact they were all men), and they showed concern for my grief, and dealt with the little coffin and with covering the little grave, made promises to remember the baby, and to take care of the grave and pray at the grave."

Her husband is not mentioned in the description of the funeral. There is a brief mention of him later: "Levochka is haggard, thin and very sad." In January 1886, Tolstoy is intensively engaged in Buddhism. He wants to set out Buddha's teachings in a book for the people. "I would like, with God's help, to create this little book," he writes to a *friend* on January 17. And in his next letter to the *friend*, he writes about his son's death: "That which left Alyosha's body, left it, and is not that which was united with God. We cannot know whether it was united, or remained what it was, without its prior connection with Alyosha. And even that is not as it should be. One cannot talk about such things. I only know that the death of a child, which seemed strange and cruel to me before, now seems both reasonable and a good thing to me." What is left after Alyosha, the child's dead body, was taken away on a sled by S.A. and the nanny. L.N. is utterly indifferent to this "subject". He's wrapped up in his thoughts and feelings, somewhere far away. And this is the very sphere which he cannot discuss with his wife. Yet he feels able to discuss it with his new and infinitely loyal *dear friend*.

The Brilliant Cavalryman

The most influential figure in Tolstoy's inner circle of friends, from the mid-80s and right up to the writer's death, was his "spiritual executor" Vladimir Grigorievich Chertkov (1854-1936).

A complex individual. It's impossible not to respect him. Yet it's difficult to sympathize with him. It's impossible not to appreciate the huge contribution he made to the preservation and systematization of Tolstoy's legacy after 1880, and above all Chertkov's "baby", an academic Jubilee Collection of the writer's works, letters and diaries, remains unsurpassed to this day. His role in the last thirty years of Tolstoy's life is so great and complex that it's impossible to imagine Tolstoy without Chertkov, just as it's impossible to imagine him without S.A. In Tolstoy's life, he was the second most important person after the writer's wife, and fans of Chertkov believed he was the most important. At the same time, it's impossible to trace his influence on the Tolstoys' family life, in which Chertkov played a very bleak role, without a degree of mental anguish and at times disgust.

The real mystery of Chertkov is not to be found in the man himself, though. Ultimately, he was just the most loyal and consistent supporter of the later Tolstoy. He devoted his entire life to the genius, subordinating every day of it to serving the man whom he regarded as a new Buddha, Christ and Muhammad. For this purpose he gave up a brilliant career, the possibility of an idle and well-to-do existence, and indeed the possibility of having a private life. A smart, energetic, educated and talented man, a man who was handsome both in his youth and his later years, a true aristocrat, an intellectual through and through, Chertkov voluntarily took on the role of the first disciple and cell-attendant of the great elder. And he did this not when the glory of Tolstoy as a teacher was at its zenith, but when Tolstoy's relatives and friends considered his views to be merely a passing fad or some kind of insanity.

The character of Chertkov himself is debatable. He remained a man of his time, a "leftist" in political opinion. He was more decisively anti-clerical than Tolstoy, a vegetarian on principle and an opponent of the idea of killing any living creature, including flies and mosquitoes. The powerful title of an anti-hunting article that he wrote, *An Evil Pastime*, suggests he was one of the forerunners of the modern 'green' movement. He was a caring father and a devoted husband. Yet for all his 'Tolstoyanism', his aristocratic habits remained with him till his dying day. His mansion in England during his period of forced emigration was far bigger and more comfortable than the home of his teacher in Yasnaya Polyana. And his house in Telyatinki, near the Tolstoys' Estate, was better and more expensive than Tolstoy's home. Even after the revolution, Chertkov attended the funeral of Sergei Yesenin, whose last wife was Tolstoy's granddaughter, with a servant in tow.

Chertkov was a man of extensive "connections", from representatives of the highest aristocratic circles in Russia and England to Bolshevik 'illegals' like Bonch-Bruyevich. Yet this apparently dubious circumstance was the very thing that enabled him to release and distribute Tolstoy's works before and after the revolution. This circumstance helped him after the revolution to get the 'Tolstoyans' and Tolstoy's daughter Sasha out of prison after the revolution. The letter he wrote to Stalin during the years when the 'Tolstoyans' were being persecuted is the perfect testimony to the conscience and courage of this man.

The role he played in the Tolstoys' family conflict was incomprehensible and mysterious. Here the figure of Chertkov unwittingly acquires a demonic character, in keeping with his surname (*chert* or чёрт is the Russian word for *devil*). Here, he isn't just a man, a companion, a translator, publisher, collector, but some kind of devil, who, as if on purpose, is around L.N. and C.A. at a time when his presence wasn't necessary, when he ought to have stood aside and allowed the spouses and their children to deal with their family affairs by themselves.

Of course, it was here that the negative side of Chertkov's nature manifested itself, with his exaggerated view of his importance near the "body" of Tolstoy. But this was characteristic of all the early pupils and cell-attendants. How Tolstoy himself perceived this is a mystery, perhaps one that cannot be solved. The riddle isn't Chertkov, but the teacher himself, in his attitude toward his first student.

In the end, Chertkov, by his presence in Tolstoy's life simply brought many of the secrets in L.N.'s relations with his family, and especially his wife, to light. If Chertkov hadn't been there, these secrets might not have become apparent or might have become apparent in other ways. Be that as it may, Chertkov was not, of course, the main reason as to why Tolstoy left his family. He instigated this departure, he was infinitely glad when it happened. But he wasn't the main propelling force behind this event.

"If Chertkov hadn't existed, he would have to have been invented." The story of Tolstoy's friendship with Chertkov is set forth in a detailed book by M.V. Muratov entitled *L.N. Tolstoy and V.G. Chertkov: Through Their Correspondence*. Published in 1934 by the Tolstoy Museum, it was not reprinted in Russia.

The first time Tolstoy heard about Chertkov was at Yasnaya Polyana, from his follower G.A. Rusanov, in August 1883. By that time, the "new" Tolstoy already had a number of followers. In October of the same year, they became acquainted in Tolstoy's Moscow home. Thenceforward, notes Muratov, "Tolstoy wrote to Chertkov more often than to anyone else, not only among his friends, but also among his family members." We know of 931 letters, including a telegram, that L.N. wrote to him. Five volumes and more than 175 printed pages were required for the publication of Tolstoy's letters to Chertkov, with commentary. Chertkov wrote to Tolstoy even more frequently, at times sending him letters with many pages.

Chertkov's first appearance at the Tolstoys' house didn't seem to foretell any danger for the family. "A brilliant horse guardsman, wearing a helmet with a double-headed eagle, handsome, son of the richest and noble family, Vladimir Grigorievich came to see Tolstoy, to tell him that he fully shared his views and wished to devote his life to them forever," Tolstoy's son Lev Lvovich recalled. "At the beginning of his acquaintance with our family, Chertkov was charming. Everyone liked him. I was close to him and on familiar terms."

There is a mistake in this recollection. In the autumn of 1883 Chertkov couldn't possibly have wanted to devote his entire life to Tolstoy's views. He first heard about these views only in July 1883, at the wedding of his friend R.A. Pisarev, from the Prosecutor of the Tula District Court, N.V. Davydov. Having spoken to Davydov, Chertkov, the twenty-nine year old officer, told him about his views, which by that time were already fairly well-formed. After listening to the strange guardsman, Davydov observed:

"Why, Tolstoy says precisely the same thing! You seem to be repeating Tolstoy's words – you absolutely must meet Tolstoy."

Davydov was acquainted with L.N. and promised to set up a meeting. In late October, Chertkov travels to Moscow specifically for this purpose, stays at the Slavyansky Bazaar Hotel, and eventually receives a telegram from Davydov: "Tolstoy is in Moscow".

The first time he set off to meet Tolstoy, Chertkov still knew nothing about his "teachings". In fact this "teaching", as such, did not yet exist. But the spiritual upheaval had already occurred within Tolstoy, and this upheaval chimed with what was going on in Chertkov's soul. Both of them were shocked by their discovery of a terrible contradiction between Christ's truth and the falsehood of modern life.

Their meeting took place in the study. They went into the "solitary, peaceful and bright room with windows overlooking the garden and the courtyard and long, green, woolen curtains which were drawn, with simple, soft black armchairs and a large writing desk, on which there were two towering candles in ancient brass candlesticks, along with a brass inkwell on a green malachite base and a pile of paper..."

Chertkov had not yet read Tolstoy's philosophical works, only his artistic ones. He therefore decided to test him first.

In the presence of this former military officer and defender of Sevastopol, the author of *Sevastopol Stories* and *War and Peace*, he began to talk about his negative attitude toward military service. Tolstoy "in response began to read to me from the manuscript of *What I Believe*, which lay on his desk," recalled Chertkov, and he "felt such joy from knowing that the period of my spiritual loneliness had finally stopped, that, lost in my own thoughts, I couldn't follow the passages he read to me after that, and only came to my senses when, having read the last lines of his book, he read out with particularly clear emphasis the words of the signature: 'Lev Tolstoy'."

A distinctive feature of Chertkov was that from the very beginning, he always "got" Tolstoy's state of mind with precision. It was late 1883. Tolstoy's first attempt to leave his family was just a few months away. S.A. is wearing herself out attending balls and the children's plays. Their eldest son is passionate about the natural sciences and the student movement. And no-one in the house wants to take Tolstoy's new writings seriously.

Chertkov doesn't just listen to him, though. His soul resonates with every word. He is much younger than Tolstoy, but they have been through similar life experiences. Chertkov is also a landowner and an officer. Not only is he equal to L.N. on the social ladder. He stands above him. He's rich, high-born, and ready to give up everything. And Tolstoy sees, in this young man, his own self from twenty years previously. But a version of himself that didn't make mistakes in life, didn't go on a false path.

There is a portrait of V.G. Chertkov that was painted by Ilya Repin in 1885. In it we see the visible embodiment of Konstantin Levin. A soft beard, big, intelligent, deep eyes. There was softness in every feature of this noble and intelligent person, but what a will as well – a benevolent will!

Chertkov was born into a noble and wealthy family. His mother, Elizaveta Ivanovna Chertkova, née Countess Chernyshev-Kruglikova, was a very influential woman in aristocratic circles in St. Petersburg. She was known in high society for her intelligence, beauty and authoritativeness. Her uncle, Count Zakhar Chernyshev, was a Decembrist who was exiled to Siberia. Her aunt was married to another Decembrist, Nikita Muravyov, and followed her husband into exile. She was brought out early into society, and at the first court ball Nicholas I asked the young beauty a speculative question about her uncle. She boldly replied to the tsar that she maintained the most cordial relations with her uncle. As a result, she was respected at court. Alexander II and Alexander III used to visit her and her husband on informal terms, without any guards. But when she was asked to become a lady-in-waiting, she refused. A few years after her marriage, she abandoned social life altogether, finding herself in religion and becoming a follower of the preacher Lord Radstock, who was fashionable at that time. Her sister's husband, incidentally, was Colonel Pashkov, whom she introduced to Radstock, thereby playing a role in the emergence of the 'Pashkovite' sect in Russia.

Elizaveta Ivanovna not only loved her son, but adored him. Her eldest and youngest sons, Grisha and Mikhail, died early, four years apart. The middle son became the idol of the family. Everyone took his will into account, everyone tried to please him.

Chertkov's father, Grigorii, served as aide-de-camp under Nicholas I and adjutant-general under Alexander II. In military circles, he was known for having the kind of special knowledge of military service which only officers who had begun their careers in the Guard under Nicholas could have. He worked his way up from regimental commander to head of a division. He was the author of the *Soldier's Instructional Booklet*, which was distributed among the troops. After having both legs amputated when they became gangrenous, he spent the last ten years of his life heading a Committee on the Ordering and Formation of Troops.

His sister was married to Count Shuvalov, the most conservative ideologue from the era of Alexander II. His brother, Mikhail Chertkov, served as Ataman of the Don Cossack Army, and then as Governor-General of Kiev and Warsaw.

The Chertkovs' permanent residence was in St. Petersburg, but they had vast areas of land in the southern part of the Voronezh Province: 30,000 desyatins.

There is a watercolor portrait by Delacroix from 1860, depicting Elizaveta Ivanovna Chertkova with her six-year-old son Volodya. She is dressed in a long velvet dress, which trails along the ground. The boy is a little angel dressed in trousers, patent leather boots and a round hat. His pose is interesting: with his powerful right hand he holds on to his mother by the pleats of her dress, and with his left he seems to be either showing her the right way to go or asking "what's that over there?..."

A distinctive feature of Chertkov's education was the fact that he grew up in a very religious atmosphere. The main "point" of Radstock's doctrine was the exclusive belief in the divinity of Christ, the power of the atonement of mankind's sins through His blood. By the time of his acquaintance with Tolstoy, Chertkov was susceptible to the influence of this faith and the 'Pashkovite' sect. Then, under Tolstoy's influence, he rejected it, but sectarian sentiments persisted in him for life. Just as his mother had been, he was prone to proselytism, obsessed with an ardent desire to "convert" the unfortunate and misguided to his beliefs.

In this respect he differed from Tolstoy, who had never been a sectarian. Any sense of belonging to a party, with its own "secrets" and "passwords", with a strict division of people into "us" and "them" and at the same time an unbridled desire to promote their own point of view, which is the only correct one, was alien to him. Tolstoy believed in man's inner spiritual resources; to be an "idol" for the "devoted" was the last thing he wanted. Compared to L.N., Chertkov was narrow, dogmatic and prone to indoctrination. But above all, he didn't tolerate inconsistencies in people's views and actions. The two most pejorative words in his vocabulary were "evade" and "shirk". He thought it undignified to shy away from the questions that arose before a person. And if he felt that someone was refusing to address these issues, he was prepared to force him to make that decision, come what may.

Chertkov's childhood was the childhood of an aristocratic baron's son: an English nanny, governesses, home schooling, lest, God forbid, he might get sick at school. His youth is very reminiscent of that of the young protagonist of *Father Sergius*, Prince Kasatsky. The only difference is that Kasatsky, just like the young Tolstoy, was not from the *crème de la crème* of St. Petersburg society and suffered as a result, tormented by vanity. Chertkov himself, by virtue of the circumstances of his birth, was spared from this vice. He didn't suffer from the complex of the poor nobleman who has no ties with which to establish himself in the world. He was very handsome – slim, slender, a head taller than other people, with large gray eyes under arched eyebrows. He was witty and loved paradoxes. He had a soft, deep voice and an infectious laugh. He was truthful and sometimes too direct. His wallet was always open to his friends. Whilst serving in the Guard, Chertkov caroused in St. Petersburg, played roulette, kept mistresses. "As a twenty-year-old Guards officer" wrote Chertkov, "I burned through my life as if there was no tomorrow." Among the duties of Guards officers were tours of duty at the hospital. In 1877 (the year in which Tolstoy's spiritual crisis began), Chertkov suffers a shock at the sight of a dying soldier; the two men read the Gospel out loud together. From that moment on, he cannot live as he did before. He cannot serve in the army, and he simply *cannot live*. How similar this is to what happens with Tolstoy, only in his fifties! When Chertkov came to him, Tolstoy, undoubtedly, must have felt jealous of the young cavalryman, who at the same time as him, had turned onto the path of truth, but was still full of physical strength, with unspent energy and plenty of time ahead of him.

This was also what predetermined L.N.'s strange dependency, as it seems to have been at first glance, on Chertkov. At first, however, the intimacy of his relationship with his "dear friend" (as Tolstoy addresses Chertkov from the first letter onwards), slightly alarms L.N. himself. He clearly doesn't warm to the idea of assuming full spiritual responsibility, as the elders do in the monasteries, for a strange young cavalryman. Tolstoy doesn't like this idea, but he can't refuse Chertkov and does not want to, because the first time he meets him, he falls under the spell of this amazing young officer, who is so like him. Meanwhile Chertkov needs Tolstoy and does not hide it. He sends to his house in Moscow not only the books he is reading, but also his diaries. Eventually he invites Tolstoy to Lizinovka.

The nuance of the invitation was the fact that in Lizinovka, Chertkov was to introduce him to three young peasants willing to share his views. But does he have the right to such spiritual guidance?

"No, Lev Nikolayevich, come, set them at ease, help them. You are needed here."

This sentence – *you are needed here* – becomes the recurring theme of the complex musical score which Chertkov begins to play in the Tolstoy family. Indeed, we might ask, where is Tolstoy needed more – in the family that doesn't understand him, doesn't appreciate his new works, or among some passionate and pure young men who are prepared to devote their whole lives to promoting his views?

However, the answer to this question, so obvious to the 'Tolstoyans', wasn't obvious to Tolstoy. And it was not only that L.N. was unwilling to give up the family, with which he was one body, but also that he fundamentally disliked the role of spiritual guide, which his dear friend was imposing on him.

"I received your letter and your book and didn't reply to the letter. I didn't reply because I don't know how to do so. It impressed me that you (my dear, accept my words seriously and humbly) that you are in doubt, and that in an internal struggle about the most personal, sincere matter of all – how to organize and lead your life – you address others, look for their support and assistance. Yet in this matter, the only judge can be you yourself and life. I cannot clearly understand from the letters what's wrong; but even if I –did – if I were with you, it's not that I would not have dared to intervene, but that I could not have done so – to approve or disapprove of your life or actions. There is only one teacher – Christ ..."

In Chertkov's language this meant "evade" and "shirk". But Tolstoy not only had doubts, but made it quite clear to Chertkov that he did not wish to be the final arbiter in solving other people's problems in life. Nonetheless Chertkov consistently and systematically brought these problems to L.N.'s attention, sometimes ignoring the problems of his own family. Sometimes he did it so tactlessly that Tolstoy's benevolent reaction to it is astounding.

Here is a telling example. In 1886, Chertkov decides to marry Anna Konstantinovna Dietrichs, a student attending the Bestuzhev of the Bestuzhev higher courses and coworker of the publishing house Mediator, created by Chertkov. Galya's (as she was called by those close to her) outward appearance is well known to us thanks to P.A. Yaroshenko's painting "Student Girl" (1883), which hangs in the Tretyakov Gallery. Beautiful, slim, rigorous and focused, Galya was a passionate follower of Tolstoy's views, and used to visit him along with another girl, which upset S.A. Before getting married, Chertkov repeatedly discussed this issue with Tolstoy in his letters, not considering himself capable of family life and afraid to repeat the "mistake" made by his teacher. But Tolstoy approved of the marriage between V.G. and Dietrichs. The new upheaval in Tolstoy's views had still not occurred, after which he had a negative attitude toward marriage in general.

In 1887, the Chertkovs had a daughter, Olga, who died in infancy.

Galya turned out to be a weak and sickly woman. In effect, V.G. had taken on a heavy cross in the shape of his constantly ailing wife, and, to give him his due, he carried this cross meekly and right to the end. With the advent of the first child in the Chertkov family, the same question came up which had once provoked those first "gashes" in the Tolstoys' domestic happiness. Galya couldn't feed the child with her own milk. A wet-nurse was needed. For some reason, a wet-nurse couldn't be found in Krekshino, in the Moscow Province, where the young couple lived. And so it comes about that V.G. appeals to L.N. with a request that he find a wet-nurse in Moscow.

It was such a delicate task that he could only ask someone to whom he was very close. At that time, however, Chertkov had lost his father and had fallen out with his mother because of Tolstoy, whose views she did not accept. "I am deeply convinced and can see from the Gospel, that anyone who doesn't recognize the Risen Savior, is imbued with this spirit, and since sweet and bitter water cannot both flow from a single source, I cannot recognize as healthy a doctrine emanating from such a source," Elizaveta Ivanovna wrote to her son.

"Dear Lev Nikolayevich," Chertkov writes to Tolstoy, "I am asking for your help yet again in a good cause, which, for those whom it concerns most closely, remains a good cause, despite the fact that the reason which compelled me to get involved is not pure. Arkhangelskaya recently had to deal with a lonely, impoverished woman who, whilst passing the city hospital, stopped and gave birth to a child there. She had decided in advance to give the child up to an orphanage, so as not to have to wander around with him in the winter. And she did it; but, after giving birth to him, she got so attached to him that when she parted with him she felt a desperate grief, yet part with him she did, she let them take him away from her to the orphanage, seeing no possibility of walking the streets with him in the winter without any kind of shelter. She has a lot of milk, and if the doctor, for whom we are waiting, recognizes the need to try the milk of another woman, then this could be very useful to us, even though we would like, if at all possible, to get by with Galya's milk... I am appealing to you again in the hope that someone from among your family or loved ones will take it upon herself to carry out this mission, so as to save you from the hassle, which would distract you from work that is more typical of you, more necessary for the people and in which no one can replace you. Here's what must be done. Go immediately with the enclosed ticket to the orphanage and tell them there that the mother of the child with such-and-such a number is taking him back home and that they should not send him to the countryside. If you have a suitable person whom you know in Moscow, then instruct him to pick up the child immediately and bring it here..."

Chertkov's nature is reflected in this letter as clearly as if in a pool of water. First of all, one's attention is drawn to the writing style: tough, enveloping, but at the same time firmly crossing the 't's and dotting the 'i's in regard to the procedure for executing the instructions. The essence of the matter is that Chertkov urgently needs a wet-nurse. Otherwise, they risk losing their first-born child. The newlyweds' panic is understandable and forgivable. But why, then, do they not say openly: Lev Nikolayevich, the little girl is dying, help us for God's sake, you are our only hope!

That would not have been Chertkov's style, though. He surrounds the question of the life and death of a child with so many confounding considerations that a stranger wouldn't immediately grasp what he was talking about. Who is Tolstoy supposed to help? What is he supposed to do? Return the child to the mother, who has come to her senses, or supply Galya with someone else's milk? The first scenario would be a good deed, the second would be immoral in Tolstoy's eyes. L.N. was fundamentally against the idea of children being fed with a stranger's milk. He considered it harmful and immoral – taking away milk that was meant for poor children for money. But he himself was fed this way, and S.A., suffering with mastitis, didn't agree with her husband and regularly paid for wet-nurses, both for their own children and for her sister Tatiana's children.

One way or another, it was a painful and delicate issue. Did Chertkov know this? In all likelihood, he did. By 1887, he had been to both Khamovniki and Yasnaya Polyana a number of times. He had made friends with Tolstoy's older sons. He would have known about Tolstoy's views on breastfeeding via the letters written to him, Chertkov, just after Olya's birth. Hence this proviso: "... even though we would like, if at all possible, to get by with Galya's milk." Hence the allusion to the impurity of the motive which had given rise to Chertkov's letter.

What was Tolstoy's reaction?

He gladly (!) throws himself into carrying out the instruction. "I just received your letter about the child (3:00), and am now going to do what I can. And I am made very, very glad by all this," he replies to his dear friend. And this is Tolstoy! The man who, according to S.A., had a "murderous" attitude toward his young wife when she refused to feed Sergei, citing unbearable pain.

All the motives for Chertkov's action, though deeply hidden in the letter, are understandable and forgivable. A young father cannot sit back and watch his child's suffering and is willing to seek immediate help from anyone, even from Lev Tolstoy. What is incomprehensible is the *joy* felt by L.N. Why was he made "very, very glad by all this"? The explanation that he was this concerned about the problem of the child's malnutrition does not ring true.

Tolstoy's "joyful" reply to Chertkov was written on December 19, 1887. And on March 31 of the following year, their son Ivan was born into the Tolstoy family. The last-born, S.A. and L.N. were especially fond of him, as was the whole big family. Immediately after his birth, however, S.A.'s old female problems began.

"Ivan is thin and is slow to regain his health," she writes from Moscow to Yasnaya on April 26. And two days later she receives this response: "Don't get fed up, my dear, about Ivan and don't disturb yourself with troubling thoughts. God has given us the baby, and He'll give him food too." The Chertkovs' family problems seem to worry L.N. to a much greater extent than the concerns of his own family. A few years later, he will be merrily looking for a home for them in the vicinity of Yasnaya, probably knowing that his wife was painfully jealous of this quest. Prior to that, he will be happily preoccupied with finding a young nurse to care for the sick Galya. After learning of Galya's critical state, he visits them in Rzhevsk in the Voronezh Province in 1894 and Galya literally comes alive upon his arrival.

The Mediator

When talking about Chertkov as a literary agent, it's impossible not to pay attention to one remarkable circumstance. Chertkov was, undoubtedly, a brilliant literary mediator for Tolstoy, particularly abroad – he was helped a great deal in this by his perfect knowledge of English, and his family ties in the highest circles of the English aristocracy. But he was an agent who, throughout Tolstoy's entire life, didn't bring him a single kopeck, not one shilling, and he himself didn't earn a single penny from his client.

This was how Tolstoy himself wanted it to be. He had once fought with Katkov and Nekrasov over the size of royalties, yet after his spiritual upheaval, he waives the rights to his works. At first without saying so explicitly, and later on a legal basis as well (as he thinks), through a waiver letter published in the newspapers in 1891. From that time onwards, any publisher who wished to do so was entitled to reprint the works he wrote after 1880, without having to pay him anything, from the moment of their first appearance in print. The works he wrote before 1881 belong to his wife – he took care of the formalities here, too, by writing out a power of attorney for his wife.

Chertkov's publishing activities before the revolution and after it stand as one of the most stand-out chapters in the book industry in Russia and worldwide. He was an outstanding organizer and mediator, and before long Tolstoy couldn't manage without him.

Tolstoy's last letter to his daughter Sasha, written on October 29, 1910 from Optina Pustyn, contains a slip of the tongue that is uncharacteristic of L.N. Speaking about the obstacles on S.A.'s side to a meeting with Chertkov, Tolstoy complains to his daughter about his wife's hatred "of the person who is closest to me and whom I need the most." Anyone who is familiar with L.N.'s letters and diaries cannot help but find the word "necessary" grating. It is not a word Tolstoy would ordinarily use in this context.

It wasn't in his nature to use people. It wasn't in his morality to divide people into those who were "needed" and those who weren't. And although here, by using the word "need", he was referring to something broader and deeper than just practical collaboration, anyone with an ear for such things will hear it: Tolstoy made a slip of the tongue (for that's precisely what it was). And this is telling.

In December 1883, Chertkov makes the acquaintance of the publisher Marakuyev, who had published books for the peasants. At this time the first entries about Chertkov appear in Tolstoy's diary. "I like him and believe in him." "He burns with enthusiasm." "I am tired, he is firm and unyielding." "He is surprisingly in convergence with me."In April 1884, Chertkov's father dies. Aware of his son's new interests, he bequeathed everything to his wife alone. Chertkov was forced to become his mother's dependent. She allocates twenty thousand annually for his allowance. This is a lot of money, but the very idea that he is dependent on money from his mother, who doesn't share his beliefs, torments him terribly. And he writes to Tolstoy about this, too, in the confessional tone that has already been adopted between them, trying to justify the fact that he's spending a part of these funds on "good works". But Tolstoy doesn't buy such a justification. He notes in his diary: "He is scared to renounce property. He doesn't know how 20,000 rubles are made. He ought to know. I know – through violence against people who are exhausted by their labors. I must write to him."

But what are these "good works"? In the summer of 1884, having returned from England with his mother, where she had tried to recuperate after the loss of her husband, Chertkov settles in Lizinovka once again. He continues to work on the trade school he founded for the peasant children, a rural school, and even tries to organize a model agricultural farmstead. But this is no longer enough for him. He dreams of creating his own publishing house for Tolstoy. At first, he goes about this in a makeshift way, making copies of the treatise *What I Believe* using a hectograph. One day, though, in a letter to Tolstoy, he advises (!) him to write stories for the people. "I would publish these stories as a series." That fall, Chertkov, while in Moscow, meets Marakuyev and the folk writers Zlatovratsky and Prugavin. They discuss the plan for a powerful national publishing house for the first time.

Such publishing houses, incidentally, already existed. But these were entirely about mass-market books, colored pictures with text-transcriptions of foreign trash like *Prince Bova* and *Milord George*, ridiculed by Nekrasov in *Who Lives Well in Russia?*. Chertkov understood, however, that in the first instance one couldn't get by without the 'mass-market' works. All that needed to be done was to convince these publishers of popular literature that publishing the works of Lev Tolstoy and other Russian writers in exactly the same way would be profitable too.

And such a publisher was duly found, the young and energetic Ivan

Sytin. In November 1884, Chertkov went into his bookshop in Moscow and met him. Sytin was interested in Chertkov's idea of publishing the most prominent Russian writers of the time on the same terms as the popular prints and sell for the same price. With his peasant wit, he realized how this might be profitable: there was no need to pay royalties, and the publisher would gain in prestige. So with Sytin's shop as its base, the Mediator publishing house came into being, which Chertkov founded with a friend of his, a former naval officer now working at an observatory, Pavel Biryukov.

The first story that Tolstoy prepared for Mediator was one that he had written earlier for the *ABC* storybook, *The Prisoner of the Caucasus*, the masterpiece of the new Tolstoy. But Chertkov himself edits the story so that it aligns with the popular taste, interferes with the text. Surprisingly, Tolstoy agrees to this readily. Chertkov gradually becomes not only a mediator, but Tolstoy's adviser. Tolstoy shares ideas for new works with him, sends him passages that he has begun or abandoned, which Chertkov rewrites, leaving spaces between the lines and large empty spaces so that Tolstoy can fill them in with new text and corrections. It had never occurred to S.A. to do such a thing!

In March 1885, the first books published by Mediator are released – three folk tales by Tolstoy in blue and red covers with black drawings, set in a very large font. They are very cheap: a kopek or a kopek and a half a book.

In May of that year, Chertkov again travels to England with his mother and reaches an agreement over the publishing in English of those of L.N.'s works which had been banned in Russia. He is helped by an English friend of his, Lord Battersby. Thus, *Confession*, *What I Believe* and *Summary of the Gospel* were released together in one volume in English. And Tolstoy is "very, very happy" about this.

With the emergence of Mediator and the first publications of Tolstoy's prohibited works abroad, a new era in the writer's life begins. The honor of opening up this era belongs entirely to Chertkov. Whilst S.A. is independently re-releasing her husband's old works, which have passed the test of time, negotiating with the typography, proofing the galleys and stocking the completed books in a shed at their Moscow home, Chertkov is opening up new horizons for Tolstoy.

And this captivates L.N. incomparably more than the endless recycling of the "old stuff", like *Childhood* and *War and Peace*, over which his wife continues to weep and which the new, spiritually fresh Tolstoy can't stand at all. And it is at home that all the "old stuff" is stored, everything that burned within him in the 60s and 70s but which he now finds stultifying, to a deadly degree. Over there, meanwhile, outside the sphere of his family, with which he had now grown bored, was the young and energetic Chertkov, who was capable of linking him with those as yet unknown progressive people of the world, of whom he had dreamed during his spiritual solitude. The choice was all too obvious, but the struggle was all too unequal.

Chapter 7

Whose Fault Is It?

The behavior of Tolstoy and his companions as they fled from Shamordino is strongly reminiscent of the behavior of refugees during a war, who suddenly break away from a place of refuge that is temporary, but to which they have already become accustomed, due to some piece of alarming news, which puts their lives under threat and forces them to run further, submitting not to a rational will, but to the logic dictated by the circumstances. Here, the lord and master is the station manager, and the book of fate is the railroad schedule.

Where did they plan to go on leaving Kozelsk? To Novocherkassk? Yet when they are already in the carriage, on the road to the station from the hotel, L.N. asks Makovitsky: "How far is it to the Annenkovs' place from the Lgov Station?" Led astray by the mistake in Bruhl's map, they still think that in order to reach Lgov, they need to go through Sukhinichi and Bryansk, i.e. due west, in the exact opposite direction to the one in which they ended up going. But the train to Sukhinichi left at 5:19 am, and they weren't going to make it. Why? They were delayed by the hapless coachmen who had been left with the two carriages in which Sasha and Feokritova had arrived the previous day.

"The coachmen were terribly slow at feeding the horses," writes Makovitsky. "It was almost six when L.N. and I got into the carriage. It was foggy and damp, the temperature may have been at freezing point, it was windless and dark." The two men's possessions were put in the second carriage. Thus, there wasn't any room for his daughter and her friend. Tolstoy had been hoping to travel in a more comfortable carriage – his sister's. To this end Makovitsky, whilst Sasha and Feokritova were packing their belongings, had gone to Maria Nikolayevna's home and woken up her daughter, Elizaveta. But at that point a misunderstanding occurred, one that seems strange from a secular point of view. L.N.'s sister was a nun, and as such she couldn't give any personal directions, even concerning her own carriage, without the permission of the Mother Superior. As for the Mother Superior herself, she was sick, and to wake her up at such an early hour would be awkward. In any case, there wasn't time to do so.

"We had no choice but to do the following: go to the farmyard, wake the two coachmen who had been retained, and hire a third one in the village, sending a worker to fetch him. And then send Maria Nikolayevna's carriage to pick her up, so that she could go to the hotel and say goodbye to her brother." She didn't get to say goodbye to her brother, finding only Sasha and her friend at the hotel, who themselves were in a desperate hurry to catch up with Tolstoy and Makovitsky.

L.N. left his sister a touching letter, which, besides showing his tender feelings for her, offers irrefutable proof that Tolstoy, even at the time of this second flight, was in his right mind and fully aware of his actions.

"Dear friends, Masha and Lizonka.

Don't be surprised and don't condemn me because we're leaving without saying goodbye properly to you. I cannot express to you both, especially to you, dearest Masha, my gratitude for your love and involvement in my trials. I don't remember, having loved you always, a time when I have felt such fondness for you as I have felt these last few days, and with which I'm leaving. We're leaving unexpectedly, because I'm afraid that Sofia Andreyevna might find me here. And there's only one train – at 8 o'clock...

I kiss you, dear friends, and I love you so joyfully.

L.T."

So, since it's already obvious that they weren't going to make it on time to catch the train to Bryansk, they planned to take the one which left at 7:40, to Gorbachevo and beyond. Beyond – to which destination?

And at this point in Makovitsky's diary there is a strange moment of confusion, which suggests that the fugitives did not yet have a clear idea about which way they were headed, let alone where their ultimate goal might be.

Lgov and Annenkova are constantly present in Tolstoy's mind, like an obsession. He tells Makovitsky about Lgov and about Annenkova's estate in the carriage on the way to the station. There, "along the road it's possible to stop and rest," he suggests to the doctor, clearly alluding to the fact that all this fleeing has tired him out and that he longs for the familiar comfort of an estate. Or perhaps he simply wants the care and concern of a kindred spirit, an experienced woman?

But Makovitsky either fails to understand this, or pretends that he doesn't understand. L.N. is also concerned by the fact that there's no sign of the carriage containing Sasha and Feokritova behind them, and they are already approaching Kozelsk. Does this mean that his daughter might miss the train?

This particular fear, it would seem, overrides all other considerations. L.N. and Makovitsky ask the coachman: will they themselves make the seven o'clock train? We'll make it, the coachman responds. Nevertheless, upon reaching Kozelsk, Tolstoy suddenly asks him about a hotel: is there a hotel? "L.N. hinted that, because of how unlikely it was that we would make the train, it might be a good idea to stop at a hotel, and he asked the coachman what sort of hotel there was in Kozelsk," writes Makovitsky. By now, this was no hint. It was the strangled cry of an old, sick man, who realizes that he doesn't have the strength to run farther, but, either out of stubbornness or out of politeness, doesn't say so.

Makovitsky was duty-bound, as a doctor, to understand this mood and, despite the fact that he was just as keen as Tolstoy himself to avoid an encounter with S.A., to make L.N. stop at the hotel. But Makovitsky hesitates. He says: "then (i.e., if they were to stop at the hotel. – P.B.), just before evening, at 4:50 we'll be able to move on." Just a moment, though – where would they move on to? Let's take a look at Bruhl's guide, the one from which the doctor took the time of 4:50. The train that stopped in Kozelsk at that time certainly didn't go to Rostov. It was the very same train to Sukhinichi on which they had travelled from Gorbachevo three days earlier. The very same freight train, with a solitary carriage for passengers, a third-class one, the one in which Tolstoy had caught a cold.

From Makovitsky's diary:

"L.N.: In the same train (carriage) in which we came here?

And you could hear in his voice that that thought frightened him. And neither of us instructed the coachman to turn toward the hotel. Had I thought to ask L.N. how he felt, perhaps he would have admitted to his ailment. L.N. sat up straight all the while, he wasn't leaning over, he wasn't looking for a way to sit more comfortably, he didn't moan, didn't sigh, didn't show any signs of fatigue or that he didn't feel well. But I didn't pay attention, it didn't occur to me that L.N. perhaps, due to his weakness, might want to stop, and so, without stopping, we went on to the station. The train was just approaching. The coachman drove the horses onwards and stopped right at the drop-off point itself."Today it is easy to condemn Makovitsky for failing to perform his medical obligations. Let's not forget, though, that we are drawing the evidence of this failure from his own diary. There were no witnesses (other than the coachman, who can hardly have been very happy to have had to wake up at such an early hour and drive the masters to the station), and nothing would have prevented the doctor, later on, when putting the diary in order, from coloring his role in Tolstoy's flight in whatever way he wanted. But he didn't do that. Yes, the doctor failed to spot his charge's illness. But he then honestly said as much to the whole world.

Besides, Makovitsky himself was horribly tired and had not had enough sleep. What's more, he did not see fit to argue with L.N.'s decisions, which he considered sacred.

Sasha and Feokritova managed to catch the train to Rostov after all. They sat together in a second-class car in which there wasn't even a free compartment. L.N. was seated next to an intelligent person from Belevo, who immediately recognized the writer and considerately freed up the compartment. They boarded the train without tickets. And only then did they "start conferring about where to go."Only then did Lgov and Annenkova slip away, of their own accord. Only then did they decide to go to Rostov, to Novocherkassk, to the Denisenkos. "We deliberated over Gorbachevo again and decided on Novocherkassk. There, at L.N.'s niece's house, we would be able to rest for a few days and decide once and for all where to go – to the Caucasus, or, after procuring passports for those of us accompanying L.N. ('You all have permits (for residency – P.B.), and I'll be your servant, without a permit,' said L.N.), go to Bulgaria or Greece." On reading Makovitsky's diary, one can't help but feel a sense of horror. So the fugitives planned to cross the border illegally, taking a sick eighty-year-old with them under the guise of a servant? It goes without saying that this would not have been possible. And it's not that they would have been found out at the border, since the news that the great

Lev Tolstoy had fled from his home, along with an imperturbable pale-faced Slovak doctor, had by then traveled around the entire world. The fact of the matter was that they were already being accompanied, on the train to Rostov, by a correspondent from the newspaper *Russian Word*, Konstantin Orlov. And Orlov, who was following hot on Tolstoy's heels, would, of course, regularly report back on the whereabouts of L.N. and his companions at every major train station. As a result, Tolstoy and his entourage would have met a crowd of reporters in Novocherkassk from all over the Southern region, so talk of a private visit to the Denisenkos couldn't even come into the equation...

Let us nonetheless consider the possible routes for Tolstoy's onward flight after Shamordino. Supposing they had obtained the passports, crossed the border and made it to Bulgaria. Was this really a way out for L.N.?

What did he want more than anything? Peace and solitude. "He didn't remember or didn't know," writes Makovitsky, "how well-known he was in Bulgaria. There wasn't a single language in the world, not excluding English and Czech, which had as many translations of L.N.'s recent writings as Bulgarian had. But none of us at that time even thought to explain to L.N. that there was nowhere where he would be able to hide for long. The only thing we were thinking about then was to avoid, at least for a few weeks (and for now, just for a few days) being sought out, being caught up with." The reception that would await Tolstoy in Bulgaria would be too warm. In particular, a passionate follower of his and a friend of Chertkov's, Hristo Dosev, who worked for the magazine *Vazrajdane*, lived in Bulgaria. In 1907, he had visited Chertkov in Telyatinki and met with Tolstoy. In Bulgaria, as in all Slavic countries, there was a 'Tolstoyan' movement, and its followers would of course carry their teacher aloft on their shoulders. But that was the very thing Tolstoy wanted least of all. The fundamental condition that he imposed on his intended place of residence was that it must not, under any circumstance, be a Tolstoyan commune. He often spoke insistently about this to his travelling companions. Anywhere at all would do – in a hut, in a hotel, only not in a commune!

How can one resist drawing the comparison with Buddha, who refused to die in a Buddhist monastery?

If that were the case, though, the Caucasus would not have seemed a good option to Tolstoy, either. There were "fellow thinkers" living in the Caucasus too, exiled 'Tolstoyans' and Dukhobors.

His daughter Sasha bought some newspapers at the Gorbachevo station that were already reporting Tolstoy's disappearance from Yasnaya Polyana. Tolstoy saw the newspapers and, according to Sasha, was very angry.

"Everything is already known, all the newspapers are full of my departure," L.N. exclaimed sadly.

Many of the passengers in the car were reading these newspapers and discussing the main story in them. "There were two young men sitting opposite me," Sasha recalled, "dressed in a vulgar manner, with thin cigars in their mouths.

'What a trick for the old man to have come up with,' one of them said. 'I don't suppose Sofia Andreyevna liked that very much,' and he gave a stupid laugh, 'him up and running away at night.'

'How d'you like that, she cared for him all his life,' said the other, 'her care apparently wasn't sweet enough for him.'"

The rumor that the guilty party in this scandal was right here among them, on this train, flew through the car like wildfire, and curious passengers began to look into the compartment at him. Try as they might, L.N.'s companions could not, on their own, contain this onslaught. At that point some intelligent conductors intervened.

"What are you bothering me for?" said one of them, a gray-haired man of respectable appearance, with a smart, penetrating expression. "I ask you, why are you bothering me? After all, I'm telling you, Tolstoy got off at the station before last."

Tolstoy, thank God, could no longer see or hear any of this. He was sleeping, covered with a blanket in an empty compartment.

And when he awoke, something became apparent to his companions: Tolstoy was seriously ill. It was as if all the resources of his powerful body, which had supported him on his journey from Yasnaya to Shamordino, had collapsed at one and the same moment. We will not speculate as to why this happened. Especially since there are several different accounts of Tolstoy's illness. Let us say only that it happened at a time when he had seemingly broken free from the traps of Kozelsk, when they had already passed the wretched Gorbachevo and the specter of S.A. posed no threat to them, in the coming days at least. But it was right there, after Gorbachevo, that he learned, via the newspapers, that whilst it was still possible to run away from his wife, it was not possible to escape his own fame. Tolstoy now knew that the whole world was watching his every move. Whichever way he turned, the tireless newspapermen would be waiting.

He was not able to take the route Father Sergius had taken. Nor, incidentally, was he able to take the same route as any of his other literary fugitives either, from Prince Olenin to the elder Fyodor Kuzmich. This last devil, his earthly fame, was one from which he could not get away. It was merely multiplied many times over by his departure.

The Ring of Fate

Tolstoy's life has tempted biographers to divide it not just into periods of time (childhood, adolescence, adulthood, early work, later works), but into segments of equal length, so that each period in his life is attributed the same number of years.

Why this should be so is difficult to explain rationally, but intuitively it is. Perhaps it is because Tolstoy lived and developed not in conventional periods, but in cycles, or, figuratively speaking, rings, like a huge tree, such as an oak. He seems to have constantly grown in his spiritual capacity, building up a new spiritual ring with each step.

These cycles don't coincide with the usual pace of human life. They have some kind of strict order, which once tempted Tolstoy himself to divide his life into time periods of equal length.

In a conversation with his first biographer, P.I. Biryukov, Tolstoy took the number 7 as his starting point. "I heard this division from Lev Nikolayevich himself, who once, during a conversation in my presence, expressed the idea that it seemed to him, that in accordance with the seven-year periods of the physical life of man, recognized by some physiologists, one could also identify seven-year periods in the development of man's spiritual life, so that it would turn out that each seven-year period corresponded to a particular spiritual state of being." In line with Tolstoy's conjecture, P.I. Biryukov divided his life into seven-year cycles. Here's what he came up with:

1) 1828-35. Infancy.

2) 1835-42. Adolescence.

3) 1842-49. Youth, education, the start of his agricultural work in the countryside.

4) 1849-56. The start of his writing, military service: Caucasus, Sebastopol and St. Petersburg.

5) 1856-63. Retirement, travel, the death of his brother, teaching activities, mediation, marriage.

6) 1863-1870. Family life. *War and Peace*. Management of the estate.

7) 1870-77. Samara famine. *Anna Karenina*. Height of literary fame, happiness and wealth.

8) 1877-84. Crisis. *Confession. The Gospel. What I Believe.*

9) 1884-91. Moscow. *What Is To Be Done?*. Folk literature. Mediator. Dissemination of ideas in society and to the people. Critics.

10) 1891-98. Famine. *The Kingdom of God is Within Us*. The Dukhobors. Persecution of the followers of these ideas.

11) 1898-1905. *Resurrection*. Excommunication. Illness. The final period. Appeal to the military, clergy and politicians. War. The revolutionary and reformist movement in Russia.

The first of the existing complete biographies of Tolstoy, written by his disciple Biryukov, begins with this chronicle. It is a wonderful biography, in many ways unrivalled to this day.

Yet it is telling that Biryukov himself describes this system of division as "provisional". The seven-year periods obviously don't reflect the most important dates in the writer's life. On the one hand, many of the time intervals are random. 1842-49, but why not, say, 1843-50? On the other hand, the key moments in Tolstoy's development, when his life literally turned 180°, are missing. There weren't many such moments, and it would be more logical to construct the cycles of L.N.'s life specifically on the bases of these.

Let's put a sheet of paper in front of us and, after the most rigorous and careful selection process, note down the most important dates in Tolstoy's life.

This is what we get:

1828 1847 1862 1877 1910

The roles of the first and last events – his birth and his departure and death – need no explanation. Their finality ("irrevocable" nature, as Tolstoy would have put it) is clear and needs no comment.

But why 1847? In this year, whilst in Kazan, the eighteen-year old Levochka Tolstoy begins to keep a diary. The early stages of his keeping a diary are, in essence, the early stages of Tolstoy's creative activity, for the diary played an almost essential role in it. This is the beginning of L.N.'s spiritual self-awareness. And as to the importance of this "irrevocable" event, one doesn't even have to mention the fact that in this same year, Tolstoy becomes the owner of Yasnaya Polyana. He abandons the university and rushes to Yasnaya to start his activity as a landowner, which he continues to carry out till the mid-80s with varying degrees of success and disappointment.

The third date, 1862, needs no commentary. It's the year of Tolstoy's marriage. Let's not forget that the very concept of an "irrevocable" event was one that he associated with marriage and death. "After death in terms of importance and before death in terms of time, there is nothing more important, more irrevocable than marriage," he wrote in his diary in 1896.

1877 marked the start of the spiritual crisis. Tolstoy turns to religion, goes to Optina Pustyn and begins work on *Confession*. He says goodbye to his old life, repents and starts a new life.

Thus, Tolstoy's biography can be divided into the following segments: 1828-47 (18 years minus a few months, because Tolstoy was born at the end of August, and the diary started in April), 1847-62 (15 years), 1862-77 (15 years) and 1877-1910 (33 years). 18 + 15 + 15 + 33. One can't help but feel tempted to name one more date so as to make the formula symmetrical: 18 +15 +15 +15 +18.

But to do this we would need the year 1892.

And then we get this:

1828 1847 1862 1877 1892 (?) 1910

In Biryukov's time-scale, this year falls into the period 1891-98. He cites the work done by L.N., his family and his brothers-in-arms to provide aid during the peasant famine in Begichevka, in the Ryazan Province, as among the most important events of this time. He also cites the book *The Kingdom of God is Within Us* and Tolstoy's selfless help in the resettlement of the Russian Dukhobors in Canada, which began in the period stated but certainly didn't end in it, its main phase coming in 1898-99, when Tolstoy puts the royalties from *Resurrection* towards this cause and sends his eldest son Sergei to accompany the Dukhobor migrants.

There's no doubt that all of these things were extraordinary events in L.N.'s life. But there is no way they can be described as irreversible ("irrevocable"). And, with the exception of the article *The Kingdom of God is Within Us*, they are not things which have to do with Tolstoy's life alone. They were collective efforts in which he played an active part.

But *The Kingdom of God is Within Us* isn't even the most important work by Tolstoy from his 'spiritual' period. Why is there no mention of *Confession*, or *Resurrection*? No mention of the diary or his letters? Thus, if we follow Biryukov's time-scale, we don't find a single irrevocable event in this stage of L.N.'s life.

Was this really how things were though?

Refusal or Separation?

In 1892, Tolstoy renounced property. Incidentally, the renunciation of property was not, in and of itself, anything new at that time. Lord Radstock, the preacher who was well-known in Russia, also renounced property. A colonel in the British Army, who had taken part in the Crimean War, he went through a spiritual upheaval at the age of thirty-three, gave away all his possessions and dismissed his servant. Renouncing one's property and giving it to monasteries was commonplace among the rich Russian merchants, when, at the end of their lives, they retreated from the world to atone for their sins. But it is the method by which Tolstoy accomplished this procedure that still raises many questions even today.

The renunciation of property was, for LN, perhaps the most painful event in his life. Something that he thought would bring him joy, spiritual relief, in fact plunged him into a real prison of endless questions and doubts.

From the very beginning of his spiritual upheaval, Tolstoy tries to prove to the family, and to his wife in particular, that property is the greatest of all evils, which must be renounced. But this must be done not in order to do good deeds for others, as his wife understood it – she accused her husband of wanting to help the poor but make his own children destitute. It is something that must be done for the family itself, since a life of luxury at the expense of the back-breaking labor of other people is not life, but spiritual death. This, indeed, became the main "discrepancy" between L.N.'s understanding of life and his wife's understanding of it after 1877.

For fifteen years (a period just as long as the time they had spent as a happy, harmonious family), L.N. tries to prove to his wife and his older children his own, as he sees it, undeniable truth. And from their side he comes up against either a deaf ear and a lack of understanding, or explicit resistance. The atmosphere in the Tolstoys' Moscow home and at Yasnaya Polyana is forever poisoned. It becomes unbearable for both sides, though it cannot always be detected by their numerous guests.

Meanwhile, the family is still growing.

In 1888, their last child is born – Vanya.

And in the same year, their second eldest son, Ilya, starts his own family.

It was the first wedding in the large Tolstoy family. Naturally, it implied the continuance and multiplication of the clan.

In accordance with the tradition established by their father, the Tolstoy children didn't marry out of monetary considerations. Ilya was no exception: he took as his bride a girl who was wonderful, but of low-income, the daughter of the famous portrait painter N.A. Filosofov, a member of the Academy of Fine Arts. Before the wedding, Ilya was "in the distracted condition in which those who are in love are". After the wedding, the young couple went to Yasnaya Polyana, where they spent their honeymoon, alone in the bottom three rooms, like the Robinsons, enjoying the freedom and independence from their parents (the Tolstoy family was living in Moscow at this time). Ilya and his young wife Sonya then moved to the Grinevka farmstead in the Chernsky District, which L.N. had acquired earlier in his wife's name. And at this point he felt his economic dependence on his parents. In effect, Ilya became the manager of the estate, which belonged to his mother, a fact which, to someone with his character, was unbearable.

The other children were slow to start families. Sergei Lvovich married for the first time in 1895 at the age of thirty-two, but the marriage did not last. Tatiana, after a long series of failures with various potential grooms, got married at the age of thirty-five to an elderly landowner named M.S. Suhotin, who already had children. Lev Lvovich married the daughter of a Swedish Doctor named Westerlund when he was in his early thirties. And finally, Tolstoy's favorite daughter, Masha, married fairly late as well, by the standards of the time. She was twenty-six years old when she became the wife of her father's grand-nephew, his sister Maria Nikolayevna's grandson, Kolya Obolensky, who was as poor as a church mouse, as the saying goes.

As for the younger Tolstoys, Sasha lived to the age of ninety-five without ever getting married. Andrei was married twice and Mikhail – once. Both of them started sizeable families.

Thus, from the late '80s onwards, a new family situation, with new concerns, including financial ones, begins to gather and grow around Tolstoy, like a snowball.

Tolstoy not only wasn't ready for this situation, but hadn't even given any thought to preparing for it. It's as though he's living on another planet. You won't find any serious reflection on the material side of life in his diary or in his correspondence with his wife. The only thing that really worries him is that the children are growing up in luxury, which is making them "parasites" on the body of the people. He is constantly voicing this criticism to his wife, and from the mid-80's onwards he also complains about it in his letters to his "dear friend" V.G. Chertkov.

Any attempt by S.A. to raise financial issues irritates her husband. In the best case she gets a condescending and lordly response. In October 1884 she sends a list of "unavoidable monthly expenses" to him at Yasnaya:

"In rubles
Englishwoman 30
Madame 50
Insurance 267
Kashevskaya 40
To the Duma 200
High school and university 47
State-owned 80
Masha's Russian teachers 36
Education 203

Salaries:
Servants' salaries 98
Cook 15
Washerwoman 40
Footman 15
Firewood 60
Coachman 16
Sergei 40
Nanny 8
Meat and food for the servants and us 150
Groundskeeper 8
Dry provisions, lighting, coal, tobacco, etc. 150
Dunyasha 8
Kitchen maid 4
Baker 25
Varya 5
Floor polishers 5
Tatiana 6
Horse, cow 75
Vlas 8
Night watchman 2
Wet-nurse 5
Given to Ilya, Tanya, Lev and Masha 12
Duties at home 50

Total for the month 910".

Tolstoy's response is startling in its lordly dismissiveness. It would be understandable if he were to point out to his wife any unnecessary or excessive items in the family budget. But he answered her by saying: "I cannot, my dear, and don't be angry – attribute to these monetary calculations any importance whatsoever. None of this is an event, such as: illness, marriage, birth, death, knowledge gained, a bad or good deed, good or bad habits in the people nearest and dearest to us; as for this, this is our structure, this is how we have arranged it and it is open to us to arrange it differently or in 100 different ways."

Tolstoy's firm belief that the life of this big, complex family, containing people of all ages and many different characters, could easily be rearranged in "100 different ways" is startling. It was as though they weren't living people with their habits and shortcomings, but the different parts of a Rubik's Cube. And the suspicion arises, not without good grounds, that by renouncing property, Tolstoy was ridding himself not only of "sin", but also of the headaches associated with those "unavoidable costs". As a philosopher, he wasn't interested in this "rat race", and he was saying to his wife, like Diogenes, "Stand a little out of my sun." Some of the elder children inherited their father's nonchalant attitude toward financial matters. His daughter Maria, for example, sided with him.

"She was a slim, rather tall and pretty blonde, whose stature was somewhat reminiscent of my mother, but her face looked more like father's, with the same clearly defined cheekbones and pale blue, deep-set eyes," her brother Ilya wrote of his younger sister. "Quiet and unassuming by nature, she always gave the impression that she was a little tired out. She felt father's loneliness in her heart, and she was the first of all of us to draw back from the company of her peers, and quietly, but firmly and definitely, move over to his side."

There is an extremely interesting entry in Tatiana's diary late in the year 1890 which indicates that their mother was the one who felt more alone in the family at that time.

"I feel more sorry for mama, because, first of all, she doesn't believe in anything – neither in something of her own, nor in what papa believes, and secondly, she is more lonely, because, since she says and does a lot of foolish things, of course, all the children are on papa's side, and she feels the pain of her loneliness. And then she loves papa more than he loves her, and delights, like a little girl, in the slightest affectionate word from him. Her main misfortune is that she is so illogical and this gives him so much material with which to condemn her."

The situation of the spouses in the early '90s is very different from the early '80s. There can no longer be any talk of Tolstoy being lonely. He feels a tremendous amount of support from public opinion in Russia and around the world. Although his new works are banned by the censors in Russia, they are distributed in lists, using the hectograph method, but above all – there are rumors about them all over the country, and in Russia, rumor is far stronger than any books and magazines. As for foreign countries, thanks to Chertkov's energetic activity, these works are published by the million (!) in many languages. L.N. goes from being a spiritual outcast to a dominant intellectual force. S.A.'s conviction in the early 80s that her husband's new works would not interest more than ten people has suffered a crushing blow.

Most importantly of all, her fortress, *her home*, is crumbling before her very eyes. It is flooded with "dark ones". In this regard, the most non-winning side of her character begins to appear in S.A., right up to class and ethnic intolerance.

"I have had to endure difficult times in my old age," she complains in her diary in 1890. "Levochka has surrounded himself with a circle of the strangest acquaintances, who call themselves his followers. And this morning one of them paid a visit, Butkevitch, who had spent time in Siberia due to his revolutionary ideas, wearing dark glasses, and dark and mysterious himself, and he brought with him his Jewish lover, whom he called his wife just because he lives with her. Since Biryukov is here, Masha went down to hover with them too, down below, and fussed over this Jewish woman. I exploded with rage at the thought that a respectable girl, my daughter, was hanging around with all manner of lowlifes and that her father seemed sympathetic to this. And I got very angry, I started shouting; I spoke harsh words to him: 'You've been used to keeping such company your whole life, but I'm not used to it and I don't want my daughters hanging around with them.' He sighed, of course, got angry in silence, and walked away." Meanwhile, Masha is in love with Biryukov and wants to marry him. Tanya is keen on Chertkov. Their son Lev befriends Chertkov. And for all of them, of course, their father's truth is much more interesting than their mother's truth. All the more so, of course, given that all of progressive humanity – and such nice people as Chertkov and Biryukov – are on his side. For S.A. the worst thing of all is beginning: she is being defeated within the family.

This was a horrible injustice! After all, she had been the family's cornerstone. In any critical family situation which L.N. created, the brunt of the responsibility fell on S.A. Unlike her husband, though, she couldn't have "dear friends" and people who might act as advisors in this struggle. Her family situation was too atypical. Every year her husband had some surprises in store for her: now he was sewing boots in his spare time, now he was writing a letter to the Tsar, urging him to release the regicides; now he was going to church every day, now he was eating meat cutlets during lent in front of the children, or tilling the land, or trying to dig up the earth under some wheat with a shovel, carried away by some unheard of form of agriculture.

Tolstoy behaves in a weird and wonderful way. He acts like a holy fool, yet formally he is still the head of a huge family and the owner of several estates, as well as the house in Khamovniki, which is also a kind of estate within Moscow, with a garden, administrative services, supplies, a cow, horses and carriages of its own. And all this is gradually being transferred, in effect, to S.A. But under the law, he might bring the question of the complete renunciation of property to a head at any time.

In February 1890, Tolstoy writes down in his diary the plot of a new play – "about life: the despair of a person who has seen the light, who brings this light into the darkness of life hoping, feeling confident that it will light up the darkness; and suddenly the darkness gets even darker." This idea would result in an unfinished play, *And the Light Shines in the Darkness*, which he would start to write, then put to one side, and he continued to work on it in this way up until the 1900's. It is the most personal of Tolstoy's plays, comparable in its autobiographical nature with the story *The Devil*. In it, he not only expressed his attitude toward the problem of renouncing property, but also tried to make sense of the drama being played out by his wife.

In the play, a rich man named Nikolai Ivanovich Saryntsev, having read the Gospel from cover to cover and decided to literally follow Christ's teachings to the letter, proposes that his family should renounce property, give everything to the poor and live by their own labor. It turns out that the suffering party here consists of his wife, Marya Ivanovna, and their children – Styopa and Ivan, Luba, Missy and Katya. There are a lot of other characters in the play – landlords, officials, priests, policemen and doctors. The most important figures among them, however, are Saryntsev's wife's sister, his sister-in-law, Alexandra Ivanovna Kohovtseva, and her husband, Pyotr Semyonovich. The prototypes of all the main characters can easily be identified. They are L.N., his wife, their children and the Kuzminskys.

Of particularly note is the character of Alexandra Ivanovna. Unlike her sister, she has no doubt whatsoever that Nikolai Ivanovich is simply being idiotic and that Marya Ivanovna must transfer all the property to herself. Thus Tolstoy gave voice to the position of Tatyana Kuzminskaya. This play provides a compelling answer to the question: what would have happened if Tolstoy had chosen not Sonya, but Tanya, after waiting for her to come of age. And here's what would have happened… Tatiana, without a moment's hesitation, would have declared her husband to be crazy when he began *being idiotic*.

The character of Maria Ivanovna (S.A.) comes across as significantly more complex. In theory, she is prepared to share her husband's beliefs because she loves him infinitely. But her *ideé fixe* is the children. They aren't property as such. Property is, to her, hateful, if anything. Both because it creates discord between her and her loved one, and because property is, for her, that cross that she must take from her husband and bear on her own shoulders for the sake of the children. Thus the essence of the conflict is not so much about the difference in moral convictions, different though these are. In essence it is about the difference in their understanding of their "cross" and of the good of the children.

In the play, Nikolai gives us a startling definition of his wife – he calls her "a cunning child":

"A child, a child is what she is, or a cunning woman. Yes, a cunning child." In terms of form the play is incomplete, but its meaning is fully conveyed by the finale. Under pressure from the family, Nikolai signs the act of transfer conferring ownership of the estate into his wife's name and tries to leave home with a mysterious fellow named Alexander Petrovich, who features in the final scene as a man "in tattered clothes". They plan to travel to the Caucasus "without a penny to their names".

Once again, however, under pressure from his wife, Nikolai Ivanovich stays at home and appeals to God:

"Can it really be that I am mistaken, that I am mistaken to believe in you? No. Father, help me!"

Before signing the act of renunciation, Nikolai Ivanovich gives his wife a very clear warning:

"If I give you this, I cannot stay here and live with you, I must leave. I cannot continue to live in these conditions. I cannot look on as the estate –

not mine any longer, but yours – squeezes all the juices out of the peasants, and puts them in jail. Make your choice.

The choice she makes means his departure. If not today, then tomorrow.

The real-life drama that was played out in the Tolstoy family in the early 1890s, though, was more complex than the literary one. By July 7, 1892, when Tolstoy signed the act which divided up his property between his wife and children, L.N. hadn't actually owned anything for almost a decade. In May 1883, in the presence of a notary from Tula named Beloborodov, a general power of attorney was given to his wife to take charge of all matters related to property, which also included her right to sell any of his property, in whole or in part, for whatever price and on whatever terms of payment she considered acceptable. She could derive income from it and spend the income however she saw fit. She could enter into any agreements of any kind and sign legal documents of any kind without the consent of her husband.

It is interesting that, despite all this, she could not move freely around Russia without her husband's consent. And when, in 1886, the need arose for S.A. to go to Yalta to see her dying mother, Tolstoy had to sign another power of attorney for his wife, giving her permission "throughout the year 1886 to seek accommodation in any of the cities and towns of the Russian Empire." Why, though, was the 1892 document needed, if Tolstoy's act of renunciation from property had been on a legal footing for almost ten years by then? It was specifically this second document that, unlike the first one, proved extremely difficult for L.N. and his family to finalize, for both moral and legal reasons (it was in the pipeline for a whole year). It was specifically this second document that created not one, but a number of fault-lines within the family. And S.A. did *not* stand to benefit from this document.

In 1883, a sweetheart contract was signed between Tolstoy and his wife, whereby she took charge of the "evil" (as L.N. saw it), or "cross to bear" (as S.A. saw it) of their property , thus liberating her idealist-husband from it. From now on, he didn't have to deal with this hateful "evil", didn't have to sign papers which ran contrary to his beliefs, didn't have to be on the lookout to make sure that no stranger came along and entrenched upon that which, as he saw it, had not been given to him by God and didn't belong to him.

His wife would now take care of everything.

What's more, Tolstoy continued to hope that he would be able to convince the family to renounce property altogether and begin to live by the fruits of their labor, setting out on a dangerous but exciting experiment in how to live. He made thorough preparations for this experiment: he sewed boots, sawed wood, worked in the fields with the plow and scythe, and built huts. His wife wasn't a shirker, either: she made clothes for the entire family. S.A never once went abroad throughout her entire life. Her fascination with balls quickly disappeared. Generally speaking, S.A. cannot be accused of having wasted her life on pleasures. And given the dedication of her love for her husband, which so angered her sister Tanya, why should we not suppose that had the family circumstances been different, she would have followed L.N. even if he had gone to live in a hut, even if he had gone to the ends of the earth?

She could not do so with the children, though! Especially children who were so different from one another, as theirs were.

Masha was the only one who was entirely on their father's side. Her brother Ilya described his sister as "a little downtrodden", and with good reason. With her angelic, unselfish character, loving disposition towards people and a willingness to serve everyone, Masha had something otherworldly about her, as did Vanya. She was capable of being spiritually led by her father whilst benefiting from financial support from her mother, whilst not being able to lead an independent life, a task which, ultimately, was beyond her.

We find a curious character trait of Masha's in her brother Lev's diary from 1890. "Masha, she is infected, no not infected, but covered all over with papa's idea, his views, with everything that might possible concern her darling father, and anything she might be able to understand from papa's infinitely complex internal machine. I'm interested to know what will come of her?"

On the very same day, he writes: "... my sister Masha is dressed in pants, covering her thin legs, she's a Christian, a vegetarian, etc., and is simply as thick as two short planks..."

Both Lev and Tatyana, however, were in principle able to accept the complete renunciation of property, as is evidenced by a diary entry made by Tatiana in that same year, 1890:

"Leva (her brother – P.B.) was very upset by this whole matter (the arguments between their father and mother – P.B.), and said that everything should be given to the devil and *que cela finisse*. I, on the other hand, if I imagine that this were to happen, nevertheless think that there wouldn't be any difference. Leva would stay on at the university on a scholarship, Sergei would continue his military service, Ilya would learn management, and Masha would get married to Posha (Biryukov – P.B.), they'd pack their children off to schools, I would become a governess, mama would run some kind of boarding house, and papa would live faithfully with Masha and Posha." So, life without property, according to Tanya, was possible. But what changes would it bring about? "We would all be left with the same ideals and aspirations, but a bitterness would probably take root in some family members over the fact that they had been put in this position." This "bitterness" had already taken root. Having been the first to marry, Ilya demanded his share of the family's property. There occurred in Tolstoy's family the same thing that happened in peasant families with a dominant male half. The adult sons, having started families of their own, didn't want to live in the family community, under their father's leadership. They certainly didn't want to live like Syutayev, the peasant whom Tolstoy so adored, with scarves and trunks shared by all. Tolstoy's new family project was doomed not because of his allegedly greedy wife, but because of his sons' natural desire to live in independent households.

Whether he intended it or not, it was Ilya who became the main reason for the family's property being divided up. This division didn't give S.A. anything, it merely took away her power over all of the family's property.

It was after Ilya's marriage that the constant conversations about the division of property began in the Tolstoy household. Ilya gets them started, but the rest of them don't remain on the sidelines either. Except, that is, for their father and Masha.

Ilya lives with his young wife in Grinevka, which doesn't belong to his father, it is registered in his mother's name. Thus it is his mother who, by making her son a mere manager of the estate, is deemed to be in the wrong.

An entry from S.A.'s diary reads as follows:

"Ilya suddenly says 'I won't give you any mares for kumis.' I flared up and said, 'I won't ask you to, I'll order the manager to do it.' He flared up too, and said: 'I am the manager.' And I said: 'But I'm the owner.' Whether because I was so very tired or because he had worn me out so with his talk of money and the estate, I got terribly angry, I said: 'How did you come to this, you begrudge your father kumis from your mare, why do you come here, go to hell, you've exhausted me!..'"

Tolstoy loved Ilya. But his relationship with his sons is a big psychological mystery.

"Father's tact in relation to us reached the point of shyness," recalled Ilya Lvovich. "There were certain matters that he didn't dare touch upon, afraid of hurting us if he did so.

I won't forget the time when, in Moscow, he sat down to write at my desk in my room, and I accidentally ran in there to get changed.

My bed was behind a screen, and from there I couldn't see my father.

On hearing my footsteps, he asked, without looking round:

'Ilya, is that you?' 'Yes, it's me.' 'Are you alone? Shut the door. Now, no one can hear us, and we can't see each other, so we won't be ashamed. Tell me, have you ever had relations with a woman?'

When I told him that I hadn't, I suddenly heard him begin to sob and cry like a little child.

I started weeping too, and we both wept good, healthy tears, long and hard, separated by the screen, and we weren't ashamed and it was so good that I think of that moment as one of the happiest of my entire life.' Ilya loved his father, too. Of all Tolstoy's sons, he bore a closer resemblance to him outwardly than all the others, and in his old age, whilst living in America, looked strikingly similar to him, which made it possible for Hollywood to draw Ilya into a venture involving a wholly unsuccessful film about Tolstoy, in which the son played his father. In his youth, however, on becoming the head of his own family, he began trying to force his mother (his mother, not his father!) to give him Grinevka, which was impossible to do without infringing upon the property rights of the other children. Entries in S.A.'s diary clearly indicate that the act renouncing ownership, signed by L.N. in 1892, was less the result of his and her will, and more an enforced situation in which the family found itself after Ilya's marriage.

"Frankly, things are difficult with Ilya alone," S.A. writes in 1891, less than a year before the formal division of property in the family, "he's horribly selfish and very greedy, perhaps because he already has a family.

The other children are all tactful and will agree to everything. Levochka always had a soft spot for Ilya and didn't see his flaws; this time, too, he wants to do everything the way Ilya wants it, and I'm afraid that there will be more endless unpleasantness. Fortunately, Grinevka is in my name, and if they don't agree to divide it up among all the children by drawing lots, I won't agree to give up Grinevka and Ovsyannikova. But I won't let the younger ones down for anything in the world… all these conversations are difficult for Levochka, but ten times harder for me because I have to protect the younger children from the older ones."

Having failed to decide the question of the renunciation of property in a radical way, Tolstoy 'washes his hands' of the matter. He renounces property, but technically this takes the form of a division of property between the family members. This was the only possible compromise solution, but we must recognize that S.A. was the injured party in this division. Her husband got what he wanted – freedom from property. The children got their shares. She received Yasnaya Polyana (on an equal footing with Vanya, who was still a minor), but at the same time retained the obligation of having to be responsible for L.N., to organize his life and remain as the tie that bound the large, splintering family together.

"In July 1891," recalled Sergei Lvovich, "all of us – the brothers and sisters – gathered at Yasnaya Polyana to discuss the division, which father proposed, of his estate among us. Father had valued his entire estate, together with the two small estates which mother bought, Ovsyannikovo and Grinevka, at about 500,000 rubles and decided to distribute all of these estates equally among nine people – our mother and his eight children. He valued each share at 55,000 rubles. After a joint discussion of this matter, the following distribution of each person's shares was agreed upon, based on father's proposal: Yasnaya Polyana was divided into two parts – one part was transferred to mother, the other – to Ivan, who, as a minor, was under her wardship; Nikolskoye-Vyazemskoye and Grinevka were divided into three parts: I was given a part of the estate, on condition that I paid 28,000 to my sister Tanya, Masha was given the middle part of Nikolskoye, whilst Ilya received the Protasov farmstead, along with Grinevka, which mother had bought, and where he settled; Tatiana received 28,000 from me and Ovsyannikovo, which mother had bought; Lev was given the Moscow house and a plot on the Samara estate; the three younger ones, excluding Ivan, who were mother's wards, got the rest of the Samara estate. Masha, who shared her father's beliefs, gave up her share, which was transferred to mother.

I then made a suggestion to mother, to which she agreed: that she give me Masha's share of Nikolskoye Vyazemsky, with the obligation to pay the cost of it, that is to say 55,000 rubles. I thus made a commitment to pay my sisters 28,000 + 55,000 = 83,000, which was about a hundred rubles per desyatin of the estate. I hoped to pay this money by mortgaging the estate and selling off the forest." Judging by the memoirs and diaries of those involved in this event, the distribution was quite a peaceful one, if we don't count Masha's rejection of her share, which caused outrage among her older brothers and older sister as a "mean trick", of sorts, against them. Note that this outrage was caused by the rejection of a share, not by a claim for an extra piece. This testifies to the lofty moral climate within the Tolstoy family.

"In Easter week, all the brothers gathered together, because it had been decided that everything would be divided up," Tatiana wrote in her diary. "This was what Papa wanted, of course, and but for that no-one would have done it. Still, it was very unpleasant for him, and, at one point, when my brothers and I had gone into his study to ask him to value everything for us, he, without waiting to hear what we wanted, quickly began saying: "Yes, I know that I must sign, that I must renounce everything in your favor." He said this to us because this was the most unpleasant thing for him and it was very difficult for him to sign and give away something that he hadn't considered his own for a long time, because, by giving it to us, he would sort of be admitting that it was his property. It was so pitiful, because it was like a condemned man hastening to stick his head in the hangman's noose, from which he knows he cannot escape. And the three of us were this noose. It was terribly painful for me to be unpleasant to him, but I knew that this division of the property would destroy so much unpleasantness between Ilya and mama that I felt it my duty to take part in it. I envied Masha, who wasn't taking part at all and had refused to accept her share."

After she got married, Masha was forced to appeal to her mother for her share of the inheritance.

Tolstoy's children felt uncomfortable dividing up their father's property, which he had dreamed of giving away to the peasants. Their father felt uncomfortable being present whilst his property was being divided up by his own children, "as if he had died" (to quote Tolstoy's exact words). Their mother was hurt by the fact that the younger children were being materially affected by the selfishness of their elder siblings. Among the older children there was a serious split, for the first time, over Masha's ill-thought-through action, which, moreover, had put them in an awkward position. The younger children, Sasha and Vanya, became owners of property against their will. As he grew up, Vanya didn't see Yasnaya Polyana as his property and, on hearing his mother say that it was his land, he stamped his little foot and said that it wasn't his, but "everyoneses". It's not difficult to imagine that if the youngest Tolstoy hadn't died at 7 years of age, there would have been serious problems with this particular "property-owner".

This distribution brought the family neither material well-being nor moral well-being. Tolstoy's sons repeated the mistakes made by their father in his youth: they loved wine, cards, gypsies, and were not renowed for any strong administrative abilities. The correspondence between mother and sons indicates that Ilya, Lev and Andrei, and even the most intelligent of the brothers, Sergei, were constantly in debt and forever asking for help from the only person who could save them – their mother.

Tolstoy considered property the greatest of all evils. He was not capable, however, of renouncing this evil and remaining spiritually at peace. The evil harassed him and even seemed to take revenge on L.N. Nowhere was this more evident than in the case of the literary rights.

An unprofitable place

In order to get a sense of the relationship between Tolstoy's properties, his assets and his literary rights, let's have a look at a few facts and figures.

The only place that was genuinely profit-making was the Samara estate. Purchased by L.N. for future use in the pristine and fertile Samara land, it grew steadily in price and did not require major capital investment. The leasing of these lands brought the family pure profit. Though their owner occasionally indulged in romantic pursuits, such as crossing English and Bashkir breeds in order to create the perfect horse for the cavalry, the land in Samara was, in its own right, the gift that kept on giving. As for the Tula estates, the situation was much bleaker.

The idle speculation to the effect that it was easy for Tolstoy to give up his literary rights, since he was a rich landowner, stems from an obvious lack of knowledge about the family's real financial situation.

Yasnaya Polyana was not a profit-making estate. On the contrary, it brought the family annual losses, which had to be covered through other sources. It modern parlance, it is fair to say that Yasnaya Polyana was like one huge summer holiday home, which put food on the table but was by no means able to provide for them in other ways. At the same time it demanded tireless farming work and annual investments of capital which were not covered by the income from the estate itself.

So as to imagine the concerns of S.A. as she ran the estate, concerns which, after her husband's renunciation of property, lay entirely on her shoulders, let's look at the "List of live and dead inventory…" of Yasnaya Polyana, which Tatiana Vasilievna Komarova, curator of the Yasnaya Polyana home, cites in an article she wrote. "On January 1, 1913 there was a large farm on the estate: 27 horses, 26 cows, 1 bull, 24 calves, 11 pigs, 9 sheep, 78 birds. On December 20, 1912 there were 880 poods of oats, 800 poods 10 pounds of rye, 800 pounds 10 pounds of rye, 6 poods 36 pounds of flour, 5 stacks of meadow hay, about 400 poods, 2 stacks of clover hay, about 1200 poods, oats in stacks, 3 stacks=130 bunches, rye in stacks, 2 stacks of hay=150 bunches, about 400 poods of potatoes." "Cabbage, cucumbers, raspberries, red and white currants, various herbs, melons and turnips were also grown," Tatyana Vasilievna reports. "One can imagine how much land was covered with cucumbers, if one considers that in 1914, 3 pounds of cucumbers were purchased." It's a real pleasure to talk to the curator of the house! In an informal, humane sort of way, one might even say in a womanly way, she feels concerned about how much work Tolstoy's companion had to do.

But at that point we looked together at the credit and debit sheets that S.A. kept in her own writing, not trusting her estate manager, Koring, with this "holiest of holies". For the sake of what was this heroic woman working so hard? From what sort of allegedly affluent estate was her great husband fleeing?

The "income" produced by Yasnaya Polyana in 1910 amounted to 4626 rubles, 49 kopecks. The "expenditure" amounted to 4523 rubles, 11 kopecks. The total annual income of the estate amounted to 103 rubles, 38 kopecks.

In 1911, business at the estate was conducted far more successfully. Expenditure stood at 5633 rubles, 46 kopecks and the income was 6371 rubles, 93 kopecks. Yasnaya Polyana brought S.A., already a widow, the tidy sum of 738 rubles, 47 kopecks. This amount is recorded as the "balance for 1912". This is the net money that she received *for the whole year* from her estate, and which, as a responsible landlady, she doesn't fritter away on dresses or leisure pursuits, but instead invests it in the development of the farmstead.

And here the most interesting part begins.

What exactly was it that constituted Yasnaya Polyana's income? The "Expenditures" were the "workers' salaries" (1690 rubles. 76 kopecks.), "day-to-day work" (576 rubles. 02 kopecks.), "repair and construction of buildings" (308 rubles. 20 kopeks.), "purchase of hay and straw" (411 rubles. 36 kopeks.), "purchase and repair of equipment" (228 rubles. 75 kopecks.), "products for workers" (114 rubles. 45 kopeks.) and even this unforeseeable expense: the "purchase of a sheepskin coat for the Circassian" (10 rubles), the man hired by Tolstoy's wife to protect Yasnaya Polyana from its own peasants.*

And the "income"? It turns out that the main source of "income" was the leasing of meadowlands, for 1200 rubles, 04 kopecks. The second most important item was the leasing of land: 342 rubles, 50 kopecks. The third was the sale of surplus dairy products - 258 rubles, 95 kopecks, followed by the sale of cattle - 147 rubles, 50 kopecks. The remaining items of income are small ones: "leather" - 13 rubles, 65 kopecks; "the sale of poultry" - 22 rubles, 60 kopecks, etc. Finally there were the fines exacted from any peasants caught by the aforementioned Circassian in the ten-ruble sheepskin, in the act of felling forests, desetroying meadowlands or other abuses: these amounted to 15 rubles in 1910.

On seeing these figures, you feel a sense of bewilderment. Can it really be the case that because of that pathetic sum of 15 rubles a year there was an out-and-out war going on between L.N. and S.A., one which eventually led to him leaving his family estate?! Was it really because of this that the great writer and humanist tormented himself so, as he watched the Circassian dragging the poor peasants out of the woods with a lasso?!

This is merely a first impression, though, and it is a misleading one. It was precisely because Yasnaya Polyana was a small and unprofitable estate that it required such rigorous accounting and control. So that the "income" at least kept pace with the "expenditure". They had to keep track not just of every ruble, but of every kopek, because it was from these kopeks that the annual financial balance was formed.

According to T.V. Komarova, S.A. had two assistants: an estate manager and a gardener/beekeeper. Twenty people handled all the housework and farming. As we have seen, about a third of all the "expenditure" went towards their upkeep (salary + food). The remaining two-thirds went towards maintaining the buildings and equipment in working order, feeding the cattle, etc., but it was certainly not spent on entertainment. It was, in essence, a subsistence economy.

Yet here in the "income" column we see that the biggest item isn't the grasslands, nor is it the land, nor the milk. This mysterious item is labelled "received from Countess S.A. Tolstoy" (written in her own hand), without any explanation as to how it was "received".

S.A. herself invests more than 2,000 rubles a year, net, in Yasnaya. In 1910, this "income" was 2521 rubles, 20 kopeks, and in 1911 it was 2491 rubles, 92 kopeks. But it is easier to understand it if you look not at the annual accounts, but at the monthly sheet for November 1912. The "income" is 256 rubles, 84 kopeks. The "Expenditure" is 256 rubles, 60 kopeks. The "Balance" is 24 kopeks. In the "income" column there is a note: "including 100 from S.A."

So, in order to get an income of 24 kopeks from Yasnaya Polyana in November 1912, S.A. spent 100 rubles on it. After the division of property between the members of the Tolstoy family, though, Yasnaya Polyana was the only thing she owned. From what source did she get her annual 2000 rubles? It is clear that after the assets were divided up, and before she began receiving an annual pension from the state (10,000 rubles) because she was a widow, this money could only have come from the sale of her husband's works.

The "Copyright" Nightmare

Before Tolstoy's death, under the general power of attorney of 1883, though it never once mentioned the words "literary rights", his wife first took charge of all her husband's works, but from 1891, at Tolstoy's behest, her "copyright" was restricted to works written before 1881. This was the source of their shared income. This money covered the cost of Yasnaya Polyana, it was used to buy everything that was needed for the upkeep of the Moscow house and many things which neither she, nor her husband, nor their children could live without.

At the same time, the value of Tolstoy's literary assets was growing exponentially. Despite the fact that in 1891 he publicly renounced all literary rights, the publishers never gave up hope of securing exclusive rights to Tolstoy's works. By the end of his life, their value was estimated by foreign publishers at ten million (!) gold rubles. As for the rights that belonged to S.A. alone, she was offered a million for them.

It is only by comparing these astronomical sums with the figures in the account book that you begin to understand what sort of booby-trap had been laid at the very foundations of the Tolstoys' family relations. Only then do you begin to understand the problematics of the family in full and, strangely enough, to respect them even more. It is easy to love and be touched by the father, who gave the shirt off his back to a beggar. Just try coming to terms with the loss of millions, though! The stakes were too high.

We ought to be surprised, not by the fact that from the beginning of the '80s onwards, arguments were continually flaring up in L.N.'s family, related to his radical-Christian attitude toward property, but by the fact that these conflicts didn't blow the family up once and for all.

The unusual nature of the conflicts in the Tolstoy family was also manifested in the fact that from the early '90 s until L.N.'s death (and for some time after his death), these problems became common knowledge. The widespread discussion of them in the press puts the family in a tortuous position. Undoubtedly, this circumstance seriously undermined S.A.'s character, already prone to hysteria, and led her, ultimately, to the brink of losing her mind.

Tolstoy's eldest sons didn't have an easy time of it, either. On May 8, 1890, an excerpt from the report by the Chief Procurator of the Synod for 1887 appeared in the *New Times*, which stated that in 1887, Tolstoy "was no longer able to provide assistance to the peasants from his estate on the former scale, as his elder sons had begun to impose curbs on his extravagance." This was a blatant lie. The sons were incensed, and on 27 May, Sergei, Ilya and Lev arranged for a rebuttal to be printed in the same newspaper, written in a very convincing way. Denials of this kind never convince the public, however, and if anything make people inclined to hold the opposite view: if they feel the need to justify their actions, then they must be guilty of something!

Relations within the family in the early '90s really do take on a dramatic character. 1891 was the Rubicon, beyond which there could no longer be peace in the family. And just as the "gash" in the family relations from the early '80s inevitably had to end in Tolstoy's two attempted "departures" from the family (1884 and 1885), so the crisis of 1891 was sure to break out in some kind of explosion, as duly occurred in 1895 and 1897.

Immediately after the family's property was divided up in April 1891 (the agreement was formally consolidated in 1892), Tolstoy raises the question of renouncing his literary rights. For his children, who at that time had nothing to do with these rights whatsoever, this question can hardly have seemed of much interest. For the writer's wife, though, this renunciation was a serious, not to say devastating blow. After all, under the power of attorney from 1883, she was in fact the holder of the exclusive rights to his works. In addition, she was his publisher and her dealings in this matter were not only motivated by mercantile interests but also by a sincerely-felt passion.

Everything significant which L.N. wrote prior to his spiritual upheaval, with the exception of the autobiographical trilogy and *Sevastopol Stories*, was written with S.A.'s direct participation. She was her husband's copyist, his advisor and even, at times, his censor. It was at her insistence, for example, that he removed from *War and Peace* a candid scene involving Helene Kuragina bathing in the bathtub. His wife managed to convince him that the scene would make it impossible for *War and Peace* to be recommended as a good book for adolescent boys and girls.

Tolstoy's renunciation of his literary rights was an attack not only on his wife's material property, but also on what she felt to be spiritually hers. At any rate, she perceived it as a personal insult. Therefore, having given up in a relatively straightforward way the lion's share of her and her husband's property for the benefit of the children, when it came to the question of literary rights, she showed a great deal of obstinacy, which came pouring out in the form of sabotage against what Tolstoy wanted to happen.

In 1883 he transferred his literary rights to his wife. Let us note that Tolstoy did this at a time when his conscience, no longer allowed him to consider himself entitled to receive income from his creative work, or indeed from his estates. Thus Tolstoy shifted the "evil" of literary rights onto his wife's shoulders and was happy for this to remain the status quo until the early '90s. Why, then, does he raise the question again in the early '90s, though clearly aware of how painful an issue it is for his wife?

On July 11, 1891, three months after Tolstoy's property was divided up, he sends a letter to Moscow from Yasnaya Polyana, in which he tries to persuade his wife gently to publish an announcement in the newspapers *herself* about his renunciation of the literary rights to all his works from 1881 onwards. *Persuasion* is the key word here, and he even resorts to sly tactics. "I've been thinking all this time about drawing up and publishing an announcement about my rejection of the rights of ownership to my recent writings, but other things kept getting in the way of my thoughts; now, though, I think that perhaps it would be a good thing as regards the charge of exploitation levelled at you by the public, as the contractor puts it in his letter, if you were to publish this announcement yourself in the newspapers: you could do it in the form of a letter to the editor: M.G. please publish the following in your esteemed newspaper:

My husband, Lev Nikolayevich Tolstoy, renounces the copyright in his recent works, enabling all those desiring to print and publish them to do so, free of charge." The contractor in question is Matvei Nikititch Rumyantsev, the man in charge of the warehouse of books written by Tolstoy and published by S.A. Negotiations had taken place between him and the writer's wife about the price per copy of the XIII volume of Tolstoy's collected works. Rumyantsev warned her that if she were to reduce the price of these copies (re-printed for retail sale) of volume XIII, which had caused a spike in interest because it contained L.N.'s most recent works, including the scandalous *Kreutzer Sonata*, then the previous buyers who had received this volume by subscription would be unhappy and would come and smash the windows of the warehouse, as had happened to Suvorin when he published cheap copies of Pushkin's works.

Tolstoy was angered by all of this price manipulation in respect of his works. The format of 'collected works' in itself seemed "vulgar" to him, calculated to appeal to the depraved urban audience, but not at all to the intellectual reader. In the letter to his wife, however, L.N. picks the most cautious of expressions and tries to base his decision on *her* interests. What's more, it wasn't as though he was giving up all his rights. Only the rights to his latest works. He considers everything that was written prior to 1881 to be the legal property of his wife, not entertaining for a moment the thought of depriving her of this source of income.

It was that unfortunate volume XIII that was the problem! It was when this volume was released that it was suddenly discovered that Tolstoy's work simply couldn't be divided into "pre-1881 and "post-1881". It's easy to do in one's head, but not in the practical world of publishing. The general public couldn't care less about the intricacies of Tolstoy's understanding of the evolution of his work. The public craves new works, new sensations. The big sensation in Volume XIII was *The Kreutzer Sonata*.

The torment that L.N. underwent when writing *The Kreutzer Sonata* is well-documented. He wasn't satisfied by any of the numerous versions of it that he wrote, and right up until the last moment he was unsure as to whether the story of jealousy described in it would end the way it did – with the wife's murder. Even after the *Sonata* was published, though, his literary conscience would not be becalmed. Bombarded by countless letters asking him to explain what exactly this story meant, Tolstoy was forced to take a step that was horrifying in terms of his literary dignity. He writes an 'epilogue' to the story, in which he clarifies its meaning "in layman's terms".

The story of the work's publication is almost more dramatic than the story of its creation. The fact of the matter is that Tolstoy's wife *hated* this piece of writing. That may be a strong word, but it would be wrong to put it more mildly. Yet she did all she possibly could – and even things that seemed impossible – to ensure that the story was published.

The trip that Tolstoy's wife made to St. Petersburg and her meeting with the Emperor in April 1891 in connection with the censors' ban on volume XIII of the collected works is described in detail by S.A. in her diary, and there is even a short story about it entitled *My Trip to St. Petersburg*. Even today, it is unbearably painful to read this work that came from the pen of Tolstoy's wife. In it, everything came together at once: fear for the family, financial considerations, the vanity of the spouse of a great writer, a strange desire on her part to prove to the public that the protagonist of this work wasn't her, since she herself was promoting its publication, and something else as well, about which we can only speculate as to what it was.

The upshot of the conversation with Alexander III was not only the fact that she got permission to sell volume XIII, but also that the Emperor agreed to become Tolstoy's personal censor. S.A. considered this to be a victory on her part. Her husband deeply resented it. The trust between Tolstoy and his wife in everything that had to do with creative matters was undermined forever.

The years 1890-91, when the *Sonata* was being completed and published, were two of the worst in the family's history. Their son Lev falls into a mental depression that is protracted and for which no medical explanation can be found. Masha wants to marry Biryukov, but not only is her mother against this, but her father is too, for all his love of the 'Tolstoyans'. Ilya selfishly demands that he be given his share of the property while his parents are still alive. Finally, the division of the property takes place. Immediately after it, Tolstoy demands to be able to renounce his literary rights, thereby prompting S.A. in the first instance to threaten to dispute this renunciation in public ("in the children's interest"), and then to attempt to throw herself in front of a train. And it's at this time that he creates *The Kreutzer Sonata* and the *Epilogue* to it, in which he pronounces his third "renunciation". This was a repudiation of the family, of this centuries-old institution itself, at the heart of which he now saw only lust and institutionalized sexual exploitation of women by men. Meanwhile women not only failed to put up obstacles to this exploitation, but from a young age, at their mother's instigation, resorted to sophisticated methods of hastening its commencement, such as baring their shoulders and chests at balls, fastening adornments to rears covered with jersey cloth, and other "abominations".

How must S.A. have felt about this tale, after thirty years of married life with its author and having given birth to thirteen children during this marriage? It's not hard to imagine how she felt. What's more, at this time her husband denies her the right to copy out his new works, sensing her hostility toward them. He cannot, however, deny her the right to proof *The Kreutzer Sonata*, since, as things stand, she is at once his publisher, his literary agent and the holder of all rights to his works. Her material interest in volume XIII is huge, because of the huge interest in it among the public. This volume is banned, though, and at the same time rumors are spreading (at the level of the Royal Court) that *The Kreutzer Sonata* is about L.N.'s jealousy in regard to his wife. This is being said of *her* – though she never once gave him cause to be jealous!

The knot in which she was entangled was terrible. It could only be untied either through a complete refusal to take part in her husband's creative process, or by coldly and pragmatically making use of her right of publication, no matter what, until such time as her husband resolved this problem.

What does S.A. do? Resenting her husband because he isn't letting her into the inner sanctum of his creative work – from now on he entrusts Masha and Tanya with the task of copying out his works – she begins, in secret, to copy out his early diaries, the ones that he made her read back in the early '60s. 30 years on from that time, L.N. forbids her from touching these diaries, sensing that something was afoot. Starting in the fall of 1890, he begins to hide the diaries from his wife, not knowing that some of them have already been hidden in her bureau and are being copied out at night.

There was a masochistic element to S.A.'s behavior. These diaries poured salt onto her old wounds, rekindled her jealousy and provoked malicious feelings about her husband.

"He didn't know how to love – not having been *accustomed* to it from an early age," she concludes in her diary.

"... How I idealized him, how I refused to see for so long that there was only sensuality in him." Finally, she finds this entry in his diary: "There is no love, there is a carnal need for interaction and a rational need for a girlfriend in life." This has an explosive effect on her! "If I had read this conviction of his 29 years ago, I wouldn't have married him, not for anything…"

And all this suddenly becomes bound up, in her mind, with *The Kreutzer Sonata*, which she is proofreading at this time. With her woman's intuition, S.A. realizes, of course, that the story is based on some sort of dark intimate experiences that L.N. went through; this is fairly clear, incidentally, even if you aren't his wife, given the extremely poignant nature of the confession made by Pozdnyshev, the main character in the story. And the chain of "jealousy-lust-murder", as per S.A.'s interpretation, can be superimposed onto the story of her relationship with her husband, especially of late. Only she understands this from a somewhat different point of view. "He is killing me very systematically and surviving thanks to his personal life," she writes in her diary. In other words, this is not about his jealousy over her, as the public thinks, but, on the contrary, about the cooling of his feelings. At the heart of this cooling, though, lies that same thing, lust – an unsatisfied lust.

"What a clear thread there is linking Levochka's old diaries to his *Kreutzer Sonata*," exclaims S.A. in her diary. "And I'm a buzzing fly in this web, having fallen into it by accident, from which the spider has sucked out all the blood."

In *The Kreutzer Sonata*, Tolstoy was opening up the black abyss and summoning up the demons from the darkness, to show the mortal danger of marital union that was subconsciously based, as he saw it, on the sexual instinct. Tolstoy's "girlfriend in life" understood this in too direct a way. Be that as it may, it became a matter of principle for her to see that *The Kreutzer Sonata* was published.

Whilst she was in St. Petersburg in April 1891 and awaiting her audience with the Tsar, S.A. conducted active negotiations with the director of the Imperial Theatres, I.A. Vsevolozhsky, regarding a production of Tolstoy's play *The Fruits of Enlightenment*. Like *The Kreutzer Sonata*, this play had been banned; it could only be put on at theaters inside private houses. After seeing *The Fruits of Enlightenment* listed as part of the repertoire of the Imperial Theatres, in an advertisement published in the *New Times*, S.A. immediately set off for the theater to assert her rights. Her conversation with the director, related in detail in her diary, calls up an uneasy feeling. On the one hand, she refused to give the theater exclusive rights to the play, citing the will of her husband, who did not wish to restrict the distribution of his works. On the other, she acted like the fully authorized and aggressive holder of these exclusive rights, "got worked up" and inwardly called the theater officials "boors". Vsevolozhsky tried to persuade her to sell the rights to stage *The Fruits of Enlightenment* in return for 10% of ticket sales, but at the same time demanded the right to bring claims against any private theaters attempting to put on the same production. If he could not secure this he could promise only 5%. S.A. was outraged by this cynical bit of bargaining. In the end, though, she managed to hold out for 10%, without conceding the exclusive right. Tolstoy's wife had behaved like an experienced literary agent.

What did she plan to do with the money, though? "My son Sergei has suggested giving this money away to the Empress Maria's charitable institutions," she writes. "I would gladly have done so, but my 9 children need so much money, and where else am I to get it?"

By what motives was Tolstoy's wife guided when, after his initial suggestion that she write a letter to the newspapers about his renunciation of the rights to his literary property, she began, in effect, to sabotage her husband's request? Was it purely for materialistic reasons? Of course not. SA was a complex character. It is more likely that at that particular time, she sensed that she was losing the last vestige of control over her great companion, over "Levochka". The success of Chertkov's Mediator and, above all, the affection and concern that her husband felt for this popular publishing house, tormented her vanity as a publisher and simply as a domineering woman, who didn't want to share her husband with anyone.

Perhaps this was where she went wrong.

By the beginning of the 1890s, Tolstoy was outgrowing himself. He was no longer just a husband and a writer. Tolstoy was becoming a spiritual celebrity of colossal fame, whose influence in Russia was comparable only to the authority of the tsar and the Orthodox Church. The esteem in which he is held around the world, not only in Europe and America but also in the East, in Buddhist, Hindu and Muslim countries, is growing at a rate of knots. He is turning into a philosopher of the caliber of Laotzu and Confucius, Schopenhauer and Nietzsche. In ten years' time, and even sooner than that, a stream of pilgrims from around the world will be streaming into Yasnaya Polyana to visit the great elder, the world's teacher.

To have "exclusive rights" over such a man was out of the question. "Not to share" him with the world was out of the question. What she needed to do was to come to terms with it. She needed to come to an agreementwith Chertkov. She needed to agree to become *one of the inner circle* around the great elder. No matter what. Regardless of the 9 children. Regardless of the farmstead. Regardless of her own wounded pride.

It would be wrong to say that Tolstoy's wife didn't understand this. In general, it's a great misconception to think that S.A. didn't understand something like that. But her complex nature, the nature of her upbringing and, finally, the womanly *resentment* she felt over the fact that her husband, who had lived with her side by side for thirty years, is *leaving* "readily" to be with other people; she hadn't been allowed to weigh up all the 'pros' and 'cons' and make an intelligent decision.

Outwardly at least, she still had to come to terms with this.

On seeing that his wife had not yet published the letter about his renunciation of his literary rights and on coming up against resistance on her part ("... all red and irritated, she started saying that she was going to publish... something to spite me," he writes in his diary), Tolstoy realised that trying to make an ally of his wife wouldn't work.

On July 21, 1891, at Yasnaya Polyana, L.N. firmly stated that he would write a letter to the newspapers himself. She knew this would happen sooner or later, but she wasn't psychologically prepared for it.

"We said a lot of unpleasant things to one another," she writes in her diary. "I reproached him for his thirst for glory, accusing him of vanity, he shouted that I needed rubles and that he had never met a more stupid and greedy woman." The quarrel ended with a shout of: "Go away, go away!" And she left having made up her mind to commit suicide. The way Anna Karenina did it – by throwing herself in front of a train.

It's hard to say just how serious she was about this decision. S.A. suffered from attacks which made her feel suicidal on a regular basis, but they never came to anything. At any rate, she wrote in her notebook that she "no longer had the strength to *decide* all the family matters alone" and was therefore going to end her life. And sure enough, after Tolstoy's renunciation of property, all the family issues did indeed lie on her shoulders alone. At the same time, her husband was depriving her of a source of income, namely his works –not the old ones, but the new ones, which the reading public was eagerly awaiting. Last but not least, the letter of renunciation amounted to a public admission of the dispute within the family. S.A. "felt all the injustice of this act in relation to the family, and sensed for the first time that this protest was a new way of making public his disagreement with his wife and family." She ran to the Kozlova Zaseka station "completely out of her mind". It was already getting dark, but she wasn't frightened. The main thing, she realized, was that now it would be "*shameful* to return home and not go through with her intention". Her state of mind at that moment was strongly reminiscent of Anna Karenina's state of mind. The only thing missing was the opium which Karenina had taken, in ample quantities, on the eve of her suicide.

By a lucky chance she bumped into her brother-in-law on the way, the husband of her younger sister Tanya, Alexander Kuzminsky. He was walking back from Kozlova after taking the evening train and was shocked to see his sister-in-law in such a state. S.A. began trying to persuade him to leave her alone, saying that she would soon return home. She was talking complete nonsense, though, and Kuzminsky insisted that they return home together...

This is how the story is told in S.A.'s diary. After parting with her brother-in-law when they reached Yasnaya Polyana, she went to the pond with the intention of drowning herself. Again, she cites the same motivation: "to leave this life with its impossible tasks". From out of the trees in the darkness, some kind of wild animal, "a dog, a fox or a wolf", lunged at her, she couldn't make out what it was due to her short-sightedness.

It was this wild animal that frightened S.A. and forced her to return to the house, where she immediately went to see her youngest son Vanya. "He had already gone to bed, he started caressing me and kept saying: "Mama, my mama!"

Then her husband came in, all animated, and kissed her, as if nothing had happened. He promised her that he wouldn't publish the letter of renunciation until she herself understood that he must do so.

The last thing that S.A. remembered about that evening was that accursed *Kreutzer Sonata*. She couldn't get it out of her mind. There was something in this work that troubled her so much that she came to this realization: her life with L.N. before *Sonata* and their life after it were two different lives. When they parted that evening, she announced to her husband that she would no longer live with him as his wife. He said he was glad to hear it. She didn't believe him.

Tolstoy's letter appeared in the *Russian Gazette* on September 19th and was reprinted by many newspapers: "I give to whomsoever may be desirous of doing so the right to publish free of charge, in Russia and abroad, in Russian and in translation, and also to perform on stage, all of the works which I wrote from *1881 onwards* and which were printed in Volume XII of my collected works, published in 1886, and in Volume XIII, published in the current year, 1891, as well as all of my works which have not been published in Russia and may be able to reappear after today." Tolstoy delayed publication of the renunciation in order to allow his wife time to sell as many copies as she could of Volume XIII, which contained *The Kreutzer Sonata*. He fulfilled this term of the agreement between the spouses. Yet he took away from her the rights to *Sonata*, to everything that was written from 1881 onwards and to everything that would be written in the future, and gave them to everyone. In effect, this was a form of "legalized piracy".

What did "everyone" really mean, though? For one thing, someone would be the first to print the new work. And someone would be first to get hold of the manuscript, in order to translate it into a different language. And that someone would be vitally interested in the writer respected this *droit du seigneur*, so to speak. This was especially true of foreign publishers, who, in being the first to print a new work by a great Russian author and paying to have the work translated, wanted to make money on it and certainly didn't want to be lumped together with the broader Russian public. A literary agent was therefore required, who would ensure that the brand new work, hot off the press, wasn't taken from under his nose by whoever happened to be passing.

Who would negotiate with the publisher about the right of first publication, before the new work started being printed by all and sundry.

Secondly, the "legalized piracy" might only last until such time as the great author died. Until such time as his eyes are closed forever to the fact that his work is being printed by everyone and no-one is paying for the privilege. As soon as the writer's eyes are closed forever, though, the "legalized piracy" would come to an end, because the writer had heirs.

By getting the letter published in the *Gazette*, Tolstoy sincerely believed that he was ridding himself of the last "evil" of property. He acted sweepingly, in the Russian way, like a *bogatyr* folk hero who, with one move of his shoulder, shakes off all the little black demons. In actual fact, though, the demons didn't go anywhere. They were lying in wait.

"Copyright" would get its vengeance on Tolstoy yet.

Whose fault was it, then?

Let us not be hypocrites though, let us ask ourselves: were the family conflicts not related to the physical cooling off of a man who was already growing old toward his own girlfriend who, though incomparably younger (the difference in age was sixteen years), was also far from the first bloom of youth? Let us take a careful look, for example, at this page from her memoirs: "Lev Nikolayevich had had all he wanted of family life. The love he felt for me, for his daughters, who were both necessary and agreeable to him, were still warm somewhere in the depths of his heart, but he was leaving us, he was quickly going away, and I felt ever greater loneliness and all the responsibility for myself and for my family." This piercingly frank feminine revelation would seem to speak for itself. Yet there is one word in that is troublesome: "quickly". This reminiscence refers to 1894. *Quickly?* Tolstoy's first departure from home took place in 1884, ten years earlier. After 1894 they had lived together for more than fifteen years. So if Tolstoy was indeed leaving them, he certainly wasn't doing so "quickly".

Tolstoy's son-in-law, M.S. Suhotin, gave an assertive answer to the question we have posed in his diaries. When was this, though? In 1910. "Oddly enough, L.N.'s complete cooling toward his wife has only been noticeable – and this is to someone living in the house, moreover – in recent years, and especially this year. Is it not something that is happening gradually, as the flesh slowly dies a death."

We don't find signs of cooling either in Tolstoy's letters or his diaries in the 1890s. A much more convincing answer to our question is to be found in a letter to his wife, written in November 1896 at Yasnaya. "You ask whether I still love you. My feelings now for you are such that, it seems to me, they cannot change at all, because they have everything in them that can possibly bind people together. No, not everything. There is a lack of outward agreement about our beliefs – I say outward, because I think that the disagreement between us is only on the outside, and I have always been confident that it will be destroyed. We are bound after all by the past and the children, and the consciousness of times when we have been in the wrong, and pity, and *an irresistible attraction* (my italics. – P.B)." What sort of "irresistible attraction" did he have in mind? It would be rude, of course, to suppose that he only meant sexual passion. Yet it would also be ridiculous to suggest that he had a purely platonic relationship with his wife, even in the late '90s, when he is moving into his seventieth year.

It was in this period that he was feeling jealous of the musician and composer S.I. Taneyev, who had begun to be a regular guest at the Khamovniki home and spent the summer at Yasnaya Polyana as if it were his holiday home. S.A.'s love of music (one she shared with her husband) and her concerns, which had never really gone away, about her abilities as a performer, inspired in her a painful passion for this brilliant musician and former pupil of Tchaikovsky's, a passion which was frowned upon even by the older children. As for LN., he, whilst outwardly being friendly toward Taneyev (he listened to his music, conversed with him and played chess with him), put the question to his wife in no uncertain terms: it's either me or him!

When S.A. was getting ready to go to St. Petersburg to watch Taneyev rehearse for a recital there in February 1897, Tolstoy wrote to her from Nikolskoye-Obolyaninovo:

"It is terribly painful and humiliatingly shameful that a complete stranger and someone who is unnecessary and in no way interesting is running our lives, has been poisoning our lives these past few years or this past year, it is humiliating and a torment, that there is a need to find out when and where he is going, what sort of rehearsals he is going to play, and where."

By May of that year, L.N.'s jealousy reaches its climax. He himself is at Yasnaya and his wife is in Moscow, but she is forced to go and see him, to soothe his rage.

Immediately after she leaves for Moscow, he sends her a letter which it would have been awkward to quote, given that it is written by a man who is almost seventy, were it not for the fact that the letter contains so much youthful poetic force.

He starts with a word of warning: "To be read when you are alone." "My awakening and your appearance is one of the most powerful, joyful feelings which I have experienced; and this at the age of 69 from a 53-year-old woman... Summer is making haste to live – the lilac is already growing pale, the lime tree is harvesting its flowers, in the depths of the garden, in the dense foliage, there are turtle-doves and orioles, the nightingale beneath the windows causes wonderment with its music. And it's night now, the stars are gleaming as though newly washed, and after the rain, the smell of lilac and birch remains. Sergei (his son. – P.B.) arrived that same evening, when you left, he knocked at my window, and I cried out with joy: 'Sonia'. – 'No, Sergei'."

Less than a week later, though, Tolstoy writes a new, angry and jealous letter, in which he clearly threatens her with divorce.

In this letter there is no talk whatsoever of spiritual differences or "misunderstandings". On the contrary, everything is all too clear.

Tolstoy demands that she cease all interaction with the man he sees as a rival.

"Your contact with Taneyev is something that isn't just unpleasant to me, it's terribly tortuous. By continuing to live in these conditions, I am poisoning and truncating my life. For the past year, I haven't been able to work and I have not been living, but rather I have constantly been tormented. You know this. I've said as much to you in irritation and with supplications, and lately I have said nothing at all. I've tried everything and nothing worked: the contact has continued and if anything grown stronger, and I can see that things will go on like this to the end." He offers her a choice of five options:

1) she curtails all interaction with Taneyev. "No meetings, no letters, no boys, no portraits ... but complete disengagement";

2) he goes abroad, having split from her forever;

3) they both go abroad and live there until such time as she manages to get Taneyev out of her head;

4) they continue to live as before, pretending that nothing is happening. But this is the most fearful scenario of all for him;

5) he will try to change how he feels about his wife's enthusiasm and will wait for things to reach their natural conclusion. Yet it is unlikely that it will be within his powers to do this.

Tolstoy didn't send this letter, and the next day went to see his brother Sergei Nikolayevich in Pirogovo, to let off steam. In July, the completely unsuspecting Taneyev arrives as a guest at Yasnaya Polyana. And during his stay at Yasnaya, Tolstoy writes his now famous letter about leaving, which is usually cited as the most extensive philosophical justification for this act.

"... Just as Indians, approaching the age of 60, depart for the woods, just as every old, religious man wants, in the last years of his life, to serve God, and not jokes, puns, gossip, tennis, so I, as I enter into my 70th year, desire with all the strength of my soul this same peace and solitude, and though perhaps not with full harmony, but at least not with screaming disharmony between one's life and one's beliefs, one's own conscience."

What grandiloquent words! With what rapture Ivan Bunin quotes them in his book *The Liberation of Tolstoy*. He not only quotes them, but uses this as the key to the mystery of the old man's departure from Yasnaya Polyana. As the Indians go into the woods. As old men wish to serve God in their final years. And this was certainly true. And it would still be true thirteen years later, when the departure finally took place.

The problem of Tolstoy's departure as seen from the perspective of his worldview is, on the one hand, so complex (dozens of studies on the subject have been written by some of the world's greatest philosophers and theologians), and the other hand so clear and sublime, like a deep lake, that one can only marvel at how Tolstoy managed to express it in just a few words in a letter written in July 1897. Therein lies the fundamental difference between genius and talent. A genius is capable of transforming the most eccentric of acts, related to the family conflicts, into a Meaning that people would ponder over for generations. They would try to interpret it as if it were a "cipher", surrounding it with all sorts of "concepts". They would measure this act against their own destinies, discuss it, sometimes replicate it, but always unsuccessfully.

Tolstoy nurtured his departure in his head for twenty-five years like a great work. He repeatedly edited it, and even did so, as we can see, on paper. In the end, though, he did it spontaneously and somehow not at an apt moment. After all, people don't just leave and head into the woods when it is chilly autumn, turning into winter, out the window.

He wrote a few other things in the letter as well, though.

"If I had done this openly, there would have been requests, condemnation, disputes, complaints, and I would have become weak, perhaps, and not have been able to go through with my decision, and I must go through with it. For that reason please forgive me if my action should cause you pain, and in your soul, above all, Sonia, let me go willingly and do not look for me, do not punish me, don't judge me." Incompatibility with his wife was one of the main reasons for this departure. It is no coincidence that all through the 1890s, the soundtrack to their family life featured sinister motifs from *The Kreutzer Sonata*. Tolstoy was renouncing, first and foremost, his family "project", which he had conceived in the '50s and which he described in a letter to Yergolskaya. This "project" had taken place, but Tolstoy himself was no longer happy with it. The role of the respectable husband and father, who saves up material treasures for his children and grandchildren in his ancestors' "chest", was no longer of interest to him. It was as repugnant to him as the grave.

The sheer scope of his field of view at this time is unbelievable. He questions the church, the government, social ideals. In a world that is about ready to collapse (and will indeed collapse!) in a cataclysm of monstrous disasters and revolutions, he searches for the solitary basis of salvation and finds it in a peasant commune which puts directly into action God's command to work by the sweat of your brow and not to seek out an opportunity to live more comfortably in a sinful, slanderous, unnatural world, in which the majority work and go hungry whilst the minority sits idly by and guzzles its food, gets dressed up, fornicates, commits the most illegitimate acts from a Christian point of view and yet is considered to be "Christian". He tries to unite the world's religions and ethical practices into one generally acceptable model of moral behavior and, of course, loses his way along this path, but goes on stubbornly every day, obeying the great piece of Chinese wisdom: start to live again every day. He searches for his own particular take on the relationship between "God and Man" and finds it in the idea that each human person is a part of the Godhead, and that only by loving one another will these suffering parts be able to achieve spiritual growth and unity as a single Whole. In light of this, the subject of procreation ceases to interest him, in the same way that he's no longer interested in the subject of breeding rabbits. But families are created for the purpose of procreation. And families are of no interest to him. He has already written *War and Peace* and *Anna Karenina*. He has already said everything there is to say on the subject. And said it better than anyone else.

And then just at this time, along comes Taneyev. Some sort of grotesque embodiment in real life of *The Kreutzer Sonata* starts to unfold. Of course, in *Sonata*, the violinist who caused Pozdnyshev's jealousy bore little resemblance to Taneyev. He was a "wretched little man", a "semi-professional" musician, a "semi-social being". Taneyev was Tchaikovsky's best student and an elite-level professional in the field of music, and on top of that an outstanding composer in his own right. But it was as if the devil himself had made Tolstoy endow the character in *Sonata* with traits that were not quite "masculine". "Moist, almond-shaped eyes, red smiling lips, a mustache that looks as if it was stuck on, the latest hairstyle, one that was in fashion, a face of vulgar prettiness, what the women call good-looking, a weak, though not ugly figure, with an especially well-developed posterior..."

Taneyev spent that summer in a wing of the Tolstoy estate; he played music, played chess with Tolstoy, engaged in pleasant conversation, but in doing so, unwittingly, he was driving Tolstoy's wife crazy. S.A. tells in her diary of how she went into the garden and talked to the deceased (!) Vanya, asking him: "is my feeling for Sergei Ivanovich wrong. Today little Vanya led me away from him, apparently he simply felt sorry for his father; but I know he doesn't condemn me; he sent Sergei Ivanovich to me and doesn't want to take him away from me." This was a form of temporary insanity, apparently associated with the recent death of her son, and with the fact that the events taking place coincided with the onset of the menopause (as she admits in the diary).

All of these diary entries are from July 5 and 6. And on July 8, Tolstoy secretly plans to leave home and writes the famous letter about the Indians. At the same time, he also writes a second letter of some sort. S.A. read both of these letters only after her husband's death. Tolstoy had sufficient common sense and morality not to leave his wife at a time when she was deeply unhappy and mentally ill. His flight remained in his head as yet another "work in progress". Nevertheless, L.N. retained both letters and hid them under the oil-cloth upholstering of a chair in the study. This was a very strange thing to do. It suggests that Tolstoy had simply postponed his departure temporarily, keeping a written justification of it in the meantime.

In 1907, Tolstoy retrieved both letters and gave them to N.L. Obolensky, his daughter Masha's husband. After Masha's death, Obolensky gave them to M.S. Suhotin. It was assumed that the two letters would be given to S.A. after L.N.'s death, and this was indeed what happened.

Having read one letter, she immediately tore it up. The second one was the one about the Indians, which she kept.

It is logical to assume that the first letter concerned the relationship with Taneyev. In 1910, this no longer had any meaning. As for the second letter, which almost completely coincides in meaning with the one L.N. left before his departure in 1910, didn't cast the slightest shadow of blame or accusation on Tolstoy's wife. Both letters portrayed the departure as an act that was carried out exclusively for ideological reasons.

The argument that took place in July 1897 was not the only "gash" in relations between the spouses in the 1890s, the decade that was probably the most complex in the family's history. In early 1895, shortly before the death of little Vanya, which brought the elderly mother and father together in shared grief, S.A. herself became insanely jealous of a young female publisher from the magazine *Northern Herald*, L.Y. Gurevich.

Northern Herald was one of the best and most artistic and radical magazines of the 1890s, in which, alongside Chekhov, Leskov and Gorky, the likes of Sologub, Balmont, Gippius and Merezhkovsky also had works published. The birth of Russian Symbolism took place in this magazine. When pressed by Gurevich, Tolstoy agreed to give her his novel *Master and Man*. This irritated S.A. beyond words!

She had not fully come to terms with the fact that she no longer had rights to her husband's works. Yet whereas it would have been difficult for her to fight against the popular booklets published by *Mediator*, released by I.D. Sytin's typography, Tolstoy's decision to surrender this new, beautiful and purely artistic work to a fashionable magazine gave her the moral right to condemn him for his inconsistency and vanity.

It would seem that in her negotiations with Tolstoy, Gurevich didn't shy away from making use of her feminine allure. And it was this that finally drove S.A. crazy. It was one thing for Chertkov and Biryukov to be printing their one-kopek books from *Mediator*, on which she couldn't earn anything. It was quite another to see that the "intriguer, the half-Jewish Gurevich, through her cunning method of flattery, was constantly eliciting something for her magazine." S.A.'s diary for early 1895 seethes with anger. She realizes, however, that her husband has written a "wonderful story". Tolstoy's wife's literary taste was still right on the money. Her assessments of L.N.'s creative works, scattered among her letters and diaries, are almost always accurate. And this "wonderful story" slips out of her grasp, just as S.A. is re-releasing volume XIII and would have liked to include *Master and Man* in it. "Lev Nikolayevich doesn't take money for his work now. He ought, then, to print a cheap little book for the publishing house *Mediator*, so that *all* of the public would be able to read it, and I would sympathize with this, would have understood. He didn't give it to me for inclusion in volume XIII, so that I wouldn't get any extra money for it; why, then, did he give it to Gurevich? Evil is taking me over, and I'm looking for a way to act fairly in relation to the public, not for the sake of Gurevich, but to spite her. And I will find it."

Here we see her jealousy as a publisher mixed with ordinary female jealousy and hurt over the fact that her husband didn't want to give in to her in anything.

Tolstoy had already made it a rule, though, that the family would not profit from his new work. Thus it was that on the one hand, male stubbornness, and on the other, a reluctance to seek a reconciliation, led to Tolstoy once again announcing, on February 21, 1895 in Moscow, that he had decided to leave home forever. To judge by S.A.'s diary, the ultimate reason for the conflict was Gurevich. "Levochka was so angry that he ran upstairs, got dressed and said that he was leaving home forever and would not be coming back."S.A.'s reaction to this is most interesting. It "suddenly occurred to me that this was only an excuse, and that Levochka wanted to leave me for some more important reason. The thought of that woman came to my mind before all else." Jealousy, jealousy, and once again jealousy tormented her. And what an immediate reaction! "I lost all control over myself, and so as not to give him the chance to leave me first, I ran into the street and ran down along the alleyway. He came after me. I was wearing a dressing gown, he was in his trousers without a shirt, in a vest. He asked me to come back, but I had only one thought – to die, one way or another. I was sobbing and I remember that I shouted out: let them take me to the police station, to the madhouse. Levochka carried me, I fell in the snow, I had nothing on my feet other than slippers, and only a nightgown under my bathrobe." At that time, Vanya had already come down with a fever, their son had only two more days to live.

A few years later, S.A. describes the death of her youngest son in her memoirs, *My Life*, and the chapter entitled *The Death of Vanyechka* will become perhaps her greatest work. This autobiographical tale is as good as some of her husband's works. The description of Vanya's funeral, who was laid to rest in the Nikolayevsky Cemetery near the village of Pokrovsky, beside the grave of his brother Alyosha, is striking in its fascinating depiction of Tolstoy. This portrait is composed of several fragments, each of which adds a new shade to the description of the inner condition of her husband, the philosopher and religious preacher, who was suddenly faced with an insoluble question: how was he to come to terms with the death of his beloved son? How was he to interpret it, within the incredible universal scope of Tolstoy's soul and thoughts? How would he have buried the boy's body, had his wife not buried him in accordance with the Orthodox rite, which Tolstoy renounced?

"Little Vanya's funeral took place. A terrible – no, not terrible, but a great spiritual event. Thank you, Father. Thank you." Two weeks later, Tolstoy interprets Vanya's death as a "joyful", "compassionate" event, which "shakes off the falsehood of life and brings me nearer to Him." At the same time, he writes of his wife: "Sonya is suffering just as much as before and cannot rise to religious heights... The reason is that she instilled all of her spiritual powers into her animalistic love for the child: she put her soul into this child, wanting to save him. And wanted to save her life with the child, and not ruin her life, not for the child but for the world, for God." These were harsh words.

One way or another, the 1890s don't show us any sort of cooling of relations between the spouses. On the contrary, this period was all too hot.

Tolstoy was not that hypothetical "Indian" who is able to turn away from the world and walk off into the forest. He was a complex Russian man, strong and weak, stubborn and sentimental, wise and jealous, tender, delicate and at times cruel to an inexplicable degree.

As for S.A., her state of mind and soul in the 90s are described from an unexpected angle by a story she wrote, her *Kreutzer Sonata*, entitled *Whose Fault Is It?* (1892-1893).

On the title page of the manuscript we read: "Whose Fault Is It?" On the subject of *The Kreutzer Sonata* by Lev Tolstoy. Written by Lev Tolstoy's wife." This already feels somewhat like overkill. The double reference to her husband, first as a writer and then as a husband, suggests that S.A. was looking at this story with double vision, as a writer-polemicist and as Tolstoy's wife, who wants to prove something to her husband. *Whose Fault Is It?* was only published more than a hundred years after it was written, in 1994, in the journal *October*. Excerpts from the tale were, however, read aloud at home.

From a literary point of view, *Whose fault Is It?* is by no means a weak work. There is a lot that is problematic in it, though. To see Tolstoy's *The Kreutzer Sonata* in the perspective in which S.A. saw it is tantamount to not seeing it at all. At the very spot where her husband had fallen into the abyss, his wife was running along the edge of the precipice and shouting: "Not everyone jumps into the abyss you know!"

The most interesting thing in the story is not its philosophical or psychological meaning, but her unexpected attitude toward her husband and the story of their marriage. *Whose fault Is It?* was a refutation not of *The Kreutzer Sonata*, but of the love story between Kitty and Levin in *Anna Karenina*, which is commonly taken to be the prototype for the love story between the young L.N. and S.A. It transpires, then, that what Tolstoy saw in one light, his wife saw in a completely different one.

The plot of the story is set out in brief below.

There is an ideal girl named Anna, from whom the thirty-five year-old Prince Prozorsky is carnally in love. The prince proposes and marries Anna. He soon realizes, however, that the image his depraved imagination painted to him, of a honeymoon with his wife of eighteen, turns out in reality to be boredom and the tortuous condition of the young woman. He dabbles in farming, they have children. It comes as a terrible blow to Anna to learn that before his marriage, the prince had a mistress – the peasant-woman Arina. Ten years pass. The prince's old friend, Dmitri Alexeyevich Behmetev, comes to see him. He has returned from abroad, where he lives with his wife, with whom he has fallen out.

He is a sickly man, but subtle in his feelings, a philosopher, an artist, and so on. Behmetev's delicate nature attracts Anna, and he is interested in her. The prince is insanely jealous. Meanwhile Behmetev is dying of consumption, and so, intending to leave the country for good, he gathers his friends together at his estate to say goodbye to them. Anna makes the journey there too, but goes without her husband, who has fallen out with his wife and with Behmetev. Behmetev asks Anna to sit in his carriage and takes her on a tour of the surrounding area, talking quietly – and nothing more. When Anna returns home, the enraged prince, who has been imagining the most depraved scenes in the interim, throws a heavy paperweight at her, fatally wounding her in the head. As she lies dying, Anna tells the prince that she is completely innocent and forgives her murderer.

It is easy to guess who Behmetev was based on: a close friend of the Tolstoy family, their neighbor Leonid Dmitrievich Urusov, whom we have already mentioned when talking about the first "Tolstoyans". He was an impeccably courteous and intelligent man who adored Tolstoy's teachings, and was the first to translate his treatises *What I Believe* and *A Summary of the Gospel* into French. Tolstoy's wife was fond of him, as were all the children and even the servants. Urusov's wife preferred to live in Paris, where her husband sometimes visited her. Urusov died of tuberculosis in 1885, in the Crimea, in the presence of his young son Sergei and no-one else. And it was Tolstoy himself who had accompanied his lonely friend to Crimea.

S.A. was in love with Urusov, in a platonic way. Yet she dedicated the story to Fet, who died in the same year that *Whose fault Is It?* was begun. S.A.'s relationship with Fet was a special romantic story, full of poetry and tender feelings.

Tolstoy's wife's fidelity is not open to the slightest doubt. What does raise doubts is the anger and contempt in the description of Prince Prozorsky, who was based on Tolstoy.

As soon as he catches sight of Anna, when she is still a girl, the prince immediately feels the dirtiest of feelings for her: "... he mentally undressed her in his imagination, her shapely legs and her supple, strong, virgin figure in its entirety." He says to himself: "I must, yes, I cannot do otherwise, than to make this child my own." None of this is in keeping with the love Levin feels for Kitty, in which L.N. put forward his version of the story of his marriage to Sonya.

The prince's characteristics as a thinker also inspire bewilderment. "He traveled a great deal, lived a tumultuous, happy youth, grew tired of everything and settled down in the countryside, studying philosophy and imagining himself to be a deep thinker. This was his weakness. He wrote articles, and it seemed to many people that he really was very clever. Only sensitive and very knowledgeable people could see that in reality, the prince's philosophy was very pitiful and absurd. He wrote articles and had them published in journals; these articles contained nothing original, but instead amounted to a re-jigging of old, hackneyed themes and the thoughts of a whole host of thinkers from ancient and modern times. This re-jigging was done so cleverly that the majority of the public read them with some enthusiasm, and this small success was infinitely gratifying to the prince..."

The characteristics of the prince, i.e., Tolstoy, are, generally speaking, awful. The looks he gives people are invariably described as "beastly"; if he stays at a hotel, he always chooses a "dirty" room.

By contrast, all of the characteristics of Anna, that is, of the author, exceed all normal standards. This isn't a woman, but a Madonna. "The highest ideals of chastity and piety." "With her characteristic artistic taste she tidied her room so beautifully and original with various little items brought by her or given to her by the Prince, that the prince was amazed by its appearance." "From a skinny girl, she developed into a strikingly beautiful, healthy and energetic woman. Always cheerful and active, surrounded by four charming, healthy children..." "She was beautiful in her indignation: her prim, pale face exuded energy and purity, and her dark eyes looked even darker and deeper because of their bitter expression." The prince has a "cynical" attitude toward his wife. In effect, he continuously rapes her, without feeling even the slightest interest in the spiritual side of her personality. She therefore wonders: "Can it really be that our womanly vocation is in this alone, to go from serving a nursing baby with our bodies to serving a husband with them too? And so on alternating between the two – forever! Where is *my* life? Where am I? That real me, who once aspired to something higher, to the service of God and ideals?"

And it is at this point that Behmetev appears.

This is the same issue that was raised in *The Kreutzer Sonata*, but seen from a female point of view. Let's not forget, though, that *The Kreutzer Sonata* is a monologue by a deeply sick and mentally shattered man, such a man as Pozdnyshev is. The tale was written, however, by the emotionally healthy Tolstoy. The paradox of the novel *Whose Fault Is It?* lies in the fact that it was written in the classic narrative language, yet it leaves one with a sense of having read something terribly delirious.

Anna's only weakness is that she is jealous. And despite all the disgust she feels at her relationship with her husband, she is terrified by the thought of him leaving the family. She is willing to do whatever it takes to stop this from happening. "She decided to hold on to her husband with all her might, to look for the ways and means by which she could attract him to her and keep him in the family. She had a vague awareness of what these means were, but they were repugnant to her, but what better option was there?"

Her jealousy of the peasant-woman Arina and of all the women with whom the Prince had had relations before the marriage, sometimes takes on a sickly-masochistic character, "and then her relationship with her husband became entirely unnatural." "Sometimes, red and flustered, she demanded that he tell her stories about his old flames." "Anna recalled everything she had done to hold on to her husband, and she felt sickened and disgusted by herself."

So the author of this story understood that the reason for the abnormal relations in the home were not only to be found in the prince? Behmetev's appearance and her friendship with him are important to Anna precisely because Behmetev is a sort of asexual being. She doesn't disturb his sexual instinct, that "beastly" thing, which has been suppressed by disease, and he doesn't excite in her pangs of jealousy and doesn't drive her crazy. Behmetev is dead as a *man*, but alive and well as a *friend*.

The story *Whose Fault Is It?* is a valuable document when it comes to understanding the real drama of Tolstoy's wife, as opposed to the invented literary one. This story was created as a literary revenge. She was attempting to turn *The Kreutzer Sonata* "the right way up", from its (dark) obverse onto its (light) front side. The tale is infused with decency and moralizing, by contrast with her husband's terrible, fascinating story, with its destructive power. She wanted to write something about an ideal woman who found herself in the grip of a male demon, then found respite in a friendship with an angel-man and was killed in "beastly" fashion by her husband. In the end, though, she wrote a story which leaves us none the wiser: who, ultimately, was to blame? And was there indeed any blame to be apportioned?

Chapter 8

The Beautiful Idol

If before the visit to Optina and the arrival at Shamordino, one can still talk about Tolstoy's departure as some sort of deliberate change of place, then after his he left Shamordino, talk of any kind of departure could not be countenanced. It was flight and flight alone. Even Tolstoy's youngest daughter Sasha, who supported her father with all her being, whilst with him on the train to Rostov, suddenly became truly frightened and sensed it: there was something amiss! He had made (or they had made) some kind of mistake, and though it wouldmight perhaps have been impossible for them not to have madeavoided making it, this did not stop it being a mistake.

Sasha clearly saw for the first time that it wasn't the great writer who had fled from their family home, treated like dirt, as it seemed to her then, by a no-good, cunning and hysterical wife, as she then judged her mother to be, but an eighty-two year old man, sick and helpless, in need of constant care from none other than that no-good wife.

The Astapovo tragedy didn't begin at Astapovo, but on the train from Kozelsk. "At four o'clock my father summoned me, he felt chilly," wrote A.L. Tolstaya. "I wrapped him up more warmly, put the thermometer in – fever. And suddenly I felt such weakness that I had to sit down. I was close to complete despair. The stuffy compartment of the smoky second-class car, surrounded by complete strangers burning with curiosity, the steady knock of the train, taking us farther and farther into the unknown, coldly and indifferently, and, under a pile of clothes, his head pressed against his pillow, a weakened, sick old man softly moaning. He needed to be undressed, put to bed, given something hot to drink… But the train is hurtling on, farther and farther… Where is it going? Where is our haven, where is our home?"

This was the moment when an uncomfortable truth dawned on her. Problems which only yesterday had seemed of the utmost importance suddenly flew away and turned to dust: the diary that Tolstoy had unsuccessfully sought to hide from his wife; the will which he had secretly signed in the forest; the enmity between S.A. and Chertkov; the supposed "life of luxury" which her father had been forced to lead in Yasnaya Polyana. There was only one question left on the agenda: what was a twenty-six year-old, single girl, with a young friend (Varvara Feokritova) of the same age and a doctor (Makovitsky) who, though he was not the best doctor in the world, displayed a loyalty that knew no bounds, to do with a fatally ill old man on board a long-distance train? Right now he needed to be "undressed, put to bed, given something hot to drink..." But this was just the beginning. After a few days in Astapovo, Sasha admits to herself in her notebook: "(Oh, how shameful). I helped with the <...>" Actually, it doesn't matter what specifically she did to help the plethora of doctors who by this time had gathered around Tolstoy. What matters is that a young woman brought up in an aristocratic family was required to do for her father what only his wife, her mother, could do. And she was deeply ashamed by this...

After Belevo, left alone in the compartment, L.N. felt good for a while. According to Makovitsky, though, he barely got up from the couch, alternating between lying down and sitting. The doctor, Sasha and Feokritova came in to see him several times (they were in the next compartment) and saw that everything was all right with the old man.

L.N. was glad to have his beloved anthology, *Circle of Reading*, which he had compiled, with him, having "rented" it from his sister in Shamordino, and Novoselov's anthology about religion, which had also been "pilfered" from his sister's library – what more could he want?

Second-class cars are comfortable: compartments with sofas, little tables, on which, if necessary, coffee could be brewed on an alcohol burner, without the need to order tea from the conductor (L.N. had long been accustomed to drinking decaffeinated coffee rather than tea), and even oatmeal and soup with crackers, which Sasha duly made immediately after they boarded the car in Kozelsk. The old man ate and drank all this with gusto and even had two soft-boiled eggs to boot.

There was, however, one unpleasant moment. As he climbed into the car, L.N. injured his finger. There was nothing unusual about this. Relations between the author of *Anna Karenina* and the railway had always been unsuccessful: one time, on a long-distance trip, he left his wallet containing the only money he had with him in the station buffet; another time, he caught his finger in the door of the on-board toilet... Yet this circumstance (the injured finger) spoke of the fact that L.N. was in a hurry, was nervous whilst boarding the car. It's possible that the lung inflammation which had been triggered was poisoning not only his body but also his brain. It is no coincidence that Makovitsky kept noticing something not quite right about Tolstoy all the way from Yasnaya: either he was shaking, or having an attack of sudden drowsiness and yawning (frequently and loudly, so that it could be heard through the wall in the hotel), or almost shouting at Makovitsky when the latter tried to wrap up the old man more warmly in his wheelchair, or not allowing Sasha to shut the window in the hotel room, though there was obviously a draft, or something else ... On climbing down from the cab after it had rolled up to the steps of the station, he stumbled on the first step of the stone staircase. This made him totter and sway.

At 5:00 pm, after they had passed Gorbachevo, but before they had reached Dankova, LN suffered an attack of drowsiness – a sure sign that he was ill. He began to shiver and asked that they wrap him up more warmly. His back was cold. There were no chest pains though, no coughing or breathlessness. Makovitsky took his temperature: 38.1°. At 6 pm it was 38.5°. The cardiac failures began. And it became clear that they would not be going to the Caucasus.

It is impossible to imagine the mood of L.N.'s fellow travelers at this moment. Their whole "project", a hastily planned one, compiled on the move, but a "project" nonetheless, the prospect of a future of some sort – was crumbling before their very eyes. And the upshot was that they had merely brought an old man – their father! – God knows where, and that under the brutal sound of the wheels of a long-distance train, something had to be done to save him.

There is no doubt that at this time Makovitsky called to mind, more than once, the hotel in Kozelsk where they had wanted to stop, but which they had sped past merely because the coachman had assured them:

they would be on time for the train. How many times, during Tolstoy's flight, had the direction of travel and even fateful decisions depended on coachmen, on conductors, on stationmasters. Even the false assertion by the lay brother Joseph, who said that the only reason the elder did not meet Tolstoy was that the attendant was unable to catch up with the coachman, seems symbolic in this context.

It was because Sasha had left their coachmen to spend the night in Shamordino that Tolstoy was tempted to make an early-morning flight. It was because of the dilly-dallying of the coachmen that they were late for one train and almost lost each other along the way, yet it was because of the alacrity of L.N. and Makovitsky's coachman that they caught the very train that they would have been better off missing, by stopping off instead at the hotel in Kozelsk.

To whom did Makovitsky go first, once he realized that Tolstoy could not go any farther? To the conductors, of course. He went to fetch some warm water and to ask: when will we reach the next town that has a hotel?

They were advised to stick it out until the train reached Kozlov.

The route of the train was as follows: Kozelsk - Belyov - Gorbachevo - Volovo - Danko - Astapovo - Ranenburg - Bogoyavlensk - Kozlov - Gryazi - Grafskaya - Voronezh - Liski - Millerovo - Novocherkassk - Rostov.

Judging by the fact that experienced conductors were advising the doctor to stay on the train until Kozlov, one can assume that neither Dankov, nor Astapovo, nor Ranenburg, nor Bogoyavlensk were the sorts of towns where one could find a decent hotel and give the patient the care he needed.

Yet judging by the fact that they nonetheless got off at Astapovo, at 6:35 pm, Makovitsky, as a doctor, had begun to panic and had decided to get off the train at the first major station. Dankov did not fit the bill. Astapovo did. Even though it did not have a hotel.

To whom did Makovitsky rush headlong, the moment he alighted on the platform at Astapovo? To the stationmaster, of course. "I hurried over to the stationmaster, who was on the platform, told him that Leo Tolstoy was on the train, that he had fallen ill, that he needed rest, to lie down in bed, and asked him to take him in at his place ... I asked him what sort of apartment he had."

The stationmaster, Ivan Ozolin, backed away in amazement from this strange gentleman with a pale, almost bloodless face and noticeably non-Russian accent, who was trying to tell him that Leo Tolstoy (!) had arrived at his station, that he was unwell (!), and that he wanted to stay in his (!) apartment. It sounded like utter nonsense. And indeed it was, all things considered. Who came to Makovitsky's aid? Again, it was the conductor, who was standing beside him and confirmed to Ozolin that the doctor was telling the truth.

Ozolin, a Latvian-born man with Lutheran and evangelical beliefs, and his wife, a German from Saratov, were both admirers of Tolstoy, who firmly believed in his call for people to "do good" in all things. He immediately agreed to accept the patient, delaying the train's departure so that Tolstoy could gather his things and get off the train in his own time. Yet he could not, of course, abandon his post immediately (at this time of day there were still a few trains that would be arriving at or leaving this junction station). Tolstoy had to be taken first of all to the ladies' waiting room, which was empty, clean and not filled with smoke. L.N. became more cheerful. He walked along the platform, leaning gently on Makovitsky's arm, the collar of his coat raised. It started to get cold, a biting wind blew. In the ladies' room, though, he sat on the edge of a narrow couch, wrapped the collar around his neck, pulled his hands into the sleeves, as though they were a muff, and began to doze off and to fall onto his side. Makovitsky offered Tolstoy a cushion, but the old man stubbornly declined to take it.

He had just pulled on a fur coat because he felt chilly and was already moaning, but still did not want to lie down. At this point, as far as Tolstoy was concerned, if he were to lie down, he would never get up again. And he was gaining strength, slowly but surely. And he would go on gaining strength for almost a week, in a lying position now, in a little room in Ozolin's house, experiencing the throes of death, but proving to everyone and above all to himself, that the transition into death is a most worthy and sublime event. One that is infinitely more majestic than our unconscious birth or our semi-conscious life. It is a time of the highest manifestation of one's personal reasoning and of the wisdom one has accumulated. It is the highest point in life.

Master and Man

When we spoke about the family rows of the 1890s, we forgot about one of the main characters – Vladimir Grigorievich Chertkov. His role in these rows was great.

There are some things that cannot be proven. They can be understood only at a psychological level. One can only wonder, for example, why Tolstoy's wife, despite being amiably disposed toward the male half of her husband's entourage and even being platonically in love with some of his friends (Fet, Urusov), hated Chertkov to such an extent?

Had she suffered from a phobia right from the outset of all those who tried to share in Tolstoy's spiritual life with her, then the likes of Fet and Strahov, Dyakov and Urusov, Gusev, Bulgakov, Biryukov and others would have experienced her jealousy and hatred too – but this wasn't the case.

The Tolstoys' homes at Yasnaya and Khamovniki were warm, open and hospitable meeting places for an extremely wide variety of people. Chertkov, in the early days of his friendship with Tolstoy, experienced this hospitality too, from the lady of the house among others. Even at a later stage, when S.A. was already at war with V.G., she showed friendly signs of concern for his family on several occasions. She kept up a correspondence with Chertkov's wife Galya (Anna Konstantinovna) and sometimes spoke to his mother, Elizaveta Ivanovna. She gave Galya valuable advice about female matters, helping to find a wet-nurse for her baby. She expressed sympathy for Chertkov's mother during her ten-year separation from her son, from 1897 to 1907. She even personally brought a doctor from Tula round to see Chertkov when he was suffering from malaria.

Chertkov constantly sought to assure Tolstoy that he had nothing against his wife. But the very fact that this issue was raised (not having anything against Tolstoy's wife) would have been simply unthinkable for the writer's other friends. After all, they understood what kind of position S.A. occupied alongside L.N. Chertkov understood this too, though. The problem was that Chertkov not only understood it, but had designs of his own on that position.

In our view, it is this specific point that was the main bone of contention between S.A. and V.G., which ended in the direst of conflicts. The struggle was not over their shares in the spiritual space alongside L.N. (this space was immense, there was enough of it for everyone), but specifically *for the place* beside Tolstoy, which S.A. and V.G., both of whom had despotic natures, could not bring themselves to share.

Tolstoy first met Chertkov in October 1883. Thereafter, V.G. travels to Lizinovka, his parents' estate in the Voronezh Province, and immediately starts sending Tolstoy not only letters, but also books, notes and even diaries. Tolstoy himself seemingly gave us the reason for this, by describing Chertkov as a man who shared the same "center" as him. He was talking, of course, about his spiritual center.

The words "brother" and "dear brother" appear frequently in Chertkov's letters to L.N. Far more frequently than in the replies to these letters. For Tolstoy, Chertkov was, first and foremost, a "dear friend". For Chertkov, Tolstoy was a brother and a teacher.

Chertkov had suddenly appeared before Tolstoy, at a time when he had barely any friends. At a time when the family treated him, with his new views, as a threat to the family. And Chertkov throws his entire being at Tolstoy's feet.

Arguments flare up between L.N. and V.G. right from the outset, incidentally. The young Chertkov isn't a blank canvas. He is a man with convictions of his own, which, in the early 1880s, differed in many ways from Tolstoy's beliefs. By way of example, their first debate about the divinity of Jesus Christ and the Resurrection, in which Chertkov still believed at the time, influenced as he was by his mother and by Pashkov, was remarkable. Tolstoy's reply was truly brilliant. He didn't try to destroy Chertkov's faith, but simply wrote about how alien to him any kind of mysticism was. Mysticism was idle curiosity.

"There are so many direct, immediate, minute-by-minute matters, and matters of such huge importance, for the students of Christ, that there is no time to engage in any of this. In the same way that a good worker probably doesn't know all the details of the life of his master; it is only the lazy worker who, whilst lingering in the kitchen to brush his teeth, chanced to find out how many children the master has, and what he eats and how he dresses. And, of course, he lied about all this and distorted it beyond recognition, but he had found out and he didn't do his work. The important thing is to acknowledge him as the master and to find out what he needs *from me*; but as for what he himself is like and how he lives, I'll never know, because I'm not his equal, I'm a worker, not the master."

Tolstoy would develop this theme of "master and man" ten years later in a story of the same name. By that time Chertkov had completely renounced the divinity of Christ, the Resurrection, and the Redemption of sin. Yet he would interpret his relationship to Tolstoy as that of the "man" to the "master". Incidentally, this would go on to become the main motif in his rebukes toward S.A.: how dare she see herself alongside Tolstoy as something more than just a "worker"! The fact that this "worker" was his wife, who slept in his bed and had given birth to his countless sons and daughters, wasn't enough to convince V.G. to acknowledge her special place.

It appears, though, that such a position suited Tolstoy. He never tried to give Chertkov a rap on the knuckles and protect his wife. All he could do was explain himself to V.G.: say why it was that in this or that case he wasn't being sufficiently brutal with respect to harsh towards his wife and family – in his renunciation of property, or of his literary rights, or when giving V.G. his diaries, etc.

We are dealing here with a surprising paradox. Whilst acknowledging his place as a "worker" beside Tolstoy, Chertkov assumes the right to *demand* "masterly" behavior of him. To demand it, no less! The "master" in this case, however, is not just a master, but a God. A God does not have, and cannot have, a wife. It was for this reason that, feeling as he did great sympathy for Tolstoy's solitude within the family, Chertkov couldn't understand L.N.'s family joys.

It wasn't all so straightforward, of course. Chertkov was friendly with Lev Lvovich for some time, took a liking to Tatiana Lvovna and Maria Lvovna, was on good terms with Sergei Lvovich and didn't immediately come into conflict with S.A. herself. There is a remarkable letter from Chertkov to Tolstoy, in which he wisely advises him not to "press" his authority on the children.

On the whole, though, V.G.'s course of conduct in respect of this family was unrelenting. Tolstoy was great, Tolstoy was the "master", and all those close to him were "workers". Tolstoy himself didn't think so – but he didn't try to alter Chertkov's opinion, either.

Yet his place in this system of coordinates turned out to be huge, beyond all proportion. The best "worker" of all alongside Tolstoy, was, without question, Chertkov.

Chertkov creates the popular publishing house Mediator for Tolstoy. He launches a massive campaign to get L.N.'s works translated and published abroad. From the late 1890s onwards, finding himself in exile in England, he creates a network of overseas publishing, magazine and newspaper projects dedicated almost exclusively to Tolstoy. Finally, he offers services to Tolstoy to help with the systematization and preservation of his legacy. Chertkov is the first to have the foresight to see that Tolstoy's manuscripts are at risk of going up in flames, unless someone takes the trouble to ensure they are preserved. The activity of S.A. herself in the preservation of her husband's legacy, first at the Rumyantsev Museum and then at the Historical Museum, was, of course, largely dictated by a sense of rivalry with V.G.

Indeed, back in December 1883 she could allow herself the luxury of writing an unhappy letter to her sister about the fact that Tolstoy's treatise *What I Believe* was being published with a print-run of fifty copies: "Instead of burning this which was banned by the censors, as they are required to do *by law*, they took it, all fifty copies of it, to Petersburg and it is being read in the highest circles for *free*. As I've been saying, they might at least have paid us 400 rubles for the printing, these are all people of means."

Chertkov, meanwhile, parts with some of his own money so as to buy a hectograph abroad and starts the dangerous activity of printing copies of L.N.'s banned works on his estate in Voronezh.

S.A. falls over herself in trying to make as much profit as possible from the sale of her husband's works, including *The Kreutzer Sonata*, which she hated. Chertkov, on the other hand, goes to see Sytin, arranges the printing of the "kopek" booklets by Mediator, and looks for sponsors so as to organize his own publishing house for Tolstoy abroad, and everything that he gets from the publications, he spends on the further development of his publishing activities. Of course, his model of the "worker" becomes incomparably more attractive than that of S.A., who is forever preoccupied with the material side of the family's life.

These are objective things. There were some subjective ones too, though. S.A. was rude and blunt with her husband, who begins with age to become increasingly sensitive. She persecutes him with her hysterics, her suicidal tendencies and all the things that Tolstoy finds it extremely difficult to bear. Chertkov, by contrast, is soft, insinuating, compliant. He agrees with Tolstoy on almost everything, more than that – he craves his advice and teachings. He only agrees to get married after hearing repeated appeals to do so from his teacher. His wife Galya adores Tolstoy. She is constantly sick, but literally comes to life when Tolstoy appears at their home. Tolstoy has a phenomenal effect on her, as an elder and healer. Yet in his own family he becomes one of the main causes of his son Lev's depression.

In the previous chapter we showed how S.A., despite being alongside a strong man, nonetheless felt an acute need for a spiritual but "asexual" friend. It turns out, though, that L.N. had an equally strong need for a "spiritual wife". And we aren't talking here about a female "worker". He needed a comforter, who would have a subtle sense of his loneliness, in all its magnitude. This place could not be taken up by another woman, though – both due to the nature of L.N.'s attitude to women (a wife and nothing more, a mother and nothing more, no emancipation at all!), and to the existence of S.A. with her jealousy.

As for Chertkov, he was a suitable friend for Tolstoy in every respect. He was of noble birth but was educated in a free-spirited way, independently. Like Tolstoy, Chertkov didn't go to preparatory school and didn't complete his university course. He was spiritual, that is, he put his spiritual needs above his material ones. He even had youth on his side, too. Chertkov could only gain from any comparison with L.N.'s young sons, who, as they grew older, had less and less desire to share their father's ideals and lived independent lives.

In Chertkov, for all his stateliness and magnificence, there was something vaguely effeminate. He was a wonderful husband and father. It is interesting, though, that in the police reports he was described as a "good, kind-hearted, weak-willed" person who "had been in the hands of women ever since he was a child." Also of interest is the fact that Tolstoy, too, observed in his diary, after the death of Chertkov's father: "His mother will twist him around her finger." And he adds: "Women are awful people, who jumped out of the yoke."

It would be too radical an assertion, of course, to say that Chertkov became Tolstoy's "spiritual wife". Yet his entire correspondence with L.N. is strangely reminiscent of the letters of a "home-wrecker" who is trying to take the husband away from his family.

The Home-Wrecker

We may be wrong. S.A., however, with her female intuition, couldn't be mistaken. "Beautiful idol", "home-wrecker" – that's what she called Chertkov to his face when the war with him was at its heightraging.

She suspected something was wrong from Chertkov's first letters to her husband, and, with her characteristic bluntness, said as much. The agreement was still in force in the Tolstoy family in the 1880s, whereby all the diaries and correspondence of husband and wife could be read by them both. Sure enough, on 30 January 1884, three months after they first met V.G., she sends her husband a letter from Moscow to Yasnaya Polyana: "I am sending you Chertkov's letter. Are you still going to deliberately turn a blind eye to people in whom you don't want to see anything other than good? After all, this is blindness!"

This exclamation is extremely interesting. Judging by the memoirs of S.A. and the Tolstoys' children, Chertkov's appearance in their home elicited an enthusiastic response. "The brilliant cavalryman", as Lev Lvovich calls him, fascinated everyone. Tolstoy's wife, brought up in a family which served the Kremlin, was far from indifferent about how well-born people were. In this respect Chertkov seemed far better than the rest of the "dark ones". Be that as it may, V.G.'s first few letters to L.N. put her on her guard, she became worried.

What was so suspect about this letter, though? Chertkov was trying to persuade Tolstoy to join him in Lizinovka, where V.G. had converted three peasant youths to his faith (as yet still a vague one). Chertkov was experiencing doubts: did he have the right to do this? "Who will correct them if I have to change my understanding of Christ? – No, Lev Nikolayevich, come and see me, encourage me, help. You are needed here..."

This was Chertkov's first tactless intrusion into the Tolstoy family's daily life. A young man who has only just met Tolstoy is insisting, a mere three months later, that the writer, who is almost sixty, rushes to him in the Voronezh Province, in winter. This letter stunned Tolstoy.

And Chertkov retreated for a while, even repented. "With regard to my last letter, you are probably right to a large extent. I remember that the day after it was sent I nearly wrote another letter as a replacement for it." V.G. himself realizes that he crossed the line. Yet he cannot and will not hide his feelings from Tolstoy: "I always want to know where you are, what you are doing..."

Tolstoy doesn't hide his emotions, either. "Any letter from you excites me."

This being said, he sees that Chertkov... isn't quite of completely sound mind. "I will tell you the feeling I have upon receiving your letters: I am terrified, horrified – lest you have lost your mind." Less than a year after he met V.G., he has a dream which he records in his diary: "I had a dream about Chertkov. He suddenly started dancing, he looked thin, and I could see that he had gone mad."

There were many who suggested that Chertkov was not a mentally healthy person. One such person was V.F. Lazursky, who taught Tolstoy's children Latin and Greek. He writes in his memoirs of Chertkov: "... he gave me the impression of being a man who had something wrong with his nerves. Chertkov said that he decidedly could not objectively judge the temperature of water, because he could not trust his sensitivity. Sometimes the state of his nerves is such that he cannot feel the cold, no matter how cold it is; sometimes he is afraid to go into the water for no apparent reason."

Chertkov himself admitted that he suffered from a persecution complex.

When choosing himself a friend for the rest of his life, Tolstoy apparently realized from the very beginning that he was dealing with a man who was mentally unstable, like his wife. Chertkov was an incredibly active person, but his bouts of activity were forever giving way to apathy. In England, he was capable of forcing his coworkers to work around the clock, through the night, without there being any need to do so, but then he would suddenly lose heart and fall into a depression. And Tolstoy knew this.

In 1898, when Tolstoy and Chertkov were engaged in the resettling of the Russian Dukhobors in Canada, the former sent a letter to him in England:

"You, due to your exaggerated carefulness, are sluggish and slow, and then look down on everything, like a grand seigneur, and because of this there is much you do not see, and, besides that, *for physiological reasons* (my italics. – P.B.) your mood keeps changing – one minute you are feverishly active, the next you are apathetic. To judge by all this I think that you, owing to your good traits, are a very precious coworker, but on your own – you're an impractical worker."

Chertkov was a man with a character that was not only difficult, but also unpleasant and repulsive, and this was not immediately detectable. Almost all of his close coworkers and even friends turned away from him sooner or later, beginning with Biryukov and ending with Bulgakov and Sasha. Only Tolstoy loved Chertkov till the end.

From the very beginning, S.A. began to suspect that Chertkov, like all the "dark ones", posed a threat to the family. After meeting him in February 1885 in St. Petersburg, however, she was once again fascinated by him. In this we see a mysterious feature of Chertkov's charismatic personality: when he met people he fascinated them with his charm, but upon parting with him, these same people might speak ironically or even with hostility about him.

In March of that year, she sends a letter from Moscow to her husband in Yasnaya Polyana: "I received the nicest letter from Chertkov today. He asks to be sent the sheets of paper with your article on, which he brought, and he says, for example: 'I always think of you and your family as relatives, and close relatives at that. Whether this is a good thing or not – I don't know – I think that it is good.' How typical of him!"

Yet this "nicest letter" ought, surely, to have put S.A. on her guard!

"Countess, I'm writing to bother you with one request: please send me the notebooks containing the first lithographed sheets of Lev Nikolayevich's last article, by mail. You will find them in the cupboard behind his writing desk. There are about 10 or 12 notebooks in all."

Chertkov had already made himself at home in the Khamovniki household, to the extent that he was now explaining where everything was to the lady of the house.

There were many who commented on the tactlessness of Chertkov's intrusion into the Tolstoys' family space. S.A. resented it – but Tolstoy couldn't see this.

Or could he?

Prior to 1887, S.A.'s attitude to V.G., though a cautious one, is also one that has a complacent and somewhat ironic character. Tolstoy's wife was not generally known for her subtle sense of humor (if anything, the reverse was true), but she knew how to appreciate other people's jokes and pranks.

In a letter to L.N. dated March 15, 1885, she quoted something Fet had once said to her: "Lev Nikolayevich wants to paint such pictures with Chertkov, that people stop believing in miracles. Why deprive the people of this happiness, that of believing in this mystery that they love so much, that he ate his god in the form of bread and wine, and was saved. It's as though a peasant were to go barefoot into a cave holding a greasy bit of candle, so as to find his way in that dark cave. And then his candle is blown out, and he is ordered to smear the tallow all over his boots... but he's barefoot!"

To joke around with Chertkov was not allowed, though. Not even Tolstoy was allowed to do so. There was a well-known instance when L.N. smacked V.G. on his receding hairline whilst they were at the table, leaving a red mark on his head. A mosquito! Everyone laughed. Chertkov indignantly exclaimed: "Lev Nikolayevich, how could you take the life of a living creature!" And it was an awkward moment for everyone.

"I am sure that ever since Chertkov began living by the principle that "thou shalt not kill", fleas, bedbugs, mosquitoes and flies have been able to torture him as much as they want, without fearing for their safety," writes V.F. Lazursky. He also tells us, in his memoirs: "Once some peasants did some work for him and, of course, once they'd finished they started asking for vodka. Chertkov came out to them and said that he could not give them money "for vodka", and instead offered to buy them some books or a Bible with the money. He then immediately took out a pamphlet about the dangers of drinking and read it to the peasants."

Chertkov was a *fanatic* in his convictions, unlike Tolstoy, the stubborn *seeker*. For some time, though, his beliefs had been nourished exclusively by Tolstoy's thoughts. Thus he was a fanatic of Tolstoy's beliefs; but Tolstoy's views at times went through a complete about-turn during his lifetime. For example, he went from the cult of the family to the renunciation of it. To be a fanatic of Tolstoy's beliefs meant only to "freeze" them at a particular point in time.

Tolstoy couldn't help but feel responsible for his beliefs, however. And therefore it was morally difficult for him to argue with Chertkov. He is forced to look on as his first disciple becomes a far more consistent "Tolstoy" than he is himself. And to obey Chertkov's dogmatism, as happened with *The Kreutzer Sonata*. After all, it was specifically on Chertkov's advice that Tolstoy "defrauded" this work with a moralistic 'Afterword'.

L.N. once asked S.A. to find a letter he had received from Repin. Among the letters she accidentally came across a letter from Chertkov, in which he praised his wife Galya and expressed *pity* for Tolstoy.

"I literally exploded with rage when I saw that letter," S.A. recalled.

She was so enraged that she still remembered this incident many years later. And one can understand why. In the letter, written by Chertkov on 18-20 February 1887, S.A. is not mentioned explicitly. Chertkov writes about Galya, about how happy he is with her. "...there isn't a single area in which we are deprived of mutual communication and togetherness. I don't know how to thank God for all the good that I get from this union with my wife." V.G. also observed: "That being said, I always think of those who are deprived of the possibility of such spiritual communion with their wives and who, as it would seem, are far, far more deserving of happiness than I am."

It was as though he had thrown a stone at S.A. She writes in her diary at the beginning of March 1887: "There was a letter from Chertkov. I don't like him: he's not clever, he's cunning, one-dimensional and not kind. L.N. is partial to him because of the way he worships him." And three days later: "The relationship with Chertkov has to stop. It's got everything in it – lies and evil, and the farther away we get from it, the better." This meant war!

A cursory glance at L.N.'s letter of reply to Chertkov, however, is all that's needed to understand that this war had clearly been lost by his wife. Not only does Tolstoy not indicate to V.G. that this invasion of their privacy is unacceptable; instead, he... thanks him. "Thank you for this. You truly cannot imagine the joy I felt on reading it. How good it all is: your life with your wife and mother, the demands of life that confront you. I'm very happy and I love you."

So on whom had S.A. declared war? On Chertkov? Or on her own husband?

From whence had it suddenly appeared, though, this tone in Chertkov's letters: pitying Tolstoy because of his wife? After all, prior to 1887 Chertkov had only been at the Tolstoys' home for short visits. Of course, he might have picked things up from rumors, but rumors would not have given him the moral right to write such a letter. Tolstoy himself had granted him this moral right.

As early as on March 27, 1884, whilst describing two terrible experiences from the day to his "dear friend" (an under-age prostitute, who had been taken to the police station, and the naked corpse of the former washerwoman, who had died of hunger and cold), he complains bitterly: "I am ashamed to write this, ashamed to live. At home a dish of sturgeon was found that had been left to go off, for the fifth time. When I talk about this to my loved ones I am met with bewilderment – why talk about it when you cannot fix it. That's when I pray: My God, teach me how to be, how I should live such that my life won't be vile to me."

At L.N.'s request, Chertkov destroyed this letter. A lengthy extract from it written down by V.G. survived, however. When they first started writing to one another, V.G., at Tolstoy's insistence, destroyed a number of his letters which were too intimate in content, and only later managed to persuade his teacher to allow him not to destroy letters which were intended for him alone, but to keep them at his home, not showing them to anyone during Tolstoy's lifetime.

During the period 1883-1887, in his letters to Chertkov, Tolstoy repeatedly complained about his loneliness in a family that doesn't understand him, and doesn't even want to listen to him. It begs the question: how was a young husband, who was genuinely happy with his young wife, supposed to respond to this? One recalls the "unutterable happiness" that L.N. himself had felt with Sonia in the early '60s.

What was the context in which Chertkov's letter and L.N.'s reply were written? Chertkov was happy with Galya. What about the Tolstoys though? Let's look at S.A.'s diary entry for March 6, 1887. "My soul is oppressed. Ilya is very upset by his secretive and unfortunate life. Idleness, vodka, often lies, bad company and above all – the lack of any spiritual life of any kind. Sergei has gone to Tula, there's a meeting tomorrow at their peasant bank. Tanya and Lev are playing vint in an irritating way. With the younger children, I have lost all ability to *educate*... I have no support in my life now whatsoever..."

In the Tolstoy family there is, if not a collapse, then a very serious crisis. It doesn't take a genius to suppose that Chertkov's letter made S.A. "explode with rage" for this reason too.

In computer terminology there is a concept known as "supporting the format". S.A., by her upbringing, habits and life experience, was unable to support, with her husband, the format of the relationship that had taken shape between L.N. and V.G. Tolstoy, in turn, as he moved from his correspondence with Chertkov to interaction with his wife, was forced to switch from one format to another. A family "malfunction".

In 1885, Chertkov writes to L.N.: "Why don't you ask your older son to help you put your papers in order and keep them in order? It is so important that these papers be kept in order by someone or other from among your relatives... Everything you write is so dear to us, so close to all that is good, all that we are aware of in ourselves, that one simply shudders at the mere thought of anything from among your writings being lost due to lack of supervision."

Tolstoy felt this lack of attention from his family toward his work acutely. How many times does he complain about his sons in his diary! Sometimes he writes long letters to them, individually and to all of them at once, trying to give them instruction on how to find the path of truth, to save them from atheism, selfishness, drunkenness and card games. It is as though he's living not in the same house as them, but on a desert island somewhere.

Chertkov, by contrast, didn't need to be instructed. He himself gladly offered instruction to all and sundry. And he is so engaged in everything in which Tolstoy is engaged that it was impossible not to recognize this.

Even S.A. admits: "I was wrong in thinking that it was *flattery* that is making Chertkov interact with Lev Nikolayevich. Chertkov fell fanatically in love with Lev Nikolayevich and has lived stubbornly, for many years, through him, through his thoughts, his writings and even his personality, which he portrays in countless photographs. In terms of his mentality Chertkov is a limited man and he *limited* himself to the writings, thoughts and life of Lev Tolstoy. I have that to thank him for, too."

This was written before Tolstoy's departure.

It is precisely because of his devotion that Chertkov can afford himself a little extra in his relations with his teacher. For example, he meddles with the text of *The Prisoner of the Caucuses* when it is re-released by Mediator. Chertkov asks L.N. to correct (!) a few lines in the story that seem ineffectual to him (!). And Tolstoy readily agrees, although he considers *The Prisoner of the Caucasus* to be his best work and ranks it far higher than *War and Peace*. "With the exception of those places that you mentioned, I very gladly agree and am grateful. Only be sure to do it yourself." In effect, he is inviting Chertkov to collaborate with him, because for Tolstoy, proofreading was an extremely important element of creative writing.

The main thing though was to preserve the manuscripts! Each line written by the genius was something that mustn't disappear! From the late 1880s until the end of Tolstoy's life, Chertkov systematically copies down everything that comes out of the writer's pen. He insistently asks L.N.'s daughter Maria, who becomes her father's secretary, to copy out all of L.N.'s new manuscripts, including his diaries and letters, and to send him copies of them. In the spring of 1890, he asks Tolstoy directly to give him his diaries so that he can copy them out and extract all the wise passages from them for a *Digest* of Tolstoy's thoughts which he has decided to compile. Tolstoy's diaries, though, as his last secretary, V.F. Bulgakov, rightly noted, "are the man in full, without reserve". Thus Chertkov begins staking a claim to the whole of Tolstoy, "without reserve".

Once again though, let's be fair. Tolstoy himself had an interest in Chertkov taking charge of his diaries and letters. He was very touched by Chertkov's idea to create a *Digest* of his thoughts. "I desire what you want to do with my letters very much..." he writes to V.G. on April 8, 1890. "The good things I have written are needed by me, even more so perhaps than by others. After all, all the good things don't come out of me, but only pass through me."

Finally, it should be said that he himself, at the beginning of his acquaintance with V.G., gave him his diary for 1884, which contained, among other things, malicious comments about his wife and his eldest son. Many years later, he remembers this, changes his mind and asks to have the diary back. Chertkov, though, is already copying it, and will keep it at his home and at the home of his friend from the Horse Guards Regiment, D.F. Trepov, the Moscow Chief of Police and from 1905 onwards – the

Governor-General of Petersburg. One of Tolstoy's most intimate diaries was being looked after by the Moscow police chief at a time when Tolstoy was under constant surveillance and 'Tolstoyans' were being exiled to the Caucasus and to Siberia, or sent to serve in disciplinary battalions.

Between 1885 and 1888, Tolstoy didn't regularly keep a diary. From 1889 onwards, though, he starts writing one systematically. Chertkov understands full well – and rightly so! – what an important part of Tolstoy's legacy these diary entries are. So, in the spring of 1890, he asks L.N. to give him *all* the diaries for safekeeping. It was assumed that Maria Lvovna would carefully forward all future entries to V.G.

And Tolstoy readily agrees once again. "... I have decided to send you my two notebooks of diaries. You take what you need. But sift out more, more."

On April 21, 1890, I.I. Gorbunov-Posadov, a writer, 'Tolstoyan' and co-worker of Chertkov's at Mediator arrives at Yasnaya Polyana. His mission is to get hold of the manuscript of the 'Afterword' to *The Kreutzer Sonata* from L.N. and take it to Chertkov in Petersburg. His second task is a more important one – to pick up L.N.'s diary notebooks. Tolstoy, though, against all expectation, refuses to give them up. He writes to Chertkov: "I have decided not to send them to you. Vanya will tell you the reasons."

There was only one reason – his wife. On learning that her husband planned to hand his diaries over to Chertkov, she was indignant and objected strongly. She did not want to relinquish her spouse, with all his intimate secrets, and put him in V.G.'s hands. And, of course, she was, in her own way, right. After all, these secrets included the "gashes" which had occurred within the family. By acquiring these diaries, Chertkov was getting his hands on all the dirt on Tolstoy's wife.

Back in July 1885, while in England, Chertkov openly advised L.N. to leave his family. S.A. didn't know about this letter; had she known about it, the storm would have broken out earlier than in 1887.

Chertkov wrote: "... get ready to hear some unpleasant things, I want to speak without reservation or mitigation, because I think that is how it should be, love dictates that I do so. You say that you are living in an environment which is utterly repellent to your faith. This is quite true. It is thus quite natural that you have, at times, formed plans to escape and overturn the whole family environment. But I cannot agree with the idea that this proves that you are weak and wretched. On the contrary, your recognition of your ability, should the need arise, to become entirely independent of the environment around you, to send your actual life in a completely new direction, proves only the presence of strength. And ... to run away or turn your life on its head – in my eyes these are not actions which in and of themselves should be deemed reprehensible in advance. Christ did this, and encouraged others to take precisely this path."

From behind V.G.'s slimy, dark-tinted style of writing, which is a feature of all his letters, the logic of his thought-process – merciless in respect of Tolstoy's family – emerges. If you, Lev Nikolayevich, are staking a claim to be Jesus Christ, appearing among us here on earth, and you have every right to make such a claim, leave the "dead to bury their dead", abandon your family!

Having not received Tolstoy's diaries from Gorbunov in April 1890, Chertkov refused to give up on the matter and sent a new agent to Yasnaya in May, the manager of his farmstead, Rzhevsk, Matvei Chistyakov. Apparently, this visit irritated Tolstoy himself. He writes in his diary: "Chistyakov arrived. He kept going on about the diaries. He, Chertkov, is afraid that I will die and the diaries will be lost. Nothing can be lost. But I cannot send them – they will cause offense..."

Offense – that is, they will offend his wife. He desperately doesn't want to offend V.G. either, though. Especially as Chistyakov had brought him a portrait of Galya – an intimate sign of attention from the Chertkov family.

In his reply, Tolstoy apologized profusely. "I am very sorry that I cannot send you the diaries. I wrote in haste back then: I did not mention the fact that it violates my attitude to this writing, I cannot send it without causing unpleasantness for my wife or creating a secret from her. I cannot do that. So as to right the wrong of not keeping my promise, I will write it out for you, as I have begun to do, and send it to you... the diaries won't be lost. They are hidden, and those at home know about them – my wife and daughters. Nothing that is of God can ever be lost. I believe this."

Chertkov could hardly have been consoled by L.N.'s assurances that his wife knew where the diaries were hidden. On the contrary, this must have scared him. And it was in vain anyway. Judging by S.A.'s diary, it was in 1890 that Tolstoy began hiding his diaries from his wife. She had to seek them out in secret and copy them out at night.

Let us allow for the fact that S.A. was a jealous and suspicious wife. In 1890, though, her daughter Maria begins to grumble too. The role of Chertkov's "agent" doesn't suit her. In addition, she notices that although her father is flattered by the attention Chertkov is showing for his legacy, the overly persistent harassment in respect of the manuscripts is preventing him from feeling free.

In the summer of 1890, she sends Chertkov two letters, in which she states that she refuses to write down excerpts from her father's letters and diaries. "In general, I hate making these excerpts, I'm ashamed to be interfering in this spiritual matter, this most cherished Godly matter. I don't ask him to write down comments. He did it that time, I shall add them, but I won't ask him again, I think he finds it unpleasant." Elsewhere she writes: "I am sure that he doesn't want just any old person reading these diaries, while he's alive."

In addition, Tolstoy himself clearly expressed his position in a letter to Chertkov. "Don't be angry with me, dear friend, but understand that it's not that it's hard, but that it paralyzes my spiritual activity, it is paralyzed by the knowledge that it will now be copied out and passed around. Don't give me various reasons, but simply, loving me, put yourself into my shoes, which is after all what love is, and reject this, and don't say that this is a deprivation for anyone and that you dislike it, and I will then be very happy. I will be able to write to you more often. Even now I often find myself thinking: I must write to Chertkov about this."

Chertkov pretended to back down. In a letter to Maria Lvovna he writes that he believes "the issue to be resolved". In a letter to L.N. he "lovingly submits" and expresses regret over the fact that due to a misunderstanding he had been the cause of an argument.

How startling, though! Even in these letters of "repentance" he continues to stick to his role as a sort of "spiritual administrator".

In a letter to L.N., he asks him to copy out and send him not his diaries this time, but letters to other people that are "substantive and of a non-intimate nature" and moreover he asks that Masha be tasked with this job. He promises not to let anyone read or copy out these letters, "until you yourself have checked them in the compilation of your thoughts that I am putting together, and that I will show you so that you can check it before it is disseminated."

How could he say no to his dear friend? In his reply, Tolstoy gave him cause for happiness: "I have asked Masha to copy out several letters and I will let you know."

In a letter sent by Chertkov to Maria Lvovna, there was "only one request": "Please write down in a consistent way, indicating the month and the date, all the people to whom he sends letters." He asked Maria Lvovna to send him these records.

Chertkov was more experienced than Tolstoy's daughters, who had taken on secretarial duties alongside their father. What's more, his daughters had got married, albeit later than expected, and they now had worries of their own. Chertkov remained as a permanent worker at Tolstoy's side. And if Chertkov and S.A. had only been able to reach an agreement and divide up the responsibilities somehow, everything would have been fine. Chertkov, however, was stubborn, corrosive and impatient, and the family resisted his intrusion. And he had no wish to have to reckon with a family which, in his opinion, was not able to reckon with the great Tolstoy.

A new row breaks out in May 1892, when Tolstoy is working with his daughters on famine relief in the village of Begichevka in the Ryazan Province, and opens a dining hall with some donated money. His wife helps him with the fundraising. Chertkov is also working on famine relief in Voronezh. This work brings the family together. Both Tolstoy, when he visits his wife in Moscow, and S.A., when she visits her husband in Begichevka, feel fondness for one another. "Sonia is very anxious, she won't let me go, she and I are friendly and loving as we have not been in a long time," he tells A.A. Tolstaya in December 1891. "The joy of the relationship with Sonia. We've never been so cordial," he writes to N.N. Ge (the son).

But relations between S.A. and V.G. are improving, as well. Business relations, at least. Tolstoy's wife sends wagons of food to his province. At this time, Tolstoy is continuing to work on his book, *The Kingdom of God is Within Us*, and he sends the manuscript for it to Chertkov, then asks him to return it for further editing. Just to be on the safe side, Chertkov sends the manuscript via S.A. – and she suddenly erupts with rage again against this "home-wrecker".

The furious letter that S.A. sent to Chertkov did not survive to this day, but its content can be guessed at on the basis of the reply. She complained that Chertkov was ruthlessly exploiting "a tired, nervous old man". Chertkov was terribly offended.

He sent S.A.'s letter to him, and his reply to it, to Tolstoy. He wanted him to witness the clear injustice that was being done to him by his wife. And Tolstoy was forced to agree with him. "You're right, but she's not at fault either. She doesn't see in me what you see..." In fact, Chertkov's verbose response was extremely unpleasant. He sought to teach the writer's wife a lesson: "In relation to everything that concerns him personally, we must see that his desires are fulfilled in the most subtle and careful way possible." He denied her right to be the arbiter of her husband's health: "In Lev Nikolayevich I not only do not see a nervous old man, but on the contrary, I am used to seeing in him – and every day I see actual confirmation of this – a man who is younger and more energetic in spirit, and less nervous, i.e. with a greater emotional balance, than every single one, without exception, of those surrounding him and of his loved ones." Finally, he openly stated his condemnation of Tolstoy's wife: "... you act in defiance of Lev Nikolayevich's wishes, albeit with the best intentions, you not only cause him great personal anguish, but even from a practical perspective, in the outward circumstances of life, you are causing him great harm." Also offended, but having sensed that she was in the wrong, S.A. complained to her husband in Begichevka: "Chertkov wrote me a nasty letter, to which I replied too heatedly. He, evidently, got mad at me because I reproached him for hurrying you with the article, and I didn't even know that you had written it out yourself. I apologized to him; but what a stupid man he is, how one-sided he is in his understanding of everything! It's a shame and a pity that people see so little and so narrowly; they're bored!" As for Chertkov, she wrote back to him with cold arrogance: " ... if I have looked after him for 30 years, then I certainly do not intend to take lessons now, either from you or from anyone else, on how to do so." In effect, after Chertkov came into the picture, Tolstoy was forced to live in two families. The attraction he feels for V.G. is made warmer still by the fact that he doesn't see him every day, but "senses" him all the time. "I wait for a letter from you every day, I dream about you and I think of you constantly. What's the latest with you? Why haven't you written a word? ... I am wondering whether I didn't perhaps anger you somehow, and I cannot guess how." This is a letter dated September 27, 1892. Chertkov had already taken the bait, though. On October 1 he sends Tolstoy a long letter with a list of complaints about his family. He accuses them of creating a "courtly atmosphere" around Tolstoy; he writes of the "bad impression" that Tolstoy's followers get on making the acquaintance of his family; he snitches to L.N. about his beloved daughter, Masha, having not forgiven her for her refusal to work for him as his "agent". And how does Tolstoy respond to this letter? One gets the impression that S.A. was right when she wrote in 1884 of her husband's "blindness" in relation to Chertkov. "Posha (Biryukov. - PB) visited us yesterday and read your last letter to me and he says: what a good letter, how right he is! And I say to him: and there I was just now thinking about you (about Posha): what a pleasant, gentle, kind man! He doesn't compromise his beliefs, doesn't try to ingratiate himself and yet doesn't offend anyone, everyone loves him ... And I love this about you." This couldn't fail to end in a row.

The incident with the photograph

In December 1894, the most prominent 'Tolstoyans' – Chertkov, Biryukov, Gorbunov-Posadov, Tregubov and Popov – proposed that L.N. be photographed with them in a group portrait at May's studio. How could Tolstoy refuse? That would have meant distancing himself from his disciples and zealous companions even in such "trifles". And he happily agreed. It was no trifling matter, though. If the picture appeared and was replicated, there would be documentary evidence that the 'Tolstoyan Party' existed. It is unlikely that Chertkov, who had ties to the royal family and senior police officials, did not realize that. After hearing about the photo, SA acted decisively. She took all the glass negatives of the group shot from May's studio and destroyed them. The 'Tolstoyans' were offended. "Posha (Biryukov. - PB) came over," S.A. writes in her diary on January 8, 1895, "and started laying the blame at my door, but I blamed all of them. By deceiving us, they had persuaded Lev Nikolayevich on the quiet to have his photograph taken with a group of all the *dark ones*; the girls (her daughters Masha and Tanya. - PB) were indignant, all our friends were horrified, Leva (her son. - PB) was angry, I fell into an angry despair. They take group photos of high school students, picnics, institutions, and so on. So it follows that the Tolstoyans are an *institution*. The public would have seized on this, and everyone would have tried to buy a copy of *Tolstoy with his disciples*. Many would have mocked them. But I didn't allow them to haul Lev Nikolayevich down from his pedestal into the dirt. The next morning I went into the studio, took all the negatives for myself, and not a single picture had been made. The delicate and clever German photographer, May, sympathized with me too and willingly gave me the negatives." On the night of 10 to 11 January, having locked herself in her room, S.A. smashed the glass negatives to pieces. In her diary, she confirms that she used a diamond earring to try to cut out her husband's face – this went badly. Tolstoy's attitude toward his wife's act is not quite clear. At any rate, this act didn't provoke his wrath. In a diary entry for December 31, 1894, he writes: "Chertkov was here. A very unpleasant clash over the portrait took place. As always, Sonia acted decisively but with no forethought and not in a good way." Besides resentment, jealousy and a despotic reluctance to share her husband with anyone, S.A.'s act was also driven by panic and fear for the family. She had in part resigned herself to the fact that she was the wife of a 'dissident', but she was also well aware of Pobedonostsev's cruelty in relation to the sectarians. All the more so given that, in high society, there was already talk of the possible expulsion of Tolstoy to the outer reaches of the empire. After a private meeting with the emperor in April 1891, S.A. hoped that she had removed the danger that her husband would suffer direct persecution on account of his articles. In 1892, though, he presented her with a new surprise. On January 14, Tolstoy's article *On the Famine*, which had been banned in Russia, appeared in the British newspaper *The Daily Telegraph*, translated into English by Emile Dillon. On January 22, the conservative *Moscow News* happily reprinted parts of the article translated back into Russian, adding these comments: "Count Tolstoy's letters... are open propaganda for the overthrow of the entire social and economic system that exists in the world. The Count's propaganda is propaganda of the most extreme kind, of the most unbridled socialism, and alongside it even our underground propaganda pales."

This was a denunciation. But it was true. Tolstoy was indeed calling for "the overthrow of the entire social and economic system that exists in the world," only not through force. It was at this time that he was working on his book, *The Kingdom of God is Within Us*, developing the well-known idea of "not resisting evil by force". Who knew this at the time, though? The fear his wife felt after the *Moscow News* published this piece is impossible to describe. She had heard, incidentally, that on January 30 the Emperor had had a conversation with the Minister of the Interior, Durnoyo, which culminated in Alexander III ordering "to leave it this time without consequences". She knew that the Emperor had spoken about Tolstoy with his aunt A.A. Tolstaya, who had defended her nephew. The Emperor had said: "I have no intention of making a martyr of him and bringing down universal resentment on myself." Yet rumors abounded... T.A. Kuzminskaya wrote to her sister: "I have heard the same thing from various sources: the Emperor is offended, and said that he had even received his wife, something he never did for anyone, and that he hadn't expected to be betrayed to the British – our enemies, no less..." It was said that the cabinet of ministers had held a meeting, so as to decide whether or not to expel Tolstoy abroad. "You'll ruin us all with your provocative articles," S.A. wrote to her husband in Begichevka, "where is the love and non-resistance here? And you don't have the right, when there are nine children, to destroy me and them. The basis may be a Christian one, but the words are bad ones. I am very worried and don't yet know what I will do, but things cannot be left as they are." On February 8 she spends the whole day writing letters to the Minister of the Interior and to the 'Official Gazette'. And she receives another letter from her sister in St. Petersburg, in which her sister writes of "some kind of danger", beseeching her to "act quickly" and come to the capital herself. Finally, the Governor General of Moscow, Grand Duke Sergei Alexandrovich, privately meets with S.A. in the Neskuchny Garden and convinces her that the Emperor is expecting a public renunciation from Tolstoy of the English text. "...They are awaiting a rebuttal from you, Levochka, at the 'Official Gazette', with your signature on it; the other newspapers are forbidden to take it, and this is what the sovereign desires, and he loves you... If in your next letter I find your letter to the newspaper or see a signed copy of the sheet I am enclosing, I will be in such a joyous, peaceful state, one in which I haven't been in a long time, but if not, then I'll probably go to Petersburg, awaken my energy once again, but I'll no doubt do something, something extreme even..." And Tolstoy gives in to his wife again. "I am so sorry, my dear friend, that you were so alarmed by the silly rumors about the articles in the *Moscow*

Gazette, and that you went to see Sergiy (*sic* - PB) Alexandrovich. Nothing new has happened, after all. What I wrote in the article about the famine was said earlier many times, in much stronger language, what is there that's new here? This is all a matter of the crowd, the hypnosis of the crowd, a snowballing effect. I have written a rebuttal. But please, my friend, don't change or add a single word, and don't even allow it to be changed. I thought carefully about every word and told the whole truth, and nothing but the truth, and I have completely rejected the false accusation."

In his letter to the 'Official Gazette' dated February 12, Tolstoy stated that "I didn't send any letters to the British newspapers", that the extract attributed to him "is a much altered (due to it having been translated twice, and the translation being very loose) part of my article" and that "the idea printed after the extract from the translation of my article, in large type, and presented as a view that I allegedly expressed… is a sheer fabrication." This was a humiliation for Tolstoy, which he endured solely for the sake of his wife. He had been personally acquainted with the British translator Emile Dillon since December 1890, when he had visited him at Yasnaya Polyana. In November 1891, tired of the censorship ordeal being endured by his article *On the Famine* in the journal 'Problems of Philosophy and Psychology', he personally asked his wife to send the text of this article from Begichevka to Dillon. "Let them print it there, from there it will get here too, the newspapers will reprint it." So he was well aware of the fact that the appearance of his article in *The Daily Telegraph* was no accident. Moreover, when he rejected his author's rights in the fall of 1891, including the rights to translated texts, Tolstoy didn't make any stipulations about the quality of the translations. What possible moral right to protest could he have now? Tolstoy was immediately punished. His letter wasn't accepted at the 'Official Gazette'. The official organ didn't publish polemics. "I have just received a letter from the 'Official Gazette' with a refusal," S.A. writes anxiously in a letter to Begichevka. "Forgive me, Levochka, for making you write it. I now vow not to meddle in any matters at all… The Grand Duke said what I wrote. So try to understand them!" The letter nonetheless appeared in other newspapers. Tolstoy, though, is entirely engaged in organizing dining halls for the hungry in the Ryazan Province (by that time a total of 170 had been opened), and he looked on all this a little condescendingly. "For God's sake, my dear friend, don't you worry about it... Please, don't adopt the tone of an accused. This is a perfect reshuffling of roles." Feeling offended, Dillon, whose honor as a translator was seriously wounded, published Tolstoy's letters to him, in which Tolstoy confirmed the authenticity of his English translation of the article, in the newspapers *Citizen* and *Moscow News*. Thus, all the accusations fell on the *Moscow News* for its incorrect Russian translation. The newspaper immediately joined in with the debate too. Chertkov acted wisely in this situation. He didn't say a single word of condemnation over Tolstoy's renunciation. He sympathized with his teacher and merely wanted to find out from him: how had this letter been written – had it been *"against your will"* or *"not at your initiative"*? He knew who the initiator of the letter was and was continuing his intrigues against her. In this context, the story of the photograph in 1894 was the straw that broke the camel's back in terms of Tolstoy's patience with his wife. She had "exploded" once again. And lost again. Tolstoy had once again been forced to apologize to his "dear friend". "I still am under the heavy impression of heartless manifestations caused in my family and they in you and our friends here by the story with a photo ... Please try to forgive both me and my family in full," he writes to Chertkov.

A short time later, Tolstoy's daughters Masha and Tanya also felt quite guilty before Chertkov. Effectively betraying their mother, they also apologized to V.G. in writing, saying that they didn't understand how such a thing could have happened. In fact, everything is very clear. If S.A.'s act was motivated by jealousy and fear, then Tolstoy's children were guided by jealousy alone. There are many well-known photographs in which Tolstoy was shown with his large family. Already gray-headed and far from physically heroic in appearance, L.N. is touchingly surrounded by grown-up sons with beards and children who are still very young – Sasha and Vanya. And of course, their mother stands in the center. The group photo of Tolstoy with the 'Tolstoyans' (or better yet, the 'Chertkovans') was also laying claim on being considered a 'family portrait'. And of course, its second focal point, after Tolstoy, would have been Chertkov.

At fault through no fault of his own

For some time, Tolstoy had begun apologizing to Chertkov suspiciously often. Sitting between two stools as he was, living in two families, he naturally couldn't fulfill all of Chertkov's wishes, or all of the demands he sometimes made, just as he couldn't fulfill all his wife's requirements. Whereas he might quarrel with his wife though, and even make a scene and threaten to leave the family, just as she had threatened him with suicide, then there could be no such "heated" interaction with Chertkov. This was the fundamental difference between his "flesh and blood" wife and his "spiritual" companion. Shortly before the incident with the photo, in October 1894, Tolstoy was forced to apologize to Chertkov for an indiscretion he had made a decade ago, when, due to the love and confidence he felt in his "dear friend", he had given him his intimate diary for 1884. Events unfolded as follows. In March 1894, Tolstoy heeds Chertkov's insistent requests to visit him and Galya at their Voronezh homestead. S.A. was firmly against this trip, and she managed to talk her husband out of it several times. Nevertheless, on March 25, L.N. leaves with his daughter Masha for the farmstead of Rzhevsk, where the Chertkovs live, and has a "happy" time there until April 1. In a letter he sends to Chertkov from Moscow, he thanks him profusely for the warm welcome he was given and writes that this time will remain "one of my dearest memories." He liked absolutely everything at the Chertkovs' place: the master of the house himself, and his mother (who was hostile toward Tolstoy because of her son), and Galya and their son Dima, who, unlike Vanya, wasn't spoilt with toys. From Moscow, he sends ten pounds of asparagus for Galya who is unwell, which he buys at the market. The asparagus turned out to be past its best, though, and Tolstoy, having given the stall-holder a stern talking to and sent endless apologies to Chertkov, sends them a new batch. At this time, at Chertkov's request, he is looking for a summer house near Yasnaya Polyana for his "dear friend" and his family. For some reason, it is suggested that the climate in the Voronezh Province is ruining Galya's health, and that it will do her good to be in the Tula Province. As it happened, Chertkov himself had a relapse of malaria in the Tula Province, which stopped immediately upon his return to Rzhevsk. The word "serve" appears several times in Tolstoy's letters to

Chertkov. The great writer wants "to serve" his dear friends. It's hard to say what was the dominating factor here: a sincere spiritual impulse or a desire to implement in practice the idea of serving other people rather than oneself. Tolstoy sends the most detailed descriptions (including floor plans) of the various houses he has found for them. S.A.'s indignation knew no bounds. After literally walking in on her husband (or rather, walking in to find him absent) when she arrives at Yasnaya from Moscow, she learns that Tolstoy is travelling all over the local area in search of a cozy summer home for the Chertkovs. Not only does she dislike this in and of itself, but on top of that her beloved younger sister Tatiana Kuzminskaya, having learned of the Chertkovs' intentions, refuses to spend the summer with her family at Yasnaya, as she had done every year until then. And S.A. again writes an indignant letter to Chertkov. It did not survive, but we know what was said in the reply. "I'm taking this opportunity to express to you, Sofia Andreyevna, how glad I am about our upcoming stay close to our dear Lev Nikolayevich." Chertkov apologizes to the Countess for having troubled the Count with the search for a summer house, but at the same time washes his hands of the matter: he had asked the Count to delegate this task to their daughters. And again, Tolstoy must awkwardly explain his wife's letter away. "She is afraid…that she'll be lonely." "If you ask me: does she want you to come? I'll say no, but if you ask me whether I think you should come, I think you should." Having been given this ultimatum, L.N. doesn't choose in favor of his wife and sister-in-law. Chertkov doesn't have enough tact to realize that he is the one who should be backing down, not the family. On May 18 Chertkov and his family settle in the village of Demenko, five versts from Yasnaya. The mountain didn't come to Mohammed, Mohammed came to the mountain. This was the beginning of S.A.'s periodically recurring nightmare, when Chertkov, whom she hated, began to make himself at home near her husband not only emotionally but also physically. Visiting Yasnaya on an almost daily basis, he is granted the exclusive right to enter Tolstoy's study whilst he is at work, a right which neither the children nor his wife had. In terms of everyday life, he proves to be just as helpless as his teacher. He forgets his suspenders while swimming in the pond and leaves a note asking Tolstoy and his family to look for them. The suspenders were never found. He asks Tolstoy to hire a carriage for him in the village of Yasnaya Polyana, so that he doesn't have to walk five versts on foot. Tolstoy gladly carries out all that he is asked to do. It is in Demenko, though, that Chertkov makes a mistake that nearly cost him L.N.'s trust. In Demenko he continues to copy out Tolstoy's diary. He also brings with him the copies of the diaries that he already had, including the diary for 1884, the original version of which is being looked after by the chief of police, Trepov. In Demenko, Chertkov became seriously ill, so ill in fact that Tolstoy's wife rushed over to Tula one day to fetch the doctor for him. During the journey back to Rzhevsk in August, V.G. feared his death might be imminent, and he handed over his suitcase containing Tolstoy's manuscripts to Maria Lvovna for temporary safekeeping. When she looked at the contents of the suitcase, Masha caught sight of that fateful diary from 1884, the darkest hour in her father's spiritual crisis, and on finding some harsh words against her mother and her brother Sergei in it, she showed it to her father. And Tolstoy got scared. His letter to V.G. in connection with this diary demonstrates once again that right from the start of his friendship with Chertkov, Tolstoy was constantly in two minds. On the one hand, he reproaches himself for the fact that ten years ago he had given that diary to V.G. without reviewing its contents carefully. On the other hand, he changes his mind about whether or not to return this diary to V.G. several times within the space of just one letter. "I tore the diary away from her and kept it for myself," writes Tolstoy. "When you send the original, which you probably have (he doesn't know that Trepov has the original - P.B.), destroy this list. Please don't allow those diaries which you have to be copied; instead, once you have written down ideas that are of a general nature, please send them to me. How many notebooks do you have?" Again, he changes his mind: "I'll send you the diary, but I ask you to destroy it." L.N.'s behavior defies common sense. It proves that Tolstoy is clearly dependent on Chertkov, not only in practice, but mentally as well. The situation in which Chertkov found himself, having revealed a secret, was extremely awkward. To choose not to admit to L.N. that the diary had been copied out, and that the original version was in the hands of a third party, was something he could not do. Afraid of losing Tolstoy's trust forever, V.G. tells the whole truth in his reply, only without explicitly using Trepov's name, replacing it with "a trusted friend". Chertkov expresses infinite remorse for his mistake, asks forgiveness, promises to be careful and, finally, states his main concern: "I confess to you, Lev Nikolayevich, that in addition to the pangs of conscience over the disappointment which I caused you, I am also plagued now by this fear: have you not lost all of the confidence you have always had in me in respect of your papers? And are you not preventing Maria Lvovna from sending me, according to your intention, the last of the notebook diaries which she has, which you gave her for safekeeping?" From this we can conclude that all of Tolstoy's later diaries were already in Chertkov's archive, with the exception of the most recent entries, which he hadn't had time to copy out due to his illness and enforced departure. Meanwhile, the earth beneath him is on fire. Searches are conducted at Biryukov's and Popov's apartments. Soon they will search his home as well and in three years he will be exiled to England. Chertkov was a brave man. He illegally distributed Tolstoy's banned works and had them published abroad. In October 1894, though, the Emperor Alexander III passed away; he had had a favorable view of Chertkov, unlike Pobedonostsev. This was another reason why Chertkov had been in such a hurry to copy out the diaries. When he was far away from Russia and Tolstoy, the only way to remain in close proximity to his teacher would be his archive. Tolstoy comes up with a compromise. "Destroy the duplicate which you copied out, and send me the ones that you do not need."

Why, though, had he not destroyed the copy when it was in his possession? Why didn't he make Chertkov send him back the original version immediately? Why, when crossing out unflattering remarks from the diaries about his wife and children, did he propose that V.G. do likewise, entrusting such intimate things to him?

More than friendship

It becomes standard practice for Chertkov to intrigue against S.A. and her children. Having snitched to L.N. on his daughter Masha in a September 1892 letter over her refusal to perform secretarial duties, not only for her father, but also for him, he tries, in January 1895, to drive a wedge between Tatiana and her father. Unable to forgive her for the incident with the photograph, he writes to L.N.: "I was wrong ... But this sin could not, or at least should not have upset Tatiana Lvovna, who consciously, continuously and in cold blood, for the benefit of her own comforts and pleasures, used your participation in the division between your children of that property which you did not recognize as yours. This was a *real*, and not an imaginary mistake on your part, one that you *consciously* recognized and recognize as such, which will serve, when it becomes known to people, as a real temptation for many, many sincere people, and yet one which Tatiana Lvovna finds it possible to continue to participate in at every moment because it is advantageous for her." "I received your cold letter, my dear friend, but it gladdened me nonetheless, because I hadn't known anything of you for a long time," Tolstoy wrote in reply. In the same year, 1895, Chertkov sends Tolstoy a jacket, not a new one, one of his own. "I am sending you my warm jacket, which we repaired here at home. (Brought by my mother at my request from abroad, it is not right at all, in spite of the fact that Vas. Alex. Pashkov fussed over it very much, on learning that it was for you.) Moreover, my old one will be more to your liking, precisely because it's so worn. It will be useful for you now in the fall, for riding your bicycle (Tolstoy was learning to ride a bike at this time. - P.B.) and horse-riding; and I find it nicer to think that it will be worn by you rather than by me." Tolstoy tenderly thanks V.G. and Galya in his reply: "Thank you for the wonderful jacket, I shall wear it and think of you both..." The 19th century was a sentimental one, of course, and there is much in people's behavior at that time that we do not understand. But it happened all too often that Chertkov and his wife would leave material evidence of their existence at Yasnaya Polyana: from jackets to suspenders, from clocks to portraits. At the end of life, Tolstoy was writing with an English fountain pen which was a gift from Chertkov – how symbolic can you get! The apotheosis of these odds and ends was... Chertkov's underwear, which was put on Tolstoy's body in Astapovo before it was laid to rest. In October 1895, V.G. suggested to L.N. that he become his, Chertkov's, "spiritual executor". He expressed his wish that Tolstoy collect, in a separate folder (which he specially mailed to him) Chertkov's letters, and also extracts from his, Chertkov's, diaries, which he would send to him. This folder was intended for "Dimochka", V.G.'s son. All this was supposed to be done "in secret". "On this folder, I have inscribed a request that no-one but you is to read its contents. This is so that I can write both my letters to you, and my diary, freely, without holding back, as if before God. So don't let anyone read anything from this folder." And again, there is not a word of reproach from Tolstoy to Chertkov over the imposition of another "secret", he didn't try to put his assistant in his rightful place. "I received your letter by special delivery, and I'll do everything in it as instructed," Tolstoy writes. 1895 is the worst year in the family's life since the beginning of its existence. In February, little Vanya dies, and S.A. starts to show clear signs of a mental illness which will start to progress from this time on. L.N. is transformed from a strong man, advanced in years, into a gray-haired, hunched-over old man. S.A. openly stated that 1895 marked the beginning of Tolstoy's old age. She can see that her husband's death is not a million miles away. And she starts – and this is excusable in a writer's wife – to think about her reputation after his death. In April, S.A. goes to see her younger sister in Kiev, to have a good cry. In a letter to her husband from Kiev, she mentions their deceased son 6(!) times. After she returns home, her passionate and painful obsession with music – and with Taneyev – begins. L.N. can see that some abnormal things are happening with his wife, and he attributes this to Vanya's death. As it turns out, though, there is also another reason. S.A. is continuing her hopeless war with Chertkov.

The war over the diaries

From the mid-1890s onwards, S.A., sensing that her husband's death will not be long in coming, begins to worry seriously about his diaries, fearing that her image in these diaries will be wrongly interpreted by the public and by her descendants. "I must keep a diary, it's too much of a pity that I wrote so little in the way of a diary during my lifetime," she writes on January 1, 1895. Aware, though not in full, of the content of L.N.'s diaries, she plans systematically to create *her* version of her life with a genius. She will go on to dedicate her unfinished memoirs, *My Life*, to this same task. Having found out that L.N.'s diaries set sail from the household in the direction of the hated "home-wrecker", S.A. began to worry. The more so because it was from her specifically that these diaries were now being hidden. And then in October 1895, at Yasnaya Polyana, before leaving for St. Petersburg for the first performance of *The Power of*

Darkness, she leaves a letter, which even today one cannot read without feeling an acute sense of pity for this strong but very vulnerable woman. "Throughout those days I went around with a heavy heart, but didn't dare to talk to you, afraid of upsetting you and bringing myself to the state I was in last winter in Moscow (when she tried to run away from home. - P.B.). But I cannot help but tell you (for the last time – I will try to make sure this is the last time) what it is that is making me suffer so much. Why are you always mentioning my name and treating me so viciously in your diaries? Why do you want all future generations and our grandchildren to revile my name, as a frivolous, malicious wife who made you unhappy? After all, if it were to add to your glory that you were a victim, then how much would it ruin me!...

After Vanya's death (remember 'papa, never offend my mother'), you promised me that you would cross out all the angry words written about me in your diaries. You didn't do this though, quite the opposite. Or are you really afraid that your posthumous fame will be the lesser for it if you don't make me out to be a tormentor, and yourself a martyr, bearing a cross in the shape of your wife... When you and I are no longer alive, this frivolousness will interpreted however people see fit, and any old person will throw dirt at your wife ..." And Tolstoy felt "guilty and softened". His diary entry for October 13 reads as follows: "...*I renounce those unkind words which I wrote about her. Those words were written in moments of irritation. I shall now repeat this once again for all those who should happen to read these diaries.* I was often annoyed with her for her quick, rash temper, but, as Fet said, every husband has the wife that is necessary for him. She, I can now see how, was the wife who was necessary for me. She was the ideal wife in the pagan sense – loyal, family-oriented, dedicated, with a familial love, a pagan one, and in her lies the possibility of a Christian friend. I saw this after Vanya's death." On October 25, having just escorted his wife to St. Petersburg, he makes an important new entry: "I feel sorry for the fact that it is difficult for her, that she's sad, and lonely. For her, I'm the one who she holds on to, and in the depth of her soul, she is afraid that I don't love her, because she didn't come to me (didn't understand his spiritual quest. - P.B.). Don't think this. I love you even more, understand everything and know that you could not, could not come to me, and that for that reason you were left alone. But you're not alone. I'm with you, exactly as you are, I love you and shall love you to the end, with a love that cannot be bettered..."

In a letter to Chertkov written on 12 October (immediately after he read the letter from his wife), he explicitly demanded the return of the diaries. "I'm writing to you today, mainly to ask you to send me those of my diaries which you have in your possession as soon as possible." And Chertkov is forced to return the diaries. He does so with an earnest request, though: that they be bound together in a single folder and "that you don't keep them with you, but give them to your daughters for safekeeping, since otherwise, in the event of your sudden death, they might be handled in a completely different spirit from the one in which they ought to be handled." Even as he returned the diaries for '89, '90 and '91, though, Chertkov didn't part with the diary for 1884, the one where Tolstoy's wife was referred to as a "cross" and "a millstone around my neck". "In accordance with your wishes," he wrote to Tolstoy, "I am re-reading it, crossing out or cutting out the undesirable parts." Thus, Chertkov had taken on full entitlement to be Tolstoy's moral censor. The war over the diaries, which had begun in the '90s, went on right up until L.N.'s departure from Yasnaya Polyana. On one side of it was Chertkov, with his passion as a collector of L.N.'s manuscripts, including those of a most intimate nature. On the other was S.A., with her desire to "edit" the living and breathing family history. In the end, this became the "cross" on which Tolstoy was crucified.

Chapter 9

Excommunication and the Will

When Tolstoy was already sitting in the waiting room at Astapovo station, Sasha and Feokritova were in the car of the train, gathering together the things laid out for the long journey to Novocherkassk. "When we arrived at the station," Alexandra Lvovna recalled, "father was in the ladies' waiting room on the couch, in his brown coat, with a cane in his hand. He was trembling from head to toe, and his lips were moving slightly. I suggested that he should lie down on the couch, but he refused to do so. The door leading from the ladies' waiting room into the hall was shut, and a crowd of curious onlookers stood near it, waiting for Tolstoy to come past. Every now and then ladies would come bursting into the room, apologize, fix their hair and hats in front of the mirror and go back out..."

"When we led father by the arm through the station hall," Sasha continues, "a crowd of onlookers gathered. They took off their hats and bowed to my father. Father was hardly able to walk, but he responded to the bows, lifting his hand to his hat with great difficulty." The crowd of onlookers features in Makovitsky's notes, too, under the heading of "people dressed like masters". The doctor at first mistook them for passengers awaiting the whistle for their train, but they were in fact railway workers. Also among them was the journalist from the *Russian Word*, Konstantin Orlov.

There was a slight hitch when they were preparing a bed for the sick man at the stationmaster Ozolin's house, and the time came to take him into the house. The right thing to do, as Makovitsky saw it, was to carry Tolstoy inside, rather than walk him in. With every independent movement, Tolstoy was losing precious strength; his heart was working at the limit. How was this to be done though, who would do it? Not a single person in the crowd, including the journalist Orlov, who was following Tolstoy incognito, volunteered to help the doctor and the two young women. Removing their hats and bowing was one thing. But they didn't dare to help. This was Tolstoy, after all! They were afraid to touch him!

Eventually, one of the workers summoned up the courage to take hold of Tolstoy from behind, under the arms. It later transpired that this man's father was a native of Yasnaya Polyana. As they left the station, another station guard had come up to them, and he took hold of L.N. under the arms from the front.

Tolstoy, Makovitsky notes, "fell forward heavily". He could no longer walk. His flight had come to an end.

At Ozolin's house, he refused to lie down in bed straight away, and sat for a fairly long time in an armchair, without taking off his coat and hat. Makovitsky's explanation for this is that L.N. was afraid of getting into a cold bed. In her memoirs, Sasha gives us a more interesting explanation.

"When the bed was ready, we asked him to get undressed and lie down, but he refused, saying that he could not lie down until everything was prepared for the night just as it always was. When he started speaking, I realized that he had started to be in an unconsciousness state. He evidently thought he was at home, and he was surprised that everything was being done in a way that was different to what he was used to…

'I cannot get into bed. Do it the way it's always done. Put the nightstand by the bed, and the chair.'

When this was done, he began asking us to put a candle on the nightstand, matches, a notebook, a flashlight and everything, just like it was at home." Sasha's recollections are corroborated by Ozolin's. It gives one an eerie feeling. Having fled from Yasnaya and ending up in another province, in someone else's house, Tolstoy thinks he is at home on his estate, and is surprised: why isn't everything as it should be in the bedroom?

Makovitsky had other concerns, meanwhile. It was necessary to warm up the oven, to heat some bricks to lay at the feet of the patient, to warm up some water. If Makovitsky is to be believed, Tolstoy, whilst sitting in the armchair, was fully conscious. He asked that Ozolin and his wife be called for. He apologized to them for the trouble he had put them to, thanked them and asked for patience. His hosts were all affection. They began to apologize themselves for the children, who were making a din in the next room.

"Oh, those angelic voices, that's nothing," said L.N.

...When his daughter Tatiana was sitting next to him several days later, Tolstoy again thought about home and said to her, "A lot falls on Sonia. We arranged things badly." She understood what her father had in mind, but asked him again: "What did you say, papa?" "On Sonia, a lot falls on Sonia..." he repeated.

And with that – he lost consciousness.

The end of the century

The end of the 19th century was a very hard time for Tolstoy. "The last five years of the 19th century was a difficult period in the life of my father," his son Sergei Lvovich writes. "In 1895, my younger brother died – the seven-year-old Vanya, a very smart boy, precocious, cordial and responsive. His mother loved him dearly, as did his father, and their love for him united them in the same feeling. And with Vanya's death, it was as if my mother temporarily lost the meaning of life, and her hysteria, to which she had been inclined before, now flared up with new strength.

Later in the same five-year period, my two sisters Tatiana and Maria got married and left home. Father, who was especially fond of his daughters, found their absence hard to bear, although he didn't say as much, and tried to fight against this feeling.

Only their youngest daughter, Alexandra, remained in my parents' house. In 1900, she was 16 years old. The sons lived elsewhere. My father felt lonely; a gloomy feeling prevailed in the house..."

The couple were in this gloomy mood on the eve of the 20th century. There weren't even any scenes of jealousy or furious quarrels between them. It became cold and dull at Yasnaya. And S.A. writes in her diary on November 23, 1900: "With difficulty I have been trying to elicit and guess, *what* it is that my husband lives for. He never tells me anything any more about his writings or his thoughts, he is less and less involved in my life." At this time, however, Tolstoy is living a very stressful emotional, literary and social life. He is studying Nietzsche and Lombroso and following with interest the wars in the Philippines and in the Transvaal. He meets with Gorky ("We had a very good chat. And I liked him. A real man of the people."). He watches Chekhov's play *Uncle Vanya* and is "outraged" by it. He continues to work with the Dukhobors, keen to know how they are arranging things in Canada. He writes articles about patriotism and "Monetary slavery". He reads the psychologists Wundt and Kefting and finds them "instructive". He re-examines Confucius. Finally, he writes his best play, *The Living Corpse*.

His diary for 1900 is over-saturated with thoughts, each of which is worth its weight in gold. For example: "Life is the expansion of the boundaries within which man is imprisoned". There is a lot of discussion in this diary about marriage and about women, but his wife is hardly mentioned in it.

At the very end of the 19th century, the Tolstoy family is dealt yet another blow. Tolstoy's grandson, the firstborn of his son Lev Lvovich and his Swedish wife, Dora, dies at Yasnaya. He too was named Lev. Lev-III. There is a touching photo in which the three Levs are all seen together. The little boy, just a short time before his death, is seen sitting on his grandfather's lap. After the death of their firstborn, the inconsolable Dora refused outright to live in Russia and went to Sweden, along with her husband.

Tolstoy's excommunication

The XX century began for Tolstoy with an event on which people have always been placed, if anything, perhaps too much importance, because of the public turmoil it created in Russia. Tolstoy was "excommunicated" from the Orthodox Church. At the end of the 20th century, it became fashionable to argue about whether this really was an excommunication or just an admission of the fact that Tolstoy was no longer a member of the Orthodox Church and that this had been the case for some time now. This activity is particularly beloved of writers and publicists who are secular but strongly oriented towards religion. "There was no excommunication!" they declare. "There was merely a defining of Tolstoy's position."

As if that changes anything.

On February 24, the *Disposition* of the Synod taken on 20-22 February and given the number 557 was published in the 'Church Bulletin', "with a message to the faithful children of the Orthodox Greco-Russian Church about Count Lev Tolstoy", which stated that "the Church does not consider him to be a member and cannot do so until such time as he repents."

Of course, the message from the Synod was far more lengthy than this. And, we must admit, it is quite convincing. Here are the points setting out the reasons as to why L.N. had "excommunicated himself":

"- Rejects the person of the living God, glorified in the Holy Trinity, the Creator of the universe and its Divine Providence,

- Denies the Lord Jesus Christ – the God-man,

- Denies Jesus Christ as Redeemer, who suffered for us men and for our salvation,

- Denies Jesus Christ as the Savior of the world,

- Denies the immaculate conception into humanity of Christ the Lord,

- Denied the virginity before the birth of Christ of the Holy Mother of God, the Virgin Mary,

- Denies the virginity at the time of the birth of Christ of the Holy Mother of God, the Virgin Mary,

- Does not recognize the afterlife or divine retribution,

- Rejects all the sacraments of the Church and the grace of the Holy Spirit within them,

- Cursing the most sacred aspects of the Orthodox faith of the people, he did not shudder to expose to mockery the greatest of the Sacraments – the Holy Eucharist." Under each of these charges Tolstoy would sign in a steady hand, without a shudder. The only thing one can say is that some of the items put forth were expressed, shall we say, not quite correctly. For example, Tolstoy did not deny the afterlife (in whatever unknown forms it took), and didn't deny "divine retribution" (during life – the pangs of conscience, spiritual emptiness). His understanding of it, though, did not correspond with the church's understanding of it, of course.

After the *Criticism of dogmatic theology*, a much earlier work written when Tolstoy was going through his "upheaval", after the string of articles and statements he had written, and finally, after the highly derisive description of the Communion in his novel *Resurrection*, it made no sense to talk about Tolstoy as an Orthodox believer or even as a believer in the church. Therein, in fact, lay the absurdity of the Synodal disposition.

To write here about Tolstoy's religion compared to the religion of Russian Orthodoxy would be to write a very different book. Today, this complex issue is being explored by the serious and authoritative researcher, Reverend Georgii Orekhanov. It is to be hoped that his work will give us answers to many of the questions that remain.

For us, what matters is that this "disposition" appeared, and that it did so at this particular moment in time.

Let us pose a simple question: why did the "disposition" appear at all? Why was there a need to "excommunicate" from the church someone who had long since ceased to be a member of it? Why was it necessary to rock the boat of public opinion in Russia – unsteady enough at the best of times – and create a problem which the Synod itself later tried, without success, to resolve? It's a mystery.

The pivotal word in the Synod's address to the children of the church is the word "faithful". With its "disposition", the Synod was in effect drawing a line between the "faithful" and the doubters. "The faithful" were supposed to recoil from Tolstoy as from an undoubted heretic. The doubters were supposed to think to themselves: whose side were they on? Were they with the church or with Tolstoy? It is here and here alone that one can find a reasonable explanation for the emergence of this "disposition" at the worst possible time for Russia.

Who, though, was at the "soul" of this reasonable action, if we can call it that? Who cared to such an extent about the "faithful children", who, it went without saying, might be troubled by the preaching of the fiery Lev? And why could Tolstoy, who *was indeed* a heretic, not be anathematized?

There is a widely held belief that the main initiator of the "excommunication" was the Procurator of the Holy Synod, K.P. Pobedonostsev. This was supposedly his personal revenge for the character of the cold and cynical bureaucrat Toporov in the novel *Resurrection*, in whom contemporaries recognized the traits of Pobedonostsev. There is no direct evidence, however, that Pobedonostsev specifically was the main driving force behind the creation of the Synodal document.

According to a well-informed Synodal official, V.M. Skvortsov, Pobedonostsev was in fact against the publication of the Synodal act concerning Tolstoy and remained unconvinced even after it was published.* Pobedonostsev's stance is well known. Pursue the 'Tolstoyans', but don't touch Tolstoy himself. The Synodal act certainly "touched upon" Tolstoy. This could hardly have been to Pobedonostsev's liking. It seems, though, that he yielded to pressure from the capital's Metropolitan, Anthony (Vadkovsky), who in turn was put under pressure by another archbishop, a passionate polemicist against Tolstoy, whom Skvortsov does not mention by name.

There were many polemicists who spoke passionately against Tolstoy's heresy at the time. For example, A.F. Gusev, a professor at the Kazan Theological Academy, wrote a series of pamphlets against the teachings of Tolstoy. He was the man, incidentally, who interviewed Peshkov (Gorky) at the Fyodorovsky Monastery, after the latter tried in the late '80s, in Kazan, to lay hands on himself and take his own life, and excommunicated him from the church for four years. It is doubtful, however, that a humble professor could have had such an influence on the Metropolitan of St. Petersburg.

A far more influential polemicist against Tolstoy was Father John of Kronstadt, Russia's most famous preacher, acclaimed by the people as a miracle-worker and later a member of the Holy Synod. For one thing, though, John of Kronstadt did not have any influence in the Synod. John was a popular priestly father, not a ranking archbishop. Incidentally, his signature does not feature on the Synodal document. Secondly, if John of Kronstadt had had his way, Tolstoy would not have been "excommunicated", but publicly hung, drawn and quartered. Father John's hatred of Tolstoy bordered on the insane. The "polemics" of St. John of Kronstadt against Tolstoy are impossible to read. It is not a polemic, but outright abuse. In a diary entry written on his deathbed on September 6, 1908, he worked himself up to the extent that he begged God to kill Tolstoy, so that the octogenarian wouldn't live to see the holiday of the Nativity of the Blessed Virgin, "whom he blasphemed terribly and continues to blaspheme." "Take him from the Earth – this stinking corpse, which with its pride has aggrieved all the land. Amen. 9 in the evening." This was Father John's evening prayer. Amazingly, we read just two days later in the same diary:

"O Lord, the seriously ill Anna (Grigorieva) prays to you passionately for her healing, through my unworthiness. Heal her, Physician of souls and bodies, and amaze us with Your grace and power." It's true what they say about the breadth of the Russian's nature.

So there weren't, most likely, any direct "services" of the Father of Kronstadt in Tolstoy's excommunication. It was a slightly different register of spiritual "polemics."

In his memoirs, V.M. Skvortsov talks about a circle of "clerics who had an influence on Bishop Anthony", mentioning Anthony (Khrapovitsky), Sergei (Stragorodsky), Innokenty (Belyaev), Antonin (Granovsky) and Mikhail (Semenov). He also alludes to the fact that the bishop's campaign against Tolstoy was indirectly a campaign against Pobedonostsev, who was thus pushed into taking stronger action against the famous writer. After all, neither two Russian emperors nor the chief prosecutor had dared to "touch" Tolstoy for some reason.

It's curious, however, that none of these "circle members" whom Skvortsov mentioned signed the Synodal act, and nor had Father John of Kronstadt.

Besides Anthony (Vadkovsky), the act was signed by Feognost, Metropolitan of Kiev and Galicia; Metropolitan Vladimir of Moscow and Kolomna; Ieroni, Archbishop of Warsaw and Holm; Yakov, Bishop of Chisinau and Khotinsk; and Bishops Boris and Markel.

Thus it remains the case that Anthony (Vadkovsky) was the figure who went out on a limb in this incident.

It is here that the most interesting part begins. According to Skvortsov, the text of the excommunication was written *by Pobedonostsev*. The members of the Synod edited it, though, so that the "disposition" didn't look like an "excommunication" and would provide evidence only of Tolstoy's own falling away from the church. That's not all: the "disposition" ended not in a curse against Count Tolstoy as a "false teacher", which was no doubt what he was in the eyes of Pobedonostsev, who had had every reason not to like Tolstoy since 1881, when they had their first struggle for influence over the still young Alexander III. It ended with a prayer. And of course, this prayer wasn't written by Pobedonostsev. "Therefore, as we testify about his falling away from the Church, we pray together, that the Lord will give him repentance and true reason. We pray to Thee, merciful God, not to want the death of sinners, hear our prayer and have mercy, and turn him to Thy Holy Church. Amen." There was a reference in the Synodal Act to Tolstoy's outstanding artistic talent, which was given to him specifically from God. Thus any attuned, attentive reader of this document could understand in its entirety the problem which the Church and Tolstoy were facing. A great writer, the glory of the Russian land, had "renounced the Mother who brought him up and nourished him, the Orthodox Church, and devoted his literary career and God-given talent to spreading teachings among the people which went against Christ and the Church, and to the destruction in the people's hearts and minds of the faith of their Fatherland, the Orthodox faith."

Who can say that there was no such problem? There was, and what a problem it was! Of course, it was a drama for Tolstoy as well, whose beloved sister lived as a nun at Shamordino, the place to which Tolstoy, ultimately, fled from Yasnaya.

Yet as it turned out, there were almost no attuned and attentive readers in Russia. Moreover, it simply wasn't the right time for the Synodal "disposition" to come out. At the beginning of the 20th century Russia was tottering and swaying. The bloody carnage of 1905-1907, and the violent measures taken by Stolypin in response, to suppress the first Russian revolution, were just a few years away. At this time, any "inflammatory" document such as this could only bring harm. Meanwhile, the authority of Tolstoy-the-teacher was approaching its zenith at this time (the Synodal act, in fact, only brought this zenith closer).

The Synodal act was an obvious mistake. In principle, it was a well-put together document, but it was published at the wrong time, *in the wrong Russia*, not in the Russia in which it should have appeared, *for the wrong Tolstoy*, not for that Tolstoy who might have taken heed of it; the document shook Russian society not because of what was in it, but because of the medieval symbolism of the act itself. After all, this act came just before the Day of the Triumph of Orthodoxy. It is on this day, the Triumph of Orthodoxy, that all heretics and rebels were traditionally "anathematized". The last time this had occurred was in the 18th century – with Hetman Mazepa. Since 1801, however, the names of heretics had not been read out in church services, and in 1869 they removed from the list of people who had been cursed by the priests even Mazepa and Otrepiev, i.e. those who were clearly state criminals.

Of course, the name of Tolstoy was not "anathematized" in the churches, as Kuprin wrote in one of his weaker stories. That's not the point though. The point is that decidedly at all levels of Russian society, from workers to students and from professors to ordinary priests, the Holy Synod's *"disposition"* was interpreted as nothing other than an *"excommunication"*. The Synodal act stirred up memories in the Russian consciousness of the time of Avvakum and the persecution of dissenters. "He's been excommunicated!" "Excommunicated!" And who was the man in question? Their greatest contemporary, the glory of the country!

On March 4, 1901, a demonstration was held in support of Tolstoy in the Kazan Square in St. Petersburg, at which many of those taking part were beaten up by the police.

At the 29th exhibition of the Association of the Wanderers, Repin's painting *Tolstoy at Prayer* was decorated with flowers. As a result, the picture had to be removed.

There were many such incidents. An endless stream of letters and telegrams was sent to Yasnaya Polyana congratulating Tolstoy (!) on having been excommunicated.

Vasily Rozanov wrote an acerbic article, the title of which speaks for itself: "On Count L.N. Tolstoy's excommunication from the church". "Meanwhile Tolstoy," wrote Rozanov, "for all his appalling errors, mistakes and bold words, is a *religious* phenomenon of vast proportions, perhaps the greatest religious phenomenon in Russian history in the 19th century, albeit a distorted one. The oak which grows in a crooked way is still an oak, and is not to be judged by a mechanical, formal institution which didn't grow at all but was made by human hands (by Peter the Great, with a series of consecutive orders). The Synod, therefore, clearly doesn't know how to approach this topic, was long wary of coming near it and, when it did so, took a step that was perhaps fatal to the Russian religious consciousness. This act has shaken the Russian people's faith more than any of Tolstoy's teachings."

The Synodal act even caused a split among the priesthood. Suddenly it became clear that were a great many admirers of Tolstoy not only among the "faithful children" of the Orthodox Church, but also among their pastors. And the Synod's decision was doubly offensive to them – they felt aggrieved on behalf of their favorite writer and on behalf of their church.

The Synodal act caused a split even among the monks, those seemingly most orthodox adherents of Orthodoxy. From the recently published letters sent by Athos the Schema-monk of Xenophont (Prince Constantine Vyazemsky) to his sister, one can judge what kind of explosion of doubt, and at times indignation too, this document caused at the holy places of Russian Orthodoxy in St Petersburg.

"The Synod's job is to act as a guardian of the Church," wrote Xenophont, "that is, to watch over the clergy to ensure they behave decently." "To curse and vilify people on account of the fact that they think differently than others does not fall within the scope of the Synod's activities." "Tolstoy himself has always declared that he does not belong to the Orthodox Church, therefore it doesn't have any rights over him, just as it doesn't have any rights over sectarians, Lutherans or Catholics." "If they want to condemn and denounce Tolstoy's religious teachings, they must convene a council and listen to what he has to say, not take decisions without him being present, as the Popes do in Rome. Incidentally, it is clear to all that personal passions and wounded pride are playing a role here." Not particularly clued-up about the intrigues of the capital, Xenophont laid most of the blame for the "excommunication" on Pobedonostsev. He also laid part of the blame on Kronstadt, whom he once known personally and didn't like, considering him to be a "harmful charlatan". These are mere details, though. The main thing that comes out of the letters is to be found in this passage: "I have precise information about everything concerning this matter, because we have many people here who get news directly from the Synod, everyone is terribly interested in this matter, and all the monasteries are divided into two camps: those who are spiteful about Tolstoy and hate him (the majority) and those who feel sympathy for him and are horrified by this struggle that has broken out in Russia."

Xenophont himself could not be objective about this issue, however. Whilst he was still Prince Vyazemsky, the writer and traveler, he visited Yasnaya Polyana on two occasions and was fascinated by Tolstoy as a man. "Am I to believe that this sweet little old man, who makes his guests' beds himself, smiles so good-naturedly as he sits by the samovar, makes fun so tactfully of newly arrived visitors who are not yet accustomed to his eccentricities, am I to believe that he is the Antichrist, an apostate, and so on and so forth. This man, who shows such love and concern for the lowliest of paupers – is it possible that he is a bad man? Ask the peasants from his province – after all, they pray for him, no-one will leave his presence without feeling consoled, he never refuses help to anyone." It appears that the attitude toward Tolstoy among the monks was even more complex than it was among the secular clergy. After all, there was a reason why Father Ambrose had three conversations with him that lasted several hours each. There was a reason why he was idolized by the nuns at the Shamordino monastery. There was a reason why such significance was attached to the fact that L.N. wasn't able to meet with Father Josif at the time of his last visit to Optina. There was a reason why the simple monks of this monastery felt such sympathy for him.

The monks sensed that he was to be looked upon as an elder. They understood that it wasn't because of his writings, but because of his way of life that Tolstoy corresponded more closely to the archetypal Christian ascetic than a great many of the official clergy, particularly those vested with higher authority. Yes, he was an "incorrect" elder, an "oak that had grown crooked", as Rozanov had put it. Yes, his writings about the church were horrifying. Never mind his writings, though; in terms of his appearance, his entire *being* – he was an *elder*.

It is no coincidence that in the first draft of Tolstoy's farewell message to his wife, written in the notebook on the eve of departure, he wrote: "I'm doing what old men ordinarily do, thousands of old men, men who are close to death, by going away from their former circumstances, which have become hateful to them, to live in circumstances which are in keeping with their mood. Most go to the monasteries, and I too would have gone to a monastery if I believed what they believe at the monasteries. Being someone who does not believe in that way, I am leaving simply to find solitude." The passage about monasteries disappeared from the final version of the letter. We must remember, though, that Tolstoy didn't walk away from Yasnaya Polyana, he ran away, fearing that he might be pursued. Might it not be that he deleted the line about the monasteries so as not to give a clue as to where they might find him? After all, that was exactly where he ended up going: to the Optina

Hermitage and to Shamordino. Indeed it's hard to imagine where else he could have gone, that would have served as his first place of refuge.

Tolstoy, it seems, felt indifferent about the "excommunication". Having found out about it, he asked only: was the word "anathema" used? And he expressed surprise that there was no mention of "anathema". Why, then, had there been so much fuss? In his diary he describes as "strange" both the "disposition" by the Synod and the ardent expressions of sympathy that were sent to Yasnaya. L.N. was unwell at the time and was continuing to write *Hadji Murat*.

Realizing nonetheless that he could not pass over the matter in silence, Tolstoy writes a reply to the Synod's decision, reworking the text numerous times, as usual, and only finishing it on April 4.

L.N.'s reply begins with an epigraph from the poet Coleridge: "He who begins by loving Christianity better than truth will proceed by loving his own sect and church better than Christianity, and end in loving himself best of all." By using this epigraph he is asserting the primacy of truth over all else, even over Christianity. And this signifies that Christianity is no longer, for him, the ultimate truth. This is Tolstoy's position.

In the text itself, he points to the ambiguity of the Synod's act. If this is an excommunication, then why have the rules not been followed. If it is just a statement to the effect that he does not belong to the church, this is already "self-evident, and such a statement can have no purpose other than to appear to be an excommunication without actually being one, and sure enough this is the effect it had, because this was how it was interpreted."

"The fact that I renounced the Church that goes by the name of Orthodox," Tolstoy agrees, "is quite true. I renounced it, however, not because I rebelled against the Lord, but on the contrary, only because I desired with all the strength of my soul to serve Him." Unfortunately, the text contains some wildly uncouth passages about the church rites. "In order for a child, if he dies, to go to heaven, one must make sure he is anointed with oil in time and save his soul via the uttering of those famous words ..." There is, alas, an obvious lie too. Or, rather, a half-truth. "I never made any efforts to spread my teachings." How can we believe this? Who was it, then, that published *What I Believe* at his own expense, using Kushnerev's printing press, and distributed it among high society in Peterburg? Who was it that gave Chertkov the manuscripts of all his anti-clerical articles, who rejoiced when they were published in England?

Tolstoy's written response, in contrast to the Synod's act, was very lengthy, suggesting that he was having difficulty setting out the main idea in it. At the end of it, though, the main idea breaks through, the one that shows its meaning. "It is for me alone to live my life, it is for me alone to die (and that will happen very soon), and for that reason I cannot believe in any other way than the way I do, as I prepare to go to that One God, from Whence I came."

In other words – leave me alone!

And that says it all about Tolstoy.

The Countess reacted differently to the Synod's decision. She remembered, of course, how bold she had been when speaking to Pobedonostsev in her time, when defending the greatness of her husband, and how affectionately Alexander III and the Empress had received her. What was some Synod or other compared to this! And the Countess decided to fight back once again.

She writes an unfortunate letter of her own, which she sends to Pobedonostsev and the three metropolitans who signed the "disposition". This letter was translated into foreign languages and widely distributed.

"There wasn't a single one of L.N.'s manuscripts that spread so rapidly and so far afield as that letter I wrote," S.A. writes in her diary. She is happy! She's experiencing some sort of exaltation. "God told me to do it, not my own will." Observing the mood she is in, Tolstoy notes sadly, "So many books have been written about this issue that you couldn't fit them all inside this house, and yet you want to teach them with that letter of yours." These were harsh words.

After all, she so wanted to feel like her husband's companion once again; she loved him ardently, but he remained indifferent to her civic impulses. In this case, however, judging by S.A.'s diary, he was affectionate and "very passionate" with her, though not in the amorous sense.

The Countess's letter was published in the informal part of the *Church Bulletin*, together with a reply written by Bishop Anthony (Vadkovsky).

"For me, the Church is an abstract concept," she writes, not realizing that by doing so she is "excommunicating" herself, too, from the church.

"Can it really be true that when I need to hold a burial for my husband and pray for him in church, I shan't be able to find either an honest priest, who isn't afraid of people before the true God of love, or a "dishonest" one, whom I shall bribe with a lot of money for this purpose?" S.A. naively admits.

The Metropolitan's response was damning. "The Church to which you consider yourself to belong consists of believers in Christ," he writes, stating the obvious. "And I don't think that any priest whatsoever, not even a dishonest one, could be found who would dare perform a Christian burial for the Count; and even if he did so, then such a burial of a non-believer would be a criminal profanation of the sacred rite. And why go against your husband's will anyway. After all, there is no doubt that he himself does not want to have a Christian burial performed for him…"

The trouble for the Countess was that, loving as she did a man who had strongly rejected the church, she wanted both to remain a church-going person and to uphold the honor of her husband.

It is at precisely this time that an event takes place in the Tolstoys' household which clearly demonstrates S.A.'s position in all its complexity. In late March, Holy Week began. S.A. had decided to prepare for Communion and wanted to make her youngest daughter Sasha do likewise, but Sasha resisted. Her mother summoned her to vespers, but Sasha announced that she was not a believer. S.A. broke into tears. Sasha went to seek advice from her father.

"Of course you should go," Tolstoy said to his daughter, "and, above all, don't do anything to upset your mother." Sasha stood through the vigil with her mother. She did not, however, prepare for Communion.

Death in the Crimea

There is one word that is particularly alarming in the "correspondence" between S.A. and Anthony. Why is there so much talk about a "burial"? It is as if Tolstoy was on the brink of dying.

In early 1901, Tolstoy was seventy-two years old. This is a ripe old age. Lev was still very strong, though. Yes, he was unwell, he was constantly experiencing weakness and depression, and thinking worrisome thoughts about his impending death. There were no signs of a *deadly* illness in March 1901, though.

In the Countess's letter to the bishops, reference is made to a "secret decree by the Synod to the priests not to read the last rites in church for Lev Nikolayevich, in the event of his death". Anthony acknowledges this fact in his letter of reply. Moreover, he suggests that this pre-dates the appearance of the "distribution". "Last year, when the newspapers carried the news of the Count's illness, the question arose for the clergy in all its starkness: should he, a man who had fallen away from the faith and the Church, be given a Christian burial and prayers? Appeals to the Synod followed, and he secretly gave the leadership of the clergy the only answer he could give them: no, he should not, if he died without restoring his relationship with the Church. There was no threat to anyone in this, and no other answer could be given." This frank admission on the part of Anthony, which was published in the newspaper, also partly explains the release of the Synod's Act in 1901, when it seemed that there was no obvious reason for it. It is interesting that in this matter Pobedonostsev's position was more "against" than "for". According to V.M. Skvortsov, who reported to the chief prosecutor a letter sent by a priest in Moscow asking whether or not he was to sing *Repose with the Saints* in church when Tolstoy died, Pobedonostsev calmly said: "Is there not enough commotion around the name of Tolstoy already, and if we now, as he wishes, impose a ban on memorial services or on reading the last rites for Tolstoy, how much unease will this cause in people's minds, and how much temptation and sin will be provoked by this unease? Whereas in my opinion, it would be better to stick to the well-known adage: don't touch it."

Generally speaking, the appearance of the "disposition" seems to have been closely linked to the possible death of Tolstoy. And this text itself, which appeared in the 'Church Bulletin', was probably addressed more to the priests than to the congregation. After the Synod's document appeared, it was already too late for there to be any talk of any funeral service in memory of the writer, anywhere in Russia, in the event that he were to die. Orthodox Russia was to meet Tolstoy's death, at best, with a mournful silence and internal regret over the loss of the "dearly departed".

Thus, the whole incident with the "excommunication" was in many ways played out as if over the "dead" Tolstoy.

Vasily Rozanov, who wrote extensively about Tolstoy's "excommunication" and knew about the circumstances of the case through his personal connections with church officials, also hints at this. In one of his articles, he wrote that the appearance of the document was provoked by Tolstoy himself, by the "listless" chapter in *Resurrection* "in which he ridiculed the liturgy". The question was raised for the first time not in the Synod, though, but at the "initiative of the local bishop, who was puzzled as to how he was to bury Tolstoy in the event of his death, and submitted this question to the Synod". In his opinion, Tolstoy's "excommunication" was something that was "unplanned".

The Synod had chased itself into a corner, though. After all, it was obvious that after Tolstoy's death, thousands upon thousands of faithful people would want to pray in churches for the much-loved writer. Tolstoy's anti-clerical writings were something that everyone had heard about, but few had seen. They had been published abroad and were only distributed in Russia by illegal means. And, of course, they were not known in detail by most of the ordinary faithful, loyal subjects of the government. Indeed, the language of these works itself was a difficult one. *A Criticism of Dogmatic Theology*, for example, requires considerable mental effort even for the well-educated reader.

The seditious chapter of *Resurrection*, with its description of the liturgy in the prison church, was, of course, deleted from the Russian edition. It was left out of most European translations, because translators received the text of *Resurrection* immediately after it was serialized in the Russian journal 'Niva'. And it was only thanks to Chertkov that the novel was published without censorship, *translated into English*, and was later released by his own publishing house, 'Free Word', in its entirety in Russian.

Interestingly, even the all-knowing Vasily Rozanov reached his verdict on the "listlessness" of the seditious chapter in the novel by hearsay, without having read it. What, then, are we to think about the vast majority of Russian readers, who were familiar with *Resurrection* only through its publication in the popular illustrated magazine 'Niva', in which the chapter about the liturgy wasn't even included?

Incidentally, this initiative by Chertkov caused outrage among L.N.'s relatives. By way of example, M.S. Suhotin, Tolstoy's son-in-law, was very unhappy about it: he wrote in his diary that Tolstoy's rejection of literary rights was now meaningless. All the rights now belonged to Chertkov, who decided where, when and in what format to print L.N's new works.

Meanwhile the matter of Tolstoy's death came up very soon; moreover, it arose *after* the Synod's decision. In the winter of 1901-1902, Tolstoy was at death's door on two occasions in the Crimea, in Gaspra, at a luxurious villa provided for him by his admirer, Countess Panina. After suffering an inflammation of the lungs (at his age and at that time, when there were no antibiotics, this was a deadly disease), he immediately contracted typhoid fever as well.

Tolstoy's recovery, and the fact that he went on to live for 8 more years, truly was a divine miracle, and can be attributed in many ways to the tireless care for him shown by his wife and family.

We won't dwell in detail on this story, in which there were many dramatic and touching moments...

Among the touching moments were the conversations Tolstoy had as he lay dying and then convalescing, with Chekhov and Gorky, to whom he was thus giving his blessing, as he "went to the grave", as it were. Admittedly, he blessed them in a very strange way. For example, he severely criticized Chekhov for his plays, which would go on to be the main source of his international fame and lead to his name being ranked alongside that of Shakespeare in the 20th and 21st centuries. Tolstoy didn't like Shakespeare either, incidentally.

One of the most dramatic moments was the arrival of his son Lev Lvovich, who had just released his novel *Searches and Reconciliation*, which went against his father from an ideological standpoint, but was clearly written under his artistic influence. Lev Lvovich wanted to know what his father thought of the novel. Tolstoy, who did not have the strength to talk to his son about a subject that he found painful and embarrassing, wrote him a letter. After reading it right then and there, in the presence of family members, his son tore the letter to shreds and left the house.

The history of the Crimea, if one were to describe it in all its detail, would take up too much space. It was here, specifically, in the Crimea, over the dying Tolstoy, that the real battle for his soul and for his legacy first got going. Besides the family, there were also people close to Chertkov staying at the house. One of these was Pavel Alexandrovich Boulanger, who genuinely idolized Tolstoy and helped him a lot in his editing of anthologies of Oriental wisdom. Incidentally, he was an employee of the railway company and provided Tolstoy with a separate carriage for the journey to Crimea. Boulanger, though, was utterly devoted to Chertkov as well.

Chertkov's sister-in-law, Olga Konstantinovna Tolstaya (née Dietrichs), the wife of Tolstoy's son Andrei Lvovich, and Anna Konstantinovna Chertkova's (Galya) sister, also nursed Tolstoy in Gaspra. In the Crimea, with the assistance of Chertkov's friend and Tolstoy's follower in Slovakia, Albert Shkarvan, D.P. Makovitsky arrived, a man who later became one of the people closest to L.N.

Chertkov's anxiety was understandable. By the beginning of the 20th century, he had become the de facto and later the legal owner of all of the works by L.N. which had been published abroad. Whilst residing in the town of Christchurch, 150 kilometers from London, in a villa which his mother had bought him, Chertkov set up a printing press there and began constructing a repository for Tolstoy's manuscripts. This repository, housed in a separate building, was equipped with state-of-the-art archiving technologies. With the aid of a gas furnace and a special ventilation system, a constant temperature and constant level of humidity were maintained. It was equipped with a fire alarm system and electrical alarm system. No-one could touch the handles of the huge strongroom at night without a deafening sound going off at Chertkov's home. The concrete repository itself was so strong that even in the event of an earthquake, it would collapse but would not be destroyed. All of this would lose all meaning to him, however, if Tolstoy had no formal will, which recognized Chertkov's rights to store and publish these priceless manuscripts. It is no coincidence that just after the events in the Crimea, Chertkov starts the battle for Tolstoy's will which ended with Tolstoy's tragic departure.

A battle for the writer's soul was taking place at the same time.

The second letter from Metropolitan Anthony (Vadkovsky) to Countess Tolstoy, which was written in the Crimea, was written at the initiative of the Bishop himself. L.N.'s son-in-law, Mikhail Suhotin, describes it as "Jesuitical", considering that it was intended as an attempt by the Synod, frightened by the results of the "excommunication", to rescue the writer's reputation and return him to the bosom of the Church on the eve of his death. Suhotin was a loyal man and didn't share the exuberant anti-clerical and anti-government fervor of his father-in-law. It is known that he met with Father John of Kronstadt. Thus, he can hardly be suspected of having a biased opinion.

Vadkovsky, however, was too strong and independent a person. A former rector of the St. Petersburg Theological Academy, with honorary doctorates from Oxford and Cambridge Universities, the Metropolitan of the Capitol and a leading figure in the Synod, Anthony could not be the "performer" of any kind of collective will. It's hard to say whether he was "moved by love of the writer", as George Orekhanov believes, but there is no doubt that the letter was written with passion and sincerity. In fact, it is this that differentiates it from the first letter to the Countess, which was intelligent but somewhat cold and a bit ironic.

The possibility that Tolstoy might actually die lent a very different tone to the "disposition". If Tolstoy were to die in the Crimea, the Synod would find itself in a difficult position. In the eyes of public opinion, this would be a heroic death for a man who had *suffered at the hands of the church authorities*.

If such a thing were to happen, it would become clear that the cunning and cautious Pobedonostsev had been right. For the imperial court and Nicholas personally, such a death would be detrimental in all respects. Besides the internal problems it would create, it would also put Russia in an awkward position in the eyes of Europe.

Vadkovsky's letter, it seems, was the result of many intertwining factors: the Bishop's personal desire, the tsar's will and the overall situation which had developed in Russia around Tolstoy after the "excommunication".

The letter isn't very long; let us cite it in full:

"February 11, 1902

Highly Respected Countess!

I'm writing you these lines, like last year as well, driven by an irresistible inner urge. My soul aches for your husband, Count Lev Nikolayevich. His age is already that of an old man. Everyone can see that persistent illness is weakening his strength. Strong rumors of his death have already been put about on more than one occasion. It is true that each of our lives is in the hands of God, and the Lord has the power to heal the Count in full and give him life for a few more years. And may God grant that such great grace manifests itself over him. God's dispositions are unbeknownst to us, however. And who knows? It may be that the Lord has already commanded the Angel of death to call him away from the land of the living in a few days or weeks.

This is where the source of my heartache over him lies. The Count broke his alliance with the Church, renounced his faith in Christ as God, thus depriving his soul of the light source of life and breaking the strong familial ties that bound him to the beloved and long-suffering Russian people. Being without Christ is like being without the sun. There is no life without the sun, there is no life without Christ. And it seems to me now that the Count, without this life in Christ, without this union with the Christ-loving people, is so miserable, so lonely ... with a coldness in his soul and with suffering!.. It is difficult in such spiritual solitude to stand and look death in the face!

Can it really be, Countess, that you will not use all of your strength, all of your love to ensure that your husband, whom you love dearly and have cherished all your life, is brought back to Christ? Will you really let him die without reconciliation with the Church, without the accompaniment of the Sacrament of the body and blood of Christ, which gives peace, joy and life to a faithful soul? Oh, Countess! Beg the Count, convince him, cajole him to do this! His reconciliation with the Church will be a bright celebration for all of the Russian land, for all of the Russian people, the Orthodox, a source of joy in heaven and on earth. The Count loves the Russian people, in the faith of the people he long sought strength for his own vacillating belief as well, but, unfortunately and most regrettably, was unable to find it. But create, O Lord, your rich mercy over him, help and strengthen him, so that he can be united, before his death at least, in his faith with the faith of the Orthodox Russian people! It is difficult to die a lonely man, torn away from the life of the people and the holy faith! And it's difficult for those who love the Count not to see him reconciled with the Church, united with them in the holy faith in Christ! Beseech him, dear Countess, to turn back to Christ, to the life and joy in Him, and to His Holy Church! Create a joyful celebration for the whole of the holy Russian land! May the Lord Himself help you in this, and may he send to you and the Count a holy joy that no-one can take away.

With the utmost respect for you
Your humble servant
Anthony, Metropolitan of St. Petersburg."

There are two parallel messages in Anthony's letter. The first is addressed to the Countess, the second – to the Count. It is not plausible that Anthony would not have assumed that S.A. would show the letter to her husband. Toward the Countess he directs the view, flattering for her, that she alone is capable of returning her husband to the bosom of the church. Only her great love and the burning strength of her convictions are capable of melting the ice in Tolstoy's heart and bringing about a new spiritual revolution within him.

The second message – about the Russian people, an "orthodox" and "Christ-loving" people – was addressed to L.N.

Vadkovsky could not have known, however, that Tolstoy, having fallen away from the Church himself, was not pleased by the fact that part of the Russian peasantry had also fallen away from it.

It was as in this that the paradox of Tolstoy's religious consciousness seemed to lie. In actual fact, there was no paradox at all. Tolstoy understood very well that by falling away from the church, the peasant falls away from faith in God in general. Unless he goes over to the dissenters and sectarians. His attitude toward the sectarians, however, was quite a complex one. He was very dubious, for example, about the skoptsy, considering this path to be far too mechanical a solution for the problem of sex. As for the Dukhobors, whom he personally helped to resettle in Canada, according to his diaries, he was cautious in his attitude to them. And finally, Tolstoy, as it is widely known, neither liked nor understood the 'Tolstoyans', with the exception of those closest to him: Chertkov, Biryukov, Boulanger, Gusev, Bulgakov, Makovitsky and a number of others. Tolstoy took a dim view of it when the peasants cursed the priests in his presence. He sensed a false note in it, a desire to please him, as the main critic of the church. At the same time, he had the utmost respect for holy fools, simple monks and rural priests.

Vadkovsky, of course, had read Tolstoy's *Confession*. He also knew that L.N. was *envious* of the ordinary people's naive belief in the church's "miracles". He interprets his religious path in *Confession* in many ways as a kind of "woe from wit".

The populist emphasis in Anthony's letters was thus addressed not so much to the Countess as to the Count. This was the only line of argument which might influence him as he lay close to death, and force him, formally at least, to be reconciled with the church. It is unlikely that Anthony seriously believed there would be any "sudden reversal" on the part of the stubborn Count.

This line of argument didn't work either, however.

The Countess found the Metropolitan's letter touching, though. She writes in her diary that, having received the letter and having told her husband about it, she asked him to seek reconciliation "all that is of this earth, the church included". This, we might suggest, demonstrates her own attitude toward the church as an institution that was "of this earth" and nothing more than that. There was, however, an impulse on her part, and she would have liked it if L.N. had returned, formally at least, to the church. And that's understandable. She had arranged funerals for all of the children who had died, including their beloved Vanya, in compliance with the Orthodox rites. And, of course, her preference would be for her husband to be laid to rest in the same way. Tolstoy stuck to his guns, though. "There can be no talk of reconciliation. I am dying without any enmity or evil at all, and what is the church after all? How can there be any reconciliation with such a vague concept." In effect, this was how Tolstoy desired things to be as he lay on his *death-bed*. On the day the Countess received the Metropolitan's letter, the patient was repeatedly injected with camphor in order artificially to support his heart, which was on the point of stopping. His hands and feet had already grown cold. He lay curled up because of the unbearable "prickly" pain in his right side. On that day, his wife saw in his eyes, for the first time, "not a somber desire to come back to life but a submissive humility", and wrote in her diary: "Help him, God, so that it is easier to suffer and to die." Nevertheless, there was yet another situation in L.N.'s life after the Crimea when one of the senior bishops of the church had the opportunity to influence the writer's beliefs directly. This was the Bishop of Tula, Parfeny (Levitsky). On January 21, 1909, he met the writer at Yasnaya Polyana and had a long conversation with him; we do not know the full version of what was said, due to the mutual desire of both men not to reveal this.

The meeting took place at Parfeny's initiative, but, importantly, L.N. undoubtedly desired it to happen. In the press, Parfeny even said that Tolstoy had spoken to him, "in the way that any Christian speaks to a pastor at confession", and attributed these words to L.N. himself. In L.N.'s diary, however, there is no mention of any confession whatsoever. It comes across more as a reverse confession. "Yesterday a bishop came round, I talked to him from the heart, but too cautiously, I didn't have my say on the sin of his business in its entirety..."

Regardless of this, Parfeny made a most favorable impression on Tolstoy's soul. The secretary Nikolai Gusev, who was present during the meeting and when L.N. said farewell to the bishop, writes in his diary that this visit "was very pleasing" to Tolstoy, that he was weeping when he said goodbye to the priest, and that he thanked him "for his courage".

Judging by the snippets of their meeting that we know about, Parfeny and Tolstoy didn't just chat about any old thing. Each of them was pursuing his own objective. Parfeny's goal was to return Tolstoy to Orthodoxy. He went about the task tactfully, though, without putting pressure on Tolstoy, and Tolstoy liked this.

Tolstoy's goal was to prove that he wasn't an enemy of the faith. When talking about the conversation with the bishop to the correspondent from *Russian Word*, S.P. Spiro, Tolstoy made a very important remark: "... I said to him: one thing I find unpleasant is that all these people (the authors – priests among them – of letters criticizing the writer's beliefs – P.B.) accuse me of destroying people's beliefs. This is a big misunderstanding, because all of my work in this regard is aimed only at rescuing people from the unnatural condition whereby they have an absence of any kind of faith whatsoever." According to Spiro, Tolstoy told Parfeny about an incident that had occurred at Yasnaya Polyana. One day he had been walking through the village and had looked in at one of the windows, where he saw an old woman who was on her knees and prostrating herself. L.N. recognized her: it was Matrona, who in her youth had had a reputation as "one of the most unvirtuous women in the village". Returning home late in the evening, he looked in through the window again. The old woman was still praying...

"Now that's praying for you! May God grant that we all pray in the same way, that is that we too are conscious of our dependency on God – and to violate that faith, which inspires such praying, is something I would consider to be the greatest of crimes. It is different with the people of our educated class – either they don't have faith, or, worse still – they have a sham faith, which plays the role of an established convention and nothing more," he said.

Tolstoy did not renounce the church faith, did not renounce the rites, but only as long as there was spiritual sincerity behind them. We recall that the communion scene in the novel *Resurrection* takes place in the church of the transit prison, where Katyusha Maslova had ended up through the fault of educated atheists, beginning with Prince Nekhludoff and ending with the judges. Against the woman they treated so cruelly and unjustly, in effect raping her both physically and spiritually, they were now committing a new act of violence, by forcing an innocent woman to confess and repent *in jail*.

Tolstoy was the rightful heir of the century of the Enlightenment, the grandson of his grandfather and his father's son. Believing in the religious ceremonies was something he simply couldn't do. He could not believe in the sincerity of the churchly faith of the educated class, either. Tolstoy said to Spiro of his conversation with Parfeny: "I told him that I receive many letters and visits from the clergy, and that I am always touched by the good wishes that they express, but that to my great regret, it's as impossible for me to do what they wish as it would be for me to fly up into the air." At the end of his life he didn't write openly anti-clerical works, dedicating himself solely to collecting worldly wisdom in the anthologies *The Circle of Reading* and *Every Day*. L.N. leaned increasingly toward the religions of the East, more ancient than Christianity: Buddhism and Hinduism. This was his path, his will.

In reply to a letter of "appeal" from the priest of the Tula prison, Father Dmitry Troitsky, with whom he was personally acquainted, Tolstoy wrote: "To what end, my dear brother, Dmitri, are you addressing such a strange proposal to me? After all, I am not appealing to you, and advising you to abandon the pernicious fallacy that you are in and into which you are diligently initiating thousands and thousands of unfortunate children and ordinary people, distorting their souls as you do so. Why won't you leave me, a man who is of such an age that he has one foot in the grave and is quietly waiting for death, alone. After all, turning me towards faith in the church would make sense if I was a boy or an adult atheist, or an illiterate Yakut, who had never heard anything about faith in the church. But I'm 82 years old, and I was brought up in the very same deception that you are in, and to which you are inviting me, and from which, with the greatest sufferings and efforts, I freed myself many years ago, when I mastered a worldview that is not of the church, but is Christian, one which gives me the possibility of leading a calm, happy life, oriented towards internal improvement and readiness for the kind of calm and joyful death, in which I see a return to that same God of love from whence I came." The end of the letter to Father Troitsky echoes almost word for word Tolstoy's reply to Metropolitan Anthony, written in the Crimea, which was dictated in S.A.'s presence, but was not sent, at the request of L.N. himself. When the Countess told her husband about Vadkovsky's letter, Tolstoy initially asked her: "write to him that my last prayer is as follows: 'From Thee I came forth, to Thee I return. Thy will be done'."

The first will

It is known that Tolstoy wrote six wills – in 1895, 1904, 1908, 1909 (two) and in 1910. If we add to this the "explanatory note" in favor of Chertkov, composed by Chertkov "from a third party" and signed in Tolstoy's hand, then there aren't six wills, but seven.

In fact, the actual number is far higher. Tolstoy's entire diary from the late '70s and early '80s is almost one long, continuous *will*, because in it he is constantly seeking to refine and clarify his spiritual legacy.

It is no coincidence that he makes his first *informal* will in the form of a diary entry. On February 21, 1895, N.S. Leskov died. In the note *My last request* he asked to be buried "in the very lowest, last category". Tolstoy knew about this note and, as he pondered it over on March 27, he decided to draw up some instructions of his own.

Tolstoy's first will is very different from his final version in 1910. Tolstoy's first will is the act of a child who doesn't know anything about how real spiritual acts are drawn up. It is for precisely that reason, though, that it is a spiritual document of the purest and most morally impeccable kind.

The first will was written in the context of a horrible period in his life, when Tolstoy's married life had lost its last chance not even of happiness, but of emotional intimacy with his wife. In February of that year, The Tolstoys' favorite child, little Vanya, had died. Tolstoy had thought of him as his only spiritual heir among the children. His mother had loved him like crazy. The last child in the family, he had also been the Tolstoys' last hope for family unity. After his death, S.A. lost the sense of any meaning in her life; Sergei Lvovich Tolstoy writes of this. For L.N., the meaning of life, of course, was not lost. For some reason, though, it seems that from that moment on, as Tolstoy forced himself to write those strange and terrible words about little Vanya's death in his diary ("Thank you, Father. Thank You"), something had broken within the great Tolstoy.

"A few days after Vanya's death, when love had begun to weaken in me..." he admits in his diary. Meanwhile his wife writes to his sister: "Lev has crumpled completely, he has aged, he walks around looking sad, with shining eyes, and it's clear that for him too, the last ray of light of his old age has gone out. On the third day after Vanya's death, he sat there sobbing and said: "For the first time in my life I feel hopelessness." There was only one way out – God. In thanking God for the death of his beloved son, Tolstoy makes an irrevocable, biblical choice. From now on, he isn't a man, but a prophet. Whatever happened, everything would now be a happy sign for him personally. What could be worse, one would think, than the death of a beloved child? Yet even from this L.N. draws a conclusion that is of spiritual use to him: "Yes, we must always live as if a beloved child is dying in the next room. He is always dying, too. I am always dying, too." To live like that is not possible, though! It would be like continuously stripping the skin off one's body. And Tolstoy, after making this entry, suddenly turns into an old man. He begins to wait for death, to chivvy it along even. And that is when the will appears.

"*My will would be roughly as follows*," L.N. writes in his diary. "*Until I have written another one, this is exactly what it would be.*"

He asks to be buried "in the cheapest cemetery, if it is in the city, and in the cheapest coffin – the way they bury the poor. Don't lay any flowers or wreaths, don't make any speeches. If possible, there should be no priest and no funeral service. But if this is unpleasant for those who will be at the funeral, let them bury me with a funeral service in the usual way, but as cheaply and simply as possible." He asks that no obituaries be written about him. He writes that his papers are to be given to his wife, Chertkov and Strahov (at first he included his daughters too – Tanya and Masha, but then he crossed this out, adding a note: "My daughters ought not to deal with this"). He doesn't give any such instructions to his sons. He loves them, but they "don't fully know my thoughts, have not followed them and may have their own particular views on things, as a result of which they might keep things that don't need to be kept or throw away things that should be kept." He initially asks that the diaries of his bachelor life be destroyed ("... not because I would like to hide my immoral life from people... but because these diaries, in which I only wrote down the things which tormented me with the awareness of sin, create a one-sided impression"), but then advises that they should be kept. "They show, at least, that despite all the vulgarity and rottenness of my youth, I was nonetheless not abandoned by God, and that, albeit in old age, I began at least a little bit to understand and love Him." Tolstoy *asks* his heirs to renounce the rights to his works. This is a *request*, not an order. "If you do this – it will be a good thing. It will be a good thing for you too; if you don't do it – that's your business. That would mean that you couldn't do it. The fact that my works have been sold for money these past ten years has been the hardest thing for me in my life." It would seem that he hadn't offended anyone, hadn't gone against anyone's will. He had given everyone a chance to come together, lovingly, in the task of disposing of his literary legacy, and he had renounced property three years previously, in favor of the family. There was a great deal of childish naiveté in this will: his desire that no obituaries should be written about him, for example, and no speeches should be made. Who could possibly have obeyed Tolstoy on this!

There were also some monstrous, gaping holes in this will from a legal perspective, though. By way of example, L.N. was convinced that everything he had written since 1881 had long belonged to everyone. He thought that the letter he had printed in the newspapers in 1891, about his renunciation of author's rights to these works, had some sort of real force, and therefore didn't even touch on this issue.

In fact, if Tolstoy were to have died in 1895, all of his writings would have been passed on, by law, to his family, and his favorite disciple and follower Chertkov would only have been allowed to access them with the family's blessing. Already, though, there could be no suggestion that S.A. would give her blessing to Chertkov, a man who had repeatedly offender her.

Moreover, Tolstoy's spouse and his sons needed the money very badly.

Tolstoy's first will didn't have any legal force at all. It was simply a heartfelt wish toward his loved ones in the event of his death. And it was not just that it wasn't notarized. The fact is that under the laws of the Russian Empire, literary rights could not belong to "everyone". They could only belong to a particular individual or legal entity.

The letter in the newspapers in 1891 with the renunciation of author's rights, in the eyes of the law, was worth nothing. All rights to Tolstoy's writings, up until his death, belonged to him. This was a matter of his own personal desire: to allow his wife to print and sell the old works, and to allow publishers to publish the new ones for free.

Meanwhile, events surrounding Tolstoy's literary rights developed rapidly even whilst he was still alive. The conflicts between his publisher-wife and 'Mediator', between Chertkov, who lived abroad, and the Russian publishers, were constantly putting him in a position whereby he had to justify an infringement of the rights of one or the other side. His wife took offense at him because he gave away new things, such as *Master and Man*, to trendy magazines ('Northern Herald'), but didn't give anything to her. The Russian publishers did not want to have to reckon with Chertkov, who lived in England, and who, in turn, was angry at the fact that the "droit de seigneur" with each new text by L.N. was not legally his exclusive right, and depended only on the writer's good will, which could easily be turned to other publishers' advantage.

"Chertkov could count on the fact that he would be able to publish new works by Tolstoy, in translations released under his supervision, only if he received Tolstoy's articles before they were published in Russian, so that they could come out at the same time in Russia and in England," writes

M.V. Muratov. This was a serious problem for Chertkov, about which he wrote to Tolstoy:

"In any case, in the interests of our international concern, 'Mediator', it is desirable that, as I've already written to you, *all* the translators who have contacted you are sent here to me, and that you don't give any of them a list without going through me. And also that I receive from you the manuscript to be translated, at least *three weeks* before publication not only in Russia, but even before it is distributed privately." One can understand Chertkov's concerns. After all, when entering into contractual relations with foreign publishers, Chertkov could not explain to them that Tolstoy had no wish to have anything to do with the legal aspect of the matter. Meanwhile any text by Tolstoy which appeared in print in Russian was immediately considered to be in the public domain. Any foreign publisher could come along and commission a translation of their own.

The problem also lay in the fact that Tolstoy was always the tireless editor of his own works. He edited not only the manuscripts, but also the proofs. For Chertkov, who was forced to work with foreign publishers and translators under trying circumstances, these editorial corrections were a serious problem. As a faithful disciple and follower, he could not violate the will of his teacher and was compelled to wait for the final edited version of the text. Yet these revisions had already been made in the galleys of the Russian versions, which threatened to appear even earlier than Chertkov received the original text. He was therefore forced to slow down the publication of the texts in Russia, by appealing to Tolstoy, and this angered the Russian publishers.

L.N. was distressed by all this. In a letter to Chertkov written on December 13, 1897, he admits: "while I was publishing for the money, the publication of any work was a joy; since I stopped taking money, the printing of any work is a series of grievances." On the one hand, then, there is Chertkov. On the other, there is his wife. Her attitude toward her husband's first will was completely negative.

A copy of the will was made by Tolstoy's daughter, Maria Lvovna, in 1901, without her mother's knowledge. S.A. knew about this diary entry in 1895, but didn't attach any significance to it: she put the diary from this period away for storage, along with her husband's other manuscripts, in the archive of the Rumyantsev Museum. The fact that neither L.N. nor Masha showed her this text, which was copied out in the form of a will and signed by Tolstoy, speaks for itself. They were both afraid of how she might react.

After events in the Crimea, however, it became difficult to keep a will hidden. Never mind months and years: Tolstoy might die on any given day. In October 1902, S.A. learned of the wills (probably from her son Ilya) and was outraged by them.

"It was extremely unpleasant for me when I found out about it by chance. I believe it is evil and senseless to give away Tolstoy's works as *common* property. I love my family and I wish it the best possible well-being, whereas by giving away these works to the public domain, we will reward the rich publishing companies, like Marx, Zetlin and others. I told L.N. that if he should die before me, I *shan't* carry out his desires and *shan't* give up the rights to his works, and that if I considered it a good and rightful thing to do, I would have given him this joy of renouncing the rights during his lifetime, but that after his death this no longer had any meaning for him."

S.A. demanded that her husband fetch his will and give it to her. L.N., as usual in such cases, couldn't say no to his wife. Masha was upset by what her mother had done. In raised voices, she and her husband told her that they had planned to publish the will after L.N.'s death.

This was a fatal mistake on S.A.'s part. She should have kept quiet at that point, should have reconciled herself to the situation! The law, after all, was on her side.

"He wanted to break humanity, but he couldn't break the family," S.A. wrote in *My Life*. Why did she use the work "break", though?

Tolstoy was trying to *convince* humanity, and was doing the same thing with his family. On every occasion, though, when he felt resistance from his family, he stepped back and made whatever compromises were necessary. The dividing up of his property between his wife and the children was a compromise. "What a great sin I committed, by giving the children a fortune," he wrote in his diary in 1910. "I hurt everyone, even my daughters. I see this clearly now." Whether Tolstoy was right or wrong is beside the point. What matters is that this tormented him all his life.

It is the same story with his first will. He was merely *asking* his wife and children not to receive monetary gain from his posthumous fame. Fifteen years later, his position on this issue was to become far tougher.

"One cannot deprive millions of people of something which, perhaps, they need for their souls... so that Andrei can drink and be caught up in debauchery and Lev can do his daubing" (diary entry, July 29, 1910).

The reasons as to why S.A. didn't accept her husband's first will are largely due to circumstantial factors. Firstly, she felt upset with her daughter, who, having refused her share of the inheritance in 1891, had later appealed to her mother to be given her share when she got married. From S.A.'s point of view, Masha was the last person who ought to be taking steps to ensure that their father deprived the family of its main source of income. Secondly, it was exactly at this time that S.A. was undertaking the publication of a new collection of Tolstoy's works, and had invested a lot of money in this project. If L.N. were to die now and his "will" bestowing rights on everyone were to appear in the newspapers, the family would suffer a severe financial crisis.

In July of 1902, N.S. Tsetlin, the owner of the publishing house 'Enlightenment', came to see S.A. "offering to buy the work, for eternal ownership thereof, for a million rubles". Tolstoy's wife turned down his offer. And now it had transpired that whilst she was turning down an enormous sum that would have provided her and the children with a comfortable existence for many years to come, her own daughter had been intriguing behind her back over her father's will. How could she endure such a thing?

Questions and answers

In May 1904, Chertkov finally decides to put his position as Tolstoy's "spiritual executor" on a legal footing. Aware, however, that to try to do so *legally* without the knowledge of S.A. and the family would not work, he sends his secretary Briggs to Yasnaya Polyana with a "questionnaire" for Tolstoy, in which he clearly crosses all the 't's and dots all the 'i's. Chertkov's questions were typed on a typewriter, L.N.'s answers were written in his own hand. Here is the document in its entirety:

"1. Would you like your statement in the 'Russian Gazette' of 16 September 1891 (containing his renunciation of his author's rights – PB) to remain in force now and after your death?

I wish that all of my works, written since 1881, as well as those that will remain after my death, shall not constitute anyone's private property, but might instead be reprinted and republished by anyone who wishes to do so.

2. Who would you like to make the final decision on the issues associated with the editing and publishing of your writings after your death, in which for any reason complete unanimity does not prove possible?

I think that my wife and V.G. Chertkov, to whom I have entrusted the task of sorting through the papers which remain after me, will come to an agreement on what to keep, what to throw away, what to publish and how to do so.

3. Is it your wish that, after your death, if I should outlive you, the authority you have given me in writing should remain in effect, as your sole representative abroad?

I wish that after my death, V.G. Chertkov alone should take charge of the publishing and translation of my work abroad.

4. Do you grant me the right, after your death, to dispose, at my own personal discretion, both for publication in my lifetime, and for the assignment by me to a trusted person after my death, of all those of your manuscripts and papers that I have received, and shall receive from you before your death?

I assign to the disposal of V.G. Chertkov all my manuscripts and papers which he has in his possession. In the event that he should die, I believe that it is better to assign the papers and manuscripts to my wife or to some Russian institution or other – a public library, an academy.

5. Is it your wish that I be given the opportunity to review, in the original, every single one, without exception, of your manuscripts, which, after your death, will go to Sofia Andreyevna or to your family?

I would like very much for V.G. Chertkov to look through all the manuscripts which remain after me and copy out from them anything that he deems it necessary to publish."

The answers were enclosed in a letter sent by Tolstoy to Chertkov on May 13, 1904, in which he made amendments to the "will" of 1895. Taken together with the answers, this letter amounted to Tolstoy's second, *informal* will. Yet it too, like the first one, didn't have any legal force, because L.N. was continuing to insist that the rights to his works from 1881 onwards belonged to "everyone". Nevertheless, a degree of "legalese" had already permeated into this will.

Tolstoy expanded Chertkov's rights so that they applied to all the manuscripts, including those which were in his wife's possession. As for the rights to his manuscript legacy, however, which was in Chertkov's possession outside the country, he assigned these to Chertkov alone. S.A. could only get her hands on these manuscripts in the event that Chertkov were to die, and even then her rights were the same as those of any public library. Not a word was said about the assignment of any manuscripts to the children.

Chertkov was already being proclaimed in this will as the only spiritual heir and manager of Tolstoy's manuscripts. He was also being appointed as chief editor and compiler. His wife was assigned the minor role of an assistant and mediator in the transfer of all the manuscripts to Chertkov. Yet she still retained the literary rights to the works created before 1881.

It is apparent from the letter and the replies to it how difficult this second will was for Tolstoy. How torturously he strove to give this "legalese" a human face. All of these instances of "I think" (instead of "I wish"), "better", "very", etc., made this document meaningless from a legal point of view, but appealed to the conscience of those to whom it was addressed.

"In addition to those papers which you have, I am sure that my wife or (in the event that she dies before you) my children will not refuse, in fulfillment of my desire, will not refuse to send to you the papers which you do not have, as well, and, together with you, to decide how to dispose of them," Tolstoy wrote. Who, though, was he really imploring to act this way? To whom was this double "will not refuse" addressed? To the family, it goes without saying...

Sensing the anxiety his "dear friend" was feeling, L.N. tries to calm V.G. with his humble answers to his remarkably tactless questions, which hint at the proximity of Tolstoy's death. The letter ends on a pretentious note:

"Thank you for all of your past labors on my writings and in advance for what you are going to do with the papers that remain when I am gone. Unity with you has been one of the great joys of the last years of my life." In fact, the matter of Chertkov's legal questionnaire was terribly unpleasant for him. So unpleasant that on this occasion Tolstoy couldn't even hide his irritation and in a second letter to his "friend", which Chertkov kept hidden and stored at his son's house, marked "secret" (it was not published until 1961), he wrote:

"I will not conceal from you, my dear friend Vladimir Grigorievich, that the letter you sent to me with Briggs was unpleasant for me ... What is unpleasant to me is not that it is about my death, about my worthless papers, to which a false importance is attached, but that there is in all this some kind of obligation, force, mistrust, ill will toward people. And I don't know how, but I get the feeling that I am being *drawn into* something hostile, into the doing of something that could cause harm. I wrote down my answers to your questions and shall send them to you. But if you should write to me that you have torn them up, or burnt them, then I will be very pleased." The stance taken by Tolstoy inspires complex feelings. Instead of immediately resolving the issue with the literary rights when he sensed something was wrong, just as he had decided the matter of his property (by gathering the whole family together and announcing his decision), he act in accordance with the principle of "non-resistance to evil" and agrees to participate in Chertkov's complex intrigues against S.A. Moreover, neither he, nor Chertkov himself are as yet aware that these intrigues, in the case in question, lack any legal footing. There still is no legally binding document. There is a humane document. And Tolstoy finds it disagreeable.

Having *dragged* Tolstoy into the world of "legal speak", Chertkov didn't stop at that and pressed ahead with the matter to the end. Half-hearted decisions and actions were not in his nature. "Whatever he wanted, he wanted very much," V.G.'s biographer M.V. Muratov wrote of him.

Who is to blame?

Tolstoy's third will was dictated to his secretary N.N. Gusev, as a diary entry once again, on 11 August 1908, two weeks before the writer's eightieth birthday. At this time, L.N. was seriously ill. His legs were giving up the ghost, and he was confined to his bed and to a wheelchair. Thinking that he was dying, he decided to edit his will.

"First of all, it would be good if my heirs gave all my writings up for general use; if not that, then certainly all of the works that are for the people, such as the *ABC* and *Books for Reading*. Secondly, although this is the most trivial of things, no rites should be performed when my body is laid to rest in the ground. A wooden coffin, and whoever wants to shall carry or convey it to the Zakaz, opposite the ravine to the place where the green stick is. At the very least, there is a reason for choosing this or that place." This was L.N.'s first will, which took effect after his death. He is referring to the place where he asked to be buried and where he was indeed buried. The story of the "green stick", a symbol of human happiness and brotherhood, buried in the Stary Zakaz woods by the brothers Levochka and Nikolenka, is well known to anyone who has read the writer's autobiographical trilogy. And now Tolstoy, both orally (to his daughters), and in writing, is asking to be buried here.

In other respects, the third will repeated the legal errors of the first two. Firstly, Tolstoy was asking for things to be done, not issuing instructions. Secondly, he wanted once again to pass on the rights to his works to *everyone*, which was impossible.

Symbolically, the diary entry for August 11, 1908 ends with a remembered story about Syutayev, the peasant-sectarian, who didn't recognize private property. "Yes, 'everything is within you and everything now', as Syutayev used to say, and everything outside of time," Tolstoy dictated to his secretary. "So what can possibly happen to what is in me and what is timeless, other than good." Tolstoy's spiritual self-centeredness didn't allow him to attach any significance to the legal aspect of the matter. This was strange, incomprehensible for loved ones, yet all the same, this was his *position*. And Tolstoy would have to stick to this position until the end, leaving it to the heirs, along with the lawyers themselves, to dispose of his literary legacy. And this, of course, is what he would have liked to do.

Yet this infringed the rights of the one and only man whom Tolstoy loved and who was not liked by the heirs – Chertkov. To go against this love was something he could not to – in his soul. Chertkov himself, for his part, could not willingly waive his rights to Tolstoy's legacy.

Firstly, this would not have been in his nature – he was a stubborn and despotic person. Many people in Chertkov's circle wrote about his difficult and despotic character: they had been pushed away from him because of it. "...love of power, love of power, founded on self-centeredness and capable at times of shifting into outright despotism", Tolstoy's last secretary, V.F. Bulgakov, wrote of Chertkov. Alexandra Lvovna, Tolstoy's daughter, also wrote in her memoirs about the oppressive influence Chertkov had on some of those who were closest to and most loyal to her father. His friend P.I. Biryukov called Chertkov "a despot".

Secondly, one must put oneself in Chertkov's shoes. He had dedicated to L.N. not just any old thing, but his entire lifetime. For him, to give up the legacy would be tantamount to renouncing his life. To reach an agreement with S.A. would be impossible because of her nature and that of Chertkov. Such an agreement would be the perfect outcome for L.N., but this outcome was something that neither side could provide.

Thirdly, S.A.'s state of mind and her boundless love for her sons inspired genuine concern that Tolstoy's legacy would not be disposed of in the way Tolstoy wanted it to be. For whose sake, then, ought V.G. to give up Tolstoy's legacy? Let us adopt his point of view for a moment. For the sake of the writer's wife, who hated Chertkov? For the sake of the sons, who drank and squandered money? And what would become of this legacy, part of which Chertkov was already looking after in England as if it were the apple of his eye? What would become of the wishes of the Teacher, who wanted his works to belong to everyone? Only Chertkov himself could make this desire become a reality. Not even his enemies could doubt that.

Ah, if only one could separate, in the story of the will, the causes from the effects, the wolves from the sheep! Everything would have been so very simple. In this story, though, there was one little lamb – Tolstoy, whom the two warring sides couldn't divide up between them. And everything in this story was so confused, from both the moral and legal perspectives, that any kind of ideal solution to the problem was out of the question.

Through his attempt to give up his literary rights in favor of "everyone", Tolstoy created an unprecedented situation. Striking proof of this is the fact that prior to 1909, none of the participants in this story, including the experienced publisher Chertkov, understood the actual legal aspect of the problem; they were all acting "blindly". Tolstoy's first three wills, which caused him such anguish, with such doubts, had no legal meaning whatsoever.

The Stockholm crisis

As he approached the boundary between life and death, Tolstoy's spiritual nature became ever softer, ever more pliable. It seemed to be melting away from the inside through his awareness of the divine origin within himself, it melted and guttered like candle wax, it streamed and flowed like the air above the candle. For Tolstoy, in the final years it would have been unthinkable not only to offend someone, but even to put them out with a careless word, and if this happened without him meaning it to, then L.N. suffered deeply and sincerely.

On May 23, 1909, after Chertkov's administrative expulsion beyond the borders of the Tula Province, Tolstoy went to the farmstead of Telyatinki, near Yasnaya Polyana, where Chertkov's wife Anna Konstantinovna (Galya) and their son, Vladimir (Dima) were still living. At the same time, A.G. Lubentsov, a colonel in the Ministry of Internal Affairs who had been sent by Stolypin, also travelled there, tasked with investigating the Chertkov case. On encountering him, L.N. did not offer his hand and instead walked briskly into the house. A short time later he came back out, apologized and struck up a conversation, trying to make amends for his actions. The colonel felt insulted, though, and the conversation didn't get going. How distressed Tolstoy was after this, how he reproached himself for having offended the man! "After all, when I was on my way there I said to myself: you're going to have to have dealings with this person, take care to treat him with love. And then that..." he said to N.N. Gusev.

"And it's terrible, it really is!" he complained to A.B. Goldenweiser about himself. "I could have told him that I consider his work harmful and evil, but I ought to have been courteous to him, as a fellow man. For me, as an old man, this is unforgivable! Afterwards, I often – you wake up in the middle of the night and remember it, and gasp (L.N. gasped): how bad that was!"

One can argue about who was most to blame for the fact that Tolstoy ultimately allowed himself to be drawn into the "legal speak" that was so hateful to him and obeyed the laws of a state which he did not recognize. When all's said and done, it was probably Chertkov. The first movement he made in favor of a legal will, however, was made not under Chertkov's influence, but because of the behavior of his wife.

And after all it cannot be said that she did not understand the spiritual and emotional processes that were taking place in her husband in his old age. She writes in her diary, for instance:

"L.N. has grown older this year (1908 – P.B.). He has moved up to the next level again. But he has aged well. It's apparent that his spiritual life is prevailing, and although he loves going riding, loves tasty food and a little glass of the wine that was sent to him by the Wine Society of St. Raphael for his birthday; loves to play vint and chess, but it's as though his body is living a separate life, whilst his spirit remains indifferent to earthly life, but somewhere higher up, more independent from the body. Something happened after his illness: something new, more alien and distant can be sensed in Lev Nikolayevich, and I am sometimes unbearably sad and sorry for what has been lost in him, in his life and in his attitude toward me and everything around him. Do others see it too?"

What a wonderful note! If only she could constantly have remained in this state of understanding of the fact that, with the approach of death, the approach of God, Tolstoy begins carefully breaking off all the ties which bind him to the outside world, and no-one must interfere to stop him from doing so!

In June 1908, Chertkov arrives with his family from England and moves into a country house near the Kozlova Zaseka railroad station.

On December 8th, S.A. writes in her diary: "Chertkov, who comes to see us every day, went into Lev Nikolayevich's room last night and spoke to him about the sign of the cross. I couldn't help overhearing their conversation from the hall. L.N. said that he sometimes made the sign of the cross out of habit, and that if his soul was not praying at that particular moment, then the body would still show the sign of prayer. In response to this Chertkov said to him that it could quite easily be that, when dying or suffering severely, Lev Nikolayevich would cross himself with his hand and those surrounding him would think that he wanted to convert or had converted to the Orthodox Faith; and so that they would not think this, Chertkov would write down in his notebook what Lev Nikolayevich had just said." Tolstoy couldn't even cross himself without people commenting on it!

Chertkov is jealous of L.N.'s Orthodoxy, and his wife is jealous of the women from his past. In early 1909, whilst copying out the story *Pavel Kudryash*, she notes in her diary:

"If he had just a little more tact in him, he wouldn't refer to those women-heroines of his by name, those Aksinyas."

The jealousy she felt over Aksinya, though (who by then was an elderly peasant woman, still living in Yasnaya Polyana) was as nothing compared to her jealousy over Chertkov. When the "home-wrecker", the "handsome idol" moves in nearby and starts turning up at their house, at *her house*, on almost a daily basis, Tolstoy's wife begins to suffer unbearably. And it's not within her emotional powers to overcome this suffering.

S.A. was passionate and inconsistent by nature. When, in March 1909, after repeated denunciations by the Tula authorities, Chertkov is banished from the Tula Province for a three-day period, S.A. is seemingly no less outraged than her husband. "Difficult news about Chertkov's expulsion from the Tula Province," she writes in her diary. "Everyone wept." She even sends a letter to the newspapers: "The expulsion of Chertkov and this punishing of someone who dares to read and distribute Tolstoy's books, is a petty insult aimed at an old man who has brought glory to Russia throughout the world through his name..."

This replicates the situation in 1901, when she fought over her husband with the Synod. And now, without feeling the slightest sympathy for Chertkov, she is again fighting not so much for him as for L.N., fearing for his mental equilibrium. "... Lev Nikolayevich is upset ... Lev Nikolayevich's leg is swollen." It's impossible to say what S.A. was guided by more when writing the letter – a sense of civic duty or concern for her husband's health. "L.N.'s heart isn't in a good way." "He is better, but he isn't taking care of himself." "Lev Nikolayevich lay down, he hasn't eaten anything all day, he's sleepy and weak, and again there is a heavy expectation of something terrible on his soul." And what's more, their granddaughter Tanya was sick; grandma Sonia, at the first sign of the March sunshine, takes her out for a walk on the terrace of Yasnaya Polyana house.

Which of them would you blame? V.G. is suffering at the hands of the authorities; L.N. is suffering because he is unable to communicate with Chertkov; his wife is suffering on account of her husband's suffering, and even more so than he is over V.G.

It was impossible to unravel this psychological knot. All that could be done was to cut through it.

And superimposed on top of all this was the awareness of the fact that L.N. would soon die, and the problem of the literary rights which arose in connection with this. Arriving in Moscow on business, S.A. doesn't fail to call in at the Historical Museum, where her share of Tolstoy's manuscripts are stored; she sorts through them and copies out excerpts. She does not yet know that Chertkov has already been granted the right by L.N. to dispose of these manuscripts too. Her daughter Tatyana rushes to St Petersburg – to appeal to Stolypin for the return of Chertkov. S.A. is anxious: "I've no way of knowing – will they let him come back or not." They refused to do so. Chertkov and his family settled on the estate of Krekshino, in the Moscow Province.

It is at this time that relations between L.N. and his son Lev, who has come over from Sweden to Yasnaya for a visit, become strained. Lev Lvovich was fond of sculpture and had begun to sculpt a bust of his father, for which Tolstoy posed. While his father is staying at Kochety, however, Lev Lvovich smashes the bust to pieces and goes back to Sweden.

This was the explanation given by Goldenweiser's wife for this act: "L.N. is still at the Suhotins, and it's still unknown exactly when he'll arrive. It was said he might come at the end of this week, but it's already Saturday and he's not here. Sofia Andreyevna continues to be displeased by this, and Lev Lvovich was so angry that papa had not shown due respect for and amazement at his sculptural endeavors, and wasn't hurrying to Yasnaya to pose for him, that he completely smashed the bust to pieces, rolled out all the clay into a pancake and, terribly offended, left for Sweden." In July 1909, L.N. himself is invited to Stockholm to give a speech at the XVIII International Peace Congress. And Tolstoy almost agrees, and writes the text of the speech. His decision causes his wife to have a nervous breakdown, however. She is afraid by the thought of him travelling abroad.

"Sofia Andreyevna didn't sleep a wink all night," Tolstoy writes in his diary. "I went in to see her. It was something crazy." Some of the reasons for S.A.'s condition can be guessed at from Makovitsky's *Notes* and the diary of the secretary, Gusev.

It turns out that Chertkov was supposed to accompany Tolstoy as an assistant on the trip to Stockholm. His other assistant was to be his youngest daughter, Sasha, who at the time was in a state of complete psychological dependence on Chertkov. S.A. couldn't interpret all this in any other way than that her husband was being *taken away* by forces hostile to her and that Tolstoy would not come back from this trip.

And at the same time, two of L.N.'s sons, Andrei and Mikhail, arrive at Yasnaya Polyana. Both are ardent enemies of Chertkov and protectors of their mother. Alas, though, they are not disinterested ones.

The attorney I.V. Denisenko, a cousin of Tolstoy's who visited Yasnaya Polyana in the summer of 1909, told Gusev of a conversation he had had with Mikhail:

"He stands in front of me with a sort of prisoner's mug and asks: 'Tell me, please, Ivan Vasilievich, can mama sell father's works without his knowledge?' I told him that this wasn't allowed, and added: 'And did you give any thought to what effect such a thing might have on your father?' He looks at me with a little smile on his face and says: 'What about his children?' Then I said to him: 'But even from a practical point of view, there is no way this can be done in secret, Lev Nikolayevich will certainly find out, and then he might say: if you abuse my power of attorney, then I shall take away it from you. All of this can be done in a quarter of an hour.'

"He was referring to the power of attorney from 1883, on the basis of which Tolstoy's wife had taken charge of his publishing activities. This document, however, did not entitle her to sell the rights to Tolstoy's works to third parties.

Their son Andrei Lvovich also feared that Chertkov might try to influence the old man during this trip and force him to draw up a will in his favor. When he heard that father had been in Gusev's room, reading out excerpts from a letter from Chertkov to Sasha and her friend Feokritova, Andrei Lvovich began questioning Feokritova about it in the dining room:

"What were you reading, then?"

"Some letter or other."

"From whom?"

"I don't know: a letter about someone's peasant bank."

"No, but what were you reading before that: wasn't it a letter from Chertkov?"

"Lev Nikolayevich only read an excerpt from it."

"He's trying to seduce papa into going to Stockholm. The bastard! It would be the death of papa."

"No, apparently Lev Nikolayevich himself had read about it in the newspapers, Chertkov didn't give him any advice on the matter at all."

"He wanted to go with him, though?"

"Apparently he did."

"And Sasha also wants to arrange a little jolly to Sweden for herself."

"Why a jolly? She's going to be travelling with her father."

S.A. suddenly gets it into her head that they want to poison her and that Tolstoy's personal physician, Makovitsky, must be the one who is going to do it. She simultaneously makes plans to go to Sweden with her husband, even ordering herself some new dresses for the journey, and tries in every way she can think of to stop her husband. S.A. had never been abroad, and this trip frightens her. She has become fixated with the idea that one of the two of them will certainly die.

And so, forcing events, she attempts, on July 27, to drink a bottle of morphine before her husband's very eyes.

L.N. seizes the bottle from her and throws it under the stairs.

The trip to Sweden had to be abandoned.

July 1909 was the moment of truth for all those interested in the matter of the will. The lawyer I.V. Denisenko, whilst visiting Yasnaya Polyana, opened the eyes of the protagonists in this story to the legal side of the issue. At this time, S.A. had come up with the idea of suing 'Mediator' and other publishers who had reprinted from the 'ABC' a few of Tolstoy's things from the '70s (such as *The Prisoner of the Caucasus*). She considered them her own property, and asked a lawyer, via a proxy, to draw up a claim. The lawyer asked: "on the basis of what document is she initiating legal proceedings? On the basis of the power of attorney. It was not possible to do so on the basis of a power of attorney, the lawyer explained. She needed a document from her husband for the transfer of rights to the publishing of his works.

Tolstoy not only categorically refused to give his wife such a document, but was also extremely angered by her behavior in relation to the publishing houses. So outraged was he, in fact, that he, in turn, decided to leave his wife without any rights whatsoever to his works.

"In July 1909," wrote Denisenko, "when I was at Yasnaya Polyana, Lev Nikolayevich Tolstoy was planning to go to the Peace Congress in Stockholm, an idea that Sofia Andreyevna was against. This caused a whole series of misunderstandings, and then Sofia Andreyevna got sick, not wanting Lev Nikolayevich go to the Congress.

One day she called me in to see her in her bedroom and, having shown me the general power of attorney for the management of his affairs, which had been given to her a long time ago by Lev Nikolayevich, asked me whether she could, under this power of attorney, sell the right to publish Tolstoy's works to a third party, and most importantly of all, whether she could initiate proceedings against Sergeyenko and some teacher at the military school for having compiled, from the works of Tolstoy, collections and anthologies, in view of the fact that these collections might cause her, S.A., a great deal of material harm ...

On the following day, I think it was, during the day, I was with his wife and children in the park, picking berries. His wife asked me to go into the outbuilding for some reason. I walked along the tree-lined path which passes between some flowers, and at that point, much to my surprise, I chanced upon Lev Nikolayevich. I was struck by his appearance. He was hunched over, his face was haggard, his eyes looked dim, he seemed weak, in a way I had never seen before. When we passed one another, he quickly grabbed me by the hand and said, with tears in his eyes:

'Ivan Vasilievich, my dear fellow, what is she doing to me! She's demanding a power of attorney from me, so as to initiate proceedings. After all, I cannot do this ... It would be against my beliefs."Then, after walking alongside me for a few paces, he said to me: "I've a huge favor to ask you, only let it just be between the two of us for the time being, don't talk about it to anyone, not even Sasha. Please draw up a document for me, in which I might be able to announce, for everyone's knowledge, that all of my works, no matter when I wrote them, I am transferring into the public domain...'"

L.N. writes in his diary on 12 July: "Last night, it was difficult due to Sofia Andreyevna's talk of publishing and court proceedings. If only she knew and understood how she alone is poisoning my last hours, days, months of life! But I do not know how to tell her and cannot hope that any words I say will have any impact on her." On the eve of this entry, Tolstoy had taken the decision to travel to Stockholm. "I have decided to go to Shtockholm (*sic* – P.B.). I have a good feeling in my soul."

PAVEL BASINSKY

In the web of "legal speak"

In 1922, Chertkov released the book *Tolstoy's Flight*, in which he tried to conceal his involvement in the drafting of Tolstoy's legal testament. He explained this document's appearance as being due solely to the immoral position of the writer's wife and several other members of his family.

Chertkov's book provoked outrage among many contemporaries, Maxim Gorky included. In the magazine 'Conversation', Gorky published a sketch of Countess Tolstoy, whom he didn't like, but whom he nevertheless tried to defend and justify.

"For me, it's unclear who, if any, of the people around Lev Tolstoy during those days was entirely normal from a psychological point of view," Gorky announced. "And I don't understand why it was that, having recognized his wife as mentally abnormal, all those normal people did not think to pay due attention to her and were unable to isolate her." This is indeed a sore point, a horrible question. Only those closest to her could have resolved this situation. For various reasons, they did not do so. This is a family problem in a deep sense, which even today one must approach with extreme caution. One thing can be said for certain though: there was no subjective guilt on the part of Tolstoy's wife. A person who is unable to control herself and is perfectly well aware of this herself, and suffers because of it, cannot be blameworthy.

Gorky, explained her position as follows:

"In the end – just what, exactly, happened?

It was only that a woman who had lived through fifty difficult years with a great artist, an extremely unique and rebellious one at that, a woman who was his only friend on his entire path through life and an active assistant in his work – had grown terribly tired, something which is entirely understandable.

At the same time, she, as an old woman, seeing that this colossal man, her husband, was breaking off from the world, felt lonely and of no use to anyone, and this angered her.

In a state of indignation at the that strangers were pushing her away from a place which she had occupied for half a century, Sofia Tolstoy, they say, behaved with insufficient loyalty in relation to the stockade of morality which had been erected for the ring-fencing of this man by people who had ill-conceived ideas about themselves.

Then her indignation took on the character of near-madness within her.

Later still, abandoned by everyone, she died alone, and after her death they remembered her so that they could take pleasure in slandering her.

That's all there was to it."

Chertkov's role of in the writing of Tolstoy's wills, was, of course, enormous.

Firstly, without Chertkov, there would have been no will. Anyone who has the slightest understanding of the psychology of Tolstoy's personality has to understand that the preparation of this legal document, which was rewritten several times (!), was for him perhaps the most difficult experience of his life. It wasn't even a matter of Tolstoy's outlook, according to which one ought not to resolve a spiritual issue by having recourse to the state. The main thing was the psychology of his personality, especially in the last years, months and days of his life. To sign a legal document against the family meant, for him, to bring out in people *evil* toward others, and moreover in the closest people of all, for whom L.N. felt responsible.

Secondly, in his book, Chertkov concealed the fact that in 1904 he had forced L.N. to answer that "little questionnaire", which *already* was a formal will in V.G.'s eyes. Prior to 1909, Chertkov didn't know that this "questionnaire" had no legal force whatsoever. Without even knowing this, though, he nevertheless *forced* Tolstoy into creating yet another formal document – the first version of the *legal* will, which was signed by L.N. at Chertkov's country house in Krekshino on September 18, 1909.

Yes, Chertkov was right, when he wrote that "his decision (Tolstoy's – P.B.) to resort to the will was taken without my knowledge and during my enforced separation from him." He neglects to mention, however, that Tolstoy's three trusted representatives were never far from his side: Sasha, Gusev and Makovitsky. He neglects to mention that Tolstoy's secretaries, Gusev and Bulgakov, were appointed to the Yasnaya Polyana house by Chertkov, moreover on conditions which cause consternation, to say the least. By way of example, Bulgakov was supposed to keep a daily log of what was going on in the house, and send this log (!) to Chertkov. In effect, this was surveillance of L.N. and his family.

Finally, Chertkov neglects to mention that throughout the entire period of his "separation" from L.N., he repeatedly harassed him with written requests concerning the legal registration of the rights to his new texts. These requests tormented Tolstoy, calling up an "unpleasant" feeling in him, but L.N. agreed to them every time.

His boundless love for Chertkov is one of the most mysterious phenomena of Tolstoy's emotional life. How many times, during their correspondence and direct communication, did Chertkov rudely intrude into family relationships, plotting against Tolstoy's wife and daughters, whom their father loved more than anything in the world! And each and every time, Chertkov not only got away with it, but emerged victorious. Every time!

"I received, my dear friend, your letter, which disappointed me in all respects. And thank you for that. It was disappointing that you did not write anything specific about yourself. And I'm still waiting. It was disappointing, and even displeased about my writings, from some years before. All of these writings fell to the "devil", all I ask is that they might not cause hard feelings," writes Tolstoy in a letter he sent to Krekshino from Kochety.

Which writings is he talking about? Chertkov had asked him to send in the story *The Devil* for the anthology which was being compiled to celebrate the fiftieth anniversary of the Literary Fund; Tolstoy had hidden this work from his wife for twenty years under the lining of a chair, but it was discovered and sent S.A. into a rage. Chertkov explained that since S.A. was publishing the story as it had been written before 1881, this might cause problems when it was published. What was this, if not an incursion into intimate family matters? This incursion was closely linked to the problem of the literary rights to which Chertkov was staking a claim.

In December 1909, at the urging of Chertkov, Tolstoy acknowledges Chertkov's exclusive rights in writing as "L.N. Tolstoy's agent in the handling of the publication of writings appearing for the first time." This was the crowning glory of Chertkov's multiple-stage attempt to become Tolstoy's *only* legally legitimate literary agent. Published in several newspapers at the same time (*New Rus*, *Russian Word* and *Russian Gazette*) with Tolstoy's approved postscript, Chertkov's *Letter to the Editor* was the visible tip of the iceberg that went by the name of 'Tolstoy's Will'.

And one final thing. When talking about the "enforced separation" with Tolstoy, Chertkov strangely "forgot" that on June 30 and July 1, 1909, he and L.N. had met in the village of Suvorovo, three and a half versts from Kochety. This "joyful meeting" was organized by Tolstoy's daughter, Tatiana Suhotina. The meeting was a secret one, for S.A. didn't know about it. Her husband was staying with their daughter in Kochety at this time. From the point of view of the law, though, the meeting would be permissible. Suvorovo was in the Orlov Province (which bordered the Tula Province) and Chertkov was only banned from entering the Tula Province.

What did he and Chertkov talk about?

According to Makovitsky, who was also staying at Kochety, Tolstoy, on his return from the last meeting, "felt weak after the stress brought on by the serious talks with Chertkov." On July 2, Tolstoy slept until 9 am, then remained in bed and barely did any work all day, played solitaire and then went to sleep again. "His pulse was irregular," Makovitsky wrote, "and lower than normal: by four in the afternoon, when L.N. lay down in bed, it had fallen to 60, with a temperature of 36, whilst the norms for L.N. were 72 and 36.6. He had heartburn, chills, back pain, and was cold all over his body." Such was Tolstoy's physical condition before he returned to Yasnaya Polyana, where the "Stockholm" family crisis was looming.

Invitation to a beheading

Who wrote the first formal will? Tolstoy had been seriously (terminally) ill for the last two years. His secretary Gusev, in his diary, describes fainting spells which occurred with L.N. and were accompanied by a partial loss of memory, when Tolstoy suddenly forgot the names of his children and grandchildren, didn't recognize their faces, asked with curiosity about where Khamovniki was, and could even ask in all seriousness whether or not his brother "Mitenka" had arrived yesterday? Dmitri Nikolayevich Tolstoy had died in 1856, half a century before Gusev became Tolstoy's secretary; his death was described in detail in *Anna Karenina*, which was written in the '70s.

In July 1909, shortly before he wrote his first formal will, Tolstoy *forgot* that he was no longer the owner of Yasnaya Polyana. He sincerely believed that he still owned the land, suffered from this knowledge and wanted to give it away to the peasants. This is hard to believe, but there were two pieces of evidence for it.

There is an entry in Tolstoy's diary for July 23: "I have decided to give the land away. Yesterday I spoke to Ivan Vasilievich. How hard is it to rid oneself of this dirty, sinful property. Help me, help me, help me." Does this mean that his conversation with the lawyer, Denisenko, was not only about literary rights? Does this mean that in his mind, the literary rights had somehow become connected to his ownership of land which he had not owned since 1892?

This is confirmed by the diary of his daughter, Tatyana Lvovna. "... when I was at Yasnaya in July and the general mood was very heavy, he told me once that land ownership was horribly difficult for him. I was taken aback.

"Papa! But you don't own anything!"

"What do you mean? What about Yasnaya Polyana?"

"No indeed! You gave it to your heirs, along with everything else."

He stopped me and said:

"Well, tell me all about it, tell me how things stand." Let us remember that at this time, L.N., accompanied by Chertkov and Sasha, was getting ready to go to Stockholm. Might it not be the case, then, that his wife's behavior, in not letting him go, wasn't so crazy after all? Might it not be that the crazy thing, on the contrary, was to provoke him to go on the trip? Why did he even want to go to Sweden at all?

On July 30, when, under pressure from his wife, he had almost abandoned the trip altogether, he and Makovitsky had a very strange conversation. The doctor was massaging L.N.'s injured leg. Suddenly, Tolstoy asked:

"I am appealing to you as to a close friend, a humble, spartan man: I want to leave home and go abroad somewhere. How do I get a passport?"

The conversation about the passport continued the next evening as well. Makovitsky told L.N. about the procedure for obtaining a passport.

"How very complicated," L.N. said. "Is it possible to do it so that it wouldn't become known?"

On August 21, in the presence of his loved ones, Tolstoy came out with a remarkable utterance which accurately reflects his state of mind at the time:

"If I could create people, I would make them old, so that they gradually became children."

On August 28th, the writer turned eighty-one. "I am three cubed," Tolstoy joked over breakfast. (Tolstoy was mistaken: 81 is 3 to the fourth power)

And on September 2nd, convulsive meetings took place at Krekshino. Convulsive because Chertkov was scaring Tolstoy with the idea that while he was away, they would conduct searches at Yasnaya Polyana and confiscate his recent writings. The scared old man tells Makovitsky, "he takes with him everything he can possibly lay his fingers on: manuscripts, articles he has begun, even the books that go with them." The route to Krekshino passes through Moscow. Tolstoy hadn't been there for many years. The city had changed beyond recognition. Horse-drawn trams and trolley cars had appeared. Zimmerman's music store was selling the latest newfangled device which recreated the playing of the most famous pianists. A telephone had been installed at the Khamovniki house. These achievements of civilization left L.N. stunned. "He looked with horror," notes Goldenweiser, "on this huge human hive, and found evidence at every step of his long-standing hatred of so-called civilization." Tolstoy nonetheless takes a childish delight in a musical device in Zimmerman's store, gasping and sighing with elation. This device is later sent to Krekshino for the duration of L.N.'s stay, for advertising purposes.

Tolstoy's Krekshino diary (from 5 to 18 September 1909) evokes some startling feelings. He is wise, but somehow too childishly so. To the uninitiated eye he really can come across as some sort of childish prattler. On God, on goodness, on love, on the meaning of dreams... Tolstoy recalls a strange dream he had, in which he and his brother Sergei had gone hunting, and L.N. for some reason had a clarinet with him instead of a gun. And so they arrived at the sea (why the sea?) and see some ships, which are actually swans. "Shoot," Sergei says. L.N. puts the clarinet to his mouth, but he can't blow into it. Then his brother fires his gun, and Tolstoy is awoken by a loud bang. Some screens which had been standing by the window had fallen down because of a gust of wind.

There is *not a single word* in this diary about what will happen on the day of the departure from Krekshino – about the will. The impression one gets is that he wasn't thinking about it at all. Or was he afraid that his wife would read the diary?

The question inevitably arises: to what extent was Tolstoy aware of what it was he had signed on September 18? There is no answer to this question, because Tolstoy doesn't comment on it in his diary. There is only a mysterious entry about a conversation with Chertkov the previous day. "Spoke to Chertkov about the children's intention to take as their own works which were given to everyone. I don't want to believe it." From this entry, one can cautiously conclude that Chertkov had raised the question.

L.N. is absent-minded, whereas V.G. is terribly businesslike. Having frightened the old man for a second time, this time with the threat of a search at Krekshino, he sends the first copies of the manuscripts brought by Tolstoy to England.

On the eve of signing the will, Tolstoy got lost in the woods. He was even scared that he wouldn't find the way back home. Suddenly, out of nowhere, V.G. appeared! He had decided to follow Tolstoy.

On the last day of his stay, Tolstoy got lost again. He was brought back to Chertkov's house once again.

Sitting on a bench after his walk, L.N. told his grandchildren Sonia and Ilyusha his "signature" story about the cucumbers. "- a little boy goes out into the garden. He sees a cucumber lying there. It's this big (he shows how big the cucumber is with his fingers). He picks it up – hap! and eats it!" "- And he's crunching it as if it's a real one," said Ilya. "But it's not, it's not a real one! I was watching grandfather so carefully and thinking, surely he'll shove a real one in. But no, he didn't." "You should be ashamed to think that grandfather was going to be devious!" Sonya, the elder child, exclaimed indignantly. "It offends grandfather!"

The will was signed that day.

"I declare that I wish that all my compositions, literary works and writings of any kind, both those that have already been released in print somewhere and those that are still unpublished, written or printed for the first time from January 1, 1881 onwards, as well as everything which I wrote before that date but which has not yet been printed, should not be anyone's property after my death, but could be published and reprinted free of charge by anyone who wishes to do so. I wish that all the manuscripts and papers which shall remain after I am gone, be transferred to Vladimir Grigorievich Chertkov, so that he might dispose of them after my death, as he disposes of them now, so that all my writings are freely available to anyone desiring to use them for publication. I ask Vladimir Grigorievich Chertkov, in addition, to select a person or persons to whom he shall assign this authority in the event of his death.

Lev Nikolayevich Tolstoy.

Krekshino, September 18, 1909

At the signing of this true will the following were present, and hereby certify that Lev Nikolayevich Tolstoy, when preparing this testament, was of sound mind and memory: Freelance artist Alexander Borisovich Goldenweiser. Tradesman Alexei Petrovich Sergeyenko. Tradesman Alexander Vasilievich Kalachev.

This true will was copied out by:

Alexandra Tolstaya."

On the way back, Tolstoy was nearly crushed by the five thousand-strong crowd which came to see the writer off at the Kursk railway station. Chertkov came to his rescue. It was Chertkov, though, who had informed the newspapers what time L.N. would be leaving Moscow. When Tolstoy got into a carriage at the Kozlova Zaseka station, he had a deep fainting spell. He only came to in the morning, on September 20. "... I don't remember anything. They said that first of all I began to speak, then I lost consciousness altogether. How simple and good it is to die like that."

Documents and people

Tolstoy's first formal will was written in his own hand. A quick comparison of the text of this document with the two wills made in the form of diary entries is enough for one to realize something: *this isn't Tolstoy's language or style*. So whose language is it?

Concerning the history of this text, Chertkov does not say at any stage of his book *The Departure of Tolstoy* that "Tolstoy *wrote* his will." He puts it more diplomatically: "He decided *to resort to drawing up* a will." Who, though, might I ask, actually drew it up?

In his book *The Departure and Death of Lev Tolstoy*, Boris Meylakh notes that the first formal will coincides, not only in terms of its content, but also in terms of its text, with the "questionnaire" which Chertkov sent from England with his secretary Briggs in 1904. Sure enough, Tolstoy's answers, which repeated the questions in an affirmative form, lay at the basis of the will.

For example:

"Questionnaire" (1904): "Do you grant me the right, after your death, to dispose, at my own personal discretion, both for publication in my lifetime, and for the assignment by me to a trusted person after my death, of all those of your manuscripts and papers that I have received, and shall receive from you before your death?"

The Will (1909): "I wish that all the manuscripts and papers that will remain after me be transferred to Vladimir Grigorievich Chertkov, so that he might continue after my death to dispose of them..."

Just what had happened on September 18th, 1909? Nothing more nor less than this: V.G. had defeated S.A. And the worst thing about it was that this had been done literally behind her back, when she had gone off to Krekshino.

After she had refused to let her husband go to Stockholm, to have refused to let him go to Krekshino would have one act of violence too many. Sure enough, she resigned herself to the trip, although she found it very hard to do so. "All these preparations Lev Nikolayevich is making to go and see Chertkov are difficult for me," S.A. writes in her "Daily diary" on September 2. "Sad farewells and departures" (an entry on September 3). On September 5, when Tolstoy arrives at Krekshino, his sister Maria Nikolayevna leaves Yasnaya Polyana for Shamordino; she comes to visit her brother, together with her daughter Liza. Yasnaya Polyana was now completely empty. Without Tolstoy, it was overwhelmingly empty, turning into a dead place that no-one wanted to visit.

"You cannot imagine how strange it is at Yasnaya Polyana without L.N.!" Goldenweiser's wife wrote in a letter to her husband in June 1909. "Such silence and lifelessness."

On the same day on which Maria Nikolayevna had left Yasnaya, the Goldenweisers had returned from Moscow. They told S.A. about how her husband had spent the time in Moscow: how he had listened to the musical device in Zimmerman's shop, how he had walked along the Kuznetsky Bridge, how the public had greeted him so rapturously at the station. S.A. was in Moscow on the morning of September 8 and set off for Krekshino. L.N. met her "affectionately" at the station, and everything in the house seemed "good, welcoming and attractive" to her. On September 10-12, she was again in Moscow. She went to the bank, put her publishing affairs in order and, as usual, went to the Historical Museum to work with her husband's manuscripts, which she had handed to the museum for safekeeping. Besides this, she also had a pain in her leg, and she went to see the doctor. On September 13th she travelled to Krekshino once again.

She already had a definite sense that something was wrong on that day. Her daughter Sasha joined her on the journey from Moscow: she had also been in the city on business, and was now returning to Chertkov and her father.

Tolstoy met them at the station again. As she took her seat in the carriage, S.A. stumbled on her injured leg and moaned loudly the whole way back. She was put to bed and the doctors were summoned. By lunchtime, she was well enough to come to the table. Goldenweiser, who was there, notes "Sofia Andreyevna's ailing and irritable condition, ready to make a scene or lapse into a fit of hysteria at any moment." On September 17, the eve of the signing of the will, a quarrel broke out between S.A. and Chertkov, about which Alyosha Sergeyenko, Chertkov's young secretary, writes in his memoirs.

The impressions Alyosha Sergeyenko picked up from his visit to Krekshino in September 1909 are extremely interesting. At the time, Alyosha understood little of the intricacies of the Tolstoys' family conflict, although he had known the writer since he was 14 due to his father's acquaintance with him – his father was the writer and Tolstoy biographer Peter Sergeyenko. In the teeming Sergeyenko family, the cult of the "great Lev" reigned supreme. Peter Alexeyevich, his wife and their eight children lived in the countryside and worked the land, and they celebrated every one of Tolstoy's birthdays in reverent contemplation of him. When he left for England, V.G. took the young 'Tolstoyan' Alexei along as his secretary.

Alyosha had an opportunity to compare the Chertkovs' lives in England and in Krekshino. As difficult and boring as things had been in England, in Krekshino Alyosha suddenly sensed the atmosphere of a *happy family*.

"I soon found out (while in England – P.B.), that in this house, in fact, there was no family, that it was more of a hotel; each person lived his own isolated life, and for me, after living to the age of twenty in a large family, I didn't quite feel at home, and was sometimes sad." The atmosphere in Krekshino was entirely different. "A completely different spirit," Alyosha notes in amazement.

Chertkov and Galya worry about the homestead, discuss the problem of the cauliflower sent to them for Tolstoy by a neighboring landowner. How are they to prepare it: "in slices", "au gratin", "in béchamel"? Chertkov is personally involved in drawing up the menu for Tolstoy. Things are fun and lively around the table.

"Lev Nikolayevich was at the end of the table, and strange to say – it seemed to me right from the first moment that these were not people who weren't related sitting there, but also something like a big family. And Lev Nikolayevich was at the head of it." "A big happy family," Sergeyenko writes.

And now try to imagine what S.A. thought of this. She could see it too. Not surprisingly, she got into a furious row with V.G. when she found out that she wouldn't even be in the same carriage as her husband on the journey to Moscow. "Sonia was very put out by the suggestion that she would travel to Moscow separately," L.N. writes in his diary. "I went to see her. I feel very sorry for her, poor thing, she's sick and weak. I didn't entirely reassure her, but later she spoke so kindly, so well, she was sorry, she said: forgive me. I was joyfully moved."

This entry was made on September 17.

L.N. signed the will the following day.

More of a royalist than the king

"Nothing at the Chertkovs' was to her liking: the "dark ones" surrounding father, the shared table, where Ilya Vasilyevich (Tolstoy's servant – P.B.) sat for meals together with her. Her nerves were in a terrible state," Sasha recalls of S.A.'s mood in Krekshino. "It is difficult to imagine what would have happened if she had found out that here, in Krekshino, father had decided to write a will... I copied out this will, father and the three witnesses signed it. I gave a copy to Chertkov, kept the original, and Chertkov asked me to go and see the barrister Muravyov in Moscow, to find out whether or not this will was valid." "His decision to resort to the will was undertaken without my knowledge and during my enforced separation from him..." writes Chertkov. "I not only did not try to persuade L.N. to write a "legal" will, but even suggested that he would not agree to do so..."

The story of this will is horribly murky. And this despite the fact that the life of the later Tolstoy was very transparent. His every word, his every gesture was recorded from various angles. This was not the case, however, in respect of that will – one of the most important acts of his life.

"I shall not touch upon a detailed history of each of these documents here, so as not to over-burden the narrative," Chertkov writes in his book *Tolstoy's Departure*. Yet for all that the book contains a very detailed account of the will from 1895 and the unseemly role played by Tolstoy's wife in keeping it concealed.

Alexandra Lvovna, who was already parting ways with Chertkov and no longer feeling any sympathy for him, is extremely sparing about V.G.'s role in the story of the will in her memoirs, written in two volumes (*Father* and *Daughter*). We find out from her memoirs, nonetheless, that Chertkov himself was the initiator of her meeting in Moscow with the lawyer N.K. Muravyov, a well-known defense lawyer in cases involving the Russian sectarians, to whom L.N. had often appealed for help. Yet it was with this meeting that the legal nightmare which eventually forced L.N. to flee from Yasnaya Polyana began.

Muravyov explained to our protagonists that literary rights, like any other form of private property, could not be transferred to "everyone". They could only be transferred to a specific person or legal entity – or to several. From this moment on, L.N.'s fourteen-year games with the laws of the Russian Empire had come to an end.

A choice had to be made. Either leave everything as it is and take no steps to create a legal will (in this case, his legal heirs would be his wife and children). Or, having promised to do one thing, do the other as well.

Chertkov denied any role in the initiation of the second formal will, written after N.K. Muravyov had subjected the first, "Krekshino" variation to much criticism. The fact remains, though: it was Chertkov's young colleague Fyodor Strahov, who twice, on October 26 and November

1, 1909, came to see Tolstoy at Yasnaya Polyana to settle this legal matter.

In Georgii Orehanov's book, *V.G. Chertkov in the Life of Lev Tolstoy*, two of Sasha's letters to Chertkov, written on 11 and 27 October, were published. They leave one in no doubt that the second legal will was carefully prepared by a "Chertkov-ite team" that was hostile toward S.A.

Oct. 11: "(Most important) The other day I was thinking a great deal about father's will, and it occurred to me that it would be better to write such a will and to certify it with the signatures of witnesses, and to declare his desire and will to his sons during his life-time. Three days ago I talked about it with papa. I told him I had been to see Muravyov, and that Muravyov had said that papa's will was not valid and that, in my opinion, he ought to do one. In response to what I said about the will being invalid, he said: well, it can be done, it can be done in Tula. As for the rest, he said he'd think about it, and that it was good in the sense that if he were to declare his desire whilst he was alive, it wouldn't be as if he suspected that the children wouldn't carry out his wishes, and that if, after his death, such a document were to be found, then his sons, Sergei for example, would be offended by the idea that their father had thought that they would not carry out his wishes without notarized papers. I took away from this conversation with father the impression that he would do everything that was necessary. Now you think about it and decide what is best. Is it impossible to raise the matter of all the works? Please don't delay. When Tanya comes, it'll be a lot more difficult, and maybe even impossible to arrange anything."

Thus, a legal testament was prepared not only behind S.A.'s back, but without the knowledge of the older children, Sergei and Tatiana, who were on their father's side in the family conflict. It was prepared with the utmost secrecy and was prepared by "Chertkov's team", which, alas, also included the Tolstoys' youngest daughter Sasha. The most unpleasant part of the letter is the part where she raises the question of depriving their mother of the rights to works written before 1881, proposing that V.G. see to this.

Sasha did not love her mother at this time, and, unfortunately, with good reason. When she was just a child, she had found out that she was born the night after her father's first attempt to leave her mother, in June 1884. She also knew that, whilst pregnant with her, her mother had gone to see a midwife in Tula to ask her to arrange a miscarriage. The midwife refused to do so; S.A. later thanked God for this. She did not spoil Sasha, however, and she did not pay her the same kind of attention which was afforded to the other children. She kept her at a distance, often got annoyed with her, insulted her and humiliated her. Her daughter responded to her mother with disobedience and insolence.

Did she herself raise the question with her father of depriving the mother and sons of all rights to L.N.'s works? However that may be, it is obvious from her letter that in the matter of the will, Tolstoy was not the master, but the slave ("... he will do whatever is necessary").

Indeed, as one immerses oneself in Tolstoy's diaries and letters from the time, we can see how far L.N. was far from making any practical decisions whatsoever on his own. At the very least, he wouldn't make any decisions himself without being prompted to do so from without.

In the memoirs of Sasha, Chertkov and F.A. Strahov, however, it looks as though her father's decision to deny S.A. of all rights to his literary legacy came as a complete surprise to them as well.

"He immediately went into his study and took Alexandra Lvovna and me in there with him," F.A. Strahov writes of his first visit to L.N. "I shall surprise you with the extreme solution I have arrived at," he said to us both, with a kind smile on his face. 'I want to be *plus royaliste que le roi* (more royalist than the king). I want to give you alone, Sasha, everything, understand? Everything, and that includes the stipulation which was made in that newspaper statement of mine.' We stood in front of him, as shocked as if we had been struck by lightning by these words of his, "you alone" and "everything". He pronounced them with such simplicity, as if he was telling us about the most trifling adventure that had happened to him whilst he was out walking."

"On November 1, 1909, father signed a new will, drawn up by the lawyer Muravyov," Alexandra Lvovna recalled. "At first, father's intention was to leave the rights to all his writings to the three of us, those who were closest to him, Sergei, Tanya and me, so that we, in turn, would pass these rights on for common usage. One morning, though, when I went in to see him in his study, he suddenly said: 'Sasha, I have decided to make a will for you alone,' and he gave me a questioning look. I said nothing. I pictured the enormous responsibility which was being put on me, attacks from the family, the offence that my older brothers and sisters would feel, and at the same time a sense of pride grew in my soul, and happiness over the fact that he was entrusting me with such a huge matter.

'Why are you saying nothing?' he said.

I expressed my doubts to him.

'No, this is what I have decided,' he said firmly, 'you're the only one now who is left to live with me, and it's entirely natural that I entrust you with this matter. In the event of your death,' and he laughed softly, 'the rights shall be passed on to Tanya."

We have absolutely no reason not to trust these recollections. The atmosphere in the Yasnaya Polyana house was such that Tolstoy might well have come to his own final decision, completely independently, concerning the transfer of all the rights to Sasha alone, the only one of his heirs whom he could not doubt.

Judging by his diary, though, Tolstoy did not get any joy out of this.

Oct. 26: "Didn't sleep until 3am, and it was sad, but I didn't give in completely. Woke up late. Sofia Andreyevna has returned. I'm glad to see her, but she's very excited... Strahov arrived. Didn't do anything in the morning. A good letter from Chertkov. He tells me in clearer terms what I myself was thinking. The conversation with Strakhov was difficult, about Chertkov's demands, because one has to deal with the government. It seems that I'll resolve everything in the simplest and most natural way – Sasha. I want the old ones too, from before '82 ... Evening. Another conversation with Strakhov. I agreed. But I regret that I didn't say that all this is very difficult for me, and that the best thing of all is inaction." S.A. returned from Moscow on the day of Strakhov's arrival. This circumstance very nearly disrupted the plan by "Chertkov's team" to decide the question of the will in her absence. Tolstoy's state of mind was "oppressive". He was having problems with his memory: he got the years 1881 and 1882 mixed up.

"...It's doubtful that I'll live: weakness, drowsiness," he writes in his diary on October 28. "... I slept a lot, an unnatural amount" (entry for October 29). "Extremely strange, a melancholy state. I cannot get to sleep, two o'clock (in the morning)" (October 31, on the eve of the signing of the will.) You will agree that people in such a physical and mental condition do not generally go about signing spiritual acts of such immense significance as Tolstoy's will was.

That is under normal circumstances, though. The situation in which Tolstoy found himself, however, was completely abnormal. This can be seen in Sasha's second letter to Chertkov, which was written on October 27.

"Vladimir Grigorievich, although Strakhov has been relating the whole matter to you, I consider it necessary to state my opinion in even greater detail.

1) This matter must not be disclosed in any way. If the family were to find out about this, then father's last days would be a torment. Remember the Stockholm incident: the hysterics, the morphine, the throwing herself on the floor, etc., and I cannot even promise that they won't demand to have the document back and tear it up. Disclosure is unthinkable. Lev Nikolayevich agrees with this.

2) Both father and I believe that Sergei, with his card-playing, is very unreliable.

As for Tanya, she once said, when I asked her once whether or not she would use these compositions, said: 'why should I decline to accept money which our brothers would spend on sprees, it's better to take it and do good with it.' I am left alone. Decide for yourselves, all of you, my friends, whether or not you can trust me with this, a matter of such great importance... I, the youngest, the least loved of all the family, and suddenly I was entrusted with such a thing, through me all of the family's money was snatched away! They'll grow to hate me, that's for certain. It's all the same to me though, I'm not afraid of that. After father's death, the only thing that will remain dear to me will be his ideas. So decide, only do so as quickly as possible so that Goldenweiser's arrival doesn't arouse any suspicions. I'll come and sign any wills and promises, if necessary."

In a letter to her brother Mikhail, written when she was living abroad many years later, before the start of the Second World War, T.L. Suhotina-Tolstaya wrote: "The person who did the most damage in this matter (relations between their parents. – P.B.) was Sasha. More so than Chertkov. She was young ... The only thing she saw was father's suffering, and, loving him with all her heart, she thought that he could start a new life away from his old friend and be happy." Sasha's letters to Chertkov inspire a sense of compassion for her. She is so overflowing with heroism, sacrifice, and at the same time blindly trusts her "friends", people from outside her family who have plotted against her own mother, such that she herself doesn't notice that she is becoming the puppet legal representative in the "case" of the transfer of all of her father's literary rights... to Chertkov.

If another person had been in Chertkov's place, someone with mercantile considerations, the whole matter would have simply been a "dirty" criminal plot. Chertkov wasn't looking for material benefits, however. At the same time, he heaped a colossal amount of moral responsibility upon himself before his contemporaries and descendants. *No normal person in their right mind would have dared to do this.* Chertkov dared to do it though. Chertkov genuinely believed that he was doing this "dirty" work so that the Teacher, after his death, would emerge in complete moral purity, would not be stained by his family's use of his great creations for material gain.

On November 1, Tolstoy writes in his diary: "Goldenweiser and Strakhov arrived today, they brought the documents from Chertkov. I redid everything. Pretty boring."

Catastrophe

If one were to read through all the evidence about life at Yasnaya Polyana after June 22, 1910, one might be at risk of damaging one's own mental health. For six months, "Chertkov's team", together with Tolstoy, managed to conceal the existence of the secret will, which would deprive the family of rights to his literary legacy. When it began to rise to the surface, however, a scandal of monstrous proportions erupted.

It makes no sense to try to determine who was in the right and who was in the wrong in this story. We must always remember that the situation in which Tolstoy and his family found themselves was unprecedented. None of the characters in this plot were prepared for it. Indeed, the plot proved to be too paradoxical: it was a combination of Shakespeare's *King Lear* and Gogol's *Taras Bulba*.

Try as Tolstoy might to "escape" from this problem, it refused to leave him in peace. He was ashamed that after his death the children would find out about their father's distrust, about the secret with which he had lived out the last year of his life. Sasha felt awkward in respect of her older sister. Finally, there was also a serious legal flaw in the second version of the formal will, signed on November 1, 1909. It didn't specify who would inherit the literary rights if Sasha were to die unexpectedly.

In the summer of 1910, Sasha showed signs of having tuberculosis. Weak lungs were the Tolstoys' hereditary nightmare. Two of L.N.'s brothers – Dmitri and Nikolai – died of tuberculosis. He suspected he had the illness himself all his life, running away from it to be treated in the Samaran steppe. The death of Chekhov, who had died of tuberculosis in 1904 and was much loved in the Tolstoy family, was still fresh in the memory.

Sasha too went off to the Crimea, where she quickly recovered. Incidentally, she gave up vegetarianism for a time in the Crimea, because it was incompatible with the treatment of tuberculosis.

Sasha's illness played a very significant role in the story of Tolstoy's departure. After all, the mere fact that L.N. chose to flee to the south (in the direction of Bulgaria or the Caucasus), had to do with his daughter's unhealthy lungs. In the summer of 1910 the question arose of its own accord: what would happen to Tolstoy's legacy in the event of Sasha's death? This must have alarmed Chertkov too. Chertkov more than anyone, in fact. Without Sasha, this puppet legal representative, L.N.'s will lost its meaning. V.G. would be cut out of everything once again. And at this point, in June-July 1910, the situation from the autumn of 1909 is repeated.

At first, L.N., tormented by his wife's behavior, goes to stay with his "dear friend", who no longer lives in Krekshino, but at the Otradnoye estate, near the village of Meshcherskoye in the Moscow Province. He is accompanied by Sasha, who has returned from the Crimea but is still physically weak, Makovitsky and the young secretary Valentin Bulgakov. As in 1909, the departure was preceded by arguments with his wife and fainting spells.

The quarrel concerned the Circassian, whom the Countess, following the example of their neighbor, the landowner Zvegintseva, had hired to protect Yasnaya. The Circassian didn't drink and thus couldn't be bribed, and he was ruthless toward the Russian peasants. Tolstoy once saw Ahmet pulling along with his lasso a former pupil of his at the Yasnaya Polyana School, the old peasant Prokofiy Vlasov. Another time, he came across a man who asked him: "is it safe to walk through the forest?" "Why wouldn't it be?" L.N. said in surprise. "The Circassian beats us mercilessly…"

Whilst in Meshchersky from June 12 to the 23rd, Tolstoy gets some good rest and is very productive: he writes two small artistic texts (including the brilliant psychological study *Inadvertently*) and makes the proofs of the book *The Path of Life*. He spends more time, though, walking around the local area and talking to people. Tolstoy visited two psychiatric hospitals located nearby, taking a keen interest in the living conditions of the patients and talking to them. Having heard and read a lot about the horrors of psychiatric hospitals (one thinks of Chekhov's *Ward 6*), Tolstoy was extremely surprised by what he saw: in Russia, the mad people were far better fed and more comfortable than the majority of the peasants! The calmest ones were even housed in peasant huts, paying 9 rubles a month for their board, which was beneficial both to the state and to the peasants. As for the violent ones, not only are they never beaten, they're never restrained either, but are instead put in special rooms with padded walls and non-shatter glass.

There is so much freedom here that a patient once simply hacked a staff member to death with an axe. Another "patient", who was obviously faking it, a murderer who had been sentenced to be hanged, boldly takes issue with Tolstoy. It transpires that he has read almost all of his articles. Tolstoy is amazed. "Ask him what his name is," the doctor says wearily. "Peter the Great," the "patient" reluctantly answers, and Tolstoy can see how ashamed he is, how tired he is of pretending.

L.N. innocently tells S.A. about this in his letters from Meshchersky: "We're fine. Yesterday I rode on horseback into a village where there were some mentally ill women… and the ill women were interesting. Back home, some doctors arrived from Troitskoye, 3 versts away, to invite me to a cinematographic show. Troitskoye is a district hospital for the mentally ill, the worst cases. There are 1000 people there. I promised to visit them…"

S.A.'s embittered mind immediately makes a logical connection: her illness, her husband's flight to Chertkov, her husband's interest in psychiatric hospital; it seems to her that he and Chertkov are planning to put her in one.

Of course, such an idea was not and could not have been in Tolstoy's mind. His interest in the issue of insanity at this time wasn't coincidental, however. This was the summer in which he was writing his article *On Madness*. On his return to Yasnaya, L.N. studies Professor S.S.

Korsakov's *Psychiatry Course* and finds clear parallels with S.A.'s illness in it.

In his diary from Otradnoye, however, Tolstoy writes: "I want to try consciously to fight Sonia with kindness and love." Soon afterwards, his wife reads this entry and sees only one thing in it: "I want *to fight* with Sonia." On June 22, S.A.'s behavior becomes unmanageable.

She sends her husband and daughter a telegram signed Feokritova (so that they wouldn't think it was just a wild guess on her part), "Sofia Andreyevna has a strong nervous disorder, insomnia, she's crying, has a pulse of one hundred, asks that you wire her. Varya." Then, under her own name, she begs her husband to come immediately. On June 23, in response, she receives a telegram: "It would be more convenient to come back tomorrow afternoon but if necessary we'll come tonight." She explodes at the words "more convenient". She sees in this turn of phrase an example of Chertkov's "heartless" style.

Feokritova claims in her diary (which one must be very cautious about believing, incidentally) that S.A.'s hysterics were caused by the problem of the will. She had made up her mind that, under pressure from Chertkov and Sasha in Meshchersky, L.N. was going to sign a will that went against the family. (She didn't know that such a document had already been signed.) She was sure that there was an ulterior motive behind Tolstoy and Chertkov's visits to the psychiatric clinics: they were looking for a place for her. She screamed at Feokritova that she would not allow this to happen, that she'd commit suicide before it could. She wrote suicide notes, which she threatened to have published in the newspapers after her death, by her sons, so that everyone would know that her husband was a murderer.

And at the same time, the "happy" news reaches Otradnoye that the authorities are allowing Chertkov to return to Telyatinki, near Yasnaya Polyana, for the duration of his mother's stay there. This was a strange way for it to be phrased. Everyone understood that this in fact meant the lifting of the ban on V.G. living in the Tula Province, and that from now on the student could live near his teacher and see him every day. Tolstoy hurries to *cheer his wife up* with this news, too.

The degree of misunderstanding between the couple, their insensitivity to the mental state of their "other half" has reached truly catastrophic proportions. S.A. sees a "conspiracy" in everything and a desire on the part of her husband to get rid of her for Chertkov's sake. L.N. is endlessly "surprised" by his wife's rude treatment of such a wonderful man. He is so blinded that he doesn't seem to notice that Chertkov is stubbornly and despotically driving S.A. away from any future involvement in the management of L.N.'s legacy, with scant regard for their marital union which has lasted almost half a century, for a mother's love for her children, or for her state of mind.

Him, her, them

On June 23, 1910, Tolstoy and Sasha return to Yasnaya Polyana. On July 27, Chertkov arrives in Telyatinki "to be with his mother" and starts visiting the Yasnaya Polyana house every day; in doing so, he literally starts to drive the Countess mad.

Tolstoy's intelligent son-in-law, M.S. Suhotin, summoned to Yasnaya together with T.L. Suhotina-Tolstaya by an anxious telegram from Sasha, tried to identify all the reasons for his mother-in-law's illness in his diary.

"1) Her love for L.N. is utterly sincere, but is somewhat pathological, as its main component part is a passion which is not quite normal in a woman of 65 toward a man of 81, a passion which, for obvious reasons, it is difficult to satisfy.

2) As a result of this passion there is jealousy. Jealousy has always been a negative trait of S.A., but in the past it was brought on by women, who, after all, might at least have been pleasing to L.N. as a man, but now it is caused by a man, Chertkov. Therefore jealousy calls up in S.A.'s feverish imagination scenes of a most shameful kind for L.N. 3) Wounded pride. This is understandable. Something that L.N. doesn't want to give to his wife, because it is very intimate, is given freely to Chertkov, then passed on by Chertkov to his "dark" secretaries to be copied out. This really is a blow to his wife's dignity.

4) Love of power. This feeling, of course, is one with which Chertkov is afflicted. S.A. realizes that Chertkov is already ahead of her.

5) Self-interest. Everything that has been written by L.N.'s hand will, of course, be of great value. S.A. exaggerates this value, too, such that in her head the value of these diaries has assumed somewhat fantastical

proportions; and what if suddenly she or her dear Andrei are left with nothing after L.N.'s death.

6) Hysteria. This, of course, plays a role. The force with which she interprets all the unpleasantness, the strength with which she expresses her feelings, it is plain to see, are abnormal, and it may be that this abnormality also borders on the area of psychopathy.

7) Fear for her posthumous fame. After all, L.N.'s diaries will be published at some point, and what if it transpires from them what kind of a person S.A. was – that in the past, too, she really had been a heavy cross in L.N.'s life?"

There is nothing to add to these seven "points". Some of the wording could perhaps be toned down. (The only thing that Suhotin for some reason neglects to mention, but that Gorky, who is far removed from the family, does notice, is S.A.'s general physical and mental *fatigue*, after she has lived for nearly half a century with the most complex man of the 19th century and borne him thirteen children). Suhotin's attempt to explain L.N.'s behavior is far more questionable.

"He is more difficult to understand. Sometimes he becomes utterly incensed, reeling, all pale and trembling, and breathlessly, with a tremor in his voice, says that *she* is throwing a tantrum. At times like this one can understand him. This is a rare occurrence though. He is far less easy to understand when he is patient, but cold, gentle with S.A., but contemptuous, loving, but under this love one senses only composure and the stubborn putting into practice of Tolstoy's ethics.

He goes out for walks in the morning just as precisely and accurately, does some work before breakfast, goes horse-riding after breakfast, has a rest before lunch and plays chess after lunch. He still loves Chertkov selflessly and still, I think, deep down, despises S.A. He once said to his daughter Masha: "when I hear her hurried step, approaching my study, my hands start to shake with anger." Over the years, I think that resentment has gradually been transformed into a calmer contempt." The problem was that S.A.'s state of mind was clear for all to see. Tolstoy himself was more reticent about how he felt about his wife. One can guess at his opinion on the basis of his diaries, especially the secret ones, which he vainly imagined that his wife would not read.

An unusually complex picture emerges from these diaries. On the one hand, Tolstoy, even before S.A. underwent an examination by the greatest psychiatrist of the day, G.I. Rossolimo, understood that his wife was mentally ill. We find entries about this in his diary from long before the nightmare that occurred at Yasnaya in the summer and autumn of 1910˚. Therefore, when L.N. wrote at Otradnoye about "the fight" which he planned to wage with his wife with "kindness and love", this was not some kind of inner revelation for him. This was the position adopted by Tolstoy, who denied that it was possible for people to be cured through psychiatric treatment and who believed that the illness could only be fought off with "kindness and love".

In this regard, his reaction to Professor Rossolimo's visit to Yasnaya Polyana is striking. Rossolimo was shocked by S.A.'s condition. He said that he had no idea how Tolstoy could live with this woman. His diagnosis was grim: "A degenerative dual constitution: paranoid and hysterical, with the former predominating." It would seem, then, that Rossolimo's diagnosis ought to have been a gift for L.N., if, as Suhotin writes, he was "contemptuous" of his wife. After all, it gave him a moral right to *demand* that S.A. be kept isolated from the older children.

How does Tolstoy relate to the diagnosis?

"Rossolimo is amazingly stupid for a scientist, hopeless," he writes in his diary on July 20. "Rossolimo's letter about Sofia Andreyevna's condition is remarkably stupid," he writes in the secret "Diary for myself alone".

The entire secret diary is dedicated to Sonia. "I can love her utterly sincerely, which I cannot do in relation to Lev (their son. – P.B.)." "The unfortunate creature, how can I not feel sorry for her." "It turns out that she found my little diary and took it away. She knows about some sort of will, leaving something to someone – obviously concerning my writings. What torture this is because of their monetary value – and she's afraid that I'll interfere in the publishing of them. She's afraid of everything, the poor thing." I kept seeing my difficult struggle with her all through the night. I

---

* For example, two diary entries from 1884: "The poor thing, she hates me so much. Lord, help me. If You want to give me a cross, let it be a cross, so that it might weigh me down and crush me. But this tugging at my soul is horrible, not only oppressive, painful, but difficult. Help me!"; "In the morning, a conversation and unexpected malice. Then she came to see me and nagged me until she drove me mad. I didn't say anything, didn't do anything, but it was difficult for me. She ran off in hysterics. I ran after her."

would wake up, fall asleep and the same thing would happen again" (this entry was made on October 27, the day before his departure).

There are some other admissions in this secret diary as well, though. "Sofia Andreyevna is calm, but just as foreign to me as before". "Today, since morning, a heavy feeling, an unkind feeling toward her, toward Sofia Andreyevna. And I ought to be forgiving and pitying her, but for the time being I cannot do so." "Nothing hostile on her side, but this pretending on both sides is painful for me". And finally: "Today I thought, as I recalled our marriage, that it was something fatal. I was never even in love. But I couldn't not get married." The last entry seemingly provides evidence to support Suhotin's opinion. Even Suhotin, though, writes in his diary: "…in him there still lives, I think, toward S.A., if not love, then something old, some sort of mixture of pity, anxiety and habit. Habit more than anything. I questioned him the other day and he said to me: "Yes, as strange as it may be to me myself, I worry about her when she's not around, and miss her."

This is confirmed by some diary entries made by Tolstoy on August 29 and 30 and September 12, the days on which his wife is away from Kochety. "Sofia Andreyevna left in tears… I am very, very tired. I read in the evening. I'm worried about her" (September 12). "She said goodbye very touchingly, asking everyone for forgiveness. I am very, very sorry for her, in a loving way… I am going to bed. I wrote her a little letter" (August 29). "It's sad without her. I am afraid for her. There is no comforting her" (August 30).

We can judge his true feelings about his wife in the last months of their life together only on the basis of Tolstoy's diaries, and certainly not on the basis of the testimony of third parties. Love and habit played a part, and there was also pity for her, horror at her behavior, the constant desire to leave, and the awareness that to depart would be a cruel act in relation to his sick wife.

Yet the presence of a "third party" in this story was precisely the thing that forced it to develop in the way it did.

This is pointed out with remarkable accuracy in letters written by T.L. Suhotina-Tolstaya in Rome to her brother Sergei in Russia in the early '30s, when Tatiana Lvovna was reading their mother's diaries, which had been published by Sergei Lvovich. Here are some excerpts from these letters.

"But he loved her tenderly and deeply. And it was only because of that that he didn't leave earlier. She annoyed him so maniacally. And it's no wonder. One needed a huge supply of patience to endure her harassment, her desire to portray herself, on the one hand, as an unfortunate victim, who had given her whole life to an evil, nasty husband, and on the other – as a youthful cutie, with high aspirations. But father saw her positive sides, which he found touching: her efforts to overcome her bad side, her efforts to be better. And to him, she was infinitely pitiful. If he hadn't loved her, he would have left the house long ago." "Of course – we both deserve the same reproach: that we didn't intervene actively enough in Sasha and Chertkov's machinations. We ought to have intervened in our parents' lives, only to allow them to come to an agreement between themselves without any intermediaries or people who wanted to keep father away from mother." "... You blame Sasha more than anyone for the events of 1910. This, in my opinion, is wrong. Take yourself back to how she was feeling at the time. She lived alone at Yasnaya and felt the drama that played out there deeply, yet on the other hand, she was very, very flattered that father had appointed her as his heir; she didn't realize that she was only a figurehead. When all's said and done, one mustn't blame anyone, not even Chertkov. What does Chertkov amount to? If he hadn't been a "friend, a publisher, who continued the work of Lev Tolstoy," he would have been nothing at all. And without a will in his favor, he would have lost the most important thing in his life, the only thing he had done in his life, and his ambition and vanity would have been dealt a severe blow. This was why he busied himself with papa and made such a big deal out of it."

Chertkov and the sons

There are various views one can take on the complex personality of Chertkov.

Here, though, is a fact which is incomprehensible from any normal, humane perspective. Knowing what sort of reaction it would provoke in S.A., he comes to the house every day (and sometimes twice a day) from the end of June 1910 onwards, conducting secret negotiations with her husband in plain sight and preparing the final text of the legal testament which is designed to go against her.

At the same time, Chertkov's active supporters and S.A.'s enemies, beginning, alas, with her daughter Sasha and ending with Feokritova, who transcribed her memoirs, either reside in the house or are there almost every day. Makovitsky and Goldenweiser are firmly against S.A. and in favor of V.G. The local peasants don't like her, for she hired a Circassian to take the fight to them. She cannot understand her husband's attitude toward her, and suffers badly from her abnormal jealousy in relation to Chertkov, which, as she herself admitted, was far stronger than the jealousy she felt over other women.

S.A.'s loneliness at the end of Tolstoy's life was as complete as L.N.'s loneliness at the beginning of his spiritual upheaval. In both cases, there was talk of "madness". Just as Tolstoy was suspected of having "gone mad", so his wife was perceived as either being mad or feigning madness.

The latter circumstance is very important. Surprisingly, in spite of the diagnosis made by Rossolimo, almost all of S.A.'s opponents, including her own daughter, were sure that she was not sick, but was merely feigning illness. This opinion is expressed most crudely in the diary kept by the stenographer, Feokritova.

Feokritova writes that S.A.'s "imaginary" madness started when she began to suspect that L.N. and Chertkov were drawing up a will against her in Meshcherskoye. At that time, she was hastily preparing a new edition of her husband's works and believed that after his death it would sell well. If L.N. were to bequeath everything to Chertkov, however, she would be livid. This was why she had such an acute interest in her husband's diaries from 1900 onwards, which were stored at Chertkov's house (she had stored away the diaries from before 1900 at the Historical Museum). Might these diaries not contain a "will", like the one in his diary for 1895 which she had hidden away at the museum? Feokritova claims that when Sasha, at Tolstoy's request, brought the diaries from Chertkov's house to Yasnaya Polyana, S.A. began to look through them, muttering, "Is there a will in here, I wonder?" According to Feokritova, she had a main goal that she wanted to achieve, either through endearment, threats, hysterics or blackmail: the destruction of the will, if there was one. When she stole her husband's secret diary and found out from it that such a will existed, the situation became unbearable. Feokritova also believed that the instigators of these actions by S.A. were her sons Lev and Andrei.

There is a reason why Feokritova's diary has not yet been published, although Tolstoy's biographer N.N. Gusev prepared it for publication in the '30s. This really is the most merciless document about Tolstoy's wife, written, what's more, by a person whom she herself had taken into her home. The trouble is that Feokritova's opinion was shared, in some shape or form, by almost all of the active participants in this story, and most importantly – L.N., who was as stubborn as Taras Bulba, but at the same time extraordinarily susceptible to being influenced by his loved ones, like King Lear, felt inclined to this point of view.

There was nothing surprising about the fact that S.A. had summoned her sons Lev and Andrei to Yasnaya. They were the only ones who defended their mother. By their presence, however, they in many ways strengthened their father's conviction that depriving the family of all rights to his literary legacy was the right thing to do.

"Lyova arrived," Tolstoy writes in his diary on July 4. "A small numerator and the denominator ∞". Tolstoy loved to define people in the form of fractions, whereby the numerator represented their spiritual qualities, and the denominator – their opinion of themselves. The relationship between the father and his sons was so strained that L.N. literally suffered as a result of their presence at Yasnaya Polyana. No matter how hard he tried to convince himself to treat them with kindness, he never succeeded.

"Our sons, Andrei and Lev, are very difficult, although they are diverse, each in their own way," writes Tolstoy. "Andrei is simply one of those about whom it is hard to believe that the soul of God is in them (but it is there, remember that)". "I can't stand Lev Lvovich. And he wants to move in here." A few days before L.N. signed a third, revised and expanded version of the formal will at Chertkov's house in Telyatinki, a very unpleasant, scandalous scene was played out between Tolstoy and his son Lev, during which the son, prompted by concern for his mother, insulted his father.

"Barely alive," L.N. writes in his diary on July 11. "A terrible night. Up until 4. And the most awful thing of all was Lev Lvovich. He told me off as if I were a little boy..."

During the night of 10 to 11 July, S.A. demanded that her husband give her the diaries which were being stored at Chertkov's house. And the request was denied. S.A. went out onto the balcony adjoining her husband's room, lay down on the floorboards and began to moan loudly. In her diary she writes that at this time, she "recalled how on the same balcony, 48 years ago, whilst still a young girl, I had felt love for Lev Nikolayevich for the first time. It was a cold night, and it was pleasing to me to think that in the same place where I had found his love, I would also find death." Tolstoy went out onto the balcony and asked her to leave. She promised to "kill Chertkov", ran into the garden and lay down in nothing but her dress on the damp ground. Several people went looking for her in the darkness, and found her with the help of the poodle Marquis. In response to all the requests that she return home, however, she replied that she would only go if L.N. came out to her.

And then Lev Lvovich went to see his father.

"'She doesn't want to come in,' I said, 'she says you threw her out.'

'Oh my God!' father shouted, 'no! No! This is intolerable!'

'Go to her,' I said to him, 'she won't come in unless you do.'

'No, no' he repeated, beside himself with desperation, 'I shan't go.'

'You're her husband, after all,' I said to him then, loudly and angrily, 'so you're the one who ought to work all this out.'

He looked at me in surprise and went shyly and silently into the garden."

This scene is unpleasant enough even in Lev Lvovich's memoirs. It looks even worse, however, in Goldenweiser's diary. "Sofia Andreyevna demanded that L.N. come for her. Lev Lvovich went in to see his father, yelled at him and told him off, and went so far as to call him a "rotter".

And on July 17 we read in Goldenweiser's diary that Tolstoy has rewritten his will in Telyatinki, listing his daughter Tatiana among the heirs, in addition to Sasha.

"Chertkov led L.N. upstairs (in the house at Telyatinki. – P.B.). L.N., when he greeted me, shook my hand firmly, twice. He sat down at the table and asked me to dictate from Muravyov's text, which was identical to the old one, but contained an addendum to the effect that if Alexandra Lvovna were to die before L.N., everything would go to Tatiana Lvovna.

L.N. was visibly uneasy, but he wrote quickly and didn't make any mistakes. When he had finished writing, he said to me:

"Well then, how wonderful!" Everything was far from wonderful, though.

In the preface to the edition of facsimile texts of Tolstoy's wills in the 'Tolstoy catalogue for 1913', Chertkov writes that this version of the text proved inadequate too, because "this time a formal error had slipped into the will, in the form of a few words being left out." What were the words in question? From the phrase "composed, written and signed by the testator, Lev Nikolayevich Tolstoy, of sound mind and firm memory," in the new version, the words *of sound mind and firm memory* had mysteriously disappeared.

Instead it read simply: "composed, written and signed by Count Lev Nikolayevich Tolstoy". The will therefore had to be redone yet again, with the phrase "of sound mind and firm memory" re-inserted.

This took another five days.

Conspirators

One might think that Tolstoy, as a superstitious person, ought to have taken note of the fact that the words "of sound mind and firm memory" had "accidentally" been omitted from the will. Yet on July 22, in a forest near the village of Grumont (alternative spellings: Grumant or Grumond*), he writes out and signs a document which, this time, is the final text of his legal testament.

The word "Grumant" is derived from the name of Greenland, which was first discovered by Europeans in the XI century. The discoverers of Greenland - the Danes - extended a long way to the East and included the islands which were later given the name of Spitsbergen (Svalbard, Grumant). The Russian Pomors therefore called the archipelago Grumant, Grunland ground. Tolstoy's grandfather on his maternal side, the owner of Yasnaya Polyana, Nikolai Sergeyevich Volkonsky, served at one time as governor-general in the Arkhangelsk region. Returning home, he decided that in commemoration of the harsh northern areas, he would rename one of the villages that belonged to him. So it was that the village of Grumant (with the stress on the first syllable) came into being, threet kilometers from Yasnaya Polyana.

The story of how this text was composed is described in detail in the memoirs of Chertkov's secretary, Sergeyenko.

"Lev Nikolayevich sat down on a stump and took out the English fountain pen attached to his shirt, and asked us to give him everything he needed to do the writing. I gave him the paper and some cardboard I had brought along for him to lean on, and Alexander Borisovich (Goldenweiser – P.B.) held the draft of the will in front of him. Having crossed his legs, and having put the cardboard and the paper on his knee, Lev Nikolayevich began to write: "The year nineteen ten, this tweny-second day of July". He immediately noticed the slip he had made, in writing 'twenty' with the letter 't' missing, and wanted to correct it or take a clean sheet of paper, but changed his mind, observing, with a smile:

'Well, let them think that I was illiterate.'

Then he added:

'I'll put it in digits too, so that there won't be any doubts.'

And after the word "July" he put in the numbers "22" in brackets.

He found it difficult, sitting on the tree stump, to follow the rough draft, and he asked Alexander Borisovich to read it out to him. Alexander Borisovich began reading the draft aloud in a clear voice and Lev Nikolayevich diligently got the words down, leaving spaces at the end and the beginning of the lines, as, it seems, they used to do in the old days, and as Tolstoy himself sometimes did in his letters, when he was trying to write particularly clearly and legibly.

At first he kept the lines compressed, but when he saw that there was still a lot of space left, he said:

'I'm going to need to make it more spaced out, if it's to go over onto the other page,' and he increased the distance between the lines.

When, at the end of the will, he was required to sign it, he asked:

'Should I write 'Count'?'

We told him that he didn't have to write it, and he chose not to.

Then we signed it too – the witnesses. Lev Nikolayevich said to us: "Well, thank you."

At the same time, Tolstoy was given a document from Chertkov, which was an extremely important addendum to the will. According to this note, all the rights to Tolstoy's compositions and manuscripts would go to Alexandra only formally. The real beneficiary was to be Chertkov.

Amazingly, on the day on which Tolstoy wrote the secret will that went against his wife, Chertkov, without wavering for a moment, turned up in the evening to visit L.N. and S.A. What a rock-solid conscience he must have had, to be able to look the lady of the house in the eye! And what his attitude toward her must have been...

Valentin Bulgakov wrote: "When I think back to that evening, I am amazed by Sofia Andreyevna's intuition: she seemed to sense that something terrible, something irreparable had just happened." She "was in the most awful mood, nervous and restless. Toward the guest, and indeed to all those present, she behaved rudely and provocatively. One can well imagine how this affected everyone. Everyone sat there feeling tense and depressed. Chertkov was as stiff as a rod: he had straightened his back, his face had turned to stone. The samovar boiled cozily on the table, a dish of raspberries stood out like a bright red stain on the white tablecloth, but those sitting around the table barely touched their cups of tea, as if denying themselves the pleasure in order to feel less guilty. And, without lingering any longer than they needed to, everyone soon left the table." This is the atmosphere, then, in which Tolstoy's will was drawn up. On one side, a mentally ill wife, in whose head things which seemed mutually exclusive had got mixed together: passion love for her husband and jealousy over him, the fear of losing him and... monetary considerations (on behalf of her children). On the other side – the impenetrable Chertkov, who had set himself the task of being the sole steward of Tolstoy's legacy, a task he saw as indispensable. Incidentally, Chertkov's mental health... also gives rise to doubt.

On one occasion, S.A. and Valentin Bulgakov ended up in the same carriage on the way to Telyatinki. The Countess was going there to meet Chertkov's mother, Elizaveta Ivanovna. Along the way she started begging Bulgakov to persuade Chertkov to return the diaries to her.

"Let them all be rewritten, copied out," she said, "and let them give me only Lev Nikolayevich's original manuscripts! After all, I'm looking after all his older diaries... Tell Chertkov that if he gives me the diaries, I shall calm down ... I shall then return the favor for him, he will be able to visit us as he did before, and we shall work together for Lev Nikolayevich and serve him... Will you tell him this? ... For God's sake, tell him!"

On arriving at Chertkov's house, Bulgakov passed on S.A.'s request to him. He then writes in his diary: "Vladimir Grigorievich is greatly agitated.

'Well then,' he asks, staring at me with his big, white eyes, darting around excitedly, 'so did you tell her just now where the diaries are?!'

As he says these words, Vladimir Grigorievich, to my complete surprise, makes a terrible grimace and sticks his tongue out at me."

"You're an idiot! Everyone knows that you're an idiot!" Lev Lvovich once shouted at V.G. in the presence of some other guests at Yasnaya Polyana.

There were just two months remaining until the departure...

"They're tearing me to pieces ..."

One of the main causes of S.A.'s emotional distress was her husband's diaries from 1900, some of which were kept by Chertkov, and some of which, on his instructions, were put in a fireproof deposit box at the "Credit Lyonnais" bank in Moscow in October 1909. After L.N.'s return from Meshcherskoye, S.A. demanded that her husband collect the diaries from Chertkov and give them to her. Tolstoy didn't agree to do so, supposing that if he were to do so, the diaries might be censored by his wife, who would destroy anything in them which, as she saw it, diminished her role alongside the great man.

On July 14, 1910, Sasha, at her father's request, collected the diaries, and his daughter Tatiana, in their mother's presence, deposited them at the Tula branch of the State Bank in Tolstoy's name.

This did not bring an end to the matter, however. The insistence with which S.A. asked her husband to give her the keys to the safe suggests that she really did suspect that there was a will in these diaries. According to Goldenweiser, the Countess was not the only one who was waiting tensely for Sasha to return home with the diaries: her son Lev was also there, standing guard in the tree-lined avenue in front of the entrance to the estate. When the diaries were put in the safe, S.A. had said to her daughter, Tatiana:

"You will all thank me for this."

The next day, she begged L.N. on her knees to give her the keys to the safe. Yet she was well aware that the texts of the diaries had been copied out by Chertkov. She therefore needed the originals. After having her request denied, she ran to her room and began shouting from inside it that she had drunk a bottle of opium. Tolstoy, who was walking past her window at the time, ran upstairs in horror, gasping for breath. S.A. admitted that she had lied to him. She herself writes in her diary that she acted *disgracefully*. But she hadn't been able to stop herself.

On July 25, having gathered her things and taken a vial of opium with her, the Countess set off for Tula in the carriage which was being sent to the station to collect her son Andrei. She had the vague intention of either leaving for good, or committing suicide. Before leaving, she wrote a note, which she intended to send to the newspapers: "An extraordinary event has occurred at peaceful Yasnaya Polyana. Countess Sofia Andreyevna Tolstaya has fled from her home, the home in which she lovingly took care of her husband for forty-eight years, giving him her entire life. The reason is that Lev Nik., having grown weak due to old age, has fallen completely under the adverse influence of Mr. C., and has lost any kind of will of his own, entrusting it to C., and is constantly conferring with him about something in secret. Having been ill for a month with a disease of the nerves, as a result of which two doctors were summoned from Moscow, the Countess could no longer stand C.'s presence and left her home with despair in her heart." At the station, Andrei, on seeing the abnormal condition his mother was in, forced her to return with him to the estate.

On July 27 Lev and Andrei interrogated Sasha: had their father drawn up a will? Finally, Andrei Lvovich went to his father and asked him straight out: had he drawn up any kind of written orders about what would happen in the event of his death? Tolstoy couldn't bring himself to lie. He couldn't tell the truth, either. If he were to do so, all the wrath of his wife and sons would fall on Sasha. He replied to his son that he did not wish to discuss the matter. Needless to say, this was seen as an indirect admission of the fact that a will existed.

From that moment on, Tolstoy was trapped. If he admitted that there was a will, he would be putting before the firing line not Chertkov (his name wasn't in the will), but the youngest member of the family – Sasha, whom they were not overly fond of already. If he did not admit that there was a will, he would have to keep lying constantly, which was unbearable.

In actual fact, Tolstoy's first attempt to flee from Yasnaya Polyana before he died occurred on August 15, when L.N. had set off to see Tatyana in Kochety for an indefinite period. This was the only place where he could take a break from his wife and also... from Chertkov, who was terribly irritated by the fact that S.A. had begged Tolstoy to promise that he would not meet up with the "home-wrecker", whom she hated.

One had to have a special sort of spiritual callousness to see any cunning will in S.A.'s actions. No, it was a dark, irrational will which was governing Tolstoy's wife, quite separate from her reason, which from time to time shone through and told her that she was acting incorrectly, doing exactly the opposite of what she ought to be doing. And Tolstoy waited patiently for these moments of enlightenment, pinning his hopes on them until the end, even after his departure.

In a letter from Shamordino written on October 31, he writes to her: "... my return *now* is completely impossible," highlighting the word "now", to stress that a return was still possible. In an unsent draft of the letter, he had written with even more clarity: "Try... to calm down, to organize your life without me, to get treated, and then, if your life really does change and I find it possible to live with you, I shall come back. To return now, though, would be tantamount to suicide, because in my present state, I could not endure such a life even for a week." Chertkov and the members of his "team", including Sasha, had a fundamentally different view of Tolstoy's wife's condition. Even Tatiana Lvovna, who was favorably disposed toward V.G., begged him in a letter to leave Telyatinki, so as not to serve as a "red rag" to her ailing mother. Instead of doing so, Chertkov started building a tenement house made of brick. Tolstoy himself took a dim view of the luxurious interior of this house, with its numerous bedrooms and a bathroom... The question one must ask is: why did V.G. need to build this house, given that Tolstoy was clearly close to death? There can be only one answer. He hoped that after L.N.'s death, some sort of 'Tolstoy Center' would be located there. Tolstoy's body would be at Yasnaya, "at the disposal" of the family. But his spirit (and the legacy of his manuscripts) would be transferred to Telyatinki. This, indeed, was almost how it happened. From the end of 1910 until the beginning of the First World War, there were two places of pilgrimage dedicated "to Tolstoy": Yasnaya and Telyatinki. The war and the revolution destroyed Chertkov's plans.

When the original diaries were taken out of Chertkov's hands, he saw it as a defeat in the war against the Countess and took appropriate action.

Valentin Bulgakov writes: "When I found out from Varvara Mikhailovna (Feokritova. – P.B.), at Telyatinki... the people closest to Chertkov hastily gathered together – his alter ego Alyosha Sergeyenko, O.K. Tolstaya (Anna Konstantinovna's sister), Alexandra Lvovna, the Goldenweisers, and also Vladimir Grigorievich himself, and everyone set to work hastily copying out the places in Tolstoy's diary which put Sofia Andreyevna in a bad light and which she, in their opinion, might destroy. The diaries were then packed away and sent to Yasnaya Polyana. Chertkov, standing on the porch of the Telyatinki house, made the sign of the cross over Alexandra Lvovna in the air with the folder of diaries, with mock solemnity, and then handed over the diaries to her. He found it hard to part with them..."

This mocking gesture on the part of Chertkov was a sort of blessing of Sasha in her war with her mother.

Before sending the diaries, Chertkov sent L.N. a letter in which she compared him to Christ. "Today I happened to think with particular vividness about the dying of Christ, about how he was vilified, insulted, how they mocked him, how they slowly killed him, how those closest to him in spirit and in the flesh could not go up to him and had to look on from afar..." And Tolstoy took this coarse flattery in the way it was intended. "A letter which touched me from Batya." Like all the 'Chertkovites', he called Chertkov "Batya" (Father).

When S.A. extracted from her husband the promise that he would not meet up with Chertkov, V.G. struck back in the form of yet another letter to Tolstoy. The aim was to "open L.N.'s eyes" to the motivation behind his wife and sons' behavior.

"The goal consisted and consists in, by distancing me, and if possible Sasha too, from you, to elicit from you, or find out from your diaries and papers, by relentless, combined pressure, whether or not you have written any kind of will which deprives your family of your literary legacy; if you have not written one, then to prevent you from doing so through relentless observation of you until your death, and if you have written one, then not to let you go anywhere until they have found time to invite the black-hundredist doctors, who would diagnose you as having fallen into senility in order to render your will invalid." This was a frank denunciation. Alas, though, it was not without an element of truth. Makovitsky wrote in his

Notes: "Sofia Andreyevna admitted her plans: if she were to have found out that Tolstoy had written a will, she would have gone to see the Tsar, declared herself to be destitute and begged for Lev Nikolayevich's will to be destroyed and for her rights to be restored. She is considering the idea, with the three younger sons, of declaring Lev Nikolayevich insane." Commenting on this note in 1933, Sergei Lvovich Tolstoy did not deny that such conversations had taken place at the house. "I was at Yasnaya at the time and I have to say that conversations about declaring that Lev Nikolayevich had senile dementia and memory loss (but not insanity) did indeed take place, but there were not, and could not have been, any serious intentions. After all, Sofia Andreyevna, Andrei Lvovich and Lev Lvovich knew that Tatiana Lvovna, Alexandra Lvovna and myself, and probably Ilya Lvovich as well, would never have allowed this. At that time, they, apparently, did not fully comprehend all the vileness and stupidity of such measures ..."

If S.A. had been acting cunningly, consciously and deliberately, though, she wouldn't have said the things she did in front of people, things that she repeated insistently, maniacally, causing antipathy towards her even among those who were sympathetic to her. Even Lev Lvovich couldn't stand it at times and shouted at his mother, trying to reason with her. She would say that L.N. was in love with Chertkov, that a living and breathing husband no longer existed as far as she was concerned, that she had been waiting for his death for a long time and that they would not be able to stop her from killing him. She wasn't allowing L.N. to get any sleep, wasn't allowing anyone to be left alone with him and was continually blackmailing him with threats of suicide. Is it really possible to conclude from all this that she had some sort of deliberate plan?

L.N. tried with great patience to explain all this to V.G. in his letters.

"Sofia Andreyevna is very calm, kind, and I'm afraid of everything that might disturb this condition, and therefore I'm not doing anything prematurely for the resumption of our meetings" (July 31).

"...She is completely beside herself, and one cannot feel anything for her except pity, and it's impossible, for me at least, it is quite *impossible* to contrecarrer her, and by so doing obviously increase her suffering" (August 14).

"...I am bound by simple pity, compassion, which I experienced particularly strongly today..." (the same day).

"What do you think, what is it like for her when she is alone at night, nights which she spends sleepless for more than half of them, with a vague but painful awareness that she is not loved and is a difficult burden for everyone except the children, one cannot but feel sorry for her..." (August 25).

"She is suffering and cannot overcome herself" (September 9).

Tolstoy was trying to speak to Chertkov in humane terms. His sentimental letters were incapable of changing Chertkov's mind, though; on the contrary, they raised the concern in him that his teacher might falter, and redo his will. These fears were not unfounded.

On July 30, P.I. Biryukov arrived at Yasnaya with his family. As a trustee, he was told about the will, and "Posha" expressed disapproval. He told L.N. that it wasn't right to keep such a document secret from his loved ones wasn't right. Apparently, Biryukov was influenced by a conversation he had with S.A., who was complaining about her position in the house. As a person capable of looking at things from the side, Biryukov was stunned by what was happening at Yasnaya Polyana, and said as much to Tolstoy. And Tolstoy himself saw that he had done something wrong.

"I understood my mistake very, very well," he writes in his diary. "I should have gathered together all the heirs and declared my intention, rather than doing it in secret. I wrote this to Chertkov." This letter was like a knife through the heart for Chertkov.

"Yesterday I spoke to Posha, and he was quite right when he told me that I was wrong to have made the will in secret. It either should have been done openly, declaring it to all those whom it concerned, or else everything should have been left as it was – *do nothing*. And he is absolutely right, I committed a mean act and now I am paying for it. What is bad is that I did it in secret, assuming ill intent on the part of my heirs, and above all, I undoubtedly did something bad in that I used the services of an agency that is part of a government which I refuse to recognize, when I drew up the will in that form. Now I see clearly that in everything that is taking place now, I have only myself to blame. I should have left everything as it was, and done nothing..."

How about that! And he wrote this to a man who for six years (!), since 1904, had led the extremely complicated conspiratorial work involved in drawing up Tolstoy's will! What did the words "done nothing" entail for

Chertkov? I'll tell you exactly what they entailed: that L.N.'s entire legacy would have gone to his wife and children.

Chertkov's response was a long letter to Tolstoy, written on August 11. It took him almost ten days to get over his shock and draw up this "memo", as he called it. In his letter, Chertkov explained to Tolstoy how the will had been prepared and what Tolstoy had been guided by when he signed it. In essence, he was telling him the story of one of the most important episodes of his life as if Tolstoy had forgotten about it. And L.N. reversed his decision once again.

"I'm writing on these leaves of paper, because I'm writing in the woods while out on a walk. Both yesterday evening and this morning, I have been thinking about the letter you sent yesterday. There were two main feelings that your letter aroused in me: aversion at those manifestations of gross selfishness and insensitivity, which I either did not see, or saw and forgot; and grief and remorse at the fact that I hurt you with my letter, in which I expressed regret about what I had done. The conclusion I have drawn from the letter is that Pavel Ivanovich was wrong and that I was also wrong to have agreed with him, and that I fully approve of your activity, but am nonetheless dissatisfied with my own activity: I sense that I could have behaved in a better way, although I don't know how." One cannot help but get the impression that Tolstoy was behaving like a weather vane, yielding to the first gust of wind that happened to pass by. In actual fact, though, his position was far more complex and reflected his general worldview. Tolstoy *didn't want to have to deal with* this accursed legal problem and believed that it ought to have been left to resolve itself of its own accord, in a "loving" way, through the as yet untapped mental resources of both the warring parties. He tried to influence these warring sides "with kindness, with love". This was his struggle, and even, perhaps, his *war* of "not resisting evil with force". And he did the same thing in 1904, when he answered Chertkov's "questionnaire" and asked that this document be destroyed *with kindness*. And now, by agreeing with Biryukov and informing Chertkov about this, he was appealing to his sense of morality, calling on him to cooperate with S.A. On receiving a negative response, he once again gave in, continuing nonetheless his quiet, unseen war.

If Chertkov had understood Tolstoy's position, he would have noticed the key passage in one of his letters. "As for the idea that robustly defending the decisions I took, which went against her (his wife's. – P.B.) wishes, might have been helpful to her, I do not believe it, and even if I did believe it, I could never have done that anyway. Above all, besides the fact that I think that I have to act that way, is that I know from experience that when I insist on something, I feel tormented, and when I concede on something, I not only have an easy feeling, but would even say I feel joyful." If Chertkov had been able to apply these words to himself, he would have realized that Tolstoy was talking to him, too, as he would to ... a madman, with whom one mustn't argue.

Wasn't Chertkov's letter of reply mad, the one in which he feverishly tried to prove that keeping the will a secret was "essential in the interests of Sofia Andreyevna herself?" "If she had found out for certain about your instructions during your life-time, she simply would not have been able to endure it, having, for so many years on end, devised, nurtured and applied her plan with such thoughtfulness, prudence and caution, to seize all of your writings after your death, that her disappointment in this respect during your life-time would have been too unbearable a blow for her, and she wouldn't have spared anyone or anything, not only would she not have spared you, your health and your life, but she wouldn't have spared herself, her own life and, worst of all, her own soul – the last remnants of conscience, in a desperate attempt to win out, to achieve her objective, whilst you are still alive..."

What difference was there, fundamentally, between the "healthy" V.G. and the mentally ill S.A., when he was effectively blackmailing Tolstoy with the threat of his wife's suicide, as he sought to ensure that a will that went against her interests was kept secret?

S.A. did the wrong thing when she refused to let her husband go to Kochety alone, forcing him to take her with him, and continuing to torment him at their daughter's estate as well. Yet was it not an act of madness, albeit a cunning and calculating one, to send Goldenweiser's letter to Kochety, containing the excerpt from Feokritova's diary which denounced the Countess's behavior at Yasnaya Polyana during her brief trip back there? M.S. Suhotin wrote of this denunciation in his diary:

"A certain V.M. Feokritova is living here at Yasnaya, S.A.'s stenographer, a confidante for Sasha and an informer, should one be needed. This V.M. keeps, like many others, a diary. The three days which S.A. recently spent at

Yasnaya were included in this diary. And this part of the diary was copied out by A.B. Goldenweiser and sent by him, together with A.K. Chertkova and V.M. Feokritova, to Lev Nikolayevich. Its contents, in brief, is as follows. S.A. is cheerful and quite healthy, she is eating and sleeping very well (we didn't see this at all at Kochety), and for no apparent reason she sort of poured out her soul to V.M., shared with her the hatred and disgust she felt for her old husband, in a word, this S.A. wasn't the usual bareheaded and talkative S.A, but some vile and spiteful Lady Macbeth.

On reading this disgusting, deceitful and boorish accusation, apparently written with the aim of frightening L.N. and forcing him to give Chertkov some kind of legally admissible permission to publish L.N.'s works, I started to feel sick, and for a long time I couldn't get off to sleep." What struck Sukhotin even more than that, however, was the fact that Tolstoy took an enormous amount of interest in this letter. This interest is recorded in Tolstoy's diary too: "A letter from Goldenweiser with an excerpt written by V.M. which horrified me." What was it exactly that horrified him, though? The content of the excerpt? The fact that it had been sent at all?

L.N.'s mood can be judged on the basis of a letter to Chertkov, written before his return from Kochety to Yasnaya Polyana. "There's one thing I'll say, and that's that lately, 'not with my brain, but with my sides', as the peasants say, things have reached the point that I have clearly understood where the boundary lies between the defiance of doing evil in response to evil, and the defiance of refusing to give in, in those activities which you recognize as your duty before your conscience and before God. I shall try my best." He writes that "I have pondered my course of action upon my return, which I am neither willing nor able to put off any longer…"

Tolstoy was returning to Yasnaya Polyana after a one-and-a-half month stay at Kochety, clearly with some kind of new plan of action. As for what it was, we can only speculate.

One thing is certain – this plan was defeated. First of all, his wife stole his secret diary, which the old man had hidden in his boot. From it, she finally found out that a will existed. Then Chertkov, who had not forgiven S.A. for the offence she had caused him by pushing him away from the physical location of his Teacher, sent him a horrible letter "with reproaches and accusations". Tolstoy exclaimed in his diary: "They're tearing me to pieces. Sometimes the thought occurs to me: to get away from them all." The next day he sent V.G. a curt reply, in which, for the first time (!) in the entire history of their correspondence, he asked him *not to interfere* in his relationship with his wife. "I alone must resolve this matter in my soul, before God, and I'm trying to do so, any kind of involvement by outsiders makes this task more difficult. I was hurt by your letter, I got the feeling I was being torn in two directions…"

He felt this feeling too late in the day. The situation had reached its final impasse. He was being bombarded on both sides by the "reproaches and accusations" of S.A. and V.G. And each of them was demanding their "exclusive rights" not only to his legacy, but also to his soul. At this time he begins his latest artistic work – the story *There Are No Guilty People*. The third draft of this unfinished work began with the words: "How strange, how remarkable my destiny is." After her mother had effectively driven Sasha out of the house, Tolstoy suffered something that was not a fainting spell, this time, but a deadly attack with terrible cramps, during which his body was thrown across the bed in convulsions and several men couldn't hold him down. After this, the mother and daughter put their differences aside. S.A. allowed Chertkov to visit Yasnaya Polyana. Then it all started again…

On the night of October 27-28, he ran away from home.

Chapter 10

Ice-cold Rain

In Astapovo, what little strength Tolstoy had left abandoned him. His eyesight, however, remained impeccable. L.N.'s route from the station building to Ozolin's house reminds one of the motion of a sick bird which is no longer able to fly, and cannot even move along the ground on its own, yet still sees everything very distinctly, because it is accustomed to having a bird's eye view of it all.

Ozolin's little house stood on a slope which had a staircase leading down it. It was already dark. "When we came out of the station building," Ozolin recalled, "and headed to the apartment, the station employee who was holding Lev Nikolayevich by the hand warned him that they were about to go down some stairs. He replied, "It's fine, it's fine, I see it." The same warning was made, and the exact same response was received, as they set foot on the stairs inside the apartment; one of the men, as he stepped into the hallway, asked for a lamp, so that the hallway could be lit up, but Lev Nikolayevich said, "No, I can see well enough, I can see everything." It is a very fortunate thing that, over the next seven days, Tolstoy couldn't see everything that was happening in Astapovo. An autumnal storm, giving a foretaste of winter, erupted on the night of November 6-7. " The weather seemed to share the people's depressed mood," the journalist V.A. Gottwald wrote of that night. "The ground froze slightly, and from above there quietly fell, by turns, small drops of rain and something that was slimy and disgustingly cold ... I cannot imagine anything worse than that night. It was dark. On the railway tracks, the red signal lights seemed to be flashing through the fog with particular malevolence. In the little garden in front of the historic house, there stood several birches. Their branches were covered with an icy crust. At the slightest gust of wind the branches would be blown against each other, their icy casings would chime and crackle, and it created a din which was reminiscent of some sort of distant, inexpressibly sad music. It was as if somewhere far away, a host of unknown beings were sobbing..."

"You are putting a difficult position before the headquarters ..."

Konstantin Orlov, the reporter from *Russian Word*, wasn't the only person who followed Tolstoy and his fellow travelers along the road from Kozelsk to Astapovo. An extremely complicated police apparatus had also joined in with the efforts to keep track of the fugitives.

Tolstoy and his companions were still on the road when a telegram was sent from Belevo to the Kurkino station: "On the arrival of train number 12, immediately establish whether or not the writer Lev Tolstoy took this train; if he did, where did he get off the train. Telegraph me. Vakh. Pushkov". The telegram was sent at 3:20 pm on October 31. The reply came through two and a half hours later from Dankov, the last major station before Astapovo: "He took train #12 on a 2nd class ticket, Rostov-Don. Non-comm. officer Dykin." Two hours later, a telegram went out from Astapova to Yelets, to Captain M. N. Savitsky, head of the Yelets Gendarmerie police department of the Railroad Administration: "The writer Count Tolstoy in transit in train 12 fell ill. The station-master Ozolin took him to his apartment. Non-comm. officer Filippov." At 10:00 am on November 1, Major General Lvov, the director of the Moscow-Kamyshinsky Gendarmerie police department of the Railroad Administration, no less, sent a telegraph to Savitsky in Yelets: "A dispatch is expected regarding number 649." Savitsky's reply was very late in coming, arriving at 7 pm: "Lev Tolstoy, accompanied by Dr. Makovitsky and two relatives, became ill on the road and is staying in the apartment of the station-master at Astapovo."

It is very difficult for the modern person to make any sense of this hierarchical, tangled maze of police reports from that time. One thing is clear, though. There could no longer be any talk of any secret onward journey to Novocherkassk, and still less – of crossing the border with false passports.

Captain Mikhail Nikolayevich Savitsky comes across as a very interesting character. In this entire story, he proved to be the most "extreme" of all the police officers who were charged not only with the duty of monitoring Tolstoy and reporting back on him to Moscow, but also with the responsibility of maintaining public order at the Astapovo station.

Being as he was in Yelets, in the Orlov Province, though, Savitsky was not controlling the situation for the first three days, and this left his bosses in Moscow displeased. Whilst the newspapers were already vying with one another to publish reports from their special correspondents in Astapovo, the captain maintained a strange silence, perhaps still not aware that he was the one who had been appointed "extreme". Astapovo was swarming with journalists from the capital and from the provincial newspapers; there was nowhere to accommodate them, so Ozolin was forced to ask his superiors to set aside a separate railway carriage for them to sleep in. Savitsky, meanwhile, was still in Yelets and on 3 November sent a telegram to General Lvov, telling him something that all of Russia had already read in the newspapers:

"After the second bell rang for train number 12, Tolstoy's daughter, in view of the doctor's statement about his extremely dangerous condition, asked the station-master to give him a room. The same was provided by the station-master, in his own apartment, there being no other room to be had." On the same day, General Lvov, in an encrypted (!) telegram, ordered him to travel personally to Astapovo with five gendarmes and take control of the situation. Lvov's telegram was sent at 3pm. Savitsky dallied for some reason, though, and remained in Yelets. In the evening of that same day he received an alarming report from Filippov, the non-commissioned officer in Astapovo: "Reporters have arrived from *Morning*, *Russian Word*, *Vedomosti*, *Speech*, *The Voice of Moscow*, *New Times* and *Petersburg Telegraph Agency*. The Governor of Ryazan will arrive in Astapovo tomorrow on train number 11." The captain tried to control the situation from Yelets: "Astapovo. Non-commissioned Officer Filippov. None of those arriving at the station are to be accommodated there. I'll be there tomorrow night. No-one is to stay in the station buildings, other than the station-master's apartment. Only the four earlier arrivals are to stay in Ozolin's apartment. Captain Savitsky." Not to provide accommodation for the correspondents who had arrived and those who were still arriving, though, was out of the question. D.A. Matreninsky, the managing director of the Ryazan-Ural Railway, who was responsible for Astapovo, was in Saratov, and was forced to send a cable to Ozolin: "I'm allowing you to grant permission for a temporary stay of one or two days for the correspondents from newspapers in St. Petersburg and Moscow and other newspapers in a second-class reserve car, with the proviso that the car may be needed to help with the start of the transportation of troops."At the same time, he cabled Klyasovsky, head of the Ryazan-Ural Railway Division at the Astapovo Station, asking him to prepare a separate building as a temporary hotel, to install heating and furnish it with beds and bed-linen. He did not give the journalists permission to move in there until further notice, however.

Having received the order from Savitsky not to let them in, non-commissioned officer Filippov prohibited the journalists from settling into the house or the railway carriage, reporting back on this to the captain in two telegrams sent on the night of November 4 and in the morning. The alarmed Matreninsky, realizing that the situation at the station in his charge was becoming critical, appealed to Savitsky by telegram on November 4: "In view of the exceptional circumstances, I humbly ask you not to prevent the relatives of Count Lev Nikolayevich Tolstoy arriving at the Astapovo station, and their entourage, from being accommodated at Astapovo in the public buildings and railway cars; it would be difficult, perhaps impossible even, to accommodate them in the village. Please send telegrams to the site and to me." "For the accommodation of individuals with passports in the shunting area, no obstacle is being encountered," the captain replied, "everything else will be decided tonight at the site." On the same day, Savitsky received a telegram from the General with an encrypted reprimand: "To date, I have not once received any information, as ought to have been done on a daily basis in detail via the post and, in emergencies, by telegram, about what is happening in Astapovo. You are putting a difficult situation before the headquarters." In the evening, Savitsky was at Astapovo and became one of the invaluable witnesses to the plotting which was taking place around the dying Tolstoy.

PAVEL BASINSKY

A shudder went through the Empire

For a period of seven days, from October 31 to November 7, 1910, the little-known station of Astapovo, on the Ryazan-Ural Railway, became a focal point for Russia, in all its vastness, and for the whole world.

The impression was created that in these seven days, it was not that a private individual – albeit a famous one – was dying at the station, but that the fate of an empire was being decided, and the entire world was watching this happen. The Astapovo site, or, to put it more accurately, the Astapovo vortex, attracted an incredibly large and diverse group of people, from all walks of life in the enormous Russian empire: railway workers and employees, peasants from nearby villages, priests, monks, doctors, journalists, police officers, telegraph operators, governor-generals, officials of all stripes, members of the Synod, Stolypin and Nicholas II.

And most remarkably of all – each and every one of them sensed their personal responsibility for Tolstoy's departure and death, experiencing it as a huge burden which had suddenly descended upon them, and, as is usually the way, tried to shift this burden onto someone else's shoulders, someone one step up or down from them. The private act of one solitary man, dictated, generally speaking, by family reasons alone, served as a test of strength for the whole empire.

On November 3rd, a reporter from *Morning of Russia*, S.S. Rayetsky, sent word to the newspaper: "The telegraph is working non-stop. Queries are coming in from the Ministry of Transportation and from the Governors of Kaluga, Ryazan, Tambov and Tula. An official sent by the Tula governor arrived and conducted an investigation. The Tolstoy family is being inundated with telegrams from all over Russia and the world." The Governor-General of Ryazan, Prince A.N. Obolensky, who arrived on the morning of November 4, tried to eject the reporters from the station. Due to end, the station canteen was closed, i.e. they clearly hoped to drive them out through hunger. The journalists were forced to appeal to Major General Lvov with a collective telegram. After that, the journalists were left alone and the focus switched to how to accommodate them. "There is a temporary requirement at the Astapovo station for a large number of beds with mattresses and all other accoutrements..." "I request that you urgently send to Astapovo ten or fifteen table lamps, strong ones, carefully packed to prevent damage on the road," wrote Volynsky, the director of business services of the Ryazan-Ural Railway, in a telegram sent from Saratov to the station-masters of the stations closest to Astapovo. Initially, the Governor of Ryazan wanted to "clear away" Tolstoy himself from the station. On November 2, General Lvov asked Savitsky, in an encoded message: "Tell me by telegram who allowed Lev Tolstoy to stay at Astapovo in a station building not intended to house the sick. The governor deems it essential that steps be taken to dispatch him to a medical establishment or permanent residence."

The position in which the Ryazan Governor found himself, now that Lev Tolstoy had for some reason taken it into his head to die in the province for which he was responsible, certainly wasn't an enviable one. Overseeing the demise of world-famous writers at random train stations was not something he had a massive amount of experience in. To get a sense of what sort of state Prince Obolensky was in, one need only read a coded telegram he sent to St. Petersburg, to Stolypin's deputy at the Ministry of the Interior, Lieutenant-General P.G. Kurlov: "Please advise, after consulting with the bishop, whether the local priest can perform a prayer service for Tolstoy's health. Yesterday he was asked to do so; he is not inclined to agree. Advise him not to allow it." And there we have it – a shudder had been sent through the empire! The matter of the prayer by the station's priest for L.N. was being decided at the level of the governor, the deputy interior minister and the bishop of the capital.

Just as had been the case in 1902, when L.N. had got sick in the Crimea, the Synod found itself in an extremely difficult position. The tsar's displeasure at Tolstoy's "excommunication", in view of the possibility that he might die, was so transparent that Stolypin kept his officer for special assignments on standby outside the room in which an emergency meeting of the Synod was being held, to discuss the departure and likely death of Tolstoy, to await a positive solution to the problem from them.

A telegram from Metropolitan Anthony arrived in Astapovo on November 4, in which he begged the Count to return to the Orthodox Church. At the same time, though, according to a telegram sent by Prince Obolensky to Kurlov, the self-same Metropolitan banned the local priest from performing a prayer service for Tolstoy's health.

Unfortunately, Nicholas's verbose response to the conflict between Tolstoy and the Synod is known to us from a not entirely reliable source – the book by Sergei Trufanov (formerly the hieromonk Iliodor) about Grigorii Rasputin, *Holy Devil*. The author cites something that Rasputin said, after he spoke to the tsar following L.N.'s death. "Papa (Nicholas II. – P.B.) said that if they (the bishops – P.B.) had loved L.N. Tolstoy, he wouldn't have died without repenting. But they treated him coldly. Throughout all that time, Parfeny was the only one who went to see him, for a heart-to-heart talk. How proud they are!"

The reference to the Bishop of Tula, Parfeny, in this context seems to stand up to scrutiny. It was Parfeny, specifically, who, having met L.N. in 1909 and made a most favorable impression on him, was summoned to St. Petersburg by the Synod and sent to Astapovo to bring Tolstoy back within the bosom of the church.

Parfeny's mission failed. It never had a chance of succeeding, incidentally, because Parfeny didn't arrive at the station until 9 am on November 7, nearly three hours after Tolstoy's death. As for the bishop, he left St. Petersburg on November 4. His lack of haste can apparently be put down to his reluctance to get involved in a hopeless affair. Besides the fact that he knew about Tolstoy's views all too well, he had been apprised of the situation at Astapovo as a whole by the newspapers. Parfeny knew that Chertkov and Tolstoy's daughter Alexandra were ever present beside the patient's bed, and that under no circumstances would they allow a meeting between L.N. and an Orthodox priest.

Before he left Astapovo, Parfeny spoke to Captain Savitsky and Tolstoy's son Andrei Lvovich, in an attempt to find out from them whether or not Tolstoy had shown any signs at all, prior to his death, of a desire to be reconciled with the church. The fact that he chose to ask these particular individuals, as opposed to those who had actually spoken to Tolstoy during those last few days, was no accident, of course. Neither Savitsky, however, nor Andrei Lvovich – the only true believer in Orthodoxy among all Tolstoy's children – were able to provide the Bishop with any evidence whatsoever of a shift in L.N.'s religious mood. More than that, Andrei Lvovich informed him of the family's unanimous collective decision to bury Tolstoy without a religious ceremony. In his report to the Synod Parfeny wrote: "Surprised by these words, I said, 'But your mother told me the exact opposite of this in person, a year and a half ago...' Andrei Lvovich replied that his mother too, devastated by grief, had changed her stance, 'besides, her nerves are currently greatly upset and it's impossible to talk to her. My brothers are probably indifferent to the matter, and my sisters decidedly don't want a religious ceremony...".

Parfeny acted judiciously and as a result was not in an awkward position, unlike the hapless Elder Varsonofy, who had to drain the cup of humiliation to the bottom.

One last try

There are a lot of myths and conjecture surrounding Varsonofy's arrival in Astapovo and his attempt to talk to Tolstoy on his deathbed, which have no direct relationship with what actually happened in Astapovo. If one were to put all this speculation together, the mythological picture that results would look roughly as follows.

When he departed from Yasnaya Polyana, Tolstoy was thinking of effecting a return to Orthodoxy. To this end, he went to the Optina monastery, where he wanted to stay on as a novice. Pride, though, did not let him reach out to the elders. Urged to leave Shamordino by his daughter Sasha, when she arrived there, he set off on his onward journey. Once in Astapovo, however, mortally ill, he repented and sent a telegram to Optina Pustyn expressing his desire to meet with Varsonofy. Chertkov and Tolstoy's youngest daughter, however, refused to allow Father Varsonofy to go in and see the dying man when he arrived with the Blessed Sacrament. These same individuals didn't let his wife, a believer and a church-goer, go in and see him, either.

It's not difficult to debunk this myth, all the facts go against it. What is harder is to identify the portion of truth that is included in it.

As he sought to make sense of Tolstoy's departure, a contemporary of his, Lev Tikhomirov, wrote: "It is a strange end to a life ... There is a sense of some kind of struggle for the soul. He wanted to be reconciled with the church, but Satan was holding on to him tightly." In these words there is a deep, though imprecise, meaning. The trouble is that people often understand "Satan" to mean very specific people from among those surrounding Tolstoy in Astapovo. At the same time, they place too much idealized significance on the arrival in Astapovo of Varsonofy.

There was no telegram from Lev Tolstoy to Optina requesting a meeting with Varsonofy. The priest Georgy Orekhanov, who looked into the matter in detail, admitted as much.

This myth arose after the publication, in an Orthodox journal released in Brazil ("Vladimir Bulletin", São Paulo, № 62, 1956), of the memoirs of a former novice monk at the Optina office, Abbot Innokenty. In them it was stated that a telegram had allegedly arrived at Optina from Astapovo, from L.N., asking *Father Josef* to come to the station. After some deliberation, the monastic brethren decided not to send the seriously ill Iosif but the Abbot, Elder Varsonofy.

"Innokenty, in all likelihood, was mistaken," writes Georgy Orekhanov, "and understandably so. In all probability, Father Innokenty had mixed up two telegrams in his head: an imaginary telegram from Tolstoy and a real one from the His Eminence Benjamin (Muratovsky), at that time the Bishop of Kaluga, requesting hieromonk Iosif, by order of the Holy Synod, to go to the Astapovo station to see Count L.N. Tolstoy, who had fallen ill during his journey..."

It would have impossible to try to keep secret any telegram sent by Tolstoy. All the telegrams sent from Astapovo, including Savitsky's encrypted ones, were stored away and later published. The Holy Synod, which came under serious pressure from Tsarskoye Selo and Stolypin, tried, through Bishop Parfeny, to discover some *indirect* signs, at least, of a desire on the part of Tolstoy to become reconciled with the Orthodox Church. Having received none, Parfeny tried, at least, to establish how Tolstoy's *relatives* felt about it: did they not wish to lay their husband and father to rest with a church ceremony? Again, he received a negative response. For the Synod, the existence of a telegram would have played into their hands! There wasn't one, though. Tolstoy couldn't have sent a telegram. The only telegram that the writer sent from Astapovo (to Chertkov) was dictated by him to Sasha.

In the Optina Pustyn *Chronicle*, there is no mention of a telegram from Tolstoy. Instead, it contains details of the telegram sent by the Bishop of Kaluga, which had served as the reason why Varsonofy was in Astapovo.

"Yesterday, on the 4th of this month (November – P.B.), in the morning, a telegram was received from His Eminence of Kaluga concerning the instruction, by order of the Synod, to the former Abbot hieromonk Iosif to go to the Astapovo Station on the Ryazan-Ural Railway, to see Count Lev Tolstoy, who had fallen ill whilst travelling, so as to offer him a spiritual conversation and religious consolation with the goal of a reconciliation with the Church. In response thereto a telegram was sent, stating that Father Iosif was unwell and was not able to go out of doors, but that it was allowed for someone to carry out this duty. At that, the Abbot of Optina was asked permission, due to the difficulty of Father Iosif going as per the instructions, for him to be replaced with Father Abbot Varsonofy. This was followed by a reply from Bishop Benjamin, to the effect that the Holy Synod permitted this. The Father Abbot then asked His Eminence by telegram whether it was sufficient, if Tolstoy were to repent, to unite him to the Church through the sacraments of the Penance and Holy Communion, to which the answer came through that the person sent to talk with Tolstoy was to inform His Grace of Kaluga of the result of this meeting, such that the Bishop could discuss it further with the Synod. On the evening of the 4th, there was a telegram from the Elder Father Iosif, asking the Astapovo station-master whether Tolstoy was there, whether it would be possible to see him on the evening of the 5th, and if he was to set off, where should he go. A reply was received, stating that Tolstoy's family requested that he should not set off. On the morning of that same day, however, Abbot Varsonofy, pursuant to the Synodal order, set off to see Count Tolstoy in Astapovo." There was no initiative stemming from Tolstoy in Astapovo; but there was no initiative that stemmed from Optina, either. The initiative came from the Synod, and the Optina Elders saw it as a *duty*.

Once he arrived in Astapovo, Varsonofy was in an excruciatingly difficult position. Firstly, his fame at the time was far less than that of Iosif, whom Tolstoy had actually wanted to meet at Optina. Secondly, if Varsonofy revealed the true motives for his arrival he would be portraying the Synod in an unpleasant light. Varsonofy was forced to remain silent. Yet he looked like an intruder. After all, not only had Tolstoy not invited him, but he hadn't been invited by the family, either, who by that time were already at the station almost in full force (with the exception of Lev Lvovich, who was living in Paris).

Varsonofy proved to be a passive character in just as extreme a way as Captain Savitsky was (Varsonofy was a former army colonel, incidentally). Responsibility for the Synod's fatal mistake in 1901 had been pinned on him, even though the elder didn't have the slightest involvement in it. In the eyes of the hundreds of journalists who covered the Astapovo tragedy, he came across as an "inept servant-boy", and they wrote about him in very humiliating terms.

According to the reporters' telegrams, moreover, Varsonofy was forced not only to remain silent, but to tell lies about the real reasons for his arrival.

A.F. Avrekh – *Early Morning*: "The Abbot of Optina Pustyn, Varsonofy, has just arrived, accompanied by hieromonk Panteleimon (the Optina doctor. – P.B.). According to the latter, Varsonofy was sent by the Synod. Varsonofy himself denies this, saying that he stopped off here whilst on a pilgrimage." P.A. Vilensky – *Kiev Thought*: "The Abbot told me that Tolstoy didn't know he was here; he was going on a pilgrimage and stopped off here."

Garness – *Saratov messenger*: "...the monks are denying the objective." A.A. Epifansky – *Morning*, "The Elder, in a conversation with reporters, says that he is on a pilgrimage, and stopped in to see Tolstoy. He told Andrei Lvovich that Tolstoy had looked for him during his trip to Optina." Garness: "The monks arrived with gifts, conferred with the local priest, and made their way home to the home in secret at night. They didn't reach Tolstoy: the door is locked, the steward only lets you pass if you know the password." One could cite similar telegrams *ad infinitum*. That candid public humiliation to which the elderly monk, who was later canonized, was subjected, was clear evidence of the Synod's fatal error of 1901. They had found someone to "excommunicate"! Tolstoy! Almost the only man of faith among the entire writing fraternity! There wasn't a single "excommunicated" man among the reporters in Astapovo.

Tolstoy's family behaved no better in relation to the Elder. Knowing that the first thing her father had done, after he ran away from home, was to go to the monastery, Sasha did everything she could to ensure that her father knew nothing at all about the arrival of the priest in Astapovo. She had a solid excuse for this: the doctors had advised against perturbing the patient in any way. On the same grounds, L.N.'s other children, including Sergei and Tatiana, who were close to their father, did not insist that L.N. should be told about Varsonofy's arrival and Metropolitan Anthony's telegram. This excuse does not seem to hold up to scrutiny, though. In the Crimea, when Tolstoy had been at death's door, the news of Anthony's letter, which his wife had informed him about, had not, for some reason, caused a cardiac arrest. Having said that, we know what Tolstoy thought of the church at that moment. We do not, however, know anything about his thoughts on this when his death was imminent.

And that is a sad fact...

On the siding

In his book *Tolstoy's Departure*, Chertkov, as one of the main arguments in support of Tolstoy's will, in which the rights to dispose of the writer's literary heritage were effectively assigned to V.G. alone, cited the fact that he was the only person L.N. summoned to Astapovo. Judging by the notes made by Sasha and Makovitsky, this was indeed the case. Yet the fact remains that there was no telegram from *Tolstoy* containing a summons for Chertkov. The telegram was *from Sasha*, who had written down what had been said by Tolstoy, who was supposedly desirous of seeing Chertkov. At the same time, however, Tolstoy himself dictated a telegram containing different content to his daughter. His daughter sent the two telegrams simultaneously at 10:30 am on November 1.

On the morning of November 1, Makovitsky writes, Tolstoy felt more cheerful. His temperature had dropped to 36.2°. "L.N. said that he felt better and that he could continue the journey." The telegram to Chertkov, which Tolstoy dictated to Sasha, was as follows: "Was sick yesterday. Passengers saw a feeble man leaving the train. Better today. We'll move onwards. Take measures. Keep me notified. Nikolayev." It cannot be concluded from this telegram that L.N. was summoning Chertkov to Astapovo. If anything, quite the opposite. Tolstoy was asking his "dear friend" to stay put and "take measures". He had written to Chertkov about these "measures" from Shamordino: monitor S.A.'s condition and mood and report back to him during his journey. Along with this telegram, though, Sasha sent one of her own: "Got off yesterday at Astapovo. High fever, unconsciousness. Temperature normal in the morning, now chills again. To go further is unthinkable. He expressed a desire to see you. Frolova." Tolstoy's summons for Chertkov, if that indeed is what it was, ran contrary to the promise L.N. had made to his wife in writing on July 14, 1910:

"...If you don't accept these conditions for a kind, peaceful life, then I will take back my promise not to leave you. I will leave. I will probably not go to Ch. I shall even set it as a prerequisite condition that he must not come and live near me, but I shall certainly leave, because to go on living the way are living now is impossible."

Of course, the condition that Tolstoy was in, both at the time of his departure and in Astapovo, doesn't allow us to draw any firm, definitive conclusions. Except for one, that is: Tolstoy clearly *wanted* to see Chertkov...

His enforced separation from Chertkov, which had been thrust on him under pressure from his wife, had been one of the main reasons for his departure. On the eve of it, on October 26, he wrote V.G. a letter which leaves us in doubt whatsoever about that.

"Today, for the first time I felt with particular clarity – to the point that it saddened me – how much I miss you ...

There is a whole sphere of thoughts, feelings, which I cannot share so naturally with anyone else, knowing that I am completely understood, as I can with you."

In a letter to the eldest children sent from Astapovo, he wrote: Seryozha and Tanya, I hope and am sure that you will not reproach me for not having summoned you. To summon you alone without mama would have been a great source of sorrow for her, as well as for your other brothers. Both of you will realize that Chertkov, whom I have summoned, is in a unique position in relation to me. He has devoted his life to the service of the cause which I too have served for the last 40 years of my life. It is not so much that this cause is dear to me, but that, as I would profess – rightly or wrongly – it is important for all people, you included." This letter gives the best sense of all of how unresolvable the family "triangle" which prevailed at the end of Tolstoy's life had become. Before his death, L.N. does not summon *a single one* of his family members to see him, attributing this to his desire not to hurt S.A. Yet at the same time he summons a man whose arrival in Astapovo is a most terrible blow for his wife. Because this person is in a *unique* position.

At the same time, if one looks carefully, one can see that there is some confusion in the dates contained in the letter. It puts the beginning of the spiritual upheaval ten years earlier than it actually was. And the entire logic of the letter (I am not summoning you so as to not offend mother, but I'm summoning Chertkov) suggests that Tolstoy at that time was already beyond the bounds of ordinary earthly reality and was thinking about something altogether different.

On the same day he dictated to Sasha: "God is that unlimited All, of which man knows himself to be a limited part. Only God truly exists. Man is His manifestation in matter, space and time. The more the manifestation of God in man (life) is connected with the manifestations (lives) of other beings, the more he exists. The connecting of one's life with the lives of other beings is carried out by means of love. God is not love, but the more love there is, the more man is a manifestation of God, the more he truly exists." It was not that the family did not fit into this "true existence", but that it was a part of it on the same terms as all other individuals. Only Chertkov alone continued to be in a unique position.

And he knew it. After her husband's flight from their home, S.A. once again tried to make peace with Chertkov. Through Bulgakov, she invited him to come to Yasnaya Polyana for talks. And her offer was refused.

"At Yasnaya Polyana," writes Bulgakov, "everyone was surprised when I came back alone. It hadn't even occurred to anyone that Chertkov might reject Sofia Andreyevna in her desire to see him and to be reconciled with him." "When Vladimir Grigorievich had heard Sofia Andreyevna's request, he wanted at first to go to Yasnaya Polyana, but he then changed his mind.

'Why should I go there?' he said. 'So that she can humiliate herself before me, and ask my forgiveness? ... This is a ploy on her part, so that she can ask me to send her telegram to Lev Nikolayevich.'"

V.G. had understood everything correctly. The main objective of Tolstoy's wife was to bring her husband back, come what may. And this was the same mistake she made when she forcibly separated him from Chertkov. Tolstoy could tolerate an infinite amount of external limitation of his freedom, and even rejoiced in it. The entire make-up of his nature, however, rejected any constraining of his inner will, any use of force against the self.

Finding himself the outright victor, V.G. continued to act prudently, but in a way that was neither noble nor even manly. He coldly (or perhaps with concealed passion) finished off his opponent by means of his refusal to enter into negotiations with her. He wrote a polite letter to L.N.'s wife, and when she had read it, the Countess said:

"Dry morality!"

Prior to this, she had prepared a telegram for her husband: "I have taken communion. I have achieved reconciliation with Chertkov. I'm getting weak. I'm sorry and goodbye." This was a desperate attempt on her part to make her husband come back. Yes, it was a cunning thing to do, yet another deception, hinting that she was dying, but had made peace with her worst enemy, his "dear friend". Chertkov had had anticipated that she would try this move. She realized this, tore the telegram up and threw it into the wastepaper basket. A photocopy of this torn up telegram is stored in Chertkov's archives.

Chertkov was the first to go and see Tolstoy. He did so before the doctors and priests, before his family members. This happened on November 2. "Vladimir Grigorievich arrived with his secretary A.P. Sergeyenko at nine o'clock in the morning," Alexandra Lvovna recalled. "His meeting with my father, after several months of separation, was very touching. They both cried. I couldn't hold back my tears, as I looked at them, and I too was crying in the next room." The meeting between L.N. and V.G. was described in the latter's memoirs: "... I found L.N. in bed, very weak but fully conscious. He was very glad to see me and offered me his hand, which I cautiously took and kissed. He wept, and immediately began to ask me lots of questions about how things were for me at home ... Soon, he began talking about the thing which, at that particular moment, was obviously bothering him most of all. With particular animation, he told me that all measures had to be taken to ensure that Sofia Andreyevna did not come to see him. He asked me anxiously several times what she was planning to do. When I informed him that she had said she would not go against his desire to secure a meeting with him, he felt a great sense of relief and did not say anything else to me about his concerns that day." It is true that Tolstoy was afraid that his wife might arrive. On the night of October 31 to November 1, he raved in his sleep:

"Run away... Run away ... Catching up..."

Did he really ask for "all measures" to be taken, though? The cold, rational expression is more consistent with Chertkov's way of speaking than Tolstoy's. And indeed, by all accounts, it was Chertkov who "took all measures" to ensure Tolstoy would not see his wife before his death, and also to prevent the other family members from coming to Astapovo.

The arrival of his son Sergei, for example, and his meeting with his father, might never have happened. The telegrams which Sasha sent to her brother before Chertkov's arrival and after it seemed to contradict each other. In the first telegram, sent on the night of November 1 to 2, she wrote:

"The situation is serious. Bring Nikitin immediately (the doctor. - PB). Wished to inform you and our sister, he's afraid of the others arriving." Since it was delivered to Moscow, this telegram didn't reach Sergei Lvovich, who had left for his place in the country. His wife sent it after him. Having received it during the journey, he turned around at Gorbachevo and headed for Astapovo.

On the morning of November 2, meanwhile, an hour and a half after V.G.'s arrival, a second telegram was sent from Astapovo for Sergei Lvovich, signed by Sasha, only not to Moscow, but via Chertkov's wife, Anna Konstantinovna:

"Father has asked you not to come. A letter from him will follow. No immediate danger. If any arises, I'll inform you*."

The last thing Chertkov wanted was for any of Tolstoy's relatives to be near him before his death. Except, that is, for Sasha, of course. And also Tatiana, incidentally, whom V.G. himself asked his wife, in a telegram to his wife sent that same morning, on November 2, to inform about his arrival in Astapovo. (She was not informed. Tatiana only learned of her father's whereabouts, just as S.A. did, from Konstantin Orlov's telegram.) Tatiana, shortly before L.N.'s departure, had been involved in the story of the will, in which she had figured as a "third party" after V.G. and Sasha. Yet she had found the whole thing unpleasant, even then. Apparently, it

---

* The story of this mysterious telegram, which Tolstoy's children, after their father's death, deemed to be "fake", and to have been sent not from Astapovo, but from Yasenki by someone in Chertkov's entourage, is set out in detail in an article by V.N. Abrosimova and G.V. Krasnov in the *Yasnaya Polyana Notebook-2006*. This story is one of the mysteries associated with the fact that Tolstoy's death took place in conditions of isolation from his wife and children.

was from her lips, and not only from Tolstoy's secret little diary, that S.A. learned of the existence of the will.

The thought of S.A. appearing beside the invalid's bedside represented a grave danger to Chertkov. He was well aware of how submissive L.N. was to his wife and of how much he had wavered in respect of the will. If S.A. were to turn up, the whole "plot" might unravel in a matter of minutes. This reminder of his children, his grandchildren and, ultimately, the sheer psychological pressure that his wife might exert on her husband, would jeopardize the work they had done to draw up the will and to dispel L.N.'s doubts.

It appears that Chertkov was not the only one who feared this eventuality. Tolstoy himself was afraid of it too. He felt a fear of seeing his wife, who might raise the matter of the will and force him either to reconsider his decision, or to say no to her in a brutal and irrevocable way, thereby tormenting the invalid and, once again, bringing him closer to Chertkov as if he were… an accomplice. In addition to being bound by spiritual ties, both of them were "bound" by this secret document as well.

In this context, one can understand the strange, conspiratorial tone of the conversation between L.N. and V.G.

"We were silent. L.N. held out his hand in my direction. I bent down to him. But he whispered sadly, "No, I just wanted to do that." Me: What is it, is it difficult for you?

L.N.: Weakness, great weakness.

Then, after a pause:

Did Galya let you go easily?

Me: Of course. She even said that she'd be glad if I took you further south.

L.N.: No, whatever for, no.

A little later he asked me whether or not a psychiatrist had gone to see S.A. When I replied in the affirmative, he said: "Was it Rossolimo?" I said no.

After a silence:

And where is your mother, Elizaveta Ivanovna?

Me: In Cannes. She sent a telegram, asking after your health.

LN: How's that, they know about everything already down there, do they?"

Not a word about spiritual matters! Everything is gloomy, secretive, everything is said in half-hints. At any rate, this is how Chertkov reports the conversation.

He kisses L.N.'s hand, having taken it in his black gutta-percha gloves which he wears because of his eczema. Tolstoy, in spite of his condition, is still very sharp-sighted and observant. The next day he sees Chertkov without his gloves on and asks after his health. This is all very touching, as is his concern for Galya and V.G.'s mother, who was in Cannes for a health treatment. Yet it all inspires complicated feelings. There was something unnatural about the fact that, at the end of his life, finding himself separated from his family, Tolstoy was so concerned about someone else's family.

After Chertkov, the other Tolstoyans arrived in Astapovo too: Goldenweiser, Gorbunov-Posadov, Boulanger ... They were able to go and see L.N. unimpeded, to chat with him and look after him. He was glad to see all of them, smiling and saying tender things.

At this time, his wife and his sons Ilya, Andrei and Mikhail were in a separate railway car on the siding. (You will recall that Sergei, Tatiana and Sasha were beside the dying man). On entering Ozolin's little house, the three sons stood in the corridor opposite the room in which their father lay, but could not go inside, and couldn't bring themselves to do so anyway. S.A., of course, was desperate to be by her husband's side, but a collective decision was taken by the doctors and all of the children to the effect that she should not be allowed inside and that Tolstoy should be told nothing about her arrival in Astapovo.

"... There is a photograph that was taken of my mother in Astapovo," Lev Lvovich later wrote. "Shabbily dressed, she is sneaking around outside the house in which my father lay dying, so as try and hear or see what was going on inside. She looks just like some kind of criminal, deeply guilty, brow-beaten, repentant, she's standing there like a beggar, under the little window of the room in which her husband is dying, her Levochka, her life, her body, her whole being."

"He's like a child, like a little child..."

Varvara Feokritova writes in her diary that Tolstoy had of course guessed that his wife had arrived in Astapovo. It is hard to try to challenge what she says in this regard. Taught by her father himself not to lie, Sasha, Sergei and Tatiana could not look him in the eyes and convince him that S.A. remained at Yasnaya as before. They had to keep quiet and ignore any temptation to discuss the subject. Even without this, Sergei was already having to lie, telling his father that he had been passing through Astapovo by chance.

Amid the general confusion they didn't notice that there was a little pillow, hand-woven by S.A., in his room. Tolstoy noticed it, though. Makovitsky, incapable by his very nature of lying, was forced to tell him that Tatiana Lvovna had brought it (she had arrived in the same railway carriage as her mother and brothers.) Tolstoy asked to see his eldest daughter.

"He began by saying, in a weak and halting voice, sounding short of breath, 'How elegant you look, and in your best light,'" Tatiana wrote in a letter to her husband. "I said that I was well aware how poor his taste was, and laughed. Then he started asking me questions about mama. That was what I feared most, because I was afraid I might tell him that she was here, and I sensed that I didn't have the strength to lie openly to him. Fortunately, he posed the question in such a way that I didn't have to tell him a bare-faced lie.

'Who has she stayed behind with?'

'With Andrei and Misha.'

'Misha too?'

'Yes. They are all very much in solidarity about not letting her see you until you want that to happen.'

'Andrei too?'

'Yes, Andrei too. They are very sweet, the younger boys, they have been tormenting themselves, poor things, trying to calm their mother whichever way they can.'

'Well, tell me then, what is she doing? How is she occupying her time?'

'Papenka, perhaps it's better for you not to talk: you'll get agitated.'

At that point he interrupted me very energetically, but nonetheless with tears in his eyes, and said with a trembling voice:

'Tell me, tell me, what on earth can be more important to me than that?' And he began asking me more questions, who was with her, whether the doctor was any good. I said no and that we had parted with him, but that there was a very good nurse, who had worked for S.S. Korsakov for three and a half years, and was therefore used to such patients.

'And she likes her?'

'Yes.'

'Come on, tell me more. Has she been eating?'

'Yes, she's eating, and she's now trying to hold herself together, because the hope of seeing you is what's keeping her going.'

'Did she get my letter?'

'Yes.'

'And how did she react to it?'

"With these questions he was torturing his children and tormenting himself. Yet it so happened that he didn't say the main thing they were expecting him to say – some with trepidation, others with hope. He didn't say that he wanted to see his wife before he died.

To say this would have been to betray Chertkov. Any conversation with his wife, if it were to be totally frank, could not but touch upon the question of the will. And it was no longer about the money. It was about the 'secret' to which he had been party behind his wife's back. This could not be left unsaid on his deathbed. It would have been impossible – *for him*, never mind her – not to raise this issue during a final farewell with the woman with whom he had lived for nearly half a century. It was so painfully embarrassing, though, that everyone tried to avert their eyes from it, to remain silent or to *keep up the pretense*.

A similar situation, only in reverse, had taken place in 1891, when, averting his eyes as he did so, he had divided his property among his wife and children, "as if he had died". That time, too, it had been excruciatingly embarrassing for him, because everyone knew that their father had not died, but was alive and well. And now everyone was pretending that he was not dying but would live on, and that the matter of a conversation with his wife could be left for later, just like the meeting with the Elders at Optina. Just as had been the case then, he hoped that the legal matter would sort itself out by itself in a morally correct way between the people he loved and the people who loved him. Just as before, he didn't want to admit that this world is a world that lies not in good, but in evil, and that human nature is sinful by its very nature.

Not only is it sinful, it is also terribly *sick*. Two people who were both of unsound mind and were infinitely dependent on Tolstoy were unable to share him with one another and hated each other, and he wanted them to love one another as he loved them. "How do you not understand. Why do you not want to understand ... It's so simple ... Why do you not want to do this," he muttered in his delirium, two days before his death. "And it seems that he was tormented and annoyed because he could not explain what it was that needed to be understood and done," Sergei Lvovich recalled. "We didn't understand what he wanted to say." On the morning of the 6th, he sat up and said in a distinct voice: "I only advise you to remember one thing: there is an abyss of people in the world, besides Lev Tolstoy – and you're looking only at Lev." What did these strange words mean?

Perhaps they simply meant: *leave me alone*?

According to Makovitsky's notes, he frequently said: "Don't wake me up," "Don't disturb me," "Don't poke it into me," (his medication).

Meanwhile, six doctors had gathered at the dying man's bedside.

When he saw them, L.N. said, "Who are these nice people?"

When Dr. Nikitin offered to give him an enema, Tolstoy declined. "God will see to everything," he said. When he was asked what he wanted, he replied: "I don't want anyone to make me fed up with them." "He's like a child, like a little child," Sasha said, when she had finished washing her father.

"I've never seen a patient like him," remarked P.S. Usov, a doctor from Moscow, in surprise. When he had lifted L.N. up during the examination, supporting him by his back, Tolstoy had suddenly embraced him and kissed him.

None of those who gathered around the dying Tolstoy and later recalled their memories of those days (some of them kept diaries) noticed the frequent presence in the room of a certain little person, a girl called Marfushka, who washed the floor in the room every day.

Tolstoy noticed her. He took an interest in her story.

"L.N. asked whether she was married or not," wrote Ozolin. "On finding out that she wasn't, he said: 'That's good.' To Marfushka herself, the dying man once advised her, tactfully: "You be careful there, else you'll knock over the little table…"

Before his death, he had visions of two women appearing before him.

He was scared by one of them, on seeing her face, and asked that the curtains be drawn across the window. Perhaps this was the ghost of his wife (perhaps, indeed, it was the living and breathing version of her). Toward the second, he was obviously trying to go toward her, when he opened his eyes and, looking upwards, exclaimed loudly, "Masha! Masha!" "It sent a shiver down my spine," wrote S.L. Tolstoy. "I realized that he had remembered the death of my sister Masha (Maria), who was particularly close to him (Masha had died in November 1906, also of pneumonia)."

In Tolstoy's life there were three Marias for whom he felt a special love: his daughter, his sister and his mother…

His mother, Maria Nikolayevna Tolstaya, had died before little Lev had even reached the age of two. He didn't know her face, and no portraits of her, besides the skillfully carved silhouette, survived. Toward the end of his life, Tolstoy began, on the one hand, to endow the image of his mother with unearthly features, and on the other – to be drawn to her just like a baby. In March 1906, he wrote on a scrap of paper: "A dull, dreary state all day long. By evening this state had turned into one of tenderness, a desire for affection – for love. I wanted, like children, to cling to a loving, compassionate being and cry tenderly and be comforted. Who, though, is that being to whom I could cling like that? I am going through all the people I love in my mind – none of them are suitable. To whom am I to cling? I shall make myself small and cling to my mother, as I imagine her to be.

Yes, yes, to dearest mummy, to whom I never even said that word, being unable to speak. Yes, her, the highest notion I have of a pure love, but not a cold, divine one, but an earthly, warm, maternal one. It is toward this that my best, my tired soul was drawn. You, mummy, you are to caress me."

On one occasion, both women appeared before Tolstoy together. Alexandra Lvovna recalled: "During the day we aired out the bedroom and took father out into the other room. When he was brought back in again, he stared fixedly at the glass door opposite his bed and asked Varvara Mikhailovna, who was watching over him:

'Where does that glass door lead?'

'Into the hallway.'

'And what is beyond the hallway?'

'The porch and the front steps.'

At that moment I entered the room.

'And is that door locked?' my father asked, turning to me.

I told him that it was locked.

'It's strange, I could clearly see that two female faces were looking at me from that doorway.'

We told him that it couldn't be so, because the door from the corridor to the porch was locked, too.

It was clear that he had not calmed down and was continuing to look anxiously at the glass door.

Varvara Mikhailova and I picked up a large covering and placed it over the door.

'Oh, that's much better,' father said, relieved. He turned toward the wall and fell silent for a while."

Here one cannot help recalling those lines by Pushkin:

I find no gladness — and softly before my eyes
Two youthful phantoms seem to appear,
Two spectres dear to me now quietly arise,
Two fate-given angels from yesteryear.
But both are winged and hold a sword most fiery,
Both guard me and to avenge me seek,
And it's of joy's secrets and the grave's mysteries
That they in a long-dead language speak.

This is from a draft version of Pushkin's *Reminiscences* from 1828 – the year of Tolstoy's birth.

It's also possible, however, that there was a more prosaic explanation for this strange vision. When they had aired out the patient's room, which was located opposite the entrance to the house, they had opened the front door for a short while (the rest of the time it was locked). And at that particular moment, S.A. had come up to the front steps. "Alexandra Lvovna and I go out onto the porch. Sofia Andreyevna was already there," writes Goldenweiser. "We persuaded her to come out. We were all extremely excited and touched by her arrival. But my God, how things transpired! Photographers from some cinematic company or other arrived in Astapovo and decided they wanted to film Sofia Andreyevna. When we opened the front door, Alexandra saw a device pointing towards the porch, heard the crackling of the wind-up handle, recoiled in horror and ran back into the house." In addition to his death throes ("How L.N. shouted, how he tossed and turned, how he gasped for breath!" wrote Makovitsky on November 6), his suffering also lay in the fact that those around him couldn't understand him. His tongue was no longer obeying him.

"Father asked us to write down what he was saying, but it was impossible, since he spoke in fragmented, incomprehensible words," Alexandra Lvovna recalled. "When he asked us to read out what had been written down, we were at a loss and didn't know what to read. But he kept on asking:

'Read it out, read it out!'

We tried to write down what he said in his delirium, but sensing that what we had written down didn't make any sense, he was left dissatisfied and asked us to read it out again." After that we tried to resort to reading aloud his anthology, *Circle of Reading*. Makovitsky's notes: "At 10 in the morning, L.N., half-delirious, insisted that there was something that we needed to "continue doing". We began to read *Circle of Reading* to him, first me, then Varvara Mikhailovna, then Tatiana Lvovna, whom L.N. asked to do it, thanking her for something, and said, 'Dear Tanya'.

We read *Circle of Reading* three times in a row on November 5.

When we had finished reading, L.N. immediately asked:

'Well then, what's next? What's written down here,' he said insistently, 'what's written here? Just look for that ... No, right now one can't get anything out of you.'" The last entry in Tolstoy's diary, on November 3, was as follows: "That's my plan. Fais ce que doit, adv...* And all for the benefit of others, and most importantly for me."

Do what you must, and let whatever happens, happen...

His last meaningful words, uttered a few hours before his death to his eldest son, who in his consternation couldn't make them out, but which Makovitsky heard: "Seryozha... the truth ... I love a lot, I love everyone..."

"Throughout his illness," Alexandra Lvovna recalled, "I was struck by the fact that, despite his temperature, the considerable weakening of activity in his heart and his severe physical suffering, father was in a strikingly clear state of consciousness the whole time. He noticed everything that was going on around him, right down to the smallest details. When everyone had left him, for example, he began to count how many people had come to Astapovo in total, and found that 9 people had come in total." This incredible clarity of mind, taken together with his inability to prove something, to express the most important thing, brought L.N. suffering which was comparable to his physical torment. He was trying to be gentle and kind to all the people who were around him and who were increasing in number all the time. He generally behaved like a gentle, albeit ever so slightly naughty child, who suddenly pushes a syringe or an enema away and asks everyone to "leave him alone". For all this, though, Tolstoy's mind was working at full capacity, and his vision remained excellent. The discrepancy between the clarity of his mind and vision and the fact that some needless (as he saw it) manipulation of his body was taking place, seems to have poisoned his final pre-death departure.

"To get away! Get away!" he kept muttering. On the evening of November 5, he did indeed try to escape...

"All that time," recalled Alexandra Lvovna, "we had been trying to keep watch over him in pairs, but then it somehow came about that I was left alone at father's bedside. He seemed to have fallen asleep. Suddenly, though, with a strong movement, he raised himself up on the pillows and began to lower his legs off the bed. I walked over to him. "What do you want, daddy," "Let me, let me go," and he made a move to get out of bed. I knew that if he got up, I wouldn't be able to hold him up and he would fall over, and I tried in every possible way to calm him down and get him to stay in bed. He tried to break away from me with all his might, however, and said: "Let me go, let me go, don't you dare hold me back, let me go!" Seeing that I couldn't cope alone with my father, since my exhortations and requests were having no effect, and I didn't have the heart to hold him back by force, I started shouting: "Doctor, doctor, come here quickly!"

Semenovsky was on duty at the time, I seem to remember. He came in together with Varvara Mikhailovna, and we managed to calm father down and keep him in bed."A very serious source of concern for him was the fact that, in addition to camphor, they also injected him with morphine. How he hated drugs, how he feared them! It was no coincidence that Anna Karenina jumped under a train after taking a double dose of opium. When Tolstoy had dislocated his arm in the early 1860s and it had been reset for him twice under anesthetic, he instinctively resisted this forcible interruption of his consciousness. His whole body rebelled against it, and he had to be given a double dose of ether on both occasions.

When the doctors, wanting to ease his death agonies, offered to inject him with morphine, L.N. said to them in a trembling voice: "I don't want paraffin... don't give me paraffin!"

"They injected some morphine," Makovitsky writes. "L.N. began to breathe with even more difficulty and, weak and half-delirious, muttered:

'I'll go away somewhere so that no-one bothers me ... Leave me alone ... I must get away, must get away somewhere ...'"

Only after an injection of morphine did they let his wife in to see him. One of the doctors, either Usov or Berkengeim suggested that she be called in. "At first she stood there and looked at father from a distance," S.L. Tolstoy writes, "then she calmly walked over to him and kissed him on the forehead, knelt down and started saying to him, 'Forgive me,' and something else that I couldn't make out."At around three o'clock in the morning on November 7, Tolstoy awoke and opened his eyes. Someone held a candle up to his eyes. He frowned and turned away.

Makovitsky walked over to him and offered him something to drink. "Moisten your lips, Lev Nikolayevich," he said solemnly. Tolstoy took a single sip. After this, life only manifested itself in him in his breathing.

At 6:05 am on November 7, L.N. passed away...

Makovitsky tied the deceased's chin with a cloth and closed his eyes. "I covered his eyes," he writes. Everyone dispersed fairly quickly after Tolstoy's death. Everyone was so tired after all those long days, they needed a rest. Tolstoy's children left, his wife left. "Makovitsky and I were the only ones left in the entire apartment," Ozolin recalled. "When I entered the room in which Makovitsky was sitting with his head bowed, he turned to me and said to me in German: "Neither love nor friendship nor devotion helped."

Epilogue

It is hard to convey the feeling one gets on leafing through a binder of Russian newspapers from November 1910. As we have already noted, their front pages were usually given over entirely to advertising, for the smallest, most piffling assortment of goods, moreover, and to personal announcements concerning lost pet dogs and so forth. Yet here is the newspaper for November 8 and as you open it, you see... an enormous portrait, covering the entire page of the newspaper, in a solemn frame, of a gray-bearded old man with a stubborn, convex and tense forehead and a harsh, intense gaze which penetrates deep into one's soul. "**LEV TOLSTOY IS DEAD**". This wasn't just news. It was a sound and a blinding light which made the whole vast country shudder and stir itself, to throw off, for one day at least, the whole fog of civilization, with its "goods", "services" and "conveniences", and remember that there were values in the world that were more important than that.

Values which are more important than life itself...

L.N.'s body was put in an oak coffin without a cross on the lid. "If they put Lev Nikolayevich in a coffin like that, then when I die, I'll have to be put in a simple timber box," the writer's widow said at this.

After her husband's death, S.A. lost consciousness several times, but then pulled herself together and sat near the head of the deceased. "She stroked with her hand the high forehead of the man who had been Lev Tolstoy," Konstantin Orlov of the *Russian Word* reported. "She keeps saying it's all over, the great light of the world has been extinguished. Gently stroking him again, she says, lowering her voice, as if whispering to the deceased: my soul, my life." One day and the night of November 7 were allotted for the station workers and the people of Astapovo and the surrounding villages so that they could say farewell to Tolstoy. The faithful asked Bishop Parfeny permission to hold a service for Tolstoy at the station church. He didn't allow it, citing the Synod's disposition. "The Synod tied my hands, it is for the Synod to untie them," said the Elder Varsonofy. He also said however strong Lev might have been, he had nevertheless been unable to escape from the cage. Before long, the elder and the bishop left.

Eternal Memory was sung almost non-stop beside Ozolin's house. According to the respondent from the *Saratov Leaflet*, on the morning of November 7 alone, three thousand people visited the room in which Tolstoy lay.

The room was adorned with flowers. There were also wreaths, though L.N. had not wanted there to be any. A note from the local intelligentsia read: "*To the apostle of love*". And – the most touching one of all – from some local schoolgirls: "*To the great grandfather from some young admirers.*" At 1:15 am the funeral train pulled out of Astapovo. The coffin containing Tolstoy's body was transported in a car marked *Baggage*. (Chekhov's body, incidentally, was transported to Moscow in a car marked *Oysters*). It turned out that Tolstoy had "departed" quite a long way from home. The journey home took more than a day. The question arose: where were they to spend the night? In Gorbachevo or in Kozlova Zaseka? They opted for Gorbachevo because several thousand people had already gathered in Kozlovka and the police feared an extreme outburst of feeling and disorder. They arrived at the Zaseka Station at 6:30 am on November 9th. The coffin was carried to Yasnaya Polyana by hand. Numerous improvised choirs sang *Eternal Memory*. Ahead of them a huge banner was carried with the handwritten words: "Lev Nikolayevich! The memory of your goodness will not die among us, the orphaned peasants of Yasnaya Polyana." It had been made by the peasants themselves, they hadn't calculated how much room they would need for all the letters and some of the words had to be shortened. At 11 am, the coffin was carried to Yasnaya.

Tolstoy was laid to rest, as he had requested in his will, "without church singing, without incense," without solemn speeches. Only a friend of the family, the theater-lover and revolutionary Leopold Sulerzhitsky, told those present why Tolstoy had been buried this way and not any other way. When the coffin was lowered into the grave, everyone got down on their knees. A policeman who was standing nearby hesitated. "On your knees!" they shouted at him. He sank to his knees at once.

The interment took place at 3 pm on November 9.

Tolstoy's sons accepted their father's will.

S.A. pursued litigation against Sasha for some time over the manuscripts which were stored at the Historical Museum. The Senate, indeed, confirmed the widow's rights to these manuscripts, which were so very dear to her. This was an unpleasant matter, and above all a scandalous one. It received wide coverage in the press. Over time, though, the mother and daughter were reconciled with one another, and the problem somehow sorted itself out. In the end, S.A. died in Sasha's arms.

After her husband's death, S.A. went through a spiritual upheaval of her own. Only it wasn't as violent and painful a one as L.N.'s had been, at the turn of the 1870s-80s. Left alone at Yasnaya Polyana, the Countess faded into old age slowly and in a very dignified manner. She survived the Revolution and the beginning of the Civil War, when fighting between the Reds and those who supported Denikin was going on literally next door to the estate.

"In recent years she has calmed down," recalled her daughter Tatiana Lvovna. "The thing that her husband had dreamed of for her was partially fulfilled; the transformation took place in her, for which he had been willing to sacrifice his fame. Now, the world-views of our father became less alien to her. She became a vegetarian… In the last period of her life, she often talked about her deceased young son (Vanechka. – P.B.), and about her husband. She told me one day that she thought about our father constantly, and added: "I did not live with him in the right way, and that tortures me." With each passing year the Countess's eyesight gradually grew worse, but she went to Tolstoy's grave every day and attended to it…

It's impossible to read the draft of her own will, which changed over the years, without emotion. What could she bequeath? Yasnaya Polyana had been purchased from her by Sasha and Chertkov with the money received from the posthumous publication of the L.N.'s works, and transferred to the peasants, as per Tolstoy's instructions. The sons, with their debts, were constantly in need of money, and their mother gradually gave away her savings to them. "They are all unhappy – and that is very sad!" she wrote in her diary. "It's not life, but some vague dream of life…"

"Ilya came to stay, I gave him 1,000 rubles. He is very pitiful, hopeless, and the bad thing is that he blames everyone in the world." "My son Mikhail came here, he elicited 1,800 rubles…"

"Andrusha was here, he took 2,000 rubles from me…"

"My sons came to visit, Andrusha, who is still unwell, and Ilya, to whom I gave as a loan (supposedly) 6,000 rubles, and he cheered up immediately." "Dora says that Lyova has lost around 50,000. Poor, pregnant, caring Dora! Lev Nik. was a thousand percent right, when he said that he had made the peasants wealthy, but not his sons. Everything would have gone on cards and carousing anyway. And that is disgusting and sad and pathetic! And what else will happen after my death!"

Seven versions of S.A.'s will survived, exactly as many as L.N. had. The first will was written in 1909. It set out who was to get what in the minutest detail. Not only the land and the house, but the belongings, tableware and jewelry. To her daughter Sasha, who had begun, that year, along with Chertkov, to prepare her father's will which went against her mother (about which the latter didn't know), S.A., for example, bequeathed "my mother's silver lorgnette and gold bracelet, a Carnelian heart of gold and a small grenade pearl brooch." Besides the children and grandchildren, the cook, steward and seamstress were also included, all referred to by their full names – they were bequeathed bonds. In the new version drawn up in 1913, her daughters Sasha and Tatiana were removed from the list of heirs. She couldn't forgive them for the fact that their father had bequeathed them his literary rights, bypassing her and their sons. Six months later, however, the new will included both Tatiana, as the heiress to the house and the plot adjoined to it, and Sasha, who was bequeathed a portion of the money. Andrei's name disappeared from the 1916 version, for he passed away that year. In the will she wrote in August 1918, *she divided everything equally between the children* and confirmed her wishes in the final document dated 16 September 1918.у

In her later years, she felt very lonely. Only Tatiana and her husband, and the little granddaughter Tanya, whom S.A. adored, lived relatively close to her, at Kochety. Sasha had left to work as a nurse on the front line. Her son Mikhail had been taken off to the war. Her grandson Andrei Ilych signed up as a volunteer. Her steward and many of the peasants were taken away from her. Her sons Ilya and Lev were touring the world giving lectures about their father. After the Revolution, during the Civil War, she experienced hardships, and even a famine, from which she was saved by the writer P.A. Sergeyenko, who had contacts in the new government, but was fairly rude toward the writer's widow.

The last entries in her diary read: "There is a war and a battle is looming near Yasnaya Polyana"; "Along the highway stretching from Tula there are carts, oxen and people. They say that they are refugees from Orel and the south." (October 1919). These refugees were to become the final image from the life recorded in her diary.

In October, she began washing the windows in the house and caught a cold. She died, like her husband, of pneumonia. And also, like him, in November. She thought about him constantly during her final years, trying to work out the real reasons for his departure. She never really managed to do so ... but one day she wrote down the most comprehensive definition of this event imaginable in her diary:

"*What* happened is incomprehensible, and will forever be beyond our understanding."

List of sources

There is a vast amount of literature on the departure and death of Tolstoy. On the other hand, the number of books in Russian dedicated exclusively to this event is fairly small. For that reason, the reader who wishes to make sense of this incredibly complex issue for himself, will have to deal not as much with the monographs as with the colossal factual material scattered across sources which are often far removed from the subject itself. What's more, the reasons for Tolstoy's departure are to be found in the earliest events of his life, starting with his birth. They cannot be understood without a very careful reading of the writer's artistic works as well.

The suggested reading list is not, of course, an exhaustive list of all the materials that the author used. Without these texts, though, the book simply could not have been written. And this, in our view, is the *minimum* with which any future researchers into this problem must be acquainted; they must not put their trust in any "*theories*" about what happened.

The list is divided into four sections. The first includes letters and diaries, published in full or partially quoted in books, by L.N. Tolstoy, S.A. Tolstaya and V.G. Chertkov. In the second, the academic material on Tolstoy's biography are listed. The third section includes various sources relating to Tolstoy's life in general, or in one way or another connected to the theme of his departure and death. And finally, the fourth section contains the literature which deals directly with Tolstoy's departure and death.

I

Tolstoy, L.N. Complete Works (Commemorative Edition) in 90 volumes, 1928 1958. Second Series. Diaries. Volumes 46-58.

Tolstoy, L.N. Complete Works (Commemorative Edition) in 90 volumes, 1928-1958. Third Series. Letters. Voume. 83-84. Letters to S.A. Tolstoy.

Tolstoy, L.N. Complete Works (Commemorative Edition) in 90 volumes, 1928-1958. Series Three. Letters. Volumes 85-88. Letters to V.G. Chertkov.

Tolstaya, S.A. Letters to L.N. Tolstoy. Moscow - Leningrad, 1936.

Tolstaya, S.A. Diaries: in 2 volumes. Moscow. 1978.

Tolstaya, S.A. My Life: [typing]. Library of the Museum-Estate "Yasnaya Polyana".

Muratov, M.V. "L.N. Tolstoy and V.G. Chertkov: Through Their Correspondence". Moscow, 1934.

Zhdanov, V.A. Tolstoy and Sofia Behrs. Moscow, 2008.

II

Biryukov, I.P. Biography of L.N. Tolstoy: in 4 volumes. Moscow. 2000.

Gusev, N.N. Lev Nikolayevich Tolstoy. Materials for his biography. 1828-1855, 1855-1869, 1870-1881, 1881-1885. Moscow, 1954-1970.

Gusev, N.N. Chronicle of the Life and Works of L.N. Tolstoy. Moscow-Leningrad, 1936.

Lev Tolstoy and His Contemporaries. Encyclopedia. Moscow, 2008.

Opulskaya, L.D. Lev Nikolayevich Tolstoy. Materials for his biography. 1886-1892, 1892-1899. Moscow. 1979-1998.

III

Arbuzov, S.P. Memoirs of S.P. Arbuzov, a former servant of Count L.N. Tolstoy. Moscow, 1904.

Boulanger, P.A. The Illness of L.N. Tolstoy in 1901-1902 / / The past few years. 1908. Number 9.

Boulanger, P.A. Tolstoy and Chertkov. Moscow. 1911.

Bulgakov, V.F. Lev Tolstoy, his friends and relatives. Tula, 1970.

Varfolomeyev Y.V. On the Spiritual Will of Lev Tolstoy / / Questions of Literature. 2007. Number 6.

Gusev, N.N. Two Years with Lev Tolstoy. Moscow, 1973.

Diary of L.L. Tolstoy / / Faces. Biographical Almanac. Volume 4. St. Petersburg., 1994.

The Spiritual Testament of S.A. Tolstaya. (Manuscript) Manuscript Division of the State Museum of L.N. Tolstoy.

Why was Lev Tolstoy Excommunicated from the Church. Collection of Historical Documents. Moscow, 2006.

Zverev, M.A., Tunimanov, V.A. Lev Tolstoy. Moscow, 2006. (Great people).

Interviews and Conversations with Lev Tolstoy. Moscow, 1986.

How L.N. Tolstoy's Will Was Written. From the memoirs of A.P. Sergeenko // Tolstoy Yearbook 1913. St. Petersburg., 1913.

Kuzminskaya T.A. My life at home and at Yasnaya Polyana. Moscow, 1986.

L.N. Tolstoy and his family. Moscow, 1986.

L.N. Tolstoy in the memoirs of contemporaries: in 2 volumes, Moscow. 1978.

Nikitina, N.A. The Daily Life of Lev Tolstoy at Yasnaya Polyana. Moscow. 2007.

Opulsky, A.I. The House at Khamovniki. Moscow, 1976.

L.N. Tolstoy's correspondence with his sister and brothers. Moscow, 1990.

L.N. Tolstoy's correspondence with Countess. A.A. Tolstoy. St. Petersburg., 1911.

Petrov, G.P. The Excommunication of Lev Tolstoy from the Church. Moscow, 1978.

Account books of Sofia Andreyevna Tolstoy. (Manuscript) Archive of the "Yasnaya Polyana" Museum-Estate.

"The path provided to us by Christ, is the way of love, not hatred ..." (Letters of the Athos monk on Lev Tolstoy's excommunication from the Church) // Yearbook of the manuscript department of Pushkin House in 2000. St. Petersburg., 2004.

Sergeyenko, A.P. Stories about L.N. Tolstoy. Moscow, 1978.

"Stand in the covenant of the...". Nikolai Konstantinovich Muravyov: A lawyer and public activist. Memoirs, documents and materials. Moscow, 2004.

Sukhotina-Tolstaya, T.L. Memoirs. Moscow, 1980.

Sukhotina-Tolstaya, T.L. Diary. Moscow, 1987.

The texts of L.N. Tolstoy's wills / / Tolstoy Yearbook 1913. St. Petersburg., 1913.

Tolstaya, A.L. The Daughter. Moscow, 2001.

Tolstaya, A.L. The Father: in 2 volumes, Moscow. 2001.

Tolstaya, S.A. Whose Fault Is It? On "The Kreutzer Sonata" by Lev Tolstoy / / Daniel Rancour-Laferriere. Russian literature and psychoanalysis. Moscow, 2004.

Tolstaya, A.L. On my father / / Yasnaya Polyana collection. Tula, 1965.

Tolstoy, I.L. My memoirs. Moscow, 1969.

Tolstoy, L.L. Yasha Polyanov. Reminiscences for children from Count L.L. Tolstoy's childhood. St. Petersburg., 1906.

Tolstoy, L.L. At Yasnaya Polyana. The truth about father and his life. Prague, 1923.

Tolstoy, M.L. My parents / / Yasnaya Polyana collection. Tula, 1976.

Tolstoy S.L. Sketches of the Past. Tula, 1975.

Tolstoy, S.M. The Children of Tolstoy. Tula, 1994.

Firsov, S.L. The Ecclesial-juridical and socio-psychological aspects of the "excommunication" of Lev Nikolayevich Tolstoy (Problems related to the incident.) / / Yasnaya Polyana Collection - 2008. Tula, 2008.

IV

Abrosimova, V.N. The Departure of L.N. Tolstoy. Based on the diary entries of M.S. Sukhotina in 1910 and the correspondence between T.L. Tolstaya and S.L. Tolstoy in the 1930s / / News from the Academy of Sciences, Department of Literature and Language Series. Volume. 55. Number 2. 1996.

Abrosimova, V.N. and Krasnov, G.V. The story of a deceptive telegram as seen through the eyes of the Sukhotins, the Chertkovs and V.F. Bulgakov / / Yasnaya Polyana Collection-2006. Tula, 2006.

Bulgakov, V.F. L.N. Tolstoy in the last year of his life. The diary of L.N. Tolstoy's Secretary. Moscow, 1957.

Goldenweiser, A.B. Near Tolstoy. Moscow, 2002.

Gottwald, V.A. The Last Days of Lev Nikolayevich Tolstoy. Moscow, 1911.

Ksyunin, A.I. The Departure of Tolstoy. St. Petersburg., 1911.

Annals of the Monastery of St. John the Baptist, located at the Optina Hermitage in Kozelsk: in 2 volumes, Moscow. 2008.

Makovitsky, D.P. At Tolstoy's. 1904-1910. The notes made at Yasnaya Polyana of D.P. Makovitsky / / Literary Heritage. Volume 90: in 4 books. Moscow, 1979.

Meilakh, B.S. The Departure and Death of Lev Tolstoy. Moscow-Leningrad, 1960.

Novikov, M.P. Taken from Experience: memoirs, letters. Moscow, 2004.

Obolensky, E.V. My Mother and Lev Nikolayevich / / Annals of the State Literary Museum. Book. 12. Moscow, 1938.

Ozolin I.I. The Last Refuge / / Literary Review. 1978. Number 9.

Official Directory of the railroad, steamship and other passenger services. Edited by N.L. Bruhl. St. Petersburg., 1910.

The Last Days of L.N. Tolstoy. An Album by Vl. Rossinsky. Moscow, 1911.

Rev. George Orekhanov. The Cruel Judgment of Russia: V.G. Chertkov in the life of L.N. Tolstoy. Moscow, 2009.

The Death of Tolstoy based on new materials. The Astapovo telegrams. Moscow, 1929.

Snegiryov, V.F. A letter to S.A. Tolstaya (Manuscipt). Manuscript Division of the State Museum of L.N. Tolstoy.

Sukhotin, M.S. Tolstoy in the Final Decade of his Life / / Literary Heritage. Volume 69. Book II. Moscow, 1961.

Tolstaya, A.L. Notebook / / Tolstoy Yearbook-2001. Moscow, 2001.

Tolstaya, A.L. On the departure and death of my father (unpublished materials). Foreword, publication and notes by N.A. Kalinina / / Tolstoy Yearbook-2001. Moscow, 2001.

Tolstaya, A.L. The Depature and Death of L.N. Tolstoy. Why L.N. Tolstoy left Yasnaya Polyana / / Tolstoy Yearbook - 2001. Moscow, 2001.

Feokritova, V.M. Diary of 1910 (manuscript) / / Manuscript Division of the State Museum of L.N. Tolstoy.

Chertkov, V.G. On the Last Days of L.N. Tolstoy. St. Petersburg., 1911.

Chertkov, V.G. The Departure of Tolstoy. Berlin, Moscow, 1922.

Dear Reader,

Thank you for purchasing this book.

We at Glagoslav Publications are glad to welcome you, and hope that you find our books to be a source of knowledge and inspiration.

We want to show the beauty and depth of the Slavic region to everyone looking to expand their horizon and learn something new about different cultures, different people, and we believe that with this book we have managed to do just that.

Now that you've got to know us, we want to get to know you. We value communication with our readers and want to hear from you! We offer several options:

- Join our Book Club on Goodreads, Library Thing and Shelfari, and receive special offers and information about our giveaways;

- Share your opinion about our books on Amazon, Barnes & Noble, Waterstones and other bookstores;

- Join us on Facebook and Twitter for updates on our publications and news about our authors;

- Visit our site www.glagoslav.com to check out our Catalogue and subscribe to our Newsletter.

Glagoslav Publications is getting ready to release a new collection and planning some interesting surprises — stay with us to find out!

Glagoslav Publications
Office 36, 88-90 Hatton Garden
EC1N 8PN London, UK
Tel: + 44 (0) 20 32 86 99 82
Email: contact@glagoslav.com

Glagoslav Publications Catalogue

- *The Time of Women* by Elena Chizhova
- *Sin* by Zakhar Prilepin
- *Hardly Ever Otherwise* by Maria Matios
- *The Lost Button* by Irene Rozdobudko
- *Khatyn* by Ales Adamovich
- *Christened with Crosses* by Eduard Kochergin
- *The Vital Needs of the Dead* by Igor Sakhnovsky
- *A Poet and Bin Laden* by Hamid Ismailov
- *Kobzar* by Taras Shevchenko
- *White Shanghai* by Elvira Baryakina
- *The Stone Bridge* by Alexander Terekhov
- *King Stakh's Wild Hunt* by Uladzimir Karatkevich
- *Depeche Mode* by Serhii Zhadan
- *Saraband Sarah's Band* by Larysa Denysenko
- *Herstories*, An Anthology of New Ukrainian Women Prose Writers
- *The Hawks of Peace* by Dmitry Rogozin
  by Leonid Andreev
- *The Battle of the Sexes Russian Style* by Nadezhda Ptushkina
- *A Book Without Photographs* by Sergey Shargunov
- *Sankya* by Zakhar Prilepin
- *Wolf Messing - The True Story of Russia's Greatest Psychic* by Tatiana Lungin
- *Good Stalin* by Victor Erofeyev
- *Solar Plexus* by Rustam Ibragimbekov
- *Don't Call me a Victim!* by Dina Yafasova
- *A History of Belarus* by Lubov Bazan
- *Children's Fashion of the Russian Empire* by Alexander Vasiliev
- *Empire of Corruption - The Russian National Pastime* by Vladimir Soloviev
- *Heroes of the 90s - People and Money. The Modern History of Russian Capitalism*
- *Boris Yeltsin - The Decade that Shook the World* by Boris Minaev
- *A Man Of Change - A study of the political life of Boris Yeltsin*
- *Gnedich* by Maria Rybakova
- *Marina Tsvetaeva - The Essential Poetry*
- *Multiple Personalities* by Tatyana Shcherbina
- *The Investigator* by Margarita Khemlin

More coming soon…

www.ingramcontent.com/pod-product-compliance
Lightning Source LLC
LaVergne TN
LVHW041957060526
838200LV00002B/51